A GUIDE TO
THE INDIAN TRIBES
OF THE PACIFIC NORTHWEST

THE CIVILIZATION OF THE AMERICAN INDIAN SERIES

A GUIDE TO
THE INDIAN TRIBES
OF THE PACIFIC
NORTHWEST

THIRD EDITION

Robert H. Ruby, John A. Brown,
and Cary C. Collins

Foreword by Clifford E. Trafzer

Pronunciations of Pacific Northwest
Tribal Names by M. Dale Kinkade
Revised and updated by Sean O'Neill

UNIVERSITY OF OKLAHOMA PRESS : NORMAN

Published with the assistance of the National Endowment for the Humanities, a federal agency which supports the study of such fields as history, philosophy, literature, and language.

A Guide to the Indian Tribes of the Pacific Northwest: Third Edition is Volume 173 in The Civilization of the American Indian Series.

Library of Congress Cataloging-in-Publication Data

Ruby, Robert H.
    A guide to the Indian tribes of the Pacific Northwest / Robert H. Ruby, John A. Brown, and Cary C. Collins ; foreword by Clifford E. Trafzer ; pronunciations of Pacific Northwest tribal names by M. Dale Kinkade. — 3rd ed. / revised and updated by Sean O'Neill.
    p. cm. — (The civilization of the American Indian ; v. 173)
Includes bibliographical references and index.
ISBN 978-0-8061-4024-7 (pbk. : alk. paper)
1. Indians of North America—Northwest, Pacific—Encyclopedias.
I. Brown, John A. (John Arthur), 1914–2004.
II. Collins, Cary C.
III. Kinkade, M. Dale (Marvin Dale), 1933–2004
IV. O'Neill, Sean, 1969–
V. Title.
E78.N77R79 2010
979.5'01—dc22

                                        2010008791

The paper in this book meets the guidelines for permanence and durability of the Committee on Production Guidelines for Book Longevity of the Council on Library Resources, Inc. ∞

*To the indigenous peoples of the nineteenth century
who, although they were pushed to the brink,
not only survived but preserved and passed
on to future generations
a remarkable heritage
of cultures, lifeways,
and history.*

*[T]he [federal] government's management of
Indian affairs was a national disgrace.*
— Gerald Ford
Interview with Charles V. Mutschler,
September 16, 2004

[The ancestors] are happy to know we are still here.
—Johnny Moses

Coast Salish storyteller, oral historian,
traditional healer, and spiritual leader

CONTENTS

The Indian Tribes

Maps

FOREWORD

Clifford E. Trafzer
University of California, Riverside

One day in 1977, I had the opportunity to fly in a small plane from Seattle to Spokane, over a great expanse of the Pacific Northwest. During that journey I saw the magnificent snow-covered mountains of the region and the great expanse of green trees west of the mountains. As we flew east toward Spokane, I marveled at the rugged mountains, the width of the Columbia River, and undulating hills of snow with shoots of green poking out here and there. Although I had never seen this ever-changing landscape, I knew that several diverse Indian tribes had inhabited the good earth long before the arrival of newcomers. Seeing the land reminded me of the close historical and spiritual relationship of the Indians of the Northwest to their homelands. That thought stuck with me when I took an academic position at Washington State University and began to study the history of the first peoples of the Northwest.

Although several people had researched and written on the history of northwestern Indians, I discovered that Robert Ruby and John Brown had conducted more research and produced more books on this subject than any other scholars. The University of Oklahoma Press had published most of their books, and I found them to be of high quality, both in content and methodology. Unlike most scholars, Ruby and Brown had listened and learned from many tribal elders. They had used the oral histories they had conducted within the body of their books, including the documentation. By doing so, they encouraged all scholars studying Native American history to learn from contemporary Indians and assess these sources alongside the written sources provided by the newcomers. It became clear to me that Ruby and Brown had a tremendous grasp of the history and culture of the tribes living along the Puget Sound and Pacific Coast. They had great knowledge of the Indian people that lived along the rivers and in the expansive plateau region. I learned much from all the books researched and written by Ruby and Brown, and I was particularly pleased when they produced a unique contribution to Native American history by writing an encyclopedic guide to the many people they had researched and written about for years.

In 1986, Robert Ruby and John Brown published the first edition of their *Guide to the Indian Tribes of the Pacific Northwest.* Although not the work of Native Americans, it was nevertheless immediately accepted as a valuable resource by scholars, Indian people, tourists, and members of the general public who were interested in American Indian history and culture. Unfortunately, John Brown died in 2004, but now historian Cary Collins has joined Ruby to update the *Guide*. They have produced a marvelous volume of great value.

Native Americans of the Pacific Northwest have not vanished as some people had predicted. In fact, Indian people are present in every part of contemporary American society. Like other Native Americans, the tribes of the Northwest survived the physical, economic, social, linguistic, and cultural genocide brought to their homelands by newcomers—including federal, state, and county government officials—bent on destroying Indian people and their cultures and languages through laws, wars, treaties, executive orders, education, and economic development. Attempts to destroy American Indian peoples significantly influenced the history of the first nations of the United States and Canada. In order to survive, Indian people changed, but they did not disappear. They rose to the challenge and endured.

Indian peoples of the Pacific Northwest survived through their strength, determination, and tenacity. They overcame numerous obstacles put before them, and they developed into unique, modern sovereign nations within the boundaries of national, state, and local governments. As detailed in the present volume, they continue to develop politically, economically, and intellectually during the early years of the twenty-first century. In large part, the innate sovereignty of Indian people of the Pacific Northwest—given to them by spiritual forces and known to them through sacred narratives, songs, and oral testimony—contributed to their survival. Tribal sovereignty emerged from Native Americans themselves, not from acts of the federal government. All of the tribes of the Pacific Northwest had their own laws by which they governed themselves as a people and as individuals. The Sahaptian-speaking peoples of the northwest plateau identified their laws as *tamanwit*, the rules by which they lived their daily lives.

Northwest Indian people had their own laws, rules, and punishments. They had their own governments long before the arrival of foreign nations. Many traditional tribal laws are extant today, and these have helped guide the people through difficult times. These laws ensured spiritual survival and allowed the people to maintain a special connection to the land, even when non-Indians forced them from their ancient homelands. The federal government moved many Northwest Indians from these homelands, thereby preventing them from obtaining their native foods and worshiping at their sacred places. Although newcomers took over Indian lands and claimed them as their own, Northwest Indians still claim these places as their own and continue their relationship with deer, salmon, huckleberries, roots, chokecherries, and other foods placed on the land for the benefit of human beings. Federal and state officials may or may not recognize Indian tribes as being "real," but Indian people continue to recognize themselves as part of the historical tribes of the greater Northwest.

The authors of this text, like the Indian people themselves, do not allow state and international borders to blur the identities of Indian tribes and people. The border between Canada and the United States is a modern invention of newcomers, not Indians. The same can be said for the borders of Washington, Idaho, Oregon, California, and other states. This *Guide* encompasses Indian people from several states. The authors use numerous sources in the creation of their narratives, including tribal documents, oral histories, government documents, and photographic evidence. In addition, over a number of years, the authors have traveled to all of the tribal lands mentioned in the volume. During the 1950s and 1960s, Ruby and Brown visited Indians living on several reservations. The authors camped out and transcribed oral histories in longhand—sources still used in the making of this new *Guide*. In recent years, Collins joined Ruby on expeditions throughout the Northwest to visit and document Indian tribes and people, obtaining new information for the revised *Guide*. The new work includes much of the information found in the first edition, but it also includes wonderful details that illuminate the growth and development of the tribes and confederated reservations found in the Northwest. The authors provide a wealth of information about each tribe and offer updates pertinent to contemporary tribes and their people. The information is current and authentic. Scholars, tourists, and laypeople will find the information accurate and fascinating. The narratives are accessible and readable, and the short bibliographies found at the end of each entry will lead readers to additional information about the tribes.

The *Guide* offers information on numerous tribes, including those that readers will readily recognize and those that seem more obscure. The authors begin with the Ahantchuyuk who lived in the Willamette Valley of Oregon and then provide useful and interesting details on the Bannock, Burns Paiute, Cayuse, Chelan, Chinook, Clatsop, Colville, Modoc, Nez Perce, Palouse, Shastas, Snoqualmie, Spokane, Tilamook, Wenatchi, Yakama, and many other tribes. The list is comprehensive and each description of a tribe offers insight and knowledge. Each entry includes historical information about the origin of the tribal name, the tribe's traditional homelands, its interactions with newcomers, and its relations with other tribes. The authors offer details, as well, on the tribe's relations with state and federal officials, on treaties, executive orders, conflicts, loss of land and resources, struggles to preserve rights, and historical change over time. They also provide lively photographs and illustrations as well as new information on contemporary Indian people. Readers will learn about Native languages, places, economic development, tribal government, and the Office of Indian Affairs.

Before the arrival of the English, Spanish, and Americans, all the tribes of the Pacific Northwest had developed successful economies, which included hunting, fishing, and gathering. Their economies required Indian people to use certain areas jointly, areas where they shared resources, the gifts of nature. Often, however, northwestern people traveled some distances to hunt, gather, and fish. But all of this changed with the arrival of newcomers, who viewed the land as private property not to be shared. Federal, territorial, and local officials and their voting constituents demanded the reduction of Indian land and access to their former domains. As a result, Northwest Indians lost millions of acres and secured for themselves only a minute portion of their former domains. In some cases, the Indian tribes lost all of their land, as the federal government opened their homelands to white settlement. Newcomers destroyed nearly all the traditional economies of Northwest Indians and forced many people onto small reservations, often with other Indians who may or may not have shared their language, religion, culture, or destiny. Other Indians moved to towns and cities to seek employment and live through wage labor.

From the *Guide* we learn that some tribes negotiated treaties with federal officials, which the Senate of the United States ratified and presidents signed into law. Other tribes agreed to executive orders that recognized portions of Indian land as reservations. Federal officials ignored other Indians altogether, refusing to recognize the right of some tribes to a square inch of ground. These Indians and their tribes became strangers in a stolen land. The *Guide* details these developments and more, offering current information on the legal status of various Northwest tribes. The authors also provide narratives about contemporary tribes, including information on powwows, rodeos, language revitalization, historic preservation, cultural programs, educational endeavors, art shows, ceremonies, dances, housing, infrastructure, libraries, health centers, repatriation, and a host of other details relevant to current times.

Some tribes in the Northwest have developed businesses in high-stakes gaming, but not all of them. Those that have developed gaming have tried to invest their capital wisely, and some tribes have been able to diversify. The *Guide* provides some information on Indian gaming, but the authors well know that, for centuries, all of the tribes had enjoyed their own forms of gaming—betting on horse, canoe, and foot races as well as hand games, and archery—if not Vegas-style gaming. After newcomers and their governments had destroyed Native economies, Indian people turned to many industries—for example, ranching, farming, fishing, and tourism—to enhance their tribal economies. Nevertheless, nothing brought the tribes out of poverty and provided sufficient economic stimulus to truly benefit the people as much as Indian gaming, which for some tribes and in some cases has provided funding for housing, health, food, roads, clean water, social services, education, and a host of other programs.

The authors recognize that many problems still exist on Indian reservations in the Northwest, including poverty, ill-health, poor housing, infant death, drug and alcohol abuse, suicide, diabetes, accidents, and short life expectancy. Tribal leaders have much work to do for the benefit of their people, and they realize that they must act carefully because of the ongoing threat to tribal sovereignty, self-determination, and economic development. Private individuals, corporations, and government groups covet Indian land, resources, and businesses. As in the past, these people pose a threat to Indian tribes and all their earnings. Some non-Indians resent the successes of Indian people and are continually challenging Indian rights. Native American leaders in the Northwest are well aware of these threats to their tribes' well-being, but the leadership is generally optimistic about the future of Indians as sovereign peoples within the United States and Canada.

Michael Finley is currently chairman of the Business Council of the Confederated Tribes of the Colville Reservation. He holds the master's degree in history from Eastern Washington University and plans to finish his doctorate one day. Finley is the coauthor, with Richard D. Scheuerman, of a groundbreaking book on Chief Kamiakin that makes use of documents Finley found on his reservation. Roberta Conner is Finley's counterpart on the Umatilla Indian Reservation, where she serves as a museum director. Conner is known worldwide for her work in preserving tribal history, culture, and language. In recent years, she has served as a member of the board for the Smithsonian's National Museum of the American Indian. Both Finley and Conner represent the new Indian leadership that follows in the old tradition, basing its service on the remarkable work of past tribal elders. The authors of the *Guide* briefly highlight the work of several such tribal leaders. They regard Indian leaders as individuals embracing their obligations for the betterment of their people, not themselves. They offer documentation showing that Indian leaders follow many old traditions, even as they deal with the modern world. The authors convey to their readers the dynamic history of Indian leadership over time. They have produced a book about people and tribes that allows readers to enter the history and culture of Northwest Indians and thereby grow in their understanding of Native Americans, past and present.

In my own research, the *Guide* has been invaluable. I have often used the first edition to learn more about the tribes, particularly about the result of claims filed against the United States under the Indian Claims Commission Act. But I have found it useful in so many other ways. It is an indispensable source for anyone interested in Native American history and contemporary society. For too many years, the general public, politicians, educators, writers, scholars, and others have not understood the history and culture of Northwest Indians. Too many people know little or nothing about the many tribes indigenous to the Northwest and their contributions to contemporary society. This *Guide* is a unique reference that will enrich the knowledge of all readers, regardless of their age. It will change the way people perceive Native nations of the greater Northwest and their significance in the history and culture of a magical region of North America.

PREFACE TO
THE FIRST EDITION

A Guide to the Indian Tribes of the Pacific Northwest is prepared for the public at large, including not only those who live in the region (many of whom are new to it) but also tourists, scholars, and interested readers. The various tribes described here live, as did their ancestors, in a vast area extending from the Rocky Mountains to the Pacific Ocean and from California to British Columbia. Although we realize that historically the habitations and the movements of the Pacific Northwestern tribes have not been confined within the state and national boundaries established by white men, we have been forced to set arbitrary geographic perimeters for our work. Despite the sedentary tendencies of the region's peoples, from a historical viewpoint they have always been in flux. Continuing archaeological studies will reveal more of that tribal ebb and flow back to the earliest times.

As in the past, there are fewer Indian tribes between the Cascades and the Rocky Mountains, but individually they are more populous than those of the coastal regions. On the coast the numerous river valleys, the lush vegetation, and the proximity of ample food supplies facilitated the formation of greater numbers of tribes. Many of the tribes described here became extinct in the nineteenth century. By contrast there has been rebirth and a regrouping of tribes in the twentieth century, a time of renewed tribalism and quests for the federal government's "acknowledgment" that assures fishing and other rights. Some formerly classified as subtribes or, in other cases, village bands, have become full-fledged tribes. To help our readers chart these transitions, we have provided comparative population figures. Those given for 1780 are from a 1928 publication by the anthropologist James Mooney. Those of 1805–1806 are from the estimates of the explorers Meriwether Lewis and William Clark. We are aware of the very tenuous nature of these population figures, yet we note that they have been used by contending parties in claims litigation and they do serve to trace the nineteenth-century decline of native populations and the reversal of that trend in the twentieth century.

In preparing the *Guide,* we have relied on standard ethnological works, such as John R. Swanton's *The Indian Tribes of North America* (1968) and Frederick Webb Hodge's *Handbook of American Indians North of Mexico* (1907 and 1971). We have also consulted numerous other sources of information and worked closely with tribal officials, whom we wish to thank for their assistance, along with the anthropologists and the historians who read portions of the manuscript and made helpful suggestions. We would not fail to thank the many librarians and government officials who aided us. Our endeavors have been exhausting and, at times, difficult, especially in sorting out linguistic families (noted in parentheses after the tribal name at the beginning of each tribal entry) and other tribal affiliations, yet these labors have been rewarding. We are especially appreciative of Dr. M. Dale Kinkade's contribution to this book of the phonetic spellings of the Pacific Northwest tribal names.

We hope the *Guide* will facilitate armchair traveling for those who are unable to visit this part of America in person. In the 1970s numerous centers were built wherein one may experience the resurgent tribal pride and museums that feature and preserve tribal cultural items and evidence of daily living. In this volume we present a sense of that history and the peoples who lived it.

Above all, we hope that because of our efforts you, our readers, will gain knowledge and understanding of the various tribes of which we write and of the many diverse and remarkable cultures that strived and struggled to exist throughout the Pacific Northwest.

ROBERT H. RUBY
Moses Lake, Washington

JOHN A. BROWN
Wenatchee, Washington

PREFACE TO THE
THIRD EDITION

"We were a proud and dignified people, and they made us nothing," lamented the Samish tribal elder Mary Hansen in October 2002.[1] Hansen was referring to the inexplicable removal of her tribe from the national register of federally recognized tribes due to a clerical error (unfathomably, the typist making up the list reputedly skipped over the Samish and the deed was done), but she could have been summarizing 150 years of American Indian and white relations. The ruling inspired the Samish to file a claim to be recognized as an endangered species and, like other tribes at the time, they were actually declared officially extinct in 1987. But that was just how it went in Indian country. Bad things happened and American Indian tribes had precious few resources or the political clout to make it any different.

That is, until recently. Fortunately, in the context of what has transpired over the last several decades, the experience of the Samish represents just one face of a double-sided coin; the other face represents one of the most remarkable economic and cultural turnarounds in American history. Make no mistake. A revolution is seemingly underway in Indian country, one that is every bit as dramatic as it is potent.

The changing landscape is impossible to ignore. Multimillion dollar casinos, luxury hotels, convenience stores and gas stations, tribal schools and colleges, health clinics, cultural centers and museums, housing programs, television channels, radio stations and newspapers, elaborate websites, language acquisition classes, the recovery of natural resources, successes in tribal recognition on the federal level and in repatriation programs, self-run tribal governments, self-written tribal histories, and more. This is not to imply that everyone is basking in the glow of all this progress—clearly they are not and, for a few, some of the achievements have proved as problematic as they have beneficial—but every tribe has felt the changes to some degree, if not simply in the diminishing level of bureaucratic involvement in their affairs by the once-omnipresent Bureau of Indian Affairs (BIA). In that regard, the following anecdote might be instructive. One of the significant changes that has taken place over the last half century is that when researchers contacted tribal groups back in the late 1950s (to

---

[1] Peggy Anderson, "Samish Tribe Keeps Up the Struggle," *Seattle Times*, October 27, 2002.

ask questions or to try to forge relationships), almost everyone with whom they spoke—at least initially—was a non-Indian federal employee. Today, in contrast, the persons answering the phones are invariably enrolled members of the tribes, an experience duplicated in our own research efforts undertaken to complete this updated volume. It may seem like a minor example, but it is indicative of the expanding empowerment of Indians to maintain control over their lives.

Several almost simultaneously occurring developments have contributed to this previously unimaginable reversal. The first impact of note is also the oldest: the emergence of the era of Indian self-determination. Beginning in the late 1960s, charging into full swing in the 1970s and 1980s, and continuing the revitalization and healing initiated in the policies of the Indian New Deal of the 1930s, self-determination reached even further by granting to tribes the freedom to manage and administer their own governments, programs, and services. Self-determination constituted a society-altering milestone, especially considering that it followed on the heels of the onerous and in many ways hurtful policies of termination and relocation, national prescriptions that were aimed at severing federal-tribal trust relationships and scaling back government services and obligations. Tribes, by running their own affairs, are now able to direct the course of current and future generations of their membership in a culturally sensitive, relevant, and responsible manner that breaks from the numbing one-size-fit-all mandates of the BIA and takes into account the unique backgrounds, traditions, and circumstances of each group.

The second advancement has been the expansion of the register of federally recognized Indian tribes. During the era of disassociation and retrenchment of the 1950s, many tribes in the Pacific Northwest lost their recognition status, while others never had it to begin with. Those communities were the unlucky victims of the vicissitudes of convoluted federal regulations, impenetrable red tape, intertribal opposition, murky reporting, and a faulty understanding by Indian Bureau administrators of those over whom they had charge. But with many tribal groups, their fortunes began to turn in the last quarter of the twentieth century. While tribes such as the Lemhis, the Snohomish, the Chinooks, the Steilacooms, and the Duwamish continue to fight for federal acknowledgment, others have found success in their legal challenges, attaining the benefits and privileges that accrue from such standing, including funding for health care, education, infrastructure, preservation of natural resources, delivery of services, and operation of programs. Federally recognized tribes, as indicated by the fact that virtually all tribes covet and hold dear such official pronouncement, have at their disposal resources and advantages that the unrecognized simply do not.

Another factor in the renaissance sweeping through Indian communities and reservations is the economic stimulus generated by Indian gaming and casinos. Many of these facilities are glamorous show palaces with construction costs that can soar into hundreds of millions of dollars. They employ workforces that number in the hundreds, often elevating a tribe to a lofty standing as the single largest employer in their region or county. The significant revenues generated from gaming have seeped into almost all facets of tribal life and beyond. Through mandatory negotiated tribal-state compacts, a portion of annual casino profits is set aside as contributions to charitable and nonprofit organizations, and many tribes disperse a percentage of their net revenue in per capita payments issued directly to enrolled tribal members. Typically, however, a greater amount is held back for underwriting cultural activities and ensuring the sustainability of tribal programs and services. Money is also invested in the acquisition and operation of businesses unrelated to gaming, those intended to be there as a buffer, or an insurance of sorts, against an always-feared dropoff in the popularity of casino gambling among the general public.

Another change among Indian tribes today is the mixed heritage and mixed affiliation that have come to exist throughout Indian country. In the original *Guide*, many tribes and bands were described as "extinct," a troublesome term that implies that the descendants of those groups no longer exist. In point of fact, they very much exist although in many instances the survivors have been absorbed into other tribes. In other cases, tribes that were once thought extinct (usually not by their memberships but by outsiders and federal agencies) have reasserted themselves in the last few decades. Many tribes have used federal acknowledgment and recognition as a springboard to this revived sense of tribal identity. But others not recognized by the federal government have overcome popular perceptions of their erasure from public memory. Tribes such as the Chinooks, the Duwamish, the Steilacooms, and countless confederated groups have, or have once been, considered virtually if not fully extinct. But as this revised volume of the *Guide* makes manifest, those groups and many others are vital and thriving members of their communities.

With all that has happened in recent decades—and there is certainly much to be celebrated—there are caveats. Tribal leaders are quick to point out that there is no small amount still to be done. In the cautionary words of the Tulalip tribal chairman Mel Sheldon, "Contrary to popular belief, the wars against Native peoples, [the wars against] our traditional cultural and spiritual lifeways and [the wars against] our simple right to exist have never been stopped. Every day here at Tulalip our legal team and scientists work to maintain treaty guaranteed rights such as access to off-reservation fishing and marine resources and protection of our area environment. We also deal with jurisdictional rights on our own reservation to include control of natural and cultural resources and the activities of people."[2] In no manner do the authors wish to overstate the achievements or present them in such a manner as to overshadow the challenges remaining.

---

[2] Mel Sheldon, as quoted in http://narfnews.bolgspot.com/2008/07/tulalip-tribes-award-50000-to-native.html.

Using financial standing as a single barometer, even among the most well-to-do tribes such as the Tulalips, there is a palpable sense that only now have they started down a road to recovery that they hope will lead to a total restoration of their cultures as well as a return to their status as fully self-supporting nations or, to couch it another way, to that broad prosperity that Indians enjoyed before coming under the strong-armed authority of the American government and the long grasp of the BIA.

Without question, there are lingering and pervasive social ills, many of which are debilitating. Poverty, especially among children, is widespread as Indians continue to rank as the poorest ethnic group in America. They experience the highest rate of unemployment and the lowest level of high school graduation. They are the worst housed and have access to the least health care. There exists a sometimes overwhelming legacy of societal corrosion that tribes are struggling to correct on a daily basis. According to a major study released in 2003, American Indians are still "at or near the bottom of nearly every social, health and economic indicator."[3] The statistics speak for themselves: "Native Americans have a lower life expectancy—nearly six years less—and higher disease occurrence than other racial/ethnic groups. Roughly 13 percent of Native American deaths occur among those under the age of 25, a rate three times more than that of the total U.S. population. Native American youth are more than twice as likely to commit suicide, and nearly 70 percent of all suicidal acts in Indian Country involve alcohol. Native Americans are 670 percent more likely to die from alcoholism, 650 percent more likely to die from tuberculosis, 318 percent more likely to die from diabetes, and 204 percent more likely to suffer accidental death when compared with other groups." According to the report, "These disparities exist because of disproportionate poverty, poor education, cultural differences, and the absence of adequate health service delivery in most Native communities."[4]

Yet for all of that, there remains an underlying optimism that in some ways things are better now than they have been in a long, long time. The problems are deadly serious and tragically real, but tribes today are more fully equipped to deal with them than they have been in the memories of some of the oldest elders. This third edition of the *Guide*, then, is presented with the hope that the advances reported herein will barely scratch the surface of those that will need to be documented when the next edition is prepared.

Originally published by the University of Oklahoma Press in 1986 as volume

---

[3] Philip Kurata, "American Indian Business Leaders Group Encourages Setting Bigger Goals," July 11, 2009, http://newsblaze.com/story/20090711132555tsop.nb/topstory.html.

[4] U.S. Commission on Civil Rights, *A Quiet Crisis: Federal Funding and Unmet Needs in Indian Country* (Washington, D.C.: U.S. Commission on Civil Rights, 2003), 34-35.

173 in their Civilization of the American Indian Series and updated and reissued with slight modifications in 1992, *A Guide to the Indian Tribes of the Pacific Northwest* has served as a valuable resource to a substantial readership for over two decades. Users have ranged from those simply wanting to look up or verify a quick fact to tourists traveling the back roads and backcountry where much of this history took place to professionals seeking a starting place for their tribal or biographical research. Describing the histories and cultures of 150 Pacific Northwest tribes belonging to fifteen language groups, the book has been a veritable treasure-trove of information. Those tribes possessing a formal government as well as social and economic structures were extensively documented with expanded entries, including census data taken at specific dates, documentation of early contacts, the effects of epidemics, the involvement of tribes in the fur trade, their encounters with missionaries, their participation in treaty negotiations and in wars and confrontations, the allotment of reservation lands, the location of Indian schools and access to education, and the outcome of Indian claims and other litigation. Also covered were the development of housing programs; the construction of medical facilities, clinics, and hospitals; the evolution of tribal enterprises and economies; and the celebration of ceremonies and cultural events, powwows, rodeos, tribal days, fishing and boating contests, and arts and crafts events.

In addition, these entries offered an array of cultural and historical facts related to language, house and dress styles, subsistence, migrations, settlement, and social, political, and kinship organization. The book was lavishly illustrated, with contemporary and historical photographs included for virtually every tribe. There was a list of pronunciations of tribal names prepared by the late professor M. Dale Kinkade, along with a series of maps indicating language families, fur and military posts, missions, and reservations. Originally intended as a companion for the popular *Indians of the Pacific Northwest: A History* (Ruby and Brown, 1981, still in print), the *Guide* was released to strong reviews—the historian Clifford Trafzer hailed it, for example, as an indispensable aid to anyone interested in American Indian and white relations—and in the two-plus decades since its first publication, it has remained a one-of-its-kind, with no comparable volume having appeared during that period.

All the background material found in the earlier editions is included in this third edition—and, in some cases, expanded. Covered as well, however, in the "Contemporary Life and Culture" sections are recent developments in the tribal life of each group. This updated version of the *Guide* had to be launched without the considerable contributions of John A. Brown, who passed away in 2004, ending a writing partnership that spanned nearly a half century. To assist with the updates and work closely in collaboration with Robert Ruby, Cary Collins was invited to join the project, and together Ruby and Collins traveled to the Indian nations of the Pacific Northwest to research and gather the information that is contained in this new volume.

Finally, we extend our sincerest appreciation to Vivian Adams, Todd Baker, Colleen Barker, Katherine Barker, Sharon Bogan, Janine Bowechop, Raymond Brinkman, Rex Buck, Jr., John Chess, James Collins, Nick Collins, Tina Collins, Roberta Conner, Jackie Cook, Michael Finley, Olive Geuer, Cecile Hansen, Jeff Heil, Steve Kent, Kathy Kiefer, Rose Krause, Mary Leitka, Charles V. Mutschler, Lynn Pankonin, David Petrie, Lawney L. Reyes, Paul Eubanks, Linda Finkle, Richard D. Scheuerman, Roxanne Southwood, Vicky S. Skane, Ursula Smith, Clifford E. Trafzer, Malissa Minthorn-Winks, Larry Workman, and Barbara J. Gallaway for their ongoing support of this project.

ROBERT H. RUBY
Moses Lake, Washington

CARY C. COLLINS
Maple Valley, Washington

PRONUNCIATIONS OF
PACIFIC NORTHWEST TRIBAL NAMES

By M. Dale Kinkade
University of British Columbia

Revised and updated by Sean O'Neill
University of Oklahoma

This list includes phonetic transcriptions both of the names by which the Pacific Northwest tribes are generally known and of their own names for themselves. In the left-hand column you will find the generally accepted tribal name. In the left-center column, under the heading "Native Phonetics," is the Native pronunciation of that generally accepted name. In the right-center column, under the heading "Native Name," is the name by which a tribe calls (or called) itself, if that is different from the accepted name. In the right-hand column is the English pronunciation of the generally accepted name printed in the left-hand column. Some of this information is simply no longer available, and blanks indicate where that is the case.

Pronunciation Key

Symbols are used following the pronunciation guide of *Webster's New Collegiate Dictionary*, 9th ed., except as follows (the corresponding symbols in the International Phonetic Alphabet are given in brackets):

ā   [eɪ] like English *day*

ä   [a] like English *bother*

äw   [aʊ] for the diphthong aủ (as in *out*)

äy   [aɪ] for the diphthong ī (as in *ice*)

a   [æ] like English *mat*

e   [ɛ] like English *bet*

ē   [i] like English *beet*

f   [f] in Indian words pronounced with lips close together [ɸ]

hl   [ɬ] a voiceless, very breathy 1

ɨ   [ɨ] a "high-central" vowel, like *i* in English *machine*, but farther back in mouth

q   [q] like k, but pronounced much further back in the mouth

kh   [x] a friction sound such as occurs at the end of 'Bach'

ŋ   [ŋ] like English *ng* in *sing*

ȯ   [ɔ] like the vowel sound in *saw, all, caught*

ō   [oʊ] like English *bone*

ȯy   [oɪ] for the dipththong ȯi (as in *boy*)

q   [q] like k, but pronounced much further back in the mouth

qh   [χ] similar to kh, but pronounced much further back in the mouth

R   [ʁ] pronounced fully in the throat, with some constriction

tl   [tɬ] a combination of t and hl

ü   [u] like English *rule*

ủ   [ʊ] like English vowel in *book*

ŭ   [ə] for the first and second vowels of *abut*

ʷ   the preceding sound is pronounced with the lips rounded

ʾ   ' the preceding sound is pronounced with glottal release

ˊ   primary stress (accent)

ˋ   secondary stress (accent)

•   the preceding vowel is about twice as long as normal

Additionally, a hook indicates nasalization. Thus, [ǫ] represents the final vowel of French *mouton*.

	Native Phonetics	Native Name	English Phonetics
Ahantchuyuk	hănchĕyŭk		ŭhắnchĕyŭk
Alsea		wüsí·ⁿ	álsē *or* ălsē *or* alsē
Atfalati	ätfắlätē		ätfắlätē
Bannock		pännäkʷatɨ	bánŭk
Boise Shoshoni			boʹysē shōshōʹnē
Bruneau Shoshoni			brŭʹnō shōshōʹnē
Calapooya	gäläpŭʹywē *or* kʼäläpúywä		kaŭpŭʹyŭ
Cascade			kaskắd
Cathlamet	gählắmät		kathlámŭt
Cathlapotle	gälhắpütl		kathlŭpŭʹtŭl
Cayuse		léksēyu	käyŭʹs *or* kắyüs
Chastacosta			chástŭkòstŭ *or* shastŭkắstŭ
Chehalis	tsʼqhíʹls		shŭhắlŭs
Chelamela			chèlŭmélŭ
Chelan	chŭlʼắn		shŭlán
Chepenafa	(che)pĕʹ·nefü		chŭpénŭfä
Chetco		chidkhu	chétkō
Chilluckittequaw	chēlüqʷʼdēgʷä		
Chimakum	chímŭkŭm(t) (*also* chŭʹbqäb)		chímŭkŭm
Chinook	chēnŭʹk		shinŭʹk *or* chinŭʹk
Clackamas		(gē)thläqḗmäsh	klákümŭs
Clallam	nŭʹkhʷ(s)tlʼŭʹyŭm		klálŭm
Clatskanie	(i)hlắtsqʼŭnäy		klátskŭnäy (*locally also* klatskắnē)
Clatsop	tlắtsᵒp	klắtsŭp	
Clowwewalla	tlắwēwälä		
Coeur d'Alene		schétsōŏmsh	kŭrdŭlắn
Colville			kắlvil
Coos	kŭs		küs *or* küz
Copalis	kʷʼpēls		kōpắlŭs
Coquille			kokél *or* kōkwíl
Cowlitz	käwlits		kắwlits
Dakubetede			

(continued)	Native Phonetics	Native Name	English Phonetics
Duwamish	dkhʷdŭw'ắbsh		düwắmish
Entiat	nt'ĕắtkʷ		ántēat
Flathead		sálēsh	flát-hed
Grand Ronde			grand rắnd
Hanis Coos	hắnēs kŭ́s		hánŭs kŭ́s
Hoh	hŏ́qhʷ		hŏ́
Hoquiam	qhʷŭ́qʷyämts		hŏ́kwēŭm
			(*locally also* hŏ́kēŭm)
Humptulips		khʷŭntŭ́läpsh, qhŭmtŭ́läpsh	hŭmtŭ́lŭps
Kalispel	qlēspel (*also* qälēspálms)		kálŭspel
Kikiallus			
Kittitas	q't̄ĕ́tä·s (*also* q't̄ĕ́tä·sh)		
		pshwắnwäpäm	kítŭtas
Klamath	hlắmähl		klámŭth
Klickitat	hlắtäqhät	qhʷ ắhlqhʷäypäm	klíkŭtat
Kuitsh			
Kutenai			kŭ́tŭnā, kü'tūnē
Kwaiailk	qʷ̈äyắyhl(q')		
Kwalhioqua			kwälēŏ́kwŭ
Latgawa			lắtgäwä
Lower Chehalis		ts'ŭqhắl's, hlŭw'l'mŭsh	lŏ́ŭr chŭhắ lŭs
Lower Elwha	'ĕ́'hlqhʷŭ, 'ĕ́'hlqhʷä		lŏ́ŭr élwä
Lower Skagit	sqắjŭt		lŏ́ŭr skájŭt
Lower Umpqua	ą̈kwä		lŏ́ŭr ŭ́mpkwä
Luckiamute	(ä)lắk'mäyŭk		lŭ́kēŭmyŭt
			(*locally also* lŭ́kēmyüt)
Lummi		nŭkhʷhlŭmŭchäsŭn	
			lŭ́mi
Makah	mắq'ắ̈ä		mŭkắ
Methow	mĕ́tqhäw		mét-häw
Mical	mēshắl		
Miluk Coos	mílŭk kŭ́s		
Mishikhwutmetunne			
Modoc		mō·wät'ắ·kknē·	mŏ́däk

(continued)	Native Phonetics	Native Name	English Phonetics
Molala	mŭlălēsh		mōlălŭ
Muckleshoot	bŭqĕlshühl		mŭkŭlshüt
Multnomah	mählnümäqh		mŭltnŏmŭ
Naltunnetunne			
Nespelem	nspélŭm		nezpélŭm
Nez Perce		nēmé·pü·	nezpŭrs
Nisqually	sqʷálē, dkhwsqwúlēäbsh		niskwálē
Nooksack	nükhʷsáʼäq		núksak
Northern Paiute	päēyü·tsēŋwɨ		páyüt
Okanagon	óʼqŭnäqán		ōkŭnágŭn
Ozette	óseʼéhlqʷ		ōzét
Paiute	päēyü·tsēŋwɨ		páyüt
Palouse	pälü·s		pŭlüs
Pend d'Oreille			pändŭrá
Pshwanwapam	pshwánwäpäm		
Puyallup	spüyálŭpŭbsh		pyüélŭp
Queets	qʷétsqhʷ		kwéts
Quileute	kʷóléʼyōtʼ		kwílēüt
Quinault	kwénäyhl		kwínólt
			or kwinólt
Sahewamish	sʼähéwäbsh, sŭhéʼwŭbsh		
Salish	sálŭsh		sálish
Samish	sʼémēsh		sámish
Sammamish	stsʼäbábsh		sŭmámish
San Juan			san wán
Sanpoil	snpŭRʷéʼlkh		sanpóíl
Santiam	säntyám		sántēam
			or santēám
Satsop	sátsäpsh		sátsŭp
Sauk-Suiattle	sáʼkʷbékhʷ		sók-süēatŭl
Semiahmoo	sŭmyámŭ		semēámŭ
Senijextee			
Shasta			shástŭ
Shoshone			shōshónē
Siletz	nsh(ŭ)láchʼ		sŭléts
Sinkaietk	(s)nqRétkʷ		
Sinkiuse	snqáʼáwʼs		

(continued)	Native Phonetics	Native Name	English Phonetics
Siuslaw	shä́'yǘ·shtl'ä·		sắyüslő or säyű slő
Skagit	sqä́jŭt		skájŭt
Skilloot	sēk'lütkt		
Skin	skē̆n		
Skokomish	sqō̆'qő̆bŭsh		skōkő̆mish
Skykomish	sqē̆khʷŭbsh		skäykő̆mish
Snohomish	sdühŭ́bsh		snōhő̆mish
Snoqualmie	sdű́kʷälbēkhʷ		snōkwálmē
Spokane	spō·qḗnē		spōkán
Squaxin	sqʷä́qhsŭd		skwä́ksŭn
Steilacoom	ch'tḗlqʷŭbsh		stílŭkŭm
Stillaguamish	stŭ̀lŭ́gʷä́bsh		stilŭgwä́ mish
Suquamish	s(y)ǘq'ʷä́bsh		sükwä́mish
Swallah			
Swinomish	swű́dŭbsh		swínŭmish
Taitnapam	tä́ytnäpäm		tä́ytnŭpŭm
Takelma	tä·kelmä'n		tŭkélmŭ
Taltushtuntude			
Tenino	tēná̆ynü		tŭná̆ynō
Tillamook	t'ēlēmüks	tílŭmúk	
Tukuarika			
Tulalip	dkhwlḗläp		tŭláĺŭp
Tututni	dōtōdŭnē		tütütnē
Twana	tüwä́'dŭkhʷ		twä́nŭ
Umatilla	ḗmätēläm		yümŭtílŭ
Upper Chehalis		qʷ"äyä́yhl(q')	ŭ́pŭr chŭhá̆lŭs
Upper Skagit	sqä́jŭt		ŭ́pŭr skájŭt
Upper Umpqua	ą̊kwä		ŭ́pŭr ŭ́mpkwä
Wahkiakum	wäqhkēäkm		wŭ̆kä́ yŭ́kŭm
Walla Walla	wäläwälä	wälǘ·läpäm	wä́lŭwälŭ
Wanapum	w ä́näpäm		w ä́nŭpŭm
Wasco	wäsq'ű́		wä́sō
Watlala	wählä́lä		

(continued)	Native Phonetics	Native Name	English Phonetics
Wauyukma	wäwyük'mä́		
Wenatchi	wēnä́·chäpäm	np'ŭsqʷä́w's	wŭnáchē
Whiskah	khʷŭ́shqä'		wíshkä
Willamette	wä́lämt		wilámŭt
Willapa	'äkhʷé·l'äpsh		wílŭpŭ
Wishram	wēshqhäm		wíshràm
			or wíshrŭm
Wynoochee	qhʷŭnŭ́hlch(ē)		wäynŭ́chē
Yahuskin			
Yakama	syä'ä́qmä'ŭkhʷ	mä́mächätpäm	yákŭmä
Yamel	yä́mhälä		yàmhíl
			or yámhil
Yaquina	yäqʷṍ·nä, yäqŭ́·nä		yŭkwínŭ
Yoncalla	yä́nkälät		yängkä́lŭ
			or yä́nkälŭ

REFERENCES

Amoss, Pamela T. "1961, Nuksack Phonemics." Master's
thesis, University of Washington, 1961.

Aoki, Haruo. *Nez Perce Grammar.* University of California
Publications in Linguistics 11 (1970).

Barker, M. A. R. *Klamath Dictionary.* University of
California Publications in Linguistics 31 (1963).

Carlson, Barry F. "A Grammar of Spokan: A Salish Language of Eastern
Washington." Ph.D. dissertation, University of Hawaii, 1972.

Frachtenberg, Leo J. *Alsea Texts and Myths.* Bureau of
American Ethnology Bulletin 67, Washington, D.C.

Golla, Victor. "Tututni (Oregon Athapaskan)." *International
Journal of American Linguistics* 42 (1976): 217–27.

Harrington, John P. Papers. National Anthropological
Archives, Smithsonian Institution, Washington.

Hess, Thom. *Dictionary of Puget Salish.* Seattle:
University of Washington Press, 1976.

Jacobs, Melville. "A Sketch of Northern Sahaptin Grammar." *University
of Washington Publications in Anthropology* 4 (1931): 285–92.

—— "Kalapuya Texts." *University of Washington
Publications in Anthropology* 11 (1945).

Powell, J. V. Personal communication, 1982.

——, and Fred Woodruff, Sr. *Quileute Dictionary.* Northwest
Anthropological Research Notes Memoir 3 (1976).

Reichard, Gladys A. "Stem-list of the Coeur d'Alene Language."
International Journal of American Linguistics 10 (1976): 92–108.

Rigsby, Bruce J. "Linguistic Relations in the Southern Plateau."
Ph.D. dissertation, University of Oregon, 1965.

Silverstein, Michael. Personal communication, 1982.

Speck, Brenda J. "An Edition of Father Post's Kalispel Grammar."
University of Montana Occasional Papers in Linguistics 1 (1980).

Vogt, Hans. *The Kalispel Language.* Oslo: Det
Norske Videnskaps-Akademi, 1940.

MAPS

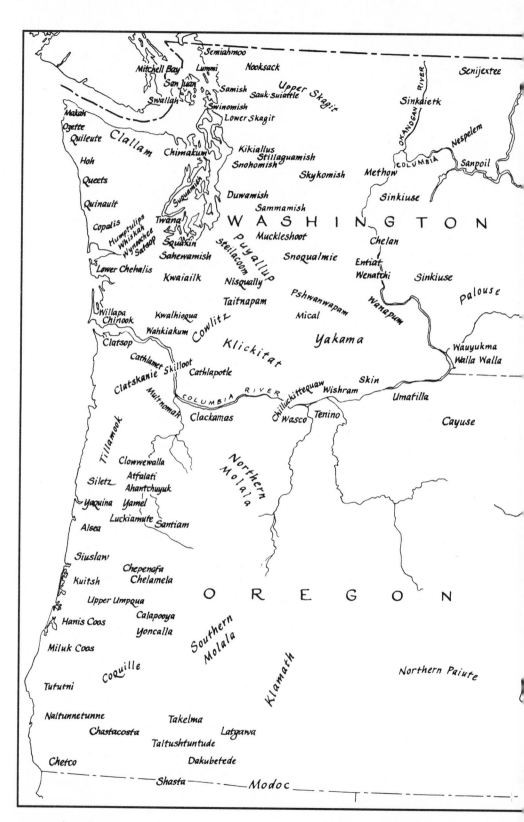

Semiahmoo
Mitchell Bay
Lummi
Nooksack
Upper Skagit
Senijextee
San Juan
Samish
Sinkaietk
Swallah
Sauk-suiattle
OKANOGAN RIVER
Swinomish
Nespelem
Makah
Lower Skagit
COLUMBIA
Sanpoil
Ozette
Quileute
Clallam
Chimakum
Kikiallus
Stillaguamish
Methow
Sinkiuse
Hoh
Snohomish
Skykomish
Queets
Duwamish
Quinault
Suquamish
Sammamish
W A S H I N G T O N
Copalis
Twana
Muckleshoot
Chelan
Humptulips
Whiskah
Wynoochee
Satsop
Squaxin
Puyallup
steilacoom
Snoqualmie
Entiat
Wenatchi
Sinkiuse
Sahewamish
Lower Chehalis
Kwaiailk
Nisqually
Palouse
Taitnapam
Pshwanwapam
Wanapum
Willapa
Chinook
Kwalhioqua
Mical
Wahkiakum
Cowlitz
Yakama
Wauyukma
Clatsop
Klickitat
Walla Walla
Cathlamet
Skilloot
Clatskanie
Cathlapotle
Skin
Multnomah
COLUMBIA RIVER
Chilluckittequaw
Wishram
Umatilla
Clackamas
Wasco
Tenino
Cayuse
Tillamook
Clowwewalla
Northern
Molala
Siletz
Atfalati
Ahantchuyuk
Yaquina
Yamel
Luckiamute
Santiam
Alsea
Siuslaw
Chepenafa
Chelamela
Kuitsh
Upper Umpqua
O R E G O N
Hanis Coos
Calapooya
Yoncalla
Miluk Coos
Southern
Molala
Coquille
Klamath
Northern Paiute
Tututni
Naltunnetunne
Takelma
Chastacosta
Latgawa
Taltushtuntude
Chetco
Dakubetede
Shasta
Modoc

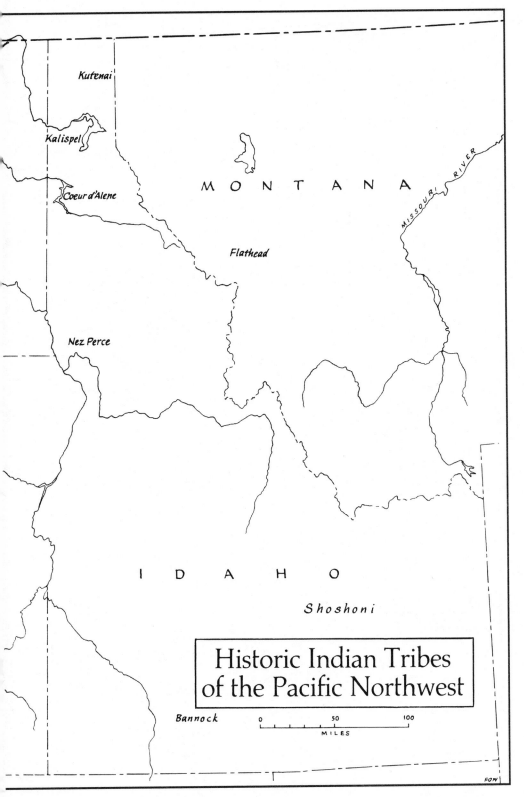

Kutenai

Kalispel

Coeur d'Alene

MONTANA

MISSOURI RIVER

Flathead

Nez Perce

IDAHO

Shoshoni

Historic Indian Tribes
of the Pacific Northwest

Bannock

0   50   100

MILES

FON

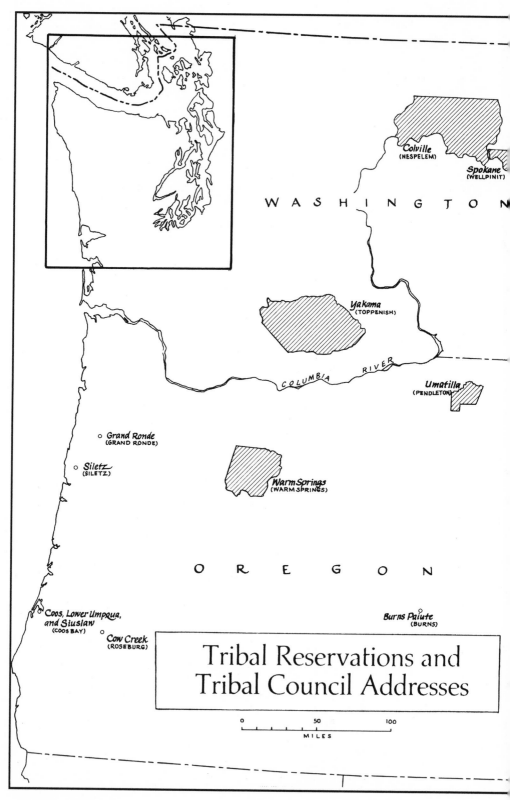

WASHINGTON

Colville
(NESPELEM)

Spokane
(WELLPINIT)

Yakama
(TOPPENISH)

COLUMBIA   RIVER

Umatilla
(PENDLETON)

Grand Ronde
(GRAND RONDE)

Siletz
(SILETZ)

Warm Springs
(WARM SPRINGS)

O R E G O N

Coos, Lower Umpqua,
and Siuslaw
(COOS BAY)

Cow Creek
(ROSEBURG)

Burns Paiute
(BURNS)

Tribal Reservations and Tribal Council Addresses

0   50   100

MILES

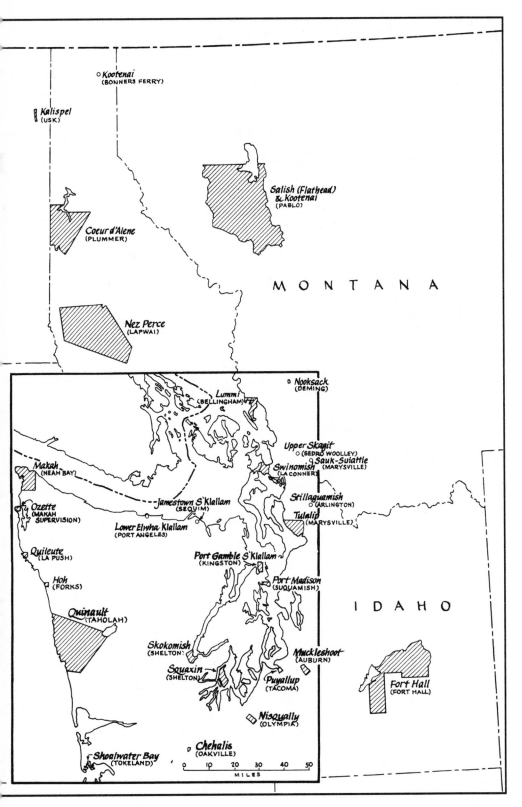

o Kootenai
(BONNERS FERRY)

Kalispel
(USK)

Salish (Flathead)
& Kootenai
(PABLO)

Coeur d'Alene
(PLUMMER)

M O N T A N A

Nez Perce
(LAPWAI)

o Nooksack
(DEMING)

Lummi
(BELLINGHAM)

Upper Skagit
O (SEDRO WOOLLEY)
Sauk-Suiattle
Swinomish (MARYSVILLE)
(LA CONNER)

Makah
(NEAH BAY)

Ozette
(MAKAH
SUPERVISION)

Jamestown S'Klallam
(SEQUIM)

Stillaguamish
O (ARLINGTON)

Tulalip
(MARYSVILLE)

Lower Elwha Klallam
(PORT ANGELES)

Quileute
(LA PUSH)

Port Gamble S'Klallam
(KINGSTON)

Hoh
(FORKS)

Port Madison
(SUQUAMISH)

Quinault
(TAHOLAH)

I D A H O

Skokomish
(SHELTON)

Muckleshoot
(AUBURN)

Squaxin
(SHELTON)

Puyallup
(TACOMA)

Fort Hall
(FORT HALL)

Nisqually
(OLYMPIA)

Chehalis
(OAKVILLE)

Shoalwater Bay
(TOKELAND)

0   10   20   30   40   50
MILES

xxxix

Early Indian Missions
of the Pacific Northwest

Saint Joachim
(LUMMI)

Saint Paul
the Apostle
(SWINOMISH)

Saint Paul
(COLVILLE)

Saint Mary
(OKANAGON)

Saint Francis
Regis (CREE)

Saint Rose
(SANPOIL)

Saint Francis
Xavier (SNOHOMISH)

Saint Peter
(SUQUAMISH)

Tshimakain
(SPOKANE)

Saint Francis
Xavier (WENATCHEE)

Saint Claire
(MUCKLESHOOT)

Nisqually

W A S H I N G T O N

Saint Francis
Xavier (COWLITZ)

Saint Joseph
(YAKIMA)

Waiilatpu
(CAYUSE)

Clatsop

Saint Rose of Chemna
(SIMCOE)

COLUMBIA   RIVER

Saint Peter
(WASCO)

Wascopam
(WASCO)

Saint Anne
(CAYUSE)

Saint Michael

Saint Paul

Willamette
Falls

Saint Francis
Xavier

Willamette
(KALAPOOYA)

O R E G O N

□ American Board
● Methodist
⚑ Mormon
■ Roman Catholic

0   100
MILES

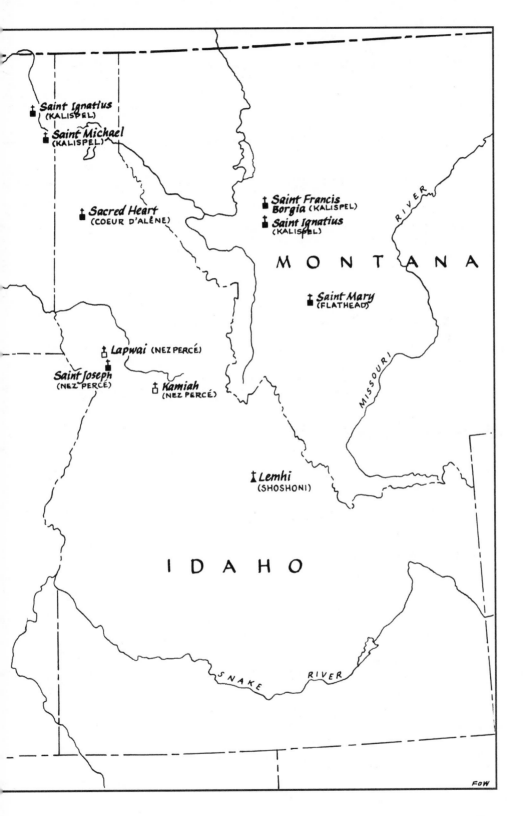

Saint Ignatius (KALISPEL)

Saint Michael (KALISPEL)

Sacred Heart (COEUR D'ALÈNE)

Saint Francis Borgia (KALISPEL)

Saint Ignatius (KALISPEL)

M O N T A N A

RIVER

Saint Mary (FLATHEAD)

Lapwai (NEZ PERCÉ)

Saint Joseph (NEZ PERCÉ)

Kamiah (NEZ PERCÉ)

MISSOURI

Lemhi (SHOSHONI)

I D A H O

S N A K E   RIVER

FoW

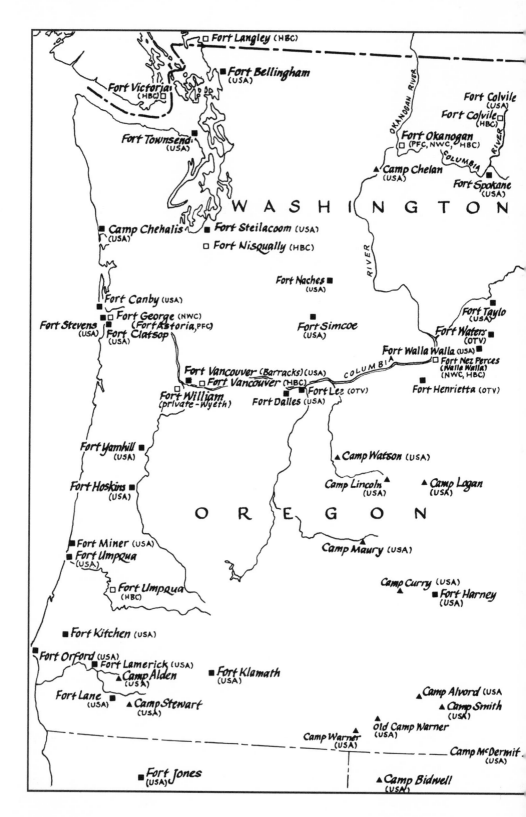

Fort Langley (HBC)

Fort Bellingham (USA)

Fort Victoria (HBC)

Fort Colvile (USA)
Fort Colvile (HBC)

Fort Townsend (USA)

Fort Okanogan (PFC, NWC, HBC)

Camp Chelan (USA)

Fort Spokane (USA)

W A S H I N G T O N

Camp Chehalis (USA)

Fort Steilacoom (USA)

Fort Nisqually (HBC)

Fort Naches (USA)

Fort Canby (USA)

Fort Taylo (USA)

Fort George (NWC)
(Fort Astoria, PFC)

Fort Simcoe (USA)

Fort Waters (OTV)

Fort Stevens (USA)

Fort Clatsop (USA)

Fort Walla Walla (USA)

Fort Nez Perces (Walla Walla) (NWC, HBC)

Fort Vancouver (Barracks) (USA)

Fort Vancouver (HBC)

COLUMBIA

Fort Lee (OTV)

Fort William (private - Wyeth)

Fort Dalles (USA)

Fort Henrietta (OTV)

Fort Yamhill (USA)

Camp Watson (USA)

Fort Hoskins (USA)

Camp Lincoln (USA)

Camp Logan (USA)

O R E G O N

Fort Miner (USA)

Camp Maury (USA)

Fort Umpqua (USA)

Camp Curry (USA)

Fort Umpqua (HBC)

Fort Harney (USA)

Fort Kitchen (USA)

Fort Orford (USA)

Fort Lamerick (USA)

Camp Alden (USA)

Fort Klamath (USA)

Fort Lane (USA)

Camp Alvord (USA)

Camp Stewart (USA)

Camp Smith (USA)

Old Camp Warner (USA)

Camp Warner (USA)

Camp McDermit (USA)

Fort Jones (USA)

Camp Bidwell (USA)

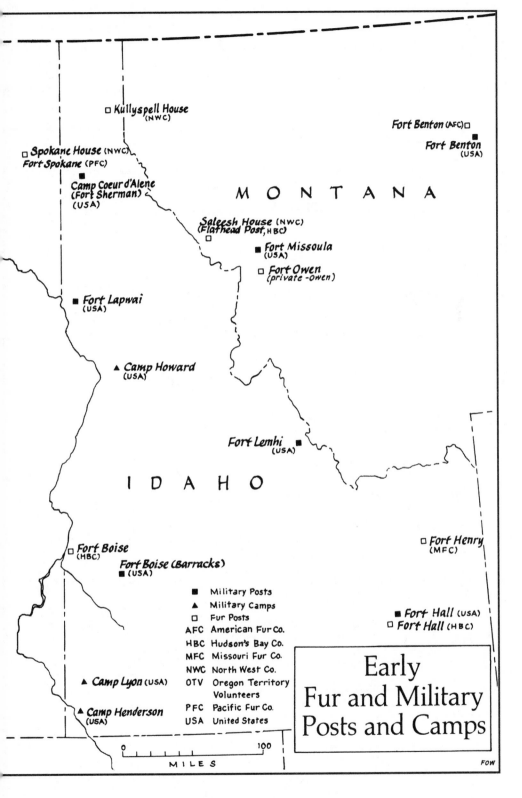

□ Kullyspell House
(NWC)

Fort Benton (AFC) □
■ Fort Benton
(USA)

□ Spokane House (NWC)
Fort Spokane (PFC)

Camp Coeur d'Alene
(Fort Sherman)
(USA) ■

M O N T A N A

Saleesh House (NWC)
(Flathead Post, HBC)
□

■ Fort Missoula
(USA)

□ Fort Owen
(private - Owen)

■ Fort Lapwai
(USA)

▲ Camp Howard
(USA)

Fort Lemhi ■
(USA)

I D A H O

□ Fort Henry
(MFC)

□ Fort Boise
(HBC)

Fort Boise (Barracks)
■ (USA)

■ Military Posts
▲ Military Camps
□ Fur Posts
AFC American Fur Co.
HBC Hudson's Bay Co.
MFC Missouri Fur Co.
NWC North West Co.
OTV Oregon Territory
Volunteers
PFC Pacific Fur Co.
USA United States

■ Fort Hall (USA)
□ Fort Hall (HBC)

▲ Camp Lyon (USA)

▲ Camp Henderson
(USA)

0   100

M I L E S

Early
Fur and Military
Posts and Camps

FOW

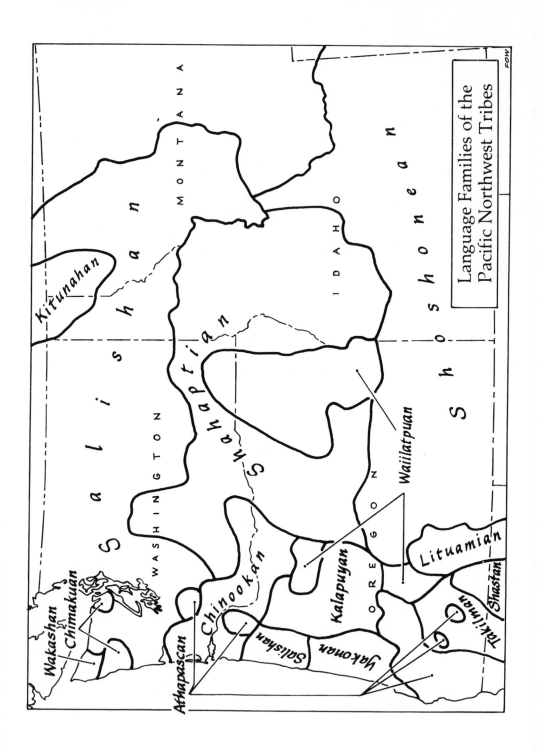

Language Families of the
Pacific Northwest Tribes

A GUIDE TO
THE INDIAN TRIBES
OF THE PACIFIC NORTHWEST

AHANTCHUYUK

(Kalapuyan)

The Ahantchuyuks were popularly known as the French Prairie Indians because that prairie lay in their homeland in the Willamette Valley north of present-day Salem, Oregon. They were also known as the Pudding River Indians for the stream that enters the Willamette River from the east about ten miles south of Oregon City. Other Indians called them the Hanchiuke. Decreased in numbers, the Ahantchuyuks were pushed from around the Molalla River (a tributary to the Willamette from the east) by the Molalas, who, according to tradition, had been driven westward across the Cascade Mountains in wars with other tribes.

Like other Kalapuyan speakers, the Ahantchuyuks were skilled hunters. They used deer-head decoys, among other devices, to catch their prey. Fur traders of John Jacob Astor's Pacific Fur Company are believed to have been the first non-Indians to enter their lands. The Ahantchuyuks were alarmed when the Astorians first came in 1812 seeking furs and venison to feed the employees at the company headquarters at Astoria on the lower Columbia River. The Natives did not wish to gather pelts for the Astorians or their successors, the Nor'Westers of the North West Company and the men of the Hudson's Bay Company, with which the North West Company later merged.

The Hudson's Bay Company operated a permanent fur trading post at Champoeg until 1825, using the Willamette Valley as a thoroughfare for its brigades traveling to and from California. On French Prairie was Chemaway (now Chemawa), one of the first permanent white settlements in the Pacific Northwest. It had received its name from former Hudson's Bay Company employees who followed Joseph Gervais, who located there in 1828. Tradition has it that a free trapper named George Montour had settled on French Prairie about fifteen years earlier. The Ahantchuyuks and other Kalapuyan speakers sold slaves to French-Canadian settlers who put these slaves to work on farms. To those settlers they also sold such goods as floormats and bed coverings.

The Ahantchuyuks witnessed the activities of the Methodist and Roman Catholic missionaries who competed for their souls when the two religious bodies established missions in their lands in 1834 and 1839. In 1841 the Ahantchuyuks were urged to send their children to the Indian Manual Labor Training School that the Methodists had opened at Chemeketa (later Salem) after they abandoned their initial Willamette mission station.

The Ahantchuyuks realized that the formation of the Oregon provisional government in 1843 presaged a flood of settlers into their homeland. Ironically, they facilitated the occupation of their territory when they signed a treaty on January 4, 1855 (10 Stat. 1143, ratified March 3, 1855), with Oregon superintendent of Indian affairs Joel Palmer, which required their removal to a reservation. Having surrendered their lands, they had little choice other than to relocate west to the

Grand Ronde Reservation, established on the west side of the Coast Range in the Yamhill River watershed.

The Ahantchuyuks numbered an estimated two hundred or more in 1780.

Suggested Readings:

> Lloyd Collins, "The Cultural Position of the Kalapuya in the Pacific Northwest," master's thesis, University of Oregon, 1951; Harold Mackey, *The Kalapuyans: A Sourcebook on the Indians of the Willamette Valley* (Salem, Ore.: Mission Mill Museum Association, 1974).

ALSEA

(Yakonan)

The name "Alsea," or "Alcea," is derived from Alsi, or Alse, the significance of which is unknown. With the Siletz and Yaquina tribes, the Alseas were sometimes called Southern Tillamooks because they had been erroneously identified in this way by Oregon superintendent of Indian affairs Joel Palmer when he negotiated a treaty with them in 1855, calling them the Alcea Band of Tillamooks. The name "Tillamook," which is sometimes applied to the Alseas, is thus a misnomer, although the Siletzes spoke a Tillamook dialect of the Salish language. Nearly a score of Alsea village sites have been identified on the Alsea River, Alsea Bay, and at nearby locations along the central Oregon coast. The name Alsea has also been assigned to a town and to an Indian reservation.

Peoples of the Yakonan linguistic stock to which the Alseas belonged totaled an estimated six thousand in 1780. The approximate number of Yakonan speakers fell sharply over the generations: to twenty-nine in 1910 and to nine in 1930.

The Alseas hunted seals and sea lions for meat and also netted salmon. Like other Indians, they coordinated food gathering with spiritual activities. Calling on animal spirits as well as other powers in nature, their shamans used their powers to promote good salmon runs. The Alseas journeyed into the Coast Range to supplement their diet with camas roots. For cooking they preferred vessels of alder and maple. Before their way of life was altered by outsiders, they flattened the heads of their infants and placed their dead in canoes at lonely points of land jutting into estuaries.

When the American trader Robert Gray sailed off the Oregon coast in 1788, the Alseas presented themselves to him and his crew in what they interpreted to be a military posture, dressed in cuirasses and allegedly shaking their spears. That they kept beyond the range of the guns on Gray's ship indicates that they possibly had had some previous unfortunate encounter with maritime visitors. By the 1820s they were trading with crewmen of the ships of the Hudson's Bay Company along their coasts.

With other western Oregon tribes, the Alseas met with Superintendent Palmer, who on August 11, 1855, negotiated a never-ratified treaty with them for their lands. Consequently, the Alseas were destined for a reservation along the coast, the southern portion of which bore their name. Nearly a century later, their descendants, along with those of other western Oregon tribes, sued the United States for compensation for lands taken from the Coast Reservation by executive order on December 21, 1865, and by an act of Congress on March 3, 1875 (Case No. 45320). On April 2, 1945, a ruling by the U.S. Court of Claims was appealed by the Justice Department to the U.S. Supreme Court, which upheld the decision of the Court of Claims on November 25, 1946. With the Siletzes, the Yaquinas, and the Neschesnes, the Alseas shared a $1,327,399.20 award. For the Alsea claims against the United States for the lands taken, *see* **Yaquina** *and* **Alsea Tribes of the Alsea Reservation.**

Suggested Readings:

> Stephen Dow Beckham, *The Indians of Western Oregon, This Land Was Theirs* (Coos Bay, Ore.: Arago Books, 1977); Livingston Farrand, "Notes on the Alsea Indians," *American Anthropologist,* 2 (1901): 239–47; Leo J. Frachtenberg, *Alsea Texts and Myths,* Smithsonian Institution, Bureau of American Ethnology Bulletin no. 67 (Washington, D.C.: Government Printing Office, 1920).

ALSEA TRIBES OF THE ALSEA RESERVATION

The Alsea Tribes of the Alsea Reservation (occasionally referred to as the Yachats Reservation) comprise Hanis and Miluk Coos, Kuitsh (Lower Umpquas), and Siuslaws. In 1859 and 1860, they were removed from their southwestern Oregon homelands to the southern part of the Coast Reservation, later called the Siletz. In 1865 the Siletz Reservation was divided into two parts by the withdrawal of a strip of land around Yaquina Bay. Those Indians in the southern part became known as the Alsea Tribes of the Alsea Reservation. For the history of their reservation, *see* **Confederated Tribes of Siletz Indians.** Most of the descendants of the Indians composing the Alsea Tribes of the Alsea Reservation live in and around Coos Bay, Oregon; *see* **Coos Tribe of Indians; Miluk Coos; Hanis Coos; Kuitsh**; *and* **Alsea.**

Suggested Readings:

> Stephen Dow Beckham, *The Indians of Western Oregon, This Land Was Theirs* (Coos Bay, Ore., Arago Books, 1977); E. A. Schwartz, "Sick Hearts: Indian Removal on the Oregon Coast, 1875–1881," *Oregon Historical Quarterly* 92, no. 3 (1991); William R. Seaburg, "An Alsea Personal Narrative and Its Historical Context," *Western Folklore* 51, nos. 3–4 (1992).

ATFALATI

(Kalapuyan)

The name "Atfalati" was sometimes shortened to Fallatah or Tfalati. The Atfalati people were also commonly known as the Tualatin or Wapato Lake Indians. They spoke the Tualatin dialect of the Tualatin-Yamhill language, one of three Kalapuyan languages. They lived in about twenty-four villages on what are now the Tualatin Plains of northwestern Oregon as well as in the hills around Forest Grove, along the shores and in the vicinity of Wapato Lake, along the north fork of the Yamhill River, and possibly at the townsite of Portland. Southwest of Portland, a town, a valley, and a river bear the name "Tualatin," which is said to mean "a land without trees" and "slow and sluggish."

As was true of other Kalapuyans, the lifestyle of the Atfalati was disrupted by non-Indians who entered their lands early in the nineteenth century. In precontact times they were fond of adornment and fancy attire and wore red feathers on their heads; long beads and bright dentalia were suspended from their pierced noses. Both sexes cut holes in their earlobes from which beads were hung. They also flattened the heads of their infants more severely than the Indians south of them did, and they raised fewer horses than the peoples east of the Cascade Mountains. Their slaves sometimes purchased their freedom with horses. The Atfalatis lived in rectangular houses containing several families. By the 1830s they had begun to clothe themselves in the manner of EuroAmericans, whose influence extended to other areas besides dress. The outsiders disturbed Indian root and hunting grounds and forced the Natives to follow EuroAmerican legal codes. Permanent Atfalati villages came to consist of little more than crude plank houses covered with dirt and bark. Contributing greatly to the changes in Atfalati culture was the decrease in their population that was precipitated by smallpox epidemics in 1782 and 1783 and by the intermittent fever that raged in the 1830s. As a consequence, the tribe was diminished in its ability to resist white encroachments.

As the Willamette watershed rapidly filled with newcomers, the Atfalatis and other Kalapuyan speakers met with American officials who were seeking to secure title to Indian lands. In a never-ratified treaty with Oregon superintendent of Indian affairs Anson Dart on April 19, 1851, the Atfalatis ceded their lands in return for a small reservation at Wapato Lake. This cession definitely reduced their homeland but it was far better than their removal east of the Cascade Mountains, as had first been demanded. Besides the reservation, they were to receive money, clothing, blankets, tools, a few rifles, and a horse for each of their headmen—Kiacut, La Medicine, and Knolah.

At the time of the treaty, the tribe numbered sixty-five persons. Under continuing pressure to relocate, they and other Kalapuyan speakers were asked to renegotiate with the government, this time with Joel Palmer, Dart's successor.

The Atfalatis were Kalapuyan speakers. The young Kalapuyan shown here was a member of one of the several tribes of his linguistic family occupying the Willamette Valley of western Oregon. The once-populous Atfalati Tribe had very few members by the middle of the nineteenth century. The sketch is attributed to A. T. Agate of the U.S. Exploring Expedition under Lt. Charles Wilkes, which was in the Pacific Northwest in the early 1840s.

Reproduced from Charles Pickering, *The Races of Men and Their Geographical Distribution* (1863). Courtesy of Harold Mackey.

Through a treaty dated January 4, 1855 (10 Stat. 1143, ratified March 3, 1855), they were to live in the Willamette Valley until a suitable reservation was designated as their permanent home. They agreed to remove to a reservation once the government provided one. From an American perspective, Palmer's benevolent influence was seen in the treaty's provisions for medical care and help for the Indians in farming and other activities. Palmer believed the Atfalatis to be one of the most influential Indian groups in the Willamette Valley. How many remained to integrate with the white community is unknown. An 1870 census cited sixty living on the Grand Ronde reservation, the permanent home assigned them by the government. The census of 1910 enumerated but forty-four persons. A publication of the Smithsonian Institution in 1914 listed only one survivor, and he was living on the Yakama Reservation in Washington. How he came to be there is not known.

Suggested Readings:

Stephen Dow Beckham, *The Indians of Western Oregon, This Land Was Theirs* (Coos Bay, Ore.: Arago Books, 1977); S. A. Clarke, *Pioneer Days of Oregon History* (Portland, Ore., J. K. Gill, 1905); Leo J. Frachtenberg, "Ethnological Researches among the Kalapuya Indians," Smithsonian Institution, *Miscellaneous Collections* 65, no. 6 (1916); John Adam Hussey, *Champoeg: Place of Transition* (Portland: Oregon Historical Society, 1967); Melville Jacobs, "Kalapuya Texts," *University of Washington Publications in Anthropology* 13 (1945); Harold Mackey, *The Kalapuyans: A Sourcebook on the Indians of the Willamette Valley* (Salem, Ore.:

Mission Mill Museum Association, 1974); W. W. Oglesby, "The Calapooyas Indians" (188?), Mss. P-A 82, Bancroft Library, University of California, Berkeley; James L. Ratcliff, "What Happened to the Kalapuya? A Study of the Depletion of Their Economic Base," *The Indian Historian* 6, no. 3 (Summer 1973).

BANNOCK

(Shoshonean of Uto-Aztecan)

The modern name "Bannock" derives from the tribe's own name of Banakwut. By early-nineteenth-century fur men and others, the Bannocks were also called "the Robbers." They were mistakenly called Snake Indians (a reference given by non-Indians to the Shoshones) because they were closely associated with the Shoshones and because they belonged to the same linguistic family. The name Bannock has been applied in Idaho to a river, a mountain range, and a county. A small community in Montana also bears the name Bannack.

The Bannock Indians were, in fact, a branch of the Northern Paiutes. They left their homelands in present-day southeastern Oregon in the eighteenth century after they had acquired horses and moved to south-central Idaho, where they associated with the Pohogwes, a branch of the Northern Shoshones, and adopted traits of horse culture. Horses enabled them to range into present-day southern Montana and western Wyoming and into the Salmon River country of Idaho. Exposed to the Indian cultures of the Great Plains, to which they traveled with their Shoshone allies to hunt buffalo, they exchanged their sagebrush and willow clothing for the skins worn by Plains Indians. They also exchanged their permanent pole-supported conical lodges of bundled grass, bark, and tule mats for skin-covered tipis. With horses at their disposal, Bannock rudimentary family units coalesced into larger groups as a means of coping with emergencies that arose on the Great Plains. Their chiefs came to be chosen for their aggressiveness and military prowess.

Estimates of the Bannock population by nineteenth-century observers are tenuous because the projections often included other allied Shoshonean peoples. In 1845 the Bannocks were said to number about 1,000 and in the late 1850s about 400 to 500. In 1870 they were placed at roughly 600 to 800; in 1901, 513; in 1910, 413 (of whom all but 50 lived in Idaho); in 1930, 415 (of whom 313 lived in Idaho); and, in 1937, 342.

In early January 1814, under a chief called The Horse, the Bannocks destroyed the Astorian fur post commanded by John Reed on the lower Boise River. The Horse led his people on other expeditions against white fur traders and their outposts until at least 1832. After that, Le Grand Coquin became the Bannocks' head chief. In 1843, during his chieftaincy, Fort Hall was constructed as a fur

Bannock woman. With the acquisition of horses, Bannocks traveled in present-day south-central Idaho and as far as the Great Plains. Bannock clothing and attire are indicative of the Plains influence.

Courtesy of the Idaho State Historical Society, Boise.

post by the American trader Nathaniel Wyeth near the mouth of the Portneuf River above Idaho's American Falls. The post was later sold to the Hudson's Bay Company. On October 14, 1863, Le Grand Coquin, with the Eastern Shoshones under their chief Washakie, signed the never-ratified treaty of Soda Springs, Idaho. The Bannock chief Tahgee (or Taghee) also touched the pen to the treaty for his people, who agreed to allow Americans to pass peacefully through their lands.

In 1864 the Bannocks were at Fort Bridger (Wyoming), where they did not receive the annuities promised them under the Soda Springs treaty. When they had agreed to that treaty they had been asked to remove to Wyoming's Wind River Reservation under Washakie. Although allied with the people of that chief, Tahgee did not want to locate his people at Wind River. Another treaty (15 Stat. 673) was signed at Fort Bridger on July 3, 1868, after a similar agreement was reached at Long Tom Creek, Idaho Territory, on August 26, 1867. The second treaty would have placed the Bannocks on a reservation, but it went unrecognized by the United States. American officials then promised the Bannocks a suitable reservation in their own country in the Portneuf and Kansas (Camas) prairie regions southeast of the Fort Hall Reservation in Idaho, at such time as they or the president deemed it wise. The same treaty set aside the Wind River Reservation for Washakie's Eastern Shoshones. Instead, by executive order on July 30, 1869, President Ulysses S. Grant assigned the Bannocks to the Fort Hall Reservation, originally established by executive order on June 14, 1867, for the Boise-Bruneau Shoshones. By the middle of the nineteenth century, these peoples from the Boise Basin in southwestern Idaho had mixed with the Northern Paiutes for mutual protection against the non-Indians who were taking their game and pasturage and other lands and were offering bounties on the scalps of local Indians. In September 1865, in council with Idaho territorial governor Caleb Lyon, the Boise-Bruneaus indicated their readiness to locate to a reservation. The area selected for them was that of Fort Hall. Compared with other Shoshonean peoples, they were relatively poor in horses. At this time the Boise-Bruneaus included 300 Boises, 850 Bruneaus, and 150 Bannocks, plus members of other tribes. They consented to remove to the Fort Hall Reservation in 1869, in part because they sought annuities like those that the Eastern Shoshones had been issued as a result of the Fort Bridger treaty. Very few Bannocks traveled to Fort Bridger to receive annuity goods, which were to be dispensed to them at that agency until an agency of their own was established.

At Fort Hall, Bannock fears of starvation were heightened when government officials urged them to abandon their off-reservation searches for buffalo and other Native foods. The tribe faced starvation when goods promised for delivery failed to arrive. Their dire situation became evident on May 30, 1878, when Indians wounded two non-Indian cattlemen in the absence of troops at Fort Hall, the military post established on May 27, 1870, about twenty-five miles from the old fur post of the same name and fifteen miles from Fort Hall Agency headquarters. The grievances of the Bannocks culminated in the Bannock-Paiute War. The first engagement occurred on June 8, 1878, when a mixed force of twenty-six volunteers and Northern Paiute scouts fought fleeing Bannocks south of the small mining town of South Mountain (Idaho). Several Bannocks were killed, including their war chief, Buffalo Horn. The Bannocks swung west from South Mountain to join some Northern Paiutes who were urged on by a subchief, the Dreamer prophet Oytes. The Bannocks and Paiutes, by then numbering about 700, included about 450 warriors. They united their forces near Juniper Lake east of Steens Mountain in southeastern Oregon. Among the assembled Indians was the peaceful Northern Paiute chief, Winnemucca, who faced Bannock threats for not joining in hostilities against the Americans. He was rescued from his predicament by his daughter, the famed Sarah Winnemucca.

Those Paiutes who had left the Malheur Reservation in southeastern Oregon to join the Bannocks fought soldiers on June 23, 1878, near Camp Curry in Silver Creek Valley, about sixty miles west of Fort Harney and thirty miles west of Burns, Oregon. After that engagement, the Bannock-Paiutes moved north. Thirty-five miles south of Pendleton, Oregon, they forced a volunteer outfit to retreat on July 4. Two days later they fought again at Willow Springs near Pendleton and on the following day, July 7, engaged volunteers and regulars at Birch Creek. From there the fighting shifted north to the Umatilla Indian Reservation, where their leader, the Northern Paiute Egan, was killed by Indians from the reservation. Some Bannocks and Paiutes were shot down by government gunboats as they attempted to escape farther north across the Columbia River. Innocent Indians of the area were also killed in the skirmish. Other Bannocks and Paiutes scattered to the south in disarray. After the war, the Bannocks assembled at Fort Hall. There they were later joined by neighboring Northern Shoshones and eventually by the Lemhi Shoshones and Bannocks after the Lemhi Reservation in east-central Idaho was abandoned in 1907.

For an account of the Bannocks on the Fort Hall Reservation, *see* **Shoshone-Bannock Tribes of the Fort Hall Reservation**.

Suggested Readings:

> George F. Brimlow, *The Bannock Indian War of 1878* (Caldwell, Ida.: Caxton Printers, 1938); Brigham D. Madsen, *The Bannock of Idaho* (Caldwell, Ida.: Caxton Printers, 1958); Omer C. Stewart, "The Question of Bannock Territory," in *Languages and Cultures of Western North America* (Pocatello: Idaho State University Press, 1970).

BOISE SHOSHONE

(See **Shoshone.***)*

BRUNEAU SHOSHONE

(See **Shoshone.***)*

BURNS PAIUTE TRIBE

The Burns Paiute Indian Colony is a sovereign tribe that originated from the homeless Northern Paiutes (Wadatikas of central and southern Oregon) who gathered in the Burns, Oregon, area where they were allotted in 1897. Their reservation was established on October 13, 1972 (Public Law 92-488), in two locations. In 1935 a 760.32-acre parcel was purchased for them under authority of Section 208 of the National Industrial Recovery Act of June 16, 1933. It lies northwest of the Burns city limits. Another parcel of approximately ten acres, known as Old Camp, is located about a half mile west of Burns. Less than twenty-five miles east of the Burns city limits, 71 scattered allotments remain of the 115 made in 1897. The allotted land totals 11,736 acres. The tribe is governed by a general council composed of all adult members, and it operates under a constitution and bylaws approved on June 13, 1968. Tribal membership stood at 223 in 1985. *See* **Northern Paiute**.

Contemporary Life and Culture: Having received federal recognition in 1968, the Burns Paiute Tribe owns and operates the 17,000-square-foot Old Camp Casino outside Burns, Oregon. The casino opened in 1998 and includes an eighty-plus-seat bingo hall, a full restaurant and lounge, a gift shop, an arcade, an events center and conference room, and an eighteen-space RV park. The tribe also operates Wadatika Health Clinic, with food distribution, child care, social services, and drug and alcohol programs. The Burns Paiutes maintain a tribal police department and a tribal court as well as a fish and wildlife department that manages the natural resources of the reservation. In total, tribal government consists of nine departments and a number of committees. The Burns Paiutes are actively retrieving their culture, sponsoring a project to gather the oral histories of elders and gathering and analyzing historical records and photographs. Tribal members also hunt and gather traditional foods. In 2009 the tribe became the first Indian community in the United States to install energy-efficient lightbulbs in and fully weatherize each of its reservation homes, part of an overall initiative by the Burns Paiutes to save money and help protect their environment.

In 2008 there were 341 enrolled members of the Burns Paiute Tribe, about a third of whom reside permanently on the reservation. The Burns Paiutes are the smallest federally recognized tribe in Oregon.

Special Events and Celebrations: The Burns Paiute Tribe has inaugurated an annual Mother's Day Powwow, and each year the Reservation Day Festival and Powwow is celebrated on October 13 in recognition of the day the land held in trust for the tribe became a reservation. October 13 is considered a Burns Paiute tribal holiday.

This Calapooya was sketched by A. T. Agate of the expedition led by Lt. Charles Wilkes in the Pacific Northwest in the early 1840s. He is wearing an elkskin robe and holding a bow and quiver made of sealskin. His cap is foxskin with the ears attached.

Reproduced from Charles W. Wilkes, U.S. Navy, *Narratives of the United States Exploring Expedition during the Years 1838, 1839, 1840, 1841, 1842* (Philadelphia: Lee and Blanchard, 1845), volume 5.

CALAPOOYA

(Kalapuyan)

The Calapooyas lived in present-day west-central Oregon. They spoke Central Kalapuyan, one of three Kalapuyan languages that shared common elements with the Takilman linguistic family. The Calapooya tribe and other Kalapuyan speakers were said to have migrated in precontact times from the south into the Willamette Valley, displacing the valley's residents identified by some early non-Indian observers as the Multnomahs, from an early name for the Willamette River. The five subdivisions of the Calapooyas were located on the headwaters of the Willamette River, on the Middle and West forks of its tributary, the McKenzie, and at the confluence of the Willamette and McKenzie rivers near present-day

Eugene, Oregon. From March to May 1812, the Astorian Donald McKenzie, for whom the river is named, explored the homelands of the Calapooyas in search of furs. Fur traders subsequently established a post at or near the mouth of the McKenzie; the post is often referred to as "the McKay old house." Geographical features bearing the tribal name are the Calapooya River on the north near present-day Brownsville, Oregon; Calapooya Creek, an affluent of the Umpqua River in southwestern Oregon; and the Calapooya Mountains in that area.

Like other Willamette Valley Indians, the Calapooyas lived by fishing, hunting, and gathering. Occasionally their seasonal rounds were interrupted, as were those of other Kalapuyan speakers, by the incursion of other Indians. Klamaths often traveled over the Calapooya Mountains to plunder and capture women.

In 1849 Oregon territorial governor Joseph Lane found that the Calapooya tribe had been reduced to only sixty members, and those sixty were living poorly. *See* **Atfalati**. Their ranks had been thinned primarily by diseases such as smallpox, which struck in the 1780s, and the intermittent fever of the 1830s.

The Calapooyas were among those involved in the January 9, 1855, treaty (10 Stat. 1143, ratified March 3, 1855). By its terms they were removed to the Grand Ronde Reservation. The move did not check their population decline nor that of other Kalapuyans sent there. In 1870 the Calapooyas numbered only forty-two. In 1880 the total of all Kalapuyan speakers on the Grand Ronde Reservation was 351; in 1890, 164; and in 1905, 130. In 1910 there were but 5 Calapooyas out of the total of 106 Kalapuyan speakers on the Grand Ronde, and the latter figure was reduced to 45 by 1930. The government allowed various peoples on the Grand Ronde Reservation to maintain their tribal identities in enclavelike settlements and their census was reported separately. In time, that segregation broke down, and by August 13, 1954, when the reservation was dissolved, the remnants of the former Kalapuyan speakers had lost much of their tribal identities. There are no Kalapuyan speakers today.

Suggested Readings:

Stephen Dow Beckham, *The Indians of Western Oregon, This Land Was Theirs* (Coos Bay, Ore.: Arago Books, 1977); S. A. Clarke, *Pioneer Days of Oregon History* (Portland, Ore., J. K. Gill, 1905); Leo J. Frachtenberg, "Ethnological Researches among the Kalapuya Indians," Smithsonian Institution, *Miscellaneous Collections* 65, no. 6 (1916); John Adam Hussey, *Champoeg: Place of Transition* (Portland: Oregon Historical Society, 1964); Melville Jacobs, "Kalapuya Texts," *University of Washington Publications in Anthropology* 11 (1945), pt. 3; Harold Mackey, *The Kalapuyans: A Sourcebook on the Indians of the Willamette Valley* (Salem, Ore.: Mission Mill Museum Association, 1974); W. W. Oglesby, "The Calapooyas Indians" (188?), Mss. P-A 82, Bancroft Library, University of California, Berkeley; James L. Ratcliff, "What Happened to the Kalapuya? A Study of the Depletion of Their Economic Base," *The Indian Historian* 6, no. 3 (Summer 1973).

CASCADE INDIANS

(See **Watlala.***)*

CATHLAMET

(Upper Chinookan Division of Chinookan)

The Cathlamets (or Kathlamets) were the westernmost speakers of the Upper Chinookan linguistic stock whose language was spoken from present-day Rainier, Oregon, down the Columbia River to the Cathlamet homelands. These lands lay on the south bank of the Columbia upstream from Tongue Point (about thirteen miles from the Pacific Ocean near Astoria, Oregon) to the vicinity of Puget Island. They also claimed lands on the Columbia's north bank from the mouth of Grays Bay (opposite Tongue Point) upstream to just beyond Oak Point. Despite the differences in languages, the Cathlamets were culturally similar to Lower Chinookan peoples. Around 1810 Cathlamet villagers traveled north across the Columbia to settle in a village of the Wahkiakums, who were Upper Chinookan linguistically but, like the Cathlamets, closely related culturally to Lower Chinookan peoples. Around the middle of the nineteenth century, some Cathlamets were still living with the Wahkiakums at Grays Bay under a Chief Selawish. Early fur men believed the Cathlamets had belonged among the Chinooks proper and with their closely related Chinook neighbors, the Clatsops, before splintering into their own villages sometime around the middle of the nineteenth century. The Astorian trader Ross Cox considered the Cathlamets who traded at Fort Astoria the most "tranquil" of the tribes around the post, which was established in 1811. In 1810 the American Winship brothers, because of alleged unfriendly Indians and high Columbia waters, had failed to establish a trading post near the Cathlamet lands.

Mrs. Wilson of the Cathlamet Tribe of the lower Columbia River, ca.1900. The image reveals evidence of head-flattening, a practice among the aristocracy of lower Columbia River peoples.

Courtesy of the Smithsonian Institution.

In a treaty dated August 9, 1851, the Cathlamets ceded to the United States the lands on which stood Fort Astoria and its British replacement, Fort George, and lands about forty miles upstream and about twenty miles to the south. In exchange, they received money, clothing, and other items and retained two small islands in the Columbia River. On August 24, 1912, the U.S. Court of Claims awarded the tribe's descendants $7,000 for loss of their aboriginal lands (37 Stat. 518). The Wahkiakums were awarded the same amount. Nonreservation descendants of Cathlamets shared in a November 4, 1971, award to the Chinook Nation (*see* **Chinook**).

The Cathlamets were estimated to number 450 in 1780. The American explorers Meriwether Lewis and William Clark counted 300 in 1805–1806. By 1849 the tribe had shrunk to 58, according to the figures given by Oregon territorial governor Joseph Lane. Since they were contemporaries of the Cathlamets whose numbers they recorded, Lewis and Clark and Governor Lane would have reported figures less tenuous than those of the ethnologist James Mooney, who published the 1780 Cathlamet population in 1928. Largely because of disease and dispersal, the Cathlamets no longer have a tribal identity.

Suggested Readings:

> Franz Boas, *Kathlamet Texts,* Smithsonian Institution, Bureau of American Ethnology Bulletin no. 26 (Washington, D.C., 1901); Melville Jacobs, "Historic Perspectives in Indian Languages of Oregon and Washington," *Pacific Northwest Quarterly* 28, no. 1 (January 1937); Albert Buell Lewis, *Tribes of the Columbia Valley and the Coast of Washington and Oregon,* Memoirs of the American Anthropological Association, vol. 2, pt. 2 (Lancaster, Pa.,1906); Fred Lockley, *History of the Columbia River Valley from The Dalles to the Sea* (Chicago: S. J. Clark Publishing, 1928); Thomas Nelson Strong, *Cathlamet on the Columbia* (Portland, Ore.: Binfords and Mort, 1906).

CATHLAPOTLE

(Upper Chinookan Division of Chinookan)

People of the Cathlapotle River

The Cathlapotles were one of several early peoples speaking the Clackamas dialect of the Upper Chinookan linguistic stock. The tribal name means "people of the Cathlapotle River." The river, now called the Lewis, is a tributary entering the Columbia near the town of Woodland, Washington, on Interstate 5. The main Cathlapotle village of Nahpooitle (or Nohpooitle) lay at the mouth of the Lewis River. Another Cathlapotle village, called Wakanasisi, was perhaps on the Columbia's north bank opposite the mouth of the Willamette River. In 1792 Lt. William Broughton, serving with the British expedition under Capt. George Vancouver, found the Cathlapotles with iron battle-axes and copper swords. Lewis and Clark noted some unusual iron swords among them in 1805–1806. The explorers estimated the tribe's population at nine hundred people, living in fourteen large wooden houses. The population had been projected at thirteen hundred in 1780. The reduction in population that continued during the nineteenth century was probably due mostly to plagues. An article appearing in the August 8, 1915, issue of the *Portland Oregonian* told of a Cathlapotle woman, Wahlla-Luk Umtux, who was among the first of her area to receive Christian baptism at Fort Vancouver. Bearing a new name, Catherine Cosike, she was one of not more than a dozen of her people remaining in 1915. Today the descendants of the Cathlapotles have been absorbed into other tribes. *See also* **Clackamas**.

CAYUSE

(Waiilatpuan)

Early-nineteenth-century French-Canadian fur men called the Cayuses the *cailloux,* a French word for stones or rocks. The name may possibly have derived from the character of the area that the tribe inhabited, or it may have been a gallicized rendering of the name by which they called themselves, which meant "superior people." Early non-Indians described them as "proud and haughty." One early American traveler called them an "imperial tribe." Closely related to the Nez Perces culturally and geographically, they eventually adopted the Nez Perce language. Like the Nez Perces, they were noted for their horse culture. Originally the Cayuses had lived in what is now north-central Oregon. After moving away from their linguistically related neighbors, the non-horse-oriented Molalas, they eventually occupied a new homeland on the upper reaches of the Walla Walla, Umatilla, and Grande Ronde rivers of present-day Oregon and Washington. Their lands stretched westward from the Blue Mountains to the John Day River, a tributary of the Columbia. Their affiliation with the Molalas has been disputed by some scholars. It was during their expansion that they abutted Nez Perce lands.

The Cayuse horse, sturdy and standing some thirteen hands high, was named for the tribe. According to tradition, the Cayuses received their first horses from the Shoshones. The horses, grazing on the lush grassy Cayuse prairielands, enabled their masters to ride down on and intimidate nearby sedentary peoples on the Columbia River. The Cayuses would force their adversaries to perform menial tasks and fish for them. With horses, the Cayuses were able to journey as far east as the Great Plains to trade and hunt. Like other Columbia Plateau peoples, they acquired cultural elements of the Plains tribes. Horses remained among the

Cayuse warriors mounted on their cayuses. The name of the breed of horse attests to the equestrian skills of the Cayuse. The Cayuses were described as an "imperial tribe" by early white travelers. The Umatilla Reservation was carved out of their lands in northeastern Oregon.

Courtesy of the Smithsonian Institution.

most prized of possessions, and it was common for warriors to be buried with their favorite mounts. Besides the Cayuse horse, a small station on the Union Pacific Railway east of Pendleton, Oregon, bears the tribal name as do many other landmarks, such as a mountain pass in Washington State.

Fur men entering Cayuse country in the early nineteenth century failed to make fur gatherers of these Indians. In 1818 personnel of the North West Company built Fort Nez Perces (later Fort Walla Walla) in the lands of the Walla Wallas, who were neighbors of the Cayuses. From that fort, men of the Hudson's Bay Company (with which the North West Company merged in 1821) sought the Cayuses' goodwill, as had the Nor'Westers, in traversing Cayuse lands and tapping the furs of the rich Snake River country on the east. Previously, at the urging of Nor'Wester officials, the Cayuses had effected a tenuous peace with enemy tribes on the upper Snake River whose furs the British sought to collect before competing Americans took them.

The Cayuse reputation among non-Indians became tarnished after their November 29, 1847, "massacre" of immigrants and missionaries of the American

Board of Commissioners for Foreign Missions, including the Reverend Marcus Whitman and his wife, Narcissa, at their Waiilatpu Mission on Cayuse lands near present-day Walla Walla, Washington. Today the massacre site is a national monument where life and death at the mission are depicted. The underlying causes of the massacre included disputes between the Cayuses and their missionaries over ownership of mission lands, Cayuse dissatisfaction at immigrants traversing their lands in the Umatilla and Walla Walla valleys, Cayuse suspicions that these travelers were carrying measles (which broke out among both the immigrants and the Cayuses immediately before the massacre), the Cayuse practice of killing doctors who failed to cure patients (Whitman was a doctor), and finally Cayuse agitation among Walla Walla Valley Indians of mixed heritage, some of whom assisted in the attack. The ensuing Cayuse War of 1848 culminated in the hanging in Oregon City on June 3, 1850, of five Cayuses whom officials of the Oregon provisional and territorial governments deemed guilty. The massacre ended the American Board's mission work among the Cayuses and other interior tribes. Roman Catholic missionaries continued ministering to Indians of the area with varying degrees of success.

Because of losses from war and disease and the inroads of Americans trying to impose their laws on them, the Cayuses, despite their frustrations and reservations, signed a treaty on June 9, 1855 (12 Stat. 945), which was ratified March 8, 1859, and proclaimed April 1, 1859. According to its terms, they submitted to the United States and were to live on a reservation to be established in their homeland. Four months later, however, some Cayuses joined an Indian confederation in fighting the Yakama War of 1855–56 against American volunteer and regular army forces. The Cayuses vented less anger toward the few remaining British with whose traders they remained on speaking terms, even tolerating British interference in the choice of their headmen. Suffering much and broken in spirit after their defeats in war, the Cayuses settled on the Umatilla Reservation with the Umatillas and the Walla Wallas.

In 1780 the Cayuses had numbered about 500. In 1904 there were 404 tribespeople; in 1923, 337; and, in 1937, 370. The merging of Cayuses with Umatillas, Walla Wallas, and Nez Perces continued into the twentieth century. Today there are no speakers of the original Waiilatpuan language. As a final blow to the Cayuses, settlers and officials rounded up and sold many of their horses and converted the lands on which these animals once grazed into wheat farms. *See also* **Confederated Tribes of the Umatilla Reservation.**

Suggested Readings:

Albert S. Gatschet, "The Molale Tribe Raided by the Cayuses," ms. no. 2029, National Anthropological Archives Collection, Smithsonian Institution, Washington, D.C.; Robert H. Ruby and John A. Brown, *The Cayuse Indians: Imperial Tribesmen of Old Oregon* (Norman: University of Oklahoma Press, 1972, 2005); Theodore Stern, Martin Schmitt, and Alphonse F. Halfmoon, "A Cayuse-Nez Percé Sketchbook," *Oregon Historical Quarterly* 81, no. 4 (Winter 1980).

CHASTACOSTA

(Athabaskan)

The name "Chastacosta" (or Shasta Scoton) derives from the tribe's name for themselves. The Chastacostas belonged to a group known as the Coast Rogues. Like other Pacific Coast Athabaskan speakers, they perhaps migrated into the region from the north at some remote time. They lived in southwestern Oregon on the lower course of the Illinois River, a tributary of the Rogue River. They also lived on both sides of the Rogue above its confluence with the Illinois and upstream on the Rogue's north bank as far as the mouth of the Applegate River. They were among those who met with Oregon superintendent of Indian affairs Anson Dart in 1851. On November 18, 1854, one or two bands of Chastacostas, along with the Grave Creek Umpquas, signed a never-ratified treaty with Oregon superintendent of Indian affairs Joel Palmer. Under its terms they agreed to go to a temporary reservation at Table Rock on the upper Rogue River until removed to a permanent reservation. Early in 1856 they joined other Athabaskan speakers in attempting to drive settlers from their lands. After futile fighting that summer, 153 Chastacostas (53 men, 61 women, 23 boys, and 16 girls) were removed northward to the Coast Reservation (later called the Siletz). Their attrition at that place, like that of the other Indians there, was marked. They and ten other Athabaskan tribes had been estimated to number 5,600 in 1780. In 1856 there were only 153 Chastacostas and in 1937 just 30, a population reduced even further by 1950.

Suggested Readings:

> Frederick Webb Hodge, ed., *Handbook of Indians North of Mexico,* pt. 1 (Washington, D.C.: Government Printing Office, 1907).

George Harvey, a headman of the Chastacostas, belonged to the group known as the Coast Rogues. In 1856 his people were involved in the later stages of the Rogue wars in southwestern Oregon.

Courtesy of the Smithsonian Institution.

CHEHALIS

(See **Lower Chehalis; Kwaiailk;** *and* **Confederated Tribes of the Chehalis Reservation.***)*

CHELAMELA

(Kalapuyan)

The Chelamelas, popularly known as Long Tom Indians, lived in the watershed of the Long Tom River, a Willamette River tributary west of present-day Eugene, Oregon. The name "Long Tom" is said to be a modification of the Native word *lungtumler.* Like other Kalapuyan speakers, the Chelamelas came into contact with white fur traders early in the nineteenth century. The traders considered them indolent because of their unwillingness to abandon their Native economy of hunting, fishing, and gathering in order to collect furs. The Chelamelas also suffered from diseases as they encountered missionaries, settlers, and other outsiders. They had already been pressured by tribes such as the Klickitats, who strengthened their position in the Willamette Valley after the ravages of the intermittent fever. They had encountered Alseas and others raiding eastward from the Pacific Coast. Meanwhile, horse-riding Nez Perces and Cayuses from east of the Cascade Mountains entered the Willamette Valley on animal hunts. Under provisions of the January 4, 1855, treaty with government agents (10 Stat. 1143, ratified March 3, 1855), the Chelamela remnant moved from its ancestral homeland to the Grand Ronde Reservation.

Suggested Readings:

Stephen Dow Beckham, *The Indians of Western Oregon, This Land Was Theirs* (Coos Bay, Ore.: Arago Books, 1977).

CHELAN

(Interior Division, Salishan)

The Chelans lived in north-central Washington east of the Cascade Mountains in the vicinity of the southern end of Lake Chelan. They spoke the Wenatchi dialect of the Interior Salishan language. The name "Chelan" has been given not only to the lake but also to a mountain range, a county in north-central Washington, a short river tumbling from the lake to the Columbia River, and the

Peter Wapato, whose father, John Wapato, fled from the Columbia River to nearby Lake Chelan in north-central Washington at the time of the great earthquake of 1872. The Wapato family came to be identified as Chelan Indians. They had a record of friendship with the non-Indians who settled in the vicinity of Lake Chelan.

Courtesy of the North Central Washington Museum Association, Wenatchee.

towns of Chelan on the lake and Chelan Falls on the Columbia (both are on or near U.S. Highway 97). The early-nineteenth-century fur trader Alexander Ross mentioned the "Tsill-anes" in his writings and grouped them with other area tribes as the "Oakinacken nation." The Chelans were known to have paddled about fifty miles to the upper end of Lake Chelan from which they crossed over a poor, steep trail to the summit of the Cascade Mountains and down the Skagit River, an affluent of Puget Sound. There they traded with the Indians of the area. According to Chelan tradition, their people in early times engaged in confrontations with tribes west of the Cascade Mountains.

Some geologists believe that the epicenter of the large earthquake of November 14, 1872, was in the Chelan area and northward. Indians in its path were frightened in the belief that the Earth Mother was angry with them. Roman Catholic priests utilized the quake to intensify their missionary efforts among the Chelans. A defender of the Native religion, Chelan chief Nmosize (Innomoseecha Bill), burned down a mission house that the Reverend Alexander Diomedi, S.J., had built during the chief's absence. Shortly thereafter, however, the Indians constructed a Catholic church along the lake near the present-day town of Manson. Chief Nmosize was greatly displeased with the behavior of white men, especially the soldiers of Camp Chelan, established in 1880 at the lower end of Lake Chelan. That post was built to oversee the Moses, or Columbia, Reservation (established April 19, 1879), which extended from the lake north to the Canadian border.

Under the terms of the Chief Moses Agreement of July 7, 1883 (approved July 4, 1884), several Chelans took up allotments around the lake and at other places on the southern end of the Moses Reservation. Under the leadership of Long Jim, about forty or fifty Chelans living on the northern shore of the lake, on the Chelan River, and at its mouth refused allotments, insisting that they were a people separate from those of Chief Moses. During further conflict between these Indians and homesteaders who claimed lands on the failure of Indians to take allotments under the Moses Agreement, three Chelans in 1890 were sent to the guardhouse on the Colville Reservation. Tensions continued over several years, reaching the U.S. Supreme Court in the case of *Starr* v. *Long Jim* (227 U.S. 613), which was ruled in favor of the settlers.

The Chelans were said to have been a numerous people in the eighteenth century, but by 1870, with the neighboring Methows and Entiats (with whom they were lumped by government officials) they had been reduced to about three hundred. During a threatened Indian outbreak in 1879, the March 27 *Portland Oregonian* stated that the Chelans could muster between fifty and a hundred warriors. Then and thereafter the Chelans, like Long Jim, fought non-Indians only in the courts. Chelan descendants live primarily in the Chelan area and in other parts of north-central Washington, including the Colville Reservation. *See also* **Confederated Tribes of the Colville Reservation.**

CHEPENAFA

(Kalapuyan)

The Chepenafas were popularly known as the Mary's River Indians because of their location at the forks of Saint Mary's Creek near present-day Corvallis, Oregon. They spoke the Mary's River dialect of the central Kalapuyan language. Some ethnologists have classified them as a subdivision of the Luckiamute Indians, another Kalapuyan-speaking people.

Like other residents of the Willamette watershed, the Chepenafas lived in harmony with their environment before the coming of settlers. Their male youths sought spirit powers by fasting five days and nights and swimming in a lake. For routine travel the Chepenafas propelled dugout canoes with long poles and decorated wooden paddles. Wood, which is abundant in their country, also figured in their ceremonials. For example, they suspended moss- and hide-covered drumsticks and boards from their lodge roofs, which they beat with fire-hardened clubs to produce humming sounds. Like other Indians between the Rogue River Valley and the mouth of the Columbia River on the north, they played a game of shinny that was much like field hockey. Pitting bands against each other, the game took several days to play amid much wagering.

Much Chepenafa culture was disrupted by non-Indians, especially settlers who began occupying their lands in the 1830s. Weakened by starvation and diseases

William Hartless, a Chepenafa, ca. 1890. The Chepenafas were unable to stem the tide of settlers into their homelands that began in the 1830s. After enduring diseases and then incursions not only by non-Indians but also by more powerful Indian tribes, the Chepenafa tribal remnant removed to the Grand Ronde Reservation in 1856.

Authors' collections.

such as smallpox and the intermittent fever of the 1830s, the Chepenafas were unable to prevent non-Indian incursions. The few Chepenafas who remained were included in the January 4, 1855, treaty with the United States (10 Stat. 1143, ratified March 3, 1855), which provided for their removal to a reservation. With other Kalapuyan speakers, they ceded their lands in the Willamette Valley to go to the Grand Ronde Reservation in 1856.

In 1870 they numbered forty-nine on that reservation and in 1910 only twenty-four.

Suggested Readings:

Stephen Dow Beckham, *The Indians of Western Oregon, This Land Was Theirs* (Coos Bay, Ore.: Arago Books, 1977); Albert Gatschet, "The Kalapuya People," *Journal of American Folklore* 12 (1899): 212–14; Harold Mackay, *The Kalapuyans: A Sourcebook on the Indians of the Willamette Valley* (Salem, Ore.: Mission Mill Museum Association, 1974).

CHETCO

(Athabaskan)

The Chetcos were among those Indians referred to as the Coast Rogues. The name "Chetco," or Cheti as they called themselves, meant "close to the mouth of the stream" and refers possibly to the tribe's forty-two-house village that lay at the mouth of the Chetco River where it enters the Pacific Ocean in extreme southwestern Oregon. The Chetcos also lived along the Winchuck River, another Pacific Ocean affluent. Their territory also included an undefined region along

Seafoods were important to the Chetcos, as demonstrated by this woman of
southwestern Oregon, who was photographed in the late twentieth century
as she gathered oysters. The basket
into which she placed the oysters and
the strap attaching it to her head were
skillfully fashioned by Chetco women.

Courtesy of the Lincoln County Historical
Society, Newport, Ore.

the coast north of the Chetco River, probably extending to Cape Farrelo. Except for those in the narrow Chetco River valley, their settlements were confined
mainly to the coast. They were closely allied with the Tolowas, a tribe of Athabaskan stock who lived in extreme northwestern California at Crescent Bay, Lake
Earl, and the Smith River. Like other Athabaskan speakers of the Pacific Coast,
the Chetcos' ancestors entered that region at some remote time, possibly from
the north.

The Chetcos lived in wood-plank houses with dirt floors and traveled in shallow Klamath-type canoes. Their country abounded in game, berries, acorns, surf
fish, molluscs, and sea mammals. They trapped deer in deep pitfalls. Like the
Tolowas, Chetco women were skilled at making baskets, which they decorated
with porcupine quills. Among their items of personal adornment were beads of
Olivella. As non-Indians increasingly traveled across their lands, the Chetcos
supplemented their livelihood by ferrying travelers across the Chetco River. Later they lost their ferrying business to settlers. Among outsiders they had a reputation for unfriendliness as early as 1828, when they abandoned several lodges at
the appearance of the north-bound Jedediah Smith party.

American settlers filed 7,437 claims on 320-acre parcels in western Oregon
Territory under the Donation Land Act (passed by Congress on September 29,
1850), appropriating 2.5 million acres of the Indian land base. Among those
claims was one filed by A. F. Miller on the site of the principal Chetco village. In
1853, after Miller and other non-Indians had persuaded the Indians to surrender

their arms, they laid siege to the village, killing twelve men and burning houses in which two other Chetcos died. In revenge, on March 29, 1856, at the mouth of the Chetco River, about sixty Chetcos attacked Lt. E. O. C. Ord and his troops, who were en route to Crescent City, California. A soldier was killed and three were wounded. After losing six of their tribe in that engagement, the Chetcos were forced from the area. Like other Coast Rogue Athabaskan speakers, the Chetcos moved up the Rogue River to help its Indians in their futile war against the Americans. Afterwards, they were removed to the Grand Ronde Reservation and then to the Coast Reservation (later called the Siletz).

Chetcos were among the Indians with whom Oregon superintendent of Indian affairs Anson Dart treated for their lands in council at Port Orford in 1851. The Chetcos also negotiated with Oregon superintendent of Indian affairs Joel Palmer in 1855. Neither treaty was ratified. After skirmishing with non-Indians between 1852 and 1856, the stubbornly resisting Chetcos were the last Indians of southwestern Oregon to surrender.

With certain western Oregon tribes, the Chetcos were plaintiffs in a case (No. 45230) tried in the U.S. Court of Claims in which the tribe sued for the loss of aboriginally owned lands that it estimated at 433,150 acres. They received an award but appealed to the U.S. Supreme Court. On November 25, 1946, that body upheld an April 2, 1945, ruling of the Court of Claims. The tribe was awarded $489,085.20 for recovery of the Coast Reservation lands that the Chetcos had lost by executive order on December 21, 1865, and by act of Congress on March 3, 1875.

In 1854 the Chetcos numbered 241, having suffered losses not only in wars but also from diseases. In 1861 there were 262 members of the tribe; in 1877, 63; and, in 1910, only 9. In 1960 fewer than five Chetco speakers remained. Their descendants try to retain their tribal heritage. For a history of the Chetcos on their reservation, *see* **Yaquina.**

Suggested Readings:

Stephen Dow Beckham, *The Indians of Western Oregon, This Land Was Theirs* (Coos Bay, Ore.: Arago Books, 1977); Joel Berreman, *Chetco Archaeology: A Report of the Lone Ranch Creek Shell Mound on the Coast of Southern Oregon,* American Anthropological Association, General Series in Anthropology, no. 11 (Menasha, Wis.: George Banta Publishing Co., 1944).

CHILLUCKITTEQUAW

(Upper Chinookan Division of Chinookan)

The Chilluckittequaws were Upper Chinookans living along the Columbia River, which divided them into two bands—those of the White Salmon estuary on the north and those of the Hood River estuary on the south.

The Chilluckittequaw population in 1780 was estimated at 3,000. Their reduction to an estimated 2,200 in 1805–1806 (of whom 1,400 were north-shore bands and 800 were Smock-shops of the south shore) suggests the prevalence of disease among them, especially the smallpox plague of 1782–83. Their Native name is not perpetuated in place-names. Non-Indians assigned to the northern division the name "White Salmon," which is also the name of a town and a river. A Chilluckittequaw remnant lived near White Salmon, Washington, until 1880 when its members removed downstream to The Cascades of the Columbia, where a few were still living in 1895. A tribal remnant was also found on the Yakama Reservation (*see* **Wishram**).

The Chilluckittequaws on the Columbia's north bank were the Woocksockwilliacums, or White Salmons. They comprised several bands whose homelands were in what are today Washington's Klickitat and Skamania counties, an area extending roughly from ten miles below The Dalles west to the White Salmon River. They were not relegated to the shores of the Columbia, for at least one of their important villages was about five miles south of the mouth of Hood River.

The Chilluckittequaws of the Columbia's south bank were called Hood Rivers. Lewis and Clark called them the Smock-shops. The photographer and observer of American Indians, Edward S. Curtis, referred to them as the Ninuhltidihs. Ethnologist James Mooney identified them as the Kwikwuilits. For the most part, the southern Chilluckittequaws lived in permanent fishing villages on the Columbia, where between May and October they caught several species of salmon. Like other Upper Chinookan peoples, they received payment from the local users of fishing stations that were passed down according to inheritance customs. The Chilluckittequaws had first use of the stations. Next were users from neighboring villages and then those from more distant points. Individuals and family groups were free to come and go from village to village within their own ethnic groups. Some would sometimes choose to remain at a village. Villages tended to be autonomous. Tribal political organization was minimal.

The Hood River Chilluckittequaws traded freely with the Shahaptian-speaking Tenino tribe. The association between the two peoples was perhaps strengthened by mutual fear of their ancient enemy, the Northern Paiutes. In time, the Hood Rivers became absorbed by and were grouped with the Wascos, another Upper Chinookan people. The few Hood Rivers remaining in the middle of the nineteenth century treated with Oregon superintendent of Indian affairs Joel Palmer on June 25, 1855. By their treaty they yielded their lands for a promised reservation. In that year they numbered eighty members. Chief Wallachin, who claimed leadership over the scattered bands that migrated back and forth across the Columbia between the Hood and Salmon rivers and downstream to The Cascades, declined to sign the treaty, saying, "I have said that I would not sell my country and I have but one talk." Most descendants of the Hood Rivers live on the Warm Springs Reservation in north-central Oregon.

Suggested Readings:

Leslie Spier and Edward Sapir, "Wishram Ethnography," *University of Washington Publications in Anthropology* 3, no. 3 (1930); Robert H. Suphan, "Ethnological Report on the Wasco and Tenino Indians," in *Oregon Indians,* vol. 2 (New York: Garland Publishing, 1974).

CHIMAKUM

(Chimakuan)

According to tribal tradition the Chimakums were a remnant of a Quileute band who had fled the Pacific Coast from a high tide that took four days to ebb. That they were of the same linguistic stock as the Quileutes lends credence to that tradition. In any case, they migrated to an area around the southern shores of the Strait of Juan de Fuca and the western shores of Puget Sound near the present-day towns of Port Townsend, Discovery Bay, Port Hadlock, Port Ludlow, and Chimacum, Washington. The latter community is located near U.S. Highway 101. A creek also bears the name "Chimakum." One of their villages, Tsetsibus, near Port Hadlock, was an important gathering place for area residents.

The Chimakums developed a reputation as an aggressive people. Shortly before 1790 they were engaging tribes such as the Snohomish, Snoqualmies, Clallams, Makahs, and Nitinats of Canada. Around 1850 they fought the Suquamish. By that time, the Chimakum population had fallen from four hundred to less than one hundred. Their headman, known as Kulkakhan, or General Pierce, was a signatory to the Point-No-Point Treaty of 1855 under which they were to remove to the Skokomish Reservation on the southern end of Hood Canal. There was, however, no viable Chimakum relocation to that place because of population decline caused by warfare and disease as well as by their absorption among the Clallams, most of whom refused to remove to the Skokomish Reservation. In 1890 the anthropologist Franz Boas found but three speakers of the Chimakum language, and they articulated it imperfectly. Yet some descendants still identify themselves as Chimakums.

This Chimakum is a descendant of a band who, according to tradition, fled the Pacific Coast from a high tide to settle on the eastern side of Washington's Olympic Peninsula. Although the Chimakums are now absorbed into the populations of other tribes, some American Indians still trace their ancestry back to the original Chimakum tribe.

Photograph by Edward S. Curtis from Curtis's *The North American Indian* (1907–1930), vol. 9.

Suggested Readings:

Franz Boas, "Notes on the Chemakum Language," *American Anthropologist* 5 (January 1892); Edward S. Curtis, *The North American Indian* (1912; New York, 1970), vol. 9; Myron Eells, *The Twana, Chemakum, and Klallam Indians of Washington Territory* (1889; Seattle: Shorey Book Store, 1971).

CHINOOK

(Lower Chinookan Division of Chinookan)

The Lower Chinooks, or Chinooks proper, were given their name by the Chehalis Indians, their Salish-speaking neighbors on the north. The Chinooks spoke the Lower Chinookan dialect of the Chinookan language and lived in what is now Washington State on the north bank of the Columbia River. Their lands stretched from the Columbia estuary to Willapa (Shoalwater) Bay on the Pacific Ocean. Some anthropologists believe that in early times Chinookan peoples had drifted down the Columbia River, making a wedge between the Salish peoples at the mouth of that river. Culturally, the Chinooks exhibited a few of the patterns of the Columbia Plateau peoples on the east as well as the patterns of peoples of the Northwest Coast.

The mouth of the Columbia River was, of course, an important entry point to the Pacific Northwest hinterland. In their villages there, the Chinooks traded

The Chinook Tribe traded extensively in their lands on the north
bank of the Columbia River near its
mouth. Much of the trading with
non-Indians was done by women.
The head of this woman reveals
head-flattening applied in infancy, a
symbol of Chinook aristocracy.

Photograph by Edward S. Curtis, ca.
1900, from Curtis's *The North American
Indian* (1907–1930), vol. 9.

with both Indians and non-Indians.
From the latter, they contracted diseases, especially those venereal in nature, and obtained liquor, which also
reduced their population.

In precontact times the Chinooks' strategic location had enabled them to maintain a mercantile hold over their homeland, but with the advent of the American and European land- and sea-based traders in the late eighteenth and early
nineteenth centuries, the economic patterns and prominence of the Chinooks
shifted. The EuroAmericans traded manufactured goods for Indian items such
as the elkhide cuirasses known as *clamons*. Then the EuroAmericans traded the
Columbia River articles to tribes on the upper northwest coast for sea otter pelts,
which they in turn traded in China for products such as teas and silks. Through
this trading the status of Chinook women evolved as they played a more active
role in interacting with white traders.

The Chinook name has been applied to a variety of features, including a
wind, a salmon, a trade jargon, a canoe, vehicles, and business establishments.

Location: Today the Chinooks live primarily in southwestern Washington State,
though their membership is widely dispersed throughout the Pacific Northwest.

Numbers: Between 1780 and 1805, the Chinook population declined from about eight hundred to four hundred. In the latter half of the nineteenth century, they numbered scarcely one hundred. In 1980, at a time of revived tribalism, Chinook membership stood at around nine hundred, which had increased to twenty-six hundred in July 2009.

History: No one knows when Chinooks first met non-Indians. Their tradition and that of the Clatsops, their Lower Chinookan-speaking neighbors on the south near the mouth of the Columbia River, tell of Spanish ships wrecking on their beaches in the second half of the eighteenth century. In May 1792, the Chinooks encountered the American trader Capt. Robert Gray, who sailed into the Columbia River in the *Columbia Rediviva,* from which the river received its name. According to the Chinooks, Gray was the first white mariner to enter the river. In 1792 they also had contact with the crew of the British vessel *Jenny,* which entered the Columbia, and the crewmen of HMS *Chatham* under the command of William Broughton, who was exploring the lower Columbia River for Britain. The Chinooks were among the Indians who traded with the American explorers Meriwether Lewis and William Clark, whose party wintered among Clatsops in 1805–1806. In 1811 the Chinooks traded with the Astorians of John Jacob Astor's Pacific Fur Company at Fort Astoria (Astoria, Oregon). Following the merger of Astor's firm with the North West Company in 1813, the Astorian post became Fort George. After the Hudson's Bay Company merged with the North West Company in 1821, Fort George became a subpost for that firm, which in 1824 moved its main operations up the right bank of the Columbia River to Fort Vancouver. As a result, the Chinooks experienced a loss of prestige as well as trade.

On August 9, 1851, agents of the United States dealt with the Chinooks for their lands in a never-ratified treaty at Tansey Point (Oregon). After that, the survivors of the once-influential tribe, bereft of members, lands, and power, dispersed to neighboring settler communities. Some others moved to local reservations.

Government and Claims: In 1953 the Chinook Tribe, with no reservation, established an organization called The Chinook Indian Tribe, Inc., for the political, educational, and social welfare of the tribe. On July 23, 1979, that group petitioned the federal government for acknowledgment, which if approved, would have bestowed fishing and other rights.

After the neighboring Tillamooks on the south were awarded a settlement of their claims in 1897 (30 Stat. 62) for lands taken by the United States, the Chinooks, Clatsops, Cathlamets, and Wahkiakums (Upper Chinookans) presented a claim to the United States on March 2 and 28, 1899, for compensation for their alienated lands. On August 24, 1912, they were awarded $20,000 by an act of Congress (37 Stat. 518, 535). After the establishment of the Indian Claims Commission on August 13, 1946, those Chinooks who were enrolled on reservations of identifiable

American Indian historian, artist, and activist Catherine Herrold Troeh (1911–2007) spent a good part of her lifetime documenting, preserving, and promoting the history and culture of the Chinook Tribe. The oldest living Chinook elder at the time of her death, Troeh was a cofounder of the American Indian Women's Service League, which was established in 1958 to counsel young Native Americans moving from the reservations to cities in the late 1950s and 1960s.

Courtesy of Charlotte Killien.

tribes filing claims were included in any forthcoming awards. The nonreservation Chinooks, Clatsops, and some Wahkiakums and Cathlamets consolidated as identifiable tribes into The Chinook Nation to press their claim (Docket 234), which they filed on August 8, 1951. In doing so, they maintained that the $26,307.95 that they had been awarded in 1912 for the 762,000 acres that they had surrendered in the unratified treaty of August 9, 1851, was unconscionable. The Indian Claims Commission, on November 4, 1971, awarded them $75,000, which, after the previous award had been deducted, entitled them to a recovery of $48,692.05. The Chinook Nation group had been organized to prosecute those claims; it was after that group disbanded that The Chinook Indian Tribe, Inc., was organized.

Contemporary Life and Culture: The Chinooks have been striving for federal recognition since 1851, which they received briefly from President Bill Clinton on January 3, 2001. That decision was reversed seventeen months later, on July 5, 2002, by President George W. Bush. In July 2008, U.S. Congressman Brian Baird, D-Vancouver, Washington, introduced the Chinook Nation Restoration Act, which, if approved, would qualify the Chinook Indian Nation for federal funding for a reservation as well as housing assistance and health care. The Chinooks would like to open a cultural center and, with restoration, envision the introduction of light industry, the construction of industrial parks, the generating of electrical energy from ocean waves, and the lending of the Chinook name to commercial merchandise. The tribe already promotes fishing enterprises, an industry as old as the Chinookan peoples themselves.

In 2001 the Chinook Tribe accepted the bones of two tribal members that had been kept by private collectors and in 2003 began working to achieve the repatriation of twenty-nine sets of bones stored in the National Museum of Natural History in Washington, D.C. In the fall of 2004 construction began on the Cathlapotle Plankhouse Project, an undertaking initiated under the Lewis and Clark Bicentennial Commemoration to erect a full-scale replica of a Chinook plankhouse at the major village site visited by the explorers in 1805–1806. In March 2009 the tribal offices were moved from Chinook to Bay Center, Washington.

Today there are no speakers of the tribal language.

Special Events and Celebrations: The only public event is the annual Labor Day Celebration held over the holiday weekend at South Bend, Washington.

Suggested Readings:

Stephen Dow Beckham, *Chinook Indian Tribe: Petition for Federal Acknowledgment* (Lake Oswego, Ore.: USA Research, 1987); Mathias D. Bergmann, "'We Should Lose Much by Their absence': The Centrality of Chinookans and Kalapuyans to Life in Frontier Oregon," *Oregon Historical Quarterly* 109 (Spring 2008); Mildred Colbert, *Kutkos, Chinook Tyee* (Boston: D.C. Heath, 1942); Yvonne P. Hajda, "Slavery in the Greater Lower Columbia Region," *Ethnohistory* 52, no. 3 (2005); Karen Huntington, *A Woman of the Clatsop Tribe of the Chinook Nation* (Pomeroy, Wash.: Sweeney Gulch Press, 2003); Melinda Marie Jette, "'Beaver Are Numerous, but the Natives . . . Will Not Hunt Them': Native-Fur Trader Relations in the Willamette Valley, 1812–1814," *Pacific Northwest Quarterly* 98, no. 1 (2006–07); Rick Minor, "Aboriginal Settlement and Subsistence at the Mouth of the Columbia River," Ph.D. dissertation, University of Oregon, 1983; Verne F. Ray, "The Historical Position of the Lower Chinook in the Native Culture of the Northwest," *Pacific Northwest Quarterly* 28, no. 4 (October 1937); William G. Robbins, "On the Banks of the Mid-Columbia: Exploring the Cultural Significance of Celilo," *Columbia: The Magazine of Northwest History* 21, no. 2 (2007); Alexander Ross, *Adventures of the First Settlers on the Oregon or Columbia River, 1810–1813* (Corvallis: Oregon State University Press, 2000); Rick Rubin, *Naked against the Rain: The People of the Lower Columbia River, 1770–1830* (Portland, Ore.: Far Shore, 1999); Robert H. Ruby and John A. Brown, *The Chinook Indians: Traders of the Lower Columbia River* (Norman: University of Oklahoma Press, 1976); James G. Swan, *The Northwest Coast; or, Three Years' Residence in Washington Territory* (1857; Fairfield, Wash.: Ye Galleon Press, 1966); Clifford E. Trafzer, *The Chinook* (New York: Chelsea House, 1990); Gray Whaley, "'Complete Liberty'? Gender, Sexuality, Race, and Social Change on the Lower Columbia River, 1805–1838," *Ethnohistory* 54, no. 4 (2007).

CLACKAMAS

(Upper Chinookan Division of Chinookan)

The Clackamases, after whom one dialect of the Upper Chinookan linguistic stock is named, occupied about twelve villages, which were located mainly on the south bank of the lower Columbia River downstream from present-day Troutdale, Oregon, roughly to a point opposite today's Kalama, Washington, and on the east side of the Willamette River from a few miles above its mouth to Oregon City and east to the Cascade Mountains. Other rivers dissecting their lands were the Clackamas, a Willamette tributary, and the Sandy, which flows into the Columbia. In addition to the Clackamas River, an Oregon county and a town bear the tribal name.

Clackamases and other speakers of their dialect lived in wooden houses; the larger of these houses sheltered three or four families of as many as twenty or more people in a communal setting. Clackamas villages varied in size but were fairly permanent. Their inhabitants migrated in summer to procure salmon, roots, and berries. An important item in their diet and trade was the *wappato* root that they harvested in swampy places along the lower Columbia. Clackamases were skilled in handling canoes fashioned from logs. From platforms erected on rocks they netted, gaffed, and speared fish as the latter tried to leap over Willamette Falls. The Clackamases and their neighbors came into contact with non-Indian traders and travelers earlier than did other Willamette Valley residents. The regional headquarters of the Hudson's Bay Company during the second quarter of the nineteenth century was at nearby Fort Vancouver, a short distance upstream on the Columbia's north bank opposite the mouth of the Willamette. In February 1841 the Clackamas headman Popoh was converted to the Roman Catholic faith by the Reverend François Norbert Blanchet. Also competing for Clackamas souls was the Reverend Alvin F. Waller of the Methodist Mission station near present-day Salem, Oregon.

A treaty that the Clackamases signed with Oregon superintendent of Indian affairs Anson Dart in the fall of 1851 was never ratified. They signed another on January 10, 1855 (10 Stat. 1143), which was ratified on March 3, 1855. At the time of the second treaty, the Clackamas signatories to it represented only eighty-eight people. By its terms, the Clackamases were promised twenty-five hundred dollars in annuities, of which five hundred dollars was to be in cash and the remainder dispersed in food and clothing. The treaty was considered one of Dart's most important because the lands obtained by the United States lay along the much-coveted south bank of the Columbia, east of the Willamette, including the Clackamas and Sandy river valleys. In the fall of 1851, twenty mills were operating in that area. Those Clackamases who were not integrating with non-Indians and other Indians in the Willamette Valley were, as stipulated by treaty, removed westward to the Grand Ronde Reservation.

There, in 1871, the Clackamases numbered but fifty-five individuals. Their population in 1780 has been estimated at twenty-five hundred. In 1805–1806 they were placed at eighteen hundred. Although early-twentieth-century newspaper accounts describing certain Indians to be the last of their tribe should be read with caution, they do reveal the decline in tribal populations evident at that time. One such article, appearing in the Portland, Oregon, *Journal,* May 9, 1915, told of Soo-sap, the "last" Clackamas, whose mother was of that tribe. His father was a Klickitat.

Suggested Readings:

Stephen Dow Beckham, *The Indians of Western Oregon, This Land Was Theirs* (Coos Bay, Ore.: Arago Books, 1977); S. A. Clarke, *Pioneer Days of Oregon History* (Portland, Ore., J. K. Gill Company,1905); John Adams Hussey, *Champoeg: Place of Transition* (Portland: Oregon Historical Society, 1967); Melville Jacobs, *Clackamas Chinook Texts* (Bloomington: Indiana University Press, 1958–59), 2 vols.

CLALLAM

(Coastal Division, Salishan)

The Strong People

The Clallams (or Klallams) called themselves by a name meaning "strong people" or "mighty tribe." The early-twentieth-century photographer-observer of Indians, Edward S. Curtis, regarded them as the most aggressive and powerful of all the Salish-speaking peoples on the coasts of Washington State, where they occupied the territory stretching along the Strait of Juan de Fuca between Clallam and Port Discovery bays, including territory formerly held by the Chimakums. Clallam tradition tells of raids and counterraids involving themselves and neighboring Makahs, Suquamish, and Chimakums, plus Canadian tribes such as the Haidas, Tsimshians, and Cowichans. To defend themselves from raiding foes, the Clallams built strong, double palisades of split logs. The fierce appearance of knife-wielding members of their Black Society was heightened by the charcoal painted on their faces.

Some scholars believe that, like the Makahs west of them, the Clallams had migrated south to their homeland on the southern shores of the Strait of Juan de Fuca. They were closely related to Canadian tribes such as the Songish of lower Vancouver Island whose Lkungen dialect was similar. Clallams continued to migrate to lower Vancouver Island and a smaller group moved to the U.S. mainland near present-day Marietta in Lummi Indian territory. One Clallam group was said to have settled on the upper west coast of Whidbey Island in northern Puget

Sound. Even into the contact period, the Clallams attempted to secure lands on that island from Skagit Indians living there. The Clallams were believed to have occupied at least fifteen villages in all, mostly in the southern Strait of Juan de Fuca area.

The Spanish explorer Manuel Quimper discovered Dungeness Bay on the Strait on July 4, 1790, marking what may have been the earliest contact of Clallams with EuroAmericans in their homelands. As later explorers did, Quimper noted the impaled heads of Clallam foes on Clallam beaches. On April 30, 1792, British Capt. George Vancouver anchored in and named Dungeness Bay.

The Clallams were tradesmen. They carried on considerable exchange with close neighbors like the Twanas and with residents of Vancouver Island. For items like skins and oils, they received goods such as blankets. Besides their trade with neighboring tribes, they would barter, for example, strings of clams for horses from the Yakama Indians east of the Cascade Mountains. The members of the Vancouver expedition were aware of the Clallams' trading prowess. They received from them venison and fish in exchange for coppers and trinkets.

During the period of the Hudson's Bay Company's dominance in the region, the Clallams came into the company's orbit but not always on congenial terms. On July 1, 1828, Bay Company trappers under Alexander Roderick McLeod killed two Clallam families in retaliation for the killing by Clallams of five company trappers. As late as 1868, as a result of Clallam-Tsimshian feuding, a party of twenty-six Clallams was taken to the Skokomish Reservation and kept at hard labor by its agent. To compensate for Tsimshian deaths in the feuding, the United States paid the Tsimshians in gold coins and other gifts. The Clallams and the United States generally remained on amicable terms because of the peaceful inclinations toward Americans of Clallam headmen like the remarkable Chitsamakkan (Chetzmokha), dubbed the Duke of York and possessed of two wives named Queen Victoria and Jenny Lind.

The ethnologist George Gibbs, when informed that the Clallams had once numbered 2,240, responded that he believed that in 1853 there were no more than 800. Official government records of that same year placed them at 400. A decade earlier, Lt. Charles Wilkes of the U.S. Exploring Expedition, estimated them at 425. During the 1850s, Clallam population losses were hastened by smallpox and alcohol, which were, according to an elderly Clallam headman, more devastating than their desultory wars.

In the Treaty of Point-No-Point on January 26, 1855, the Clallams were scheduled to remove to the Skokomish Reservation at the southern end of Hood Canal. They shunned that reservation because of its poor soils and its distance from their own lands and because it lay in the territory of their traditional rivals, the Twanas. Very few Clallams removed to the Skokomish Reservation. Many Clallams were scattered in small villages around Hood Canal, Puget Sound, and the Strait of Juan de Fuca at distances from 50 to 150 miles from the Skokomish Reservation. Some Clallams acquired land by purchase or homestead entry. One

The image of this Clallam couple, Charles and Nellie Jackson, reveals the influence of Americans, ranging from mill owners to missionaries, who had come among the powerful tribes of the Strait of Juan de Fuca. The picture, taken ca. 1890, is typical of those posed by photographers in studio settings.

Courtesy of Whitman College, Walla Walla, Wash.

small group purchased 210 acres of land at Jamestown on the Strait of Juan de Fuca, where they managed their holdings as a communal venture. A less ambitious village undertaking was that of a Clallam band at Port Gamble. Available statistics indicate that before 1914 the average Clallam population at Jamestown was about 240 and at Port Gamble about 90. Many Clallams worked in sawmilling, fishing, and canoeing and were characterized by Indian agents as independent, self-supporting, industrious, and relatively prosperous.

Bearing the tribal name are a town, a bay, a river, and a county.

In 1936–37 the United States purchased and placed in trust 1,604.44 acres of land for the Clallams. The historic relative independence of the Clallam bands from each other came into play in the division of the trust acreage. In essence, the United States recognized the de facto Clallam separateness in the establishment of reservations for the Lower Elwha Klallam Tribe and the Port Gamble S'Klallam Tribe.

As a result of a relief act of March 3, 1925 (43 Stat. 1102, 44 Stat. 173), the Clallam band received $399,277.68. The Indian Claims Commission did not consider this a gratuitous offset to the claim (Docket 134) that the Clallams had filed for themselves and the Chimakums for additional compensation for lands ceded to the United States. The Clallams had claimed that, at the time of the Point-No-Point Treaty, the few Chimakums who remained had been absorbed within the Clallam tribe that had occupied the Chimakum lands and claimed those lands as well as their own. On December 2, 1957, the commission recognized the Clallam claim that they had taken possession of the Chimakum lands between 1855 and 1857. Finding the claim to have involved 438,430 acres, the commission, on October 1, 1970, awarded the Clallam bands $440,000. After excluding $39,180 because of a previous consideration, their award was $400,820. The commission then deducted from that sum the value of aboriginal Clallam land holdings, or $15,000, which the United States had paid for the Port Gamble Reservation tract, making for a net award of $385,820.

A small group of Clallams, apart from the other three groups (Jamestown, Lower Elwha Klallam, and Port Gamble), are organized as the Clallam General Council but are not federally acknowledged. *See also* **Jamestown S'Klallam Indian Tribe; Lower Elwha Klallam Tribe;** *and* **Port Gamble S'Klallam Tribe, Port Gamble Reservation.**

Suggested Readings:

> Myron Eells, *The Twana, Chemakum, and Clallam Indians of Washington Territory* (1889; Seattle: Shorey Book Store, 1971); Robert H. Ruby and John A. Brown, *Myron Eells and the Puget Sound Indians* (Seattle: Superior Publishing Company, 1976); Erna Gunther, "Klallam Ethnography," *University of Washington Publications in Anthropology* 1, no. 5 (1927).

CLATSKANIE

(Athabaskan)

The Clatskanies split off from a band of Athabaskan speakers, the Kwalhioquas, who lived in the hills north of the lower Columbia River in present-day Washington State. Probably before 1775 a band of these Kwalhioquas migrated to the south side of the Columbia River in search of more favorable subsistence and became the Clatskanies. Their Kwalhioqua relatives, languishing in their homeland, eventually disappeared, while the Clatskanies flourished a while longer. The migrants explained their exodus from their homelands in one of their traditions. According to legend, some young men with a magic spindle had started a forest fire that burned for two years, driving the elk away. About five years later, after the grass returned, some hunters following the trail of the elk crossed the Columbia River on a raft. After they had gotten over and before moving south, they sent a messenger north with the news of their success.

About fifty miles east of the mouth of the Columbia, an Upper Chinookan people, the Skilloots, eventually moved south across the river, pushing the Clatskanies back about twenty miles. Those Clatskanies remained primarily a hunting people. The Clatskanies on the river were possibly a mixed group of Chinookan and other speakers. Among Native and white traders they developed a reputation for violence because of their attempts to exact tribute from those passing their shores. Like other white fur traders before them, the men of the Hudson's Bay Company traveled past the Indian shores only in large, armed convoys. While the Lewis and Clark expedition wintered at Fort Clatsop in 1805–1806, the Clatskanies allegedly planned to storm the fort. Clatsops seem to have thwarted the plan.

Some anthropologists maintain that the Clatskanies were the "Clackstar Nation" whose numbers Lewis and Clark placed at 1,200. The anthropologist Herbert C. Taylor, Jr., has estimated them at that time more conservatively at 400. George Simpson of the Hudson's Bay Company placed their population at 175 in 1825. Oregon territorial governor Joseph Lane stated in 1849 that they numbered about 300 on lands stretching along the coast northward to the Columbia River. It is very likely that Lane included Clatsops in his enumeration. According to Oregon superintendent of Indian affairs Anson Dart, with whom they signed a never-ratified treaty on August 9, 1851, ceding their lands, the Clatskanies numbered no more than 3 men and 5 women in 1851. In 1910 they were said to number only 3. Diseases such as smallpox and the intermittent fever, desultory fighting, and interspersing with others had finally taken their toll.

Suggested Readings:

Melville Jacobs, "Historic Perspectives in Indian Languages of Oregon and Washington," *Pacific Northwest Quarterly* 28, no. 1 (January 1937); Herbert C. Taylor, Jr., and Lester L. Hoaglin, Jr., "The 'Intermittent Fever' Epidemic of the 1830's on the Lower Columbia River," *Ethnohistory* 9, no. 2 (Spring 1962): 165.

CLATSOP

(Lower Chinookan Division of Chinookan)

Today an Oregon town and county bear the name "Clatsop," which is derived from a Native word for dried salmon. Culturally, the Clatsops were much like the Chinooks proper across the Columbia River on the north. Both peoples held slaves and flattened the heads of infants of the aristocracy. Both performed similar rituals, such as those associated with the first salmon runs. The Clatsops were more dependent on hunting than the Chinooks to whom they sold elk skins for processing into cuirasses *(clamons).* Reputedly less skilled in trade than the

This mother and child, photo-graphed ca. 1880, are representa-tives of those Clatsops who, after extensive non-Indian contact, remained in their tribal home-land on the south bank of the Co-lumbia River at its entrance into the Pacific Ocean. The Ameri-can explorers Lewis and Clark wintered among the Clatsops in 1805–1806.

Courtesy of the Oregon Historical Society, Portland.

Chinooks, the Clatsops none-theless competed with them in such endeavors and occasionally engaged them and their other neighbors in petty conflicts. The Clatsops' exposure to Eu-roAmericans was also similar to that of the Chinooks, though the earliest ships entered the Columbia at Baker Bay in Chinook waters. Later, these craft crossed the treacherous bar of the Columbia and passed into the stream along its southern shores where the Clatsops resided.

The Clatsops stole a march on the Chinooks when the Lewis and Clark party camped in their country at Fort Clatsop during the winter of 1805–1806. In 1811 Astorians of John Jacob Astor's Pacific Fur Company established Fort Astoria in Clatsop country at present-day Astoria, Oregon. Two years later, British fur traders of the North West Company founded Fort George at that same place. The post was under Hudson's Bay Company management after 1821, and, save for a few buildings, it was moved up the Columbia's right bank to Fort Vancouver in 1824.

Disease and other issues rendered the Clatsops unable to recover their popula-tion. They struggled to survive by trading with non-Indians, butchering whales cast up on their beaches, and salvaging goods from wrecked ships. In 1829 their appropriation of goods from the Hudson's Bay Company ship *William and Ann* caused that firm to send a punitive expedition against their villages. Cold sta-tistics reveal their continuing relentless decline: 220 in 1841, 180 in 1848, 56 in 1871, and 26 in 1910.

Attempting to save Clatsop souls were the Reverend John E. Frost and others of the Missionary Society of the Methodist Episcopal Church, which ministered to tribal members beginning in 1840. Like Pacific Northwest Methodist missions in general, the Clatsop Mission ended in failure. Frustrating such activity was the continuing Indian attrition from liquor-induced violence and the loss of Indian lands. As missionaries shifted their focus from the Indians to white settlers, some Clatsop families, evaluating their situation, married their daughters to non-Indians, including French-Canadian former fur men such as those who settled on French Prairie in the Willamette Valley.

On the heels of the settlers, the United States sent an Indian subagent to Astoria. On August 5, 1851, Oregon superintendent of Indian affairs Anson Dart signed a never-ratified treaty with most of the Clatsops. Two days later, he concluded another with a small Clatsop band known as the Nucqueclahwemuks. On August 24, 1912, Congress awarded these two Clatsop bands fifteen thousand dollars and fifteen hundred dollars, respectively (37 Stat. 518), to satisfy claims arising from nonratification of their treaty. A descendant of a Clatsop signatory to the treaty named Dunkel claimed that none of Dunkel's heirs had received the moneys due them under its terms. Clatsops who intermarried with members of other tribes were also involved in claims against the United States. In 1897 the Nehalem "band" of Tillamooks, which included Indians of Clatsop heritage, was awarded a ten-thousand-dollar settlement by the government for its unratified treaty of August 6, 1851. This was one of many belated adjustments that the government made to descendants of the Clatsops who had extended hospitality to Americans in their lands. Nonreservation Clatsop descendants also shared with Chinooks, Wahkiakums, and Cathlamets a November 4, 1871, award (*see also* **Chinook**).

By 1980 the Clatsops had not regained the status of a viable or identifiable tribe, but those remaining members attempted to retain the memory of their ancestry and complained of intrusion of industrial firms on ancient tribal burial places. *See also* **Clatsop-Nehalem Confederated Tribes.**

Suggested Readings:

Franz Boas, *Chinook Texts,* Bureau of American Ethnology Bulletin no. 20 (Washington, D.C., Government Printing Office, 1894); Grace P. Morris, "Development of Astoria, 1811–1850," *Oregon Historical Quarterly* 37, no. 4 (December 1937); Verne F. Ray, "Lower Chinook Ethnographic Notes," *University of Washington Publications in Anthropology* 7, no. 2 (1938) and "The Historical Position of the Lower Chinook in the Native Culture of the Pacific Northwest," *Pacific Northwest Quarterly* 28, no. 4 (October 1937); Robert H. Ruby and John A. Brown, *The Chinook Indians: Traders of the Lower Columbia River* (Norman: University of Oklahoma Press, 1976).

CLATSOP-NEHALEM CONFEDERATED TRIBES

(Lower Chinookan Division of Chinookan)

The Clatsop-Nehalem Confederated Tribes organized in 2001 with seventy members as a nonprofit group seeking federal tribal recognition. The Clatsop-Nehalems applied for membership in both the Confederated Tribes of Siletz and the Confederated Tribes of Grand Ronde but were denied. The tribal offices of the Clatsop-Nehalem Confederated Tribes are located in the Port of Astoria Building in Astoria, Oregon. In addition, twenty acres of oceanfront property has been secured in Tillamook County on which the Confederated Tribes plans to construct a cedar-plank longhouse to serve as a tribal headquarters and museum.

CLOWWEWALLA

(Upper Chinookan Division of Chinookan)

The Clowwewallas were of the Clackamas division of the Upper Chinookan linguistic stock. They lived along the Willamette River from its mouth south about twenty miles to and around Willamette Falls. They were found on the west bank of the falls across from present-day Oregon City. At the falls they built platforms from the rocks from which they netted, gaffed, and speared the fish trying to leap up the falls. They also traded with such peoples as the Tillamooks on the west from whom they obtained oil from sea animals. Because they lived in the lower Columbia-Willamette river area, the Clowwewallas, like their neighbors, came into early contact with white fur traders. Until truces were effected, they were initially on poor terms with non-Indians.

One consequence of their contacts with fur traders, and later with settlers, was a severe population loss due to the epidemics that followed the Columbia and Willamette river valleys in the late eighteenth and early nineteenth centuries. In 1780 the Clowwewallas numbered roughly 300 and in 1805–1806, 650. The latter estimate probably included others of the Clackamas division of Upper Chinookans. Those living at the Willamette Falls were said to have numbered only 13 in 1851.

Clowwewallas and Clackamases, along with Kalapuyan speakers such as Molalas, were included in treaties effected with Oregon superintendent of Indian affairs Anson Dart on January 10 and 19, 1855 (10 Stat. 1143, ratified March 3, 1855). In accordance with the terms of their treaty, a Clowwewalla remnant was removed west to the Grand Ronde Reservation, where its members were absorbed into that community. *See also* **Clackamas.**

COEUR D'ALENE

(Interior Division, Salishan)

Schítsu'umsh or Skitswish

Those Who Are Found Here or The Discovered People

Originally the Coeur d'Alenes called themselves Skitswish, a word believed to be simply the name of one place, perhaps meaning "foundling." The name "Coeur d'Alêne," translated from the French as "heart of an awl," was said to have been given the Skitswish by early-nineteenth-century French-Canadian fur traders who thought them to be stingy-hearted with a sharpness in trade like that of a pin or an awl. They were a fiercely independent people who ranged over 4 million acres, from Spokane Falls in present-day Washington State on the west to the Clark Fork River in today's Montana on the east and from Lake Pend Oreille in present-day Idaho on the north to the Clearwater River in Idaho on the south. They were composed of three major bands based in the present state of Idaho on Coeur d'Alene Lake, the Coeur d'Alene River, and the Saint Joe River. Bearing their name today, besides the lake and the river, are the Coeur d'Alene Reservation, a mountain range, and a city on Interstate 90 on the northern shores of the lake. The successor to the original Coeur d'Alene tribe is known today as the Coeur d'Alene Tribe, Coeur d'Alene Reservation.

Location: The Coeur d'Alenes settled on and in the environs of their reservation of about 345,000 acres, which is located in the panhandle of northern Idaho about thirty-five miles south of the city of Coeur d'Alene. Principal settlements include Benewah, Desmet, Plummer, Sanders, Tensed, and Worley.

Numbers: In 1827 a Hudson's Bay Company trader, John Warren Dease, documented the Coeur d'Alene population at 400, about 600 less than an estimate in 1780. In 1835–36 Samuel Parker, a missionary for the American Board of Commissioners for Foreign Missions, placed them at 700, but Parker was prone to exaggeration. In 1841 Lt. Charles Wilkes, commanding a naval expedition to the Pacific Northwest, listed them more realistically at 450. In 1870 they were officially enumerated at 300 and in 1888 at 516. The 345,000-acre Coeur d'Alene Reservation is home today to 6,500 residents, 19 percent of whom are American Indian, and almost half of those are under the age of twenty. In 1998 the Coeur d'Alene Tribe counted approximately 1,400 enrolled members, a number that had climbed to 1,900 in 2006 and to 2,000 in 2009.

History: As noted, the Coeur d'Alenes were an independent people. Occasionally, they engaged in hostilities with other tribes such as the Nez Perces on the

Chief Seltice of the Coeur d'Alenes
of northern Idaho, photographed ca.
1890. Like his forebears, he vigorously
sought to protect his people from the
encroachment of outsiders on their
lands. The Coeur d'Alenes possessed
a reputation among non-Indians as
shrewd traders.

Courtesy of Jerome Peltier.

south and the Spokanes on the west,
but generally they enjoyed amicable
relations with their neighbors, with
whom they shared fishing, gathering, and gaming sites. Although
they discouraged non-Indian traders
from entering their lands, the Coeur
d'Alenes in the early nineteenth century traded with them outside Coeur d'Alene
country at posts such as Fort Spokane and Fort Colvile and Kullyspell (Kalispel)
House and Spokane House. Three Coeur d'Alene Indians visited the American
explorers Meriwether Lewis and William Clark in Nez Perce country as those
men journeyed homeward in 1806.

In April 1842 the Reverend Pierre De Smet, S.J., laid the groundwork for a
Coeur d'Alene mission, which began operating in November of that year when
the Reverend Nicholas Point, S.J., and a Brother Huet built a log church on the
St. Joe River. Point characterized his Native parishioners as noted for "dissimu-
lation, egotism and cruelty." The clerics, to whom the Indians confessed their
"pagan" practices, set about immersing them in the Catholic faith. Despite the
opposition of some Coeur d'Alenes, such as Chief Stellam, in response to the efforts of churchmen to have them become farmers, the priests held fast. In 1879,
one priest hailed them as "the tribe which has now made the greatest advance in
civilization."

In May 1858, the Coeur d'Alenes led neighboring tribes in repulsing the command of U.S. Army Col. Edward Steptoe, which was moving northward toward
the Canadian border. During the Yakama War, which broke out in 1855, the Coeur d'Alenes remained neutral, but in September 1858, along with several other
interior tribes, they unsuccessfully engaged the army command of Col. George
Wright in two encounters in Spokane country. One provision of a "treaty" that
Wright blustered from them was the right to build the Mullan Road through
their lands. In 1859 they submitted to the building of the road, despite threats of
some tribal members to kill its builder, Capt. John Mullan.

Coeur d'Alene Chief Peter Moctelme. After early difficult years, Roman Catholic fathers persuaded many Coeur d'Alenes, such as Moctelme, to become farmers. Around the turn of the century, he opposed allotment on the Coeur d'Alene Reservation in northern Idaho.

Courtesy of the Eastern Washington State Historical Society, Spokane.

With the executive orders of June 14, 1867, and November 8, 1873, the tribe ceded to the United States 2,389,924 acres, while assuming possession of the 598,500-acre Coeur d'Alene Reservation, which extended from the central Idaho panhandle west ten or twelve miles into Washington Territory, east to the Bitterroot Mountains, north to the Pend Oreille River, and south to the dividing point between the drainage basins of Coeur d'Alene Lake and the Snake River. The Coeur d'Alene Reservation was established only after the failure (for lack of ratification by the United States) of the agreement into which the Coeur d'Alenes had entered on July 28, 1873, to relinquish their right and title to their lands. After petitioning for a commission to treat for their lands outside the reservation, the tribe ceded to the United States 184,960 acres of the northern part of the reservation for $231,884.97 by an agreement dated March 26, 1887 (26 Stat. 989, 1027, ratified March 3, 1891). The pact opened those acres to non-Indian occupancy and settlement under U.S. mineral laws. By an agreement concluded at Spokane Falls in Washington Territory a week earlier, on March 18, 1887, the nonreservation Spokanes living in the vicinity of Spokane Falls, after deeding to the United States all right, title, and claim that they had or ever would have to any and all lands outside the Spokane Reservation, agreed to remove to the Coeur d'Alene and Flathead reservations. In exchange, the United States agreed to assist them in moving and becoming established in their new homes. Thus, in January 1894, thirty-two largely Roman Catholic Spokane families were relocated on the Coeur d'Alene Reservation, which some of them later vacated. Between 1905 and 1909, 97 Spokanes and 541 Coeur d'Alenes were allotted quarter sections, despite the opposition of important Coeur d'Alenes such as Chief Peter Moctelme.

Government and Claims: On November 17, 1934, the successor of the historic Coeur d'Alene tribe, the Coeur d'Alene Tribe, Coeur d'Alene Reservation, rejected by a narrow margin the Indian Reorganization Act (48 Stat. 984). The tribe has a council from which its principal officers are elected. Committees deal with issues related to land, law and order, education, welfare, credit, and domestic affairs.

The Coeur d'Alene Tribe, Coeur d'Alene Reservation, claimed (Docket 81) additional payment for the 2,389,924 acres that the tribe had ceded to the United States for $231,884.97 pursuant to the agreement of March 26, 1887. The Indian Claims Commission decided that, as of March 3, 1891 (the ratification date of the 1887 agreement), the value of the land had been $4,659,663 and ordered that the tribe be paid this amount minus the previous award, or $4,427,778.03. With twenty-four other tribes throughout the western United States, the tribe in 1970 filed claims (Dockets 523-71 and 524-71) with the Court of Claims for mismanagement of Indian Commission judgment funds and other moneys such as Individual Indian Money accounts held in trust by the United States. The Coeur d'Alene Tribe in 1981 was awarded $173,978.79.

Contemporary Life and Culture: Of great importance to the Coeur d'Alene Tribe is its Development Enterprise. Instituted in 1970 and boasting one of the largest farms in northern Idaho, profits from this undertaking were used in initiating the Swine Enterprise. Other businesses under the Development Enterprise are the Utility Service Enterprise (a construction company), the tribal service station at Tensed, the Timber Enterprise, and the Tribal Distributors. The tribe has sought to repurchase as much land as possible, and members lease their lands. Tribal members continue to participate in traditional means of livelihood such as hunting, fishing, and gathering. Nearly everyone speaks English. To preserve the fast-disappearing Native language, a tribal language program was adopted. Children attend the Sacred Heart Mission School at Desmet and public schools in reservation towns and at Tekoa, Washington. Tribal officials are encouraging continuing school attendance.

The Coeur d'Alene Tribe has operated the Coeur d'Alene Casino Resort Hotel since 1993 at Worley, realizing in its first several years of operation $8 million to $10 million in profits annually, including bingo revenue, a figure that had climbed to $20 million by 2008. The facility operates with a paid staff of approximately nine hundred. Five percent of gambling profits are earmarked for distribution among the region's schools, collectively totaling $10 million from 1994 to 2008. In the summer of 2009 the tribe announced a $75-million project to increase the size of its casino hotel by 50 percent, while adding a luxury spa, several restaurants, an outdoor amphitheater, and other amenities. Besides new conference and events centers that are in the works, other tribal enterprises include the Circling Ravens Golf Course facility north of Worley and the Benewah Automotive Center, the Benewah Market, and Ace Hardware located in Plummer. A producer of wheat, barley, peas, lentils, and canola, the tribal farm encompasses about six thousand acres. Two other tribal businesses in which the Coeur d'Alenes are a majority shareholder include a manufacturing plant known

Lawrence Aripa (1926–1998) of the Coeur d'Alene Tribe. An author, linguist, storyteller, artist, and painter, Aripa designed the Coeur d'Alene tribal seal and one side of the Idaho state centennial coin. In addition to his cultural leadership, Aripa also served for over a decade on the Coeur d'Alene tribal council.

Courtesy of Larry Reisnouer, *(Spokane) Spokesman-Review.*

as BERG Integrated Systems and HearthBread BakeHouse bakery, with more than $300,000 in monthly sales. BERG has a $400-million contract with the U.S. government to make fuel bladders for the military. In 1998 the tribe launched U.S. Lottery, the first pari-mutuel lottery accessible by both telephone and the Internet.

The Coeur d'Alenes also operate a bus system and have constructed a new preschool, senior center, and Community Technology Center with an Internet Café of forty computers offering free broadband access. The tribe is striving as well to bring broadband WI-FI to all six thousand homes on the reservation. In fiscal year 2007 tribal enterprises generated $300 million in total revenue, with approximately $100 million in earnings. Employing fourteen hundred, the tribe is the second largest employer in the five northern counties of Idaho. Unemployment among the members has shrunk from 70 percent in 1989 to single digits in 2008. At Plummer, the tribe recently built a new Tribal Wellness Center and provided principal funding for the Benewah Medical Center.

The Coeur d'Alenes also operate a substantial Early Childhood Learning Center for infant, toddler, and preschool development (Early Head Start and Head Start), and they hold control over Coeur d'Alene Tribal School (founded 1978) in Desmet, an eighty-student, K-8 grant school funded by the Bureau of Indian

Affairs (BIA). A fraction of Coeur d'Alene students attend public schools in the St. Maries School District, but most are in the Plummer-Worley Joint School District. The Coeur d'Alene Tribal Institute, in coordination with North Idaho College, offers dual-enrollment high school classes through which students can receive both high school and college credit. In addition, the tribe maintains multiple programs in adult general education, adult vocational education, and higher education support, including employment training for job skills and acquisition.

The tribe has successfully litigated to regain possession of the lower one-third of Lake Coeur d'Alene and other related waters and has assumed a leading role in the potentially billion-dollar cleanup of the Coeur d'Alene River. The Coeur d'Alenes are the only people to harvest *sqiqwts*—water potato—along the southern shore of Lake Coeur d'Alene.

Special Events and Celebrations: The Whaa-laa Days, held during the second week of July at Worley, features Indian games and war-dance contests. The annual Julyamsh Powwow, sponsored by the Coeur d'Alene Casino, is held in Post Falls on the fourth weekend of July and is considered the largest outdoor powwow in the Northwest. Water Potato Day, an annual tribal holiday in which elementary- to college-age students and the public are invited to participate, is held on the days leading up to and on the fourth Friday of October.

Suggested Readings:

Ross R. Cotroneo and Jack Dozier, "A Time of Disintegration: The Coeur d'Alene and the Dawes Act," *Western Historical Quarterly* 5, no. 4 (October 1974); Jack Dozier, "Coeur D'Alene Country: The Creation of the Coeur D'Alene Reservation in Northern Idaho," *Idaho Yesterdays* 6, no. 3 (Fall, 1962); "The Coeur d'Alene Indians in the War of 1858," *Idaho Yesterdays* 5, no. 3 (Fall, 1961); "The Coeur d'Alene Land Rush, 1909–10," *Pacific Northwest Quarterly* 53, no. 4 (October 1962); and *The Coeur D'Alene Indian Reservation* (1970); John Fahey, *Joe Garry and the Battle to Be Indian* (Seattle: University of Washington Press, 2001); Ted Fortier, *Religion and Resistance in the Encounter between the Coeur d'Alene Indians and Jesuit Missionaries* (Lewiston, N.Y.: Edwin Mellen Press, 2002); Rodney Frey, *Landscape Traveled by Coyote and Crane: The World of Schitsu'umsh* (Coeur d'Alene Indians) (Seattle: University of Washington Press, 2001); William T. Geoffroy, "The Coeur d'Alene Tribe: A Contemporary View," *Idaho Heritage* 1, no. 10 (October 1977); Richard E. Hart, "The Coeur d'Alene Tribe's Claim to Lake Coeur d'Alene," *American Indian Culture and Research Journal* 24, no. 1 (2000); Sven Liljeblad, "The Indians of Idaho," *Idaho Yesterdays* 4, no. 3 (1960); Lawrence Palladino, S.J., *The Coeur d'Alene Reservation and Our Friends the Coeur d'Alene Indians* (Fairfield, Wash.: Ye Galleon Press, 1967); Jerome Peltier, *A Brief History of the Coeur d'Alene Indians, 1806–1909* (Fairfield, Wash.: Ye Galleon Press, 1982) and *Manners and Customs of the Coeur d'Alene Indians* (Moscow, Ida.: Peltier Publications, 1975); Gladys A. Reichard, "An Analysis of Coeur D'Alene Myths," *Memoirs of the American Folklore Society* 41 (1947); Joseph Seltice, et al., *Saga of the Coeur d'Alene*

Indians: An Account of Chief Joseph Seltice (Fairfield, Wash.: Ye Galleon Press, 1990); Jill Maria Wagner, "Language, Power, and Ethnicity on the Coeur d'Alene Reservation," Ph.D. dissertation, Washington State University, 1997; John V. Wood, *Railroads through the Coeur d'Alenes* (Caldwell, Ida.: Caxton Printers, 1983); Laura Woodworth-Ney, *Mapping Identity: The Creation of the Coeur d'Alene Reservation* (Boulder: University Press of Colorado, 2004) and "Negotiating Boundaries of Territory and 'Civilization': The Coeur d'Alene Indian Reservation Agreement Councils, 1873–1889," *Pacific Northwest Quarterly* 94, no. 1 (Winter 2002–2003).

COEUR D'ALENE TRIBE, COEUR D'ALENE RESERVATION

The Coeur d'Alene Tribe, Coeur d'Alene Reservation, is composed of Coeur d'Alenes and those Spokanes who wish to live on the Coeur d'Alene Reservation. The Spokanes, by a treaty of March 18, 1887, were allowed their choice of living on the Coeur d'Alene or the Flathead reservation. Those Spokanes who joined the Coeur d'Alenes were for the most part Upper Spokanes of the three Spokane groups living nearest to the Coeur d'Alenes. Many Upper Spokanes shared the Roman Catholic faith with the Coeur d'Alenes.

In 1960 approximately 400 tribal members were listed as living on the Coeur d'Alene Reservation. In 1965 about 360 people were living there. As of 1982 there were about 822 enrolled tribal members, and in 1985 there were 853. Since 1984 one-quarter Indian blood degree has been required for tribal enrollment. *See also* **Coeur d'Alene.**

COLVILLE

(Interior Division, Salishan)

The Colvilles were called by other Salishan peoples a name that has been written Scheulpi, or Chualpay, in English letters. French-Canadian fur men called them La Chaudières, or Kettles, for the kettlelike depressions in the rocks at Kettle Falls on the Columbia River just south of the Canadian border in present-day Washington State. Besides living at the falls, the Colvilles also lived south of them, farther down the Columbia River to today's Hunters, Washington, and in the Colville River valley a short distance to the east. The designation "basket people," given them by a white observer in 1846, refers to the fifteen- to twenty-foot baskets of woven osiers, roots, and hard, twisted cords in which they netted up to three thousand salmon daily at Kettle Falls. Their name, "Colville," is

Chief Oropaughn of the Colvilles proper, a very popular leader of the 1880s and 1890s. His people lived in the general area of Kettle Falls on the Columbia River, below the Canadian border. They are not to be confused with other Indians of the Colville Reservation, also called Colvilles, though the Colvilles proper did live on the reservation bearing their name, which derives from the personage of Andrew Colvile, a governor of the Hudson's Bay Company.

Authors' collections.

derived from that of a Hudson's Bay Company governor, Andrew Colvile, after whom a nearby company post, Fort Colvile, established in 1825, was named. The U.S. military's Fort Colville was constructed nearby in 1859. Also bearing the name Colville are a river and its valley, a reservation, and a town on U.S. Highway 395.

Colville numbers in 1780 have been estimated at 1,000. In 1882 only 6 or 7 were reported by a reservation census taker. The number of Colvilles was 321 in 1904, 334 in 1907, and 322 in 1937. It would seem that those figures included people from other tribes on the Colville Reservation. Among the causes of attrition among the original Colvilles was a smallpox epidemic in 1782–83 and subsequent outbreaks of that disease—which would have been more widespread if some Indians in the Kettle Falls area had not been vaccinated by their Roman Catholic priests.

No one knows for certain when Colvilles first met non-Indians. Two whom they very likely encountered around 1800 were the trappers Le Blanc and La Gasse, sent westward by David Thompson of the North West Company. A Colville Indian, Alexander Daylight, who died in 1913, claimed to have talked with Thompson at Kettle Falls in July 1811. Because of the falls, the area was not only a fishing, trading, and military center but also a hub for missionary activity. Three years after meeting the first Catholic missionaries near the falls in 1838, the Colvilles were ministered to by the Reverend Pierre De Smet, S.J., then the best-known cleric of his faith in the interior of the Pacific Northwest. For years Indians from miles around visited the St. Francis Regis Mission near the falls. Although opposed to miners, soldiers, and settlers in their country, the Colvilles abstained from participating in the Indian wars of the 1850s, at least partly because of the influence of their priests. Their chiefs also concluded that with such a small population, they stood little chance of success in combat against soldiers possessing superior weapons.

An executive order dated April 8, 1872, established the Colville Reservation east of the Columbia River for tribes of the area. Before that year had ended, settlers in the fertile Colville Valley within the reservation had pressured the government into opening it again to settlement and setting aside another reservation for the Colvilles. This second Colville Reservation was created by executive order on July 2, 1872, west of the Columbia River. The tribal members belonging to this Colville Reservation are today called Colvilles and are incorporated as the Confederated Tribes of the Colville Reservation. *See* **Confederated Tribes of the Colville Reservation.**

Suggested Readings:

David H. Chance, "Balancing the Fur Trade at Fort Colville," *The Record* (Washington State University) 34 (1973); Edward S. Curtis, *The North American Indian* (1912; New York: Johnson Reprint Corporation, 1970), vol. 7; Pierre Jean De Smet, S.J., *Life, Letters, and Travels of Father Pierre-Jean De Smet, S.J., 1801–1873*, ed. Hiram Martin Chittenden and Alfred Talbot Richardson (New York: Francis P. Harper, 1905), 4 vols.

COLVILLE CONFEDERATED TRIBES

(See **Confederated Tribes of the Colville Reservation.***)*

CONFEDERATED SALISH & KOOTENAI TRIBES OF THE FLATHEAD RESERVATION

The roots of the Confederated Salish & Kootenai Tribes of the Flathead Reservation in Montana lay in the Hell Gate, Montana, tribal council of July 16, 1855, during which the Flatheads (Salish), Pend d'Oreilles (or Upper Kalispels), and Kutenais signed with the Washington territorial governor and superintendent of Indian affairs Isaac Stevens a treaty that was ratified on March 8, 1859. The Flatheads and Pend d'Oreilles were of the Interior Division of the Salish linguistic stock. The Kutenais were of Kitunahan linguistic stock. The treaty provided the tribes with a reservation called the Flathead, or Jocko, on the western slopes of the Continental Divide in western Montana. The original Flathead Reservation totaled 1,242,969 acres, but by a government act of April 23, 1904, 2,378 of its Indian residents were allotted 80 or 160 acres each, while 404,047.33 acres were patented to settlers, 60,843.04 acres were granted to the state of Montana for school

Johnny Arlee, 1982, a shaman who practices Native traditional religion and healing. Catholics have been reconciled to the practices after once scorning them. Arlee uses the sweat house and incorporates the elements of rock, earth, fire, and water in the rites. Today's Salish and Kutenai tribal members are descendants of the Flathead and Kutenai peoples, who were distinct linguistic groups when removed to the Flathead Reservation in western Montana.

Courtesy of Larry Reisnouer, *(Spokane) Spokesman-Review.*

purposes, 18,523.85 acres were reserved for the United States, and 1,757.09 acres were reserved for the tribes for church, school, agency, railroad, and biological-station purposes. The total acreage thus disposed of was 485,171.31 in 4,834 parcels. Allotting was completed in 1908. Eighty acres were allotted if the lands were classified as agricultural, and 160 acres were allotted if the lands were classified for grazing. Before the opening of the reservation, some Indian families had as many as three thousand head of horses.

By proclamation on May 22, 1909 (36 Stat. 2494), the president opened to entry and settlement all nonmineral and unreserved reservation lands classified as agricultural lands of the first class as well as agricultural lands of the second class and grazing lands. The reservation was officially opened to holders of lands in those categories on May 2, 1910. Although the reservation's boundaries remain as originally designated, its Indian-owned lands, as of September 30, 1977, had been reduced to 618,758.51 acres because of allotment and homestead sales. Of that acreage, 567,319.54 acres were in tribal ownership. The balance, except for 1,017 acres in government reserve, was in individual ownership. In 2009 the Flathead Reservation encompassed 1.314 million acres, just over 790,000 of which were owned and managed by the Tribes and its members.

Among those who later came to live on the reservation were some ninety Upper Spokanes, who relocated there in 1887 under the leadership of Baptiste Peone. They subsequently signed an agreement with the United States that allowed them to remain.

Location: The majority of the enrolled tribal members live on the Flathead Reservation. Those off the reservation reside principally in the Pacific Northwest but also in other areas, such as California.

Numbers: Tribal membership in 1980 was approximately 5,937; in 1985, 3,225; and in 1989, 6,669. In 2007 the Confederated Tribes had 7,180 enrolled members, 4,500 of whom were living on the Flathead Reservation. Of those, 1,550 were under the age of eighteen.

Government and Claims: The Confederated Salish & Kootenai Tribes of the Flathead Reservation were organized under the Indian Reorganization Act, and their constitution and bylaws were approved by the secretary of the interior on October 28, 1935. Their corporate charter was ratified on April 25, 1936. The governing body is a council whose members are nominated reservationwide. Elections of council members are held biennially. Many tribal members have held public office at the state, county, and local levels.

A compromise settlement between the petitioning Confederated Tribes and the defending United States was reached for an entry of a final judgment by the Indian Claims Commission in the amount of $4,431,622.18 on the condition that the claim (Docket 61), which had been appealed to the Court of Claims (Docket 1-66), be dismissed and remanded to the commission. This was done. For 12,005,000 acres of ceded lands under the 1855 treaty, a final judgment was entered on August 5, 1966, based on the value of the land as of March 8, 1859. This amounted to $5.3 million, less the consideration that had already been paid the tribes ($593,377.82) and an offset of $275,000. Thus, the final award totaled $4,431,622.18. On July 24, 1951, the tribes filed a claim with the Indian Claims Commission (Docket 156) for an accounting of their trust funds, erroneous boundary surveys, the opening of the Flathead Reservation, and the taking of lands and waters. The docket was dismissed because the claims were similar to those filed with the Court of Claims (No. 50233) under the act of July 30, 1946, which had authorized the suit by the tribes a year before the Indian Claims Commission was established. The claims for compensation for waters and lands taken were for the waters of Hell Roaring Creek, which had been appropriated for a power plant for the city of Polson, Montana; for reservation lands seized without adequate compensation for a power site under an act of March 3, 1909; and for waters from Flathead Lake used for constructing and operating the Flathead Irrigation Project under the act of April 3, 1908, without the compensation agreed upon. The court dismissed those claims, but on December 18, 1967, it awarded the tribes $190,399.97 as reimbursement for the expenses of surveys and classification of tribal lands sold and otherwise disposed of under the act of April 23, 1904 (33 Stat. 302) in breach of the Hell Gate treaty. On March 8, 1971, a judgment was rendered for $6 million that was a compromise settlement for the general accounting of tribal monies and property. On April 23, 1971, a judgment of $7,410,000 was issued. It included the 1912 value of 485,171.31 acres of reservation land, minus the $1,343,331.22 already paid, plus interest of $16,294,880.29, for a total award of $22,361,549.07. On November 11, 1971, a judgment of $550,000 was approved for erroneous surveys of the northern and southwestern reservation boundaries.

Contemporary Life and Culture: Much of the tribal land consists of valuable stands of timber, the sales of which have averaged about $3 million annually. Two large sawmills, which are of non-Indian ownership but located on the reservation, provide employment to tribal members who also work in other area mills and in allied logging operations. Additional tribal revenue comes from yearly rent paid for the site of Kerr Dam, a hydroelectric facility built by the Montana Power Company on the Flathead River on reservation lands. The Tribes continues to lease waters from the dam to power companies in the state. The BIA operates an irrigation system on the reservation that serves about 125,597 acres. The project was established in 1908 to help the Indians become farmers. As of 1980, less than 12 percent of the lands irrigated by the project belonged to tribal members. The Tribes owns a tourist resort at Blue Bay on Flathead Lake as well as recreational facilities at Hot Springs. Points of interest on the reservation include the National Bison Range at Moiese, waterfowl refuges, and historic St. Ignatius Mission, established in 1854. Tribal children have attended both mission and public schools since both began operations on tribal lands. Two cultural committees, one formed by the Salish and one by the Kootenais, have been gathering several hundred cassette tapes of tribal stories, songs, and general language information. The committees work with the Northwest Reading Laboratory in developing Indian literary materials. The involvement of youth in these activities—part of a trend toward "being Indian"—is a source of great satisfaction to their elders.

The Confederated Tribes operates Gray Wolf Peak Casino (opened 2007) in Evaro and KwaTaqNuk Resort and Casino at the south end of Flathead Lake in Polson. Together, the two casinos provide full-time jobs to 150 employees. In total, the Confederated Tribes employs about 2,200 people, 73 percent of whom are tribal members. In recent years, the annual operating budget of the CSKT reached $112 million. In addition to gaming and timber enterprises, CSKT owns S & K Technologies, a premier information technology and aerospace company that in May 2007 entered into a renewable $2.2-million annual contract with Lockheed Martin to supply couplers used in the manufacture of F-16 fighter jets. The Confederated Tribes is also engaged in banking, tourism, manufacturing and fabrication, and a marina operation. From all operations, CSKT generates $160 million annually in goods and services.

The Information Technology Program operated by CSKT on the reservation forms one of the largest computer networks in Montana and is the largest of any tribe in the state. Early Head Start and Head Start centers are operated in five reservation communities, providing services to children aged birth to five years. Elementary and secondary students attend the twenty-five public schools in the localities where they live (there are six high schools within the boundaries of the reservation), but through BIA contract, the Confederated Tribes now operates the all-Indian Two River Eagle School (grades 7–12), which is located four miles north of Ronan in Pablo. CSKT also operates Salish Kootenai College in Pablo and supports the higher education pursuits of tribal members, with up to five thousand dollars in unmet need per school year. Self-governing since 1981 and one of the first Indian community colleges in the United States, Salish Kootenai is open to all races and has an enrollment of about 1,750.

Kicking Horse Job Corps Center is the longest-running federally contracted program operated by CSKT, having been in continuous service since November 1970. In 2006 there were about fifty fluent Salish speakers still living, but the language is being revived through the *Snqwiiquo* immersion school, where specialist elders like Johnny Arlee teach children ages three through eleven. The cultural heritage of the Flathead Reservation is preserved through The People's Center (opened 1991) in Pablo, which combines education programming with museum exhibits and a gift shop. CSKT also operates one of the most active, successful, and technologically advanced repatriation programs in the country. The CSKT Tribal Historic Preservation Department currently maintains a staff of twenty-eight, while the Salish-Pend d'Oreille Culture Committee has amassed one of the largest oral history collections in America. In 2007–2008 CSKT tribal members took part in the first buffalo hunt near Yellowstone National Park in a hundred years, taking thirty-three animals. The *Char-Koosta News* is the official publication of the Flathead Reservation.

Special Events and Celebrations: On a weekend near the second week of May a Cherry Festival is held at Polson, as is the Blue Ray Regatta on Memorial Day weekend. In June at Hot Springs, Homesteader Days features an Indian rodeo and powwow. Also held at that time is Pioneer Days in Ronan, with a rodeo and powwow. Around the Fourth of July, the Arlee Powwow (the oldest powwow in North America to be held continuously at the same location) is put on at Arlee. At about the same time, the Babb Rodeo is held at Babb. In mid-July the Wagon Burner Regatta is staged at Polson. On Labor Day weekend the Indian Summer Regatta is held, also at Polson.

Suggested Readings:

Robert J. Bigart and Clarence Woodcock, *In the Name of the Salish & Kootenai Nation: The 1855 Hellgate Treaty and the Origin of the Flathead Indian Reservation* (Pablo, Mont.: Salish Kootenai College Press, 1996); Robert J. Bigart, ed. *Zealous in All Virtues: Documents of Worship and Culture Change, St. Ignatius Mission, Montana, 1890–1894* (Pablo, Mont.: Salish Kootenai College Press, 2007); Bonnie Bozarth, "Public Law 280 and the Flathead Experience," *Journal of the West* 39, no. 3 (2000); Heather M. Cahoon, "'For Better or for Worse': Flathead Indian

Reservation Governance and Sovereignty," Ph.D. dissertation, University of Montana, 2005; Confederated Salish and Kootenai Tribes, *Ktunaxa Legends* (Pablo, Mont.: Salish Kootenai College Press, 1997); Confederated Salish and Kootenai Tribes, *The Salish People and the Lewis and Clark Expedition* (Lincoln: University of Nebraska Press, 2005); James D. Keyser, *The Five Crows Ledger: Biographic Art of the Flathead Indians* (Salt Lake City: University of Utah Press, 2000); Theresa DeLeane O'Nell, *Disciplined Hearts: History, Identity, and Depression in an American Indian Community* (Berkeley: University of California Press, 1996); Jaakko Puisto, "'We Didn't Care for It': The Salish and Kootenai Battle against Termination Policy, 1946–1954," *Montana: The Magazine of Western History* 52, no. 4 (2002) and "'This is My Reservation; I Belong Here': Salish and Kootenai Battle Termination with Self-Determination, 1953–1999," *American Indian Culture & Research Journal* 28, no. 2 (2004); Patrick Impero Wilson, "Tribes, States, and the Management of Lake Resources: Lakes Coeur d'Alene and Flathead," *Publius* 32, no. 3 (2002).

CONFEDERATED TRIBES OF THE CHEHALIS RESERVATION

People of the Sand

The Confederated Tribes of the Chehalis Reservation originated from the establishment of the 4,224.63-acre Chehalis Reservation for Kwaiailks (Upper Chehalises) and Lower Chehalises at the confluence of the Chehalis and Black rivers in southwestern Washington State.

Location: Tribal members live on the Chehalis Reservation or nearby in towns such as Oakville, Rochester, and Elma, which are west of the cities of Chehalis and Centralia. Some live at points as distant as the state of Florida.

Numbers: In 1906 there were about 149 Chehalises. By 1984, the tribe numbered 382 and in 2005, 700.

History: The area designated for the Chehalis Reservation was selected by the government as early as 1860. Two years later, 230 Chehalises were living in the area, which was established as a reservation by executive order on July 8, 1864. In 1868 there were only forty families on the reservation, but many more Chehalises lived close by. Those on the reservation became concerned about the uncertain status of their lands. In 1873, when their agent, R. H. Milroy, requested that the reservation be enlarged, the commissioner of Indian affairs replied that additions were impossible because parcels of the land earmarked for the expansion had already been granted to the Northern Pacific Railroad. As a nontreaty people, the Chehalises received less federal assistance than did treaty tribes. Because of their nontreaty status they were not issued patents for the lands allotted them, and they therefore had to apply for lands under the homestead laws. By an executive order signed by President Grover Cleveland on October 1, 1866, 3,753.63 acres of the reservation were restored to the public domain for homestead entry, and 471 acres were set aside for school purposes. Thirty-six Indians on the reservation selected homesteads. A third executive order, dated November 11, 1909, restored an additional section of the reservation to the public domain.

Government and Claims: The Confederated Tribes of the Chehalis Reservation is a self-governing, independent political unit within the United States, with a constitution and bylaws adopted on July 15, 1939, and approved by the commissioner of Indian affairs on August 22, 1939. The Tribes had voted to reject organization under the Indian Reorganization Act of 1934 (48 Stat. 984). The governing body, the Chehalis Community Council, is composed of all qualified voters. It elects a business committee, which manages all of the Confederated Tribes' real property and other assets and administers the funds within tribal control. The committee also enforces tribal ordinances.

In 1906, because of diminishing natural resources on the reservation due to encroaching homesteaders, the Chehalis Tribe petitioned the U.S. government for payment for the lands that the United States had appropriated. Not having signed a treaty relinquishing the lands, the Chehalises had to wait a considerable time for compensation for their loss. In a 1908 report, the acting commissioner of Indian affairs, C. F. Larrabee, denied the validity of the Chehalis claims, maintaining that the Chehalises had participated in the Tansey Point (Oregon) treaties in 1851. Those treaties had been drawn up by Oregon superintendent of Indian affairs Anson Dart. Several Chehalises complained bitterly in depositions in an 1929 investigation of Native land use that was a part of the Indian claims case *Duwamish et al. v. the United States* (No. F-275). On August 8, 1951, a century after the Tansey Point treaties, the Chehalis Tribe again filed a petition with the Indian Claims Commission against the United States (Docket 237) for lands that the United States had appropriated, including 3,753.63 acres removed from the Chehalis Reservation by executive order in October 1886. The plaintiffs were the Upper and Lower Chehalis, Satsop, Humptulips, Upper and Lower Chinook, and Clatsop tribes as well as the Confederated Tribes of the Chehalis Reservation. Complications arose when the Claims Commission initially questioned the plaintiffs' right to prosecute the claim on behalf of the various tribes. Finally, however, the commission decided that the Confederated Tribes of the Chehalis Reservation was the successor in interest to the tribes who were the original owners of lands. The Confederated Tribes was seeking compensation for the lands because the government in the 1860s had ordered the Indians to locate on the Chehalis Reservation.

There is no proof that the Satsops, Humptulipses, Wynoochees, and Lower Chehalis villagers (such as Hoquiams, Ohyuts, and others) ever merged with the Chehalises on the Chehalis Reservation after those groups were directed by the government to remove there. Even the Lower Chehalises did not, for the most part, relocate there. In 1873 the Humptulipses still refused to leave their lands for the reservation. In 1879, the 164 Lower Chehalises living along the Pacific Coast on the tributaries of Grays Harbor refused to remove. In 1885 most of the Lower Chehalises were reported to be under the jurisdiction of the Quinault Agency, and many of their families eventually moved to the Quinault Reservation. Some Lower Chehalises were on the Shoalwater Reservation. Some Kwaiailks refused to remove to the Chehalis Reservation, though it lay in their territory. Instead, they chose to live with the Cowlitz and Nisqually Indians. Thus, contrary to government reports of the period, the Chehalises were not all brought together on the reservation as the government planned that they would be. The Indian Claims Commission, unable to determine who the claimant Indians or their ancestors were, decided unfavorably for the petitioners. The latter then took their case to the U.S. Court of Claims (140 C.Cl. 192), which returned the case to the Claims Commission for reconsideration. The petitioners at that juncture changed their case to delete the Clatsops and Chinooks, as directed by the Court of Claims. The Claims Commission reheard their case and determined that the band of Kwaiailks had held aboriginal title to 320,500 acres and the Lower Chehalises to 517,700 acres. The final judgment, entered October 7, 1963, was an award of $754,380 to the Confederated Chehalis Tribes.

Contemporary Life and Culture: Many Chehalises are engaged in the timber and fishing industries, the building trades, social services, and education. Some Chehalises carve wood pieces and craft beadwork and basketry for sale. Much reservation land that once produced good timber has been cleared for pasture and other agricultural uses. Some Chehalises lease individual allotments on the reservation, of which about 1,780 acres remain in trust or otherwise restricted in status. One source of tribal income was eliminated, as on other reservations, by a June 1980 U.S. Supreme Court ruling forbidding the sale of non-state-taxed cigarettes to non-Indian buyers at reservation smoke shops. The first major reservation housing program was begun in 1976 and completed in 1978. In 1980 another housing project was undertaken. Among other tribal projects are water-system and river-cleanup operations. A tribal center was built in the mid-1970s with facilities for children, a health clinic, a meeting room for the elderly, a library, classrooms, and tribal offices. Law enforcement is delivered through the Chehalis tribal police, a force that consists of six officers and a chief. Medical and dental services are provided by visiting doctors and nurses. The Tribes has produced Chehalis history films and published a tribal history.

In June 1995 the Confederated Tribes opened the Lucky Eagle Casino, a $13-million, 50,000-square-foot facility with a bingo hall, restaurant, and gift

After graduating from Chemawa Indian School in Salem, Oregon, Hazel Pete (1915–2003) spent a lifetime promoting the culture and history of the Chehalis Tribe. She was a master basket weaver and almost single-handedly revived the craft form among Chehalis tribal members in the second half of the twentieth century.

Courtesy of Paul D. G. Eubanks.

shop located on the western edge of the reservation. The casino employs seven hundred people, nearly three hundred of whom are members of the Confederated Tribes. A profit was realized for the first time in 1999. In January 2008 the Chehalises embarked on a major $14-million expansion of the Lucky Eagle, doubling square footage, increasing the number of slots to nearly eight hundred, and adding sixty new jobs. Eighty-five percent of casino revenue is set aside for economic development; the remainder is disbursed in per capita payments. The Tribes belongs to the Northwest Coalition of Gaming Tribes.

In 2005 the Confederated Tribes partnered with Great Wolf Resorts, Inc. of Madison, Wisconsin, to build a four-story, 51,000-square-foot indoor water park, a $100-million lodge, and a 399-room hotel sitting on forty-three acres of Chehalis tribal trust land located near Interstate 5 at Grand Mound. Adjacent to the main facility, which opened in March 2008 to twenty-three sold-out days, is a separate 40,000-square-foot conference center with six meeting rooms. The Confederated Tribes opened the sixty-nine-room Eagles Landing Hotel next to their casino in July 2005, adding it to the two construction companies and three convenience stores already operated by the Chehalises, one of which houses the MexiGo Mexican restaurant (opened March 31, 2009). In July 2009, a new community center opened on the reservation with classrooms, a regulation-size gymnasium, and a swimming pool. The Confederated Tribes has also built a new public safety building and a wellness center. It is the fourth largest employer in Thurston County.

Chehalis students attend public schools in the nearby communities of Oakville and Rochester, and a Head Start program is operated on the reservation. There is a program to preserve the Native language. In the summer of 2007 the Confederated Tribes, in conjunction with The Evergreen State College in Olympia, completed a curriculum of the Tribes' history designed for K-12 use in social studies classes. The Confederated Tribes supports forty tribal members with college tuition and books.

Special Events and Celebrations: The Chehalises hold their annual Tribal Days around the last weekend of May.

Suggested Readings:

> Cary C. Collins, "Art Crafted in the Red Man's Image: Hazel Pete, the Indian New Deal, and the Indian Arts and Crafts Program at Santa Fe Indian School, 1933–1935," *New Mexico Historical Review* 78, no. 4 (Fall 2003) and "A Future with a Past: Hazel Pete, Cultural Identity, and the Federal Indian Education System," *Pacific Northwest Quarterly* 92, no. 1 (Winter 2000/2001); Carolyn Marr, Donna Hicks, and Kay Francis, *The Chehalis People* (Oakville, Wash.: Confederated Tribes of the Chehalis Reservation, 1980); Herbert C. Taylor, "Anthropological Investigation of the Chehalis Indians Relative to Tribal Identity and Aboriginal Possession of Lands," in *Coast Salish and Western Washington Indians,* vol. 3 (New York: Garland Publishing, 1974), 117–58; Edwin VanSyckle, *The River Pioneers: Early Days on Grays Harbor* (Seattle, Wash.: Pacific Search Press, 1982).

CONFEDERATED TRIBES OF THE COLVILLE RESERVATION

The Confederated Tribes of the Colville Reservation is composed primarily of descendants of the following Salish and Shahaptian-speaking peoples: Colvilles, Entiats, Methows, Nespelems, Nez Perces, Sinkaietks (Southern Okanagons), Palouses, Sanpoils, Senijextees, Sinkiuses, and Wenatchis.

Location: A large portion of tribal members live on the Colville Reservation in north-central and northeastern Washington State. A slightly higher number reside off the reservation, particularly in bordering towns such as Omak, Okanogan, Brewster, and Grand Coulee.

Numbers: In 1985 tribal membership stood at 3,799; in 1989 it was 3,880; by 2007 it had grown to 9,065; and in July 2009 it was 9,365.

History: The Confederated Tribes of the Colville Reservation was formed by the April 19, 1872, executive order of President Ulysses S. Grant, which established the Colville Reservation east of the Columbia River. The boundaries of the reservation were changed by another executive order on July 2, 1872. The western boundary was then the Okanogan River; the eastern and southern boundaries were the Columbia River; and the northern boundary was the Canadian border.

The entry onto the reservation of the bands of chiefs Moses and Joseph in the 1880s caused considerable anguish, especially among the Sanpoils and the Nespelems, the original residents of the reservation.

In an agreement completed May 23, 1891, that was never ratified by the U.S. Senate, the Okanagons, Sinkiuses, Nez Perces, Colvilles, and Senijextees agreed to sell to the United States 1.5 million acres, the North Half of the reservation, for $1.5 million to be paid in five annual installments of $300,000. An act of July 1, 1892 (27 Stat. 62), restored the North Half to the public domain and provided that Indians not wanting to move to the South Half of the reservation be allotted from the vacated lands in the North Half. Before the North Half was opened to settlement on October 10, 1900, six hundred Indians had been allotted 51,653 acres by a presidential proclamation dated April 10, 1900. The North Half had been opened for mineral entry by an act of February 20, 1896. The 1,449,268 acres of the diminished reservation (its South Half) were opened to mineral entry on July 1, 1898 (30 Stat. 571). On December 1, 1905, 350 of the estimated 551 adult Indians living on the reservation signed the so-called (James) McLaughlin Agreement, relinquishing to the United States all rights, title, and interest to lands within the diminished reservation. The agreement also provided that the Indians be remunerated the as-yet-unpaid $1.5 million for the North Half. An act of March 22, 1906 (34 Stat. 80), allowed for the allotment of eighty acres to each Indian belonging to the reservation and for the sale of the surplus lands. The act was amended August 31, 1916, to reserve lands for schools, mills, cemeteries, and missions. By presidential proclamation on May 3, 1916 (39 Stat. 1778), the unallotted, unreserved nontimber and mineral lands within the diminished reservation were opened to white settlement. As a result of the Indian Reorganization Act of 1934, undisposed lands (about 818,000 acres) within the Colville Reservation were temporarily withdrawn from further disposition or sale by a Department of Interior order of September 19, 1934. An act of July 24, 1956 (70 Stat. 626–627), restored to the Confederated Tribes ownership of the undisposed lands.

Government and Claims: After considerable intratribal conflict, the Business Council of the Confederated Tribes of the Colville Reservation, Washington, was established. The council derived its powers from the constitution and bylaws of the Confederated Tribes, which were adopted by referendum vote on February 26, 1938. A serious point of contention in the 1950s and 1960s was possible termination of the relationship of the Confederated Tribes with the federal government. Termination was generally favored by tribal members living off the reservation and others who possessed a lesser Native blood quantum. Today, the Colville Tribal Council opposes termination. It does, however, seek sovereignty in tribal matters in which state and federal governments have heretofore been involved, such as law enforcement and protection of water rights.

After the Yakama Tribe filed a claim (Docket 161) for additional recovery for

Mel Tonasket, a tribal official, who in 1979 reflected the progressiveness of the Confederated Tribes of the Colville Reservation in north-central Washington, The Confederated Tribes is an amalgam of nearly a dozen Pacific Northwest tribes. Not all of the tribal members live on their reservation.

Authors' collections.

lands ceded to the United States in the June 9, 1855, Yakama Treaty, the Confederated Tribes of the Colville, on its own behalf and that of the thirteen other tribes under that treaty, filed two intervenor claims for additional compensation for ceded lands of five of the fourteen tribes. One of the intervenor claims (Docket 222) was on behalf of certain Palouses and others who had removed to the Colville Reservation. The other (Docket 224) was filed on behalf of Sinkiuses (such as the Moses Columbia Tribe et al.). The intervenor dockets were consolidated with Docket 161 on July 28, 1959, and November 10, 1961. Among the various tribes besides the Moses Columbias were Chelans, Entiats, and Wenatchis. They all had been represented at the Yakama treaty council by chiefs Tecolekun and La-Hoom, who signed for them. (In 1954, five years before the Confederated Tribes had been permitted by the Indian Claims Commission to intervene, there were 301 Sinkiuses, 113 Entiats, and 253 Wenatchis on the Colville Reservation.)

The Yakama Tribe attempted to block the claims filed by the Confederated Tribes of the Colville, maintaining that the fourteen tribes assigned to the Yakama Reservation (of which eleven are now identifiable) were a confederation for which the Yakamas were the spokesman. The Indian Claims Commission, opposing the Yakama convention, asserted that the lands of the various tribes had been ceded to the federal government, which had tried unsuccessfully to force the fourteen Salishan tribes and certain Palouses to remove to the Yakama Reservation, as provided by treaty. In 1883, when peoples under the Chief Moses agreement had not relocated to the Moses, or Columbia, Reservation, the government had made an agreement with them to remove to the Colville Reservation. The commission decided that they were entitled to additional compensation separate from that of the Yakamas, whose nation the commission found to be nonexistent, should the compensation of $593,000 for the combined cession of 8,176,000 acres, plus additional gratuities of $48,300, be found unconscionable. After it was so found, the commission awarded the tribes concerned $4,088,000, less offsets, making its final April 6, 1965, award $3,446,700.

On July 31, 1951, the Confederated Tribes filed a claim (Docket 178) before the Indian Claims Commission for mismanagement of Colville funds and property held in trust by the United States. An agreed-upon settlement of $5,540,598 was reached by the Confederated Tribes and the defending United States and approved by the commission in a final judgment on September 17, 1970. The order allowed the Colvilles to file a claim for accounting from July 1, 1951, which was to be set in a separate docket (178-A). This claim was transferred to the Court of Claims on February 24, 1977. In 1982, the tribes accepted an out-of-court settlement of $7 million for mismanagement of range and forestry lands and fiscal mismanagement from 1952 to 1982 (Docket 178-A). On July 31, 1951, the Colville Tribes filed a petition (Docket 177) alleging that the BIA had accepted insufficient compensation for lands sold on the South Half of the Colville Reservation and that the handling of the funds had been improper. Docket 177 had also stemmed from the act of March 22, 1906, whereby the government had reduced the payments it required for surplus lands and had permitted entry on them before they were paid for, thus violating its fiduciary duties as trustee for the Indians and injuring them. The Claims Commission dismissed that claim because of its similarity to Docket 181-B described below. Also filed on July 31, 1951, was a petition (Docket 181) of multiple claims made not only by the Confederated Tribes but also by individuals. The claims were subsequently put into separate dockets (181, 181-A, 181-B, and 181-C).

Docket 181 was for loss of aboriginal lands to the United States: 130,590 acres taken from the Colvilles proper; 513,050 acres taken from Sanpoil-Nespelems; 395,152 acres taken from the Okanagons; 379,665 acres taken from the Methows; and 311,305 acres taken from the Senijextees. The lands alienated were calculated as those that the tribes claimed at the time of the executive order of July 2, 1872, by which the tribes were to remove to the Colville Reservation. On March 1, 1960, the Claims Commission awarded the Colvilles proper $104,600, the Sanpoil-Nespelems $410,900, the Okanagons $223,400, the Methows $143,300, and the Senijextees $117,800. Total recovery by the Colville Tribes was $1 million after offset deductions, which amounted to $61,000.

In Docket 181-A it was claimed that certain tribes under Chief Moses of the Sinkiuses (referred to as Columbias, Chelans, Entiats, and Wenatchis) who had received his Moses, or Columbia, Reservation (established by executive order April 19, 1879, and amended by executive orders March 6, 1880, and February 23, 1883) had been forced under the agreement of July 7, 1883, to leave that reservation for the Colville. As the Columbia Reservation had been restored to the public domain by executive order on May 1, 1886, the Colville Tribes claimed that the removal had been uncompensated.

Docket 181-B had its roots in an agreement dated May 9, 1891, whereby the North Half of the Colville Reservation was ceded to the United States. The agreement was to have gone into effect after ratification by Congress, but by an act of July 1, 1892 (27 Stat. 62), Congress opened the North Half to settlement without

The Confederated Tribes of the Colville Reservation operates several businesses on the reservation, and Michael O. Finley is chairman of the Business Council. He is also coauthor of *Finding Chief Kamiakin: The Life and Legacy of a Northwest Patriot* (2008). Finley holds a master of arts degree in history from Eastern Washington University in Cheney and has been active in tribal historic preservation and in safeguarding the natural resources of the Colville Reservation.

Courtesy of Michael O. Finley

ratifying the agreement, while delaying the payment of the agreed-upon compensation of $1.5 million until June 21, 1906. The Colville Tribes contended that the payment was, in retrospect, unconscionable. A portion of the same docket (181-B) also alleged that the act of March 22, 1906 (34 Stat. 80), provided for sale of surplus lands on the South Half of the Colville Reservation and that the government had failed to provide adequate and fair compensation for those lands. For purposes of a final judgment, the Claims Commission consolidated dockets 181-A and 181-B, making an award of $3.5 million.

Docket 181-C was for several claims: for spoliation and depletion of fisheries due to construction of Grand Coulee Dam; for removal of resources (this claim is sometimes labeled "Docket No. 181-C, Mineral Claims"); for failure to safeguard hunting grounds; and for failure to safeguard rights to compensation for the taking and using of lands for railroads. The last two claims were not compensated, but in 1980 the Court of Claims heard the docket (because by law the Claims Commission had ceased to exist) and awarded the Colville Tribes compensation plus interest amounting to $3,257,000 for loss of fisheries and $140,000 for loss of mining operations. One claim, the Grand Coulee Dam claim (Docket 181-D), had been separated from Docket 181-C to allow the above award to be made. Docket 181-D originally included claims for the taking of tribal lands in connection with the construction of the Chief Joseph Dam on the Columbia as well as the Grand Coulee, but it was later amended to exclude reference to the former project. With twenty-four other tribes throughout the western United States, the Confederated Tribes filed other claims (Dockets 342-70 and 343-70) that reached the Court of Claims for mismanagement of Individual Claims Commission judgment funds and for other funds such as Individual Indian Money accounts held in trust by the United States. The tribes were awarded $1,213,027.79 in 1980 for their claim in Docket 181-D.

Contemporary Life and Culture: The effort to acquire power revenues from Columbia River dams is part of a wider effort by the Colville Tribes to control resources that include not only the waters of the Columbia and other rivers but also a variety of wildlife. In 1981 the Colville Tribes budgeted $4 million for land purchases.

A failed molybdenum mining venture dashed the Colvilles' hopes for economic stability. Other failed enterprises were Package Log Cabin sales, a meatpacking plant, and a modern greenhouse operation. After ridding the reservation of non-Indian businesses in 1973, the Colville Tribes started a thriving Trading Post. Timber is a viable resource. In 1984 the tribes dedicated their new $10 million sawmill located near Omak. In 1991 they continued an ongoing fight of federal (tribal) versus state jurisdiction—for example, the right of the State Highway Patrol to arrest drivers on reservation highways.

In 1984 the Colvilles established the Colville Tribal Enterprise Corporation (CTEC), which is headquartered at Coulee Dam, Washington. In the beginning, the corporation employed one hundred people; it now employs eight hundred and manages seventeen tribal enterprises, including gaming, recreation and tourism, retail, and construction and wood products. In 2007 CTEC ranked as the largest and most diverse American Indian business in the state of Washington and was the largest single employer in north-central Washington, generating over $140 million in annual revenue. In 1987 the Okanogan Bingo-Casino opened, followed in 1994 by the construction of the first gaming facility, Mill Bay Casino in Manson on Lake Chelan, and then the Coulee Dam Casino in Coulee Dam. In 1998 and 1999, CTEC acquired the Barney's Junction restaurant and motel in Kettle Falls and the Rainbow Beach Resort in Twin Lakes. And in July 2008 the Colvilles broke ground on a third, $24-million, 58,000-square-foot casino, which opened a year later on reservation land located near Omak.

In 2009 CTEC formed a new electrical company in Nespelem to provide power and communications services. The Confederated Tribes also owns and operates the Colville Indian Plywood and Veneer, which employs more than 230, and Precision Pine mills, with 120 employees, in Omak. The Confederated Tribes operates four Head Start centers on the reservation. In 2004 the Tribes assumed ownership of Pascal Sherman Indian School, a former Catholic Indian boarding school, now operated as a pre-K-9 residential and day facility located at St. Mary's Mission near Omak. One goal of the school is the perpetuation of tribal heritage. High school students attend school at Grand Coulee, and an increasing number of young people attend higher education centers such as community colleges and state universities. In 2005 the Colvilles opened a corrections center and the year after that a new health clinic, both in Nespelem.

The Colvilles are active in retrieving their own history and culture, introducing in 1984 a history-archeology program and opening a tribal repository to begin curating federal archeological collections. In 2004 the Colvilles observed a First Salmon Ceremony, which celebrated the first salmon to return up the Okanogan River in forty years. The tribe also promotes salmon runs on the upper Columbia River and has announced the construction of the $41-million Chief Joseph

Bernie Whitebear (1937–2000), a member of the Sin Aikst (now Lakes) Tribe who grew up on the Colville Indian Reservation, ranked among the most prominent Indian leaders, both in the Pacific Northwest and nationally. Whitebear, whose birth name was Bernard Reyes, founded the Seattle Indian Health Board, the United Indians of All Tribes Foundation, and the Daybreak Star Cultural Center in Seattle.

Courtesy of Paul D. G. Eubanks.

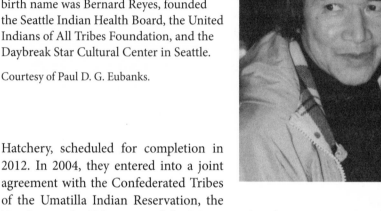

Hatchery, scheduled for completion in 2012. In 2004, they entered into a joint agreement with the Confederated Tribes of the Umatilla Indian Reservation, the Nez Perces, the Yakamas, and the Wanapum bands to initiate intertribal repatriations. In June 2006 the Colvilles participated in a joint intertribal repatriation ceremony at Palus Cemetery at the confluence of the Palouse and Snake rivers at the Lyons Ferry. Here they reburied over 37,000 funerary objects and the remains of 143 individuals that had been disinterred by the Army Corps of Engineers during the construction of the Lower Monument Dam in 1968.

Special Events and Celebrations: The Ground Hog Day Powwow at Nespelem Community Center is held in February and the Nespelem Junior Rodeo, Nespelem Rodeo Grounds, is held in April. Celebration of the Nez Perce Longhouse Root Feast is determined by the season of the roots. Commemorated at the end of May at Mission Point is the "Ceremony of Tears," which honors the Last Salmon Ceremony at Kettle Falls. The annual First Salmon Ceremony is held at the Omak Longhouse in June. Mill Pond Days at Nespelem City Park is held annually in the third week of June. The Circle Celebration, featuring Indian stick games and tribal dances, continues for several days in early July. Another rodeo is held on the reservation at Inchelium on the Fourth of July, followed by a powwow the week after that. The Fourth of July Powwow is held on the original Chief Joseph encampment site. There is an Indian powwow at the Omak (Washington) Stampede, which is held on the weekend falling nearest to mid-August. Indians from the Colville Reservation also participate in the Suicide Race Run in conjunction with the Stampede, and another celebration centers around the historical significance to the Colvilles of Soap Lake, Washington. Even after non-Natives settled around that place in the 1900s, the Confederated Tribes continued to return annually in the summer to celebrate the lake's spiritual and healing powers. But in 1970, because of cultural differences, the Colvilles stopped coming. They were invited to return and join in the 2008 Fourth of July parade in Soap Lake, and in 2009 they were there for the dedication of a large sundial with a sculpture of two Indians looking out over the lake.

Suggested Readings:

Laurie Arnold, "The Paradox of a House Divided: The Colville Tribes and Termination," Ph.D. dissertation, Arizona State University, 2005; Ann Briley, *Lonely Pedestrian: Francis Marion Streamer* (Fairfield, Wash.: Ye Galleon Press, 1986); David H. Chance, *People of the Falls* (Kettle Falls, Wash.: Kettle Falls Historical Center, 1986); Kathleen A. Dahl, "The Battle over Termination on the Colville Reservation," *American Indian Culture & Research Journal* 18, no. 1 (1994); John Fahey, "Power Plays: The Enigma of Little Falls," *Pacific Northwest Quarterly* 82, no. 4 (1991); M. Gidley, *Kopit: A Documentary of Chief Joseph's Last Years* (Seattle: University of Washington Press, 1981) and *With One Sky above Us: Life on an Indian Reservation at the Turn of the Century* (New York: Putnam, 1979); Rickard D. Gwydir, *Recollections from the Colville Indian Agency, 1886–1889* (Spokane, Wash.: Arthur H. Clark Co., 2001); Alexandra Harmon, "Tribal Enrollment Councils: Lessons on Law and Indian Identity," *Western Historical Quarterly* 32, no. 2 (2001); Lawney L. Reyes, *White Grizzly Bear's Legacy: Learning to Be Indian* (Seattle: University of Washington Press, 2002) and *B Street: The Notorious Playground of Coulee Dam* (Seattle: University of Washington Press, 2008); Robert H. Ruby and John A. Brown, *Half-Sun on the Columbia: A Biography of Chief Moses* (Norman: University of Oklahoma Press, 1965); Ruth Scofield, *Behind the Buckskin Curtain* (Seattle, Wash.: Seattle Pacific College, 1977); Jerry M. Scott, "A History of the Formation of the Colville Indian Reservation," master's thesis, Washington State University, 1992.

CONFEDERATED TRIBES OF COOS, LOWER UMPQUA AND SIUSLAW INDIANS

The three tribes were interrelated through marriage and trade for countless generations. The Pacific Ocean and its beaches offered a transportation route north and south linking the ancestral territories of the Coos, Lower Umpqua and Siuslaw. In 1917 the Coos, Lower Umpqua and Siuslaw, who had operated as a confederated group ever since the treaty of 1855, established an elected government with a tribal council. The Confederated Tribes ceded nearly 1.9 million acres as required in the 1855 treaty in exchange for a permanent reservation and government services to ease the transition to their new home. But the treaty never became a binding legal document. The United States Senate never ratified it. All of the tribal lands on the southern Oregon coast were taken without formal codified treaty.

Chief Edgar Brown of the Confederated Tribes is of Coos descent. In 1984 the tribe obtained federal recognition entitling them to government services, and serving as a catalyst for the tribal rejuvenation that has taken place in recent decades.

Courtesy of the Confederated Tribes of Coos, Lower Umpqua and Siuslaw Indians.

Location: Most of the membership lives within a five-county service area, including Coos, Curry, Douglas, Lane, and Lincoln counties.

Numbers: Tribal membership in 1986 stood at 248; in 2009 it was 934.

History: In 1850 Congress passed the Oregon Donation Land Act, which provided 320 acres of free land to each man and woman over the age of eighteen who had settled in the territory prior to 1850—or 160 acres if they had arrived after 1850. By 1854 a number of those lands taken under that law were along the margins of Coos Bay and the lower Umpqua River. In August and September 1855, meetings were held at Winchester Bay and also near Empire City on Coos Bay to negotiate a treaty for formal land cession. The treaties, duly signed, provided for the creation of a large reservation in coastal Oregon as part of the exchange for the cessions of land that reached as far east as the Coast Range. By that agreement, the Coos, Lower Umpqua, and Siuslaw tribes ceded nearly 1.9 million acres.

In October and November 1855 companies of volunteers, self-styled protectors of the new communities in the Rogue River valley, attacked the Indians on the Table Rock Reservation and fermented what became known as the Rogue River Indian War of 1855–56. The Coos, Lower Umpqua and Siuslaw Indians did not participate in any hostilities against the pioneer generation that moved in on them. While engagements were occurring just to the south, they remained peaceful. In late February 1856, the Coos County volunteers surrounded the local tribes and confined them to a village on the beach at Empire City. Native peoples were all herded together and impounded under armed guard, with the anticipation that they would be removed to the reservation that the treaties of the previous summer had called for. The tribes who had lived there for centuries became prisoners in their own homeland.

By late summer, the Coos Indians from the Coos Bay Estuary were moved north. They were marched through the sand dunes, forced to abandon their villages, their canoes, and most of their possessions to be colonized on a windswept 18,000-acre spit on the north side of the mouth of the Umpqua River. Meanwhile, the U.S. Army established a fort at a place that had been laid out as a small town called Umpqua City. Fort Umpqua became the new garrison at the southern end of the Great Coast Reservation. The Siuslaws were allowed to remain in their homeland, which fell within the boundaries of that reservation.

For the Coos and the Lower Umpquas it was a dreadful situation. The prospect for survival on the sand spit was very limited, but for the next two and a half years they were relegated to that location. This was a period of starvation and death through malnutrition and exposure as well as a time of waiting and confinement.

Then, in 1859, the BIA decided to remove the Coos and Lower Umpquas again. They herded them north along the coast, marching them over the trails around the Sea Lion Caves and Haceta Head over Cape Perpetua to Yachats Prairie, where they were to establish a new colony on the southern part of the Great Coast Reservation. The Yachats years would be remembered for the failure of its agricultural and educational programs as well as for the continuing abuse and death of Native peoples. With each passing season pressures on the land mounted. There were farmers living in Lynn and Benton counties in the mid-Willamette Valley who wanted a corridor to the sea. That led in 1865 to an executive order that cut a swath right through the center of the Great Coast Reservation and left a northern section that reached toward the Salmon River and a southern section that became known as the Alsea Subagency. Finally, in 1875 Congress threw open the whole southern part of the Coast Reservation for pioneer settlement. The amendment to close the southern portion and thereby eliminate the Alsea Subagency was presented as an economic measure. The chairman of the Indian Affairs Committee objected and moved to insert at the end of the amendment a proviso: "*Provided, that these Indians shall not be removed until their consent has been obtained.*"

A conference was held in June 1875 at Yachats. Indian agents argued the case for the removal to the tribes. Not a single tribal leader consented to the opening of that part of the reservation. Numerous attempts were undertaken by the Indian agents to secure the needed approval of the tribes for removal. Although the tribes remained steadfast in their resistance, Ben Simpson, the surveyor general of Oregon, certified to Congress on October 28, 1875, that the Indians had given their assent for removal.

During the reservation years over 50 percent of the people died from starvation, exposure, and disease. Without a treaty, the tribes had no protection whatsoever, and they were eventually forced off the lands they had spent sixteen years improving. Once again, they lost all they had struggled and worked for. Many found their way back to the lands of their ancestors, eking out a living on the fringes of the new culture that had displaced them. They became a homeless people in their own homelands.

In 1931 the Confederated Tribes of Coos, Lower Umpqua and Siuslaw Indians won permission to file a land claims case. Several tribal elders testified at the hearings to the extent of the holdings of the tribes, the locations of villages and other important sites, and of their forced removal to Yachats. Several testified in their Native language, using other tribal members as translators. In the end, the court rejected all of the testimony and ruled against the land claims. But the lessons learned by the defeat enabled other Oregon tribes to win their cases. Using expert witnesses culled from the fields of anthropology and linguistics, they avoided the pitfalls of the trail blazed by the Confederated Tribes. Despite the setback, the Confederated Tribes did not give up. Several tribal members worked throughout the 1930s and 1940s on land claims. In 1941, on six donated acres in Empire, the BIA built a hall for the general use of the tribes. Here the Confederated Tribes held many meetings.

Federal Indian policy kept evolving, usually in ways not beneficial to tribes. With the Eisenhower administration in the 1950s, conservative thinkers simply declared that tribes did not exist and severed all government-to-government relationships with them. This policy, adopted in 1954, was called termination. By 1956 Congress had passed a bill terminating all the tribes of western Oregon, plus the Klamaths. The Confederated Tribes of Coos, Lower Umpqua and Siuslaw vigorously opposed termination and a new battle was on: the fight to reverse termination.

Eventually, the federal government altered its policies and disavowed termination. After extensive efforts, restoration was achieved for the Confederated Tribes in 1984. Since restoration, tribal members have been working to improve the social, economic, and educational status of their people. The work of recapturing tribal culture, history, and heritage continues, and thanks is given to the hard work and strength of their ancestors.

Children of the Confederated Tribes of Coos, Lower Umpqua and Siuslaw Indians in traditional cedar-bark dresses and holding a shinny stick. Shinny is a game similar to field hockey.

Courtesy of David M. Petrie, Confederated Tribes of Coos, Lower Umpqua and Siuslaw Indians.

Contemporary Life and Culture: Since restoration in 1984, the Confederated Tribes has experienced tremendous growth. The Health Department was opened in Tribal Hall in 1987 to promote programs that empower tribal families and improve their health status and quality of life. The Education Department opened in 1990 with a commitment to help tribal members attend universities around the United States. Over the past ten years the Confederated Tribes has assisted more than 150 tribal members with educational goals. Today there are over forty tribal members attending college full-time. In 1998 the Tribes acquired a loan from the USDA Community Facilities Loan Program and renovated an existing building for administrative office space. In 2000 they completed their seventeen-unit Qaxas Housing Development project. That same year they were awarded the HUD Best Practices Award for Outstanding Achievement in the Nation for the Qaxas project.

The Confederated Tribes owns and operates the Three Rivers Casino and Hotel, which was opened in 2004. This facility is the largest employer in the city of Florence. The casino includes four restaurants and an events center, while the hotel offers ninety deluxe rooms and three suites. Adjacent to the casino, hotel, and 9,000-square-foot special events center is a 15,000-square-foot administration building. In 2003 the Confederated Tribes cosponsored the "Weaving Our Past into the Future—Cultural Education Workshop." This workshop promoted the study, cultivation, and utilization of native plants, barks, and grasses and their uses in the construction of traditional south coast Native basketry and clothing.

In 2005 the U.S. government returned the forty-one-acre Coos Head site, which was taken in 1855. In late 2008 President George W. Bush signed a bill restoring twenty-four acres considered sacred by the Confederated Tribes. The property included Chief's Island and the ancient village site of Bal'diyaka near

Charleston, which will be placed in trust for the Confederated Tribes. Currently the Tribes has 7.4 acres of reservation land, 130.5 acres of trust land, and 205 acres of fees land. This is what is left to them of the 1.9 million acres that was once their ancestral territory.

Special Events and Celebrations: The Salmon Ceremony is held on the first Sunday in August at the Tribal Hall in Coos Bay. Annual Restoration Days is celebrated on October 17 or the closest weekend to that date. The Confederated Tribes observes summer and winter solstices and, depending on the weather, sponsors seasonal events for hunting and gathering.

Suggested Readings:

> Stephen D. Beckham, *Indians of Western Oregon: This Land Was Theirs* (Coos Bay, Ore.: Arago Books, 1977) and *Land of the Umpqua: A History of Douglas County, Oregon* (Roseburg, Ore., Douglas County Comissioners, 1988); Friends of South Slough, *South Slough Adventures: Life on a Southern Oregon Estuary* (Charleston, Ore.: Friends of South Slough, 2006); Michael Wayne Simpson, "The Kusan People: A Systematic Cultural History," Ph.D., dissertation, University of Hawaii, 1990; Mark Axel Tveskov, "The Coos and Coquille: A Northwest Coast Historical Anthropology," Ph.D. dissertation, University of Oregon, 2000; Lionel Youst, *She's Tricky Like Coyote: Annie Miner Peterson, an Oregon Coast Indian Woman* (Norman: University of Oklahoma Press, 2005).

CONFEDERATED TRIBES OF THE GRAND RONDE COMMUNITY

The Confederated Tribes of the Grand Ronde Community of Oregon grew out of several tribes representing a half-dozen linguistic groups on the Grand Ronde Reservation. They were confederated under the 1934 Indian Reorganization Act (48 Stat. 984). On March 8 and 9 of that year the tribes met at the Chemawa Training School near Salem, Oregon, where they were reported to be eager for self-government and the reestablishment of their Native identity. After receiving a charter of incorporation on May 13, 1935, they expected many governmental aids and the restoration of their alienated reservation lands. Their expectations were not realized. Their disappointment was perhaps one reason why they voted to terminate their relations with the government under a congressional act of August 13, 1954 (68 Stat. 732). With termination on August 13, 1956, they lost health and school funds and other government-supported programs. In the 1970s the successors of the Confederated Tribes of the Grand Ronde Community came together as the Confederated Tribes of Grand Ronde Indians, a loosely organized group not acknowledged by the federal government.

Jackie Colton and Clara Riggs, 1981. In 1983 these women and their fellow residents of the Confederated Tribes of the Grand Ronde Community received the recognition of the federal government after having previously had their relations terminated with the United States.

Authors' collections.

Numbers: In 1856, after most of the tribes assigned to the Grand Ronde Reservation had been removed there, a census revealed that there were 1,925 Indians on the reservation, of whom 909 were Takelmas, Latgawas, or Shastas. In May 1857, after most of those three groups had relocated to the Siletz Reservation, 922 Upper Umpquas, Kalapuyan speakers, and Molalas remained on the Grand Ronde with a few Takelmas, Latgawas, and Shastas. A small number of Clatsops was added to Grand Ronde membership rolls in 1875, making for a total enrollment from all tribes of 424 in 1886. In 1902 there were 398. In 1984 the population of the Confederated Tribes of Grand Ronde Indians was about 1,500, a number that had grown to 5,111 enrolled members by 2008, making it the largest tribe in Oregon.

History: The organization of the Confederated Tribes of Grand Ronde Indians has a history that dates to January 11, 1856, when eight wagons carried some elderly and infirm Upper Umpquas and Kalapuyan speakers from the Umpqua River valley north to the Grand Ronde. These Indians had been gathered on the temporary Umpqua Reservation from which a remainder, numbering about three hundred, walked to the Grand Ronde through winter cold and snow. In February 1856 the bands composing the Rogue River Indians were moved from the Table Rock Reservation to the Grand Ronde. The Molalas and Kalapuyan-speaking tribes of the Willamette Valley were also removed there. Then, in late summer two boatloads of Rogues and coastal Indians were brought to the Grand Ronde, where they remained until May 1857, at which time the coastal Indians and over half of the Rogues were moved to the Siletz Reservation. In order to establish a military presence near the Grand Ronde and to prevent clashes with settlers, Fort Hoskins was established on July 26, 1856, in Kings Valley (near Hoskins, Oregon) on the Luckiamute River, close to the mouth of Bonner Creek. In that same year, Fort Yamhill was established a half mile north of Valley Junction. After 1866, when those posts were no longer manned, the whiskey trade became rampant, exacting its toll on the Indians.

The first schools on the Grand Ronde opened in August 1856. Unlike the Kalapuyan speakers and Umpquas, the Takelmas and Latgawas asked for payment to send their children to school. Such institutions were established to destroy Indian cultures. Use of Native languages was discouraged and children were forced to cut their hair, wear shoes, and abandon much of their Native culture. Their male elders were taught farming and the women to do household chores. Unsuitable conditions on the Grand Ronde produced intertribal conflict among elderly traditionalists. When, for example, a Molala killed an Umpqua on the reservation, the matter was settled by payment of blood-feud money to the victim's relatives. The establishment of the Manual Labor Training School early in 1880 at Forest Grove was an amalgamating catalyst among Pacific Northwest Indians. (Within five years the school would be relocated near Salem, as Chemawa Indian School.) Marriages further broke down intertribal barriers. During the 1870s, in the Peace Policy era of President Ulysses S. Grant, the Grand Ronde was administered by officials of the Roman Catholic faith.

In 1871 about thirty families on the Grand Ronde were given individual plots to farm. Property ownership and manual labor, government officials believed, would help instill in Indians those qualities needed to assimilate successfully into American society. As the system of land tenure was unfamiliar to the Indians, the plan failed. Under the Dawes Indian Severalty Act of February 8, 1887 (24 Stat. 388), Grand Rondes took up 33,148 acres on the reservation. Three years after a June 1901 conference, on April 21, 1904, the Indians, with government approval, ceded 26,111 acres of the reservation to the United States. By 1928 the land base of these reservation Indians was virtually nonexistent. Most of the allotments had been sold off, and only sixty-seven allottees remained, holding a mere 440 acres.

Government and Claims: On August 26, 1935, a congressional act (49 Stat. 810) was passed pertaining to the western Oregon tribes. Those with whom unratified treaties had been made in 1851 and 1855 were to bring suit for certain lands taken from the Siletz Reservation. The Confederated Tribes of the Grand Ronde Indian Community was included with the petitioners from the Siletz Reservation (Case No. 45230). Because the Grand Ronde Indians were not coastal tribes formerly affected by the withdrawal of the tracts from the Siletz Reservation, the Court of Claims excluded them from the suit, along with certain petitioning Chinooks and Clatsops and the Willamette Valley Confederated Tribes, a loosely organized group of nonreservation Indians.

The Grand Ronde tribes were included with petitioning Kalapuyan-speaking descendants and others in filing a claim (Docket 238) with the Indian Claims Commission on August 8, 1951. Their case was dismissed on November 17, 1954. After termination, and emulating other Oregon tribes that had restored themselves as separate and legal entities, the present-day Tribes of the Grand Ronde Indians Incorporated effected a similar restoration by formally orga-

Kathryn Harrison (b. 1924) is former chair of the Confederated Tribes of the Grand Ronde, having guided them into the era of cultural revitalization and casino ownership in the late twentieth century.

Courtesy of the Oregon Historical Society, Portland.

nizing and holding regular meetings. Their loose organization lacked federal acknowledgment until November 1983, when Congress voted to recognize the Grand Ronde Indians, paving the way for them to receive federal aid for housing, health, and education and to develop a plan for the establishment of a reservation on Bureau of Land Management (BLM) land. Thus, their termination status was ended. Today, over eleven thousand of the sixty thousand acres that belonged to the Grand Rondes before termination have been restored.

Contemporary Life and Culture: Having been restored in 1983, the Confederated Tribes of Grand Ronde was reported in 1998 to be the wealthiest tribe in Oregon, with a net worth of $100 million and the most successful casino, Spirit Mountain, not only in the state but in all of the Pacific Northwest. In addition, the Tribes operates Grand Ronde Industries and Spirit Mountain Logistics, providing inventory management and support services to manufacturers, as well as Spirit Mountain Environmental Services, an environmental consulting and management enterprise. The Confederated Tribes now employs some seventeen hundred Oregonians, boasts investments in real estate and other commercial ventures, and provides thousands of dollars annually in pensions, scholarships, and charitable contributions. By April 2009 the Spirit Mountain Community Fund had given some $60 million to charities since its inception in 1997.

To retrieve and preserve their culture, the Confederated Tribes maintains an archives and library, teaches immersion classes in their traditional languages, is active in reclaiming ancestral remains and other funerary and significant objects (sending out four thousand letters to museums and other institutions requesting holdings lists), and is partnering with other organizations and institutions to promote and share Indian art and culture among all peoples. The Confederated Tribes operates a health and wellness center with a full pharmacy, an optometry clinic that dispenses glasses and contact lenses, a dental clinic with two dentists and two hygienists, a wellness and prevention department that provides education and promotes healthy lifestyles, and a behavioral department that addresses mental health and drug and alcohol addiction. The Tribes also employs chiropractic and podiatrist physicians and publishes a tribal newspaper, *Smoke Signals*. In 2003, tribal member Elvin Butler, Sr., commented, "We've come a long way from a tribe that was supposed to be exterminated, but we made it."

Special Events and Celebrations: In November 2008, the Confederated Tribes of Grand Ronde celebrated the twenty-fifth anniversary of their restoration with a powwow. Annual events include the Veterans Powwow, held the second weekend in July on the Uyxat Powwow Grounds, and the Contest Powwow, one of the largest powwows in the western United States, which is held the third weekend in August.

Suggested Readings:

Stephen Dow Beckham, *Oregon Indians: Voices from Two Centuries* (Corvallis: Oregon State University Press, 2006); Laura Berg, *The First Oregonians: Second Edition* (Portland: Oregon Council for the Humanities, 2007); Tracy Neal Leavelle, "'We Will Make It Our Own Place': Agriculture and Adaptation at the Grand Ronde Reservation, 1856–1887," *American Indian Quarterly* 22, no. 4 (1998); Kristine Olson, *Standing Tall: The Lifeway of Kathryn Jones Harrison* (Seattle: University of Washington Press, 2006).

CONFEDERATED TRIBES OF SILETZ INDIANS

The Confederated Tribes of Siletz Indians initially evolved from several tribes representing about a half-dozen linguistic groups on the Siletz Reservation. They took their name from the reservation that had been named for the Siletz Indian tribe. Their relationship with the federal government was terminated on July 20, 1956, by an act of Congress (Public Law 588, signed August 13, 1954), which declared in essence that on August 13, 1956, there would be no Indian tribal entities in western Oregon. A nucleus of the former Confederated Tribes reorganized in the 1960s, and in 1973, endeavoring to regain federal recognition, they filed as a nonprofit corporation. On November 18, 1977, an act (91 Stat. 1415) called for the secretary of the interior to submit to Congress within two years a plan for locating a reservation in Oregon's Lincoln County for the Confederated Tribes. That reservation, held in trust by the United States, was established on September 4, 1980 (Public Law 96-340; 94 Stat. 1072). The tribes were given two parcels: 3,633 acres of BLM timberlands in Lincoln County and 38.44 acres of the original Siletz Reservation, known as Government Hill, where the town of Siletz is located. The November 18, 1977, act had allowed transfer of public-domain lands from the BLM to the BIA to be held in trust for the Confederated Tribes of the Siletz Indians of Oregon. By that act, tribal members were to receive the federal services and benefits awarded other Indians of that status. Tribal holdings in 2006 totaled 4,204 acres.

Location: Tribal members live in the area of their reclaimed holdings in such towns as Newport along the north-central coast of western Oregon.

Numbers: In 1857 there were 590 Latgawas and Takelmas, Shastas, and a few Umpquas on the Siletz Reservation, this from a total of the 909 who had been on the Grand Ronde Reservation the previous year. By July 1858, 205 of the 590 had died and 35 had returned to the Grand Ronde. Of the Indians on the Siletz at that time, only 259 treaty Takelmas received subsistence support. That left 1,766 others there in a starving condition. Included among the latter were 279 Kuitsh (Lower Umpquas) and Coos and 181 Siuslaws and Alseas, most of whom did not become part of the Siletz Confederated Tribes. In 1865 there were 123 Chastacostas and Umpquas, 121 Takelmas, and 1,824 coastal Indians, including Chetcos, Tututnis (Rogues), Yaquinas, Upper Coquilles, and others, on the Siletz Reservation. All of these peoples were greatly reduced from the time when they had first come into contact with non-Indians.

At the time of termination in 1956 the Confederated Tribes numbered 929. When a new tribal council was formed in the fall of 1973, the population stood at 200. By 1985 there were 867 registered Confederated Siletzes, but many more were unregistered. In 1989 the membership numbered 1,309; in 1994 the number was approximately 2,200; in April 2006, 4,400; and, in 2008, 4,574.

History: In 1856, at the end of the Rogue wars, the Tututnis, Takelmas, Shastas, Latgawas, and a few Dakubetedes and Taltushtuntudes were all counted as Rogues. After removal to reservations, they were included with the Takelmas. Members of those tribes, plus Chetcos, Chastacostas, and Upper Coquilles, were rounded up at Port Orford as combatants in the war. From there, 600 were shipped on the steamer *Columbia* in June 1856 up the Pacific Coast and the Columbia and Willamette rivers to Dayton, Oregon. From there they were marched to the Grand Ronde Reservation. In July another boatload of 592 Rogues was transferred north in the same manner. Another 215 Indians, mostly from coastal tribes, walked the 125 miles to the north portion of the Coast Reservation (the future Siletz Reservation) north of Yaquina Bay. Some Latgawas and Takelmas from the Table Rock Reservation reached the Grand Ronde via the Willamette Valley by walking or riding in wagons. By May 1857 nearly all of the Rogues and Shastas had been moved to the Coast Reservation except for Chief Sam and 58 of his men and their families, who remained on the Grand Ronde. Sam had remained neutral during the Rogue wars.

The original Siletz Reservation, established by executive order on November

9, 1855, had been designated as the "Coast Reservation." It contained 1,383,000 acres running roughly 102 miles north and south along the Oregon coast and 20 miles east and west between the summit of the Coast Range and Cape Lookout on the north to about midway between the Siuslaw and Umpqua rivers on the south. In August 1856 the Siletz Agency was staffed at headquarters north of Yaquina Bay. By 1860 the reservation had come to be called the Siletz. A sub-agent, stationed at Yachats Prairie in 1861, oversaw Indians on the southern portion of the reservation, which became known as the Alsea. The Indians of that southern portion, including Coos and Kuitsh along with the Siuslaws, were removed to near the Yachats River estuary on the coast where the Alsea Indians were. The Umpqua Subagency (located in 1856 on the south near the mouth of the Umpqua River), which formerly had supervisory control, was closed late in 1859.

By executive order on December 21, 1865, a strip of land about twenty-five miles wide, running from east to west across the Siletz Reservation, including Yaquina Bay, was withdrawn to give settlers the lands that they wanted. This cut the Siletz Reservation in two. The south half, which then became the Alsea Reservation, ran about thirty-one miles from north to south. On March 3, 1875, it was turned over to the public domain (18 Stat. 420). After the withdrawal of the Alsea Reservation and the Yaquina strip, the Siletz was reduced to about 223,000 acres. Acts of October 31, 1892 (28 Stat. 286 and 323), and August 15, 1894 (28 Stat. 236 and 323), ceded to the public domain 191,798.80 acres from the Siletz. This was the total unallotted acreage except for five sections withheld for the Confederated Tribes. A proclamation by President Grover Cleveland on May 16, 1895, ceded the remaining lands of the Siletz to the public domain after its Indians were allotted. When terminated in 1954, the reservation comprised approximately 7,900 acres. All but 38.44 of those acres reverted to the public domain for sale, while the 38.44 acres were eventually given to the town of Siletz in lieu of payment of taxes.

The first year after removal to the Coast Reservation, 1856–57, was disastrous. Several hundred Indians died from exposure, starvation, and disease. Future prospects were no better. In 1865, for example, the Siletz agent spent $46.23 on each of the treaty Chastacostas and Umpquas and the 121 treaty Takelmas. Each of the other 1,824 Indians, parties to unratified treaties, received a mere $2.50 per year. The disparity in the amount of Indian goods and services aggravated intertribal conflict. Troubles increased when relatives sought revenge on Indian shamans who had failed to cure the diseases that ran rampant on the reservation. By 1859 about a hundred of these healers had been killed. The government sought to reduce such killings by seizing Indian weaponry, a step that served only to inflame attitudes. To control the Indians, prevent them from escaping, and lessen the burden on the agents, the military established two forts, Hoskins in Kings Valley (closed 1866) and Yamhill near Valley Junction (also closed 1866). A third post, Fort Umpqua (abandoned 1862), had been constructed near the mouth of the Umpqua River during the Rogue wars. Despite the efforts of the military at containment, Indians continued to flee down the coast or across the Coast Range. For example, in 1857 after the Rogue wars, about a hundred Rogues, Coos, and Umpquas were gathered up. In July 1864 a hundred Coos and Umpquas were captured in the mountains of southern Oregon and at Coos Bay. The military proved as objectionable to the Indians as the reservations, the troopers harassing their women and introducing diseases among them.

Helping to make reservation life unbearable were agents who stole from the Indians on the Siletz. The few treaty goods supplied to the Indians were of poor quality. In the schools the children learned only the English language and other aspects of American culture. By the twentieth century the tribal languages had virtually disappeared. The efforts of officials to curb alcohol consumption proved ineffective. The requirement that Indians obtain passes when leaving the reservation in no way reduced their access to strong drink secured from liquor dealers who had appropriated old village sites. Only in 1871, when Gen. Joel Palmer became agent, was the whipping post, which was used whenever Indians failed to follow orders or participated in old tribal practices, abolished. Also abolished was the chieftaincy. Instead of headmen acting as spokesmen for their people, tribal courts and juries were instituted. In the 1870s, during the era of the President Ulysses S. Grant Peace Policy, when churches ran the agencies, the Methodist influence on the Siletz, like that of other churches at other agencies, only served to hasten the process of acculturation. To help prevent reversion by the Indians to old ways, the church tried to neutralize the teachings of the messiah cults that surfaced during this period. An Indian police force established on the Siletz on August 15, 1878, was also used as an instrument of acculturation, as was a boarding school founded there the following year.

Government and Claims: On March 3, 1901, after Indian allottees on the Siletz had petitioned Congress for full titles to their properties, that legislative body passed a law ending trust control of allotted lands. By 1953 only seventy-six allotments remained on the Siletz, or 5,390 acres of the lands formerly held in trust for individuals. Of a voting population of 233 members in April 1935, 53 voted to accept the Indian Reorganization Act (48 Stat. 984), while 123 members voted against it. On October 31, 1892, the Confederated Tribes of Siletz Indians had been party to an agreement ratified by an act of Congress on August 15, 1894 (28 Stat. 286, 323), to cede to the United States the unallotted lands on the Siletz Reservation—with the exception of five timbered sections near the Siletz River, which were reserved as tribal land. For a total of 191,798.80 acres ceded, the Confederated Tribes was paid $142,600. The ceded portion had been opened to homestead entry by presidential proclamation on May 16, 1895. At first, the land was disposed of only gradually, since a fee of $1.50 per acre was required in addition to the regular Homestead Act filing fee. Once Congress removed this acreage fee on May 17, 1900, the land sold more rapidly.

Art Bensell, shown in 1980 as chairman of the Confederated Tribes of Siletz Indians, which received federal recognition in 1977. Bensell was inducted in 1987 into the American Indian Athletic Hall of Fame. Before him, Rube Sanders from the same tribe received the same honor.

Authors' collections.

Eventually the Confederated Tribes attempted to sell the five reserved timbered sections except for one section at Depoe Bay. An act of Congress of May 13, 1910 (36 Stat. 367), and amended May 18, 1916 (39 Stat. 123, 149), permitted the government to offer the timbered sections for sale. Only one was sold; the other four were disposed of at the time of termination. The Confederated Tribes claimed (Docket 239) that the $142,600 that they had received for the 191,798 acres was far too little. The Indian Claims Commission ruled on November 23, 1955, that the Confederated Tribes was entitled to a payment of $573,396, less their original payment of $142,600. Some of the individual tribes composing the Confederated Tribes of Siletz Indians were petitioners for various claims before the Court of Claims and the Indian Claims Commission. (*See* **Coos Tribe of Indians; Coquille; Hanis Coos; Siuslaw;** *and* **Tututni.**)

On August 13, 1954, President Dwight D. Eisenhower signed Public Law 588, which terminated forty-three bands west of the Cascade Mountains in Oregon, effective August 13, 1956. Although the Confederated Tribes of Siletz Indians and the Grand Ronde Indian Community had passed resolutions favoring termination, other Indians opposed it, including the Coos, Kuitsh, and Siuslaws as well as the Chinooks and several Tillamooks. After termination, the Indians were expected to become taxpayers, which resulted in the sale of some allotments and further alienation of Indian lands. In the fall of 1973, two hundred persons of the Siletz formed a new council. Their objective was to move toward the restoration of their Indian status. The minimum Native-blood quantum for membership was established at one-eighth. On March 30 and 31, 1976, Siletz council members testified in Washington, D.C., before the Senate Subcommittee on Indian Affairs. Despite the opposition of commercial and fishing interests, Congress passed an act (91 Stat. 1415) on November 18, 1977, which, when signed by President Jimmy Carter, restored the Confederated Tribes of Siletz

Indians of Oregon as a federally recognized Indian tribe. It was the first tribe in Oregon and the second in the United States to be restored. The act permitted them to receive the federal services and benefits accorded recognized tribes and their members, but it did not provide a reservation for the Siletz Indians or restore hunting and fishing rights. However, on October 4, 1980, 3,630 acres of land in scattered blocks were transferred from the BLM for the reservation described above.

Contemporary Life and Culture: In 1975, the Siletzes opened a manpower office with a Comprehensive Employment Training Act (CETA) grant. They also operated an alcohol- and drug-abuse program. Recognition followed in 1977, when the federal government reversed the 1956 termination of the Siletzes, but self-governance did not come until 1992. Only then were services and programs placed under tribal control in an extended service area that encompassed eleven Oregon counties. In 1985 the Confederated Tribes formed the Siletz Tribal Economic Development Corporation (STEDCO) as an independent entity to oversee and foster economic opportunity.

The Confederated Tribes owns and operates the $20-million Chinook Winds Casino Resort and Convention Center, which opened 1995 and is the single largest employer in Lincoln County. The resort includes a $26-million, 227-room oceanfront hotel and the 18-hole Chinook Winds golf course. The casino is extremely ecologically friendly, operating on significant quantities of renewable wind energy; it reduces its carbon emissions by 900 tons annually. In addition, the Siletzes operate two RV parks—Logan Road in Lincoln City and Hee Hee Illahee RV Resort at Salem. In the past decade, the Confederated Tribes has acquired several multimillion-dollar properties. It operates a dredging and salvage company as well as the Siletz Gas & Mini Mart. Not including the casino and resort, the Confederated Tribes employs approximately 250 people.

Comprehensive health services (direct care, contracts, and agency referral) are delivered through the Siletz Community Health Clinic, which opened in 1991. Education is provided through Head Start (ages three and four), a school of 190 students from kindergarten through eighth grade, and the Siletz Valley Early College Academy School (65 students in grades 9 to 12). In 2006–2007 Siletz Valley School was one of two such schools selected in Oregon to receive a Bill & Melinda Gates Foundation grant, which allows students to simultaneously earn high school and college credits. Siletz Youth Center offers tutoring assistance and a place for students to complete homework. The Confederated Tribes also supports with scholarships eligible tribal members pursuing higher education. Since 1998, the Confederated Tribes has received over $15 million in funding under the Indian Housing Block Grant Program, and since restoration the Siletzes have built a tribal services building, a 13,500-square-foot medical clinic, and both a social services and a child-care facility. In 2006 the Confederated Tribes distributed nearly $825,000 through its Siletz Tribal Charitable Contribution Fund.

In 1994 the Confederated Tribes established the annual Run to the Rogue in which tribal members volunteer to carry the tribal feather staff in a 240-mile relay that stretches from Siletz to ancestral lands located at Agness near the Rogue River in the Siskiyou Mountains. In 2003 the Siletzes inaugurated the Siletz Language and Traditional Arts program to promote and teach the use of the Siletz Athabaskan language and tribal traditional arts. In 1994 fewer than a dozen tribal members possessed a working knowledge of the Siletz dialect. By 2007 there was only a single speaker left of Siletz Dee-ni, the last of twenty-seven languages once spoken on the Siletz Reservation. The Siletzes partnered with the Confederated Tribes of Grand Ronde to develop a 15.6-acre site at Keizer into a business park. In 2007 the Confederated Tribes assumed title to 3,900 acres of Oregon coast-range forest, which they will manage in perpetuity for the purpose of restoring the marbled murrelet population lost in a 1999 oil spill.

Special Events and Celebrations: On the second weekend of August, tribal members and visitors gather for the Nesika Illahee Powwow in Siletz, Oregon. This powwow is considered one of the premier powwow events in the Pacific Northwest. After mid-November, the Confederated Tribes holds its annual Siletz Restoration Powwow.

Suggested Readings:

Stephen Dow Beckham, *The Indians of Western Oregon, This Land Was Theirs* (Coos Bay, Ore.: Arago Books, 1977) and *Oregon Indians: Voices from Two Centuries* (Corvallis: Oregon State University Press, 2006); Edwin L. Chalcraft, *Assimilation's Agent: My Life as a Superintendent in the Indian Boarding School System*, Cary C. Collins, ed. (Lincoln: University of Nebraska Press, 2004); Laura Berg, *The First Oregonians: Second Edition* (Portland: Oregon Council for the Humanities, 2007); J. Owen Dorsey, "Indians of Siletz Reservation, Oregon, 1856–1877" *The American Anthropologist* 2 (January 1889); Jane Marie Harger, "The History of the Siletz Reservation, 1856–1877," master's thesis, University of Oregon, 1972; William Eugene Kent, "The Siletz Indian Reservation, 1855–1900," master's thesis, Portland State University, 1973; Lee Sackett, "The Siletz Indian Shaker Church," *Pacific Northwest Quarterly* 64, no. 3 (1973); E. A. Schwartz, *The Rogue River Indian War and Its Aftermath, 1850–1880* (Norman: University of Oklahoma Press, 1997); Coquelle Thompson, *Pitch Woman and Other Stories: The Oral Traditions of Coquelle Thompson, Upper Coquille Athabaskan Indian* (Lincoln: University of Nebraska Press, 2007); Charles Wilkinson, *The People Are Dancing Again: The History of the Siletz Tribe of Western Oregon* (Seattle: University of Washington Press, 2010); Lionel Youst and William R. Seaburg, *Coquelle Thompson, Athabaskan Witness: A Cultural Biography* (Norman: University of Oklahoma Press, 2002).

CONFEDERATED TRIBES OF THE UMATILLA INDIAN RESERVATION

The roots of the Confederated Tribes of the Umatilla Indian Reservation date to the June 9, 1855, Walla Walla Treaty (12 Stat. 945, ratified March 8, 1859) between the Cayuses, the Umatillas, and the Walla Wallas and the United States. In that treaty those tribes agreed to remove to the Umatilla Reservation in northeastern Oregon. They also ceded to the United States 2,151,680 acres in Oregon Territory and 1,861,120 acres in Washington Territory to create the 245,699-acre reservation. For a time, each of the tribes maintained a measure of individual identity on the reservation while sharing the name "Umatilla." Late in the nineteenth century, in addition to the descendants of the three tribes, a few Northern Paiutes were removed to the reservation. On November 4, 1949, the Umatilla Tribes became officially confederated with the adoption of a constitution and bylaws, which were approved by the Department of the Interior on December 7, 1949.

Location: Approximately half of the total tribal membership lives on the Umatilla Reservation. Agency headquarters are just east of Pendleton on Interstate 80 and U.S. Highways 395 and 37.

Numbers: In 1985, tribal membership stood at 1,578. In 1989, it was 1,652; in 2002, 2,350; and, in 2008, 2,719.

History: Before the introduction of wheat farming on the reservation, Indians used its lush grasslands primarily as range for horses. In the later nineteenth and early twentieth centuries, many of those animals were rounded up and slaughtered for animal food or used for other purposes, such as pulling trolley cars in Chicago. The Indians also grew gardens along the Umatilla River. The Slater Act of March 3, 1885, reduced the reservation and provided for allotment of the lands to the Indians residing on it, but it also limited allotment to 120,000 acres. An act of October 17, 1888, replaced that legislation, allowing the secretary of the interior to set aside more lands for Indians on the eastern part of the reservation. A total of 82,742 acres was allotted to 1,118 allottees, and an additional 980 acres were reserved for school and mission purposes. Acts of July 1, 1902, and March 2, 1917, provided for allotment of 73,130.76 more acres between 1921 and 1926. By an act of May 29, 1928, about 7,000 acres of the reservation were reserved for tribal grazing purposes. By an act of August 5, 1882, 640 acres had been withdrawn from the reservation and added to the existing townsite of Pendleton. A cession on December 4, 1888, removed a considerable portion of the southern part of the reservation. Of the roughly 157,000 acres reserved for the Indians, by 1969, only 95,273 remained, of which 15,438 were tribally owned and 79,835 were allotted. Tribal holdings in 2006 totaled 172,882 acres.

David Steve Hall (1921–1996), a leader among the Confederated Tribes of the Umatilla Indian Reservation, 1968. The reservation, which was originally occupied mainly by Umatilla, Cayuse, and Walla Walla Indians, lies just east of Pendleton, Oregon.

Authors' collections.

For the early histories of the tribes composing the Confederated Tribes of the Umatilla Reservation, Oregon, *see* **Cayuse; Umatilla;** *and* **Walla Walla.**

Government and Claims: Before adopting their constitution and bylaws, the Umatilla Tribes rejected the Indian Reorganization Act (48 Stat. 984). Tribal affairs are administered by a general council of adult enrollees and a nine-member board of trustees elected from the council.

On August 9, 1951, the Umatilla Tribes filed four claims against the United States. Assigned under Docket 264, they were later separated. The first and fourth claims in that docket were for additional compensation for lands ceded to the United States under the 1855 treaty. One claim was for compensation for three parcels of land totaling approximately 3,840,000 acres outside the ceded area for which aboriginal title was claimed. The Indian Claims Commission found insufficient evidence that the Umatilla Tribes held aboriginal title to, and nonexclusive use of, the parcels. This docket was heard by the Claims Commission with Docket 198 filed by the Confederated Tribes of the Warm Springs Reservation, Oregon, because the same area was in dispute. The rulings on the two dockets were issued separately, however. An unfavorable decision by the commission on the issue of title, entered June 10, 1960, caused the Umatilla Tribes to file a motion for a rehearing. The 1960 verdict was vacated and new findings were entered. The petitioner appealed these to the U.S. Supreme Court (Appeal Docket 1-65), but on November 24, 1965, petitioner and defendant agreed to dismiss the appeals pending before the Court of Claims and to combine separated claims (Dockets 264, 264-A, and 264-B) to make one lump settlement. The final judgment entered with the commission favored the tribes, who were awarded $2,450,000 after all allowable deductions, credits, and offsets. Docket 264-A was a claim for loss of salmon, steelhead, and eel due to the construction of diversion dams on the Umatilla River and for the loss of Umatilla River water rights in a 1916 state court decision. Docket 264-B was a claim for an erroneously established boundary survey in 1871 that excluded about 19,000 acres promised to the tribes under their 1855 treaty. Final judgment of the three dockets was entered on February 11, 1966.

In 1970 the tribes filed in the Court of Claims Dockets 342-70 and 343-70 for petitions claiming damages arising from government policies and practices in the investment of tribal trust funds and Individual Indian Moneys. The tribes combined with twenty-four others with similar claims. A judgment for $172,059.39 was awarded in November 1981. For still another loss, that of fishing rights at Celilo when The Dalles Dam was constructed in 1957, the tribes received $4,198,000.

Contemporary Life and Culture: Most tillable Umatilla Reservation lands are leased to farming, as is the McNary Dam townsite near Umatilla, Oregon, to which the Umatilla Tribes obtained title under the provisions of Public Law 85-186—a transaction effected after the dam was built in 1957 on the Columbia River. On February 18, 1959, the Indians leased the townsite to S & S Steel Products, Inc., of Los Angeles, a manufacturer of ten-by-fifty-foot mobile homes. Under the lease provisions, tribal members were accorded first preference for employment with the company, while other Indians were given second preference. An on-the-job training contract with S & S provided training for other Indians as well. Indians made up more than 50 percent of S & S employees in 1983.

That some elders speak the Nez Perce and other Shahaptian dialects affords the reservation residents a measure of unity. The tribes administer a scholarship fund for enrolled members to pursue academic and vocational-technical training. The latter has helped tribal members to find work on logging and construction projects. Special tribal committees manage enrollment, credit, recreation, and summer-work programs. The reservation maintains an office for general and adult education, a daycare center, employment and health facilities, alcohol and drug treatment programs, a housing authority, and an educational program for the elderly. A forest and range enterprise is tribally owned, as are a store and a lake for camping and fishing. The tribe has received a half-million-dollar grant from the Meyer Memorial Trust for the Oregon Trail Interpretive Center under development. There are Roman Catholic and Presbyterian denominations on the reservation, though some tribal members follow the traditional *washat* religion. A few are Shakers.

In 1994 the Confederated Tribes began publishing the *Confederated Umatilla Journal*, a monthly tabloid-sized paper with a circulation of six thousand to seven thousand. That same year the Tribes inaugurated a language-restoration program. In 2006 CTUIR published *Wiyaxayxt/Wiyaakaaʾawn/As Days Go By*, a history of the Cayuse, Umatilla, and Walla Walla peoples. CTUIR owns a low-frequency FM radio station, KCUW—101.1. After operating a temporary casino for several months, CTUIR opened Wildhorse Casino in March 1995 with

Roberta (Bobbie) Conner, speaker and writer, is recognized as a leader on the national and local level. She is the museum director and curator of the Confederated Tribes of the Umatilla Indian Reservation. Since 1998, Conner has served as director of Tamástslikt Cultural Institute, one of the premier American Indian tribal museums and archives in the United States. She served as vice president of the Lewis and Clark Bicentennial Commission and is a board member of the Smithsonian Institution's National Museum of the American Indian.

Authors' collections.

a one-hundred-room hotel. In May 2009 a $45-million expansion was approved that included a doubling of the number of hotel rooms, the addition of a six-screen movie theatre, and the creation of a new 15,000-square-foot multievent center. (The anticipated completion date is March 2011.) To house government staff, a new 90,000-square-foot, $21.9-million Tribal Services Center is scheduled for completion in March 2010. In August 1997, the one-hundred-site Wildhorse RV park and eighteen-hole golf course was completed, and in October 2000 the Confederated Tribes purchased Arrowhead Travel Plaza. Gross revenues from the facility in 2008 amounted to $17 million; the next spring it reopened in a new and greatly enlarged structure. The Tribes also operates Mission Market.

Meanwhile, on July 31, 1998, Tamástslikt Cultural Institute opened, one of the premier American Indian culture centers in the United States. It encompasses a museum, a library, an archive, and 45,000 square feet of exhibit space. Currently, CTUIR is attempting to locate the graves of the Cayuse 5, those tribal members hanged in Oregon City, Oregon, in 1850 for their alleged involvement in the Whitman Massacre. In 2004 Nixyaawii Community High School was dedicated, the only such tribally operated facility in the state of Oregon, while the former St. Andrew's Catholic boarding school complex on the reservation is now operated by CTUIR as the Crow's Shadow Institute of the Arts. In October 2007 CTUIR opened Cayuse Technologies, a state-of-the-art technology company employing 150 people and the first company to locate in CTUIR's Coyote Business Park, a 140-acre master-planned light-industrial park. For the past decade, CTUIR has operated the Business Service Center, which assists entrepreneurs in starting new businesses.

CTUIR is the largest single employer in northeastern Oregon; in May 2007, it was providing jobs for 1,135 people. From January 1992 to January 2000 the unemployment rate on the reservation decreased from 37 to 17 percent, while the total annual payroll of CTUIR between January 1992 and January 2007 increased from $2.5 million to $35 million. The total operating budget of CTUIR in 1992 was $7.5 million; in 2007 it was $145 million, and in 2009 it was almost $200 million.

CTUIR supports ongoing repatriation efforts, and in April 2008 reburied human bones uncovered during an excavation near Richland, Washington. That same month, the National Park Service announced its plans to repatriate unassociated funerary objects in possession of the Maryhill Museum of Art in Goldendale, Washington, and CTUIR is working to save the ancient, 2,500-year-old tribal village of matalam near Umatilla, Oregon. In 2008, thirteen tribal members gathered roots at the Tuulikeecetpe area in Union County, the first time they had done so in years, and the Umatillas joined with the Nez Perces and the Colvilles to help purchase the sixty-two-acre Marr Ranch property that adjoins the Old Chief Joseph Cemetery and national park in Wallowa County, Oregon. Perhaps most notably, CTUIR has been intimately involved in the Kennewick Man controversy, in which the skeletal remains of a prehistoric man were discovered in 1996 on a bank of the Columbia River near Kennewick, Washington. CTUIR contested rights to the remains but was defeated when the U.S. Court of Appeals for the Ninth Circuit ruled that a cultural link between the remains and the Confederated Tribes had not been established.

Special Events and Celebrations: The Umatillas observe their annual Root Feast Celebration Powwow in May. Usually in June CTUIR stages Treaty Days, commemorating the signing of the Walla Walla Treaty of 1855. Indians of the Umatilla participate in the Wildhorse Powwow, which is conducted on the weekend closest to the Fourth of July, as well as the Pendleton (Oregon) Round-Up, held during the second full week in September. The Salmon Walk at Tamástslikt Cultural Institute is an annual event scheduled the fourth weekend in August.

Suggested Readings:

Larry Cebula, *Plateau Indians and the Quest for Spiritual Power, 1700–1840* (Lincoln: University of Nebraska Press, 2003); Albert Furtwangler, *Bringing Indians to the Book* (Seattle: University of Washington Press, 2005); Steven L. Grafe, "Lee Moorhouse: Photographer of the Inland Empire," *Oregon Historical Quarterly* 98, no. 4 (Winter 1997–98) and *Peoples of the Plateau: The Indian Photographs of Lee Moorhouse, 1898–1915* (Norman: University of Oklahoma Press, 2006); Eugene S. Hunn, *Nch'i-Wána, "The Big River": Mid-Columbia Indians and Their Land* (Seattle: University of Washington Press, 1989); Jennifer Karson, ed., *Wiyaxayst/Wiyaakaaʼawn/As Days Go By: Our History, Our Land, Our People—The Cayuse, Umatilla, and Walla Walla* (Seattle: University of Washington Press, 2006); Robert H. Ruby and John A. Brown, *The Cayuse Indians: Imperial Tribesmen of Old Oregon* (Norman: University of Oklahoma Press, 1972, 2005); Clifford E. Trafzer, *Yakima, Palouse, Cayuse, Umatilla, Walla Walla, and Wanapum Indians: An Historical Bibliography* (Metuchen, N.J.:

Scarecrow, 1992); Charles Wilkinson, "Celilo Falls: At the Center of Western History," *Oregon Historical Quarterly* 108, no. 4 (2007).

CONFEDERATED TRIBES OF WARM SPRINGS

The Confederated Tribes of the Warm Springs Reservation of Oregon had its origin in the treaty of June 25, 1855 (12 Stat. 963, ratified March 8, 1859), where Oregon superintendent of Indian affairs Joel Palmer, representing the United States, signed with the Teninos—including Teninos proper, Tyighs of the upper Deschutes River, Wyams of the lower Deschutes, and Dockspuses (Tukspush) of the John Day River—and the Wascos of the Kigaltwalla, Dog River, and Dalles bands. These peoples were confederated with a view to locating them on the Warm Springs Reservation south of The Dalles of the Columbia River in Jefferson and Wasco counties of north-central Oregon.

Location: Many members of the Confederated Tribes reside near the Warm Springs Agency headquarters about fourteen miles northwest of Madras on U.S. Highway 97. Tribal members also live as far away as Simnasho, twenty-five miles north of agency headquarters.

Numbers: After the 1855 treaty, the Indians scheduled to go on the Warm Springs Reservation numbered 1,355. In 1985 there were 2,200 enrolled members of the Confederated Tribes; in 2003, 4,200; and, in 2008, 4,306.

History: The treaty with the tribes and bands destined for the Warm Springs Reservation was precipitated by the increasing number of settlers who wished them removed from their ancestral lands. With promises of government payments and of retention of fishing and hunting privileges, they were induced to surrender title to about 10 million acres in exchange for a reservation of about 464,000 acres. The area was later increased after long-festering disputes over the northern and western reservation boundaries were settled in 1972. In 2006, tribal holdings encompassed 644,000 acres. Fortunately for the Warm Springs Tribes, the treaty (14 Stat. 751) signed on November 15, 1865, with Oregon superintendent of Indian affairs J. W. Huntington and ratified on March 2, 1867, did not threaten their right to fish in traditional places along the Columbia River. The peoples of the Warm Springs continued fishing there, and on February 9, 1929, a government act (45 Stat. 1158) set aside a village site near Celilo Falls for a small band who had been assigned to the Warm Springs.

In addition to harassment from non-Indians, the tribes on the Warm Springs Reservation were subjected to Northern Paiute raids as early as 1859. Those continued until 1866 when the army began a campaign to exterminate or subdue the Paiutes. Warm Springs Indian scouts served the army in offensives against the Paiutes and in operations in 1873 against the Modocs of southern Oregon and northern California.

During the Peace Policy era of President Ulysses S. Grant in the 1870s, Warm Springs agent Capt. John Smith tried not only to advance the EuroAmerican style of education among Indians but also to eliminate Native practices such as slavery, shamanism, and polygamy. The economic standing of the Confederated Tribes remained low. They tried to subsist by fishing, which became more tenuous each year, and by farming lands poorly suited to agriculture. After the Bannock-Paiute War of 1878, thirty-eight Paiutes were moved in September 1879 to the Warm Springs from Vancouver Barracks in Washington Territory, where they had been imprisoned since as early as 1866 to 1868 during the Snake War to exterminate the Paiute raiders. After Gen. Nelson Miles, commanding the Department of the Columbia, recommended that the Paiutes captured in the Bannock-Paiute War and still held on the Yakama Reservation be allowed to leave, about seventy under their leader Oytes went to the Warm Springs in August 1884. That, in essence, completed the establishment of the more recognizable tribes on the reservation: Teninos, Wascos, and Northern Paiutes.

Government and Claims: After adopting the Indian Reorganization Act (48 Stat. 984) in 1937, the Confederated Tribes incorporated itself the following year with a constitution that recognized self-management while retaining the BIA in an advisory capacity.

Because the ancient Columbia River fishing grounds at Celilo Falls were inundated by the waters behind The Dalles Dam, the Confederated Tribes in 1958 received a $4 million indemnity. A part of that sum was distributed to tribal members on a per capita basis, but most of it was held in the tribal treasury. The Tribes submitted a claim (Docket 198) to the Indian Claims Commission to recover additional compensation for lands in north-central Oregon ceded to the United States on June 25, 1855. For what was determined to have been the Tribes' aboriginal ownership of 1,605,000 acres, it was awarded by the Claims Commission on October 17, 1973, a compromise settlement of $1,225,000. A related claim, separated from Docket 198 and docketed 198-A, was dismissed on the motion of the Tribes. The Warm Springs Indians also filed a claim (Docket 524-71) that reached the Court of Claims for mismanagement of Indian Claims Commission judgment funds and other moneys such as Individual Indian Money accounts held in trust by the United States. The Tribes was awarded $88,249.98 in 1981 for its claim per Docket 524-71.

Contemporary Life and Culture: Because of the demand for lumber during World War II, the Tribes in 1942 entered into its first contract for the sale of timber logged along the western edge of the reservation. Revenues derived from such sales raised per capita payments. Members also receive pensions beginning at age sixty. In 1967 the Tribes purchased a privately owned sawmill on the reservation and a plywood plant operating under the name of Warm Springs Forest Products Industries. With the $4-million settlement from 1958, the Confederated Tribes opened a resort and convention center, Kah-Nee-Ta Lodge, in the early 1970s, increasing employment and revenues. Later, the Kah-Nee-Ta High Desert Resort & Casino was added at a cost of $6 million. The casino offers lodging, camping, RV parking, pools, a health-and-beauty spa, an eighteen-hole golf course, tennis courts, horseback riding, and kayaking, hiking, and rafting. The operation generates about $4 million in annual profits. Additional income is derived from employment in a small electronics plant on the reservation and the sale of wild horses.

The Tribes authorized the building of Pelton Dam by the Department of the Interior on the Deschutes River and shared in some of the expense. On July 16, 1982, the $30-million Pelton Reregulating Dam hydroelectric project was dedicated. Its license was the first issued to an Indian tribe by the U.S. Federal Energy Regulatory Commission, and the dam was the first low-rise hydroelectric project ever built by an Indian tribe. The generated power, which is sold to Pacific Power and Light Company, is produced from waters reserved by the Pelton and Round Butte dams on the Deschutes.

In 1995, the Warm Springs Plaza was built, which includes such businesses as Warm Springs Ventures, Eagle-Tech Technology Center, Nathan's Business Services, Visions of the West, and Wild Rye Bead Gallery. Among various other projects are a modern administrative and tribal center, a housing program, and a $5.5-million trout and salmon hatchery near Kah-Nee-Ta. The Tribes administers its own laws for fish and game management, and tribal members maintain fisheries and fishing sites along a number of rivers for ceremonial, subsistence, and commercial purposes.

Warm Springs children attend Jefferson County district schools in Madras. There are on the reservation a Catholic and an Indian Shaker church and churches of Protestant denominations. The Confederated Tribes owns and operates KWSO 91.9 FM, a community radio station that first broadcast in 1986 and transmits from Eagle Butte with 4,300 watts of power. The *Spilyay Tymoo* is the newspaper of the Warm Springs Indian Reservation. The Confederated Tribes maintains a 25,000-square-foot museum, constructed in 1993 in the form of a traditional encampment at a cost of $7.6 million. Since about the time the museum was built, the Tribes has been negotiating with the Smithsonian Institution to acquire twenty-eight sets of ancestral skeletal remains gathered from Lower Memaloose Island in 1934. The Tribes also operates a police force, a fire and safety department, health and wellness and early childhood centers, and a senior center.

Special Events and Celebrations: Warm Springs tribal members practice the *washat,* a religious ceremony in which drums and feathers are used at funerals,

These children of the Confederated Tribes of Warm Springs of Oregon, photographed in the 1970s, are typical of Indian youth who receive lessons both in the three Rs and in their tribal history and culture.

Courtesy of Rockey/Marsh Public Relations, Portland, Oregon.

feasts, and Sunday services. There is also an Indian feather religion whose rituals are closed to the public. A First Roots Feast is usually held in early spring at Warm Springs. In the second or third week of May, the Tygh Valley All-Indian Rodeo and Celebration is held. In late June, the Pi-Ume-Sha Treaty Days Powwow at Warm Springs and Kah-Nee-Ta features competitive dancing. Fun Days is staged at Warm Springs around the Fourth of July. There is also a Huckleberry Feast in early fall at the He-he Mill. Rodeos are often held in conjunction with those celebrations. Other gatherings and powwows are scheduled at Thanksgiving and Christmas and on New Year's Day. Lincoln's Birthday is celebrated at Simnasho, and there is an Indians' Night Out honoring the elderly.

Suggested Readings:

George W. Aguilar, Sr., *When the River Ran Wild!: Indian Traditions on the Mid-Columbia and the Warm Springs Reservation* (Seattle: University of Washington Press, 2005); Katrine Barber, *Death of Celilo Falls* (Seattle: University of Washington Press, 2005); Michael Baughman and Charlotte Hadella, *Warm Springs Millenium: Voices from the Reservation* (Austin: University of Texas Press, 2000); David S. Boyer, "Warm Springs Indians Carve Out a Future," *National Geographic* 155, no. 4 (April 1979); David Braly, *Crooked River Country: Wranglers, Rogues, and Barons* (Pullman: Washington State University Press, 2007); Confederated Tribes of the Warm Springs Reservation of Oregon, *A Brief Look at the Warm Springs Indian Reservation* (Portland, Ore.: Confederated Tribes of the Warm Springs Reservation, 1975); Andrew H. Fisher, *Shadow Tribe: The Making of Columbia River Identity* (Seattle: University of Washington Press, 2010); Bill Mercer, *People of the River: Native Arts of the Oregon Territory* (Seattle: University of Washington Press, 2005): Cynthia D. Stowell, *Faces of a Reservation* (Portland.: Oregon Historical Society Press, 1987); Eugene S. Hunn, *Nch'i-Wána, "The Big River": Mid-Columbia Indians and Their Land* (Seattle: University of Washington Press, 1989); Margaret Ann Knox, "Identity, Territory and Place: Insights from the Warm Springs Reservation," Ph.D. dissertation, University of Oregon, 2005; Martha (Ferguson) McKeown, *Come to Our Salmon Feast* (Portland, Ore.: Binfords and Mort, 1959); Gordon MacNab, *A History of the McQuinn Strip* and *A Short History of the Confederated Tribes of the Warm Springs Reservation* (both published by the Tribal Council of the Confederated Tribes of the Warm Springs Indian Reservation, Portland, Ore., 1972); Ralph Shane and Ruby D. Leno, *A History of the Warm Springs Reservation, Oregon* (Portland, Ore.: U.S. Department of the Interior, Bureau of Indian Affairs, 1949); Cynthia D. Stowell, *Faces of a Reservation: A Portrait of the Warm Springs Indian Reservation* (Portland: Oregon Historical Society Press, 1989); Charles Wilkinson, "Celilo Falls: At the Center of Western History," *Oregon Historical Quarterly* 108, no. 4 (2007).

CONFEDERATED TRIBES AND BANDS
OF THE YAKAMA NATION

The origins of the Confederated Tribes and Bands of the Yakama Indian Nation of Washington lay in the Yakama Treaty signed in the Walla Walla Valley on June 9, 1855. After that treaty, some of the signatory bands, primarily Klickitats, joined the Yakamas proper on the Yakama Reservation of the Simcoe Agency. Most of the tribes who belonged to what the Yakama Tribes call the Yakama Nation subsequently located with and became associated with other tribes. Today the Yakama Tribes stresses nationhood and protecting their sovereign status.

Location: Members of the Yakama Indian Nation live on their reservation of over 1 million acres in south-central Washington State as well as on farms in the Yakima River valley or in reservation towns such as Toppenish, Wapato, Parker, and White Swan. Others reside in off-reservation communities in the valley such as the city of Yakima.

Numbers: In 1984 tribal membership was about 6,853, more than double the 3,000 estimate of the number of Yakamas proper in 1780. In 2008 there were nearly 8,400 enrolled members, a population that was approaching 10,000 by July 2009. Among the reasons for the increase is the inclusion of peoples such as the Klickitats, who historically did not belong to the Yakama tribe. Less exposure to endemic diseases than other tribes also helped to sustain their population.

History: Under the Yakama Treaty of 1855, the Klickitats became the most numerous people, next to the Yakamas proper, on the Yakama Reservation. Many Klickitats were removed there in 1867 under the pressure of settlers who wanted them out of the Willamette Valley of Oregon, where for many years they had gone to trade, hunt, and farm. An indication of the close cultural link between Klickitats and Yakamas was the election of the influential Klickitat, White Swan, or Joe Stwire, as head chief of the Yakamas during the early reservation period. During that time Yakama Reservation peoples came under the strong hand of the Reverend James ("Father") Wilbur, a Methodist minister who became agent in 1864. Except for a brief period, the Reverend Wilbur retained that office throughout the Peace Policy era of the 1870s and early 1880s. Wilbur ruled under the standard of "The Plow and the Bible," and his administration was regarded by the Protestant community as a model of Indian agency management and efficiency. The Indians, however, were unenthusiastic about accepting farming, and the teaching of the Bible led to Protestant-Catholic friction over management of the Simcoe Agency. Initially, clerics of the latter faith had worked among the Yakama peoples. Tension also developed between the original inhabitants of the reservation, their descendants, and the Northern Paiutes, of whom 540 were exiled to the Yakama Reservation in the wake of the Bannock-Paiute War of 1878. The Paiutes' stay was brief, lasting only from early 1879 into the early 1880s.

In the late nineteenth century, non-Indians began encroaching on the Yakama Reservation with projects such as a dam that was built across the Yakima River in 1891 for irrigation purposes. In 1894 the agent, L. T. Erwin, attempted to elevate his charges in their acculturation by constructing the Erwin Ditch with funds secured from the sale of the Wenatshapam Fishery, which had been reserved for the Indians under the Yakama Treaty (*see* **Wenatchi**). Controversies among Yakamas and settlers over fishing, water, and land-use rights continued into the

Watson Totus of the Yakama Indian
Nation, 1977. Totus was renowned
in business and in religious affairs
and was a leader of the Seven Drum
religion, which is deeply rooted in
Yakama worship.

Authors' collections.

twentieth century, when evolving
technology and increasing in-migra-
tion aggravated the problems.

Allotment of the reservation began
in the early 1890s and was mostly completed by 1914. Between 1892 and 1915
about 4,506 allotments were made. By 1914, 440,000 acres of the reservation had
been allotted, with 798,000 acres remaining unallotted. As the twentieth century
advanced, Yakama peoples were brought more closely into the non-Indian world
but not always on friendly terms. During World War I, for example, Yakama
traditionalists believed their youth were being sent to the battlefields so that
Americans could destroy them. In the twentieth century, the relationship of the
Yakama tribes with the federal government centered on the arbitration of tribal
claims.

Government and Claims: Despite pressures on them to do so, the Yakama peoples did not formally organize their government until 1935. One reason they
initially rejected organization under the Indian Reorganization Act of 1934 (48
Stat. 984) was a long history of dissatisfaction with and distrust of the United
States.

The council of the Confederated Tribes and Bands of the Yakama Nation of
Washington is composed of fourteen members representing the fourteen tribes
and bands signatory to their treaty. A general council includes all tribal members over eighteen years of age. A close liaison exists between these two bodies. The tribal and agency headquarters are located at Toppenish, Washington,
about twenty miles south of Yakima on U.S. Highway 97 and Interstate 82. Under
Washington State law (Chapter 36, *Laws of Washington,* dated March 13, 1963)
and federal law (Public Law 280, 83rd Congress, 1st Session, passed August 15,
1953), the state assumed jurisdiction over Yakama Indians on tribal and allotted lands held in trust by the United States. The jurisdiction extended to eight

categories of activity: compulsory school attendance, public assistance, domestic relations, mental health, juvenile delinquency, adoption proceedings, dependent children, and operation of motor vehicles on public streets, alleys, roads, and highways.

On June 21, 1949, the Yakama Tribes filed a claim (Docket 47) with the Indian Claims Commission for compensation for, or recovery of, any of five areas on and adjacent to the Yakama Reservation. Restricting the claim to one tract, designated as Tract A and located adjacent to the eastern reservation boundary in the Mabton area, the commission accepted the boundary line established by the Harry A. Clark survey of 1885. The commission also denied the Tribes' claim to two other tracts (designated B and D) but established the value of the 17,669.10-acre Tract C in the Ahtanum Creek area at $22,086.38, plus interest dating from 1923. Tract C lay north of the pre-1953 western end of the northern reservation boundary, which began at the confluence of Reservation Creek and the South Fork of the Ahtanum and extended up Reservation Creek to its headwaters and thence in a straight line to Spencer Point. The acreage in Tract C had been involved in a dispute over which fork of Ahtanum Creek served as the western portion of the northern boundary. That creek has a very small branch now designated as the North Fork. Upstream, the South Fork has a large tributary, now known as Reservation Creek. In his 1890 survey, George A. Schwartz had established the boundary along today's Reservation Creek, which he called the South Fork. In an 1899 survey, E. C. Barnard had followed Schwartz's definition of the boundary along Reservation Creek, which he too called the South Fork of the Ahtanum. In his report, Barnard wrote that he thought that the boundary should follow a natural line west from the headwaters of the creek. That "natural line" was from the crest of the divide around the headwaters of the Klickitat River via Darling (or Darland) Mountain to Spencer Point.

At the time of the hearings, the Claims Commission possessed the map drawn for the 1855 treaty council, a document which had been lost until 1930. The commission sided with the Yakamas by establishing the present-day South Fork of the Ahtanum as the boundary and by designating natural contours between the present South Fork headwaters and Spencer Point as the boundary. This placed the boundary north of the old one, adding 18,094.42 acres to the reservation. This additional acreage had been taken up by settlers, except for a 425.32-acre land grant that the Northern Pacific Railroad had received under the act of July 2, 1864 (13 Stat. 365). Those 425.32 acres were returned to the Yakamas, since the patent had not been finalized by the General Land Office. Schwartz had also surveyed the western and southwestern boundaries of the reservation. His surveys were accepted by the General Land Office on October 21, 1891. The southwestern boundary followed the crest of the Simcoe Mountains. Barnard's surveys, accepted by the General Land Office on April 7, 1900, pushed the boundary line farther west in a straight line from Spencer Point to Goat Butte (usually referred to as The Hump) just east of Mount Adams and from there to Grayback Peak, adding 293,837 acres to the reservation. Within the area between the two lines, formerly believed to be public domain and sold to settlers, lay 27,647.7 acres in a twenty-square-mile area within the southwestern corner of the reservation. About three-fifths of this acreage formed an almost solid block in Klickitat County. The rest was scattered in Yakima County. The acreage was mountainous between Simcoe Ridge on the south and Toppenish Ridge on the north. On November 6, 1953, the Claims Commission fixed the value of those lands at $69,119.28 as of December 21, 1904, when the settlers' rights to ownership were validated.

On November 29, 1957, the Claims Commission entered an interlocutory order for an award for the Tract C lands of $22,086.38 plus interest from 1923, and for the Cedar Valley tract, the value plus interest from 1904. On November 6, 1953, after the commission denied the Yakamas any recovery for Tracts A, B, and D, the Indians appealed the decision to the Court of Claims (Appeals Case No. 4-61, 158 C.Cls. 672). That body affirmed the decision of the Claims Commission in all cases except those of tracts B and D, in which two considerations were reversed and remanded to the commission for consideration of the liability of the United States. On its return from the Court of Claims, Tract C was redocketed 47-A; and on June 25, 1965, the Yakamas were awarded $61,991.40 for the 17,669.10-acre tract. The commission later found that 121,465.69 acres in Tract D should be added to the Yakama Reservation. Tract D, shaped in the form of an isosceles triangle, lay on the southwestern boundary of the reservation on a line running southeast from a terminal point of the western boundary west of the summit of Mount Adams in the Cascade Range to a point beginning on the southern boundary at Grayback Mountain, in lands between the watersheds of the Klickitat and White Salmon rivers south of Mount Adams. The commission found that the boundary had been laid out erroneously in 1907 by the Campbell, Germond, and Long surveys, which had followed the survey of Barnard, who used the so-called White Swan map that Governor Stevens had made of the reservation in March 1857, just four years before the unreliable first survey of the reservation's eastern and southeastern boundary lines by Thomas F. Berry and James Lodge in 1861. The commission determined that in Tract D the Yakamas were entitled to compensation for 97,908.97 acres that had been sold to settlers. To be returned to the Indians were 2,548 acres of vacant and unpatented lands as well as 21,008.66 acres of the Gifford Pinchot National Forest, including the eastern half of Mount Adams. The treaty had placed the western reservation boundary just east of that mountain, but the original map (which was discovered in 1930 filed with maps from Montana in the National Archives) placed the boundary west of the mountain. The Department of Agriculture reluctantly released the acreage, claims for which were redocketed separately (Docket 47-B). That docket was dismissed when the defending United States agreed to transfer the 21,008.66 acres to the Yakamas by executive order on May 26, 1972. Claims for recovery of the remaining 97,908.97 acres in Tract D and the Cedar Valley tracts were consolidated with the claim (Docket 164) for the erroneous allotment of nearly 411 eighty-acre tracts to non-Yakamas on the reservation. Finally, $2,160,000 was awarded for the remaining portions of Dockets 47 and 164, less $60,000 that the Yakamas had retained from other claims (Dockets 161, 222, and 224). The settlement called for dismissal of Dockets 147 and 160. Docket 147 had been a claim for loss of fish in the Yakima River.

For a second time the Claims Commission denied the Yakama claim for Tract B, which is known as the Lake Walupt area. This 7,705-acre, pear-shaped section west of the western boundary of the reservation included the lake and berry grounds. The E. D. Calvin survey of 1939, however, found the lake area to be on the western slopes of the Cascade Range and thus outside the reservation, established by the 1855 treaty at the crest of those mountains. The Tract B claim was denied by the commission in a decision dated February 25, 1966. The Chester W. Pecore boundary line was established as the western reservation boundary. This line dated from a 1920–24 survey along the western edge of the Cascade Range that had been accepted by the General Land Office on August 6, 1926. Thus, 47,593 acres were added to the reservation. This addition included 346.44 acres of Northern Pacific Railroad mineral lands that that company had filed on. The filing was withdrawn and the land returned to the Yakamas. The company released its claim to the 346.44 acres on March 28, 1941.

The Yakama Tribes filed a claim (Docket 162) for additional compensation for 23,000 acres of timber land near Leavenworth, Washington, where the Wenatchi Tribe (one of the fourteen Confederated Tribes under the 1855 Yakama Treaty) resided and maintained their fishery. On January 8, 1894, by an agreement with the United States, the Yakamas had signed away the land for $20,000. Money from the sale, as noted above, had been used to build the Erwin Ditch. The Indian Claims Commission decided that the lands had been worth $69,000 in 1894 and on August 31, 1965, awarded the Yakamas an additional $49,000. With twenty-four other tribes throughout the western United States, the Yakama Tribes filed a claim (Docket 310-74) that reached the Court of Claims. The claim was for mismanagement of Individual Claims Commission judgment funds and for other moneys held in trust by the United States, such as Individual Money accounts. The Yakama Tribes was awarded $1,306,390.11 in 1980.

On behalf of the Wishram Tribe, one of the fourteen groups under the Yakama Treaty, the Yakama Tribes filed a claim (Docket 165) on July 24, 1951, alleging that after the 1855 treaty the United States had not intended to pay for the lands ceded by the tribes and thus had forced the tribes into war with that country. Although the Wishrams had remained peaceful, turning over their weapons to the commandant at Fort Dalles at his request, they had been mistakenly attacked by American troops, who destroyed much of their properties in the belief that they were combatants. Despite promises by the military command that the Wishrams would be compensated for their losses, that never happened, nor were their weapons ever returned. When the defending United States asked for an accounting of Indian losses, none was forthcoming. The Claims Commission dismissed the docket.

The Yakama Tribes also filed a claim (Docket 161) for additional recovery for lands ceded to the United States by the fourteen tribes confederated under the Yakama standard. *See* **Confederated Tribes of the Colville Reservation.**

Contemporary Life and Culture: In 1975, 1,118,149.04 acres of tribal lands were held in trust on the Yakama Reservation. In 1983 about 15,000 acres were under cultivation. No other Pacific Northwest tribe has been more active in promoting business enterprises than the Yakamas. About 150 million board feet of timber are taken annually from their sustained-yield-managed reservation holdings. A tribal furniture manufacturing operation bears the name of their sacred mountain, Mount Adams. Other enterprises involve tribal heritage, agriculture, fishing, and banking. The oldest and largest reservation irrigation undertaking is the Wapato Project, which delivers water to nearly 150,000 acres of croplands, including 90,000 acres of Indian lands. Reservation lands include more than 2.7 million acres of range for domestic livestock. The Yakama Tribes also derives income from claims for lost fishing rights and lands taken without compensation. On November 8, 1979, the Tribes succeeded in convincing the Ninth Circuit Court of Appeals to order returned to it some legal ground lost in a Supreme Court decision ten months earlier. The circuit court ruled that in several reservation matters the Tribes held concurrent jurisdiction with the State of Washington.

There is a Yakama Tribal Housing Authority. Health needs are met primarily through facilities operated by the Indian Health Service. For years the Yakamas opposed nuclear waste dumping at nearby Hanford. In 1992, the 6,706-member tribe fought the U.S. Supreme Court ruling that owners of fee patent Yakama Reservation lands were subject to property taxes levied by the county. In 1989 the Yakamas blamed a smaller salmon run (by 100,000) on the March 24 Exxon oil spill at Valdez and filed suit for $25 million. That same year they became aware of a $123-million loss through BIA mismanagement of their timber sales. A November 1990 judgment given in Yakima County Superior Court to a case filed in 1977 limited tribal irrigation rights, while prescribing and assuring a stream flow sufficient to maintain fish life. A suit for 2.5 million acre-feet of Yakima River water was kept at 655,000 acre-feet.

In 2008 the Yakama Indian Nation announced plans to spend more than $32 million over the coming decade to expand its coho salmon reintroduction program in the Wenatchee and Methow river basins, an objective the Tribes has been working toward since 1996. If successful, it is hoped that the program can be phased out in twenty years. The Fisheries Department of the Yakama Nation operates with about forty employees. In 2008 the Yakama Tribes began restoration of three generators acquired from the BIA, generators it plans to use to increase local irrigation and produce electrical power. The Yakama Tribes operates Yakama Nation Radio, KYNR 1490-AM and maintains substantial business interests through the Yakama Nation Land Enterprise, including an RV park and resort; 2,000 acres planted in apples, cherries, and asparagus; timber harvests; land leases; and other revenue-generating enterprises. In 2008 the Yakama Nation helped fund a $660,000 plant that manufactures fiberglass and plastic products for military and mass-transit purposes.

From 2005 to 2008 the Yakama Nation owned the Yakama Sun Kings (purchased for $140,000), a franchise of the Continental Basketball Association. Operations were discontinued after three seasons because of mounting financial losses. To promote cultural awareness and preservation, the Yakama Nation operates Yakama Nation Museum & Cultural Heritage Center at Toppenish. The facility, which opened on June 9, 1980, includes a museum, gift shop, restaurant, theater, longhouse, offices, and library. The Yakama Tribes is also involved in a $12.5-million project to reconstruct a longhouse and village site at Celilo Falls on the Columbia River. The tribally owned and operated Yakama Nation Legends Casino, established in May 1998, donated $233,684 to nonprofit groups in 2008. Many other businesses owned and operated by the Yakama Tribes are emerging, including Yakama Juice, purchased in 2004 and employing thirty full-time workers. It is the first Native American–owned juice plant in the United States. The Tribes also operates the Yakamart Convenience Store, based in Toppenish; the Mount Adams Furniture Factory; the Real Yakama Fruit Stand; the Heritage Inn Restaurant, and the Yakama Nation Credit Enterprise. Since 1994, Yakama Forest Products manages 309,000 commercial acres of sawlog timber and operates a fully modern small-log sawmill. In 2005 two tribal members founded the King Mountain Tobacco Company, which employs twenty people and manufactures 140,000 cartons of cigarettes a month. In the budding field of tribally owned utilities, Yakama Power provides energy purchased from the Bonneville Power Administration to the tribe's casino, sawmill, administrative building, health clinic, and some homes. The Yakamas also maintain a bison herd.

The Yakama Tribes funds an array of cultural and youth programs, among them projects for restoring and sustaining horse and buffalo on the reservation; species, range, and habitat programs; and a Wildlife Youth Camp for boys and girls ages fourteen to seventeen. In 2008–2009 the University of Oregon began offering Yakama Sahaptin language classes. From the late 1960s to 2005 the Yakama Tribes operated a fifty-bed tribal jail in Toppenish. The Yakama Tribal School, established in 1980 in Toppenish, has an enrollment of eighty-nine students in grades 7 through 12 and offers a culture-based curriculum. Yakamas also attend public schools in Yakima, Toppenish, White Swan, and other communities located on or near the reservation. During the summer, children prepare for fall public school at Camp Chaparral on the reservation near Mount Adams.

Special Events and Celebrations: The Yakama Tribes has a full schedule of cultural events. These include the annual George Washington Birthday Celebration at Toppenish Longhouse in the third week of February; the Speely-mi Annual Arts and Crafts Fair at Toppenish on a weekend near the middle of February; the annual Celilo Wy-Am Salmon Feast & Powwow at Celilo, Oregon, in April; the Rock Creek Root Feast at Rock Creek in April; the Satus Powwow at Satus on the fourth weekend of April; the Weaseltail Club event at White Swan on the Memorial Day weekend; the Treaty-day Golf event in the first week of June; the Tiinowit Powwow at the ancient ceremonial grounds at White Swan during the first weekend of June; the All-Indian Rodeo and Yakama Nation Treaty Day at White Swan on the first weekend of June; the American Indian Days Celebration at White Swan on the third weekend of September; the annual Veterans Day Celebration at Toppenish in the second week of November; the Christmas and New Year's Powwow at Wapato, of which the final night's activities are held at White Swan.

Suggested Readings:

Virginia Beavert and Sharon Hargus, *Ichishkiin Sinwit Yakama / Yakima Sahaptin Dictionary* (Seattle: University of Washington Press, 2009): Carol Craig, "WY-AM: Echo of the Falling Waters—Celilo Falls," *Columbia: The Magazine of Northwest History* 21, no. 1 (2007); Richard D. Daugherty, *The Yakima Peoples* (Phoenix, Ariz.: Indian Tribal Series, 1973); Andrew H. Fisher, "The 1932 Handshake Agreement: Yakama Indian Treaty Rights and Forest Service Policy in the Pacific Northwest," *Western Historical Quarterly* 28, no. 2 (1997) and " 'This I Know from the Old People': Yakama Indian Treaty Rights as Oral Tradition," *Montana The Magazine of Western History* 49, no. 1 (1999); Donald M. Hines, *Ghost Voices: Yakima Indian Myths, Legends, Humor, and Hunting Stories* (Issaquah, Wash.: Great Eagle, 1992); Eugene S. Hunn, *Nch'i-Wána, "The Big River": Mid-Columbia Indians and Their Land* (Seattle: University of Washington Press, 1989); Melville Jacobs, *Northwest Sahaptin Texts* (New York: Columbia University Press, 1934–37), 2 vols.; Barbara Leibhardt, "Allotment Policy in an Incongruous Legal System: The Yakima Indian Nation as a Case Study, 1887–1934," *Agricultural History* 65, no. 4 (1991); Lucullus V. McWhorter, *The Crime against the Yakimas* (Yakima, Wash.: Republic Printers, 1913); Robert E. Pace, *The Land of the Yakimas* (Toppenish, Wash.: Yakima Indian Media Services, 1977) and *Yakima Indian Nation Bibliography* (Toppenish, Wash.: Yakima Indian Media Services, 1982); Click Relander, *Strangers on the Land* (Yakima, Wash.: Franklin Press, 1962); Richard D. Scheuerman and Michael O. Finley, *Finding Chief Kamiakin: The Life and Legacy of a Northwest Patriot* (Pullman: Washington State University Press, 2008); Helen Hersh Schuster, *The Yakimas: A Critical Bibliography* (Bloomington: Indiana University Press, 1982) and "Yakima Traditionalism: A Study in Continuity and Change," Ph.D. dissertation, University Microfilm International, Ann Arbor, Mich., 1977; A. J. Splawn, *Ka-Mi-Akin, The Last Hero of the Yakimas* (Yakima, Wash.: Binfords and Mort, 1944); Clifford E. Trafzer, *Death Stalks the Yakama: Epidemiological Transitions and Mortality on the Yakama Indian Reservation, 1888–1964* (East Lansing: Michigan State University Press, 1997) and "The Legacy of the Walla Walla Council, 1855,"

Oregon Historical Quarterly 106, no. 3 (2005); Clifford Trafzer and Robert R. McCoy, *Forgotten Voices: Death Records of the Yakama, 1888–1964* (Lanham, Md.: Scarecrow Press, 2009); Roberta Ulrich, *Empty Nets: Indians, Dams, and the Columbia* (Corvallis: Oregon State University Press, 2007); Charles Wilkinson, "Celilo Falls: At the Center of Western History," *Oregon Historical Quarterly* 108, no. 4 (2007).

COOS

(*See* Coos Tribe of Indians, Hanis Coos, Miluk Coos, *and* Confederated Tribes of Coos, Lower Umpqua and Siuslaw Indians.)

COOS TRIBE OF INDIANS

The Coos Tribe of Indians originated from four tribes: the Hanis Coos, the Miluk Coos (or Lower Coquilles), the Kuitsh (or Lower Umpquas) and the Siuslaws. The present-day Coos Tribe is composed for the most part of descendants of members of those tribes who lived on the Alsea Reservation.

Location: The Coos Tribe of Indians lived mainly around Coos Bay, Oregon.

Numbers: In 1975 tribal membership numbered approximately 125.

Government and Claims: In 1938 the Coos Tribe adopted its first constitution and bylaws. There was a schism in the tribe in the 1950s when a few members were included in an award to the Upper Coquilles and other tribes of the Siletz Reservation, lumped together as Tillamooks for payment. In 1851, when Oregon superintendent of Indian affairs Anson Dart had made his two treaties with Athabaskan-speaking tribes at Port Orford, Oregon, he had gathered Indians as far north as the estuary of the Coquille River. A few Nasomahs of the southernmost division of the Miluk Coos were in the group near today's Bandon. Also in the group who treated with Dart were Upper Coquilles, who through intermarriage were related to certain Nasomahs. Thus, as successful litigants before the Court of Claims (Case No. 45320), the Upper Coquilles, the Chetcos, the Tututnis, and the Alcea Band of Tillamooks received awards, and those Coos who could prove Upper Coquille ancestry became eligible for some compensation as well. Since the 1950s those Coos have broken away from the now-incorporated

Coos Tribe of Indians and joined the Coquille Tribe. The relationship between the two groups is uneasy because the Coos Tribe of Indians failed to receive a judgment from the United States for its land cession. Even before the Coquilles did so, the Coos Tribe had petitioned the Court of Claims for a settlement (Case No. K-345) but received none. When the Coquilles subsequently petitioned the Court of Claims, they were successful. The Coos Tribe then petitioned the Indian Claims Commission again, but the commission refused to hear its case. Continuing tension between members of the Coos Tribe and Coos members of the Coquille Indian Tribe has also stemmed from competition for federal programs. The Coquille Indian Tribe has a small reservation and is federally recognized. The Coos Tribe has 6.1 acres of land and several cemeteries. Believing that its claims were strengthened by this land case, it sought federal acknowledgment in 1975. Today the Coos have federal recognition within their confederation with the Lower Umpquas and Siuslaws. *See* **Confederated Tribes of Coos, Lower Umpqua and Siuslaw Indians;** *and* **Hanis Coos.**

Suggested Readings:

> David R. M. Beck, *Seeking Recognition: The Termination and Restoration of the Coos, Lower Umpqua and Siuslaw Indians, 1855–1984* (Lincoln: University of Nebraska Press, 2009).

COPALIS

(Coastal Division, Salishan)

The Copalises lived on the Pacific Coast of Washington State from north of the entrance to Grays Harbor to the lands of the Quinault Indians and in the valley of the Copalis River, a Pacific Ocean affluent. In 1805–1806 Meriwether Lewis and William Clark reported that the "Pailsk," who were perhaps the Copalis, numbered two hundred and were living in ten houses. Not only does the Copalis River bear the tribal name but also the towns of Copalis, Copalis Beach, and Copalis Crossing.

The Copalis River yielded what were regarded as the most succulent of all Pacific Coast salmon. The Copalises ate other fish as well, including sculpin that were noted for their large heads and wide mouths. Neighboring tribes came to the Copalis villages to obtain razor clams, which today are as highly prized as they were in prerecorded times. It is said that the Copalises never let their fires die out because they always expected visitors. Contact of the Copalises with whites was evident in the potatoes grown in the 1850s by one of their headmen, Herkoish.

In the 1850s the Copalises had no special designation in most official tabulations. As a nontreaty people, their few remaining members depended on the Quinault Agency for such aids as medicines and vaccinations against smallpox. The Chehalises alleged that the Copalises were a subdivision of their tribe, although they attacked the Copalises so often that the latter had deserted some of their villages. The Quinaults also claimed the Copalises as part of their tribe, a conclusion not shared by the Indian Claims Commission in *The Quinault Tribe* v. *United States* (Docket 242). Archaeologists have unearthed old Copalis villages in recent years.

COQUILLE

(Athabaskan)

Originally the Coquilles were known by their Native name, which in English was spelled as "Mishikhwutmetunne" and meant "people living on the stream called Mishi, or Misha." Whites called them Upper Coquilles and Coast Rogues. Although Athabaskan speakers at some early period entered southern Oregon from the north, the Coquilles are believed to have migrated into the valley of the Coquille River only shortly before contact. The Coquille River flows into the Pacific Ocean where the town of Coquille, Oregon, is located today. The origin of the tribal name is disputed. Some say it is the French word meaning "shell." Others believe that it is a Native word with a French spelling.

The dwellings of the Coquilles were made of willow frames covered with sod or grass reeds over wood-frame poles. Some houses were lean-tos of cedar planks. During the precontact period, females were matched with spouses in arranged marriages. Although women had no role in village government, they did go out on spirit quests, and some women became shamans. During the precontact period, governance operated at the village level. Later, non-Indians grouped the Indian villagers together to better administer them. After the Coquilles moved away from the coast, they depended on acorns and deer for much of their subsistence, hunting the latter with dogs. They fished occasionally for salmon along the coast near present-day Port Orford, using nets and baskets. They also caught eels in willow-twig baskets.

The Coquilles had little contact with coastal Indians, although they did raid the Coos for slaves. Coquille tradition, however, explains that during early times a marriage united the Coquille and Coos peoples when a Coos headman, Kitzunginum, took a Coquille woman, Nestilcut, as one of his five wives. To commemorate their marriage, the couple marked a cedar tree as high as they could reach. Eventually, Kitzunginum's own people killed him during an elk hunt, shooting him with arrows when his back was turned. Another tradition has it that the chief had forcibly wrested tribal leadership from his brother.

Coquille contacts with non-Indians were especially unfriendly. After an Indian guide misled W. G. T'Vault and his party, who were searching for an overland route between the coast and the Willamette Valley, the Coquilles engaged them on September 14, 1851, with bows and arrows, war clubs, and knives fashioned from iron seized from the vessel *William G. Hagstaff*, which had previously wrecked near Port Orford. Wading into the water, the Indians (who may, in fact, have been Lower Coquilles, or Miluk Coos) attacked the party before it could ready its rifles. (For an account of this incident, *see* **Miluk Coos.**) Aggravating the conflicts between the tribes of the upper and lower Coquille River were the unratified treaties effected with them by Oregon superintendents of Indian affairs Anson Dart and Joel Palmer in 1851 and 1855. The Coquilles and other so-called Rogue peoples were rounded up in June 1856 and moved mostly by ship from Port Orford to Portland and then to the Grand Ronde Reservation, where many succumbed to smallpox. Eventually, those who did not escape from the reservation to their homelands were moved to the Siletz Reservation. Those who got away had previously buried their canoes in the sand in their homelands, hoping to find them on returning there. After fleeing the reservation, they discovered that they could no longer live in a traditional manner because settlers had occupied their old lands. Many intermarried with whites.

With certain other descendants of western Oregon tribes, the Coquilles were plaintiffs in Case No. 45230 in the Court of Claims seeking compensation for lands taken from the Coast Reservation by executive order on December 21, 1865, and by an act of Congress on March 3, 1875. After receiving an award that did not include interest, the Coquilles appealed to the U.S. Supreme Court for payment of the same, but on November 25, 1946, that court upheld the April 2, 1945, ruling of the Court of Claims. In the end, the Coquilles received an award of $847,190.40. For the history of a suit brought before the Court of Claims in which the Coquilles were named as defendants, *see* **Yaquina** *and* **Alsea.** For other claims, *see* **Confederated Tribes of Siletz Indians.**

Anthropologist John R. Swanton reported that the 1910 census listed fifteen Mishikhwutmetunnes under the name Upper Coquille. Today there are no full-blood-degree Coquilles. *See also* **Coquille Indian Tribe.**

Suggested Readings:

Stephen Dow Beckham, *The Indians of Western Oregon: This Land Was Theirs* (Coos Bay, Ore., Arago Books, 1977); Roberta L. Hall, *Oral Traditions of the Coquille Indians* (Corvallis: Oregon State University, 1978) and *The Coquille Indians: Yesterday, Today and Tomorrow* (Lake Oswego, Ore.: Smith, Smith and Smith Publishing Company, 1984); Beverly Mecum Ward, "White Moccasins," n.d., manuscript in possession of author.

Jerry Running Foxe, a modern Coquille of the Oregon coast, ca. 1980. His ancestors vigorously opposed invasion of their coasts by outsiders.

Authors' collections.

COQUILLE INDIAN TRIBE

The Upper Coquilles (*see* **Coquille**) were Athabaskan speakers. The Lower Coquilles, or Miluk Coos (*see* **Miluk Coos**), were Yakonan speakers. According to those identifying themselves today as Coquilles, the spelling of their tribal name until the early twentieth century was Coquelle. In 1952, Indians of Coquille descent organized with a few Coos to seek a judgment from the Court of Claims in a land claims case. The tribe disbanded in 1956 but reformed in 1975 as the Coquille Indian Tribe. On July 28, 1989, President George H. W. Bush signed Public Law 101–42, restoring Coquille tribal status after thirty-five years of nonrecognition. Their tribal status had been lost with the 1954 Western Oregon Termination Act. The 631-member tribe acquired a gift of 1.2 acres from the Port of Bandon, and the tribe purchased four acres adjacent to that.

Numbers: Nearly two-thirds of tribal members are under the age of thirty, and 38 percent are under the age of eighteen. In 2000 the resident population of their 10.404-square-mile reservation was 258 persons. In 2008 there were 888 enrolled tribal members.

Contemporary Life and Culture: With the restoration of the Coquille Tribe, the Coquille Economic Development Corporation was established in 1992 to expand and manage tribal businesses. Today the largest tribal enterprise is The Mill Casino-Hotel and RV Park in North Bend. The casino opened in May 1995, and the 115-room hotel opened in July 2000, with a major $40-million, seven-story tower completed in July 2008. The casino-hotel operation immediately boosted the local economy, providing five hundred jobs and $25 million spent on goods and services annually. By 2001, 577 jobs in Coos County—one of every forty-two jobs in the county—paying an average of $21,560 per year, were attributable, either directly or indirectly, to The Mill Casino-Hotel. That year one-quarter of the economic output of the entire county was connected to tribal businesses, and the tribe ranked as the second-largest employer in the county, not to mention the hundreds of thousands of dollars contributed to local nonprofit groups.

Besides The Mill, tribal enterprises include an assisted living and Alzheimer's facility called Heritage Place, which opened in 1994, and the Coquille Tribal Community Health Center, which opened a year later; Coquille Cranberries, an organic cranberry-growing and -packing operation in North Bend; ORCA Communications, a high-speed broadband telecommunications provider; and other business entities. In 1996 Congress passed the Coquille Forest Act, restoring 5,410 acres of ancestral homeland and timberland to the tribe, whose holdings in 2006 totaled 6,512 acres.

The tribe has set education as its foremost priority and through its educational department it maintains both Head Start and after-school programs. Teenage students can also gain practical experience through a summer youth program at the Mill Casino-Hotel, and tribal members may apply to the tribe for financial assistance to attend college or vocational school. In 2008 the Coquille Tribal Community Fund distributed $590,000 in donations to forty-two organizations, including $150,000 toward building a new museum in Coos Bay.

Special Events and Celebrations: The Mill-Luck Salmon Celebration is held annually the second weekend in September at the Mill Casino Hotel in North Bend, Oregon.

Suggested Readings:

Roberta Hall, *People of the Coquille Estuary: Native Use of Resources on the Oregon Coast* (Woodlands, Tex.: Word & Pictures Unlimited, 1995); Roberta L. Hall and Don Alan Hall, "The Village at the Mouth of the Coquille River: Historical Questions of Who, When, and Where," *Pacific Northwest Quarterly* 82, no. 3 (1991); Mark Axel Tveskov, *The Coos and Coquille: A Northwest Coast Historical Anthropology* (Eugene: University of Oregon, 2000); George Bundy Wasson, Jr., "Growing Up Indian: An Emic Perspective," Ph.D. dissertation, University of Oregon, 2001; Jason Younker, "The Southwest Oregon Research Project: Strengthening Coquille Sovereignty with Archival Research and Gift Giving," *American Indian Culture and Research Journal* 29, no. 2 (2005) and "Coquille/ Ko'Kwel, A Southern Oregon Coast Indian Tribe: Revisiting History, Ingenuity, and Identity," Ph.D. dissertation, University of Oregon, 2003; Lionel Youst and William R. Seaburg, *Coquelle Thompson, Athabaskan Witness: A Cultural Biography* (Norman: University of Oklahoma Press, 2002).

COW CREEK BAND OF UMPQUA
TRIBE OF INDIANS

The Cow Creek Band of Umpqua Tribe of Indians was created when Oregon superintendent of Indian affairs Joel Palmer affixed his signature to a treaty on September 19, 1853 (10 Stat. 1027), which was ratified on April 12, 1854. That was the second ratified treaty in the Pacific Northwest to be negotiated with Indians of several villages of different linguistic groups. In this case, the villages were along Cow Creek, a tributary of the South Fork of the Umpqua River in southern Oregon. Among the Indians included in the treaty were Athabaskan-speaking Upper Umpqua Targunsans and Miwaletas. The Miwaletas took their name, meaning "small, long-time-ago people," from that of their chief. Also included in the treaty were Takilman speakers and possibly a few Waiilatpuan-speaking Southern Molalas.

Location: The descendants of those Cow Creek peoples, who form the nucleus of the present-day tribe, reside in towns such as Drew, Tiller, Riddle, and Canyonville in Oregon. The Cow Creeks formerly lived on the creek that bears their name. The Upper Umpquas were their downstream neighbors on the South Fork of the Umpqua River. Beyond them were the Yoncallas. The Southern Molalas lived far into the nearby Cascade Mountains along the headwaters of the North and South Umpqua rivers.

Numbers: In 1985 the Cow Creeks numbered 221; in 1990, 755; in 1992, 831; and in 2008, 1,471.

History: By the terms of their 1853 treaty, the Indians ceded nearly 800 square miles of land for $12,000, dispersed in twenty-one payments, and a small temporary reservation on their lands on Cow Creek. Later, on the decision of the federal government, they were removed to another reservation. In contrast to such confinement, they had previously been a mobile people who moved their villages seasonally. When the Rogue wars were renewed in October 1855, many Cow Creeks escaped to the hills, joining others who had fled when the government threatened to move them to the temporary reservation established for Upper Umpquas (*see* **Upper Umpqua**). Those who left had no desire to be moved north with Upper Umpquas, Yoncallas, and Southern Molalas to the Yamhill country, where the Grand Ronde Reservation was to be established for them. The journey to the reservation in January 1856 was indeed very arduous for those who endured it. Many were forced to walk because the eight wagons commissioned to transport them were inadequate. Many of those who did remove later managed to get away and return to their former homes, where, hiding out in the mountains, some died from starvation and exposure. Half the Miwaletas perished,

Susan Thomason of the Cow Creek Band of Umpqua Tribe of Indians of the southern Oregon coast. This picture was taken about 1860, a few years after her people signed a treaty with the United States in which they yielded their lands.

Courtesy of the Douglas County Museum, Roseburg, Ore.

some expiring so fast that the survivors could not bury them but had to burn the bodies instead. Several were killed by Oregon mounted volunteers scouting through the hills.

After 1868, settlers pushed the Cow Creek Indians ever farther up the South Umpqua, where they finally came to rest in headwater country above and around Canyonville along the route of north-south travel between the Pacific Northwest and California. Some of their women married French-Canadian fur trappers. The settlers who occupied their former home built fences to prevent Indians from burning their lands, as they had for generations, to promote berry growth, thus depriving them of that food source. Two attempts were made to capture the still-at-large Cow Creeks. In May 1856 agent James P. Day failed to seize those Cow Creeks who were around Canyonville. In 1860 the military was likewise unsuccessful in attempting to confine them. Faced with starvation, the Cow Creeks raided the farms of Douglas County settlers, killing their livestock. When the searches of volunteers finally tapered off, the Indians emerged from hiding. They also sent runners to the Grand Ronde Reservation to ascertain the condition of the Indians there. The messengers returned with reports of starvation and exposure.

Government and Claims: The Cow Creek Band of Umpqua Tribe of Indians is a nonprofit organization incorporated in the state of Oregon. Although landless and without a reservation, the tribe has, since late 1910, sought through legislation to obtain payment for their lost ancestral lands. In 1932 President Herbert

Hoover vetoed a bill that would have compensated the tribe. In 1936 the Cow Creeks were named in the group of litigants in *Rogue River Tribe of Indians* v. *United States* (64 F. Supp. 339, Ct. Cl.); four years later they were named in a second suit (89 F. Supp. 789, Ct. Cl.). The Cow Creek Band of Umpqua Tribe of Indians alleges, however, that it was in error to list them as litigants because they lacked knowledge of the case. They had not, they said, negotiated a contract with an attorney. Of the seventeen petitioning tribes, only two proved successful. The Cow Creek claim was dismissed.

The tribe argued that those Cow Creeks listed in the petition were descended from the Cow Creeks who were on the Grand Ronde Reservation before removal to the Siletz. The Court of Claims decided on April 3, 1950 (Case No. 45231), that the total of $12,000 paid in installments to the Cow Creek Band that had removed to the Grand Ronde constituted adequate compensation for the Cow Creek lands, and thus tribal members were not entitled to any further awards. In fact, most of the tribe had received the first two payments before the band was removed to the Grand Ronde. The Cow Creek Band of Umpqua Tribe of Indians failed to petition the Indian Claims Commission (established by an act of Congress on August 13, 1946) before August 13, 1951, the deadline for the renewal of past claims. The Cow Creeks asserted that not only had they not been notified but they were also unaware of the existence of the commission. For those reasons they sought congressional approval to litigate their claim before the Court of Claims. Their request, in the form of Senate and House bills (S. 688 and H.R. 2882), was for Congress to extend for them the statute of limitations in the Indian Claims Commission act for filing claims against the government, thus permitting them to bring suit. The tribe insisted that the majority of its ancestors had fled and had therefore received none of the eighteen remaining payments, which it claimed were paid to only about forty-five members of the tribe residing on the Grand Ronde. Both the congressional bills finally passed on May 26, 1980 (94 Stat. 372), giving the tribe authorization to sue the United States in the Court of Claims for compensation for its alienated lands—for which, the tribe maintained, the previous payment was unconscionably low. (*See* **Upper Umpqua.**)

By a congressional act dated December 29, 1982, the tribe was granted federal recognition. A decade later, the tribe was seeking a means to produce tribal income, one of the considerations being a bingo parlor.

Contemporary Life and Culture: The Cow Creeks operate a number of businesses, including the 68,000-square-foot Seven Feathers Hotel & Casino Resort, which opened in 1992 as the first high-stakes Indian gaming facility established in Oregon. Today, more than 1 million guests visit the casino per year, and the hotel offers 147 deluxe guest rooms. An expansion is underway by which the facility will have five floors and an additional 154 rooms. Other enterprises supported by the tribe include Seven Feathers Truck and Travel Center; Seven Feathers RV Resort; Umpqua Indian Foods; Umpqua Indian Utility Cooperative, the first utility in the Pacific Northwest both owned and operated by an Indian tribe; and a communications business called Rio Networks. The tribe also operates two motels, a mini-storage, a graphics design business, a self-funded tribal health insurance program, and a 4,000-acre cattle ranch. In 2001 the Cow Creek Band was listed as one of the region's largest employers, with more than a thousand employees working in a dozen businesses with an annual payroll exceeding $20 million.

As of January 2008, the Cow Creek Umpqua Indian Foundation, a private enterprise founded in 1997 that represents the tribe, had funded 815 grants for a total of $8,797,146. In 1999 the Cow Creeks challenged the use of the Indian image as the trademark of a motorcycle manufacturer, a complaint centered on who has the power to determine how American Indian names and images are appropriated.

Special Events and Celebrations: The tribe holds its annual Cow Creek Band of Umpqua Powwow, usually in the last two weeks of July at South Umpqua Falls. Land of Umpqua Discovery Days is celebrated the third weekend in June in Roseburg, Oregon.

Suggested Readings:

Stephen Dow Beckham, "Lonely Outpost: The Army's Fort Umpqua," *Oregon Historical Quarterly* 70, no. 3 (1969), *The Indians of Western Oregon: This Land Was Theirs* (Coos Bay, Ore.: Arago Books, 1977), and *Land of the Umpqua: A History of Douglas County, Oregon* (Roseburg: Douglas County Commissioners, 1988).

COWLITZ

(Coastal Division, Salishan)

The name "Cowlitz" is said to mean "capturing the medicine spirit" because the Cowlitzes visited a small prairie on the Cowlitz River, a Columbia River affluent in Washington State, to commune with the spirit world and receive "medicine" power. During the early nineteenth century the Cowlitzes became divided into four groups. One group, the Lower Cowlitzes, occupied the middle and lower courses of the Cowlitz River from Cowlitz Landing south to the mouth of the river, plus the river's tributaries and adjacent lands. Because their lands bordered on the Columbia River, these Cowlitzes relied more on salmon for subsistence than did other Cowlitz groups. Another group was the Mountain Cowlitzes. They combined with the Kwalhioquas, who subsequently gave up their language for that of the Cowlitzes. The Mountain Cowlitzes lived on the upper reaches of the Chehalis River and eventually united with the Kwaiailks (Upper Chehalises). The Upper Cowlitzes (sometimes called the Stick Indians) lived on the upper Cowlitz River and below Mount Rainier. They intermarried with the Sha-haptian-speaking Klickitats and adopted their language. The western movement of the Klickitats from just east of the Cascade Mountains was accomplished by individuals, mostly women, and not by the tribe at large. The Upper Cowlitzes traveled widely for mountain game and grazed horses on their mountain meadows. Another Cowlitz group, the Lewis Cowlitzes—so named because of their location on the Lewis River, a Columbia affluent—coalesced as well with the Klickitats and adopted the Klickitat language.

Without access to the sea, the Mountain and Upper Cowlitz groups became skilled hunters. The anthropologist Verne F. Ray found the Cowlitzes to be the most cohesive tribe in western Washington, partly because of their isolation. Their women were excellent basketweavers, who worked cedar roots horizontally and bear and straw grass vertically in their manufactures. Possibly those techniques were learned from the Klickitats or at least improved on by the association of the Cowlitzes with that tribe. The Cowlitzes held and traded slaves, who were obtained mostly through barter and war.

In addition to the Cowlitz River, Cowlitz County, Washington, bears the tribal name.

Location: Many Cowlitzes remain in the general area of their ancestral homelands. Others have dispersed, especially to western Washington and into Oregon.

Numbers: In 1780, the tribal population, along with that of the Chehalises, the Humptulipses, and some others, numbered about 1,000. In 1842 there were 350 Upper Cowlitzes, about 100 Mountain Cowlitzes, and 330 others, presumably including the Lower Cowlitzes and perhaps the Lewis River group. Epidemics, such as the intermittent fever of the 1830s, reduced the total Cowlitz population to less than 1,000. In the 1850s, smallpox diminished them to between 600 and 700. In 1879 there were only 66 Cowlitzes near the mouth of the Cowlitz River under the supervision of a Nisqually agent. In 1887 there were 127 Cowlitzes whom the government classified as part of the Chehalis tribe. In 1893 the Puyallup agent reported that those Cowlitzes had scattered onto small farms or had been absorbed within the white community.

Today, the Cowlitz Tribe accepts as members those having one-sixteenth or more Cowlitz heritage. In 1973 the tribal population was 278; the following year, it stood at about 320 adult Cowlitzes. In 1980 tribal enrollment was 1,689, and by 2008 it had grown to over 3,600.

History: During the early contact period the Cowlitzes could be unfriendly to outsiders. One special agent wrote that they were "independent, fearless and aggressive and refused to subordinate themselves to the white man." Because they were also on poor terms with the Indians on the Pacific Coast, the Cowlitzes in 1813 asked the traders of the North West Company's Fort George near the mouth of the Columbia River to trade with them in their own lands, where such activity could be carried on more safely. In 1818, after a party of Iroquois in the employ of the North West Company massacred thirteen innocent Cowlitzes, the chief trader at Fort George brought the Cowlitz headman, How How, to the post, hoping to arrange a marriage between his daughter and one of the men. Thinking that the chief and his people had come to attack them in retaliation for the killings, the Indians at the post confronted them until the matter was resolved. During the 1830s, the Lower Cowlitzes acted to possess the environs of the mouth of the Cowlitz River, replacing the Chinookan speakers formerly there. Intermarriage continued between Cowlitzes and Chinookan peoples, as it did between Cowlitzes, Klickitats, and Chehalises. During this period the intermittent fever struck with great ferocity.

In December 1838 the Roman Catholic priest François Norbert Blanchet established the St. Francis Xavier Mission near today's Toledo, Washington, on the route between the Columbia River and southern Puget Sound. In that same year, the Anglican minister, Rev. Herbert Beaver, vaccinated nearly 120 Lewis River Cowlitzes. Others of the tribe were vaccinated by a Hudson's Bay Company medical officer. In February and March 1855, the Cowlitzes attended the Chehalis River treaty council with Washington territorial governor and superintendent of Indian affairs Isaac Stevens, but they did not sign a treaty. They were dissatisfied that the proposed treaty did not provide for a reservation in their own country. With most of the other mountain tribes, like the Snoqualmies, the Upper Cowlitzes opposed the Americans in the 1855–56 Indian wars. In 1856, other Cowlitzes, under the watchful eye of Indian Agent Sydney S. Ford, were collected on a temporary reservation, on the lands of one Simon Plomondon, a former Hudson's Bay Company employee who was the first settler on Cowlitz Prairie. During the wars, large numbers of Lewis River Cowlitzes were confined at Fort Vancouver. During their captivity, their horses and other properties were stolen or destroyed. In 1860 the Indian agent of the Columbia River District, R. H. Lansdale, removed Lewis River Cowlitzes because of conflicts with non-Indians, who were driving them from place to place, seizing their lands, and burning their properties. Among those relocated were forty-three Cowlitzes, who, with their livestock, were sent eastward across the Cascade Mountains to the Yakama Reservation.

On March 20, 1863, a presidential proclamation offered Cowlitz lands for public sale, even though the tribe had never signed a treaty relinquishing them. Subsequently, tribal members defied the wish of the government that they remove to the Chehalis Reservation, established on July 8, 1864, between the Chehalis and Black rivers. The Cowlitzes never recognized the reservation and continued to hold out for one of their own. In 1868 they refused presents offered them by government officials, fearing that acceptance would mean surrender of their lands. In 1872, when it was definitively ascertained that the Chehalis Reservation was

Joseph E. Cloquet, former chairman of the Cowlitz Tribal Council, photographed ca. 1980. The Cowlitzes were among the southwestern Washington tribes who opposed removal to reservations outside their homelands. The Cowlitz Tribe has sought to maintain tribal traditions and to obtain settlement of claims.

Authors' collections.

for all nontreaty Indians of southwestern Washington Territory, the Cowlitzes continued to reject it as their home.

Government and Claims: The Cowlitz tribe is an unincorporated association formed by a group of Cowlitz Indians to maintain tribal traditions and to obtain settlement of tribal claims. The association's constitution and bylaws provide that membership should consist "solely of Cowlitz Indians and their descendants." The constitution and bylaws also provide for an executive committee of five to supervise tribal affairs. The organization accepts for its membership those persons claiming Cowlitz descent.

In 1931 the U.S. Supreme Court ruled in *Halbert* v. *United States* that the Cowlitzes were entitled to take allotments on the Quinault Reservation and that the Cowlitz tribe was recognized and protected under the Treaty of Olympia (1855). On June 23, 1971, the Indian Claims Commission (Docket 218) determined that the United States had exercised such "domination and control" over Cowlitz lands that the tribe had been deprived of its aboriginal title without its consent and without any payment of consideration. On April 12, 1973, the tribe entered into a compromise settlement for which the Claims Commission, on July 1, 1973, awarded it $1,550,000—fifty-eight years after the tribe's first bills for a settlement had been introduced. A total of 280 members voted to accept the award. Wanting land instead of money, forty voted to reject it. The group voting negatively broke from the Cowlitz Tribe of Indians to become the sovereign Cowlitz Tribe. A controversy with the government over plans for the distribution of funds followed, especially to Cowlitz-descendant members of the Yakama Tribe who under federal legislation were eligible for Cowlitz tribal enrollment. Meanwhile, many of the Klickitats who had formerly lived in the Cowlitz country and with whom the Cowlitzes had intermarried, had removed eastward across the Cascade Mountains and joined other Klickitats on the Yakama Reservation. *See* **Klickitat** *and* **Taitnapam.**

Contemporary Life and Culture: After twenty-one years of struggle, the Cowlitzes gained federal recognition in February 2000 (upheld on appeal in January 2002). They have since opened health clinics in Longview and Vancouver and are converting a schoolhouse in Toledo into an apartment complex for elders. They are the only federally recognized tribe in Washington State without a reservation, but the Cowlitzes maintain administrative offices in Longview and have applied to the federal government to turn 152 acres of tribally purchased land near La Center into trust land on which they hope to construct a Las Vegas-style casino at a projected cost of $500 million, with an estimated employment of between three thousand and five thousand people. A hotel, restaurant, shops, cultural center, and tribal offices and service buildings would be included in the project. In 2005 the tribe entered into preliminary discussions with NASCAR officials to bring a speedway to southwestern Washington. The late Cowlitz tribal chairman John Barnett said, "After all these years, justice has finally been done. We're not extinct. They are finally recognizing that we've always been here and always been an historic tribe."

Special Events and Celebrations: The Honoring the Spirit of All Cowlitz People Powwow is held annually in September at the St. Mary's Center near Toledo, Washington. A First Salmon Ceremony is also observed each year.

Suggested Readings:

Darleen Ann Fitzpatrick, *We Are Cowlitz: A Native American Ethnicity* (Lanham, Md.: University Press of America, 2004); Judith Irwin, "The Cowlitz Way A Round of Life," *Cowlitz Historical Quarterly,* Spring 1979, 5–24; M. Dale Kinkade, *Cowlitz Dictionary and Grammatical Sketch* (Missoula: Linguistics Laboratory, University of Montana, 2004); Judith W. Irwin, "The Dispossessed," *Columbia: The Magazine of Northwest History* 8, no. 2 (1994); John C. Jackson, "Mixed-Bloods on the Cowlitz," *Columbia: The Magazine of Northwest History* 12, no. 1 (1998); Verne F. Ray, "Handbook of Cowlitz Indians," in *Coast Salish and Western Washington Indians,* vol. 3 (New York: Garland Publishing, 1974), 245–315; Brett Rushforth, " 'The Great Spirit Was Grieved': Religion and Environment among the Cowlitz Indians," *Pacific Northwest Quarterly* 93, no. 4 (2002); State of Washington Indian Affairs Task Force, *Are You Listening, Neighbor?. . . The People Speak. Will You Listen?* (Olympia: State of Washington, 1978); Roy I. Wilson, *Historical Overview of the Cowlitz Tribe* (Seattle, Wash.: Talking Stick Press, 1988) and *Legends of the Cowlitz Indian Tribe* (Bremerton, Wash: Cowlitz Indian Tribe, 1998).

DAKUBETEDE

(Athabaskan)

The Dakubetedes lived in southwestern Oregon on the Applegate River, an upper Rogue River tributary that enters that stream from the south. They were also called the Applegate River Indians. They spoke a dialect similar to that of the Taltushtuntudes, who were Athabaskan speakers living on nearby Galice Creek. The Dakubetedes were also neighbors of the Shastas, whose lands extended from Oregon into California. The history of the Dakubetedes during the latter half of the nineteenth century parallels that of the Takilman-speaking Takelmas with whom they became culturally assimilated. The Dakubetedes have always been counted in conjunction with other tribes. The ethnologist James Mooney estimated their 1780 population at 3,200, which included Taltushtuntudes and a portion of the Umpquas (probably that element that spoke the Athabaskan tongue). For an account of Dakubetedes' interactions with non-Indians, including their wars, treaties, and removal to a reservation, *see* **Takelma**.

DUWAMISH

(Coastal Division, Salishan)

Dkhw'Duw'Absh
People of the Inside

The name "Duwamish" is said to mean "inside [the bay] people." The tribe lived in autonomous winter villages on the Duwamish, Black, and Cedar rivers and their tributaries as those watercourses existed before the changes wrought by the U.S. Army Corps of Engineers in 1916. According to the nineteenth-century ethnologist George Gibbs, their "proper seat" was at the outlet of Lake Washington and along the Duwamish River, where their most important villages were located.

A prominent subdivision, the Sammamish, was autonomous as well, as were all other groups within the Duwamish River basin. The Sammamish spoke a dialect similar to that of the Duwamish proper and were intimately connected with other bands and tribes of the area. It was reported that instead of locating on the Suquamish (Port Madison) Reservation, as other Duwamish subdivisions did, the Sammamish were assigned to the Tulalip (Snohomish) Reservation, but apparently they did not remove there either.

In the Duwamish homelands, because of the changes brought by engineer-

George, a Duwamish who lived in the general area of Seattle, which was named for the Duwamish chief Sealth (Si'ahl). Today many Duwamishes are assimilated within the greater Seattle community, though they seek to retain their tribal identity.

Courtesy of the Smithsonian Institution.

ing, the Black River no longer exists, while the northern half of the Duwamish River, transferred to the Duwamish Waterway, serves as a vital link in the busy waterfront complex of Seattle. The Duwamish left their mark not only on that waterway but also in the names of several other landmarks such as the large boat moorage area Shilshole Bay and the city of Seattle, which was named for their headman Sealth, or Seattle.

Because of the flexibility of Duwamish resident kinship ties, it was common for individuals to affiliate with other bands and tribes. Upper-class Duwamish frequently married into other groups, a practice followed by Chief Seattle. His father was a Suquamish headman and his mother was a Duwamish woman.

Location: Many Duwamish are descended from those who remained in their aboriginal homelands. They are assimilated within the greater Seattle community and the Pacific Northwest and the nation.

Numbers: In 1854 Washington territorial governor and superintendent of Indian affairs Isaac Stevens placed the Duwamish at 162, far short of the rough estimate of 1,200 listed for 1783. A census in 1856 enumerated them at 378, while one completed in 1910 counted only 20. In 1980 the Duwamish Tribe claimed about 325 active members, from a judgment roll of 1,200. As of August 2008, the tribe counted about 600 enrolled members, who were dispersed throughout the Puget Sound region, Washington, Oregon, California, Alaska, and other states.

History: After providing leadership in wars against neighboring peoples, Chief Seattle signed the Point Elliott Treaty in 1855. At that time, he reaffirmed his friendship with Americans, including those who were settling on his people's lands. From a Duwamish winter village that became Pioneer Square, white men laid the foundations of Seattle. Several Duwamish worked for non-Indians in the Seattle area and traded such items as potatoes to them.

When Duwamish, Taitnapam, Puyallup, Nisqually, and Suquamish elements attacked the fledgling Seattle community in 1856, Chief Seattle proved his loyalty to the settlers. To remove the Duwamish from the Indian-white hostilities on the mainland, the tribe was assigned by their treaty to the Fort Kitsap (later the Suquamish and Port Madison) Reservation on the Kitsap Peninsula that lies across Puget Sound from Seattle. They were anxious to leave the reservation, not only because of barely being able to subsist there but also because they were on poor terms with the Suquamish for whom the reservation came to be named. They also infringed on the rights of the Suquamish to have total access to their homeland. In the summer of 1856, all but four or five Duwamish families vacated the reservation. They remained on the eastern shores of Bainbridge Island for five months before moving to the western shores of Elliott Bay, from which they were removed to Holderness Point (Duwamish Head). By that winter, the Duwamishes had returned to their old homeland on the Duwamish River. Under pressure from local settlers, the agent assigned the Duwamish to the Muckleshoot Reservation because the Indians there were from the nearby Green and White rivers and were related to the Duwamish. Some Duwamish did settle on the Muckleshoot. In 1893 a large group gathered on Ballast Island in Seattle in order to avoid confinement after settlers had burned them out of their homes in west Seattle. In 1910 the Duwamish still had a village at Foster, south of Seattle.

Government and Claims: In 1925 the Duwamish adopted a constitution and formed a government. Like so many other landless tribes, under the direction of their tribal council they sought acknowledgment by the federal government. A proposal that they join with the Suquamish to obtain recognition was opposed by some members of the latter tribe. In seeking acknowledgment, the Duwamish strove to attain rights enjoyed by certain other Puget Sound tribes, including eligibility to catch up to 50 percent of the annual harvestable salmon and steelhead trout of Washington State. In a 1974 decision, they were denied those rights because of lack of acknowledgment and their landless status.

After Congress authorized some Puget Sound tribes on February 12, 1925 (43 Stat. 836), to take legal action for compensation for the loss of their lands, *Duwamish et al.* v. *U.S.* (79 C. Cls. 530) was filed in 1926. The case remained in the Court of Claims for over a decade. During that time the Duwamish conducted business with the federal government through the Tulalip Agency. Their case, which involved a claim of nine hundred dollars for each of fifty-six longhouses destroyed, was dismissed without recovery. The court determined that the sums that had been appropriated for and disbursed to the Duwamish by the United States had exceeded their legal and equitable claims. In 1946 the tribe filed a

Since 1975 Cecile Hansen has been the chairwoman of the Duwamish Tribe. Under her leadership, the Duwamish have continued to fight for federal recognition. They have also opened the Duwamish Longhouse and Cultural Center in the city of Seattle.

Courtesy of Paul D. G. Eubanks.

claim (Docket 109) with the Indian Claims Commission for additional compensation for lands ceded to the United States. The commission ruled that the tribe's aboriginal lands had comprised 54,790 acres as of March 8, 1859. On July 20, 1962, the commission issued a final award, after a $12,000 offset, to the Duwamish of $62,000. The payment amounted to $1.35 for each acre lost—in essence, for acreage that had become the city of Seattle. The tribe appealed to the Court of Claims, which on July 12, 1963, confirmed the commission's findings and dismissed the Duwamish appeal on motion of the tribe on December 10, 1963. The commission entered an amended final judgment the following day.

Contemporary Life and Culture: The Duwamish Tribe remains federally unrecognized, although it continues to seek such status and was briefly granted acknowledgment in the waning hours of the Bill Clinton administration. The designation was overturned within forty-eight hours by President George W. Bush, who cited procedural errors after his inauguration in January 2001. On May 7, 2008, the tribe—its members are often known as the "First People" but also the "Forgotten People"—filed an appeal in U.S. District Court against that decision and is currently awaiting judgment.

Some members of the Duwamish tribe are enrolled on the Suquamish and Muckleshoot reservations. By the BIA they are treated as either Suquamish or Muckleshoots—not Duwamish. If they were to identify themselves as members of the Duwamish tribe, they could not receive the services of the BIA or the Indian Health Service, though some Duwamish Indians not enrolled on a reservation have received some federal services. Like the Puyallups who are assimilated in the Tacoma community, many Duwamish are assimilated into the society of the greater Seattle area.

Besides its efforts to achieve acknowledgment and fishing rights, the tribe has established a nonprofit corporation to facilitate the retention and reclamation of tribal culture and the development of self-determination projects. In the late 1970s, archaeologists unearthed some Duwamish settlements. Others, however, were beyond recovery because of industrial development. *See* **Suquamish Tribe, Port Madison Reservation.**

The land base of the tribe is a three-quarter-acre parcel located along the Duwamish River in Seattle near the ancient village of hah-AH-poos, upon which in November 2008 they constructed a 6,044-square-foot, $4-million cedar longhouse and cultural center—their first erected since 1894 and the first in Seattle in 150 years. It serves the dual purpose of tribal headquarters and cultural center. Since the founding of their first tribal office in Burien in 1976, at a cost of a hundred dollars, the Duwamish have relocated their central office five times. Duwamish youth attend public schools in the communities where they live. The tribe does not operate a casino, nor does it enjoy fishing rights on the river that bears its name, and there are no tribally operated businesses, although the Duwamish plan to sell smoked fish and seafood in their new longhouse.

Special Events and Celebrations: The Annual Duwamish Tribe Gala Dinner & Art Auction: Honoring Seattle's First People is held in June at the Duwamish Longhouse and Cultural Center.

Suggested Readings:

Jerry L. Clark, "Thus Spoke Chief Seattle: The Story of an Undocumented Speech," *Prologue* 17, no. 1 (1985); Denise Low, "Contemporary Reinvention of Chief Seattle: Variant Texts of Chief Seattle's 1854 Speech," *American Indian Quarterly* 19, no. 3 (1995); Albert Furtwangler, *Answering Chief Seattle* (Seattle: University of Washington Press, 1997); Catherine D. Lucignani, "Seattle's First People: An Ethnohistory of Washington's Duwamish, 1850–1900," master's thesis, University of Wyoming, 2005; Patricia Hackett Nicola, "Rebecca Lena Graham's Fight for Her Inheritance," *Pacific Northwest Quarterly* 97, no. 3 (2006): 139–47; Coll Thrush, *Native Seattle: Histories from the Crossing-Over Place* (Seattle: University of Washington Press, 2008); Kenneth D. Tollefson, "Political Organization of the Duwamish," *Ethnology* 28, no. 2 (1989) and "The Political Survival of Landless Puget Sound Indians," *American Indian Quarterly* 16, no. 2 (1992).

Entiat Chief Shilhohsaskt and his wife, Spokokalx. The Entiats were an Interior Salish people of the Entiat River, a Columbia River tributary in north-central Washington. Shilhohsaskt died ca. 1900, shortly after this photograph was taken.

Courtesy of the North Central Washington Museum Association, Wenatchee.

ENTIAT

(Interior Division, Salishan)

The Entiats, also known variously as the Sintiatqkumuhs and the Intietooks, lived mainly along the Entiat River, of which the lower banks at the confluence with the Columbia River were known to Canadian voyageurs as *Point de Bois*. The Entiat River drainage area in north-central Washington extends from the Columbia west into the Cascade Mountains between the drainage areas of the Wenatchee River and Lake Chelan. One Entiat band, the Sinialkumuhs, lived on the Columbia between the Entiat and Wenatchee rivers. The Entiats have been classified as a subdivision of Wenatchis, although Verne Ray, a leading student of Pacific Northwest Indians, believed they were a separate people.

During the spring and fall, the Entiats were at fishing stations, catching mainly salmon. At other seasons they gathered roots and berries or hunted deer, bear, and other game at higher elevations. Their first contacts with non-Indians were with fur men, missionaries, and government explorers in the early and middle nineteenth century. An Entiat chief, La-Hoom, or La Hoompt, signed the Yakama Treaty of 1855. Some Entiats removed off their lands and took allotments on

Lake Chelan. One who moved there was Wapato John (Nicterwhilicum), who abandoned a store on the Columbia River upstream from the Entiat River when the earthquake of 1872 dislodged what became known as Ribbon Cliff along today's U.S. Highway 97, temporarily damming the Columbia and flooding him out. One Entiat chief, the centenarian Shilhohsaskt (Standing Cloud), remained near the mouth of the Entiat River until he died around 1900. Today some Entiat descendants live on the Colville Reservation. *See* **Confederated Tribes of the Colville Reservation.**

FLATHEAD

(Interior Division, Salishan)

The Flatheads were known by various names, including Selish, or Salish, a designation that came to be applied to their linguistic family. In somewhat the same manner, the term "Flathead" was used to delineate any of the Native peoples who practiced head flattening of their infants. The Flatheads, however, denied that their ancestors flattened heads. They believed that they were called Flatheads because the sign language identified them by pressing both sides of the head with the hands. A mountain man claimed that the Salish meant "we the people," which was signified by striking the head with the flat of the hand; from this gesture the Flatheads were said to have received their name. It has also been alleged that the tribe was called Flatheads because, unlike other tribes west of them, they left their heads in the normal configuration, flat on the top, instead of pressing them to slope toward the crown. Translating the English name, the French-Canadian fur traders called them *Têtes-Plates.*

For hundreds of years, the Flatheads were among the Salish peoples living west of the Rocky Mountains. Some scholars believe that it was after they traveled east of those mountains that they came under pressure from the Blackfeet Indians who possessed firearms and in the early eighteenth century drove the Flatheads west across the Rocky Mountains to what became their homeland in the Bitterroot Valley of western Montana. Other authorities believe smallpox plagues on the plains were a more powerful force pushing the Flatheads toward the Bitterroot.

It was at the head of the Bitterroot that their chief Three Eagles (Cheleskaiyimi) met the American explorers Meriwether Lewis and William Clark in 1805. The two explorers noted that the Flatheads had about 450 lodges and about 500 horses. Their population in 1780 has been estimated at 600. After obtaining horses, mainly from the Shoshones, the Flatheads became expert horsemen and hunters. Despite Blackfoot hostility, they routinely traveled across the Rocky Mountains and onto the plains in pursuit of buffalo. In the late eighteenth century, the father of Three Eagles, Chief Big Hawk, was killed in the buffalo country of the upper Missouri River. The Flatheads also journeyed to the plains to steal horses, avoiding whenever possible conflict with their owners. They not only bravely faced Plains Indians, but also were a buffer separating their Salish allies from them. Over the years, the Flatheads impressed whites with both their courage and their friendliness. During the Indian wars of the nineteenth century they remained loyal to Americans.

In the first half of the nineteenth century the Flatheads were involved in the fur trade. Saleesh House, later called the Flathead Post, operated to the northwest of their country. Fur trapping by the Flatheads was mainly in the spring, when the Blackfoot raids abated. In retaliation for those raids, the Flatheads and other Salish peoples fought the Blackfeet whenever the latter interrupted their hunting and horse-stealing enterprises on the plains. The British fur men with whom the Flatheads did their early trading tried to keep them from the American traders approaching from the east.

It was from the east that an important personage came to the Flatheads, Shining Shirt, possibly an Iroquois who reportedly antedated the acquisition of horses in the eighteenth century. He was said to have been the first to introduce them to Christianity, prophesying the coming of white men with long black robes "to teach them religion." Other Iroquois followed. Relocating from Quebec, they lived among the Flatheads in the early nineteenth century after their defeat in the War of 1812 as partisans of the British. Under their leader, Old Ignace La Mousse, two dozen of them came to live among Flatheads in 1820 and exerted considerable influence. Through intermarriage, these Iroquois eventually lost their tribal identity. Their Christianity had a strong nativist cast, and it was among Salish peoples that the nativist Prophet Dance resurged. In the 1830s Flathead delegations, usually led by Iroquois, visited St. Louis seeking the Black Robes. As white publicists described their quest, the predictions of Shining Shirt were fulfilled in the person of the Reverend Pierre De Smet, S.J., who established the St. Mary's Mission in the lower Bitterroot Valley in 1841. From the Bitterroot, De Smet and his associates worked among the Natives in a wide area, the Blackfeet numbering among those receiving their ministrations. That set poorly with the Flatheads, who associated the Christian faith with the "medicine" power needed to overcome their plains foes. The church fathers sought to make farmers of the Flatheads to keep them from their dangerous buffalo-hunting ventures. By the 1850s, Blackfoot attacks both east and west of the Rockies had reduced the Flatheads to a population of three hundred or four hundred, or roughly half the numbers given by the Hudson's Bay Company trader John Warren Dease in 1827.

Under their chief Victor, the Flatheads and the Pend d'Oreilles (or Upper Kalispels) met in council with Washington territorial governor and superintendent of Indian affairs Isaac Stevens at Hell Gate near Missoula, Montana, in July 1855. From that council, a treaty was effected setting aside the 2,240-square-mile Flathead, or Jocko, Reservation north of the Bitterroot Valley. An important con-

Chief Charlot, also known as the Bear Claw. For a considerable period he refused to remove from his homeland in Montana's Bitterroot Valley to the Flathead Reservation to the north. He finally located there in 1891. He died in 1910.

Courtesy of the Smithsonian Institution.

sideration in its establishment was the presence there of the Jesuit St. Ignatius Mission. Initially, most Flatheads opposed removing to the reservation. On November 14, 1871, James Garfield, later president of the United States, was empowered to represent the government to negotiate a contract with the Flatheads for their removal. Victor's successor, his son Charlot, refused to sign that document, despite government proddings and promises. Finally, in 1891, as more non-Indians entered the Bitterroot Valley, Charlot removed to the Flathead Reservation, where he regained his head chieftaincy and remained a traditionalist until his death in 1910. *See* **Confederated Salish & Kootenai Tribes of the Flathead Reservation.**

Suggested Readings:

Robert Bigart, "The Salish Flathead Indians during the Period of Adjustment, 1850–1891," *Idaho Yesterdays* 17, no. 3 (Fall 1973) and "Patterns of Cultural Change in a Salish Flathead Community," *Human Organization* (Fall 1971); W. L. Davis, S.J., "Peter John De Smet: The Journey of 1840," *Pacific Northwest Quarterly* 35, no. 1 (January 1944); John Fahey, *The Flathead Indians* (Norman: University of Oklahoma Press, 1974); Olga Wedemeyer Johnson, *Flathead and Kootenay: The Rivers, the Tribes, and the Region's Traders* (Glendale, Calif.: Arthur H. Clarke Co., 1969); Gloria Ricci Lothrop, *Recollections of the Flathead Mission* (Glendale, Calif.: Arthur H. Clark Co., 1977); Peter Ronan, *Historical Sketch of the Flathead*

Indian Nation (1890; Helena, Mont., Ross & Haines, 1965); Claude Schaeffer, "The First Jesuit Mission to the Flathead, 1840–1850: A Study in Culture Conflicts," *Pacific Northwest Quarterly* 28, no. 3 (July 1937); Allan H. Smith, "The Location of Flathead Post," *Pacific Northwest Quarterly* 48, no. 2 (April 1957); Harry Holbert Turney-High, "The Flathead Indians of Montana," *American Anthropologist* 39, no. 4, Pt. 2 (1937).

GRAND RONDE CONFEDERATED TRIBES

(See **Confederated Tribes of the Grand Ronde Community.***)*

HANIS COOS

(Yakonan)

The Hanis Coos (Kowes) constitute the northern dialect division of the Kusan linguistic family of which the Miluk Coos are the southern division. The Hanis Coos lived around Coos Bay on the southern Oregon coast. They also claimed lands beginning at Ten Mile Creek (ten miles south of the Umpqua River) and extending down the coast to Coos Bay and east to the summit of the Coast Range. The word "*coos*" is said to mean "on the south," "lagoon" or "lake," and "place of pines." Although no present-day places bear the name "Hanis," Coos Bay, Coos County, and the city of Coos Bay all carry the tribal name.

Combined with the Miluk Coos, the Hanis Coos were estimated to have numbered 2,000 in 1780, about 500 more than were believed to have existed in 1805 and 1806. In 1871 there were 136 Coos on the Alsea Subagency of the Siletz Reservation. In 1910 the population of the combined Coos tribes was given as 93; in 1930, as 107; and, in 1937, as 55. Like the Miluk Coos, the Hanises depended on foods from the sea for subsistence, skillfully operating their canoes in carrying out seasonal harvests. In summer they camped in the Coast Range to hunt, fish, pick berries, and dig roots.

When Congress passed the Donation Land Act on September 29, 1850, settlers staked out claims to Coos Bay without having to make any purchases of land or to enter into any treaty with the Indians. Like the Miluk Coos, the Hanises, despite provocations, remained noncombative toward whites during the Rogue wars, which lasted through 1856. On August 11, 1855, Coos groups, along with several other tribes on the Oregon coast, demonstrated their peaceful disposition by signing a treaty with Oregon superintendent of Indian affairs Joel Palmer,

Chief Daloose ("Jack") Jackson, in the 1890s. In the early part of the twentieth century his descendants suffered several reversals as they sought compensation from the United States for the lands in southwestern Oregon that had once been theirs. In 1972 the Hanis, along with other Coos, incorporated as the Coos Tribe of Indians and instituted tribal programs.

Courtesy of the Coos-Curry Museum and Historical Association, North Bend, Ore.

even though settlers had staked out Coos Bay after passage of the Donation Land Act. During the Rogue wars, Coos peoples were under the guard of Coos County Volunteers of Empire City (present-day Coos Bay). After the wars, the Hanis and Miluk Coos were rounded up and brought to a temporary reservation on the north side of the Umpqua River at its mouth, where they were kept under military surveillance. With closure of the Umpqua Subagency on September 3, 1859, they were marched north to the mouth of the Yachats River where, with the Kuitsh (Lower Umpquas) and Siuslaws, they were placed under the newly located (1861) Alsea Subagency (sometimes referred to as the Yachats Reservation) on the Siletz, or Coast, Reservation. In April and May 1864, soldiers from Fort Yamhill rounded up thirty-two families at Coos Bay and returned them to the mouth of the Yachats River on the reservation. In 1875, while they were living on the southern portion of the Coast Reservation, which by then had been named the Alsea, that reservation was turned over to non-Indians, forcing the Hanis Coos, the Kuitsh, and a few Siuslaws to return to their original homelands.

In 1916 and 1917 the descendants of the Coos, who had organized before 1900, met with a remnant of Kuitsh and Siuslaws at Coos Bay to initiate a suit against the government for claims for lands lost. Their claim (Case No. K-345) was not decided until May 2, 1938, when the U.S. Court of Claims handed down an opinion that their Indian testimony was inadmissible. Oblivious to records of fur trappers, diarists, Indian agents, and others, the U.S. Supreme Court, on November 14, 1938, refused to hear their appeal. The Coos experienced a similar refusal by the Indian Claims Commission between 1947 and 1951, despite the presentation of additional evidence. The commission maintained that they had already had their day in court. After those defeats, the Coos, Kuitsh, and Siuslaws unsuccessfully petitioned the United Nations to permit them entrance into that organization. Having acquired a 6.1-acre "reservation" and a tribal hall at Coos Bay, the Hanis and Miluk Coos, joined by others of Kuitsh and Siuslaw ancestry, opposed termination under the congressional enabling legislation during the 1950s. In 1975 a bill (S.B. 945) was drafted to reopen the case of the Coos, Kuitsh, and Siuslaws, but it did not pass.

The failure of the three tribes to win those claims did not deter them from instituting programs on their own. In 1972 they incorporated as The Coos Tribe of Indians under the laws of the State of Oregon. In 1973 they opened the Tribal Trading Post to sell groceries at low cost to low-income families. In 1974 the Willow River Benevolent Association secured a Comprehensive Employment Training Act (CETA) grant and became a clearinghouse for a manpower program, establishing a successful job-placement staff run by Indians. Also in 1974 the Indians established the Coos and Curry County Indian alcohol- and drug-abuse program and a detoxification center in Coos Bay.

In 1967 only one Coos spoke the Native language, but in the 1970s several programs were begun to preserve Coos culture. In 1974 the Coos Tribe of Indians formed the Oregon Coast Indian Archaeological Association, perhaps the first such society organized by Native Americans. In January 1975 a Native American research group opened the Research Center Museum in the Indian hall on the reservation belonging to the Confederated Tribes of the Coos, Lower Umpqua and Siuslaw. Wishing to preserve and share the endangered culture of her people, Esther Waters collected baskets, artifacts, photos, and other materials for the museum. The tribe also secured the services of Peter J. Stenhouse, who in 1974 began excavating a former Indian village situated on private land on the lower Umpqua River estuary. The artifacts retrieved were deposited in the Research Center Museum in Coos Bay. In 1975, Indians of southwestern Oregon began stressing in the Coos Bay public schools the importance of Indian history and culture by instituting a series of mini-courses, including demonstrations of basketmaking, dancing, storytelling, and other folklore programs. In 1977 the program was expanded to other areas of Coos County. In 1976 a Cheyenne, James Thornton, was hired to initiate and coordinate programs relating to Native Americans. Among other activities, he edited a newsletter, *Indian Education. See* **Confederated Tribes of Coos, Lower Umpqua and Siuslaw Indians,** *and* **Coos Tribe of Indians.**

Suggested Readings:

Stephen Dow Beckham, *The Indians of Western Oregon: This Land Was Theirs* (Coos Bay, Ore.: Arago Books, 1977); Leo J. Frachtenberg, *Coos Texts,* Columbia University Contributions to American Anthropology, vol. 1 (New York, 1913) and *Lower Umpqua Texts and Notes on the Kusan Dialect,* Columbia University Contributions to American Anthropology, vol. 4 (New York, 1914); Melville Jacobs, "Coos Myth Texts," *University of Washington Publications in Anthropology,* vol. 8, no. 2 (Seattle, 1940) and "Coos Narrative and Ethnologic Texts," *University of Washington Publications in Anthropology* vol. 8, no. 1 (Seattle, 1939); Henry Hull St. Clair and Leo Frachtenberg, "Traditions of the Coos Indians," *Journal of American Folklore* 23 (1909).

HOH

(Chimakuan)

Chalá-at

People of the Hoh River

The Hohs were formerly considered a band of the Quileute Tribe, who are also of Chimakuan linguistic stock. The Hoh Tribe, Hoh Indian Reservation, Washington, is today the successor of that band.

Location: The members of the Hoh Tribe primarily live on and around their 443-acre reservation that was established by executive order on September 11, 1893. The reservation lies on the Pacific Coast of the Olympic Peninsula of northwestern Washington, about fifteen miles south of the Quileute Reservation and about twenty-five miles from the town of Forks, near U.S. Highway 101.

Numbers: The Hohs and Quileutes combined were estimated to have had a population of 500 in 1780. By 1905 the Hohs had been reduced to 62, primarily due to disease and their assimilation with others. In the early 1970s there were about 15 or 20 permanent residents of the Hoh Reservation. In 1985 the tribe numbered 91. By 2008 tribal membership had climbed to 240, but only four elders over the age of sixty lived on the 133-resident reservation, and 60 percent of the reservation residents were under the age of eighteen. In the summer of 2009 enrolled membership was estimated to be between 250 and 300.

History: According to Indian tradition, the Hohs, Quileutes, and Quinaults of the Olympic Peninsula managed their own affairs in a confederation that was strong enough to virtually control all of the tribes from Cape Flattery at the entrance to the Strait of Juan de Fuca on the north to Grays Harbor along the

Pacific on the south. Centrally located in this confederation, the Hohs and the neighboring Queets Indians dominated the hunting grounds of the area, guarding them from the encroachments of other peoples like the Clallams. Like the other tribes of the confederation, the Hohs had both war and peace headmen. In July 1787, they encountered the British trader Charles Barkley, who dispatched a boat up the Hoh River to trade. It never returned. Natives allegedly killed all of the hands aboard. The Hohs were among the tribes who fought a party of about twenty Russians and Aleut Indians late in 1808, holding them captive before trading them among the coastal tribes, as was their custom with captured Natives. The prisoners were finally ransomed by an American trader in May 1811.

The Hohs were among the tribes north of Grays Harbor who met with Washington territorial governor and superintendent of Indian affairs Isaac Stevens to effect the Quinault River Treaty, which was negotiated on July 1, 1855, and signed by Stevens at Olympia on January 25, 1856 (12 Stat. 971, ratified March 8, 1859). By executive order on September 11, 1893, a small reservation was set aside for the Hohs at the mouth of the Hoh River. It was insufficient for allotment. On March 4, 1911, Congress passed an act (36 Stat. 1345) directing the secretary of the interior to make allotments to Hohs, Quileutes, and Ozettes on the Quinault Reservation, as stipulated in their 1856 treaty, rather than having them allotted on the reservations set aside for them. By 1913 lack of farming and grazing lands had halted allotment on the Quinault Reservation.

Government and Claims: The Hoh Tribe, Hoh Indian Reservation, Washington, having approved the Indian Reorganization Act of 1934 (48 Stat. 984), adopted a constitution on May 24, 1969. Elections of tribal officers are held biennially. The Hoh Tribal Business Committee is the governing body. Under the 1963 Washington State Indian Jurisdiction Act, the state assumed control over several social programs. Some services are provided by the federal government.

With the Quileutes, the Hohs claimed (Docket 155) additional compensation for the lands ceded to the United States under the Quinault River Treaty. The Hoh, Quileute, Queets, and Quinault tribes had each received $25,000, which they claimed was an unconscionably small amount. The Indian Claims Commission determined that the four tribes had held aboriginal title to 688,000 acres as of March 8, 1858. On April 17, 1963, it awarded the Hohs and Quileutes $112,152.60 as their share of compensation for those lands. Congressional legislation on October 14, 1966, provided for division of the funds between the two tribes on the basis of the total tribal memberships.

Contemporary Life and Culture: The Hoh Tribe received federal recognition on July 1, 1969. The tribe occupies a small reservation on the far Pacific Coast at the mouth of the Hoh River. In 2008–2009 the Hohs acquired an additional 460 acres in anticipation of relocating their principal village inland and out of the Hoh River floodplain.

The Hoh Tribe, to which this man belonged, lived on the Pacific shores of Washington's Olympic Peninsula. Today the tribe occupies a tiny reservation in that area and depends heavily, as its ancestors did, on fishing.

Photograph by Edward S. Curtis from Curtis's *The North American Indian* (1907–1930), vol. 9.

Hoh Reservation residents rely heavily on fish in the Hoh River for their income. To help maintain fish production, the tribe has constructed enhancement facilities. The reservation, which was logged in 1954, provides merchantable timber at decades-long intervals. Some Hoh men supplement their incomes by logging on the Olympic Peninsula. The tribe's picturesque ocean frontage has potential for economic development. In the 1980s one or two Hohs were still manufacturing traditional dugout canoes for river and ocean travel, and some women weave baskets to sell to tourists. Religious preference is Protestant, and some Hohs are Shakers.

There is no tribal school on the Hoh Reservation, but children attend Quileute Tribal School as well as schools in the Forks school district; Clearwater School (K to 7), located about twenty minutes south of the reservation; and Lake Quinault High School. Some students attend off-reservation boarding schools such as Chemawa in Oregon and Riverside in California. Early childhood education is delivered through Head Start programs located at Queets and Quileute. The Hohs do not operate a casino and have no tribally owned or operated businesses. The tribe is the major employer on the reservation, maintaining about thirty paid positions. There is no museum or cultural center, although the Hoh favor the development of such a facility. Health care is accessed through contract with the Indian Health Service in the nearby town of Forks, and in June 2008 the tribe opened a small reservation clinic, providing counseling and diabetes programs. In June 2009 the tribe took delivery of two large cedar logs, which will be used for carving totems and other carving projects.

Special Events and Celebrations: Hoh River Days has been celebrated in the past and the tribe hopes to have it revived in the future. Tribal members participate annually in the Canoe Journey.

Suggested Readings:

George Gibbs, *Tribes of Western Washington*, vol. 1 of Smithsonian Institution, *Contributions to North American Ethnology* (Washington, D.C.: Government Printing Office, 1877); Harry Hobucket, "Quillayute Indian Tradition," *Washington Historical Quarterly* 25, no. 1 (January 1934); Albert B. Reagan, "Tradition of the Hoh and Quillayute Indians," *Washington Historical Quarterly* 20, no. 3 (July 1929); Steve Wall and Harvey Arden, *Wisdomkeepers: Meetings with Native American Spiritual Elders* (Hillsboro, Ore.: Beyond Words Publishing, 1990).

HOQUIAM

*(See **Humptulips**.)*

HUMPTULIPS

(Coastal Division, Salishan)

The name "Humptulips" derives from a Native word said to mean "chilly region." The tribe was also called the Grays Harbor Indians because it held the north shore of that body of water in Washington State from near the middle of North Bay to possibly as far east as Junction City, plus Hoquiam Creek and the Humptulips and Whiskah rivers, which are affluents of Grays Harbor. Besides the river, a town on U.S. Highway 101 bears the name Humptulips. Because of their location, the Hoquiam and Whiskah groups of Indians were classified by ethnologist John R. Swanton as Humptulips villagers. Some scholars regard the Humptulipses as having been closely related to the Lower Chehalises. They spoke a dialect of the Lower Chehalis language, but politically they were a separate people. Like the Chehalis peoples, they had no treaty with the United States, though, like other nontreaty peoples, they were given some government assistance. Several received vaccinations and other medical aids from the Quinault Agency on their north. Their nineteenth-century chief Chinoose rejected government goods, fearing that if the Humptulipses accepted them, the items might be construed as payment for their lands. The Humptulipses kept a semblance of tribal identity by having their own headmen and by refusing to remove to a reservation as late as 1873. Through disease and assimilation with other peoples, they were reduced to sixteen tribespeople in 1885 and twenty-one in 1904. *See* **Confederated Tribes of the Chehalis Reservation**.

Cookhouse Billy, his wife (with beaded bag), and Mary Hall Hunter (seated with baby). They were of the Jamestown S'Klallam Tribe, which received its name from their settlement, Jamestown, near Sequim, Washington, on the southern side of the Strait of Juan de Fuca.

Courtesy of Virginia Keeting.

JAMESTOWN S'KLALLAM INDIAN TRIBE

The Strong People

The Jamestown S'Klallams received their name from the settlement of Jamestown, which was seven miles north of Sequim, Washington, on the upper Strait of Juan de Fuca. The S'Klallams called the place *nuxia'antc,* or "white firs." Formerly, most Jamestown S'Klallams lived at nearby Dungeness, from which whites pressured them to remove. Some lived at Washington Harbor and Port Discovery. Like other Clallams, they did not wish to go to the Skokomish Reservation, where they were scheduled to remove under the provisions of the Point-No-Point Treaty of 1855. In June 1874, under their headman Lord Jim Balch, they bought 210 acres of logged-off land for five hundred dollars. This they surveyed and divided among themselves according to the amount contributed by each purchaser. The new site of Jamestown was named in honor of Balch, who had engineered the transaction.

According to the late-nineteenth- and early twentieth-century missionary Rev. Myron Eells of the Congregationalist Church, which maintained a mission station among the Jamestown S'Klallams, they were the "most civilized and prosperous band" of the Clallam peoples. In 1892, a Clallam named Jacob Hall established a prosperous business selling crabs in the Seattle market. Other Clallams fished, farmed, and worked for local whites in various occupations, including canoeing. About 1890 the Indian Shaker religion was introduced into Jamestown, from where it spread to nearby places such as Neah Bay in the lands of the Makahs.

Location: About 75 percent of the Jamestown S'Klallam Indian Tribe lives in or within a 150-mile radius of Port Angeles, which lies about twenty miles east of the old Jamestown location on U.S. Highway 101 and is the largest city in the area. The remainder are dispersed throughout the Pacific Northwest and as far as the east coast of the United States.

Numbers: In 1985 there were about 188 tribal members. A century earlier there had been about 100. In 1989 there were 389 and, in 2008, 530.

Government and Claims: In 1981 the Jamestown S'Klallams joined the Port Gamble S'Klallams and Lower Elwha Klallams and Skokomish as members of the Point-No-Point treaty council, which makes fishery management decisions. On February 10, 1981, the Jamestown S'Klallam Indian Tribe was acknowledged as an entity having a government-to-government relationship with the United States. That acknowledgment accorded it fishing treaty rights and other privileges. With the success in self-governance by the Hoopa Tribe of California, the Mille Lacs of Minnesota, and the Cherokees and Absentee-Shawnees of Oklahoma, the Jamestown S'Klallam Indian Tribe, along with the Quinaults and Lummis of Washington State, declared their independence from BIA paternalism, a system they claim gave them only eleven cents of every dollar appropriated for them. The balance, they say, was spent on administration. For claims *see* **Clallam.**

Contemporary Life and Culture: Though the Jamestown S'Klallams achieved federal recognition in 1981, they do not have a reservation. Their administrative offices and businesses are located on trust lands. They operate the 7 Cedars Casino overlooking Sequim Bay on the Strait of Juan de Fuca. In 2007, the tribe invested in a California medical-supply company, now called the Jamestown Health and Medical Supply Company, a certified buy-Indian business that services medical, dental, and housekeeping needs at effective prices with an inventory of over 100,000 products. In 2008, the tribe opened the lavish Longhouse Market and Deli, which has twelve gasoline pumps, a wine shop, a walk-in cigar humidifier, an in-store café, and fireplace—built at a cost of $12 million. The Jamestown S'Klallams are also constructing a luxury $100-million, 175-room destiny hotel and 500-room conference center that is scheduled to open in 2010. They have taken over, renamed, and revamped the $3-million, eighteen-hole Cedars at Dungeness golf course, with an additional half-million-dollar investment in electric carts and course improvements. JKT Development, Inc., oversees economic enterprises for the tribe and has business divisions in residential, commercial, and industrial construction, excavation, and information technology support. Other tribal businesses include Jamestown Fireworks, a major seller of local pyrotechnics; Northwest Native Expressions, which offers traditional and contemporary art forms; and an oyster processing and sales plant; a business park building; and a telecommunications firm.

The tribe has financed construction of a $1.5-million Clallam County fire station near their casino. For cultural and family gatherings, it has built the water-

Elaine Grinnell (b. 1936). An elder of the Jamestown S'Klallam Tribe and the great granddaughter of the Prince of Wales and the great-great-granddaughter of headman Chetzemoka, Grinnell is a teacher, historian, storyteller, and traditional cook. She is past president of the Native American Basket Weavers Association and is currently an advisory board member for the Northwest Indian Storytellers Association.

Courtesy of Paul D. G. Eubanks.

front Jamestown S'Klallam Community Center. The Jamestown S'Klallams do not have a Head Start program, but operate Building Blocks, which provides support to families with children from birth to age four. Elementary and secondary students attend the public schools in the nearby Port Angeles and Sequim school districts. At the rate of $19,138 per year, the tribe funds full assistance for the cost of higher education; thirty-five tribal members were enrolled in college in 2008. It also supports adult education enhancement at a rate of $5,000 lifetime or $1,000 per year maximum per individual. Health care for tribal members is provided through the Jamestown Family Health Clinic and the Jamestown Family Dental Clinic.

The Jamestown S'Klallams are involved in several environmental restoration projects on local waterways and, in August 2003, while building a dry dock on the Port Angeles waterfront, Washington State Department of Transportation workers unearthed Tse-whit-zen village. The site has yielded human remains, artifacts, and archeological evidence of human activity there dating back at least 2,700 years.

Said W. Ron Allen, chairman of the Jamestown S'Klallam tribal council, "The ability of the tribes to become more self-reliant based on business opportunity has emerged in the last 10 years. . . . Now we are addressing generations of need in our communities, providing housing opportunities, jobs, health care, and education for our people."

Special Events and Celebrations: The Jamestown S'Klallams Annual Potluck Tribal Picnic is held in August.

Suggested Readings:

> Virginia Keeting, ed., *Dungeness: The Lure of a River* (Sequim, Wash.: Sequim Bicentennial Committee, 1976); Joseph H. Stauss, *The Jamestown S'Klallam Story: Rebuilding a Northwest Coast Indian Tribe* (Sequim, Wash.: Jamestown S'Klallam Tribe, 2002).

KALISPEL

(Interior Division, Salishan)

The Kalispels, or Pend d'Oreilles, were called "boat" or "canoe people" and "paddlers" by other Indians. The designation "Pend d'Oreille" was given them by French-Canadian fur men. It means literally either "to hang from, at, or around the ear" or "ear pendants." The Kalispels were divided into upper and lower groups, with little dialectic variation in their common language. The Lower Kalispels were known for their low-riding canoes, which had distinctive snubbed prows to meet the buffets of gusty winds on Lake Pend Oreille in northern Idaho. They were also noted for their horsemanship and for their proficiency in making a bread out of the camas root, which caused them also to be called "camas people." The Upper Kalispels were sometimes referred to by a name meaning "people of the confluence," alluding to a place at the outlet of Lake Pend Oreille where a large band formerly wintered.

It was said that at one time the Upper Kalispels lived east of the Rocky

Louis Male Wolf. Although there is no record of it, this photograph was probably taken by Frank A. Rinehart of the Bureau of American Ethnology in Omaha, Nebraska, in 1898. The Kalispels are an Interior Salish people. In precontact times, the Upper Kalispels, also known as the Upper Pend d'Oreilles, lived east of the Rocky Mountains but they were driven west into modern-day Washington, Idaho, and Montana.

Courtesy of the Smithsonian Institution.

Mountains but were driven west by Blackfeet to become the neighbors of the Lower Kalispels, or Kalispels proper, who lived in the Pend Oreille River valley in northeastern Washington State and northern Idaho. The Lower Kalispels also lived in northern Idaho on Lake Pend Oreille, from which the Pend Oreille River flows, and on Priest Lake and in Montana and Idaho along the lower Clark Fork River, which flows into Lake Pend Oreille. The Upper Kalispels lived east of the Lower Kalispels in Montana; on Thompson Lake and the Flathead Lakes; on the Flathead River, west past Thompson Falls to Lake Pend Oreille; on Horse Plains; and around present-day Missoula.

Some have considered the Chewelahs of northeastern Washington (sometimes called the Slate'use or Tsent) a Kalispel group. They were culturally related to the Kalispels but spoke a slightly different dialect. The Chewelah Mountains east of the upper Colville Valley in Washington have also been called the Calispell Mountains. A city in western Montana also bears the name Kalispell. There is a Calispell Lake in Washington State.

The Kalispel population (both Uppers and Lowers) in 1780 has been estimated at 1,600. In 1805–1806 they were placed at 853 and in 1850 at 1,000. In recorded times the Kalispels hunted as far east as the Great Plains, as far north as Canada, and as far south as the Salmon River country of Idaho. The organization and development of the Kalispels resembled that of their Kutenai neighbors. Both tribes were divided into upper and lower branches, and both came under the influence of white fur traders after David Thompson of the North West Company selected the site of his Kullyspell House on the eastern shores of Lake Pend Oreille in September 1809. Like the Kutenais, the Tribes were visited by the Roman Catholic missionary, Rev. Pierre De Smet, S.J., who established St. Ignatius Mission near what is now Cusick, Washington, in 1846. In the spring of 1845 the Reverend Adrian Hoecken, S.J., had begun St. Michael's Mission on the Pend Oreille River at Albeni Falls. From there it was removed downstream a short distance and renamed St. Ignatius. The mission was moved to the Flathead, or Jocko, Reservation in Montana in 1854. The Upper Kalispels followed the mission, unlike the Lower Kalispels, who refused to vacate their homeland. Also unlike the Lower Kalispels, the Upper Kalispels, under their chief Alexander, were among those who met Washington territorial governor and superintendent of Indian affairs Isaac Stevens in council at Hell Gate, Montana, in July 1855. After that negotiation concluded, they were assigned with the Kutenais and the Flatheads to the Flathead Reservation. From that point forward, developments among the Upper Kalispels followed closely those of the other peoples on that reservation. *See* **Confederated Salish & Kootenai Tribes of the Flathead Reservation.** *See also* **Pend d'Oreille.** For the history of the Lower Kalispels thereafter, *see* **Kalispel Tribe of Indians.**

Suggested Readings:

Robert Carriker, *The Kalispel People* (Phoenix, Ariz.: Indian Tribal Series, 1973).

KALISPEL TRIBE OF INDIANS

The Camas People

The Kalispel Tribe of Indians, or the Kalispel Indian Community, Kalispel Reservation, is descended from the Lower Kalispels, or Lower Pend d'Oreilles, who lived in what is now northeastern Washington State and northern Idaho.

Location: The members of the Kalispel Tribe of Indians live on and near their reservation, which contained 4,620 acres when established by executive order on March 23, 1914, on the western shores of the Pend Oreille River about forty miles north of Spokane.

Numbers: In 1985 tribal membership stood at 259 and in 1989 at 232. In January 2000 the Kalispels counted about 240 enrolled members, a number that had grown to 393 in 2008 and to over 400 by 2010.

History: The Yakama Indian War, which broke out in 1855, prevented Lower Kalispels, Spokanes, Coeur d'Alenes, and Colvilles from meeting with Dr. R. H. Lansdale, whom Washington territorial governor and superintendent of Indian affairs Isaac Stevens had instructed to effect a treaty. The Upper Kalispels, or Upper Pend d'Oreilles, however, were among those who negotiated with Stevens at Hell Gate near Missoula, Montana, where on July 16, 1855, they signed a treaty that consigned them, the Kutenais, and the Flatheads to the Flathead, or Jocko, Reservation in Montana. Advised that the St. Ignatius Mission had been moved to the Flathead Reservation, Stevens assumed that the Lower Kalispels would also sign a treaty to relocate there. In August and September 1855, some of both Kalispel branches moved to the area around the transplanted mission. Victor, or Happy Man, was the successor of the Roman Catholic chief Loyola, or Standing Grizzly, of the Lower Kalispels. Both Victor and his son, Marcella (Masselow), disliked living on the Flathead Reservation with Indians of other tribes, and for the most part the Lower Kalispels remained in their homeland. Ironically, at that time the Lower Kalispels were an amalgam of Kalispel, Spokane, and Flathead peoples.

During the Spokane–Coeur d'Alene phase of the Indian War of 1858, most Kalispels abstained from hostilities. In the 1880s, despite the pressure of railroad surveyors and white settlers in the Pend Oreille River valley, about four hundred Kalispels still remained in that country. Their days of freedom were in jeopardy because of such developments as the Northern Pacific Railroad's acquisition of their lands under that railroad's 1864 congressional charter. By 1881, about seventy-five miles of track had been laid around Lake Pend Oreille, and the railroad was selling its government-granted lands to settlers. In 1884, under such pressures, Victor requested compensation for the lands lost. He also appealed for a reservation located in the homeland of his people. Public land surveys followed in 1886, and in that same year cavalry troops arrived to control Indian-white conflicts over lands. Chief Marcella refused to remove to the Flathead Reservation, though one band of sixty-three Kalispels under Chief Michel relocated to that reservation after Michel agreed with the government, in 1887, to sell his lands. Michel's band feared that if they did not move, they would be forced onto the Coeur d'Alene Reservation. A white traveler among the Lower Kalispels—or Calispels, as he termed them—noted that though they were a small tribe they had powerful relatives and backers among other tribes, who would not let them be "eaten up by their enemies." In 1890 large numbers of non-Indians entered the Pend Oreille country. By then, the Indians were concentrated on the eastern shores of the Pend Oreille River opposite Usk, Washington.

As the twentieth century neared, nontreaty (nonreservation) Lower Kalispels were displaced by settlers. In 1895 the Indian commissioner therefore ordered their lands surveyed and legal descriptions filed with the General Land Office. Most Kalispels did not live on the lands surveyed for them; rather, they joined in communal enclaves that moved about on these lands. A problem arose when it was realized that the Northern Pacific Railroad had been granted odd sections on which some Kalispels lived. In 1906 Congress gave the Northern Pacific lands in lieu of 2,711 acres occupied by Kalispels, thus minimizing the threat of their removal to a reservation. Ongoing land pressures exerted by non-Indians in the early twentieth century precipitated renewed surveys and allotting. Since the time of the 1895 surveys, the deaths of over a score of Kalispels had been offset by births; hence, only forty acres of agricultural or eighty acres of grazing lands could be allotted each member. In December 1911, the Spokane agent was ordered to allot them following the resurvey the next year. Individual trust patents were not issued, since many allotted lands were withdrawn for power-site development on the Pend Oreille River. Nevertheless, as noted, a reservation was established in 1914 on the allotted land, even before land patents were issued. The first patents were received in May 1924 and the remainder nine years later.

Government and Claims: With but two of their thirty-eight members voting against it, the Kalispels accepted the Indian Reorganization Act of 1934 (48 Stat. 984). In 1939 they chartered themselves under a new constitution, which was approved in 1938, as the Kalispel Indian Community. Known more commonly today as the Kalispel Tribe of Indians, the community's governing body is the Kalispel Indian Council. Their constitution was revised on July 27, 1967. In 1974 the Kalispel federal tribal jurisdiction was transferred from the Northern Idaho Indian Agency at Lapwai to the Spokane Indian Agency at Wellpinit.

In 1927, the Kalispel Indian Community filed a claim (Docket 94) with the Indian Claims Commission and on March 21, 1963, was awarded $3 million for 2,247,000 acres, which had been taken mostly in northeastern Washington and the Idaho panhandle, as well as 126,000 aquatic acres. In 1970 the tribe, along with twenty-four other western tribes, filed claims (Dockets 532–71 and 524–71) with the Court of Claims for mismanagement of Indian Claims Commission judgments and other funds such as Individual Indian Money accounts held in trust by the United States. The tribe was awarded $114,127.80 in 1981. In 1991 the U.S. Supreme Court ruled for the Kalispels that they had lost a ten-mile strip along the Pend Oreille River between Usk and Cusick when the Box Canyon Dam was built (1955).

Contemporary Life and Culture: As late as 1950 many tribal members were jobless and lived in houses built by the Civilian Conservation Corps. Public assistance and land leases to local cattlemen were the sole sources of individual and tribal support. As late as 1965 only one tribal member had graduated from high school, and an interpreter was required at tribal meetings. The key to the tribe's development is the Kalispel Indian Development Enterprise, which seeks to acquire for the Kalispel Tribe of Indians a manageable land base (in addition to its own 4,557.41 acres of trust land) on which to preserve for future generations the soils, water, plants, animals, and Kalispel lifestyle. A gift of 436 acres from the Northwest Power Planning Council has gone toward establishing a wildlife refuge. The Kalispels belong to the Upper Columbia United Tribes, which is a fish and wildlife management program, and they have developed a fish hatchery and aqua farm for raising perch, which they package for market.

The Kalispels consider their Northern Quest Casino, which opened in December 2000 and now employs some fifteen hundred people, the backbone of their economic resurgence as well as the economic underpinning of "Camas Institute," the Kalispels' vision for opportunity through education. The Camas Institute provides tribal members and the members of other tribes a vehicle to improve every individual in a positive and culturally

Renee Pierre, a candidate for Queen of the Kalispel Tribe of Indians in northeastern Washington, 1980.

Authors' collections.

sensitive learning environment. Founded in February 2001 and addressing issues of behavioral health, education and career counseling, goal setting, reading, and community involvement, the institute offers enrichment and a spirit of lifelong learning aimed at the whole person.

In addition to their casino, with its adjoining ten-story, 350-room hotel tower completed in December 2009, Kalispel tribal enterprises include Kalispel Case Line, a manufacturing operation established in 1974 that produces condensed-foam-lined aluminum cases for electronic instruments, cameras, rifles, pistols, and custom use. Gun cases crafted by the tribe are considered among the premier of those made in America. Kalispel Agricultural Enterprise maintains a herd of about a hundred buffalo, the meat of which is used by the elders and is also prepared and sold. Along with buffalo ranching, the tribe keeps six hundred acres of hay in production and is looking to start up a custom meat-cutting and -wrapping operation.

Indigenous Learning Company, the first Native-owned Internet publishing company and one of the world's only web-based educational publishing companies, provides Indian learners and instructors with outstanding, culturally appropriate educational and vocational programs and is helping integrate Kalispel culture and history into the Cusick public school curriculum. Kalispel Natural Resources Department, established in 1993, has over twenty full-time employees in the areas of fisheries, wildlife, culture, and water quality.

Available to the tribe are child welfare and mental health and community outreach services, a nutrition program for the elderly, and a substance abuse program. A community health nurse is contracted to provide WIC (Women, Infants and Children) services once a month. The $18-million, 7,700-square-foot Camas Center for Community Wellness includes an early learning center, walk-in child care, medical and dental clinics, a café serving healthy foods, water slides and lap pools, a three-hundred-seat gymnasium, and meeting rooms and offices. In 2007, the Kalispel Charitable Fund contributed approximately $700,000 to over two hundred nonprofit organizations.

Special Events and Celebrations: In early August, the Kalispel Powwow Days, featuring Indian games and war dances, is held near Usk. The Kalispel Salish Fair and Buffalo Barbecue is also held at that time.

Suggested Readings:

Robert Carriker, *The Kalispel People* (Phoenix, Ariz.: Indian Tribal Series, 1973) and "The Kalispel Indian Tribe and the Indian Claims Commission Experience," *Western Historical Quarterly* 9, no. 1 (January 1978); O. J. Cotes, ed., *The Kalispels: People of the Pend Oreille* (Spokane, Wash.: Kalispel Tribe, 1980); John Fahey, *The Kalispel Indians* (Norman: University of Oklahoma Press, 1986); Sonny Tuttle, *Kalispel Indian Development* (Usk, Wash.: Kalispel Indian Community, n.d.).

KIKIALLUS

(Coastal Division, Salishan)

The Kikiallus Tribe of Indians descended from the Kikiallus subdivision of the Skagits. The Skagit River, a Puget Sound affluent in northwestern Washington, was formerly called the Kikiallus River. The Kikialluses lived primarily in two villages in the Fir-Conway area south of today's Mount Vernon and on nearby Camano Island. They also migrated beyond present-day Arlington on Jim Creek on the Stillaguamish River, another Puget Sound affluent. Thus, they maintained close ties with the Stillaguamish Indians on the Stillaguamish.

Location: Tribal members today live at various places in the Pacific Northwest, particularly in northwestern Washington State.

Numbers: In the middle of the nineteenth century, the Kikialluses numbered about 140. In 1980 they were placed at roughly 150.

History: The Kikialluses did not have slaves. In that respect they differed from other coastal peoples who held slaves as a part of their class system. At the time of the white settlement of the Conway area, the tribe lived in four longhouses. The Kikiallus chief Sd-zo Mahtl signed the Point Elliott Treaty with the United States in 1855. Their last headman was Bill Jack. The Kikialluses were helped in their assimilation with non-Indians through the marriage of a daughter of the Jack family to an Irishman, John O'Brien, who came to the tribe's homeland in the late 1850s. From that marriage came many children.

Government and Claims: The Kikialluses have a tribal organization, but by 2010 they still had not received federal acknowledgment.

In 1951 they filed a claim (Docket 263) with the Indian Claims Commission for additional payment for the 8,060 acres that they had ceded to the United States under the Point Elliott Treaty in 1855 and for which they had been paid $5,973.31. Their aboriginal lands had consisted of two tracts: 4,560 acres on the northern tip of Camano Island and a 3,500-acre, heart-shaped tract on the mainland abutting Skagit Bay. The commission found the tribe entitled to a payment of $12,000 for their lands and, after deducting the amount already paid, awarded them on June 7, 1972, an entitled recovery sum of $6,026.69.

Suggested Readings:

Martin J. Sampson, *Indians of Skagit County* (Mount Vernon, Wash.: Skagit County Historical Society, 1972); "Susie Sampson Peter—Oldest of the Kikiallus," (Spokane) *Spokesman-Review*, November 2, 1959.

KITTITAS

(See **Yakama***)*

KLAMATH TRIBES

(Lutuamian)

The anthropologist A. L. Kroeber suggests that the name "Klamath" possibly stems from the Calapooya name, "Athlameth," for this people. Anthropologist Albert Samuel Gatschet reported that the tribe's own name for themselves, Maklaks, means "people," "community," and similar descriptors. It has also been reported by anthropologist Leslie Spier that the name Klamath is reserved for the Klamath-Marsh–Williamson River subdivision—the Auksni. Other Klamaths use the name only by courtesy. From the Canadian trappers has come down a hybrid French-English name, La Lakes.

Oregon's Klamath Lake and Klamath County bear the Klamath name today. Within Klamath County, on Interstate 97, is the city of Klamath Falls. A river in Oregon and California and a town in the latter state also bear the name. Before their treaty with the United States in 1864, the Klamaths—with two other tribes who signed the treaty, the Modocs and the Paiute Yahuskins—claimed over 20 million acres in present-day Oregon and California. The Klamaths gained much attention when the United States terminated its trust relationship with them by an act dated August 13, 1954 (25 Stat. 718 USC X 564).

Location: In 1957, 404 of the 2,038 Klamaths lived outside Oregon. Three hundred of those who remained in Oregon lived mostly in the south-central part of the state but off the reservation. In the post-termination era, the Klamaths have tended to locate in the general area where the Klamaths proper formerly lived. The former village sites were on Klamath Lake and Klamath Marsh and on the Williamson and Sprague rivers. In 2006 the landholdings of the Klamath Tribes numbered 290 acres.

Numbers: Estimates of the Klamath 1780 population have varied from 400 to 1,000. In 1848, their numbers stood at roughly 1,000. In 1923 there were 1,201 Klamaths, Modocs, and other Indians under the Klamath superintendency. In 1930, 2,034 were listed as Klamaths and Modocs, and in 1937 there were 1,912 enumerated Klamaths, which likely included members of other tribes. On the final tribal roll at the time of termination in 1958 there were 2,133 members. In 1977, the same number was listed for the Klamaths, but in 1990 there were 3,147 members of the Klamath Tribes. In 2008 enrolled tribal membership stood at 3,669.

Yu-mai-poo-tas, also called Tecumseh or Medicine Man. When this photograph was taken in 1875, the Klamaths of south-central Oregon were becoming less isolated from settlement. In 1864 they had signed a treaty with the United States, which provided them with a reservation.

Courtesy of the Klamath County Museum, Klamath Falls, Ore.

History: Because of their interior location in today's south-central Oregon and north-central California, the Klamaths were able to avoid contact with non-Indians longer than other groups. The Hudson's Bay Company trader Peter Skene Ogden, who met them in 1826, called them a "happy race." They would not be so for long, he believed, after they began associating with whites. Among the goods that the Klamaths obtained from non-Indians were guns and horses. At The Dalles they acquired from other Indians horses, blankets, buffalo skins, and dried salmon in exchange for slaves captured from California tribes. They also traded beads and the seeds of the *wocus,* which they gathered in marshy places in their homelands. They processed the seeds into a nutritious food used in soups or mixed into flour to make cakes. The Klamaths also met annually with other tribes to trade at such places as Yainax, east of Klamath Lake. They harpooned fish and shot waterfowl with bows and arrows. The clothing of both sexes consisted of fiber skirts and basket caps. In cold weather, they added tule leggings and sandals, mantles of skin and fiber, and fur mittens. Not until early in the nineteenth century did they adopt buckskin clothing and footwear, which they obtained through trade. They wore dentalia shells in nasal-septum perforations and flattened the heads of their infants. They also adopted the practice of tattooing their bodies. Their winter habitations were semisubterranean earthen lodges, which were circular pits up to four feet deep.

On October 14, 1864, the Klamaths' treaty (16 Stat. 718) was signed by twenty-one of their headmen, along with four Modoc and two Yahuskin leaders. These peoples traded to the United States their high, semiarid lands east of the Cascade Mountains for the Klamath Reservation. This reservation of about 1,107,847 acres was proclaimed on February 17, 1870 (16 Stat. 383). The Klamath Agency had been established on May 12, 1866, at the upper end of Agency Lake, a few miles south of Fort Klamath and north of Klamath Lake. The Klamaths settled at the agency with a few disgruntled Modocs. Most of the latter tribe refused to join the Klamaths on the reservation, preferring to remain in their own home-lands. Because of intertribal friction, the Modocs and some Upland Klamaths and Yahuskins were placed at Yainax, where a subagency was created in 1870 some thirty-five miles east of the main Klamath Agency.

The boundaries of the Klamath Reservation had been established by surveys in 1871 and 1888 and were reported on December 18, 1896. An act (30 Stat. 571) was passed on July 1, 1898, authorizing negotiations for a settlement with the Klamaths for the lands that had been excluded from the reservation by errone-ous surveys. It was agreed on June 17, 1901, that the Klamaths were to be paid $537,007.20 for 621,824.28 acres of "Klamath Reservation-Excluded Lands." Because many Klamaths sought allotments on sections of the reservation that originally had been intended for a military road company, the allotment process that began on the reservation in 1895 was interrupted two years later by conflicts that remained unresolved until 1906. Allotment resumed three years later. By an act of May 27, 1902 (32 Stat. 260), Klamath children born after the completion of allotment in 1895 were authorized to receive further allotments, but elders were unhappy that those born after April 15, 1910, could not do so, even though as tribal members they retained an equity in tribal properties.

In 1902 the Modocs, who had been exiled to the Quapaw Agency in Oklahoma after their defeat in their 1872–73 war with the United States, sent representatives to the Klamaths, seeking permission for certain of the Modoc Tribe to receive al-lotments on the Klamath Reservation if they returned to the area. The Klamath Council approved the request, and in 1903 twenty-one Modocs settled at the up-per end of the northeast portion of the reservation. Forty-seven others wanted to come at a later time. In 1909 Congress authorized allotments to Quapaw Modocs on the Klamath Reservation, but by then the Klamaths opposed letting them have the land. Sixteen Modocs, however, were certified for allotments when allotting re-sumed in 1909. In all, 177,719.62 acres were allotted to 1,174 Indians, and 6,094.77 acres were reserved for agency, school, and church purposes.

Unlike most Oregon Indians, the Klamaths were not ravaged by great epidem-ics nor did they come into violent confrontations with non-Indians. Yet in the roughly one-hundred-year history of the Klamath Reservation Indians, perhaps nothing changed their lives more than the termination of their trust relationship with the United States in 1954. *See also* **Modoc.**

Government and Claims: The roots of the modern Klamath General Council, as the tribe was called, lay in the creation in 1909 of a council to deal more effec-tively with agency staff. In 1929 the tribe established a business committee. On June 15, 1935, a majority of Klamaths voted to reject the provisions of the Indian Reorganization Act (48 Stat. 984). The termination of the 861,125-acre Klamath Reservation came about as members were permitted to vote for themselves and for their children to be either "withdrawing" members (who would receive about $50,000 each for their share of the tribal assets) or "remaining" members (who would hold tribal interests in common under state law). There were two factions that supported termination. One represented advocates of individual Indian rights, dissolution of the tribe, and distribution of its assets. The other, the tribal governing body, favored the recognition of tribal identity and the upholding of tribal rights. Of the 2,133 members on the final roll in 1958, 1,660 elected to withdraw and 473 voted to remain. The individual holders of lands no longer in trust became subject to taxation. In 1980 the "remaining" Klamaths and their heirs, a total of about 600, received about $173,000 for each of the remaining 473 shares in the thousands of acres of forest lands taken by the federal government through condemnation in 1974 and added to the Winema National Forest.

Before the treaty with the Klamaths, Modocs, and Yahuskins, Congress, by an act on July 2, 1864 (13 Stat. 355), granted the State of Oregon three alternating sections of public lands on each side of a military road that was to be constructed from Eugene to the eastern boundary of the state. Having been assigned by the Oregon legislature to build the road, the Oregon Central Military Road Company began the project. In 1867, 1871, and 1873 the State of Oregon issued patents to the company for a total of 402,240.67 acres, which by conveyances became vested in the California & Oregon Land Company. Of that acreage, with the exception of that required for a right-of-way for the road, 111,385 acres lay within the Klamath Reservation. Before the establishment of the Indian Claims Commission in 1947, Indian tribes were permitted to sue the United States for recovery of losses only on the consent of the Congress. An act of May 26, 1920 (41 Stat. 623), permitted Klamaths, Modocs, and Yahuskins to bring suit. The government would not stop tribal attempts to reclaim that portion of the reservation given to the Military Road Company.

The tribe's long journey to recovery began after the United States unsuccessfully instituted three suits against the company to annul patents to the Indian lands that the company held. In February 1904, the U.S. Supreme Court ruled that the Indians had indeed lost 111,400.48 acres. Congress therefore passed an act (33 Stat. 1033) directing the secretary of the interior to ascertain the value of the acreage and to ask the California & Oregon Land Company how much it would be willing to accept in return for the lands or whether it would accept in exchange other unallotted lands within the reservation. Eventually, the land company conveyed to the United States the 111,400.48 acres, accepting in their place 86,418.06 acres of unallotted choice timber lands near Yamsey Mountain. That transaction was concluded on August 22, 1906, in accordance with provisions of the act of June 21, 1906 (34 Stat. 325, 367), without the knowledge of, or any compensation going to, the tribe. In 1913 the Internal Revenue Service valued the tribe's timber at $3,550,000. That land exchange had reduced the reservation by considerable acreage. On November 2, 1907, the secretary of the interior authorized paying the Indians $108,750 for the lost acreage, and on April 30, 1908, Congress appropriated the moneys (35 Stat. 70, 92). In councils, about 150 of a total of 287 adult Klamath males signed the release that relinquished lands for the moneys offered. After the May 1920 act enabling the Klamaths to sue for a more equitable payment for the 86,418.06 acres, the case was argued in 1934 before the Court of Claims. On April 8, 1935, that body decided against the Indian plaintiffs. An act of May 15, 1936, authorized and directed the Court of Claims to reinstate and rehear the case. On April 25, 1938, the Supreme Court confirmed a Court of Claims award of $2,980,000 for the lands, plus interest, for a total of $5,313,347.32. Ironically, the military road that set off all of the above-described developments was never used.

On January 31, 1964, one hundred years after their initial treaty with the government, the Klamaths—after presenting to the Indian Claims Commission their claim (Docket 100) for lands ceded in 1864—were awarded $2.5 million for which Congress specified methods of distribution in an act of October 1, 1965 (79 Stat. 879). Various other claims were put into separate dockets. The Klamaths filed a claim (Docket 100-A) for additional compensation for the 621,824.28 acres of the reservation excluded by erroneous surveys. An award was made by the Claims Commission on September 2, 1969, for $4,162,992.82 above the original consideration paid for the boundary-survey errors. For mismanagement of their funds and properties, the Klamaths filed a claim (Docket 100 B-1) on which the commission issued final judgment on January 21, 1977, by awarding the tribe $18 million after the case had been appealed to the Court of Claims (Docket 389-72). A claim for mismanagement of tribal forest and sawmill operations was filed (Docket 100 B-2), and on May 1, 1982, by a twelve-vote margin, the members accepted the government's offer of $16.5 million to settle the claim. The moneys, a far less amount than the tribe sought, were distributed to those 2,133 members of record on August 13, 1954, who were still living or to their descendants. Claims for mismanagement of Klamath grazing and agricultural lands and irrigation projects, as well as for rights-of-way conveyed through tribal lands at less than fair market value (Docket 100-C), were disposed of by a final award of $785,000. The Klamath Executive Committee passed a resolution on January 16, 1976, asking that the proceeds from the docket be disbursed to pay off tribal loans used as litigating funds.

After Congress had twice delayed the termination of federal supervision as a result of the Termination Act of August 13, 1954 (from the initial date of August 13, 1958, to August 12, 1961), two suits were filed before the Court of Claims in 1961 and 1962 for additional compensation for the tribal lands disposed of during termination—that is, Antelope Desert, Klamath Marsh, and ten units of Klamath forest land. The property selected for sale as a result of termination constituted 77.825 percent of the value of the total estate. Of that, 78 percent was forest land, which had the greatest value. These suits, Dockets 125-61 and 87-62, were consolidated, becoming Docket 387-72. The result was an award to the majority of Klamaths of $21,235,496.80 (Docket 125-61). The other 162 tribal members (represented by Docket 87-62) were awarded $2,220,793.20.

Contemporary Life and Culture: The problems attending termination were severe for the Klamaths. Congress, claiming no responsibility for the effects of the policy, had made no provision for a follow-up program for the tribe, except to assist the Klamaths in hunting and fishing activities through BIA contracts, since with termination there was no abrogation of those contracts. Receipt of the monetary awards made many recipients victims of non-Indians wishing to cash in on the Indians' payments. Individual tribal identity problems followed in the wake of termination. The withdrawal of federal services aggravated the situation, as many BIA programs came to an end.

In 1969, the remaining and withdrawing Klamaths and three non-Indians formed the Organization of Forgotten Americans, which sought social benefits for the Klamaths, including their tribal reinstatement. The organization also tried to protect Klamath tribes from squandering compensation from any future claims. Most important, it worked toward restoration of the tribe to make it eligible to receive federal funds and services of the BIA. In the early 1980s, a court ruling required the U.S. Forest Service to consult the tribe over land-management issues. The tribe also entered into an agreement with the Forest Service to establish traditional cultural camps at the head of the Williamson River in the Winema National Forest. In 1985, one tribal member began keeping a fire that he vowed never to extinguish until his people regained their lost lands.

Public law restored the tribal status of the 2,313 Klamaths on August 27, 1986.

In the summer of 1997, the Klamath Tribes opened Kla-Mo-Ya Casino. The 15,000-square-foot facility, set on forty acres along the Williamson River at Chiloquin, employs 150 and offers amenities of a deli, a buffet, and a nonsmoking gaming area. The casino is second only to Crater Lake as the most popular tourist attraction in Klamath County, attracting 300,000 visitors each year. In the future, the Klamaths are hoping to expand the casino, adding a hotel, an RV park, and a truck stop. Klamath Family Health & Tribal Services was established on January 1, 1992, in Klamath Falls. Providing comprehensive coverage to Klamath tribal members, it employs a staff of over sixty and operates with a $4-million annual budget. It manages medical and dental clinics in Chiloquin and a pharmacy. The tribe is one of the largest employers in Klamath County and contributes over $25 million each year in goods and services to the local economy. The Klamath Tribe recently purchased a site on which they propose building an $8-million to $12-million biomass energy plant that, at full capacity, could provide energy to four thousand homes and provide two hundred jobs. The Klamaths are concurrently working to raise nearly half a million dollars to purchase the largest artifact collection on their history and culture in the world.

In late 2008 the George W. Bush administration reached a nonbinding agreement with PacifiCorp to remove four dams from the Klamath River. The agreement included a $21-million congressional appropriation to the Klamath Tribes over the next four years to purchase 90,000 acres of private forestland, part of a plan by the Tribes to restore the reservation lost to termination.

Special Events and Celebrations: The Return of the *C'waam* Ceremony honors the annual migration of the Lost River Sucker up the Sprague River to Spawn. Held annually the fourth weekend in August in Chiloquin is the Restoration Celebration, which features a youth rodeo and powwow and commemorates the anniversary of Klamath federal recognition.

Suggested Readings:

S. A. Barrett, "The Material Culture of the Klamath and Modoc Indians," *University of California Publications in American Archaeology and Ethnology,* no. 5 (1907–1910), 239–92; Charles Crane Brown, "Identification of Selected Problems of Indians Residing in Klamath County, Oregon—An Examination of Data Generated Since Termination of the Klamath Reservation," Ph.D. dissertation, University of Oregon, 1973; Luther Sheeleigh Cressman, *The Sandal and the Cave: The Indians of Oregon, Studies in History,* no. 8 (Corvallis: Oregon State University Press, 1981); Douglas Deur, "A Most Sacred Place: The Significance of Crater Lake among the Indians of Southern Oregon," *Oregon Historical Quarterly* 103, no. 1 (2002); Michelle Durant, "The CCC on the Klamath Reservation: An Introduction," *Journal of the Shaw Historical Library* 20 (2006); Albert Samuel Gatschet, *The Klamath Indians of Southwestern Oregon,* vol. 2 of Smithsonian Institution, *Contributions to North American Ethnology* (Washington, D.C.: Government Printing Office, 1890), pts. 1 and 2; Patrick Haynal, "Termination and Tribal Survival: The Klamath Tribes of Oregon," *Oregon Historical Quarterly* 101, no. 3 (2000); Patrick Mann Haynal, "From Termination through Restoration and Beyond: Modern Klamath Cultural Identity," Ph.D. dissertation, University of Oregon, 1994; Carrol B. Howe, *Ancient Tribes of the Klamath Country* (Portland, Ore.: Binfords and Mort, 1968); Lee Juillerat, "Edison Chiloquin: Klamath Indian Won Honors as a World War II Warrior," *Journal of the Shaw Historical Library* 17 (2003); Stephen Most, *River of Renewal: Myth and History in the Klamath Basin* (Seattle: University of Washington Press, 2006); Leslie Spier, "Klamath Ethnography," *University of California Publications in American Archaeology and Ethnology,* vol. 30 (Berkeley, Calif., 1930); Theodore Stern, "The Klamath Indians and the Treaty of 1864," *Oregon Historical Quarterly* 57 (March 1956–December 1956) and *The Klamath Tribe: A People and Their Reservation* (Seattle: University of Washington Press, 1965); Ward Tonsfeldt, "Selling Klamath Reservation Timber, 1910–1935," *Journal of the Shaw Historical Library* 16 (2002); Edward C. Wolf, *Klamath Heartlands: A Guide to the Klamath Reservation Forest Plan* (Corvallis: Oregon State University Press, 2004); "The Klamath Tribes: A Photo Essay," *Journal of the Shaw Historical Library* 13 (1999).

KLAMATH AND MODOC TRIBES AND
YAHOOSKIN BAND OF SNAKE INDIANS

The Klamath and Modoc Tribes and Yahooskin Band of Snake Indians is composed of descendants of the Klamaths, Modocs, and Yahuskin Paiutes who treated with the United States on October 14, 1864. Under provisions of their treaty,
the three tribes were assigned to one reservation, the Klamath. For an account of
this tribe *see* **Klamath Tribes.**

KLICKITAT
(Shahaptian)

It is believed that the Klickitats (Klikitats), or the Wah-how-pums as they were
called by explorers Meriwether Lewis and William Clark, were given the name
by which they are known today by Chinookan peoples. The name "Klickitat" is
derived from one village name meaning "beyond the [Cascade] Mountains." The
Klickitats were said to have moved in precontact times either from the south
or the western slopes of the Rocky Mountains to their lands near the Cascade
Mountains of Washington State. Their removal was hastened by pressures from
the Cayuse Indians. After coming to their new homeland, they divided into eastern and western divisions, both of which retained their Shahaptian language.
Besides the Klickitat River, a town and a county in Washington bear the tribal
name.

The Western Klickitats (also called the Cowlitz Klickitats) mixed with the
Cowlitzes west of the Cascade Mountains and became the Taitnapams. They
settled on the headwaters of such streams as the Cowlitz and Lewis rivers, Columbia River tributaries in southwestern Washington. The Eastern Klickitats primarily occupied the upper drainage systems of two other Columbia tributaries,
the Klickitat and White Salmon rivers of south-central Washington. They were
fine horsemen and noted for their weaponry, especially their superb bows and
arrows, which helped earn them the reputation of good hunters. They were also
skilled traders, acting as intermediaries between interior and coastal peoples.
Their women were experts at basketry.

After the epidemics of the 1820s and 1830s had reduced the populations of the
Willamette Valley tribes, the Klickitats' aggressiveness strengthened their posi-
tion in that valley, where they migrated to hunt and trade. They were also found
as far south as the Umpqua River of southern Oregon and as far west as Puget
Sound and the Coast Range of Oregon. Among Indians of the lower Willamette
Valley they developed a reputation as robbers and plunderers. Under their chief

The Klickitat Tribe, to which this early-twentieth-century man belonged, lived mostly in south-central Washington, but a branch of the tribe lived on the west in the foothills of the Cascade Mountains and hunted extensively in the Willamette Valley of Oregon. Many Klickitat descendants live on the Yakama Reservation and have been prominent among its leaders.

Photograph by Edward S. Curtis, from Curtis's *The North American Indian* (1907–1930), vol. 7.

Socklate Tyee, and armed with Hudson's Bay Company guns, they fought the Rogue Indians of Oregon in the 1840s. During the Rogue wars of the 1850s under their chief Quatley (Quarterly), they scouted for the U.S. military. When the United States subsequently consummated treaties with Oregon Indians, the Klickitats unsuccessfully sought redress in American courts for their losses of lands in the Willamette Valley. The Eastern Klickitats were one of fourteen tribes under the Yakama standard to sign a treaty on June 9, 1855, with Washington territorial governor and superintendent of Indian affairs Isaac Stevens. Angered at the treaty, some of them confronted Americans in the ensuing Yakama and Puget Sound wars of 1855 and 1856. Under the pressure of settlers in the Willamette Valley, where the Western Klickitats had returned after the war, they were sent up the Columbia to the Yakama or Simcoe Agency in 1867. Evidence of their close alliance with the Yakamas was the election of one of their headmen, Joe Stwire, or White Swan, to the Yakama chieftaincy during the reservation era. The government had handpicked his predecessor, the Klickitat-Yakama Spencer, for the position.

Lewis and Clark estimated the Klickitat population at 700 in 1805 and 1806. The 1910 census listed them at 405, a reduction less dramatic than that suffered by other tribes who had greater exposure to the diseases of non-Indians. In 1962 there were between 10 and 20 Klickitats in Washington. In 1970 there were only 21 remaining, of whom 5 were on the Yakama Reservation. Their reduction appears to have been primarily due to intermarriage with other peoples, such as the Yakamas with whom they were confederated. *See* **Yakama** *and* **Taitnapam.**

Suggested Readings:

Katrine Barber and Andrew H. Fisher, "From Coyote to the Corps of Engineers: Recalling the History of The Dalles-Celilo Reach," *Oregon Historical Quarterly* 108, no. 4 (2007); Delia M. Coon, "Klickitat County: Indians of and Settlement by Whites," *Washington Historical Quarterly* 14, no. 4 (October 1923); Melville Jacobs, *Northwest Sahaptin Texts* (New York: Columbia University Press, 1934–37), 2 vols.; H. O. Lang, ed., *History of the Willamette Valley* (Portland, Ore.: G. H. Himes, 1885); Lucullus V. McWhorter, *The Crime against the Yakimas* (Yakima, Wash.: Republic Printers, 1913); J. G. Maddock, "The Klickitat Indians," *Travel,* August 1895, 306–11 (University of Washington Pacific Northwest Collections); Selma Neils, *The Klickitat Indians* (Portland, Ore.: Binford & Mort Publishing, 1985); Click Relander, *Strangers on the Land* (Yakima, Wash.: Franklin Press, 1962). For a bibliography of the Yakamas (with whom the Klickitats were assimilated), see Robert E. Pace, *Yakima Indian Nation Bibliography* (Toppenish, Wash.: Yakima Indian Media Services, 1978); Helen Hersh Schuster, *The Yakimas: A Critical Bibliography* (Bloomington: Indiana University Press, 1982).

KOOTENAI TRIBE OF IDAHO

The Kootenai Tribe of Idaho (also known as Kootenay or Ktunaxa Nation) is made up of Lower Kutenais who did not join others of the tribe living in Canada nor unite with Upper Kutenais who had located on the Flathead Reservation in Montana. In 1984 tribal membership stood at 60 and in 1989 they numbered 108. In August 2007 the enrolled membership was given as 164 people, 15 to 20 of whom held dual U.S.-Canadian citizenship.

On September 21, 1974, the then-sixty-seven surviving members of the Kootenai Tribe of Idaho declared and fought a victorious three-day war against the U.S. government that won for them 12.5 acres, the basis for their current reservation of 18.922 acres. Tribal recognition by the BIA followed in 1979.

In 1986 the tribe opened what is now the Kootenai River Inn, Casino & Spa. The original facility included a forty-seven-room hotel with a restaurant, a gift shop, and a recreation center. The casino part opened in 1996 and underwent renovation in 2005, with the addition of a luxury spa and an expanded hotel. Kootenai Tribal School (K-12) is a three-classroom facility with three teachers and six staff members servicing approximately thirty-six students. Since 1993 the tribe has operated an on-site health clinic. In 1989 the tribe contracted with the Bonneville Power Administration to fund construction of a white sturgeon hatchery program on the Kootenai River. Then, in the summer of 2009, the tribe announced a major habitat restoration plan to protect fifty-five miles of the Kootenai River, while promoting the white sturgeon population, a species of great cultural significance but much reduced in numbers in recent decades. In February 1991 the Kootenai Tribe of Idaho joined other area tribes in special ceremonies honoring Indian troops in the Persian Gulf War (Operation Desert Storm). *See* **Kutenai.**

KUITSH

(Yakonan)

The Kuitsh, commonly referred to as Lower Umpquas, lived on the lower Umpqua River of Oregon. Sand dunes along the coast separated them from their neighbors on the south, the Coos. The Kuitsh seem never to have been enumerated separately before modern times. The estimate of their population in 1780 included members of Yakonan stock—Coos, Siuslaws, Alseas, and Yaquinas. Only nine Kuitsh were counted in the 1930 census.

Because of their coastal location, the Kuitsh were exposed to EuroAmerican culture sooner than Indians of the interior on the east. At an early date they adopted American culinary utensils and styles of dress. Before coming under white influences, they had worn skirts and basket hats. Large beads worn in their noses concealed their mouths. They flattened the heads of their infants. The double-pitch roofs of their houses resembled those of non-Indians. Like white men, they wrapped their dead and enclosed them in boxes or, in Native fashion, in inverted canoes. They placed burial containers beneath small plant shelters.

One summer day in 1791 the Kuitsh discovered the British schooner *Jenny* lying at anchor in the estuary of the Umpqua River. During her stay of several days, they traded some sea otter skins to her captain, James Baker. The following year, they were contacted by the British vessel *Ruby,* commanded by Charles Bishop. This vessel entered Winchester Bay at the mouth of the Umpqua River. In 1821 they were visited by J. Birnier of the Hudson's Bay Company, who was said to be the first white man to descend the course of the Umpqua River. Five years later, still embittered by the killing of several Indians along the Umpqua by some Iroquois Indians who had been gathering furs to sell to the Hudson's Bay Company, the Kuitsh chased a free trapper upstream. On July 14, 1828, they pounced on the north-bound party of seventeen Americans led by Jedediah Smith, killing all but four of its members. Before that attack, after a headman had stolen an axe from the party, Smith had ordered him tied as though to be hanged. The axe was recovered, but the chief had been humiliated and was resentful. Smith, absent at the time of the killings, finally reached Fort Vancouver with the help of Tillamook Indians. Sanctuary was provided to them by the chief factor, Dr. John McLoughlin.

The Kuitsh succumbed at an alarming rate to the intermittent fever outbreak of 1829 and 1830. Angered by their attrition, they ascended the Umpqua River

Mid-nineteenth-century headman Solomon Riggs of the Kuitsh tribe. The Kuitsh inhabited the southern Oregon coast and in 1860 were removed north to coastal reservations. Before coming under EuroAmerican influence, they wore skirts and basket hats and flattened the heads of their infants.

Authors' collections.

in 1838, traveling about forty miles from the Pacific Ocean to the mouth of Elk Creek, where they attacked the Hudson's Bay Company post, Fort Umpqua. In the confrontation no fort personnel were killed but three were wounded. The hostilities caused the Methodist missionaries, Rev. Jason Lee and Rev. Gustavus Hines, to cancel a trip to the mouth of the Umpqua in 1840. Because of their losses from disease and the marriage of their women to Caucasian men, the Kuitsh were largely immobilized during the Rogue wars of the 1850s. On July 28, 1856, the American military established Fort Umpqua on the Rogue River two miles upstream from its mouth. It was intended to keep the Indians submissive and protect miners and settlers. Because of such measures, promoters entered Kuitsh country. Samuel Roberts penetrated the Umpqua River on August 4, 1850. Herman Winchester and others of the Umpqua Land Company settled in the Lower Umpqua country at Umpqua City, Scottsburg, Elkton, and Winchester. When they were too weak to repel a marine invasion of about seventy-five vessels calling at the Umpqua River, the Kuitsh elected to board the craft peacefully. During the gold discoveries in the Rogue River valley and the ensuing Rogue wars, they and some Coos and a few Siuslaws were expelled from Scottsburg and forced onto the beach at Empire City (present-day Coos Bay), where they were guarded by the Coos County Volunteers.

Immediately after the Rogue wars, the Kuitsh were moved north to the Umpqua Subagency, one of four such jurisdictions in western Oregon in 1856. There, a village of Kuitsh, Coos, and Siuslaw refugees was established on the right bank of the Umpqua, extending about two miles upstream from its mouth. The village houses, furnished by the agency, were of split-cedar planks atop three- to five-foot pits. They were walled a short way above ground and covered with gable roofs. From fires on the mat-covered ground, smoke escaped through rooftop apertures. Occupants slept in bunk beds. The Indians aspired to own tables and other furniture in the manner of whites. In 1858, two years before their removal to the Coast Reservation (later to become the Siletz and the Alsea), the villagers numbered about 460, over half the number that had belonged to the Umpqua Subagency. Two years after the September 3, 1859, closing of that subagency, the Kuitsh were marched north to the Yachats River, where the Alsea Subagency was established on the Siletz Reservation.

Artifacts unearthed in former Kuitsh lands near Reedsport in 1979 were heralded as the oldest ever found on the Oregon coast.

For information about Kuitsh land claims, *see* **Hanis Coos** *and* **Siuslaw.** For more information about more recent cultural developments among them, *see* **Confederated Tribes of Coos, Lower Umpqua and Siuslaw Indians,** *and* **Hanis Coos.**

Suggested Readings.

Stephen Dow Beckham, *Requiem for a People: The Rogue Indians and the Frontiersmen* (Corvallis: Oregon State University Press, 1996); Joel V. Berreman, *Tribal Distribution in Oregon,* American Anthropological Association Memoir no. 47 (Menasha, Wis.: George Banta Publishing Co., 1937); Leo J. Frachtenberg, *Lower Umpqua Texts and Notes on the Kusan Dialects,* Columbia University Contributions to American Anthropology, vol. 4 (New York, 1914); Leslie Spier, "Tribal Distribution in Southwestern Oregon," *Oregon Historical Quarterly* 28, no. 4 (December 1927).

A Kutenai woman of the early twentieth century. The Kutenais were among the tribes pushed west by the Plains Indians. Their homes were mainly in today's northern Montana and British Columbia. They were divided along geographic and economic lines. The Upper Kutenais were influenced by Plains culture; the Lower Kutenais were oriented toward rivers and lakes in seeking subsistence.

Photograph by Edward S. Curtis from Curtis's *The North American Indian* (1907–1930), vol. 7.

KUTENAI

(Kittinahan)

The Kutenais (Kootenays) called themselves by a name meaning "people of the waters, or lakes." Like other tribal names, Kutenai has been the subject of various interpretations. Some authorities allege Kutenai is a Blackfoot term meaning "big stomach." In that vein, Indians of the Great Plains were said to have referred to the Kutenais as "those who are soft" because by Plains standards they lacked aggressiveness. Many authorities agree that the word *Kutenai* stems from the Piegan word *ktonai, or ktunai.* Although there is consensus that the tribe migrated west across the Rocky Mountains and subsequently became a linguistic island, there is some question when they migrated. Some scholars, disputing the claim that they were pushed west by armed Blackfeet, argue that their migrations were too ancient for their traditions to be historically valid. One Kutenai tradition has it that they migrated from around Lake Michigan about six hundred years ago.

After the migration across the Rocky Mountains, the parent Kutenai villages and activity centers were said to be on Tobacco Plains on the Kootenai River of Montana and on that same river in southeastern British Columbia. From those points, their migrations resumed as they splintered into upper and lower divisions. The Upper Kutenais were influenced by the horse-buffalo-hunting Plains Indian culture complex. In contrast, the Lower Kutenais were a sedentary people who, to a great extent, subsisted on fish, roots, and game. Before about 1850 the Upper Kutenais of the aboriginal Agiyiniks, or Jennings band, numbered more than seven hundred. They lived in the area of Jennings, Montana, and migrated east to today's Kalispell and then south to Elmo. Their descendants live on the Flathead Reservation in Montana. Another Upper Kutenai band, the Aganahoneks, or Tobacco Plains band, live on a reservation in Canada. A third band, the Agukuatsukings, or Tweed-Warlands, once lived on the Kootenai River between Tweed and Warland, Montana, but are now absorbed among other tribes. Yet another band, the Libby Montanas, moved to the Fort Steele area near Cranbrook, British Columbia. Before the 1855 treaty of the Kutenais with the United States, the Libby and Jennings bands had moved to the upper Flathead Lake country of Montana.

The Lower Kutenais were known as canoe Indians. They were also called Arc-à-plats, meaning "flat bows," by French-Canadian fur men because their bows were straight, broad, and flat. They were also called the Skalizises. One Kutenai group broke away from those in the area of Bonners Ferry, Idaho, and went north to Creston, British Columbia. Some Lower Kutenais of the Arrow Lakes of the Columbia River became part of the Senijextees, a Salishan people. After experiencing poor relations with the Salish speakers, most of these Lower Kutenais moved to Kootenay Lake in southeastern British Columbia. The few who remained with the Senijextees went on the Colville Reservation in north-central Washington State.

Location: Today the primary centers of Kutenai population are southeastern British Columbia at Creston, Cranbrook, Windermere, and Grasmere; western Montana on the Flathead Reservation; and northern Idaho around Bonners Ferry.

Numbers: At the time of the 1855 treaty, the Kutenais numbered about 500, about 130 less than the figure given by the Hudson's Bay Company trader John Warren Dease in 1827. In 1881 the Kutenais on the Flathead Reservation numbered 395. Their population increased between 1895 and 1910, with migrations of Kutenais to the reservation from Bonners Ferry, Idaho, and Libby, Montana. At the middle of the twentieth century, most of the 600 Kutenais lived in Montana and British Columbia. A smaller number, about 99, lived near Bonners Ferry.

History: The Kutenais became exposed to the white fur trade early in the nineteenth century. They frequented various posts after July 1807 when David Thompson of the North West Company surmounted Piegan opposition to establish his Kootenay House north of Lake Windermere in British Columbia. At that time the Upper Kutenais had many horses, which they introduced to other Indians. Ironically, they were subsequently relieved of many of their horses by raiders of the plains. Like other horse peoples, the Kutenais used the animals variously as a means of transportation and a source of wealth. Horses facilitated their travels to the plains from whose peoples they adopted secret societies. Their sun dance was less complex than that of the Plains tribes and lacked the element of self-torture. The last such dance among the Kutenais is said to have been held around the beginning of World War I.

It was through the fur trade that the Kutenais came into contact with Christianity. They were introduced to that faith by Iroquois Indians whom the trading companies had brought west. Two Kutenai youths were among the first to attend an Anglican mission school near the Hudson's Bay Company's Fort Garry (later Winnipeg, Manitoba). Among the early Roman Catholic clerics who ministered to them was the venerable and seemingly ubiquitous Pierre De Smet, S.J. The Kutenais were attracted to the St. Ignatius Mission in the lower Flathead Valley in Montana, where they raised crops. Their move to that place early in 1855 had been facilitated by the marriage of Kutenai women to white men. In July 1855, Washington territorial governor and superintendent of Indian affairs Isaac Stevens met with Kutenais, Flatheads, and Kalispels at Hell Gate near Missoula, Montana, to treat for their lands. Absent from the council was Edward, or Edwald, who had been the chief of the original Tobacco Plain Kutenai tribe before it separated into the Upper and Lower divisions. Attending the council was a Tobacco Plains band under Michelle, who after unsuccessfully seeking to have one large reserve established for all Kutenai bands, became disillusioned with the promises of white men and relocated north to Canada with his band. Claiming that Michelle had not represented them at the council, the Lower Kutenais retained a nontreaty status. Gold discoveries in the 1860s proved a mixed blessing to them and to the other Kutenais.

After they refused to remove to the Flathead Reservation, the Kutenais near Bonners Ferry (later the Kootenai Tribe of Idaho) were allotted by the government in 1895. Each family received an eighty-acre tract.

Government and Claims: The constitution of the Kootenai Tribe of Idaho was approved on June 16, 1947.

Tribal members filed a claim (Docket 154) with the Claims Commission asserting title to 1,160,000 acres in northeastern Idaho and northwestern Montana because their aboriginal title had been extinguished by the United States on March 8, 1859, without treaty or compensation. A judgment was rendered on April 25, 1960, in which members of the Kootenai Tribe of Idaho were awarded $425,000. (For other Kutenai claims, *see* **Confederated Salish & Kootenai Tribes of the Flathead Reservation.**)

Contemporary Life and Culture: On September 20, 1974, the tribe gained national attention by its "Declaration of War . . . between the Kootenai Nation and the United States of America." In October of that year President Gerald Ford signed a bill creating a 12.5-acre reservation for the tribe. As a result of the "war," these Kootenais also received some new houses, paved roads, and a community center. Tribal membership in 1982 was 115. The tribe has done considerable planning under the direction of its council, which is notable for the youth of its members. Education is conducted through the Boundary County and Bonners Ferry school districts of Idaho.

Suggested Readings:

Paul E. Baker, *The Forgotten Kutenai* (Boise, Ida.: Mountain States Press, 1955); Franz Boas, *Kutenai Tales,* Bureau of American Ethnology Bulletin no. 59 (Washington, D.C.: Government Printing Office, 1918); Clara Graham, *Fur and Gold in the Kootenays* (Vancouver, B.C.: n.p., 1945); "An Interview with Joe Mathias (Director of Kootenai Tribe, Outreach)," *Idaho Heritage* 1, no. 10 (October 1977); Olga Wedemeyer Johnson, *Flathead and Kootenay: The Rivers, the Tribes, and the Region's Traders* (Glendale, Calif.: Arthur H. Clark Co., 1969); Frank B. Linderman, *Kootenai Why Stories* (New York: Scribners, 1926); Carling Malouf, "Early Kutenai History," *Montana The Magazine of Western History* 2, no. 2 (Spring 1953); Harry Holbert Turney-High, *Ethnography of the Kutenai,* Memoirs of the American Anthropological Association, no. 56 (Menasha, Wis.: George Banta Publishing Co., 1941).

KWAIAILK

(Coastal Division, Salishan)

The Kwaiailks were also known as Upper Chehalises. The name "Kwaiailk" was that of one of at least four bands in the upper Chehalis River country, an area that extended from Cloquallam Creek to the upper reaches of the Chehalis River in southwestern Washington State. The name is now used to designate those bands collectively. They all spoke dialects distinct from those of Lower Chehalis peoples. The boundary dividing the Kwaiailk and the Lower Chehalis dialects was at the confluence of the Chehalis and Satsop rivers. If dialect is considered to mean mutually intelligible forms of the same language, it may be said that the Kwaiailks spoke at least two distinct dialects, though the variations between them were not great. The boundary between the two Kwaiailk dialects was at Grand Mound; Chehalis 1, or Oakville Chehalis, was spoken west of the mound; Chehalis 2, or Tenino Chehalis, was spoken southeast of that point.

While the Lower Chehalises depended primarily on the sea and the lower Chehalis River country for subsistence, the Kwaiailks in the prairie and foothill country subsisted on roots, game, and berries as well as fish. To encourage growth of berries and camas roots, they burned prairie lands every two or three years. Such areas were shared by peoples from several villages. The Kwaiailks fished for salmon and traveled up the Black River to Mud Bay on southern Puget Sound to gather clams and catch flounder. Among the game they hunted were deer and elk. Successful hunters feasted their friends and relatives. Well-established trade routes lay between the Lower Chehalis and the Kwaiailk lands. Over those routes the Kwaiailks obtained goods such as dentalia and seal oil, which were traded along the Pacific Coast from Neah Bay southward to the Columbia River. Trade routes also ran from the Kwaiailk country to east of the Cascade Mountains.

At some time before 1800 the Kwaiailks acquired horses, which they grazed on their prairie lands. In 1824 the Hudson's Bay Company trader John Work noted that, unlike the peoples near the coast, those inland, including a people whom he called the Halloweena Nation, which some believe to have been a Kwaiailk band, had horses. When, nine years later, Work's company established Fort Nisqually on the southern reaches of Puget Sound, the Kwaiailks began to trade there as well as at another company post on the Columbia River. Some Kwaiailks tended sheep for the Puget Sound Agricultural Company, a subsidiary of the Hudson's Bay Company.

Among the Indians with whom Kwaiailks had close ties were the neighboring Cowlitzes and Nisquallis. Combined with them and other nearby tribes, the Kwaiailks were believed to number about 1,500 to 2,000 at the beginning of the nineteenth century. Epidemics reduced them to about 215 shortly after midcentury. The survivors of those plagues sometimes burned entire villages in trying to escape the contagion. American naval Lt. Charles Wilkes estimated Kwaiailk and Lower Chehalis numbers at 700 in 1841, prior to a severe smallpox epidemic of the early 1850s. The ethnologist George Gibbs placed Kwaiailk numbers at 216 in 1854.

The Kwaiailks were among the Natives who, in February and March 1855, met Washington territorial governor and superintendent of Indian affairs Isaac Stevens, who sought unsuccessfully to treat with them for their lands. During the Indian war that immediately followed, some Kwaiailks in the vicinity of present-day Centralia, Washington, were moved by their agent, Sydney S. Ford, to a temporary reservation on Ford's Prairie. Among the four hundred Indians confined there were some who had served as scouts for the Americans during the war. After the hostilities ended, the government succeeded in obtaining title to Kwaiailk lands with neither their consent nor compensation. Finally, the 4,224.63-acre Chehalis Reservation was set apart physically at the confluence of the Chehalis and Black rivers and established by executive order on July 8, 1864, for Chehalises, Chinooks, and other small bands. By an executive order dated October 1, 1886, 3,753.63 acres of the reservation were restored to the public domain for Indian homestead entry, and 471 acres were set aside for school purposes. Thirty-six Indians on the reservation selected homesteads covering all of the lands not reserved for school purposes. Many Natives who had been scheduled to remove to the reservation became absorbed within the white community or were removed to other reservations. Today, no Kwaiailk tribe exists as such, but Kwaiailks are among the members of the Chehalis Confederated Tribes. *See* **Confederated Tribes of the Chehalis Reservation.**

Suggested Readings:

George Gibbs, *Tribes of Western Washington and Northwestern Oregon,* vol. 1 of Smithsonian Institution, *Contributions to North American Ethnology* (Washington, D.C.: Government Printing Office, 1877); Hermann Haeberlin and Erna Gunther, "The Indians of Puget Sound," *University of Washington Publications in*

Anthropology 4, no. 1 (1930); Carolyn Marr, Donna Hicks, and Kay Francis, *The Chehalis People* (Oakville, Wash.: Confederated Tribes of the Chehalis Reservation, 1980); Leslie Spier, *Tribal Distribution in Washington,* American Anthropological Association, General Series in Anthropology, no. 3 (Menasha, Wis.: George Banta Publishing Co., 1936); Herbert C. Taylor, "Anthropological Investigation of the Chehalis Indians Relative to Tribal Identity and Aboriginal Possession of Lands," in *Coast Salish and Western Washington Indians,* vol. 3 (New York: Garland Publishing, 1974), 117–58.

KWALHIOQUA

(Athabaskan)

The name "Kwalhioqua" (also Quillequeoqua or Willopah) is a Chinookan designation meaning "at a lonely wooded place." The Kwalhioquas were unique in that, as Athabaskan speakers, their language was, for a period, an isolate among other tongues. They were of the Pacific division of the Athabaskan language, one of three Athabaskan language divisions in North America. Like others of the Pacific division, they are believed to have migrated into the Pacific Northwest in the distant past. In the eighteenth century, they moved into the Willapa Hills of southwestern Washington State. Probably before 1775 one of their bands pushed to the south and became the Clatskanies. Those who remained suffered a decline in their population. Others meanwhile had relocated to the Chehalis and Cowlitz river watersheds and eventually came to rest on the upper reaches of the Chehalis River as part of the Cowlitz tribe living there. As they slowly mixed with the Cowlitzes, those Kwalhioquas assumed their language and lost their own. This intermingling, which began in the 1820s and 1830s, was complete by the end of the century when they became indistinguishable from Cowlitzes. Those few who did not mix with the Cowlitzes moved west to Shoalwater (Willapa) Bay on the Pacific Coast, where they intermarried with Chinooks and Chehalises and adopted the Chehalis dialect of the Salishan language. Some anthropologists have speculated that the Kwalhioquas had been unable to secure footholds on the lands of the once-populous lower Columbia River and coastal peoples. Having no seines for fishing, they borrowed such implements from those peoples and arranged with them for brief stays in their lands. In their own lands, the Kwalhioquas subsisted by hunting, fishing, and gathering.

On August 9, 1851, Oregon superintendent of Indian affairs Anson Dart treated with the Kwalhioquas at the Willapa River. He erroneously called them the "Wheelappa Band of the Chinook Indians." They ceded to the United States their lands: those between Willapa Bay and the Cowlitz Valley, those in the hill country between the Chehalis and Willapa valleys, and those bordering on the lands of the Cathlamets on the Columbia River. In 1853 an Indian agent listed the Kwalhioqua population as probably numbering no more than ten or fifteen, no doubt because of a smallpox epidemic that had sharply reduced them. About that time, only two or three Indians among the tribes at Shoalwater Bay were identified as Kwalhioquas, and in 1856 only three or four families on the head-waters of the Chehalis River so identified themselves. In 1910 there were said to be but two survivors, a woman on the Nisqually Reservation and her aunt living near Rochester, Washington.

Suggested Readings:

Jean Hazeltine, *The Historical and Regional Geography of the Willapa Bay Area, Washington* (South Bend, Wash.: South Bend Journal, n.d.); Frederick Webb Hodge, *Handbook of American Indians North of Mexico,* pt. 1 (Washington, D.C.: Government Printing Office, 1907); Melville Jacobs, "Historic Perspectives in Indian Languages of Oregon and Washington," *Pacific Northwest Quarterly* 28, no. 1 (January 1937).

LATGAWA

(Takilman)

The Latgawas lived in southwestern Oregon on the upper Rogue River around Table Rock and Bear Creek on the east and in the neighborhood of Jacksonville. The tribal name, deriving from their location on the upper Rogue, means "those living in the uplands." They have also been called Upland Takelmas, but they were culturally distinct from the Takelmas and spoke a different dialectic as well. In precontact times, the Latgawas often raided the Takelmas for slaves, whom they then traded to the Klamaths. The Takilman linguistic stock to which they belonged numbered an estimated 500 in 1780, but in 1910 only one remained. A 1937 enumeration counted 104 "Rogue River" Indians. The Latgawas' history from the middle of the nineteenth century parallels that of the Takelma bands, with whom they had become closely associated and intermixed when the two tribes united to confront settlers and gold miners. Both resisted treaties with the United States, fought against non-Indians, and opposed removal to the Siletz Reservation. For an account of those developments, *see* **Takelma.**

Suggested Readings:

Stephen Dow Beckham, *Requiem for a People: The Rogue Indians and the Frontiersman* (Corvallis: Oregon State University Press, 1996); Nathan Douthit, *Uncertain Encounters: Indians and Whites at Peace and War in Southern Oregon, 1820s–1860s* (Corvallis: Oregon State University Press, 2002).

This man, John Ponsee, was classified as a Rogue River Indian because his tribe, the Latgawa, was located on the upper Rogue River in southwestern Oregon. In 1910 only one Latgawa remained.

Courtesy of the Lincoln County Historical Society, Newport, Ore.

LEMHI

See **Shoshone-Bannock Tribes of the Fort Hall Reservation, Idaho.**

LOWER CHEHALIS

(Coastal Division, Salishan)

People of the Sand

The Lower Chehalises lived in what is now southwestern Washington. Their name derives from *tshels,* a Native word meaning "sand." Tshels was also the name of a large village at Hanson's Point at the entrance to Grays Harbor, near the modern-day town of Westport. The Chehalis name is now applied to formerly autonomous villagers who spoke a similar language in a much wider area along the Chehalis River and around Grays Harbor. The Lower Chehalises lived principally around the south banks of the Chehalis River and Grays Harbor. In later times, after the Chinookan speakers had been reduced by epidemics, such as the intermittent fever of the 1830s, the Lower Chehalises occupied territory to and around Shoalwater (Willapa) Bay that had been held by the Chinooks. Among the pressures to which the Lower Chehalises were subjected in early times, according to some anthropologists, were the movements of Chinookan peoples down the Columbia River, which pressed the Lower Chehalises into their historic homelands.

Besides being culturally if not linguistically related to the Chinooks, the Lower Chehalises were closely associated with other peoples of the lower Chehalis River watershed and Grays Harbor, into which the Chehalis River flows. These peoples included the Humptulipses, Copalises, Wynoochees, and Satsops. Some ethnologists considered the Satsops a subdivision of the Lower Chehalises because they were part of the same political group. The Satsop language, however, was a Kwaiailk (Upper Chehalis) dialect. The Lower Chehalises had close ties with the Quinaults on the north, along the Pacific Coast, and with the Chinooks on the south. They maintained close relations with Kwaiailks, but spoke a distinctly different Salish language.

The Lower Chehalises' villages were their largest social groupings and their only political and land-use units. In contrast to the Kwaiailks, they subsisted primarily on seafoods. They traded such products as dried sturgeon, clams, and seal oil to their inland neighbors. During the maritime fur-trading era, they encountered non-Indian mariners such as the American Robert Gray, who in 1792 sailed into the harbor bearing his name. They also were among those who traded with Meriwether Lewis and William Clark in 1805 and 1806 at the American ex-

Tillie Atkins, a Chehalis woman of the 1890s, shows evidence of EuroAmerican influences in her dress. The Chehalis peoples lived along the lower Chehalis River and the adjoining Washington coast. They were first exposed to non-Indian mariners and traders late in the eighteenth century.

Courtesy of Whitman College, Walla Walla, Wash.

plorers' winter quarters near the mouth of the Columbia River. During the early nineteenth century, the Lower Chehalises traded with Astorians of John Jacob Astor's Pacific Fur Company at Fort Astoria and with employees of the North West and Hudson's Bay companies. Indicative of their importance to foreign traders, the latter sometimes set aside rooms on their ships anchored in Baker Bay on the lower Columbia River for important Chehalis men and women. In the latter part of 1824, a Hudson's Bay Company trader, John Work, found the usually friendly Lower Chehalises not so congenial because of rumors that non-Indians planned to attack them. By distributing tobacco among them, Work quickly dispelled the rumors. In 1858 an Indian agent complained that Lower Chehalises were intermediaries in a liquor trade that extended from Shoalwater Bay to the Quinault country.

The Lower Chehalises and neighboring peoples, including those of the upper Chehalis River, were estimated at between 1,500 and 2,000 at the beginning of the nineteenth century and at 400 shortly after midcentury. In 1854 the ethnologist George Gibbs placed their numbers at 100 in Grays Harbor and on the lower Chehalis River. The estimate of 217 in 1855 may have included other peoples of the lower Chehalis River country.

In February and March 1855, Washington territorial governor and superintendent of Indian affairs Isaac Stevens met in council with the Lower Chehalises and neighboring tribes to treat for their lands. Although the negotiations ended in failure, the government later succeeded in obtaining title to the Lower Chehalises' lands without compensating the tribe. Without their consent and with no treaty, it also determined that a reservation should be established for them. Few Lower Chehalises removed to the 4,224.63-acre Chehalis Reservation created by executive order on July 8, 1864, farther up the Chehalis River at its confluence with the Black River.

Today, the Lower Chehalises do not exist as a tribe, having been incorporated within other tribes (primarily with those near them). Some Lower Chehalises have assimilated into non-Indian communities. The Lower Chehalises were grouped with their non-Quinault neighbors (Chinooks, Humptulipses, Hoquiams, and Satsops) who took allotments on the Quinault Reservation. Their descendants belong to the Quinault Allottees Association, which is opposed by the Quinault tribal government. At the time of the allotting, only about 10 percent of the original Quinaults took allotments on the reservation that bore their name. *See* **Confederated Tribes of the Chehalis Reservation.**

Suggested Readings:

George Gibbs, *Tribes of Western Washington and Northwestern Oregon,* vol. 1 of Smithsonian Institution, *Contributions to North American Ethnology* (Washington, D.C.: Government Printing Office, 1877); Hermann Haeberlin and Edna Gunther, "The Indians of Puget Sound," *University of Washington Publications in Anthropology* 4, no. 1 (1930); Leslie Spier, *Tribal Distribution in Washington,* American Anthropological Association, General Series in Anthropology, no. 3 (Menasha, Wis.: George Banta Publishing Co., 1936); Herbert C. Taylor, "Anthropological Investigation of the Chehalis Indians Relative to Tribal Identity and Aboriginal Possession of Lands," in *Coast Salish and Western Washington Indians,* vol. 3 (New York: Garland Publishing, 1974), 117–58.

LOWER ELWHA KLALLAM TRIBE

The Strong People

The Lower Elwha Klallam Tribe was formerly one of three Clallam bands. Like the other two, the community is today recognized by the federal government as a tribe. The others are the Port Gamble and the Jamestown S'Klallam bands. The Lower Elwha Reservation was created in 1936–37 when the United States purchased and put into trust for the tribe 372.74 acres of land on the northeastern Olympic Peninsula in Washington State. The purchase, amounting to $58,701.54, was made pursuant to section 5 of the Indian Reorganization Act of June 18, 1934 (48 Stat. 984). The tract, known as the Lower Elwha Tract, lies on aboriginal Clallam lands. It consists of fifteen parcels near the mouth of the lower Elwha River, west of the city of Port Angeles.

Location: The Lower Elwha Klallams live primarily on or adjacent to their Lower Elwha Reservation in Clallam County, Washington, where the Elwha River, flowing north from the Olympic Mountains, enters the Strait of Juan de Fuca. The reservation, consisting of bottomlands, possesses about a mile of beach along the strait. The nearest city, Port Angeles, lies about nine miles to the east on U.S. Highway 101.

Numbers: Tribal membership was given as 250 in 1978, 413 in 1984, and 1,099 in 1989. In 2009 there were 776 enrolled members.

Government and Claims: The reservation, originally assigned to fourteen families living on a sand spit, was proclaimed on January 19, 1938. On it, the Lower Elwha Klallams developed their own constitution and bylaws, which they adopted on April 6 and approved on April 29, 1968. Their governing body is the Lower Elwha Klallam Tribal Council composed of all of the qualified voters of the community. Officials are elected from among the council members to a business committee for two-year terms.

To seek compensation from the United States for alleged wrongs, the three Clallam groups consolidated their claims. *See* **Clallam.**

Contemporary Life and Culture: The religious preference of tribal members has been Protestant. Children attend public schools. Local, state, and federal agencies provide health care and other services. Residents earn their livelihood by fishing, logging, and performing seasonal farm labor. The Tribal Community conducts a fisheries enhancement and management program, which is coordinated through the Point-No-Point treaty council. The tribe is working to have two dams removed from the Elwha River in order to restore salmon runs, a project that was put to bid in April 2010 and constituted the largest such demolition in U.S. history. *See* **Clallam.**

In August 2003, some State of Washington Department of Transportation workers accidentally unearthed human remains on the Port Angeles waterfront, where the ancient 2,700-year-old tribal village of Tse-whit-zen once stood. Three years later, the tribe gained control over eleven acres of land at the site, and 335 intact skeletons were reburied in September 2008. The Lower Elwha Klallams eventually hope to build a cultural center and museum to re-create Tse-whit-zen as it was before it was razed for a sawmill in the early twentieth century. The tribe is also involved in the cleanup of the old Rayonier mill site near the Klallam ancestral village of Y'Innis.

The Lower Elwha Klallams initiated a language retrieval program in 1991, and at Port Angeles High School Klallam is now one of the elective languages offered. In 2007 Elder Walt Bennett passed away at age eighty-eight. He was the last man of his generation to actively teach his tribal language, and before his death, he was contributing vocabulary for the tribe's first written dictionary. On April 20, 2009, Bea Charles died at eighty-nine. She had been working with a linguist in recording and analyzing the language.

The first tribe to sign a gaming compact with the State of Washington (1989), the Lower Elwha Klallams broke ground on a new $4-million, 7,000-square-foot casino on the reservation in January 2009. They maintain a reservation police department and operate a $2.9-million, 15,000-square-foot health center. Another planned project is the opening of a skills center for youth recovering from drug and alcohol addiction.

Special Events and Ceremonies: Tribal members participate in Canoe Journey,

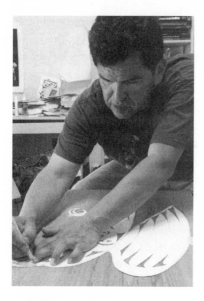

Roger Fernandez is the renowned Coast Salish artist of the Lower Elwha Klallam tribe. He practices and teaches Puget Salish art and design, a form overshadowed by those of British Columbia and Alaska and a traditional style nearly lost. Fernandez is also a performer of traditional songs and stories.

Courtesy of Paul D. G. Eubanks.

which the Lower Elwha Klallams hosted in 2005. That year the annual theme for the intertribal event was "Reflections on Our Past: Honoring Tse-whit-zen Village."

Suggested Readings:

Jeff Crane, "Finding the River: The Destruction and Restoration of the Kennebec and Elwha Rivers," Ph.D. dissertation, Washington State University, 2004; Lynda V. Mapes, *Breaking Ground: The Lower Elwha Klallam Tribe and the Unearthing of Tse-whit-zen Village* (Seattle: University of Washington Press, 2009).

LOWER SKAGIT

(Coastal Division, Salishan)

The meaning of the name "Skagit" is unknown. The Skagits proper, or Lower Skagits (sometimes called the Whidbey Island Skagits), were one of several peoples to whom the name was applied. They occupied land in what today is the central portion of Washington's Whidbey Island in Puget Sound, and they lived on a tract on the mainland at the mouth of the Skagit River and a triangular 56,300-acre area adjacent to the North Fork of that stream. They were hostile to northern British Columbia tribes, who raided them for slaves, and to the Clallams on the south shore of the Strait of Juan de Fuca, who encroached on their homeland. The Hudson's Bay Company trader John Work described them as a fine-looking people whose heads were not so flattened as were those of the Chinooks and who went unclothed, save for blankets or small fur or feather cloaks.

During the fur-trading era, they traded at Hudson's Bay Company posts such as Fort Langley (founded in 1827 on the lower Fraser River of British Columbia), Fort Nisqually (founded in 1833 on southern Puget Sound), and Fort Victoria (founded in 1843 on lower Vancouver Island). Roman Catholic priests began ministering to the Lower Skagits in their homelands early in the 1840s. Like other Puget Sound Indians, they were wary of non-Indians. In the later nineteenth century, they struggled to stem the tide of settlers occupying their lands, especially the fertile bottomlands of the lower Skagit River valley, some of which had been reclaimed from Puget Sound. In 1853, the ethnologist George Gibbs believed that, when their headman S'neet-lum had died, they had lost much of their former prestige. One of their prominent leaders was Goliah, who signed the Point Elliott Treaty of January 22, 1855. At the time of that treaty, government officials reported that the Lower Skagits numbered around three hundred. As a result of the treaty, they were placed under the Tulalip Agency and removed to the Swinomish Reservation, which was set aside in western Skagit County by

A woman, ca. 1900, of the Lower Skagit Tribe of the lower Skagit River of the upper Puget Sound basin. She is completing a mat that might have served for many purposes, including the preparation and consumption of foods. Among the materials from which mats were made were rushes and the inner fibrous layers of bark. Mats were also an item of trade.

Courtesy of the Skagit County Historical Museum, La Conner, Wash.

executive order on September 9, 1873. The descendants of the Lower Skagits and other Indians on that reservation are members of the Swinomish Tribal Community.

One of twelve Skagit subdivisions listed by ethnologist John R. Swanton was the Nuwahas (Duwahas), who figured prominently in Skagit history. The division of Skagits into an Upper Skagit Tribe and a Lower Skagit Tribe is a separation of modern origin. While some believe the Nuwahas were a subdivision of the Upper Skagits, the Claims Commission, in hearing the Upper Skagits' suit (Docket 92) for compensation for lost lands, found the Nuwahas not to be Upper Skagits. At the time of the Point Elliott Treaty, the Skagit and Samish tribes were organized for mutual defense under Satbabutkin, the leader of the peoples around present-day Concrete, Washington, in the middle-upper Skagit watershed. Satbabutkin was the son-in-law of the Nuwaha headman Pattehus Pateus, who lived around Bay View on the eastern shores of Padilla Bay across from Anacortes. The Lummi, Nooksack, and Semiahmoo Indians called the Nuwahas "cliff dwellers." The Swinomish, Samish, and other Indians called them Stucktabshes, which non-Indians translated as "Stick Samishes" because the Nuwahas were from the forested mainland.

Under a former headman, Sathill, the Nuwahas fought the "last war" between the Puget Sound tribes and those of Vancouver Island when Sathill and his men invaded that island near present-day Sydney, British Columbia. In an ensuing confrontation, the Nuwahas recovered the head of a former headman, Chadaskadim, which had been stolen the previous year by a Canadian tribe. These events were said to have occurred in the eighteenth century after a great plague, perhaps the smallpox, which destroyed most of the Nuwahas except those in the upland reaches of their territory. Other epidemics of the early nineteenth century also decimated them, reducing their population to about two hundred. At one time they were said to have numbered several hundred. The succeeding generations were powerless to resist the settlers who arrived in the latter part of the nineteenth century and occupied the Nuwahas' lands, which today are considered among the most fertile in America. The Nuwahas were converted to Roman Catholicism, and their descendants are proud that Chief Pattehus signed the Point Elliott Treaty. The "up Samish River" Nuwahas have become associated with Upper Skagit peoples. The Lower ("Samish Flat") Nuwahas merged with the Samish about 1918. (*See* **Samish**.) Although efforts toward federal recognition have failed, a Nuwaha remnant seeks to keep their tribal history alive and maintain an identity. Descendants live on reservations such as the Lummi and at such places as the Bow-Edison area below Bellingham.

The Lower Skagit aboriginal lands totaled 56,300 acres, including 50,300 acres on central Whidbey Island and the triangular 6,000-acre mainland tract extending along Skagit Bay from the mouth of Brown's Slough to north of the mouth of the North Fork of the Skagit River. In the middle of the nineteenth century, these lands were valued at $100,188. As the Lower Skagits had received $25,331.50 as a result of the Point Elliott Treaty, they were entitled to a recovery of $74,856.50. The Indian Claims Commission on October 13, 1971, ordered them paid that amount for the acreage they had yielded. *See* **Swinomish Indian Tribal Community.**

Suggested Readings:

Lee Ann Bennett, *Effect of White Contact on the Lower Skagit Indians,* Occasional Paper no. 3 (Seattle: Washington Archaeological Society, 1972); Martin J. Sampson, *Indians of Skagit County* (Mount Vernon, Wash.: Skagit County Historical Society, 1972).

LOWER UMPQUA
(See **Kuitsh.***)*

LUCKIAMUTE
(Kalapuyan)

The Luckiamutes were one of the Willamette Valley tribes. They spoke one of several dialects of Central Kalapuyan, one of the three Kalapuyan languages. There were probably six Luckiamute bands living on the Luckiamute River, a Willamette River tributary in west-central Oregon. Like other Kalapuyan peoples, they obtained their subsistence directly from nature, depending mainly on roots, especially the camas, which they cooked in holes dug for that purpose. They ate fish, but any salmon that they consumed had to be caught north of their country, because the species could not ascend above the Willamette Falls. The Luckiamutes also subsisted on insects, berries, and nuts. Excellent bowmen, they hunted deer and bear, plus smaller game and wildfowl. Since they owned but few horses, they crossed rivers on reed mats and conducted their hunts largely on foot. Like other Kalapuyan peoples, their women were expert makers of baskets, buckskin clothing, and robes of fine otter and weasel fur. They imported garments of mountain-sheep wool and clothing ornamented with porcupine quills and beads. Wealthy Luckiamute men often possessed multiple wives and, as further evidence of their well-developed class system, held slaves. The men wore buckskin headbands with redheaded-woodpecker scalps attached. To match that ostentatious adornment, they wore necklaces, wrist bands, and plugs fastened in their earlobes.

On April 30, 1851, the Luckiamutes met with federal commissioners who, though they did not know it themselves, were no longer authorized by Congress to treat with Oregon Indians. Luckiamute headmen Daboe (or Jim), Scholaque (or John), and Nuhkow staunchly opposed the plan to move their people east of the Cascade Mountains. On May 2, 1851, they agreed to terms with the United States that included a clause that they would never countenance or aid other tribes or bands hostile to America. With various Kalapuyan peoples, they consented to settle on a small reserve, but it turned out that those lands had already been taken under the terms of the Donation Land Act of September 29, 1850, which, in essence, granted lands to settlers even before those lands had been ceded. In exchange for surrendering their homeland, the Luckiamutes were to receive money, clothing, and a few farming tools. Oregon superintendent of Indian affairs Anson Dart attempted to resettle them on the agreed-upon tract, even though their treaty was never ratified.

Increasing emigrant pressure rendered it impossible for officials to isolate the Indians. Consequently, the Luckiamutes were asked to negotiate a new treaty. With the Molalas and a few Clackamases from below Willamette Falls, they met in council at Dayton, Oregon Territory, where on January 4, 1855, they effected a treaty (10 Stat. 1143, ratified March 3, 1855) with Oregon superintendent of Indian affairs Joel Palmer, who promised to assist them with medical care and other aids. They agreed to relocate to a reservation at such a time and place as the government designated. As a result, they were moved to the Grand Ronde, which lay immediately north of the Luckiamute homelands. On that reservation they numbered thirty-six in 1870. In 1910 only eight Luckiamutes remained. Confederated with other peoples and depopulated by disease, they lost their tribal identity. On June 30, 1957, the Grand Ronde Reservation itself was terminated.

Suggested Readings:

Stephen Dow Beckham, *The Indians of Western Oregon: This Land Was Theirs* (Coos Bay, Ore., Arago Books, 1977); S. A. Clarke, *Pioneer Days of Oregon History* (Portland, Ore., J. K. Gill Company, 1905); Leo J. Frachtenberg, *Ethnological Researches among the Kalapuya Indians,* Smithsonian Miscellaneous Collections 65, no. 6 (1916); J. A. Hussey, *Champoeg: Place of Transition* (Portland: Oregon Historical Society, 1964); Melville Jacobs, "Kalapuya Texts," *University of Washington Publications in Anthropology* 12 (1945), pt. 3; Harold Mackey, *The Kalapuyans: A Sourcebook on the Indians of the Willamette Valley* (Salem, Ore.: Mission Mill Museum Association, 1974); W. W. Oglesby, "The Calapooyas Indians," [188?], Mss. P-A 82, Bancroft Library, University of California, Berkeley; James L. Ratcliff, "What Happened to the Kalapuya? A Study of the Depletion of Their Economic Base," *The Indian Historian* 6, no. 3 (Summer 1973).

LUMMI

(Coastal Division, Salishan)

Xwlemi or Nuglummi
The People

The Lummis spoke the same Straits, or Lkungen, dialect as the Songish of southern Vancouver Island, who, according to anthropologist Franz Boas, called themselves Lkungen. Another anthropologist, Wayne Suttles, has determined that the name is derived from that of a Native house on Gooseberry Point, west of Bellingham, Washington, which was in Lummi territory. Possibly the name of the house came to designate the peoples of a larger area after their concentration on the Lummi Reservation across from Gooseberry Point.

Location: Successors of the Lummis, the Lummi Tribe, Lummi Reservation, Washington, live primarily in northwestern Washington in the general area of Bellingham on Interstate 5 below the Canadian border. The largest population of Lummis reside on their reservation on the mainland on the northwestern shores of Bellingham Bay and along the eastern shores of the Strait of Georgia.

Numbers: Including neighboring Samish and Nooksacks, the Lummis numbered about 1,000 in 1780. In the 1850s they were listed variously from 386 to 500, and in 1905 the number was given as 412. According to the 1910 census, the population had decreased to 353. In official reports, there were 505 in 1923 and 661 in 1937. Estimates during the 1950s stood at around 400. As of 1989, tribal membership was 2,846, and in April 2005 the enrolled Lummi membership was listed at 4,219.

History: Sometime before 1850 the Lummis, who were primarily a fishing people, abandoned their settlements in the San Juan Islands and established their main villages on and adjacent to the mainland on the east. They moved because of smallpox and raids of other tribes, especially those from present-day British Columbia. They also sought the lands and the fishing places of other peoples, for example, on the Nooksack River, where they defeated and absorbed the Hulhwaluqs and neighboring Skalakhans. Despite such conflicts, the Lummis and other Indians of northwestern Washington maintain heritage ties today with northern Indians. After moving to and near the mainland, the Lummis built stockades, as did other area tribes, to protect themselves from northern tribes. Under their headman Chowitsoot, they became signatory to the Point Elliott Treaty, which was concluded on January 22, 1855 (but was not proclaimed until April 11, 1859). By its terms, they and other northern Puget Sound Indians relinquished their rights to a large area west of the Cascade Mountains and north of today's Seattle.

In 1857 one of the Lummi agents reported that there were three Lummi bands, one at each of the three mouths of the Lummi, or Nooksack, River. Each acknowledged the headship of Chowitsoot. Four years earlier, the ethnologist George Gibbs had stated that Chowitsoot led a southern band, while a chief named Chilleuk headed a northern one. The Lummi Reservation was established by the Point Elliott Treaty. Originally consisting of 12,562.94 acres, it was enlarged by executive order on November 22, 1873, to approximately 13,600 acres. Although set aside for Lummis, Nooksacks, Samish, and other local Indians, it was occupied primarily by Lummis. Many of the Indians who were scheduled for relocation declined to go to the reservation, and some vacated it after having been removed there.

Shortly after the treaty signing, Rev. Eugene Casimir Chirouse, O.M.I., and Rev. Louis J. D'Herbomez of the same order established a mission among the Lummis, introducing a Roman Catholic influence that remains to the present. At that time the Lummis came into contact with not only missionaries but also the military, which in 1856 established Fort Bellingham three and a half miles northeast of Whatcom Creek. The garrison was maintained until the spring of 1860, when it was abandoned. It was officially decommissioned in 1868. In 1858 the Lummis furnished goods and services to miners en route to the Fraser River goldfields in Canada. Gold seekers and other non-Indians often harmed the Lummi. In 1856 a Lummi headman had to canoe to Victoria on lower Vancouver Island to purchase blankets because those that his tribe had received from the government had been traded for alcohol. After the Point Elliott Treaty, the Lummis pleaded with government officials to send an agent to protect them from outsiders. They continued to fish for subsistence, but they also began to work for settlers and in their businesses. In 1871, for example, the monthly payroll for Indians employed in the nearby Bellingham Bay coal mines was seven hundred dollars in coin. From around the turn of the century, the Lummis were embroiled in controversy with white fishermen. Among other problems at that time, an 1897 adverse legal decision in *United States* v. *Alaska Packers' Association* had kept them from removing the Alaska Packers from one of their ancient tribal fisheries at Point Roberts near the Canadian border. In 1974 some of the fishing rights of the Lummis and other treaty tribes were restored by the decision of federal judge George Boldt, which provided them with legal protections.

Government and Claims: A new constitution adopted in 1970 by the Lummi Tribe, Lummi Reservation, Washington, conveyed broader powers to the tribe's business council. Eleven persons are elected to three-year terms on the council, which selects the principal tribal officers from among its own members and establishes committees to study and make recommendations pertaining to business and social services.

A Lummi, ca. 1920, in the warrior clothing that the tribe wore in engagements against Indians from as far away as northern British Columbia. As in the past, the Lummis are today a marine-oriented people. On their reservation, located just west of Bellingham, Washington, they have inaugurated an ambitious aquaculture program.

Courtesy of the North Central Washington Museum Association, Wenatchee.

The Lummis filed a claim (Docket 110) to recover additional moneys from the United States, alleging that the amount paid them for their lands under the Point Elliott Treaty was unconscionably low. On October 30, 1957, the Indian Claims Commission determined that a gross total of 107,500 acres had been taken from them. After the acreage of their reservation and the waters in the claimed territory were excluded, the net land area claimed amounted to 72,560 acres. On March 2, 1962, its fair market value was determined by the commission to have been $52,067. It was difficult to ascertain the amount of money that the Lummis had received, because the Point Elliott Treaty had not specified exact amounts for the twenty-three signatory tribes. Thus, the Lummi case was combined with those of ten other tribes for the limited purpose of determining the amount due each petitioner (*Upper Skagit Tribe of Indians et al. v. United States,* 1964). In absence of proof of the amount paid each tribe, allocation of moneys was based on each tribe's proportion of the estimated tribal populations on the effective date of the treaty. It was determined that the Lummi Tribe had received $33,634.13. The difference between the amount paid the tribe and the fair market value of $52,067 was not considered unconscionable. Thus, the commission issued no additional award to the Lummis. The tribe appealed the commission's decision to the Court of Claims (197 C. Cl. 789), which ruled in 1972 that the valuation that the commission had placed on the Lummi lands constituted the bare minimum fair-market value in 1859. It thus reversed the Claims Commission's judgment and remanded the case for further proceedings. The commission then set the fair market value at $90,634.13 and on October 22, 1970, awarded the tribe $57,000.

Contemporary Life and Culture: The Lummi Reservation lands rise gently from Puget Sound. Most of the acres are timbered. There are some patches of fertile soil, but when the reservation was established, it was purposely separated from the rich Nooksack Valley lands, which today lie on the opposite side of Slater Road. By the summer of 1950, 10,162 acres of the reservation had been allotted, of which 2,040 were patented in fee, and 2 were reserved by the government. Sales of approximately 4,824 acres have reduced the allotted lands in trust to about 7,598 acres. There are about 20 acres of tribally owned trust lands.

In 1970, to help ease unemployment problems, the Lummi Business Council, in cooperation with other governmental agencies, instituted its Aquacultural Project to cultivate and harvest food from nearby coastal waters, though pollution entering Puget Sound from the Nooksack River posed a danger to the project. In the middle 1980s, the Lummis controlled the largest tribal salmon fleet on Puget Sound, comprising approximately 600 gillnet boats and 40 seiners. By 2003, following the collapse of the salmon fishery, those numbers had been reduced to between 150 and 200 gillnetters and 3 or 4 seiners. Meanwhile, in response to highly diminished salmon runs experienced throughout much of the 1990s and following the complete failure of the 2001 commercial season, the Lummi Indian Business Council passed a resolution in September 2001 declaring the Lummi Nation an Economic Fisheries Disaster Area and, through a Department of Labor grant, initiated a Dislocated Fishers Program to retrain idle fishermen. The tribe owns the third largest oyster factory on the West Coast.

The tribe has developed Head Start and daycare centers. The formal education of Lummi children is provided by the schools at nearby Ferndale. Some children attend a Catholic parochial school in Bellingham. Lummi Nation Tribal School (K-12) opened in September 2004. Costing $21 million, the facility comprises three buildings sitting on a ninety-acre site. Four years later, the Lummi Youth Academy opened, offering grades 9 through 12. At a cost of $2.1 million, it is a forty-bed residential facility available to all high-school-age Lummis. With a goal of strengthening families and ties to Lummi heritage and culture, the academy offers social programs for at-risk teenagers. Northwest Indian College, which was founded on the reservation in 1973 as Lummi Indian School of Aquaculture to provide training in fishing and shellfish hatcheries, is today the only accredited tribal college in the states of Washington, Oregon, and Idaho.

The Lummi Tribe operates an ambulatory direct care facility in Bellingham. Employing a staff of twenty-nine, the center offers comprehensive medical and dental care as well as health and substance abuse counseling.

In 1992 the Lummi Casino boasted 450 employees and was the second-largest employer in Whatcom County, but it closed in August 1997 because of increasing competition from Canadian gambling houses and losses of some $2 million. Then, in 2002 the facility reopened as the Silver Reef Casino. A year later it underwent an $11-million expansion that included a forty-seat steakhouse, an indoor terrace, a cocktail bar, and a four-hundred-seat pavilion for special events.

The Lummis also operate Portage Bay Construction, which builds residential homes in Ferndale and Bellingham. A home-improvement program has been operating since 1969. The Nooksack River flooded out fifty-seven families in 1975, causing great need for reservation housing. The poor perking qualities of the reservation soils create sewage disposal problems that bring the tribe into conflict with Whatcom County officials.

In July-August 1999, twenty-eight burials of Lummi ancestors were unearthed near Blaine. When city officials failed to properly notify tribal authorities of the discovery, the Lummis brought suit and the city eventually paid damages of $1.2 million. In the summer of 2007, the Lummis hosted their first potlatch since 1937.

Special Events and Celebrations: An important event is the annual Lummi Stommish Water Carnival, which features canoe racing between Lummi Island and the mainland. Coastal tribes, including those of British Columbia, compete in the eleven-man "war" canoes, which can measure fifty feet in length. The celebration is held near the middle of June, the date being contingent on the tides. Established by Lummi World War I veterans to honor tribal members returning home from service in World War II, the event today honors Native American veterans of all wars. Also included in the celebration are salmon feasts and Indian games and dances in which participants wear colorful costumes.

Suggested Readings:

BIA Planning Support Group, Portland Area Office and the Western Washington Agency, *The Lummi Reservation: History, Present, Potential,* Report no. 220 (1974); Daniel L. Boxberger, *To Fish in Common: The Ethnohistory of Lummi Indian Salmon Fishing* (Seattle: University of Washington Press, 1999) and "The Lummi Indians and the Canadian/American Pacific Salmon Treaty," *American Indian Quarterly* 12, no. 4 (1988); Barbara Lane, "Anthropological Report on the Identity, Treaty Status, and Fisheries of the Lummi Tribe of Indians," submitted in *United States v. Washington,* May 10, 1973; Michael Marker, "Lummi Stories from High School: An Ethnohistory of the Fishing Wars of the 1970s," Ph.D. dissertation, University of British Columbia, 1995; Edmond S. Meany, "Legends, Traditions, and Present Condition of Lummi Indians," in Bagley Scrapbook no. 12 (1905), Pacific Northwest Collections, University of Washington; Ann Nugent, *The History of Lummi Fishing Rights* (Bellingham, Wash.: Lummi Communications, 1979) and *Lummi Elders Speak* (Lynden, Wash.: Lynden Tribune, 1982) and *Schooling of the Lummi Indians between 1855–1956* (Bellingham, Wash.: Lummi Communications, 1981); Lottie Roeder Roth, *History of Whatcom County* (Chicago: Pioneer Historical Publishing Co., 1926); Bernhard J. Stern, *The Lummi Indians of Northwest Washington,* Columbia University Contributions to

Anthropology, no. 17 (1936; New York: AMS Press, 1969); John Stolpe, *A Look at the Lummis* (Bellingham, Wash.: Goliards Press, 1972); Wayne P. Suttles, *The Economic Life of the Coast Salish of Haro and Rosario Straits,* vol. 1 of *Coast Salish and Western Indians* (New York: Garland Publishing, 1974) and "Post-Contact Changes among the Lummi Indians," *British Columbia Historical Quarterly* 18 nos. 1 and 2 (January–April 1954); David G. Tremaine, *Indian and Pioneer Settlement of the Nooksack Lowland, Washington, to 1890,* Center for Pacific Northwest Studies Occasional Paper no. 4, (Bellingham: Western Washington State College, 1975).

Pauline Smith, 1989, of the Lummi Tribe of Indians. The tribe declared its independence of BIA paternalism in 1991. The first tribal college established in the Pacific Northwest, the Northwest Indian College in Bellingham, Washington, is located on the Lummi Reservation.

Authors' collections.

LUMMI TRIBE OF INDIANS

Under the Point Elliott Treaty on January 22, 1855, many tribes of northern Puget Sound were assigned to the Lummi Reservation. For an account of the ancestry of this group, known today as the Lummi Tribe of Indians, *see* **Lummi**.

These Makah women, ca. 1900, are cutting up halibut that their people caught in the Pacific Ocean. The Makahs of northwestern Washington reportedly were one of only a few whale-hunting Indian tribes in the United States. Other tribes traded for whale products or processed animals that were cast up on their beaches by storms. The Makahs are among the Pacific Northwest tribes on whose lands archaeologists have worked in recent years.

Authors' collections.

MAKAH
(Wakashan)

Kwih-dich-chuh-ahtx
People of the Cape

With the exception of their southern branch, the Ozettes, the Makahs were the only people of Wakashan linguistic stock in the United States. Their name, originally a derisive Clallam word for them meaning "the cape people," comes from their location at Cape Flattery, the very tip of the continental United States in Washington State. They were also called by a name meaning, in the Wakashan tongue, "people who live on a point of and projecting into the sea." The Makahs came to that area from Vancouver Island about five hundred years ago. Archaeological excavations and carbon-14 dating, however, indicate that the coastal village of the Ozette branch was occupied as long as fifteen hundred to two thousand years ago. Another Makah village, Wa'atch, is believed to have been occupied fifteen hundred years ago and its beach may have been used a thousand years earlier than that.

The Makahs are remembered for their intrepidity in hunting whales, which they canoed far out in the Pacific Ocean to harpoon. They buoyed up their catches with skin floats and towed them ashore where they processed and distributed them with much ceremony according to tribal custom. There was considerable interaction among the peoples of the five permanent Makah villages, leading some anthropologists to believe they exhibited more elements of tribal organization than other Native peoples of present-day Washington State. In historical times, Makah villagers took slaves from other Natives but generally not from each other. Because they were isolated for so long from white settlement, the Makahs maintained a higher Native blood quantum than did most other Pacific Northwest peoples.

Location: Most Makahs today are members of the Makah Tribe, Makah Reservation, Washington. Their reservation, lying at the northwest tip of the Olympic Peninsula, fronts both the Pacific Ocean and the Strait of Juan de Fuca.

Numbers: In 1805–1806, the Makahs were estimated to number 2,000. In 1853 the ethnologist George Gibbs placed their population at about 500. One cause of the severe decline was the smallpox that struck in 1853. Some Makahs reportedly carried it home aboard ship from California. In 1861 the noted observer of Indians, James Swan, recorded 654 Makahs living in permanent villages. His figure was slightly higher than that given in government reports in 1870. Census returns counted 435 Makahs in 1905, 407 in 1937, and 550 in 1950. Tribal membership in 1985 was 919, and in 1999 it was 1,214.

History: The Makahs were similar in language and other cultural traits to the Nootkas, Wakashan speakers on Vancouver Island on the north. That suggests that the Makahs drifted south in precontact times, possibly five hundred years ago. Their early Nootkan association did not prevent them from joining their Ozette allies in conflicts with Nootkan peoples like the Nitinats on the southwest coast of Vancouver Island. The Makahs also fought tribes on the south, such as the Quileutes, the Hohs, the Quinaults, and the Queetses.

In 1788, during the early contact period, the British sloop *Princess Royal*, commanded by Charles Duncan, anchored within the Strait of Juan de Fuca at the Makah village of Classet. On April 3, 1789, Neah Bay, whose name derives from that of the Makah village Deah, was visited and described by the Boston trader Robert Haswell. In 1790 under their chief, Tutusi, Makahs traded at Neah Bay with some Spaniards under their commander, Manuel Quimper. Impressed with a Spanish show of force after the Natives allegedly wounded a soldier who had strayed from camp to molest an Indian woman, Tutusi kept on peaceful terms with his white visitors. In 1791 the Spanish explorer Francisco de Eliza anchored in Neah Bay, where for thirty-three sheets of copper he allegedly purchased twenty small boys and girls. In 1792 the Spaniards returned aboard the brig *Princesa* and established the colony of Núñez Gaona, primarily to check British movements across the strait. From these Spaniards, the Makahs received what was perhaps their first significant introduction to European culture. Conflict between them and the Spaniards caused the commander, Salvador Fidalgo, to abandon the place to the Indian residents. Conflicts followed with other white mariners such as the British Capt. George Vancouver in 1792. With the decline of the sea-otter trade in the early nineteenth century, Makah contacts with outsiders became less frequent. During the Hudson's Bay Company era, they occasionally traded with personnel aboard the Bay Company's ships and at Fort Nisqually, which the company established in 1833 at the southern end of Puget Sound. Also in 1833 the Makahs enslaved three of the crew of a wrecked Japanese junk, holding them until they were ransomed by a Bay Company official. Around 1840 a Russian vessel beached on Makah shores, one of many shipwrecks off their coast.

The Makahs are party to a treaty that was effected with Washington territorial governor and superintendent of Indian affairs Isaac Stevens at Neah Bay on January 31, 1855. Among its provisions was the establishment of the Makah Reservation, which was enlarged by executive orders on October 26, 1872, and January 2 and October 21, 1873. On their reservation, the Makahs failed to become the agrarians that the government wished them to be. Not only was their land unsuited for such purposes but also elderly Makahs, having faced the dangers of whaling and other kinds of hunting, ridiculed younger men for "digging in the earth" like women.

Government officials pressured the unwilling Makahs to send their children to agency schools. At the same time the officials came to realize that it was almost impossible to alter the ways of the elderly. Enrollment in an industrial school at the agency was seventy. A police force was established, and in 1882 an attempt was made to establish an Indian court. There was friction not only between tribal members and agency officials but also among the officials themselves. In 1869 Makah agent Henry A. Webster traveled to Washington, D.C., to defend himself from the charge, among others, that he had traded with Natives for dogfish oil and furs at his store on the edge of the reservation. Until the latter half of the nineteenth century, the Makahs dispatched war parties against other American tribes such as the Clallams and Canadian tribes such as the Sookes and Nitinats of Vancouver Island.

The Makahs' economy continued to center around the sea. In the late 1880s they hunted seals from aboard ships owned by whites. By the end of the century they not only owned their own schooners but also hired whites to work for them. By then, some of the traditions and ceremonials attending their maritime pursuits had disappeared. Allotment of agricultural lands on the reservation was delayed until 1907, when each Indian received ten acres. Tracts were reserved for schools and other purposes on lands adjoining the townsite of Neah Bay. In 1931 the relative isolation of the reservation and its peoples was broken by the completion of an automobile road to Neah Bay.

Government and Claims: In 1934 the Makah Tribe, Makah Reservation, Washington, voted to accept the Indian Reorganization Act (48 Stat. 984). They received their constitution in 1936 and their tribal charter the next year. The first tribal chairman was Maquinna Jongie Claplanhoo, whose first name had been passed down from a powerful eighteenth-century Nootka chief. At the time of the passage of the Indian Reorganization Act, the trust period for the Makah Reservation had not expired. The land, reconverted into a tribal trust, was protected from alienation—an important reason why the tribe accepted the act. It had feared that when the trust period expired individual members would sell their holdings to non-Indians eager to acquire valuable tribal holdings and fishing sites. The governing five-member Makah Tribal Council is elected for staggered three-year terms. Among the more active appointed committees are those dealing with timber, leasing, enrollment, law and order, fishing, and labor.

The Makahs filed with the Indian Claims Commission (Docket 60) a suit for $1 million in compensation for lands ceded by them under their 1855 treaty. They also sought $10 million in damages for deprivation of fishing and hunting rights guaranteed them under article 1 of the treaty. Their land claim was separated, becoming Docket 60-A. Docket 60 remained for the deprivation of their rights to take halibut and seal.

In 1912 the United States had entered into an agreement with Canada, Japan, and Russia to preserve and protect fur seal and sea otter, and in 1924 it became party to a convention with Canada to establish the International Fisheries Commission to administer a program to preserve halibut in the North Pacific. The Makahs contended that that agreement and convention had reduced their harvests of fish and furs and were abridgements of their inviolable rights under article 4 of the 1855 treaty. The defending United States contended that it possessed a paramount right and duty to act in its sovereign capacity to protect and conserve game and wildlife. The petitioning Makahs countered, contending that in so doing the United States had an obligation to compensate them for damages. The United States further argued that the fishing rights claimed by the Makah under the treaty had been given gratuitously and that the rights of the Indians were merely "coequal in extent with rights of other citizens, and as such [were] subject to interference and control by necessary conservation measure[s]." The Indian Claims Commission ruled against the Makahs, following a U.S. Supreme Court interpretation that the treaty rights of Indians may be abridged to some extent by state regulations to conserve fish. As for the international agreement to remove the threat of extinction of seal and otter, the commission was informed by the United States that the convention allowed the Makahs to engage in pelagic sealing in open waters, where they had hunted with firearms and open canoes at the time the treaty was ratified. The commission finally concluded on April 15, 1959, that the Makahs were not entitled to recover for loss of halibut and seal hunting. On April 15, 1959, the commission dismissed Docket 60. The Makahs appealed the ruling to the Court of Claims, which affirmed the commission's decision. Concerning Docket 60-A, the commission wrote into its findings that, along with a consideration of the payment to the Makahs for their land cession, there should have been a review as to whether or not the United States had breached its treaty obligation to supply fishing gear to the tribe. The Makahs contested the October 15, 1976, award of $29,734.60, and on May 4, 1977, a rehearing was granted. As a compromise settling Docket 60-A, the government returned to the Makahs Waadah and Tatoosh islands just off their shorelines by an act of May 14, 1984 (98 Stat. 179) and by Public Law 98-282.

Contemporary Life and Culture: In 1991 nearly three-quarters of all Makahs lived on the reservation. A considerable portion of the Makah economy continues to center around commercial fishing. Some Makahs rent cabins to commercial and sports fishermen. Included in the tribe's enhancement program is a major federal hatchery and a very sophisticated fisheries management program through which advanced research is carried out by the tribe to maintain their vast treaty fishery, which has the largest number of species taken in the state. Some Makahs engage in logging on the heavily timbered reservation where their ancestors selectively logged yellow cedar to make canoes. Several Makahs engage in service-oriented jobs. From their beaches Makahs harvest rare Olivella shells to make jewelry, an operation that is administered through the National Park Service. But because of their location on the ocean, Makah beaches are often the site of oil spills, which require frequent cleanups.

Janine Bowechop is the executive director of the Makah Cultural and Research Center at Neah Bay. She is also the historic preservation officer for the tribe, in which role she has worked closely with historians and writers researching the history and culture of the Makah people.

Courtesy of Paul D. G. Eubanks.

In the summer of 1952 the Makahs organized a craft club to revive and maintain lost skills. Three decades earlier, a youth group had requested tribal council permission to use a community hall to hold Makah language classes. Makahs have since accepted grants from the National Endowment for the Humanities to revive and preserve the use of their language, which the government at one time discouraged or forbade in schools such as those at Neah Bay and Chemawa, Oregon. The Makah Cultural and Research Center (MCRC), which opened in 1979, hosts a Language Preservation Program, and the tribe continues to document, analyze, develop, and teach Makah language to preschool-age through adult learners. Today, there are no fluent-speaking elders alive on the Makah reservation. MCRC added an 8,100-square-foot storage facility in 1993, the largest artifact repository in western Washington State. The tribe offers a wide range of cultural interpretive programs through their cultural and research center, which was chartered by the tribe, but is independently governed by a board of trustees. MCRC also runs a summer dance program to prepare students up to fourteen years of age for Makah Days. On May 17, 1999, the Makahs made national headlines when they took their first gray whale in some three-quarters of a century.

With the abandonment of the Ozette Reservation, which had been established by executive order on April 12, 1893, some Makahs moved to the former Ozette site because of their opposition to non-Indians on their own reservation. As relations with whites improved, they returned to the Makah reservation. Activities at the ancient Ozette whaling village resumed in the 1970s as archaeologists excavated houses that mud slides had covered and preserved. Thousands of items from the excavation have been placed in the tribal museum in Neah Bay, which also houses a few items repatriated through NAGPRA. The excavation site at Cape Alava, four miles west of Lake Ozette, has become a tourist attraction.

Many educational opportunities are made available to members of the Makah Tribe. A Head Start and child-care facility is operated for preschoolers. K-12 education is provided to approximately three hundred Makahs by three public schools under the jurisdiction of the Cape Flattery school district. The tribe also funds the unmet college needs of about thirty tribal members per year, to a total sum of $100,000.

The reservation has no casino, although there is Makah Bingo. There are twenty-two small businesses—both private and tribal—including a motel and campground. The 210-slip Makah Marina opened in 1996. The tribe owns the Warmhouse Café and the Makah Mini Mart. In addition, the tribe owns and leases the land on which the Washburn Store sits. Earth Resources, a rock quarry, is also tribally owned.

The Makahs recently started self-governance of the Sophie Trettevick Health Clinic, the only health care facility on the reservation, while hospital care is available in the nearby communities of Forks and Port Angeles. Makah Housing Authority strives to improve opportunities, and most tribal members end up owning their own homes. Looking ahead, the tribe is hoping to build a Wellness Center and in 2010 will host Tribal Journeys, with Neah Bay scheduled as the destination of the largest gathering of canoes from throughout the Pacific Northwest.

Special Events and Celebrations: A two-day celebration, Makah Days, is held annually at Neah Bay on the weekend falling nearest August 26. It features canoe races, Indian dances in costume, Indian games, and salmon barbecues. The occasion, first celebrated on August 26, 1926, marks the extension of American citizenship to Makahs in 1924. In 2009, the tribe held its first Eagle Festival, which is planned to be an annual event.

Suggested Readings:

Cary C. Collins, "Subsistence and Survival: The Makah Indian Reservation, 1855–1933," *Pacific Northwest Quarterly* 87/4 (Fall 1996): 180–93; Elizabeth Colson, *The Makah Indians: A Study of an Indian Tribe in Modern American Society* (Westport, Conn.: Greenwood Press, 1974); Charlotte Coté, *Spirits of Our Whaling Ancestors: Revitalizing Makah and Nuu-cha-nulth Traditions* (Seattle, University of Washington Press, 2010); Philip Drucker, *Indians of the Northwest Coast* (New York: McGraw-Hill, 1955); Patricia Pierce Erikson, et al., *Voices of a Thousand People: The Makah Cultural and Research Center* (Lincoln: University of Nebraska Press, 2002); Alice Henson Ernst, *The Wolf Ritual of the Northwest Coast* (Eugene: University of Oregon, 1952); Linda Goodman, *Singing the Songs of My Ancestors: The Life and Music of Helma Swan, Makah Elder* (Norman: University of Oklahoma Press, 2003); Samuel Hancock, *The Narrative of Samuel Hancock, 1845–1860* (New York: R. M. McBride, 1927); Ruth Kirk, *Tradition and Change on the Northwest Coast: The Makah, Nuu-chah-nulth, Southern Kwakiutl, and Nuxalk* (Seattle: University of Washington Press, 1986); James G. McGurdy, *Indian Days at Neah Bay* (Seattle: Historical Society of Seattle and King County, 1981); Alan D. McMillan, *Since the Time of the Transformers: The Ancient Heritage of the Nuu-chah-nulth, Ditidaht and Makah* (Vancouver: University of British Columbia Press, 1999); Beatrice D. Miller, "Neah Bay: The Makah in Transition," *Pacific Northwest Quarterly* 43, no. 4 (October 1952); Carroll L. Riley, "The Makah Indians: A Study of Political and Economic Organization," *Ethnohistory* 15, no. 1 (1968); Robert Sullivan, *A Whale Hunt* (New York: Scribner, 2000); James G. Swan, *The Indians of Cape Flattery at the Entrance to the Strait of Fuca, Washington Territory,* Smithsonian Contributions to Knowledge (Washington, D.C.: Government Printing Office, 1869); Herbert C. Taylor Jr., *Anthropological Investigation of the Makah Indians Relative to Tribal Identity and Aboriginal Possession of Lands,* in *Coast Salish and Western Washington Indians,* vol. 3 (New York: Garland Publishing, 1974), 27–115; Ann M. Tweedie, *Drawing Back Culture: The Makah Struggle for Repatriation* (Seattle: University of Washington Press, 2002); T. T. Waterman, "The Whaling Equipment of the Makah Indians," *University of Washington Publications in Anthropology* 1, no. 1 (June 1920).

METHOW

(Interior Division, Salishan)

The Methows (or Mitois) lived mainly on the river bearing their name that enters the Columbia River in north-central Washington at the town of Pateros on U.S. Highway 97. Besides the river, a valley and a town in that valley bear the tribal name. The Methows spoke an Okanagon dialect of the Interior Salishan language. Earlier, before they lost their old speech forms, their dialect belonged to the Columbia-Wenatchi dialect cluster.

Some have it that Methows inhabited the eleven scattered lodges of the Metcowwees that the American explorers Meriwether Lewis and William Clark encountered on the north bank of the Columbia, a few miles above and across from the John Day River. That seems unlikely, though upper Columbia River peoples sometimes traveled as far south as the John Day River to trade. In 1811 the North West Company trader David Thompson visited the tribe at their salmon fisheries at the mouth of the Methow River. He called them Smeathhowes and wrote that they knew little of the Columbia River below their own lands. In 1814 Alexander Ross of the North West Company contacted the Methows, whom he called the Battle-le-mule-emauhs on the Salmon Falls (later the Methow) River. He described them as "in all respects exceedingly kind." Thompson had characterized them in a similar manner.

The Methows' population in 1780 numbered an estimated 800, including the Sinkiuses (Moses Columbias). In the early 1870s they were listed at 300, a misleading figure because it included other bands located between the Methow and Wenatchee rivers. Because of their small population, the Methows played only a minor part in nineteenth-century Indian and white conflicts. In the latter third of the century, the tribe came under the jurisdiction of the Colville Agency, but wishing to retain their traditional independence, they kept apart from agency officials. One Methow band, the Chilliwists, wintered on the Lower Okanogan River, wedged between two Sinkaietk bands.

After their contact with non-Indians, the Methows maintained small farms and enclosures in which they planted corn and potatoes. Around 1870 a Methow band traveled to Walla Walla to purchase agricultural tools. The Methows also carried out considerable trading with settlers in Ellensburg in the Kittitas Valley on the south. Some Methows, whose tribal lands lay within the Moses, or Columbia, Reservation, accepted 640-acre allotments under provisions of the Moses Agreement of July 7, 1883. Accepting Chief Moses' leadership, other Methows settled with him and his people in the Nespelem Valley of the Colville Reservation. Today there is no formally organized Methow Tribe.

From early times until the later nineteenth century, the Methow Valley had been the tribe's homeland and gathering place, where local Indians had collected on their return from fall hop picking in the Yakima Valley. Today the Methow

Methow George and his wife, Jennie, ca. 1910. George drowned in the Methow River, a Columbia affluent in north-central Washington. At the time of his death he was reported to be 104 years of age. Among the first white men to visit his people was the fur trader-explorer David Thompson in 1811.

Courtesy of the North Central Washington Museum Association, Wenatchee.

Valley is filled with orchards, small farms, towns, and tourist facilities. In an attempt to preserve the Methow language, courses have been offered at a nearby community college. *See* **Confederated Tribes of the Colville Reservation.**

Suggested Readings:

> James A. Teit, "The Middle Columbia Salish," *University of Washington Publications in Anthropology* 2, no. 4 (1928); James A. Teit, "The Salishan Tribes of the Western Plateaus," *Forty-fifth Annual Report of the Bureau of American Ethnology* (Washington, D.C.: Government Printing Office, 1930).

MICAL

(Shahaptian)

The Micals lived on the upper courses of the Nisqually River, a Puget Sound affluent in Washington State. Their dialect of the Shahaptian language closely resembled that of the Pshwanwapams, a Kittitas band of Upper Yakamas who were located just east of the Cascade Mountains in the upper watershed of the Yakima River, a Columbia River affluent. It also resembled that of the Shahaptian-speaking Klickitats and Taitnapams. Some anthropologists believe that the Micals were joined by some Pshwanwapams migrating west over the summit of the Cascade Mountains and by others of that cluster of tribes of similar dialect. The Micals have been absorbed by other tribes in the region of their homeland.

Suggested Readings:

> Melville Jacobs, "A Sketch of Northern Sahaptin Grammar," *University of Washington Publications in Anthropology* 4 no. 2 (1931), 85–292; Leslie Spier, *Tribal Distribution in Washington,* American Anthropological Association, General Series in Anthropology, no. 3 (Menasha, Wis.: George Banta Publishing Co., 1936).

MILUK COOS

(Yakonan)

The Miluk Coos (or Koweses) were also called Lower Coquilles. They formed the southern dialect division of the Kusan linguistic family of which the Hanis Coos spoke the northern dialect. Both Coos tribes lived in what is now southwestern Oregon. The word *"coos"* is said to mean "on the south," "lagoon" or "lake," and "place of pines." The Miluk Coos had two villages. The Miluks proper lived on the north, up the Coos River estuary from the Pacific Ocean and the Nasomahs lived on the south, as far as the estuary of the Coquille River, a Pacific Ocean affluent near today's Bandon. Some authorities maintain, however, that there were two other Miluk Coos villages. A bay, a county, and a city in southwestern Oregon bear the Coos tribal name.

The Miluk and Hanis Coos population was estimated to have been 2,000 in 1780, about 500 more than were believed to exist in 1805–1806. In 1871 there were 136 Coos at the Alsea Subagency of the Siletz Reservation. In 1910 the combined Coos population was given at 93; in 1930, at 107; and in 1937, at 55.

The Miluk Coos obtained subsistence from the sea from which they gathered foods such as clams. From the land they harvested camas and other roots and berries. Wood was important not only for housing but also for transport in their canoes dug out of logs. These craft were of the Klamath type, shorter and shallower than those of the Chinooks and with no distinct bows. The Miluks buried their dead in graves that they often lined with cedar planks and accoutered with possessions of the deceased. Like other Oregon coastal peoples, they held slaves and on occasion were in turn enslaved by Indians such as the Coquilles who raided them.

At least from the time that Capt. George Vancouver visited them in 1792, the Coos traded with the crews of foreign ships. They traded with Hudson's Bay Company fur men after 1826, when an employee of that company, Alexander

The ancestors of this Miluk Coos family of southwestern Oregon had traded with white mariners at least from the time of Capt. George Vancouver, who visited them in 1792. This posed studio portrait was taken ca. 1893.

Courtesy of the Coos-Curry Museum and Historical Association, North Bend, Ore.

McLeod, traveled overland to their country. Shortly after their encounter with him, they were observed with metal weapons, including an occasional gun, and wearing European clothes. A few Miluk Coos of the Nasomah branch and their relatives, the Upper Coquilles (Mishikhwut-metunnes), along with other Athabaskan-speaking peoples of the area, signed a treaty with Oregon superintendent of Indian affairs Anson Dart on September 20, 1851.

After an Indian guide misled W. G. T'Vault and his party as they searched for an overland route between the coast and the Willamette Valley, some Indians, most probably Miluks, attacked the party at the mouth of the Coquille River on September 14, 1851. Their weapons—bows and arrows, war clubs, and knives—proved that they had had access to iron from the vessel *William C. Hagstaff,* which previously had wrecked near present-day Port Orford. Wading into the water, the Indians overwhelmed them before the T'Vault party could ready their rifles. It is said the Indians killed or drowned eight in the assault. T'Vault escaped by swimming to the opposite shore. In late November 1851, as a result of the retaliatory measures of non-Indians, fifteen Indians were killed and many others were wounded. Their villages and stores were also destroyed. In the ensuing months, non-Indians, mostly miners, continued to strike back. With little provocation, they shot and hanged Indians. In response to a message from the settler camp, early in 1854 Chief Tie-John vowed to kill every one of the foreigners coming against him. On the night of January 28, 1854, a group called Minute Men from the nearby town of Randolph surprised a Coquille village. Randolph, previously called Whiskey Run, lay six miles north of the mouth of the Coquille River, where gold had been discovered. In an ensuing attack, the Minute Men killed sixteen and wounded four others, many of whom were women and children. The vengeful miners also captured some elderly men and put to the torch their village and canoes. Chief Tie-John and those with him escaped. Shortly after that, the headman was forced to sue for peace. Hanged at Randolph were three captured Indians. In another confrontation in the spring of 1855, fifteen Indian men were killed, and thirty-two women and children were captured. In November of that year an Indian agent, Ben Wright, circumvented an armed party of Coos Bay settlers from destroying Coos camps, but later that month the pioneers, on rumors of an Indian attack, assaulted the Coos on the lower Coquille, killing four and hanging four others.

Aware that the diggings would soon be exhausted, gold miners turned to opportunities for settlement in the fertile lands of the Coquille River valley. On August 11, 1855, Oregon superintendent of Indian affairs Joel Palmer consummated a treaty with several tribes of the Oregon coast, including Coos peoples. During the Rogue wars, which ended in 1856, Coos were generally peacefully disposed, despite their enduring harassment by non-Indians. During the war years, they remained under the guard of the Coos County Volunteers at Empire City (Coos Bay). At the end of the war, they were temporarily held under the picket of a subagent stationed on the north side of the mouth of the Umpqua River. They were also kept under surveillance by troops from nearby Fort Umpqua.

With closure of the Umpqua Subagency on September 3, 1859, the Coos, with some Umpquas, numbering about 460 in all, were sent northward to Yachats on the Siletz Reservation (later the Alsea) to live among the Siuslaw Indians. Their prescribed mode of life there included garden cultivation, but repeated crop failures reduced these nonfarmers to starvation. With the 1875 closure of the Alsea Reservation, the Coos and Kuitsh moved down the coast to Coos Bay, where early in the twentieth century they purchased a 6.1-acre reservation on western Coos Bay.

With Kuitsh and Siuslaws, the Coos met at Coos Bay in 1916–17 to organize and to prepare a suit against the federal government for compensation for lost lands. Their case (No. K-345) was not decided until May 2, 1938, at which time the Court of Claims ruled the Indian testimony inadmissible due to inadequate documentation. On November 14 of that year, the U.S. Supreme Court refused to hear their subsequent appeal. Between 1947 and 1951, despite additional evidence based on the words of fur trappers, diarists, Indian agents, and others, the Indian Claims Commission declined to hear their case, maintaining that they had already had their day in court.

The descendants of Miluk Coos, who until the midtwentieth century had been members of the Coos Tribe of Indians and were able to prove Coquille (Mishi-khwutmetunne) ancestry, shared in an award of $847,190.40 by the Court of Claims (Case No. 45230) for the Coquilles' land cession after a Supreme Court ruling on April 6, 1951, disallowed the payment of interest. This award immediately produced a schism in the Coos Tribe of Indians. Those participating in the award became affiliated with the Coquille Indian Tribe also based at Coos Bay.

(*See* **Coos Tribe of Indians** *and* **Coquille Indian Tribe.** For information on current Coos social programs, *see* **Hanis Coos.** For details of their reservation life and claims *see* **Siuslaw.**)

Suggested Readings:

Stephen Dow Beckham, *The Indians of Western Oregon: This Land Was Theirs* (Coos Bay, Ore.: Arago Books, 1977); Leo J. Frachtenberg, *Coos Texts,* Columbia University Contributions to American Anthropology, no. 1, (New York, 1913) and *Lower Umpqua Texts and Notes on the Kusan Dialects,* Columbia University Contributions to American Anthropology, no. 4 (New York, 1914); Melville Jacobs, "Coos Myth Texts," *University of Washington Publications in Anthropology,* 8, no. 2 (Seattle, 1940) and "Coos Narrative and Ethnologic Texts," *University of Washington Publications in Anthropology* 8 no. 1 (Seattle, 1939); Henry Hull St. Clair and Leo Frachtenberg, "Traditions of the Coos Indians," *Journal of American Folklore* 13 (1909), 25–44.

MISHIKHWUTMETUNNE

(See **Coquille.***)*

MITCHELL BAY

The Mitchell Bay Indians are descendants of Indians who lived for generations in the San Juan Islands of Washington State and on lower Vancouver Island in British Columbia. Their name, apparently given by a special Indian agent in 1919, refers to a tribal settlement on Mitchell Bay on the northwestern shores of San Juan Island, the largest in the archipelago of that name.

The Mitchell Bays still live primarily in the San Juan Islands and at other places in the Puget Sound area. Their ancestors spoke a Lkungen dialect of the Coastal Salishan language. They claim that the ancestral village, Taleqamus, was composed of three Songish subdivisions. It lay on the western shore of San Juan Island. Archaeologists have found it to have been very populous. Other Songish villages were on Open Bay on Henry Island, on Garrison and Wescott bays on San Juan Island, and opposite Spieden Island on San Juan Island.

In the 1850s and 1860s, during the controversy between Great Britain and the United States over the location of the international boundary, the Pig War was "fought" mainly on San Juan Island. Ancestors of the Mitchell Bays remained friendly to representatives of both nations, trading with each. After the Fraser River gold discoveries in Canada in the late 1850s and early 1860s, non-Indians settled in the San Juan Islands. Their presence contributed to the decline of the already dwindling Indian population. In 1919, 181 Mitchell Bays were reported. In 1980 the tribe numbered over 100.

Apparently the first federal mention of a Mitchell Bay tribe was in a report for the Office of Indian Affairs (OIA) prepared by Charles Roblin, who conducted a survey between 1916 and 1918 of homeless and landless Indians. Operating under a five-member council, the tribe today seeks federal acknowledgment and accompanying fishing rights. The economy of the Mitchell Bays, like that of their ancestors, depends principally on fishing. In 1982 the Department of the Interior defined the Mitchell Bay Indians as a "group" of Indians similar to the "San Juan Island Indians." In 1957 the group filed a claim under the latter name with the Indian Claims Commission (Docket 214). It was denied on the grounds that the litigants were descended primarily from Lummis and Samish, and therefore the claim was covered under the claims of those tribes. Presumably, the group is quite fluid, having included members from Canadian tribes. *See* **San Juan Tribe of Indians.**

MODOC

(Lutuamian)

The name "Modoc" stems from the Native word for "southerners," indicating that it may have been ascribed to the tribe by their northern neighbors, such as the Klamaths. Today a county bears the name as well as Modoc Point, Oregon. Formerly, Tule and Clear lakes were known as the Modoc Lakes. Several places in the central and southern United States carry the name Modoc.

The Modocs lived in what today are the Oregon-California borderlands, on Lower Klamath, Modoc, Tule, and Clear lakes and in the Lost River valley. At times, their territory extended to Goose Lake. Historically, they were closely associated with the Klamaths and perhaps drifted with them into the lakes district of southern Oregon and northern California as early as the fifteenth century. The two peoples separated after the middle of the eighteenth century, but were later rejoined.

The Modocs are remembered for their spirited but stubborn and futile resistance to American troops and their Indian scouts in the Lava Beds of northern California in 1872 and 1873. Their 1780 population has been variously estimated at from 400 to 800. In 1905 there were 56 on the Quapaw Agency in Indian Territory (Oklahoma), where, except for the 223 who remained on the Klamath Reservation, they were consigned after their defeat. Of 282 Modocs in 1910, 212 lived in Oregon, 33 in Oklahoma, and 20 in California. The remainder were scattered among at least five other states. In 1937 there were a reported 329 Modocs. Today they are incorporated with other tribes, especially the Klamaths, under whose standard Modoc descendants were involved in the mid-twentieth-century termination of the Klamath Reservation.

The Modocs hunted deer, antelope, and mountain sheep as well as rabbit and squirrel. They also gathered roots and seeds, most commonly the *wocus*, a species of water lily that was also utilized by the Klamaths. They caught and dried fish, and in precontact times they fashioned their clothing from grass or tule fiber and animal skins decorated with shell beadwork. They wore belts of braided grass. By the middle of the nineteenth century, they had adopted European-style clothing. Before 1800 they set their lodges in excavations that were a half foot to four feet deep and from twelve to twenty feet across. The frameworks of willow poles were covered with tule matting and layers of earth. They traveled on their lakes in dugout log canoes or rafts of tule bundles. They did not acquire horses until about 1825.

The Modocs' initial contacts with non-Indians were with fur traders around 1825 when Hudson's Bay Company brigades traversed their lands. For the next fifteen years the brigades, mostly en route to California, only marginally altered Modoc living patterns.

During a severe winter around 1830, tribal food caches were lost in deep snow drifts that obliterated natural landmarks. Consequently, many Modocs, huddling in their lodges, died of starvation. On one occasion some Modocs were saved when an antelope herd plunged into Tule Lake directly in front of their village.

Not until around 1835 did some Modocs travel northward to The Dalles of the Columbia River. Although impressed with the goods traded there, they initially had little to exchange for them. Later they learned that female slaves brought good prices at that market. In the following decade, Modocs mercilessly raided neighboring California tribes, the Pit Rivers and the Shastas, for human spoils, the sales from which they used to acquire horses. Usually their slaves were not taken to The Dalles, but traded to middlemen like the Klamaths and the Teninos who frequented that location.

During the 1840s and 1850s, non-Indian contact by the Modocs was sporadic. Among the travelers they did meet was Capt. John C. Frémont, who entered their lands in December 1843 and again in May 1846. In 1846 Frémont's party ventured northward to around Klamath Marsh, where Klamaths attacked and killed four of the Americans. Accompanying Frémont was the noted western scout Kit Carson, who in retaliation returned to burn the Klamath village. In July of that same year, a fifteen-man party worked its way east from the Willamette Valley through the Klamath and the Modoc lands, laying out the Scott-Applegate Road, which was a circuitous southern detour from the main Immigrant Road (the Oregon Trail) by which settlers usually entered the Willamette Valley. In the late summer and early fall of 1846, Modocs attacked immigrants traveling the route.

In 1847 and 1848 many Modocs succumbed to the measles that non-Indians carried into their land, but by 1849 the survivors were strong enough to resume raiding white travelers. On one occasion, they killed eighteen at a place known to Oregon pioneers as Bloody Point, where the Applegate Road first intersects Tule Lake after its long descent from the highlands around Clear Lake. Equally troubling to Modocs were the miners who crossed their lands en route to California after gold was discovered in 1848. Two years later, gold was found near Yreka, California, near the Modoc country, and more miners trespassed on their lands. By the summer of 1851 hundreds of non-Indians were occupying Modoc lands, many with the intention of farming the homesteads they had claimed. Indian and white confrontations caused the settlers to organize vigilante groups against which the Modocs retaliated with more attacks at Bloody Point. Despite provocations, they kept out of the Rogue wars of the 1850s. They did not, however, escape unscathed, because the Americans, after defeating the Indians of the Rogue country, more easily imposed their culture on the other tribes in southern Oregon. The Modocs abandoned the slave trade, but some of their women drifted into prostitution and others performed domestic tasks for whites in exchange for money, much of which went for liquor.

When the Americans grew adamant about removing Indians to reservations, some Modocs, like Old Schonchin and his band, were willing to relocate, but not Captain Jack (Keintpoos) and his band, who knew that settlers coveted their lands in the Lost River and Tule Lake regions on which the white men wanted to graze their stock. The result of such pressures was a treaty effected on October 14, 1864, with the Modocs, Klamaths, and Yahuskins (Northern Paiutes), by which those tribes agreed to a reservation in the Klamath country. Since the reservation was outside the borders of their lands, the Modocs and Yahuskins signed reluctantly. They were perhaps influenced to do so because the Walpapis (Northern Paiutes) under Chief Paulina were attacking the Modocs and Klamaths, who perceived a possible ally in the U.S. military. American officials preferred to deal with Chief Schonchin instead of his rival, Captain Jack, who repudiated his own signature on the treaty and vacated the Klamath Reservation in 1865. Despite pressures from the white community for his return, Jack remained apart from the reservation, while Schonchin relocated his people from the main Klamath Agency to that at Yainax about thirty-five miles to the east. There they suffered starvation and opposition from the Klamaths. In council on Lost River on December 23, 1869, Jack and forty-three of his band agreed to remove to the Klamath Reservation, where they too suffered starvation and coolness from the Klamaths. In April 1870 Jack and nearly all the Modocs, about 375 in all, abandoned the reservation for the Lost River country. To survive in that barren region, they demanded rent from area settlers. When the latter refused to pay, Jack and his men raided the stock of immigrants passing through. He wished to remain off the Klamath Reservation and insisted on one established in his own region, a request refused by American officials.

Late in 1872 troops closed in on Jack's camp. Thus began the Modoc War in which three Modoc bands of only 170 members withstood 1,000 American

Hooka (or Hooker) Jim, a Modoc prisoner taken in the war between his people and American troops in the Lava Beds, today a national monument in north-central California. After eluding the troops, the Modocs under Captain Jack were forced to surrender, but unlike Captain Jack, Hooka Jim escaped trial and punishment after the war.

Authors' collections.

troops and settlers, who for several months tried to dislodge them from what is now the Lava Beds National Monument in the Tule and Klamath lake basins. The Modocs, worn down by attrition, ended their war on June 1, 1873, after Jack and his chiefs were captured and confined at Fort Klamath. There he and three others were hanged and two had their death sentences commuted to life imprisonment on Alcatraz Island. In October 1873, 153 Modoc prisoners were settled on the Quapaw Agency in Indian Territory.

In 1902 the Modocs in Indian Territory sent representatives to the Klamaths, seeking their permission to return to the Klamath Reservation. Twenty-one came back in 1903 to take up residence on the northeastern portion of that reservation. In 1909 the Modocs who had remained on the Quapaw were given the option of selling their lands and returning to Oregon to take allotments on the Klamath, or keeping and leasing their lands on the Quapaw. The modern Modoc Tribe of Oklahoma, which maintains a government-to-government relationship with the United States, is descended from Modocs who remained in Oklahoma and some of the others who went west but returned to Oklahoma to join tribal members living there.

After the return of forty-seven Modocs to the Klamath Reservation from Oklahoma, the Modocs and Klamaths in time became integrated. In 1964 there were but seven or eight Modocs who spoke their Native language and today, largely through intermarriage, there are none of full-blood degree. As people of the Klamath Reservation, Modoc descendants shared in the termination of the Klamath tribe's trust relationship with the United States in 1954. In the 1980s,

300 Modocs were living in the area of Chiloquin, about thirty miles north of Klamath Falls, Oregon. In 2009 there were approximately 600 Modocs living in the state of Oregon. *See* **Klamath Tribes.**

Suggested Readings:

S. A. Barrett, "The Material Culture of the Klamath and Modoc Indians," *University of California Publications in American Archaeology and Ethnology* 5 (1907–1910); Jeremiah Curtin, *Myths of the Modocs* (New York: B. Bloom, 1912); Ivan Doig, "[Edward] Fox among the Modocs," *Pacific Search about Nature and Man in the Pacific Northwest* 10, no. 7 (May 1976); A. B. Meacham, *Wigwam and War-Path; Or The Royal Chief in Chains* (Boston: John P. Dale, 1875); A. B. Meacham, *Wi-Ne-Ma (The Woman-Chief) and Her People* (Hartford, Conn.: American Publishing Co., 1876); Keith A. Murray, *The Modocs and Their War* (Norman: University of Oklahoma Press, 1959); Verne F. Ray, *Primitive Pragmatists: The Modoc Indians of Northern California* (Seattle: University of Washington Press, 1963); Jeff C. Riddle, *The Indian History of the Modoc War and the Causes That Led to It* (Eugene, Ore.: Urion Press, 1914).

MOLALA

(Waiilatpuan)

In early times the Molalas were neighbors of the Cayuses and were thought to have shared the same linguistic stock with them. Anthropologists now disagree with this contention. The Molalas lived near the eastern slopes of the Cascade Mountains of central Oregon near the Warm Springs River, a tributary of the Deschutes, which in turn flows into the Columbia. Perhaps more passive than the Cayuses, the Molalas were moved westward sometime after 1780 by more aggressive tribes of the Oregon interior. Some anthropologists once believed those aggressors to be Northern Paiutes migrating north, but now it is understood that pressure came from even more assertive Teninos pushing south on the horseless Paiutes.

The Molalas split into two groups. The Southern, or Lower, Molalas relocated to lands around the headwaters of the Umpqua and Rogue rivers of southern Oregon. The Northern, or Upper, Molalas remained primarily in the Willamette watershed west of Mount Hood in the Molalla River country and on the south in the Santiam River watershed. Even in their new homes they were still occasionally raided by the Cayuses. Besides holding the northeastern slopes of the Willamette country, the Northern Molalas claimed its bottomland hunting grounds, which they left in the hands of the peacefully disposed Kalapuyan peoples. Today the river and city of Molalla in the region bear the tribal name.

The Molalas lived in mat houses in summer and in mud-covered semisubterranean houses in winter. Both the Northern and the Southern Molalas were closely related to the Klamaths, who called them a name meaning "people of the serviceberry tract" and in early times ridiculed them for their incorrect use of the Klamath language. From the Molalas, the Klamaths obtained elk-horn spoons in exchange for the *wocus* lily roots of the Klamath Marsh.

In 1780 the combined Molalas and Cayuses numbered an estimated 500; and in 1848, 200. In 1851 there were 123 Northern Molalas. In 1870 there were 74 Molalas on the Grand Ronde Reservation and, in 1881, 55 on the Klamath Reservation. In 1910 there were but 31 Molalas, 6 of whom lived outside Oregon.

After a disturbance between non-Indians and Molalas in 1846, a volunteer company marched to a Molala settlement, where the dispute was resolved. In March 1848, when some Klamaths traveled north along the Klamath Trail to the Silverton, Oregon, country to camp with some Molalas, frightened settlers, wanting them removed, confronted them in what was known as the Abiqua War. In two days of fighting, thirteen Klamaths were reported killed and one was wounded in addition to a single white man.

Molala subsistence patterns were disrupted not only by encroaching whites but by laws such as that passed by the Oregon Territorial Legislature in 1854 prohibiting sales of firearms to Indians. Such a ban forced Molalas and other Indians to resort to their traditional weapons to secure what little game remained.

On May 6 and 7, 1851, at Champoeg, Oregon Territory, two land-cession treaties were entered into with the Northern Molalas. Effecting the treaty on behalf of the United States was a commission under superintendent of Indian affairs Anson Dart, which, unbeknownst to its members, had been stripped of its authority by Congress two months earlier. Signing on May 6 for the fifty-eight-member "main band" of Molalas were their headmen, Quai-eck-e-ete, Yal-kus, and Crooked Finger. The latter was killed in Clackamas County, Oregon, by a settler. Signing on May 7 for the sixty-five Santiam Molalas was their headman, Coast-no. It had been the original intent of Superintendent Dart to obtain the consent of Indians west of the Cascade Mountains to be moved east of that range, but the Molalas, like other Willamette Indians, refused to leave their homes. That they had previously lived east of the Cascade Mountains was of little importance to them. On January 9, 1855, with the Clackamases, Clowwewallas, and others, they signed a treaty (10 Stat. 1143, ratified March 3, 1855) that ceded all of the Willamette Valley to the United States. They also agreed to relocate to a reservation at such time and place that one should be made available for them. On October 13, 1855, before they were removed, and as war clouds were forming over the Yakama country in the interior on the northeast, Oregon superintendent of Indian affairs Joel Palmer issued a proclamation, ordering the Willamette Valley Indians to remain in temporarily designated areas. Settlers regarded their absence from those places without permission as endangering the peace. Indians who were unable to account for their presence were to be arrested, retained in custody, and sent to county jails or to the military's Fort Vancouver.

Fred Yelkis, a Molala. The Molalas originally lived in central Oregon but were pushed west of the Cascade Mountains by other Indians. Once there, they divided into northern and southern branches of the tribe.

Courtesy of the Smithsonian Institution.

The temporary reservation of the main band of Northern Molalas was located on Silver Creek at the base of the Cascade Mountains. The reservation of the Molalas in the Santiam area was quite mountainous with some agricultural lands, parts of which settlers claimed as their own. When, on October 8, 1855, the Rogue wars flared anew, Superintendent Palmer persuaded the Southern Molala chief and about thirty of his tribe to go on the Umpqua Reservation in the Umpqua Valley. The group arrived there on November 7, 1855. Because of actual and potential conflicts with whites, the Southern Molalas signed a treaty on December 21, 1855 (12 Stat. 981, ratified March 8, 1859 and proclaimed April 27, 1859) by which they were required to cede their lands, confederate with the Yoncallas and the Upper Umpquas, and remove with those tribes to the headwaters of the Yamhill River, an area later known as the Grand Ronde Reservation. Having set out on January 10, 1856, these peoples finally arrived on the Grand Ronde on February 2, 1856. They were later moved to the reservation established on November 9, 1856, on the coast that was to be called the Siletz.

On April 3, 1950, descendants of the Southern Molalas were awarded $34,996.85 by the Court of Claims (Case No. 45231) for recovery of the Umpqua Reservation lands reserved for them by the December 21, 1855, treaty in which they had confederated with the Umpquas and the Yoncallas. That treaty had stated that they would share in the Umpqua Reservation, but in fact they never occupied any portion of it. After only two months' residency there, they were removed to the Grand Ronde.

There are no modern speakers of the Molala language. Pacific Northwest newspapers at one time carried stories of the last of various Oregon Indians. One such story appeared in the *Portland Journal* on July 3, 1957, reporting Fred Yelkis to be the last of the Molala tribe.

Suggested Readings:

Albert S. Gatschet, "The Molale Tribe Raided by the Cayuses," Ms. no. 2029, National Anthropological Archives Collection, Smithsonian Institution, Washington, D.C.

MOSES COLUMBIA
(See **Sinkiuse.***)*

MUCKLESHOOT TRIBE, MUCKLESHOOT RESERVATION

The name "Muckleshoot" derives from the Buklshuhls, a Puget Sound-basin Salish people who formerly lived in the White and Green river valleys of western Washington State. The Muckleshoot tribe was an amalgam of several peoples. The tribal name first appeared in government records about 1868 denoting the Indians on the Muckleshoot Reservation. There was controversy later as to whether the Muckleshoots were, in fact, a treaty tribe, a dispute that had significant implications for the Muckleshoots in their dealings with the State of Washington over fishing rights. One group from which the Muckleshoot Tribe was formed was the Skopahmish, or Green River Indians, who had formerly occupied the central Green River valley and later moved to the Muckleshoot Reservation. Another group, the Smulkamish, had inhabited the vicinity of today's Enumclaw before they too relocated to the Muckleshoot Reservation. Another group, the Skekomish (Stakamish), or White River Indians, moved to the Port Madison Reservation. Important Muckleshoot villages were the Yelaco, formed of seventeen houses at the confluence of Green River and Suice Creek; the Quiats on the Green River; and the Cublokum, which consisted of one large building on Boise Creek. The present Muckleshoots are known officially as the Muckleshoot Tribe, Muckleshoot Reservation, Washington.

Unlike many Coastal Salish peoples, the Muckleshoots did not live on the shores of Puget Sound but were located a few miles inland. Nonetheless, salmon fishing was important in their economy, which was based on other types of fishing as well and on hunting and gathering. The Muckleshoots traveled eastward to the Cascade Mountains to trap goats from whose wool they made blankets and burial robes. Hunting in that area also were the Klickitat Indians, to whom the Muckleshoots were related, as they were to the Puyallups.

Location: The irregularly shaped 3,440-acre Muckleshoot Reservation lies near the city of Auburn, Washington, and along the White River, which was formerly called the Stokamish, or Smalhko, by Indians.

Numbers: In 1854 Washington territorial governor and superintendent of Indian affairs Isaac Stevens reported the Smulkamish at 50, the Skopahmish also at 50, and the Skekomish at 30. However, at that time the ethnologist George Gibbs listed the Smulkamish at 8, the Skopahmish at 50, and the Skekomish at 30. In 1937 the U.S. Office of Indian Affairs reported 194 Muckleshoots. In 1996 there were 1,200 enrolled members of the Muckleshoot Tribe. As of February 2008, the tribe counted approximately 2,100 members, with an on or near the reservation population of about 3,300 in 2009.

History: The Muckleshoot Reservation in essence grew out of the Medicine Creek Treaty of December 26, 1854, when Governor Stevens effected a treaty with bands of Nisquallis, Puyallups, and other Indians of lower Puget Sound. No mention in that treaty was made of the Muckleshoots per se, but the treaty scheduled tribes from the Green and White rivers to remove to the Nisqually Reservation. The treaty also provided that, for their welfare, they could be relocated to a more suitable place, and on December 5, 1856, Stevens recommended the establishment of the Muckleshoot Reservation between the Green and White rivers on Muckleshoot Prairie. The president approved that plan on January 20, 1857. The reservation had formerly been a military tract. An executive order on April 9, 1874, gave definite metes and bounds to the reservation, which at the time consisted of 3,532.72 acres. Thirty-nine Muckleshoots were later allotted 3,191.97 acres of the reservation. During the Indian War of 1855–56, the Muckleshoots, under headmen Kitsap and Nelson, joined the warring coalition against the Americans. They were involved in the so-called White River Massacre of October 28, 1855, in which eight Americans were killed. After the war, a Roman Catholic church was built on the reservation. The Indians complained of the encroachments of settlers, a problem that was particularly acute on the Muckleshoot Reservation because of its fragmented and irregular configuration, which caused its residents to enter into disputes with the government over its dimensions.

Government and Claims: The constitution of the Muckleshoot Tribe, Muckleshoot Reservation, Washington, since amended, was approved on May 13, 1936, under the Indian Reorganization Act (48 Stat. 984). Its charter was ratified on October 21, 1936. The governing body is the Muckleshoot Indian Tribal Council, to which three new members are elected annually. The Muckleshoot Reservation is one of several under the jurisdiction of the Western Washington Indian Agency located at Everett, Washington, which is staffed to provide professional and technical services in connection with reservation tribes and their economic development. The Muckleshoot Tribe is also a member of an intertribal court system formed in 1978 by several reservation tribes. The tribe levies taxes on liquor, depositing the moneys into either a general fund for its members or a fund set aside for land acquisition. Tribal members also operate a fish hatchery. The tribe has business licensing, zoning, land-use ordinances, and a water code. They run a bingo operation.

The Muckleshoots were denied their land claim in the Court of Claims in their suit *Duwamish Indians* v. *United States* (79 C.C1. 530) (1934) on the grounds that the United States had no basis on which to award judgment, because it had no treaty with them. The Indian Claims Commission, however, found (in Docket 98) that the tribe had possessed 101,620 acres of aboriginal land valued at $86,377, and consequently, on March 8, 1959, the commission ordered that the Muckleshoot Tribe be awarded that amount.

Contemporary Life and Culture: As of 1975 there were 1,201.26 acres of trust lands on the reservation. The allotments are covered with second-growth timber, save for small cleared homesites interspersed with non-Indian farmlands. Some Muckleshoots are employed by industries in the city of Auburn or by tribal government in various state and federal programs. Some engage in fishing, logging, and agriculture. As mentioned, the tribe manages fish-hatching facilities. It also has a community center, community housing, Head Start facilities, a library, a medical-dental clinic, an educational training program, a fisheries patrol, and a youth group program, including foster care. It has a water system and various housing improvement programs, one that is called House My People. Cooperation exists between the tribe and the public school system in Auburn. The reservation has a Pentecostal and an Indian Shaker church, and a Catholic church that was restored in 1980.

In April 1995 the tribe opened the Muckleshoot Casino on twenty-five acres in Auburn, Washington. Since then, the facility has undergone four expansions with the addition of a seven-floor, 2,700-space parking garage. Twenty percent of all tribal gaming revenue is set aside for educational purposes. In 2003 Muckleshoot Seafood Products entered into agreement with Safeway, whereby the large food chain began carrying fresh, tribally caught coho salmon in five western states. This agreement marked the first time that a Pacific Northwest tribe has marketed its own brand of fresh wild salmon through a major retailer. In June 2006, the Muckleshoots concluded an agreement with the Seattle City Council for $42 million for the protection of the Cedar River and a year later purchased the historic Salish Lodge & Spa near Snoqualmie for $62.5 million. At the same time, they invested another $3 million in a manufactured-home company op-

Eva Jerry (1915–1992) pictured here at the age of seventy-two in 1986. She was a member of the Indian Shaker Church and raised ten children. She had thirty grandchildren and eleven great-grand-children. She taught the Muckleshoot language in the Auburn, Washington, school district and in the tribal school. Jerry served as judge for the tribal court. The Muckleshoot Reservation southeast of Seattle, Washington, is characterized by its highly irregular configuration. One must have one-eighth-degree Muckle-shoot blood quantum to be a member.

Courtesy of the Muckleshoot Tribe.

erating out of California as well as putting additional money in the Four Seasons Hotel and Residences in downtown Seattle. Already the owner of the land on which the Emerald Downs Racetrack sits, the Muckleshoots in September 2007 offered to donate twenty-six acres—which the tribe had purchased in 2005 for $3.2 million—for a new arena for the Seattle SuperSonics. The maneuver, which ultimately failed, was intended to keep the National Basketball Association (NBA) franchise in Seattle. In early 2008 the Muckleshoots contacted several other tribes concerning the feasibility of forming a consortium to purchase seventy acres on the south end of the Las Vegas strip in Nevada for the purpose of opening the first Native-owned casino there. The Muckleshoots also operate the 20,000-seat White River Amphitheatre, Muckleshoot Bingo, Muckleshoot Smoke Shop and Liquor Store, a video store, the $1.7-million Muckleshoot Mall, and Muckleshoot Market & Deli. The total workforce of the tribe is around twelve hundred employees, making it the second-largest employer in southeast King County, behind only the Boeing Company.

Education for young tribal members, from birth through age three, is delivered through Muckleshoot Child Care. Muckleshoot Tribal School, which opened in 1984, places an emphasis on Native history, art, dance, and customs and the tribe's Whulshootseed language. In 1997 high school grades were added, and four years later the first two graduates received their diplomas. The tribe broke ground in November 2007 on a new $40-million, 107,000-square-foot K-12 school that opened with 500 students in the 2009-10 academic year. The tribe also operates Muckleshoot Tribal College through which students can earn their associate's degree.

Medical care is provided to tribal members through the on-site Muckleshoot Medical Center. Services include comprehensive medical, behavioral, dental, clinical, and diabetic care.

Special Events and Celebrations: Skopabsh Days is held each year in August, attracting thousands of visitors for the three-day event that features Indian arts and crafts, traditional clothing, and Native cooking. Each July the Muckleshoots host their Muckleshoot Sobriety Powwow.

Suggested Readings:

American Friends Service Committee, *Uncommon Controversy: Fishing Rights of the Muckleshoot, Puyallup, and Nisqually Indians* (Seattle: University of Washington, 1970); Marke Dickinson and Bill Wiggins, *A Single Acre, A Sovereign Effort: A Model for Muckleshoot Land-Use and Economic Development* (Cambridge, Mass.: Malcolm Weiner Center for Social Policy and John F. Kennedy School of Government, 1995); Barbara Lane, "Anthropological Report on the Identity and Treaty Status of the Muckleshoot Indians: Political and Economic Aspects of Indian-White Culture Contact in Western Washington in the Mid-19th Century, May 10, 1973," photocopy in Washington State Library, Olympia; Kent D. Richards, "Agrarianism, United States Indian Policy, and the Muckleshoot Reservation" in William L. Lang, ed. *Centennial West: Essays on the Northern Tier States* (Seattle: University of Washington Press, 1991); Patricia Slettvet Noel, *Muckleshoot Indian History* (Auburn, Wash.: Auburn School District, 1980); Leslie Lincoln, et al., *Native American Canoes: Paddle to Seattle, 1989* (Olympia: Washington State Centennial Commission, 1989); Kenneth D. Tollefson, "Remembering the Old Ways," *Columbia: The Magazine of Northwest History* 7, no. 3 (1993); Muckleshoot Tribe, *The Muckleshoot Tribe* (Auburn, Wash.: The Muckleshoot Tribe, 1999).

MULTNOMAH

(Upper Chinookan Division of Chinookan)

The Multnomahs, whose name means "down river," lived on Sauvies Island on the lower Columbia River. Portland lies on the south in the county in Oregon that bears their name. The Multnomahs were of the Clackamas division of the Upper Chinookan linguistic stock. Early writers called the Willamette River the Multnomah. Tradition has it that in the distant past Kalapuyan peoples from the south displaced Multnomahs, presumably those of the Willamette Valley, though it is also said that the two peoples fought a battle for possession of Sauvies Island. Some ethnologists have grouped lower Columbia River Multnomahs into ten bands, one of which was the Multnomahs proper. The American explorers Meriwether Lewis and William Clark observed one of those bands, the Clahnaquahas of Sauvies Island. Under the heading Wappatoo Indians, the ethnologist James Mooney estimated the population of the Multnomahs and neighboring tribes at thirty-six hundred. In 1805–1806 they were listed by Lewis and Clark at eight hundred. The Reverend Samuel Parker visited their homelands in 1834 and found that they had suffered catastrophic losses from the epidemic diseases that had raged along the Columbia River in the late eighteenth and early nineteenth centuries. Some ethnologists believe that they had become absorbed into other tribes as late as 1910. In 1907 the number of the once-populous Wappatoo Indians was given as ten individuals. *See* **Clackamas**.

NALTUNNETUNNE

(Athabaskan)

The Naltunnetunnes spoke an Athabaskan dialect distinct from that of the Tututnis (Coast Rogues). They lived along the Oregon coast between the Tututnis and another Athabaskan people, the Chetcos, until they were collected and moved north to the Siletz Reservation. Like their neighbors, they experienced a population decline, numbering only seventy-seven in 1877.

NESPELEM

(Interior Division, Salishan)

The Nespelems lived in what is now north-central Washington State, primarily on the Nespelem River (a Columbia River tributary), on which today there is a town called Nespelem. They also lived downstream along the Columbia to its confluence with the Okanogan River. The tribe's name derived from their Native word meaning "large open meadow," "barren hill," or "prairie of flat open country." The Nespelems were among the Indians of the northern interior whose traditions told of an ash fall from an eruption of Mount Saint Helens in about the year 1802. In their eagerness to appease the Great Spirit for that catastrophe, they neglected to gather food, and some reportedly starved to death.

The Nespelems were closely related to the Sanpoils, who lived primarily along the river that bears their name, which enters the Columbia a few miles upstream from the mouth of the Nespelem. Because of the cultural similarity of the two peoples, anthropologists grouped them together for study, as did government officials for purposes of enumeration. Like the Sanpoils, the Nespelems had no treaty with the United States and remained outside the control of agency officials. Both tribes were angered when the federal government in the 1880s permitted other Indians to move onto the Colville Reservation,

Que-Que-tas-ka, a woman of the Nespelem Tribe of north-central Washington. Her husband, Nespelem George, had a reputation among government officials in the early twentieth century as a progressive. By contrast, the Nespelems traditionally avoided accepting government aid or control.

Courtesy of Frank Avery.

which was located on the homelands of the two tribes. On the reservation, the Nespelems and Sanpoils declined annuities and other government aid and refused to reveal their population. To a considerable extent, their lack of cooperation was to a considerable extent due to their nativist Dreamer religion, against which Roman Catholic missionaries competed for converts. By the beginning of the twentieth century, the Nespelems were recognized as a tribal entity separate from the Sanpoils. At that time, their economies varied somewhat: whereas the Sanpoils sought to remain independent largely through hunting, fishing, and farming, the Nespelems, characterized by some as industrious and thrifty, pursued the same goal mainly by raising grain and other crops.

The differing economies might help explain why the censuses of the two tribes were recorded separately. The Nespelems were said to number sixty-two in 1892 and forty-five in 1910, a date by which the Indians acknowledged there were but few still living. In 1959, statistics revealed only seventeen full-blood-degree Nespelems on the Colville Reservation and eight of that blood quantum outside it. *See* **Confederated Tribes of the Colville Reservation.**

Suggested Readings:

Verne F. Ray, "The Sanpoil and Nespelem Salishan Peoples of Northeastern Washington," *University of Washington Publications in Anthropology* 5 (1933); Robert H. Ruby and John A. Brown, *Half-Sun on the Columbia: A Biography of Chief Moses* (Norman: University of Oklahoma Press, 1965); James A. Teit, "The

Middle Columbia Salish," *University of Washington Publications in Anthropology* 2, no. 4 (1928) and "The Salishan Tribes of the Western Plateaus," *Forty-fifth Annual Report of the Bureau of American Ethnology* (Washington, D.C.: Government Printing Office, 1930).

NEZ PERCE

(Shahaptian)

Nimiipuu

The People or Children of the Coyote

Some scholars believe the name "Nez Perce" derived from *nez pres,* meaning "pierced nose," given by early-day French-Canadian trappers. According to tradition the tribe first heard their name applied to them when some of their members traveled to St. Louis a quarter century after their 1805–1806 meeting with the American explorers Meriwether Lewis and William Clark, who referred to them as the Chopunnish. They called themselves Nimiipuu (variously spelled), meaning "we the people" or "the real people." They were also called Tsoop-Nit-Pa-Loo or "the walking out people." The tribe's language consisted of two dialects, Upper and Lower Nez Perce, of the Shahaptian linguistic family.

According to tribal understanding, this most numerous branch of Shahaptian speakers was created at Kamiah on a branch of the Clearwater River, a Snake River affluent in central Idaho. They believed that the ark of the Flood rested on a mountain in that vicinity. The Nez Perces lived in at least twenty-seven permanent villages on the Clearwater River and its branches. There were eleven villages on the Snake River between the mouths of the Clearwater and Imnaha rivers, three permanent villages on the Salmon River and its tributaries, six permanent villages south of the Grande Ronde River (the area of Oregon's Wallowa Mountains and river valley, where the famed Nez Perce, Young Chief Joseph, lived) and on the western Snake River, and three permanent villages between the Grande Ronde and Snake rivers west of the Idaho-Washington border. There were also several villages along the Snake between the Clearwater and Tucannon rivers.

The Nez Perces acted as intermediaries in trade between the Flatheads on the northeast and the residents of the Columbia Plateau on the north and west. They were generally on favorable terms with those peoples but much less so with tribes to the south, such as the Bannocks and Shoshones, and with the Blackfeet to the east. A handsome and hardy people, the Nez Perces were noted for several things: their traditional friendship with Americans, a posture that some believe began with their meeting Lewis and Clark; their horsemanship, which they developed after acquiring that animal around 1720; and finally, the poignant story of Young

Joseph and a small Nez Perce band fleeing government troops in 1877.

Before they had horses, the Nez Perces lived in separate but ethnically and culturally related villages. With horses they tended to coalesce into larger and more cohesive settlements organized along the same sociopolitical pattern. Lapwai Creek, a Clearwater tributary, was considered the dividing line between the buffalo-hunting Nez Perces and their primarily fishing and hunting neighbors. With horses the buffalo hunters traveled mainly the ancient well-known Lolo Trail through the Bitterroot Mountains that Lewis and Clark followed and that U.S. Highway 12 follows today. Sometimes the Nez Perces moved north through the Bitterroot Valley into the country of the Flatheads, whom they joined for a time on buffalo hunts. From the peoples of the Great Plains who hunted buffalo, the Nez Perces acquired certain cultural traits. Their intratribal organization was especially strengthened by the use of horses in times of war, replacing the old village controls that prevailed in times of peace. In terms of decision making, the Nez Perces acted in councils under rules of unanimity. Chiefs and headmen were elected on the basis of merit.

Location: Formerly the Nez Perces lived in numerous scattered and independent communities in a wide area of present-day north-central Idaho and parts of southwestern Washington and northeastern Oregon. Today most of their descendants are members of the Nez Perce Tribe of Idaho, Nez Perce Reservation, and live on or near the reservation on farms and in towns and cities such as Lapwai, Spalding, Culdesac, Craigmont, Ferdinand, Ahsahka, Orofino, Kamiah, Kooskia, Stites, Nezperce, Winchester, Lewiston, Grangeville, and Cottonwood. The last three communities are not located on the reservation.

Numbers: In 1805–1806 Lewis and Clark estimated the Nez Perce population at 6,000, 2,000 more than their approximated numbers of a quarter century earlier. In 1827 a Hudson's Bay Company official placed them at 1,450. In 1901 they numbered 1,567. The constancy of their population is partially a reflection of their relative isolation, which spared them from the epidemics that proved so disastrous to Indians living on or near routes of American travel and settlement. Further evidence of that isolation was seen as late as 1950 when their census revealed 608 full-blood-degree Nez Perces in Idaho. That was a higher Native blood quantum than existed in most other Pacific Northwest tribes. Since then, however, there has been considerable intertribal and interracial mixing. In 1950, there were 1,261 Nez Perces on their reservation—in addition to 15 enrolled on the Colville Reservation and 115 on other reservations. In 1985, the Nez Perces numbered 2,015 and in 1989, 2,455. Today there are approximately 3,100 enrolled members, about 1,800 of whom live on the reservation.

History: During the precontact and early contact periods the Nez Perces were involved in conflicts with powerful Plains tribes on the buffalo ranges that extended at one time west from the Rocky Mountains into the intermontane Nez Perce homelands. As the buffalo retreated eastward during the first half of the nineteenth century, the Nez Perces allied with other Shahaptian and Salish peoples, and with them they hunted buffalo east of the Rockies, where they were challenged by Blackfeet and other Plains tribes. On the south they traded with and fought against the Bannocks, the Paiutes, and the Shoshones. At a very early time they were obtaining Native goods from great distances. When Lewis and Clark were among them, they exhibited goods acquired from the Spaniards far to the south and from white mariners along the Pacific Coast. At that time they possessed few firearms but acquired more shortly afterward with the advent of the inland fur trade.

In 1831 the Nez Perces were among the Native delegations who traveled to St. Louis to receive the "White man's Book of Heaven," the Bible. Among those who responded to their plea were missionaries of the American Board of Commissioners for Foreign Missions, including the Reverend Henry H. Spalding and his wife, Eliza, who in 1836 established a mission at Lapwai. Spalding introduced them to such novelties as domestic animals and a printing press. Another mission was established among them in 1839 at Kamiah under the Reverend Asa Bowen Smith. One of Spalding's first converts was Old Joseph, father of the Young Joseph who helped lead his band in retreat from army forces in 1877. In December 1842, the Nez Perces met with Indian agent Dr. Elijah White to ratify his laws, which to a great extent imposed American legal mores on them. At that time, the first head chieftaincy of all the Nez Perces was established. The American Board mission was terminated shortly after the 1847 killing of the Reverend Dr. Marcus Whitman, his wife, Narcissa, and others at their Waiilatpu Mission in the Walla Walla Valley.

Left unchanged was the division of the Nez Perce peoples into Christian and nativist blocs. Intratribal conflict between pro-American Christians and the anti-American nativist faction rose to the fore in the brief Cayuse War that followed the Whitman affair and in the Indian War of the middle 1850s. At the 1855 Walla Walla treaty council, dissatisfaction with the terms offered, which precipitated the war, was evident among traditionalist Nez Perces who were embittered by the pro-American faction that had secured tribal adherence to the treaty. The Nez Perces recorded the treaty council proceedings on paper in their own language. Under the treaty, they yielded their vast homelands of about 11 million acres in Idaho and Oregon for a reservation of about 7,694,270 acres. After gold was discovered on the reservation in 1860, Americans were permitted to intrude on it, and the town of Lewiston was founded. On April 10, 1861, government officials effected an unratified agreement whereby that portion of the reservation lying north of the Snake and Clearwater rivers was to be opened in common to Americans and Indians for mining purposes, but Indian root grounds on the reservation were not to be occupied. No Americans were permitted residence on the reservation south of the above-mentioned line except on a right-of-way lead-

Silas Whitman, 1977, at the White Bird (Idaho) battle-field, site of the 1877 confrontation between the Nez Perces and the U.S. military. Whitman comes from a strong Nez Perce Presbyterian Church background, but like other American Indians today, he has turned to traditional Native religion. Nez Perces had a reputation for friendliness toward Americans from the time of Lewis and Clark's visit in 1805. Their one conflict with the United States, in 1877, involved only a portion of the tribe who were seeking to escape from army troops.

Courtesy of *Lewiston (Ida.) Tribune.*

ing to the mining district. In keeping with a provision that a military patrol force could be stationed on the reservation, troops were sent there. Commissions sent by the government to negotiate with the Nez Perces for their reservation secured the cession of June 9, 1863 (14 Stat. 647, ratified April 17, 1867), that left the tribe with a reservation consisting of only 1,182.76 square miles, one-tenth of its original size.

Traditionalist opposition to that land loss caused the Nez Perces to abandon the head chieftaincy established by Dr. White. In the early 1870s, the Reverend Spalding, who had returned among the Nez Perces after a long absence, conducted revival meetings that strengthened the Protestant-Presbyterian Nez Perce community in the face of the Roman Catholic and native traditionalist intrusions. Presbyterian control was bolstered under the Ulysses S. Grant Peace Policy of the 1870s, which gave that church management over the Nez Perce Agency. Unhappy with what he saw as contradictions between Christian American preachments and practices, Old Joseph tore up his New Testament, while Young Joseph, also embittered, tried unsuccessfully to retain his ancestral homelands in the Wallowa country. A reservation had been established there by executive order on June 16, 1873, but had been withdrawn by another order on June 10, 1875. Such developments led to the involvement of Young Joseph and his band in the Nez Perce War with the United States. In 1877, during that conflict, the Indian chiefs with Young Joseph— Looking Glass and White Bird— engaged the army in several bloody encounters as they retreated about eighteen hundred miles, generally in a northeasterly direction. Although a small number escaped to Canada, 375 others were captured and herded to the Indian Territory (Oklahoma). After great suffering there, some returned to Lapwai, but 118 adults, including Young Joseph and Yellow Bull, with 16 children and 14 infants were moved to the Colville Reservation, where they settled under the nominal authority of Chief Moses.

Government and Claims: The Nez Perce Tribe of Idaho, Nez Perce Reservation, has a constitution and bylaws that were approved by the United States on April 2, 1948, and ratified by the tribe in general assembly on April 30, 1948. The governing body is the Nez Perce Tribal Executive Committee whose members are elected at large by the General Council. The Executive Committee administers and guides tribal economic development, improvement of human and natural resources, and the investment of income and assets of the tribe.

In July 1951, the Nez Perces filed three petitions with the Indian Claims Commission. One claim (Docket 175) was for additional compensation for the 1855 cession of their aboriginal lands. At the same time the Colvilles, or (Chief) Joseph Nez Perces of the Colville Reservation, filed a claim (Docket 180) for compensation for the loss of the same lands in the same cession. At the order of the commission, the claims were combined in a new docket (175) on February 27, 1953. On August 25, 1971, the commission awarded the Nez Perces $3,550,000, of which 86.5854 percent went to the Nez Perces of Idaho. A third claim (Docket 179), filed in July 1951 by the Confederated Tribes of the Colville on behalf of the Colville Nez Perces, was for governmental mismanagement of tribal funds and assets. On November 5, 1968, those of Joseph's band living in Idaho filed an intervenor claim. On April 29, 1970, the commission issued an award of $119,071.78, of which the Colville Nez Perces received two-thirds and the Idaho Nez Perces received the remainder. An additional claim (Docket 179-A) was filed by the Nez Perce Tribe of Idaho alone for mismanagement after June 30, 1951. Since the claim was not settled by September 30, 1978, when the life of the Indian Claims Commission had expired, it was transferred to the Court of Claims.

Another claim (Docket 186) was filed for compensation for the withdrawal of the reservation in the Wallowa country, which had resulted in the ultimate destruction of the Wallowa, or Joseph Band, as a viable economic, social, and political entity. That band had originally brought a claim before the Court of Claims (95 C.Cl. 11) in 1941, but the court had held that they were not representative of the "roaming bands" for whom the reservation had been established and that the 1873 order creating the reservation did not imply their exclusive aboriginal claim to the land because the reservation had been conceived for so-called "nonroaming" Nez Perces as well as the Joseph Band. The Indian Claims Commission decided that the executive order of 1873 did give the Joseph Band a compensable interest on the Wallowa Reservation, even though the bands under

Joseph of Looking Glass, Big Thunder, White Bird, and Eagle from the Light had not accepted the 1873 order. On October 31, 1974, the commission awarded these Nez Perces $725,000, of which 150/268, or $406,542.07, went to the Joseph Band on the Colville Reservation and the balance to the Nez Perces of Idaho.

A claim (Docket 175-A) was separated from Docket 175 and filed as such on December 4, 1957, for additional compensation for 6,932,270 acres of the Nez Perce Reservation ceded to the United States on June 9, 1863. The consideration that the petitioners had received had been $352,394.94. From an award of $4,650,000 from which that consideration would be deducted, plus a compromised value for offsets of $140,000, the Nez Perces received an award on June 17, 1960, of $4,157,605.06. On April 7, 1964, the Indian Claims Commission dismissed a claim (Docket 175-B) for an additional payment for the cession in 1894 of 549,559 acres from the 762,000-acre reservation after allotments had been agreed to on May 1, 1893. The commission decided that the consideration the Nez Perces had received for that cession was not unconscionable. The Nez Perces then took their case to the Court of Claims as Appeal No. 5-64 (decided July 15, 1966, 176 C. Cl. 815), wherein the court found that the compensation allowed for the cession was the minimum amount and referred the case back to the commission. On November 14, 1969, the commission approved a final award of $3,022,575, minus the consideration of $1,634,664 paid after the 1894 cession. On the $1,387,911 due the tribe from 1894, the Claims Commission allowed 5 percent interest. The defending United States then appealed to the Court of Claims, which ruled against payment of interest to the tribe. Of the remaining reservation lands, 180,657 acres were allotted and the other lands placed in trust for the tribe.

A claim (Docket 180-A) separated from Docket 180 was for compensation for trespass on and gold taken from the reservation before the cession of a large part of it to the United States. The Nez Perces had previously litigated such a claim before the Court of Claims (95 C.Cl. 1). The decision on October 6, 1941, had been favorable to the tribe. The Claims Commission, accepting the petitioner's argument that the Court of Claims had no jurisdiction to determine equitable claims of Indians, on December 31, 1959, awarded the Nez Perces $3 million, of which the Idaho Nez Perces received $2,168,761 and the Colville Nez Perces received the balance. The tribe has also been awarded $2.8 million for loss of fishing rights at Celilo Falls on the Columbia River, which are now covered by the waters of The Dalles Dam. The cash allotments of $1,400 to each tribal member were to be spent on home improvements, farm machinery, and similar purposes. The tribe, with twenty-four others throughout the western United States, filed claims (Dockets 523-71 and 524-71) that reached the Court of Claims for mismanagement of Indian Claims Commission judgment funds and for mismanagement of other funds such as Individual Indian Money accounts held in trust by the United States. The Nez Perce Tribe was awarded $232,905.25 in 1980.

Horace P. Axtell, or Isluumts (b. 1924), is a Nez Perce writer, linguist, movie advisor, and teacher. Axtell served in the army during World War II, and his great-grandfather fought at the battle of the Big Hole and died at the battle of the Bears Paw during the Nez Perce War of 1877.

Courtesy of Steve Hanks, *Lewiston (Ida.) Tribune.*

Contemporary Life and Culture: About two-thirds of the Nez Perce Reservation is in individual allotments, some of which have been sold to non-Indians. Trust lands as of 1975 totaled 87,015.39 acres. About 80 percent of the total reservation acreage is leased to non-Indians. Farm and timber lands produce most of the tribal income.

Head Start early-childhood-education programs are maintained for children ages birth to five. Children attend public schools located in their respective communities such as Lapwai and Kamiah, and an increasing number are completing high school and pursuing advanced academic and vocational training. The tribe, like several others in the Pacific Northwest, administers a scholarship fund for the postsecondary education of qualifying students and, in some cases, provides direct assistance for the unmet financial needs of college students. Since 1995, the tribe has operated a "Students for Success" program that aims to immerse youth in cultural practices and knowledge as a strategy for preventing tobacco, alcohol, and drug abuse.

The Nez Perces operate a printing plant that does job printing for the tribe and others. They also have a marina at Dvorshak Dam on the Snake River, and there is a limestone quarry on the reservation. Among the tribe's cultural achievements was the completion in 1961 of a translation into the Nez Perce language of *Webster's Collegiate Dictionary* by Corbett Lawyer, a grandson of the famous Chief Lawyer. The Nez Perces were among Shahaptian speakers who, in the later 1970s, alphabetized their language. By 1980 linguist Haruo Aoki had completed the transcription of Nez Perce texts, a dictionary, and the first authoritative Nez Perce grammar.

In 1977, as evidence of their newly revitalized tribal identity, the Nez Perces commemorated the conflict between Chief Joseph's band and the United States in sacred rites on the battlefield at White Bird, Idaho. From that event they returned to their homes resolved to conduct their own affairs and create their own destiny in an atmosphere of revived spiritism and tribalism.

Clearwater River Casino & Resort outside Lapwai includes a fifty-room luxury hotel with suites, an arcade, a restaurant, deli, and lounge, bingo parlor, events center, gift shop, and RV park. Nearby is the Nez Perce Express gas station and convenience store. A second casino, It'se Ye Ye, is operated at Kamiah. Departments of fisheries, forestry, wildlife, water, land, and natural resources manage and preserve the resources of the reservation. Law enforcement is through the Nez Perce Tribal Police Department.

Established in 2003, the Nez Perce Tribal Children's Trust Fund is a self-sustaining and comprehensive children's service program that includes the Nez Perce Tribal Children's Home and Advocacy Center, Child Protection Services, Foster Care Placement, support services, youth development and eventually internships and college scholarships for specified social service needs. Joining with six other Inland Northwest tribes, the Nez Perce helped to establish The Healing Lodge of the Seven Nations in Spokane, a drug and alcohol treatment center. The Pi-Nee-Waus (Lapwai), Teweepuu (Orofino), and Wa-a'yas (Kamiah) community centers provide recreational, athletic, educational, and cultural opportunities to tribal members of all ages. In 1997 Nimiipuu Health assumed charge of tribal health from the BIA and maintains clinics in Lapwai in a 43,000-square-foot facility that opened in 2004 and in Kamiah in a 7,000-square-foot building that opened in 2001.

In July 2008 the Nez Perces and the State of Idaho signed an agreement whereby, for the first time in fourteen years, state lottery tickets could be sold on the reservation. Through a joint project with the University of Idaho, Nez Perce elders have been contributing to an oral history website designed to preserve Indian history and culture. Another major Nez Perce repository is the Nez Perce National Historical Park museum and visitor center, which is located north of Lapwai at the Spalding Mission site. In the past decade, the Nez Perces have experienced a growing presence in the Wallowa region of Oregon. For example, in 1997 they participated in what has come to be known as "Nez Perce homecoming" and accepted 160 acres on which they maintain an interpretive center, a permanent campground, and powwow sites. The tribe has also been reviving their renowned horse culture, beginning in 1994 with a breeding program that has expanded to include the introduction of a new breed that crosses their Appaloosa with a lean, central-Asian breed. In 2008 the Nez Perce tribe was seeking to expand its bison hunt in Montana.

Special Events and Celebrations: On Lincoln's Birthday games and war-dance contests are held at Kamiah. In the first week of March the tribe sponsors the E-pah-tes championship Indian games and war dances at Lapwai. The Spring Root Festival is held in the first week in May at Lapwai, followed by the Talmaks in early summer at Craigmont, an annual camp meeting of religious services. Games and races are put on in conjunction with Talmaks on the Fourth of July. In the second week in August Pi-Nee-waus Days is celebrated at Lapwai. It features parades, war dances, Indian games, and tribal exhibits. In the third week of August at the Mud Spring Camp at Craigmont, Indian games and feasts are enjoyed. Observed in late November at Lapwai is the Thanksgiving Day celebration during which games and war dances are staged by the tribe. *See also* **Confederated Tribes of the Colville Reservation.**

Suggested Readings:

Horace Axtell and Margo Aragon, *A Little Bit of Wisdom: Conversations with a Nez Perce Elder* (Lewiston, Ida.: Confluence Press, 1997); Dennis Baird, et al., *The Nez Perce Nation Divided: Firsthand Accounts of Events Leading to the 1863 Treaty* (Moscow: University of Idaho Press, 2002); Francis Haines, *The Nez Percés: Tribesmen of the Columbia Plateau* (Norman: University of Oklahoma Press, 1955); Bette Lynch Husted, *Above the Clearwater: Living on Stolen Land* (Corvallis: Oregon State University Press, 2004); Elizabeth Jean James, "Forging an Indigenous Future: The Nez Perces, 1893–1934," Ph.D. dissertation, Arizona State University, 2002; Alvin M. Josephy, Jr., *The Nez Perce Indians and the Opening of the Northwest* (New Haven, Conn.: Yale University Press, 1965) and *Nez Perce Country* (Lincoln: University of Nebraska Press, 2007); Robert R. McCoy, *Chief Joseph, Yellow Wolf, and the Creation of Nez Perce History in the Pacific Northwest* (New York: Routledge, 2004); Kent Nerburn, *Chief Joseph and the Flight of the Nez Perce: The Untold Story of an American Tragedy* (New York: HarperSanFrancisco, 2005); J. Diane Pearson, *The Nez Perces in the Indian Territory: Nimiipuu Survival* (Norman: University of Oklahoma Press, 2008); Archie M. Phinney, "Numipu among the White Settlers," *Wicazo Sa Review* 17, no. 2 (2002); Allen P. Slickpoo, *Noon nee-me-poo (We, the Nez Perces)* (Lapwai, Ida.: Nez Perce Tribe of Idaho, 1973); Scott Thompson, *I Will Tell of My War Story: A Pictorial History of the Nez Perce War* (Seattle: University of Washington Press, 2000); Deward Walker, *Conflict and Schism in Nez Perce Acculturation: A Study of Religion and Politics* (Pullman: Washington State University Press, 1968); Elliott West, *The Last Indian War: The Nez Perce Story* (New York: Oxford University Press, 2009); Lee Whittlesey, "The Nez Perces in Yellowstone in 1877: A Comparison of Attempts to Deduce Their Route," *Montana The Magazine of Western History* 57, no. 1 (2007); Charles Wilkinson, "Celilo Falls: At the Center of Western History," *Oregon Historical Quarterly* 108, no. 4 (2007).

NISQUALLY

(Coastal Division, Salishan)

Squalli~Absch

The People of the Grass Country, the People of the River

The name "Nisqually" is said to derive from that for the Nisqually River, which flows into southern Puget Sound in western Washington. Some anthropologists suggest that there is no basis in fact for the tradition that the name came from *nez quarrés,* meaning "square noses," which supposedly was given by French-Canadian fur men. The Nisquallis spoke the Nisqually dialect of the Coastal Salishan language. They believed, as did other Puget Sound Natives, in the deity Dokibatt (variously spelled among the tribes) the Changer, who was the son of a woman and of a star. They held that Dokibatt had much to do with the world as it existed. The trickster Coyote, who figures prominently in the mythology of Indians east of the Cascade Mountains, appeared occasionally in Nisqually mythology. Some scholars see in that a cultural link between the Nisquallis and the peoples of the interior such as the Klickitats and their subdivisions west of the Cascade Mountains and the Yakamas with whom, like the Klickitats, the Nisquallis traded marine products and intermarried. From the Klickitats, the Nisquallis purchased horses that they pastured on their prairies, keeping more of these animals than did most tribes west of the Cascades.

Location: In former times the Nisquallis occupied at least forty villages on both banks of the Nisqually River and extending nearly thirty miles upstream from its delta. Today Nisquallis of the Nisqually Indian Tribe, Nisqually Reservation, Washington, live on their reservation on the west side of the Nisqually River in Thurston County or in the lower Nisqually Valley. Others live in the town of Yelm, about fifteen miles southeast of Washington's state capital, Olympia. Some tribal members have intermarried with Puyallups, Muckleshoots, and members of other tribes.

Numbers: The Nisquallis were said to have numbered 258 in 1838–39 and 200 five years later. At the time of their treaty with the United States at Medicine Creek in 1854, their population was less than 300. Some enumerations, not only in early times but also in the early twentieth century, recorded a census as high as 1,000, a figure that probably included other speakers of the Nisqually dialect of the Coastal Salishan language. As it did with those other speakers, disease played a major role in the Nisqually decline. In 2002, Nisqually tribal membership was listed at 507.

History: The first major contact between Nisquallis and whites occurred with the establishment of the Hudson's Bay Company's Fort Nisqually, which was erected in their homeland in 1833. Besides purchasing furs from the Nisquallis and surrounding tribes, the post traders tried to instruct them in the doctrines of the Christian faith. In 1839 the Roman Catholic secular priest, Father Modeste Demers, met several Nisquallis at Fort Nisqually, where he had gone to prevent the establishment of a Methodist mission. Two Methodist missionaries, John Richmond and William Wilson, came to Fort Nisqually in 1840 but remained only two years. A Catholic priest, Pascal Richard, established an Indian mission north of today's Olympia in 1848.

Around 1825 the Nisquallis and other Coastal Salish peoples attacked Cowichans of the southwestern coast of Vancouver Island, with the Nisquallis and their allies suffering heavy losses. At nearby Butlers Cove in 1855, Stikine Indian war parties from Canada raided Puget Sound settlers after a white man had murdered a Stikine chief in his employ.

The Medicine Creek Treaty of December 26, 1854, concluded with Washington territorial governor and superintendent of Indian affairs Isaac Stevens, established the original Nisqually Reservation. It consisted of 1,280 acres on Puget Sound near the mouth of Shenahnam Creek. By executive order on January 20, 1857, it was enlarged to 4,717 acres on both sides of the Nisqually River, a few miles above its mouth. Since the Nisqually Reservation lay on both sides of the river, the tribe claims the river, which comprises 210 additional acres, securing for its people the right to take fish, in the words of the treaty, "at usual and accustomed places." This provision has embroiled the Nisquallis and other tribes in controversy with state and federal governments.

A Nisqually headman, Leschi, was the leader of the Indian coalition against the Americans in the middle 1850s. To his death he declared that he had never signed the treaty. During the negotiations, when each headman was expected to make a map of his country in preparation for a composite one, Leschi reportedly refused to complete his, and he tore up a paper commissioning him as chief. He was angered that under the treaty his people were scheduled to settle at the mouth of McAllister Creek, a heavily wooded area and a poor place for them because they were accustomed to gathering marine foods at places such as the mouth of the Nisqually River. It also had been their practice to pasture their horses in the Nisqually Valley, the prairies of which they set afire to prevent forest growth and to promote the growth of grasses. As a result of Leschi's participation in the Yakama Indian War in 1855 (also known as the Puget Sound Indian War), in which Leschi was accused of killing an officer of the territorial militia, the headman was sentenced to hang on February 19, 1858. His people came to his defense, as did prominent members of the American community. But their support could not save him. He was condemned in the white men's court, and, as a white historian later recorded, "strangled according to the law." Not all of the Nisquallis were combatants during the war. Many were among the Indians of the lower Puget Sound whom an acting Indian agent, J. V. Weber, confined to Squaxin Island in 1855 to quarantine them from the hostilities.

On September 30, 1884, the acreage set aside for the Nisqually Reservation was divided into thirty family allotments distributed on both sides of the Nisqually River. The acreage did not include the river itself. After that, the tribe lived in peace for some time, harvesting fish from the Nisqually River and growing potatoes on prairie tracts. Tribal members received few government rations. Among other foods, they consumed as many as five hundred salmon annually per family. In the winter of 1917, the U.S. Army, without warning, moved onto Nisqually lands and ordered the residents from their homes. The army later condemned about two-thirds (3,353 acres) of the Nisqually Reservation in order to expand

George Kalama, former Nisqually tribal chairman active in national Indian politics. The Nisquallis, traditionally a fishing people, confronted state and federal officials in conflicts known as the Fish Wars.

Authors' collections.

its Camp (later Fort) Lewis base. Replacement lands were secured for the Nisquallis at points as distant as the Quinault River on the Olympic Peninsula. Other lands were purchased for displaced Nisquallis at such places as the Puyallup, Skokomish, and Chehalis reservations. The Nisquallis were also paid $75,840 for their lands and improvements. On April 28, 1924, Congress belatedly awarded them $85,000 as compensation for the hunting rights that they had lost with their lands as well as for lost access to lakes and streams.

In the post-World War II period, the focus of Washington State action centered on Frank's Landing, a six-acre tract on the Nisqually River just below the reduced Nisqually Reservation, which Willie Frank had purchased to replace, in part, lands that had been lost in the government's Fort Lewis acquisition. In the 1960s, Frank's Landing was the scene of sometimes violent confrontations between state police and game officials and the Nisquallis. Helping to focus national attention on the conflict was the symbolic arrest there of actor Marlon Brando during a "fish-in" and the appearance of Dick Gregory, a well-known entertainer and civil rights activist. (For an explanation of the background of the conflict, *see* **Puyallup.**)

Government and Claims: The Nisqually tribe was organized under provisions of the Indian Reorganization Act (48 Stat. 984) as the Nisqually Indian Community, Nisqually Reservation, Washington. Its constitution and bylaws were approved on September 9, 1946.

After filing a claim (Docket 197) with the Indian Claims Commission, the Nisquallis received a final judgment of $80,013.07, for which funds were appropriated on September 30, 1976. The moneys awarded by the Claims Commission were set aside for land acquisition. This award did not include compensation for land within the Fort Lewis Military Reservation, for which Nisquallis later sought payment.

Nisqually tribal elder and visionary Billy Frank, Jr. (b. 1931) has served since 1981 as chairman of the Northwest Indian Fisheries Commission and has been a leading activist since the 1960s in the struggle to secure tribal fishing rights.

Courtesy of the Northwest Indian Fisheries Commission.

Contemporary Life and Culture: The reservation is the focus of the Nisqually Community. Today, the reservation acreage is as follows, excluding, as noted, the Nisqually River of 210 acres: allotted lands in trust or in restricted status, 715 acres; alienated lands, 392 acres; tribally owned lands and those in trust, 247 acres (including a cemetery of 2.5 acres); and an additional 45 acres because of a change in the reservation boundary.

In recent years, the tribe has enlarged its on-reservation housing by forty-eight units and has erected a tribal center. The major source of tribal income is fishing, which is a pivotal cultural and identity touchstone for tribal members. One tribal spokesman, writing of the favorable decision by Judge George Boldt in 1974 and the *U.S.* v. *Washington* fishing cases, stated that those decisions had gone far beyond the improvement of Nisqually fisheries by reinforcing and validating tribal members' knowledge of themselves as Nisqually Indians, their fishing way of life, and their community. The predominant religion in the Nisqually Community is Roman Catholic. There are also adherents of the Indian Shaker Church.

On May 2, 1997, the Nisqually Tribe opened the Red Wind Casino fifteen miles east of the city of Olympia, making them the twelfth tribe in Washington State to offer Las Vegas-style gaming. At the end of 2004 a $31-million expansion of the casino was completed, transforming the establishment from a 9,000-square-foot bingo hall to an 85,000-square-foot Vegas-style gaming facility with cabaret, meeting rooms, restaurants, and gift shop. The tribe also operates Nisqually Rez Mart, which opened in 1997 with eight employees and $950,000 in annual sales. In April 2008 the Nisquallis spent $6.8 million to acquire a 9.6-acre parcel of development property outside Olympia and near Interstate 5, where they hope to develop a shopping center. Nisqually Aquatic Technologies is a commercial diving enterprise founded in the mid-1990s by the tribe to increase shellfish harvests. The business generates $750,000 in annual revenue. The Nisquallis hope to expand its jail to house prisoners from other jurisdictions. In 1991 the tribe dedicated a salmon hatchery on Clear Creek.

A significant milestone was achieved by the tribe in December 2004 when a Historical Court of Inquiry and Justice exonerated Chief Leschi of the charge of murder that had led to his conviction and execution in 1858, the judges ruling that the Nisqually leader's actions were carried out during a time of war and should have been treated as such. The verdict was not legally binding, but represented a major personal and public relations victory for the tribe and the families involved. In late 2007 the tribe repatriated six sets of skeletal remains of tribal members, some of which had been stored in wooden boxes at the Smithsonian Institution's National Museum of Natural History since 1855. The tribe maintains a culture center and a library in the renovated former health building.

The Nisqually Tribe operates Wa He Lut School (K-8), which opened in 1974 with ten students. Enrollment has now grown to approximately 120 students. Named after a warrior closely associated with Chief Leschi, and located at Frank's Landing on the Nisqually River, the school is open to the enrollment of children from all tribes. Subjects taught include Native languages, sign language, traditional ceremonies, and Indian history and culture. In 1998 a new 18,000-square-foot structure designed in the shape of a longhouse replaced the original school that had been destroyed by flood. The tribe also maintains a branch of the Northwest Indian College.

Primary care, mental health, social services, substance abuse, and dental care are available through clinics maintained on the reservation. Other tribal enterprises include law enforcement, a youth center, and an economic development center.

Special Events and Celebrations: The Nisqually and Puyallup tribes have alternated hosting the Leschi-Quiemuth Honor Walk/Run in February. Each year the Nisqually Tribe holds its Red Wind "Wellbriety" Powwow to increase awareness of the social and economic costs of substance abuse.

Suggested Readings:

American Friends Service Committee, *Uncommon Controversy: Fishing Rights of the Muckleshoot, Puyallup, and Nisqually Indians* (Seattle: University of Washington Press, 1970); Cecelia Svinth Carpenter, *The Nisqually—My People: The Traditional and Transitional History of the Nisqually Indian People* (Tacoma, Wash.: Tahoma Research Service, 2002); Cecelia Svinth Carpenter, et al., *Nisqually Indian Tribe* (Charleston, S.C.: Arcadia, 2008); George Pierre Castile, "The Indian Connection: Judge James Wickersham and the Indian Shakers," *Pacific Northwest Quarterly* 81, no. 4 (1990); Della G. Emmons, *Leschi of the Nisquallies* (Minneapolis: T. S. Denison, 1965); Alexandra Harmon, *Indians in the Making: Ethnic Relations and Indian Identities around Puget Sound* (Berkeley: University of California

Press, 1998), and *The Power of Promises: Rethinking Indian Treaties in the Pacific Northwest* (Seattle: University of Washington Press, 2008); Richard Kluger, *The Bitter Waters of Medicine Creek: A Classic Collision between White and Native America* (New York: Alfred A. Knopf, 2011); Alexander Olson, "Our Leschi: The Making of a Martyr," *Pacific Northwest Quarterly* 95, no. 1 (2003–2004), 26–36; Maria Pascualy, "Klee Wyk: Artists on the Nisqually Flats," *Columbia: The Magazine of Northwest History* 12, no. 4 (1998–99); Weldon Willis Rau, "Frontier Conflict," *Columbia: The Magazine of Northwest History* 7, no. 1 (1993); SuAnn M. Reddick and Cary C. Collins, "Medicine Creek to Fox Island: Cadastral Scams and Contested Domains," *Oregon Historical Quarterly* 106, no. 3 (2005); Henry Sicade, "Hard Lessons in America: Henry Sicade's History of Puyallup Indian School, 1860 to 1920," *Columbia: The Magazine of Northwest History* 14, no. 4 (2000–01) and "In a Familiar Yet Foreign Land," *Columbia: The Magazine of Northwest History* 19, no. 2 (2005); Marian W. Smith, *The Puyallup-Nisqually,* Columbia University Contributions to Anthropology, vol. 32 (New York 1940); Jamie Sanchez, "The Nisqually Indian Reservation," *The Indian Historian* 5, no. 1 (Spring 1972); Charles Wilkinson, *Messages from Frank's Landing: A Story of Salmon, Treaties, and the Indian Way* (Seattle: University of Washington Press, 2000).

NOOKSACK

(Coastal Division, Salishan)

Noxwsá7aq

Nooksack was the name of one of the tribe's villages. White men applied the name indiscriminately to all of the Indians in the valley of the Nooksack River, a Puget Sound affluent. The word means "bracken-fern roots." It is also said to be a corruption of Kunuhsaack, the name of one of the tribe's several bands.

In the middle of the nineteenth century, the Nooksacks lived in three main villages northeast of present-day Bellingham in northwestern Washington. One of those villages was near today's Deming; another was near present-day Goshen; and a third was near present-day Everson and Nooksack. Besides the town, a river bears the tribal name.

The Nooksacks are of mixed lineage, having been allied and intermarried with such tribes as the Lummis on the west, the Skagits on the south, and the Chilliwacks in British Columbia. Their dialect, but not their culture, was closely related to that of the Squawmish of British Columbia. The Nooksacks were a riverine people. Although they hunted game in the Cascade Mountains and gathered plant foods on natural prairies, it has been estimated that at least 50 percent of their food was obtained from fishing, especially during annual salmon runs on the Nooksack River and its branches in the area stretching upriver from Ferndale

Phyllis Roberts at the Deming, Washington, location of the Nooksack tribal headquarters, 1987. The Nooksacks live primarily in Whatcom County, Washington. Historically they have been a fishing people, but since contact have supplemented their incomes by farming, logging, and other occupations. Tribal members have been especially active in the past several decades practicing their revived traditional Spirit Dancing.

Authors' collections.

(once generally recognized as the Nooksack-Lummi boundary). They fished especially on the north and south forks of the Nooksack, but they were also active at the mouth of that river; around Bellingham and Chuckanut bays, as well as on the Sumas River and Sumas Lake; on the Samish, Fraser, and Skagit rivers; and on Lake Whatcom. They gathered seafoods from Bellingham Bay northward along the coast.

Location: Most of the successors of the Nooksacks are members of the Nooksack Indian Tribe of Washington, as the tribe is officially known, and they live in the general area of Deming, Nooksack, and Everson. They have no contiguous land base. The land base of the tribe is estimated to be 444.53 acres.

Numbers: In 1856 there were 376 Nooksacks by official count. In 1864 an agent wrote that this "stubborn and desperate tribe" could field about 65 warriors. In 1906 there were 200 Nooksacks by official count. The ethnologist Charles Hill-Tout alleged that in the early twentieth century there were but a half-dozen Nooksack males of full-blood degree. In 1978 tribal membership stood at 425, and in 1984 it was 453. In 2008 the Nooksacks counted over 1,900 enrolled members and in 2009, approximately 2,000.

History: In the contact period, the Nooksacks communicated very little with American settlers around Puget Sound, but, as noted, they did not isolate themselves from Native peoples. They fashioned fishnets of cedar and nettle roots. To make their sinew-backed bows, they obtained glue from the sturgeon in Canada's Fraser River, traveling over three trails to reach the river. Like many tribes during the fur-trade era, they traded with the Hudson's Bay Company at Fort Langley, established in 1827 on the lower Fraser. There they purchased, among other goods, guns, powder, and lead. An early-day shifting of the Nooksack River cut them off from riverine travel to the mouth of that stream. Like other Natives of the Puget Sound basin, the Nooksacks raised potatoes on the rich bottomlands in a culture that they probably had learned from Hudson's Bay Company personnel. In 1856, an American agent reported that they had a patriarchal government under chieftains who held considerable power. He noted the absence of slaves, an indication to him of the lack of the class structure common among the saltwater tribes.

Inclement weather prevented the Nooksacks from attending the Point Elliott Treaty Council held near Mukilteo, Washington, on January 22, 1855. The treaty authorized the establishment of the Lummi Reservation to which the Nooksacks had little wish to remove. Some of the tribe did settle there, but later left. In 1858, the tribe was much dissatisfied by the development of a ferry over the Nooksack River for miners en route to the newly discovered goldfields on the Fraser and Thompson rivers. Farther upstream, in the Mount Baker country, however, some Nooksacks served as guides and sold potatoes to the prospectors probing that region for gold. Among the ill effects of the Nooksacks' confrontations with whites was smallpox, or "Nooksack sickness," as the Skagit Indians called it. In the 1870s the Nooksacks along the lower and middle Nooksack River again clashed with settlers who homesteaded both on tribal lands and on the lands of Nooksacks who had severed tribal relations.

Government and Claims: Business is conducted by the Tribal Council of the Nooksack Indian Tribe of Washington, which was established after the tribe was federally recognized in 1971.

With several Puget Sound tribes, most of whom had been signatories to the Point Elliott Treaty, the Nooksacks were party in 1934 to a suit (*Duwamish Indians v. United States,* 79 C.C1. 530) in which they sought payment for lands taken by the government. Not being a signee of the Point Elliott Treaty, the Nooksacks were not officially recognized as holding original title to the lands involved. Because the Court of Claims took the position that it could not deal with them, the Nooksacks then filed a claim (Docket 46) with the Indian Claims Commission for the loss of their lands. The commission decided that the tribe did have aboriginal ownership of 80,590 acres. On October 20, 1958, it awarded the Nooksacks $52,383.50, the 1858 value of their lands. Finally, on February 9, 1962, the commission awarded the tribe $49,383.50, after deducting a $3,000 counter claim.

Contemporary Life and Culture: In 1971 the Nooksack Tribe received federal recognition status, along with the acquisition of a one-acre reservation. Virtually a landless tribe insofar as their reservation is concerned, the Nooksacks live on fragmented allotments totaling about 2,906 acres, which are mostly in second-growth upland timber- and bottomlands, some of which are river-washed. Some holdings are nontrust homesteads that escaped jumping by non-Indians before the legal titles were obtained by Indian homesteaders. Much land is used for subsistence gardening. Small incomes are derived from rentals to non-Indians. Most of the income of tribal members comes from fishing, logging, and seasonal farmwork. Tribal goals have been established, with much attention given to youth, land, housing, health, education, and fishing. One objective, the establishment of a tribal center, was achieved by the construction of an impressive complex at Deming.

In 2008 the Nooksack River Casino in Deming celebrated its fifteenth anniversary of operation, as the Nooksack Tribe ranked as the largest employer in eastern Whatcom County. The tribe also operates the Nooksack Northwood Casino, which opened in November 2007 north of Lynden. In addition to the casinos, the tribe owns the Nooksack Market Centre, which opened in 2002 and sells cigarettes, snacks, pizza, sub sandwiches, beer, and gasoline; a liquor store; a gas station; and a tribal smoke shop. Recently, the Nooksack Business Corporation announced a $20-million community development project along the Mount Baker Highway.

The tribe operates Head Start programs in Deming and Everson and an after-school tutoring program called Tsiyettsotkwan. The Nooksack Tribal Youth Employment Program pairs high school students with tribal jobs and training. Nooksack students attend public schools in the Mount Baker and Nooksack Valley school districts and are supported by the tribe in their pursuit of higher education.

The Nooksack Tribal Police Department consists of four officers, a sergeant, and a chief. A comprehensive health clinic operated by the Nooksack offers primary care, substance counseling, mental health services, nutrition counseling, and dental care. The tribe also provides an elders program, social services programs, and youth and family services. Outreach to families to strengthen relationships among children, parents, and the larger community and culture is supported by The House of Children.

The Nooksack language is taught through the tribe's Upriver Salish Halq'emeylem classes, and the tribe maintains a small library. *Snee-Nee-Chum*, the newsletter of the Nooksack Tribe, is published quarterly.

Special Events and Celebrations: The tribe holds an annual Mother's Day Canoe Race. Each year in July the Nooksacks host the Nooksack Genesis II Sobriety Powwow. Nooksack Days is held each September to commemorate the 1971 federal recognition of the tribe.

Suggested Readings:

Pamela Amoss, *Coast Salish Spirit Dancing: The Survival of an Ancestral Religion* (Seattle: University of Washington Press, 1978); Robert Emmett Hawley, *Skqee Mus or Pioneer Days on the Nooksack* (Bellingham, Wash.: Miller and Sutherlen,

1945); P. R. Jeffcott, *Nooksack Tales and Trails* (Sedro-Woolley, Wash., *Courier Times,* 1949); Nooksack Tribal Council, *Nooksack Tribal Planning Project Phase I: A Report to the Community* (Sedro-Woolley, Wash.: Nooksack Tribal Council, 1974); Allan S. Richardson, "Longhouses to Homesteads: Nooksack Indian Settlement, 1820 to 1895," *American Indian Journal,* August 1979; Lottie Roeder Roth, *History of Whatcom County* (Chicago: Pioneer Historical Publishing Co., 1926); David G. Tremaine, *Indian and Pioneer Settlement of the Nooksack Lowland, Washington to 1890,* Center for Pacific Northwest Studies Occasional Paper no. 4 (Bellingham: Western Washington State College, 1975).

NORTHERN PAIUTE

(Shoshonean)

The term "Paiute," though of uncertain origin, has been interpreted to mean "water Ute" or "true Ute." The Northern Paiutes were called the Paviotso by the scientist Maj. John Wesley Powell. Their language was referred to as Mono-Paviotso by the anthropologist A. L. Kroeber. They were also designated as "digger" Indians to distinguish them from the horse-riding peoples of the plains. In scanty clothing of brush and willow bark, they struggled for subsistence, migrating to the mountain tops to gather nuts and berries and returning to the valleys to dig roots and to fish. They occupied lands in northwestern Nevada, in southwestern Idaho, in central and southeastern Oregon, and in California east of the Cascade and Sierra Nevada mountains and north of Owens Lake.

Some ethnologists have applied the term "nation" to collective Shoshonean linguistic groups and the term "tribe" to individual groups. In this guidebook, however, we follow those ethnologists who consider the Northern Paiutes to be a tribe and the groups to be bands.

Geography influenced the organization and development of the twenty-one Northern Paiute bands, which had political autonomy and internal organizations that were outwardly simple. Because of the vastness of their lands, the Northern Paiute population, though of low density per square mile, was large by Pacific Northwest standards. With the Southern Shoshoneans (the Ute-Chemehuevis of western Utah, northwestern Arizona, southeastern Nevada, and parts of southeastern California), the Northern Paiutes numbered about 7,500 in 1845 and 5,400 in 1903. They have always been an independent people.

History: Before the eighteenth century, the Paiutes of central and southeastern Oregon were encroached on by the Teninos and Wascos, who previously had lived on the north bank of the Columbia River for protection from the Paiutes.

Old-style nobees alongside canvas tents in a Paiute encampment.

Courtesy of the Nevada Historical Society, Reno.

The Northern Paiutes' conflicts with those tribes was noted by the American explorers Meriwether Lewis and William Clark in 1805. Lacking European weapons and horses and also the war complex of their enemies of the plains, the Paiutes were unable to retaliate against their Columbia River adversaries. Thus around 1810, they accepted a buffer zone between themselves and Columbia River peoples.

The following subdivisions, or bands, of the Northern Paiute peoples in the Pacific Northwest were sometimes designated as "diggers" or "Snakes":

- The Hunipuitokas (Walpapis) occupied about 7,000 square miles on streams that eventually enter the Pacific Ocean or that feed the Great Basin lakes with no drainage to the sea. Paulina and Weahwewa were important among their chiefs. In 1870 the Hunipuitokas numbered ninety-eight on the Klamath Reservation.

- The Goyatokas (Yahuskins), or "crawfisheaters," inhabited a 5,000-square-mile region around the Silver, Summer, and Abert lakes in Oregon. Under Chief Moshenkosket, they numbered about one hundred on the Klamath Reservation in 1867.

- The Wadatokas, or "seedeaters," lived in a 5,250-square-mile area around Burns, Oregon, in a land of streams flowing into Harney and Malheur lakes and the Malheur River. They were one of four bands living on streams in the Pacific watershed. Among their chiefs were Oytes and Egan, who was also the chief of the Weiser Indians.

• The Koaagaitokas, or "salmoneaters," possessed lands in southern Idaho. Since numerous claims by Northern Paiutes and western bands of Northern Shoshones placed both tribes in southwestern Idaho, neither owned that area to the exclusion of others. The peoples of the Koaagaitoka subdivision intermixed and intermarried with some of the people from the sedentary western bands of Northern Shoshones, who were primarily fisheaters. By historic times and certainly by the middle of the nineteenth century, the two peoples had banded together for mutual protection from the whites invading their lands. The Shoshones were the Wararereekas and Wihinashts (Winnases). Combined, they were popularly called by the name of the local river, the Weiser, and were perhaps predominantly Northern Paiutes with a few Boise and Bruneau Shoshones.

• The homelands of the Tagotokas, or "tubereaters," were roughly 7,500 square miles, mostly in the Owyhee River watershed of Oregon and Idaho. Among their chiefs were Paddy Cap and Leggins. The descendants of the band live on Nevada's Duck Valley Reservation, established on April 16, 1877.

• The Tsosoodos tuviwarais, or "cold dwellers," of Oregon's Steens Mountain were possibly the "berryeaters" under Chief Winnemucca by reason of his marriage to a woman of their group.

• The Kidutokados, or "woodchuckeaters," occupied a territory of about 5,000 square miles, including Surprise Valley on the border of northern California and Warner Valley in Oregon as well as the valley along the eastern slopes of Oregon's Warner Range. Their chiefs were Ocheo and Howlark (Howlah). Howlark, who lived around the Sprague River, was one of those with whom the United States attempted to effect a treaty in 1865. Probably the Kidutokados were a band of 150 "Snakes" on the Klamath Reservation whose descendants live at Fort Bidwell, California, and in settlements around their homelands.

• The Agaipaninadokados ("fish lakeeaters"), or Moakokados ("wild onioneaters"), lived around Summit Lake, Nevada, and along the southern Idaho border east of the Kidutokado lands in a roughly 2,800-square-mile region. One of their chiefs, Sequimata (Chiquite, or Little Winnemucca), was noted for his leadership when miners attacked the Pyramid Lake Reservation and precipitated the Pyramid Lake War of 1860.

• The Atsakudokwa tuviwarais, or "red butte dwellers," occupied roughly 2,700 square miles in northwestern Nevada but did not extend above the southern Idaho border. Slated for removal to the Pyramid Lake Reservation in 1870, their chief, Itsaahmah, refused to lead his 140-member band to that place.

- The Yamosopo tuviwarais, or "half-moon valley dwellers," lived within roughly 2,000 square miles east of the Atsakudokwas in the Little Humboldt River drainage area of Nevada's Paradise Valley.

The Hunipuitokas, more popularly known as Walpapis, were the most familiar to Oregon settlers of all the Northern Paiute bands because they most often came into conflict with Americans during the later nineteenth century. Also familiar to whites for the same reason were the Goyatokas, better known as Yahuskins (Yahooskins). The latter designation was of fairly recent mid-nineteenth-century origin. The Goyatokas' name, meaning "people far off below," was perhaps given them by Klamaths. About 22 of them were present with 710 Klamaths and 339 Modocs at a treaty council with U.S. officials on October 14, 1864, when they ceded their lands (16 Stat. 407) and agreed to live on the Klamath Reservation. *See* **Klamath.**

The Walpapis occupied lands that encompassed the Crooked River valley and extended as far north in Oregon as the headwaters of the John Day River and as far south as Two Buttes. In 1864 the population of the band was about 500. Those under Chief Chocktoot numbered 100 in 1872 and 128 the following year. Their head war chief, Paulina, signed a treaty with the United States on August 12, 1865 (14 Stat. 683), mainly to obtain release of several of his people who were being held hostage by the military, including members of his own family. Paulina agreed to cede his lands and live on the Klamath Reservation, where he, four of his men, and eighteen women and children remained during the winter of 1865–66. However, they abandoned the reservation at the urging of the Kidutokado chief, Howlark, to wage full-scale war against whites. They also agreed to cease skirmishing against other tribes. For some time, Paulina eluded the troops sent to capture him and raided mines and miners as well as immigrants and their trains in a swath that cut across south-central and eastern Oregon. In attempting to capture him, the military established several camps in the area, including Bidwell in Surprise Valley, Alvord east of Steens Mountain, and the Old Camp Warner north of Lakeview, Oregon. Other Paiute bands of that Oregon region, as well as those of southwestern Idaho Territory, confronted Americans in the Snake War of 1866–68. Paulina also fought the Modocs under their chief, Schonchin, and attacked the Klamath Agency.

During that time, the Paiutes' ancient foes, the Teninos, were recruited from the Warm Springs Reservation in Oregon by the military as scouts in the fighting that had begun as early as 1854 when Paiute bands accosted the Ward party on the Immigrant Road (Oregon Trail) in southern Idaho. Having killed most of their horses for food, the Paiutes, starving and war-weary, finally surrendered. After the whites had killed Paulina in April 1867, his people were led by Ocheo and Weahwewa. During the Snake War, the military conducted campaigns to round up the Oregon Paiutes and place them on the Klamath Reservation. In July 1866, 16 Walpapis were marched to that reservation and 60 more came there the following month. Most escaped its confines. In September 1867, 19 Walpapis were brought to the Klamath Reservation by the military, who in August 1868 seized a few more from the Silver Lake area, including Chocktoot and his band, making a total of 130 Walpapis on the reservation. Starvation subsequently drove the Walpapis, except for Chocktoot and about 100 others, to vacate the Klamath in search of subsistence. Ocheo moved to the Klamath in November 1869. In March 1870, 12 more Walpapis were relocated there from the Silver Summer lakes area.

As a result of the Snake War campaigns and starvation, perhaps two-thirds of the Oregon Paiutes perished. A treaty that had been negotiated with three bands under Egan, Oytes, and Weahwewa on December 10, 1868, at Fort Harney was never ratified. Consequently, the government made no treaty with them. An executive order dated March 14, 1871, set aside lands in southeastern Oregon to keep them out of the public domain, and on September 12, 1872, the Malheur Reservation was created by executive order in eastern Oregon from those lands. On that reservation, certain Walpapis, except for Chocktoot and those with him on the Klamath Reservation, were joined by other free-ranging Paiutes of southeastern Oregon. Because they had not been assigned to a reservation, the Paiutes were sent to the Malheur, whose 2,775 square miles was increased on May 15, 1875, to 1,778,580 acres. On January 28, 1876, a subsequent order diminished and redefined the reservation.

About two hundred independent Paiutes and Shoshones in the lower Weiser country of Idaho went to live on Miner Creek at the northern end of the Duck Valley Reservation on the Idaho-Nevada border. Most refused to remove to the Malheur when it was initially designated for them. Today their descendants are a fragmented amalgam of Egan's Weiser Paiutes and a few Shoshones. With other Northern Paiutes, the Weisers fought in the Bannock-Paiute War under Chief Paddy Cap. For an account of Paiute participation in that war, *see* **Bannock.**

At the end of the war, Paddy Cap's people scattered to the following reservations: the Malheur in Oregon, the Fort Hall in Idaho, the Yakama in south-central Washington, and the Warm Springs in Oregon. Separated from whites and from so-called progressive Shoshones and Paiutes, they adhered longer to traditionalism than did others. Paddy Cap and certain of his followers located on the Duck Valley Reservation on lands that were withdrawn from the public domain and set apart as an addition to the Duck Valley Reservation by executive order on May 4, 1886. In 1887 there were 115 Paiutes on the Duck Valley Reservation.

On September 27, 1879, 38 Paiutes, following imprisonment at Fort Vancouver, Washington Territory, were taken to the Warm Springs Reservation, among

Winnemucca, sometimes called The Giver, was chief of one of the twenty-one Northern Paiute bands who migrated through parts of Idaho, Oregon, California, and Nevada. A city in Nevada bears the chief's name.

Courtesy of the Oregon Historical Society, Portland.

them the prophet and war instigator, Oytes, who later left for the Yakama Reservation to visit Paiutes there. On February 2, 1879, 540 scattered combatant and noncombatant Paiutes who had been rounded up after the war arrived on the Yakama Reservation after a long march from southern Oregon through deep winter snows under their leader Leggins, a noncombatant from western Nevada. Oytes was detained on the Yakama Reservation, as were others at Fort Harney under the watchful eye of the military.

The noncombatant Paiutes, under the western Nevada Paiute chief Winnemucca, clustered at Camp McDermit in Nevada. Winnemucca and the Kidutokado chief, Ocheo, kept their people mostly at Camp McDermit and Camp Bidwell. Many Paiutes drifted south from the Yakama Reservation after they were permitted to leave it in 1883. Of that group, about 300 went to the Bend, Oregon, area. Some of those soon moved to Nevada because the Malheur Reservation was being usurped by white farmers and stockmen. Executive orders on September 13, 1882, and May 21, 1883, restored the Malheur to the public domain—except for 317.65 acres that were reserved from the reservation's North Half for the Camp Harney military post, which itself was restored to the public domain by executive order on March 2, 1889. The Malheur Agency office had been discontinued on December 23, 1880, though the reservation existed until September 13, 1882. In June 1884 Paddy Cap and about fifty of his people moved from the Yakama Reservation to the Duck Valley Reservation. In August 1884 Oytes and about seventy of his people left the Yakama Reservation for the Warm Springs Reservation.

In 1945, 145 Paiutes of full- or mixed-blood degree were listed on the Umatilla Reservation; in 1950 there were over 500 on the Duck Valley Reservation; and in 1960, 207 were recorded on the Warm Springs Reservation.

Government and Claims: The approximately twenty-three hundred Shoshone-Paiutes living on the Duck Valley Indian Reservation form the only self-governance tribe in the state of Idaho. The reservation is administered by a council. Approximately $6 million is received annually from the BIA, which the Shoshone-Paiute Tribes then distributes as it chooses.

In 1969 a settlement was reached with a per capita payment of $741 to nearly 850 Paiutes who were able to prove that they were related to Indians formerly located on the Malheur Reservation. That payment was the award from a claim (Docket 17) filed on December 4, 1959, for Paiute descendants of former Malheur residents. The Indian Claims Commission determined that Paiutes held title to that reservation as described in the executive order of January 28, 1876, and that the area under consideration comprised 1,449,304.77 acres. That was the acreage after deduction of 120,019.43 acres for road grants across the confine; 17,541.96 acres in allotments to Indians after 1879; and 10,000 acres that were in question in the location of the southern boundary of the reservation. To the descendants of those who were party to the unratified treaty of December 10, 1868, the Claims Commission awarded $579,722 because those descendants had held original title to the Malheur Reservation.

Another claim (Docket 87) from petitioning Paiutes on six reservations in Nevada was decided on November 4, 1965. Among those filing from those reservations were Paiutes who (except for descendants of the Malheur Walpapis and Yahuskins) had shared in awards to the Paiutes of Owens Valley in California and Nevada of $935,000, the fair market value of their aboriginal lands as of March 3, 1953; plus an award to the Paviotsos of $16 million, the fair market value of their lands in Nevada and California as of December 31, 1962; and a judgment to Pacific Northwestern Paviotsos of $3,650,000 for the "Snake Tract" in Oregon, which also included lands in southwestern Idaho and northeastern California. The Walpapis and Yahuskins were recipients of an award to Klamath Reservation Indians covered under Docket 100 (*see* **Klamath Tribes**).

In 1897, 115 homeless Paiutes of Oregon had received individual allotments east of Burns. Three-quarters of a century passed before they had a reservation, the Burns Paiute Indian Colony. Tribal government had evolved there through agreements from 1936 to 1938 between the Burns Paiute Colony and the BIA. Three-fourths of the members live on or adjacent to the reservation. Operating under a business committee, the Colony generates income from a 110-acre tribally owned farm. (*See* **Burns Paiute Tribe.**)

Contemporary Life and Culture: On April 16, 1977, the governor of Nevada proclaimed Duck Valley Indian Reservation Day in commemoration of the hundredth birthday of the original 312,320-acre reservation, which was enlarged to a half-million acres by executive order on May 4, 1886.

In 1980 the main sources of revenue for about 1,200 tribal members were ranching and farming. There is also considerable fishing in reservoirs. The Shoshone-Paiutes are working to maintain the streams and water habitats of their 453-square-mile (289,819-acre) reservation, especially the freshwater salmon and steelhead stocks. Irrigation is made possible by the waters from reservoirs, such as the Wild Horse and Sheep Creek in Nevada and the Mountain View in Idaho.

A tribal complex was constructed with federal funds at the state line. In 1956 the reservation BIA school system was consolidated into the Elko County School District of Nevada, which operates today as the Owyhee Combined Schools (K-12), Owyhee being the only townsite on the reservation. A Community Education Center in Owyhee offers GED and higher education courses. Health care, dental, optical, mental and social services are provided through Owyhee Community Health Facility. Economic development has remained limited on the isolated reservation, with the rate of unemployment continuing to hover between 40 and 75 percent. Recently, a new fire station was built, and the Shoshone-Paiute Tribes operates a store and fuel pumps. In the planning stages is a $2-million commercial center that would include a grocery store, barbershop, and retail center. A juvenile detention center, once completed, is estimated to provide fourteen jobs. A casino built on reclaimed tribal land near Boise would be twice as large as the Coeur d'Alene facility and bring seven hundred new jobs.

In 1998 the Shoshone-Paiute Tribes began a catch-and-release fly-fishing operation on the manmade, 430-acre Lake Billy Shaw. Due to its isolated location, the Duck Valley Reservation has no cell phone or radio service and in the winter suffers intermittent power outages. In 2008 there were approximately 2,300 Shoshone-Paiute members at Duck Valley.

Special Events and Celebrations: The Shoshone-Paiute Tribes celebrates its annual Fourth of July Rodeo and Powwow in Owyhee as well as their Veterans Day Powwow each November.

Suggested Readings:

"An Interview with Thurman Welbourne," *Idaho Heritage* 1, no. 10 (October 1977); David Braly, *Crooked River Country: Wranglers, Rogues, and Barons* (Pullman: Washington State University, 2007); Gae Canfield, *Sarah Winnemucca of the Northern Paiutes* (Norman: University of Oklahoma Press, 1981); Verne F. Ray et al., "Tribal Distribution in Eastern Oregon and Adjacent Regions," *American Anthropologist* 40, no. 3 (July–September 1938); Omer C. Stewart, "Culture Element Distributions: XIV Northern Paiute," *Anthropological Records* 4, no. 3

(1941) and "The Northern Paiute Bands," *Anthropological Records* 2, no. 3 (1939); Virginia Cole Trenholm and Maurine Carley, *The Shoshonis: Sentinels of the Rockies* (Norman: University of Oklahoma Press, 1964); Erminie Wheeler Voegelin, "The Northern Paiute of Central Oregon: A Chapter in Treaty-Making," *Ethnohistory* 2, nos. 2 and 3 (1955), and 3, no. 1 (1956); Robert H. Ruby and John A. Brown, *Indians of the Pacific Northwest: A History* (Norman: University of Oklahoma Press, 1981).

OKANAGON

(See **Sinkaietk.**)

OZETTE

(Wakashan)

The Ozettes (Hosetts) lived on the western Olympic peninsula of present-day Washington State on the lake and river that bear their name and at Flattery Rocks. Ozette Island, reportedly their burial grounds, was discovered on March 22, 1778, by the British naval explorer Capt. James Cook.

The Ozettes were a Makah group, who, like other Makahs in early times, migrated southward from the west coast of Vancouver Island. In their new home they sometimes fought peoples from the north, such as the Nitinats, a Nootkan people of southwestern Vancouver Island. Sometimes they fought Makah villagers, but they just as often joined them in confronting their southern neighbors, particularly the Quileutes. With other Makah peoples, the Ozettes traded such items as dentalia shells and Hudson's Bay Company blankets with their erstwhile Quileute foes in exchange for whale oil and dried fish, which they in turn traded to the peoples of Vancouver Island. Archaeological excavations begun in the 1970s at Usaahluth (Usahl), the ancient Ozette village at the mouth of the Ozette River, revealed the importance of whaling and other maritime pursuits to its inhabitants. Many artifacts were unearthed that were once used in hunting and processing game and in rituals associated with those activities. Several houses of the village were covered by mud slides from as long as five hundred to eight hundred years ago to as recently as the middle of the nineteenth century. The village was reoccupied after each slide. In 1872 an Indian agent reported two hundred Indians living there. In August of that year those villagers killed as many as nine whales.

An 1870 census reported 188 Ozettes. During the 1880s, their population increased, mostly from an influx of families from Neah Bay whose elders opposed sending their children to boarding school there. The excavated Ozette village was the population center of the 640-acre Ozette Reservation along the Pacific Ocean at Cape Alava, about fifteen miles south of the tip of the Olympic Peninsula. The reservation was established by executive order on April 12, 1893. Its population declined from 91 in 1888 to 44 in 1901 and 35 in 1906. In 1914 seventeen people were reported to be living in the Ozette village.

On March 4, 1911, Congress passed an act (36 Stat. 1345) directing the secretary of the interior to make allotments to Ozettes, Hohs, and Quileutes on the Quinault Reservation, as stipulated in an 1856 treaty. With the Makahs, the Ozettes had treated with the United States on January 31, 1855. Lack of farming and grazing land on the Quinault stopped the allotting process there in 1913, but that did not halt the exodus from the Ozette village. Among those abandoning it were some who returned to Neah Bay and reluctantly faced the white influence there. In 1923 there were said to have been only eight Ozettes. In 1937 only one Ozette was reported living on the reservation. When he later moved to the Makah Reservation, he was described by the press as the "last living Ozette." *See* **Makah.**

PAIUTE

(See **Northern Paiute.***)*

PALOUSE

(Shahaptian)

The Palouses comprised three autonomous Shahaptian-speaking bands along the lower Snake River from Alpowa west to the Columbia-Snake confluence. Between those two points and in adjacent areas, usually on sandy terraces or in sheltered canyons, lay over forty Palouse winter villages. The Palouses called themselves the Nahaum, or Palous, after the "standing rock," a massive basaltic outcropping at the mouth of the Palouse River near the Middle Palouses' main village, which was also called Palus. The Palouses explained the rock variously as a remnant of a wicked woman whose defiance had led to her transformation into stone, the heart of a giant beaver, or the boat of the mythical trickster Coyote.

In the nineteenth century, the Palouse lands were divided into three general areas on the lower Snake. There were not only slight differences in the climates of the three areas but also different dialects were spoken by the three Palouse (Upper, Middle, and Lower) bands who inhabited them. In the Upper Palouse villages, more food and animal resources supported larger populations. Besides the Palouse River, the spectacular Palouse Falls and a town bear the Palouse name. The name of the Appaloosa horse might possibly stem from the name of the tribe.

The ethnologist James H. Teit believed that the Palouses were a Yakama people, or closely related to the Yakamas, and that they once occupied the lower-middle Columbia River, from which some of their tribe had moved to the lower Snake and Palouse rivers. In 1780 the Palouses numbered roughly eighteen hundred. In 1805–1806 they were estimated at sixteen hundred and in 1854 at about five hundred. Besides villages on the Snake River upstream from the mouth of the Palouse, there were at that time several lodges farther downstream under a Chief Quelaptip, others under So-ei on the north bank of the Snake thirty miles below its confluence with the Palouse, and yet others, under Tilcoax, at the mouth of the Snake.

When visited by the American explorers Meriwether Lewis and William Clark, the Palouses lived in wooden houses in contrast to the mat tipis of their neighbors. The explorers noted some neighboring Nez Perce wooden houses, a type of construction that the Nez Perces may have adopted from the Palouses. The Palouses were primarily a piscatory people, but they migrated from their permanent salmon-fishing villages to gather roots and berries and to hunt. Early-nineteenth-century fur traders en route to posts in the upper interior traversed the Palouse country and continued northward across the Columbia Plateau. For that part of their journey, they often purchased horses from the Palouses, who managed their herds with a skill equal to that of the Nez Perces.

The Palouses were one of the tribes whom white treaty makers designated as members of the Yakama Nation in the Walla Walla Treaty of 1855. During the 1855–58 war that followed the treaty signing, the Palouses fought against the Americans. The leader of the Indian coalition in the Yakama phase of the war (1855–56) was Kamiakin, who was of Palouse-Yakama ancestry. In September 1858, U.S. Army Col. George Wright invaded the Spokane–Coeur d'Alene country in retaliation against the Palouses and other tribes for their part in the defeat of the army command of Col. Edward Steptoe the previous May. To put his Indian adversaries afoot, Wright ordered the killing of about eight hundred horses, which were reported to have belonged to Tilcoax but were probably those of the Palouse chief Poyakin.

In the immediate postwar period, the Britisher John Keast Lord wrote: "The Pelouse [sic] Indians were at one time numerous, predatory, and always at war, but this once-dreaded tribe has dwindled away to a mere remnant." Living at the center of a triangle at whose points lay the Nez Perce, Yakama, and Umatilla reservations, the Palouses were urged by government officials to remove to one of them. They not only declined to do so but also rebuffed government aid. They also refused to reveal the population of their tribe. They claimed that the United States had been negligent in its treaty obligations by failing to evaluate and compensate them for their properties. Especially zealous in seeking their removal to the Yakama Reservation was its agent, the Methodist Reverend James Wilbur.

Harlish Washshomake, or Wolf Necklace, also known as Tilcoax the Younger. Although small in numbers, no Indian people resisted white influence more than did Washshomake's Palouses.

Courtesy of Richard Scheuerman.

In 1872, at the beginning of the Ulysses S. Grant Peace Policy era, the Palouses had numbered 150, a population large enough to cause white settlers to seek their removal so that they could appropriate their lands. Although some Palouses had agreed at a Spokane River council on August 18, 1877, to remove to either a proposed Spokane reservation or to the Coeur d'Alene Reservation, they continued subsisting on small farm patches in their homelands until the end of the nineteenth century. Some Palouses of the Dreamer religion, called "renegades" by white men, fought alongside the Nez Perce Chief Joseph against American forces in 1877 and accompanied him into exile in Indian Territory (Oklahoma), from where they returned to settle on the Colville (Washington) Reservation in 1886. Traps and wheels on the Columbia River deprived the Palouses of the salmon so vital to their existence. Encroaching ranchers and farmers also denied them their traditional sources of food.

In 1919 the Palouses numbered only eighty-two. Today, Indians of Palouse ancestry are living on several reservations.

Suggested Readings:

Angelo Anastasio, "Intergroup Relations in the Southern Plateau," master's thesis, University of Chicago, 1955; Albert W. Thompson, "The Early History of the Palouse River and Its Names," *Pacific Northwest Quarterly* 62, no. 2 (April 1971); Richard D. Scheuerman and Clifford Trafzer, "The First People of the Palouse Country," *The Bunchgrass Historian* 8, no. 3 (Fall 1980); Clifford Trafzer and Richard D. Scheuerman, *Renegade Tribe* (Pullman: Washington State University Press, 1986) and "'This Land Is Your Land and You Are Being Robbed of It': Dispossession of Palouse Indian Land, 1860–1880," *Idaho Yesterdays* 29, no. 4 (1986).

PEND D'OREILLE

(Interior Division, Salishan)

On the basis of linguistic similarity, anthropologists and ethnologists such as John R. Swanton, Frederick Webb Hodge, Leslie Spier, and James Mooney classified the Upper Pend d'Oreilles, or Upper Kalispels, and the Lower Pend d'Oreilles, or Lower Kalispels, as one tribe. This approach is followed in this guide. Certain anthropologists, ethnologists, and field observers such as Edward S. Curtis, Verne F. Ray, and James H. Teit have considered the two groups to have always been two tribes with distinct cultural and political characteristics. The two groups lived contiguous to each other (*see* **Kalispel**). Today, however, the groups are separated. After the midnineteenth century the Upper group located to Flathead Lake in the eastern part of their territory and became part of another tribe. (*See* **Confederated Salish & Kootenai Tribes of the Flathead Reservation**). The Lower group, holding nontreaty and nonreservation status, moved to the western part of its area and refused to join any tribe on a reservation. Near the end of the century, the U.S. government granted the Lower Pend d'Oreilles, or Lower Kalispels, a reservation in their own homeland, and they achieved tribal status as a sovereign political entity. *See* **Kalispel Tribe of Indians**.

PORT GAMBLE S'KLALLAM TRIBE, PORT GAMBLE RESERVATION

The Port Gamble S'Klallam Tribe, Port Gamble Reservation, was formerly one of three Clallam bands but has since obtained formal tribal status. In the latter half of the nineteenth century, some Clallams from the country around the Elwha River (a tributary to the Strait of Juan de Fuca) returned from fishing on Hood Canal and stopped to work at a sawmill at Port Gamble. They stayed to settle near the mill, established in 1853. Their settlement became known as Little Boston. Under the Point-No-Point Treaty of 1855, they, like other Clallams, were scheduled to remove to the Skokomish Reservation, but they remained instead in their Port Gamble community. They were autonomous but were without a reservation until the 1930s, when the federal government provided them one. The Port Gamble Reservation originated in 1936–37 when the United States purchased and put in trust 1,231.70 acres for them in the Little Boston area. The purchase, amounting to $15,000, was made pursuant to section 5 of the Indian Reorganization Act of June 18, 1934 (48 Stat. 984). Known as the Port Gamble Tract, it was located across a small inlet from the town of Port Gamble, approximately three miles from original Clallam lands.

Location: The center of the Port Gamble S'Klallam Tribe is the Port Gamble Reservation on the northern Kitsap Peninsula of northwestern Washington State.

Numbers: In 1985 there were 534 Port Gamble S'Klallams enrolled in the community. About 375 were living on the reservation. In July 2008 there were 1,131 members, about half of whom were living on the reservation.

Government and Claims: A tribal constitution was adopted on September 7, 1939. It provided for a business council, which meets regularly and appoints standing committees to deal with education, health, planning, housing, and personnel. The Community also conducts a fisheries enhancement program coordinated through the Point-No-Point treaty council of January 26, 1855.

For the purpose of recovering additional compensation for lands ceded to the United States, the three Clallam bands consolidated their claims against the government (*see* **Clallam**).

Contemporary Life and Culture: The Port Gamble S'Klallam Reservation consists of 1,340 acres from which all tribal services are delivered. Administrative offices are housed in the Tribal Center, including an annex for the Natural Resources Department and the tribal education facility. Nearby is the Little Boston Library, the Housing Authority, and the S'Klallam Arts Building. A new housing office was completed in early 2002, and the reservation has both a youth center and a senior center. All businesses on the reservation are owned by the Community, including a mobile home park, the Gliding Eagle Market Place, and the 17,000-square-foot Point Casino (formerly Point No Point Casino), which opened in 2002 at Kingston. There are also forestry, craftshop, and silk-screen enterprises. Fishing is done on an individual basis, but there are tribal fish hatchery facilities.

Among the programs conducted for the benefit of the Community are those pertaining to justice, fire prevention, education, food service, and community and environmental health, including a wellness center focusing on mental health and prevention of and treatment for chemical abuse. There is also a four-chair dental clinic. There is a Young Adult Conservation Corps and a preschool. Most elementary students attend the David Wolfe School. Other students attend the North Kitsap middle and high schools in nearby Poulsbo.

Several members of the Community are employed in a nearby sawmill. Members also work at government projects in the area and for the tribe. Law enforcement is largely in tribal hands but the office of the Kitsap County sheriff is called in emergency situations. Religious preference is predominantly Protestant.

A new casino is currently under construction. It will replace the Point Casino with a new $100-million, 100,000-square-foot facility that will include restaurants, lounges, a live-entertainment center, and a thirteen- to fifteen-floor luxury hotel with a dance club. The tribe is negotiating to purchase an additional 120 acres on which to construct a shopping center that will be surrounded by walking and hiking trails. In 2004, the tribe finished construction on a new $1.2-million longhouse, the first traditional gathering place built on the Port Gamble reservation in more than a century. The plankhouse is the cornerstone of a larger $4.5-million House of Knowledge project designed to celebrate S'Klallam culture and promote education and future opportunity. It is the catalyst for the cultural renaissance taking place on the reservation, which includes reviving skills of carving, drum- and basket-making, and beadwork; restoring old songs and dances; resurrecting canoe protocols; and introducing culture and arts classes. "We want our young people to know who they are, where they come from, why things are made the way they are—not just as decoration but as something that's usable and to be proud of," said Francine Swift, coordinator of the S'Klallam Longhouse Project.

Special Events and Celebrations: The Stan Purser Memorial Powwow is held each February. The S'Klallam Elders Honoring Powwow is put on in August. S'Klallam Days is celebrated annually in September. *See* **Clallam**.

Suggested Readings:

Jacilee Wray, *Native Peoples of the Olympic Peninsula: Who We Are* (Norman: University of Oklahoma Press, 2002).

PSHWANWAPAM

(Shahaptian)

The Pshwanwapams lived just east of the Cascade Mountains on the upper courses of the Yakima River, a Columbia River affluent in Washington. They gave themselves their name, which means "stony ground." Their language was speculated to have been in the Yakama dialectic division of the Shahaptian group. They were reported as closely related culturally and possibly politically to the Upper Yakamas (Kittitas). Some anthropologists believe that the language of the Pshwanwapams was similar to that of the Shahaptian-speaking Klickitats, Micals, and Taitnapams. At one time, individuals from those tribes probably moved freely from one band to another and intermarried. Today they are generally accepted by anthropologists as having been a band of Kittitas.

Suggested Readings:

Melville Jacobs, "A Sketch of Northern Sahaptin Grammar," *University of Washington Publications in Anthropology* 4 (1931), 85–292; Leslie Spier, *Tribal Distribution in Washington,* American Anthropological Association General Series in Anthropology, no. 3 (Menasha, Wis.: George Banta Publishing Co., 1936).

PUYALLUP

(Coastal Division, Salishan)

S'Puyalupubsh

Generous and Welcoming Behavior to All People
(Friends and Strangers) Who Enter Our Lands

The derivation of the name "Puyallup" has been traced to a Nisqually Indian word for the mouth of the Puyallup River, along which the Puyallup villages extended for about fifteen miles east from Commencement Bay on which lies the city of Tacoma, Washington. The name Puyallup has also been associated with a Native word meaning "shadow" because of the dense forest shades of Puyallup lands. It is also said to mean "crooked stream." At certain seasons the Puyallups were found at various places besides the Puyallup River such as Carr Inlet and southern Vashon Island in Puget Sound. A reservation, a city, and a valley near Tacoma also bear the tribal name.

The Puyallups were primarily a piscatory people. They supplemented that diet with berries and, after contact with fur traders, with potatoes. The original 1,280-acre Puyallup Reservation was established by the Medicine Creek Treaty of December 26, 1854. It was later enlarged to 18,062 acres by executive orders on January 20, 1857, and September 6, 1873. Some Nisquallis, Cowlitzes, Muckleshoots, Steilacooms, and Indians of other tribes also lived on the reservation. Although many of the Pacific Northwest Indian reservations were located at some distances from large population centers, that was not true of the Puyallups. The city of Tacoma, which borders the reservation, was at one time larger than Seattle farther north. The proximity of the reservation to an urban center affected not only its eventual size but also cultural developments among its inhabitants.

In the 1960s and 1970s the contemporary Puyallup Tribe, Puyallup Reservation, Washington, was in the forefront of the fish wars with the State of Washington over Indian off-reservation fishing on the Puyallup River, whose waters the state regulated for purposes of conservation. Once an abundant resource, salmon was the measure of wealth for many Pacific Northwest Indians. By the early twentieth century, this natural resource was diminished through overharvesting and the alteration of streams for power production and irrigation. The artificial means used to revive the runs were insufficient to meet the demands of white and Indian sport and commercial fishermen. Indians were losing out in the competition for fish, which led the Puyallups and other Indians of the Pacific Northwest coast, Puget Sound, and Columbia River, including the Nez Perces of Idaho, to assert their rights under their treaties with the United States. Major combatants in this new type of legal warfare were the Puyallups, who fished in defiance of state laws. The clash was publicized when Hollywood personalities joined them in the "war," which involved verbal and sometimes physical confrontations with state officials on the Nisqually River south of the Puyallup Reservation. On October 13, 1965, at Frank's Landing on the Nisqually River, six Puyallups were the first Indians arrested and jailed for illegal fishing. Their trial was delayed until January 15, 1969. Other litigation involving fishing cases followed. Finally, the federal government sued the State of Washington on behalf of the Indians for their rights to fish. In 1974, a federal judge, George Boldt, ruled that federally recognized western Washington Indian tribes were entitled to take from many western Washington streams 50 percent of the harvestable runs of salmon and steelhead trout (*United States* v. *State of Washington*, 384 F. Supp. 312, 1974).

Numbers: In 1853 the Puyallups had a reported population of 150; three years later, the number had reportedly risen to 550, but the latter figure may have included members of other tribes. In 1929 the base tribal roll stood at 344. In 1937 it was listed at 322. In 1984 the Puyallup Tribe numbered 1,286, and in 2008 tribal membership had increased to more than 3,800.

History: In Puyallup mythology, as in that of other nearby tribes, Dokibatt the Changer, or Transformer, was held to have created everything, from language to roots and berries. It was believed that Dokibatt had removed life from stones, had rendered the insects small and less harmful, and had taught the people how to make fire, clothing, fish traps, and medicines. In modern times, the greatest "changer" for the Puyallups was the white man, especially Americans. Attempting to interfere as little as possible with Indian mores, the British Hudson's Bay Company had been content simply to draw the Puyallups and other tribes of the region into its trading system. But from the time of their first settlement on southern Puget Sound in 1845, Americans had pressured their government to effect a treaty with these Indians. The result was the Medicine Creek Treaty of 1854, to which the Puyallups were a party. In the war that broke out the following year, the Upper Puyallups joined other Indian combatants in futile resistance to the Americans. In 1855 many Puyallups were among the 530 Indians whom an acting agent, J. V. Weber, confined to Squaxin Island in Puget Sound to separate them from the "hostiles" in the war.

The Puyallups first came under Roman Catholic influence in the 1840s, but under the Puyallup Agency they were supervised by Protestants because of the President Ulysses S. Grant Peace Policy of the 1870s. During this period, the cultivated acreage on their reservation increased from 291 acres in 1871 to 1,200 in 1880, a significant increase considering the difficulty of clearing land. The Puyallups raised wheat, oats, and hay on natural meadows near tidal flats. An American traveler among them in 1884, on observing the efforts of their schoolchildren and other signs of Puyallup "progress," termed the Puyallups the "most creditable specimens of civilized Indians to be found in the West." Among the

A Puyallup couple, Burnt Face Charley and his wife, photographed ca. 1895. The homeland of the Puyallups was on Puget Sound, primarily along the river bearing their tribal name. Much of their lands near Tacoma have been appropriated for commercial and industrial enterprises.

Courtesy of the Washington State Historical Society, Tacoma.

various schools established over the years on the Puyallup Reservation was the Puyallup Indian School, earmarked after 1906 as a trade school for Indians of all tribes. In 1910, as the Cushman Indian Trade School, it enrolled Indian youth of various tribes. There was also a Catholic boarding school, St. George's Mission.

Increasing incursions into the Puyallups' marine food sources hastened the allotment process on their reservation, for which provision had been made in their Medicine Creek Treaty. Allotting and patenting were completed in 1886, one year before the enactment of the General Allotment, or Dawes Severalty, Act of 1887. The continued growth of Tacoma, which by 1890 had a population of forty thousand, caused its citizens to seek removal of the restrictions on allotted reservation lands. Their first maneuver resulted in the establishment by Congress on August 19, 1890 (26 Stat. 354), of a commission to authorize sale of Puyallup Reservation tracts. An act of March 3, 1893 (27 Stat. 612, 633), provided for another commission to select and appraise portions of allotments not required for Indian homes and part of an agency tract that was not needed for school purposes. The commission was then to arrange for the sale by public auction of the lands so selected. The 1893 statute provided that the land not chosen for sale remain in Indian hands and not be sold for ten years. When that time expired in 1903, buyers were able to negotiate directly with the Indians. Before that time, Indian signatures were required for sale of their lands. The sales, begun in May 1895, were conducted by agency personnel, and approximately half of the reservation was sold under the authorization of the commission. The Indians claimed that they were coerced into signing permissions for the sales. A railroad company that had located its western terminus near the Puyallup Reservation in 1873 was said to have obtained its lands through improper means. By congressional action on March 2, 1899 (30 Stat. 990), railroad companies received blanket approval from the secretary of the interior for rights-of-way through Indian lands. Among the Puyallup lands sold by the commission were valuable waterfront tracts that were concentrated in the possession of railroad, lumber, and land companies and other businesses and industries. In 1903, when the ten-year restriction against selling their lands had expired, the Indians had little choice but to succumb to whites and lose their lands. By 1909 their losses were nearly complete.

Government and Claims: The Puyallup Tribe, Puyallup Reservation, Washington, owns 66.9 acres of land in several parcels. It maintains a tribal organization provided under its constitution, which was approved by the secretary of the interior on May 13, 1936. The Puyallup Tribal Council is the designated governing body.

In 1909 the Puyallups tried to regain their tidelands in a lawsuit, *U.S.* v. *Ashton* (170f. 509, 1909), but lost their case. For decades the tribe continued to bring suits against the American government and other jurisdictions for recovery and/ or compensation of alienated lands. In 1984 they won a major judgment when they received a $162 million settlement for usurpation of an area that extended southeast from Tacoma's Commencement Bay to the limits of the city of Puyallup. The federal government paid $77.25 million of the sum, while the balance consisted of $43 million from the Port of Tacoma, $21 million from the State of Washington, $11.4 million from private businesses, and $9 million from local governments. From that settlement, each tribal member received $20,000.

Contemporary Life and Culture: Many tribal members are employed as skilled and semiskilled workers in lumbering, fishing, and other industries. After its victory in the contest for fishing rights on its ancestral fishing grounds on the Puyallup River, the tribe started a salmon business. It also operates a fish hatchery. Work on a 350-bed hospital began in 1941. Later, the facility became a diagnostic center run by the State of Washington, but after confrontations less violent than those attending the fish wars, the center was returned to the Indians in 1980.

With their $162-million settlement in 1989, the Puyallups began their first housing project. A $5-million commercial marina with 298 moorings was also built.

As of 2003 the Puyallups were one of the few tribes in the United States to successfully reclaim Indian remains categorized as unidentifiable and thereby by law not required to be returned. That year the bones of twenty unknowns were claimed by the tribe from three Puget Sound museums. The tribe has also invested in retrieving their culture through such programs as the Puyallup Tribal Language Program and the teaching of the Twulshootseed dialect. A tribal archives-museum is maintained. The Puyallup Tribe operates the Puyallup Tribal Health Authority and Takopid Health Center. In 1996 the 200,000-square-foot Chief Leschi Schools opened with a pre-K through 12 enrollment of seven hundred students. Puyallup schools provide students with culturally relevant curricula, and the tribe makes available $25,000 in annual support per student to those pursuing higher education. Departments within the tribe deliver cradle-to-grave services, including funeral assistance. The tribe has its own police department and court system. In the developmental stages are the construction of an elders' activity center and a community/youth center. The cost of these two projects is estimated at $15 million. Meanwhile, a site has been selected and plans drawn for a new $15-million, 50,000-square-foot tribal jail and justice center, and $8.9 million has been set aside for a new children's services center to be built in the next several years.

In conjunction with a world leader in container shipping, the tribe began planning in 2008 for the establishment of an underwater seaport, while also investing in a $300-million, 180-acre container terminal at the Port of Tacoma. At the same time, the Puyallups donated $685,000 to the Point Defiance Zoo in Tacoma to help finance a new exhibit of red wolves, a species that through federal recovery efforts had been brought back from the brink of extinction. The tribe maintains the Chinook Landing Marina and two gasoline stations, with plans to acquire two more gas stations.

In 1992 the Puyallups built a 36,993-square-foot, $2.1-million, 1,500-seat bingo hall. Today they operate two gaming facilities—the Emerald Queen Casino I-5 in Tacoma and the Emerald Queen Hotel and Casino in Fife—which together generated $126 million in net revenue in 2005. (In 2008 the tribe erected, at a cost of over $1 million, a huge, 140-foot-tall electronic sign along Interstate 5, advertising these casinos.) An events pavilion at the Tacoma facility hosts professional boxing and top-drawer musicians and entertainers. Two percent of profits from the casinos funds infrastructure projects and supports services for nearby communities; 1 percent of the profits is donated to qualifying nonprofit charitable organizations. Total allocations to these two accounts are in the tens of millions of dollars. As of 2006, $280 million had been paid to tribal members from gaming revenues.

The 2008 fiscal budget for the Puyallup Tribe was $232.6 million. Free enterprise is encouraged among tribal members. There are 17 licensed smoke shops on the reservation, and in 2008 alone, over 150 permits were issued to operate summer fireworks stands. In that same year, the Puyallup Tribe ranked among the five largest employers in Pierce County.

Special Events and Celebrations: Each Labor Day weekend the Puyallups hold their Puyallup Tribal Powwow, which features traditional dances and ceremonies and attracts visitors from around the region.

Suggested Readings:

American Friends Service Committee, *Uncommon Controversy: Fishing Rights of the Muckleshoot, Puyallup, and Nisqually Indians* (Seattle: University of Washington Press, 1970); George Pierre Castile, "The Indian Connection: Judge James Wickersham and the Indian Shakers," *Pacific Northwest Quarterly* 81, no. 4 (1990); Alexandra Harmon, *Indians in the Making: Ethnic Relations and Indian Identities around Puget Sound* (Berkeley: University of California Press, 1998), and *The Power of Promises: Rethinking Indian Treaties in the Pacific Northwest* (Seattle: University of Washington Press, 2008); Richard Kluger, *The Bitter Waters of Medicine Creek: A Classic Collision between White and Native America* (New York: Alfred A. Knopf, 2011); Jay Miller, "Inflamed History: Violence against Homesteading Indians in Washington Territory," *North Dakota Quarterly* 67, nos. 3–4 (2000); Alexander Olson, "Our Leschi: The Making of a Martyr," *Pacific Northwest Quarterly* 95, no. 1 (2003–04); Maria Pascualy and Cecelia Svinth Carpenter, *Remembering Medicine Creek: The Story of the First Treaty Signed in Washington* (Fairbanks, Alas.: Fireweed Press, 2005); Weldon Willis Rau, "Frontier Conflict," *Columbia: The Magazine of Northwest History* 7, no. 1 (1993); SuAnn M. Reddick and Cary C. Collins, "Medicine Creek to Fox Island: Cadastral Scams and Contested Domains," *Oregon Historical Quarterly* 106, no. 3 (2005); Henry Sicade, "Hard Lessons in America: Henry Sicade's History of Puyallup Indian School, 1860 to 1920," *Columbia: The Magazine of Northwest History* 14, no. 4 (2000–01) and "In a Familiar Yet Foreign Land," *Columbia: The Magazine of Northwest History* 19, no. 2 (2005); Marian Smith, *The Puyallup-Nisqually,* Columbia University Contributions to Anthropology, vol. 32 (New York, 1940); State of Washington Indian Affairs Task Force, *Are You Listening Neighbor? . . . The People Speak: Will You Listen?* (Olympia, Wash., 1978).

QUEETS
(Coastal Division, Salishan)

The People Made from Dirt

The name of the Queets (formerly also called the Quaitso) is said to stem from a word meaning "people made of dirt." The tribe lived on the Queets River and its branches on the Pacific side of Washington's Olympic Peninsula. They were closely related to their neighbors on the south, the Quinaults, who claimed the lands south of the Queets River.

Location: Descendants of the aboriginal Queets tribe live mainly in the towns of Queets and Taholah within the Quinault Reservation, where the Queets received allotments. They have intermingled with the peoples of the Quinault Reservation.

Numbers: Never a numerous people, the Queets were enumerated by the American explorers Meriwether Lewis and William Clark in 1805–1806 as 250 Indians living in eighteen houses. As a separate tribe in 1885, they numbered 85. In 1936 a census recorded 82 members of the Queets Tribe. In 1998 approximately 300 residents lived at the village of Queets on the Quinault Indian Reservation, a population that had grown to between 400 and 500 by the summer of 2009. *See* **Quinault.**

History: The Queets Indians were often on poor terms with the neighboring Quileutes to the north and also occasionally with the Quinaults. Informants told of an abortive Queets invasion of Quinault lands around 1800, at about the time the Queets Indians suffered attacks by the Chehalises, who burned several of their villages and killed many of their people. Often the Queets and the Quinault Indians would vent their aggressive feelings in a rough-and-tumble game of shinny. At other times, the two peoples peacefully gathered roots at such places as Baker Prairie, halfway between Moclips and Point Grenville on the coast. Perhaps conflict was kept in check between the Queets and the neighboring Quileutes, Hohs, and Quinaults because those tribes were in a confederation to oppose such tribes as the Clallams, Makahs, Ozettes, Satsops, and others who lived farther south, as far as the mouth of the Columbia River. The Queets Indians were geographically central in the confederation and in a trading complex that stretched from Vancouver Island south to the Columbia River and beyond.

During the contact period, the Queets Indians were wary of white traders, having learned of the conflicts between whites and Natives at various places along the coast. In 1854, brandishing guns and knives, Queets Indians prevented an Indian agent and his party from passing through their lands. At about that time, one Howyatchi (Hoo-e-yas'lsee), or Sampson, received from a government official a commission recognizing him as the Queets head chief. With Quinaults and others, the Queets Indians met with Washington territorial governor and superintendent of Indian affairs Isaac Stevens at the abortive Chehalis River treaty council early in 1855. A white settler who attended the council, James Swan, stated that a Chehalis shaman with great bravado shot a young Queets headman because his people and the Quinaults had favored the treaty. Opposed to such violence were followers of the Indian Shaker faith, which was carried to the Queets by Quinaults after a Squaxin Indian, John Slocum, had founded the church in 1882.

Government and Claims: With the Quinaults, the Queets Indians petitioned the Indian Claims Commission (Docket 242) for additional remuneration for the lands that they, along with the Quileutes and the Hohs, had surrendered to the United States under their so-called Quinault River Treaty on July 1, 1855 (12 Stat. 971), signed January 25, 1856, and ratified March 8, 1859. The Quinault Reservation had originated under that treaty but was subsequently enlarged by executive order on November 4, 1873. After an appeal to the Court of Claims, which that body dismissed, the Queets and Quinault petitioners finally received a compromise settlement from the Claims Commission, which on June 25, 1962, approved a judgment against the United States of $205,172.40. Both tribes shared in the settlement.

Contemporary Life and Culture: In 1998 the Quinault Indian Nation opened a $750,000 convenience store at Queets with gasoline and diesel pumps, air and water service, a self-serve laundromat, and handicapped-accessible restrooms and showers. It replaced an earlier business that had closed six years previously. A year before the convenience store was built, a medical-dental clinic had opened in the village, and a bike and sidewalk path was dedicated. The tribe operates a Head Start and daycare facilities and a senior center. Queets Fish House and Queets Fisheries both involve local Queets fisheries. Queets students attend the Clearwater public school on Highway 101, six miles from Queets, and Lake Quinault High School on Highway 101, twenty-seven miles north of Queets.

Special Events and Celebrations: There are no tribally sponsored events, but tribal members participate annually in the Canoe Journey.

Suggested Readings:

Russel L. Barsh, "The Economics of a Traditional Coastal Indian Salmon Fishery," *Human Organization* 41, no. 2 (1982).

QUILEUTE

(Chimakuan)

The name "Quileute" (Quillayute) is said to mean simply "name." According to the photographer and observer of American Indians, Edward S. Curtis, the tribal name was applied originally to residents of the village of Ziliyut (now La Push, Washington) at the mouth of the Quillayute River. Some scholars maintain that its meaning is unknown. Other names were given the Indian village at the mouth of the Quillayute River. Besides the Hohs, the only linguistic kin of the Quileutes south of Vancouver Island were the Chimakums, who were said to have fled eastward from huge tides in early times *(see* **Chimakum**). Quileute family-unit settlements extended for thirty miles up the Quillayute, which tumbles from the Olympic Mountains in Washington west to the Pacific Ocean.

The Quileutes believed that they had been created from wolves by Dokibatt the Changer, or Transformer, who looms large in Pacific Northwest coastal mythology. Among the Quileutes' legends, like those of other tribes of the region, was the story of the huge whale-snatching bird, Tistilal, whose flapping wings were thunder and whose yellow feathers were lightning. In early times there were six Quileute societies: for the fisherman, the elk hunter, the whale hunter, the weather predictor, the medicine man, and the warrior (the latter society performed the wolf dance). The societies reflected the nature of Quileute life. With the vast Olympic Peninsula at their backs, the Quileutes turned to the Pacific Ocean as the main source of their subsistence, becoming proficient seal and whale hunters. They never achieved the reputation enjoyed by Makahs for whale hunting, and it was probably from them that they acquired the techniques of the hunt, which they in turn passed on to the Quinaults.

Location: The modern Quileute Tribe, Quileute Reservation, Washington, live on or near their 593.84-acre Quileute Reservation, which was originally 837 acres when established by executive order on February 19, 1889. It is situated on a beautiful stretch of ocean about fourteen miles west of the logging community of Forks on U.S. Highway 101 and about a hundred miles north of the Grays Harbor cities of Hoquiam and Aberdeen. The largest numbers of Quileutes live in the reservation town of La Push, which is on the south side of the Quillayute River, about thirty-eight miles south of Cape Flattery at the northern tip of the Olympic Peninsula.

Numbers: With the Hohs, the Quileutes were estimated to have numbered about 500 in 1780. In 1888, when the two tribes were enumerated separately, 64 Quileutes were counted. In 1962 their recorded population varied from 10 to 100. The

Quileutes were listed at 383 in 1985. In 2005 tribal membership was estimated at more than 750.

History: More study is needed to ascertain the times and the routes of the early migrations that brought the Quileutes to their historic location, where they occasionally fought other tribes like the Makahs. When attacked by superior numbers, the villagers at the mouth of the Quillayute River took refuge on the impregnable nearby James Island, from which a Quileute village was moved to the mainland in the nineteenth century. The Quileutes faced in warfare nearly every saltwater tribe between Vancouver Island and the Columbia River. According to their tradition, their last major confrontation occurred on the Grays Harbor mudflats when they engaged a Chinook-Clatsop coalition. Intertribal strife, especially with the Makahs, continued into the latter half of the nineteenth century, but such conflicts did not prevent the intertribal trade by which the Quileutes obtained such goods as dentalia and blankets from the Makahs and the Ozettes. They in turn traded those goods to the Quinaults for that people's highly prized salmon. The Quileutes and their neighbors also exchanged whale products with the residents of Vancouver Island. Like other Indians of the region, the Quileutes held potlatch ceremonies at which a man's wealth was measured not by what he possessed but by what he gave away.

Quileute tradition tells of shipwrecked Spaniards, the "drifting white people," who lived among them in early times. In May 1792 they traded with the American Capt. Robert Gray at their main village, today's La Push. They were among the Natives who attacked and, for a time, enslaved persons from a Russian vessel that wrecked near the mouth of the Quillayute River on November 1, 1808. In the 1840s the Quileutes survived a severe famine. From the time of Captain Gray's visit until 1855, when they were contacted by Americans seeking to effect a treaty with them, their encounters with whites appear to have been few. Indian Agent M. T. Simmons, representing Washington territorial governor and superintendent of Indian affairs Isaac Stevens, was among the first to break their relative isolation. On January 25, 1856, Chief How-yaks (How-yat'l) and two subchiefs whom Simmons appointed were in the territorial capital of Olympia to sign officially the Quinault River Treaty, which they and others had informally accepted on July 1, 1855. In 1863, an agency was established at the Makah Reservation, and in 1864 another was authorized on the Quinault Reservation. The Quileutes were administered variously from the town of Taholah on the Quinault Reservation and from the community of Neah Bay on the Makah Reservation. According to their 1856 treaty, they were to live on the Quinault Reservation, but they chose not to, even after its establishment on November 4, 1873. After they refused to remove to the Quinault, they settled on their own Quileute Reservation, created in 1889.

In 1866 twenty soldiers were dispatched to the Quileute country to arrest three Natives accused of killing a white man. Ten others were seized for offenses that ranged from slave trading to the murder of another white man some years previously. The prisoners were incarcerated at the U.S. Army's Fort Steilacoom, from which they escaped in 1867. The Quileutes had much trouble from the invading white settlers, who, in 1867, tried to establish a "Quilehuyte County" government and petitioned the American government to confine the Quileutes to a reservation. In 1882 whites requested that the Quileute shaman Obi, who had opposed them, be removed from the territory as a "troublemaker." Obi appears to have been at the root of violent quarrels over the Quileute chieftaincy. He was finally arrested by his son, an agency policeman. In 1889, while the Quileutes were away hop picking, a white man seeking to appropriate their properties burned down twenty-six of their houses at La Push. The Quileutes were forced to build new ones on the beach, which was flooded during storms and high water.

The establishment of the first school among the Quileutes in 1883 set poorly with them. One task of its first teacher was to assign the children Christian, or what he called "civilized," names. The Quileutes were relatively free of white pressures during the first decade of the twentieth century. Until then, there were but two wagon roads in the entire western Olympic Peninsula. In 1912 whites constructed a salmon cannery on the Quillayute River and infringed on Indian fishing by appropriating their ancient fishing sites. Indians were treated as noncitizens and declared ineligible to obtain licenses. By an act on March 4, 1904 (36 Stat. 1346), the commissioner of Indian affairs declared the Quileutes eligible to obtain allotments on the Quinault Reservation, as stipulated in their 1856 treaty. (The first allotments on the reservation had been made to Quinaults in 1892.) A reverse decision two years later denied the Quileutes their allotments. But the ruling was again reversed. On March 4, 1911, by congressional action, the secretary of the interior was directed to allot land to all Quileutes, Hohs, and Ozettes on the Quinault Reservation, as authorized in the Quinault River Treaty, even though the various tribes had reservations of their own. Lack of farming and grazing land on the Quinault brought allotting there to a halt in 1913. The remaining 168,000 acres of the Quinault Reservation were timbered and were to be held by the Quinault Tribe as a whole. Finally, in 1928, the government completed the allotment by granting 165 Quileutes each an 80-acre timbered tract on the Quinault Reservation.

Government and Claims: The Quileute Tribe voted to organize under the Indian Reorganization Act (48 Stat. 984, 1934) and adopted a constitution and by-laws approved by the secretary of the interior in 1936. The governing body is the Quileute Tribal Council, which elects the principal tribal officers from among its members. The Quileute Tribe has gained several important powers, including the authority to veto any sales, disposition, lease, or other encumbrance of tribal lands; to advise on and approve appropriations; to levy and collect taxes and license fees from nonmembers doing business on the reservation; to enforce ordinances involving visitors, trespassers, and tribal membership; to establish a tribal court; and to maintain law and order.

Today members of the tribe of this early-twentieth-century Quileute man live on their nearly 600-acre Quileute Reservation on the Pacific Coast in northwestern Washington, earning their livelihoods mainly by fishing and logging.

Photograph by Edward S. Curtis, from Curtis's *The North American Indian* (1907–1930), vol. 9.

With the Hohs, the Quileutes claimed (Docket 155) additional compensation for lands that they had ceded to the United States under the Quinault River Treaty. With Quinault and Queets Indians, they and the Hohs had received $25,000 as stipulated by treaty, and they claimed that compensation was unconscionably small. The Indian Claims Commission determined that all four tribes had had aboriginal title to 688,000 acres as of March 8, 1858, and on April 17, 1963, the commission awarded the Quileutes and Hohs $112,152.60 for their share. At the time of white contact the Quileutes had claimed about 900 square miles as their homeland.

Contemporary Life and Culture: Many Quileutes earn their living by fishing and logging. Some receive income from land and timber sales, though in 2002, the tribe suffered a 70 percent unemployment rate. As of 1973 there were 393.84 acres of trust lands on their tribally owned and unallotted reservation. As noted, reservation residents live primarily in the village of La Push on the Quillayute River, which provides a harbor for fishing boats as it is sheltered by a breakwater and permits safe passage to and from the Pacific Ocean. The predominant religious orientation is Protestant. An Indian Shaker church was established shortly after the founding of the faith in 1882. Social services are provided through local and federal agencies. During World War II twenty-two Quileutes served in the American armed forces. A 14,000-word Quileute dictionary and study manual have been prepared. Considerable attention has also been given to preserving traditional crafts and culture. The Quileutes are one of few tribes requiring a 50 percent Native blood quantum and birth on the reservation to qualify for membership.

The Quileute Tribe does not operate a casino, but in 2001 it began leasing gaming machines to tribes with casinos. From this venture, the tribe realizes $1 million in annual revenue. Since 1978 the tribe has owned and operated the Ocean Park Resort at La Push, which includes fifteen cabins constructed in 2002, at a cost of $1.8 million, in a design reflective of Quileute culture. Placing tourism at the center of its economy, the tribe also operates the riverfront River's Edge restaurant and the Lonesome Creek convenience store.

In 1992 there were only three fluent speakers of the Quileute language, but the tribe has introduced language acquisition classes. Quileute Tribal School (K-12) has been run by the tribe since 1979. At one time it was one of only thirty schools in the United States overseen by a Native American school board. In 2002 the tribe opened a new school facility—A-Ka-Lat Center—built at a cost $3.7 million. It replaces a tribal school abandoned in 1927 and also serves as a community center, providing a full-service kitchen, classrooms, auditorium, library, and culture room. The Quileutes also operate a Head Start program and Quileute Higher Education, a program that offers precollege and college training. High school students may also attend the Quillayute Valley public school in Forks. Similar to the Hoh Tribe, the Quileutes are in negotiations with the National Park Service to acquire acreage that would allow them to move their school, senior center, and other buildings to higher ground and out of a tsunami zone.

In 2005 the Quileute Tribe gained popular notoriety with publication of the best-selling novel *Twilight,* the plot of which is set in the nearby community of Forks. Some characters in the book are fictionalized members of the Quileute Tribe.

Special Events and Celebrations: The annual Quileute Days is usually held on the first weekend of August. Each April the tribe hosts Whale Welcome, commemorating the annual migration of these mammals off their coast.

Suggested Readings:

Edward S. Curtis, *The North American Indian* (1912; New York: Johnson Reprint Corp., 1970), vol. 10; Philip Drucker, *Indians of the Northwest Coast* (New York: McGraw-Hill, 1955); Harry Hobucket, "Quillayute Indian Tradition," *Washington Historical Quarterly* 25, no. 1 (January 1934); Ronald L. Olson, *The Quinault Indians: Adze, Canoe, and House Types of the Northwest Coast* (Seattle: University of Washington Press, 1967); George A. Pettitt, "The Quileutes of La Push, 1775–1945," *Anthropological Records* 14, no. 1 (1950); J. V. Powell, et al., "Place Names of the Quileute Indians," *Pacific Northwest Quarterly* 63, no. 3 (July 1972); Jay Powell and Vickie Jensen, *Quileute: An Introduction to the Indians of La Push* (Seattle: University of Washington Press, 1976); Albert B. Reagan, "Tradition of the Hoh and Quillayute Indians," *Washington Historical Quarterly* 20, no. 3 (July 1929); *Seattle (Wash.) Times,* Pictorial, June 25, 1978; "Teacher 22 Years among Quillutes," *Tacoma (Wash.) News Tribune,* February 17, 1963; Robert E. Steiner, "Shipwrecks & Promises," *Columbia: The Magazine of Northwest History* 9, no. 2 (1995).

QUINAULT

(Coastal Division, Salishan)

The Canoe People, the People of the Cedar Tree

The name "Quinault" (Quinaelt) derives from that of the tribe's largest settlement, which was on the site of present-day Taholah, Washington, at the mouth of the Quinault River on the Pacific Coast of the Olympic Peninsula shores. The Quinaults' homelands were the Quinault River valley and the coast between Raft River and Joe Creek. Like their neighbors, they were intermediaries in the cultural flow between Indians of the Strait of Juan de Fuca on the north and the tribes of the Columbia River on the south. The Quinaults were the southernmost peoples along the coast who hunted whales, but they did so less intensively than the Makahs north of them. They secured the other requirements of their subsistence not only from the sea but also from the forests and rivers. Their most important food source was the succulent salmon that they caught in the Quinault River. They also fished for salmon and sturgeon in the Columbia River, and, like other salmon-fishing peoples, they observed social taboos that attended the catching of that fish. For instance, Quinault mothers sent their daughters off to a village so that their menses would not frighten salmon away. Understandably, fish were also important in their mythology and influenced how they were perceived by outsiders. Their ease in obtaining fish and other foods caused some early non-Indians to regard them as lazy. The customary flattening of the heads of high-born children and such practices as shamanism also encouraged the opinion among whites that Quinaults were a "barbarous" people.

Location: Today most Quinaults are members of the Quinault Tribe, Quinault Reservation, Washington, and live on the tribe's 189,621-acre reservation, which lies on a coastal plateau extending east from the Pacific Ocean to the foothills of the Olympic Mountains. Most residents of the reservation live in the towns of Taholah (on U.S. Highway 109) and Queets (on U.S. Highway 101). A few families live on allotments and some live off the reservation.

Numbers: In the early contact period, the Quinaults were estimated conservatively at about 2,400. In 1885 they numbered 102. In 1984 the tribe counted 1,623 members, about 440 more than in 1912. In 1989 there were 2,260, a decade later about 2,500, and another decade after that, in July 2009, 2,848.

History: The Quinaults usually kept on friendly terms with their neighbors, to whom they extended their hospitality. Sometimes they engaged in conflicts with other Pacific Coast groups and with tribes to the east such as the Twanas, who traveled through the Olympic Mountains onto Quinault lands. The first recorded contact between Quinaults and non-Indians occurred on July 13, 1775, when

Johnnie Saux, a Quinault, holding a dog salmon in 1936 at Taholah on the Quinault Reservation on Washington's coast. The salmon caught by the Quinaults in their homeland were said to have been the most succulent of all Pacific Coast salmon.

Courtesy of the National Archives.

they visited the Spanish vessel *Sonora* in their canoes. On the following day, emerging from the forest, they killed five Spaniards but lost several of their own people in an ensuing fight. As late as 1854, the early white settler James Swan was of the opinion that there were Quinaults living farther up the Quinault River who had never seen white men. It is possible that Swan was the first non-Indian to see Lake Quinault. It is an indication of the Quinaults' isolation that white settlers did not arrive among them in appreciable numbers until the late 1880s. Foreign hunters also entered Quinault territory from the sea at Point Grenville to shoot sea otters, whose valuable furs they sold to others at handsome prices. The very existence of these animals was endangered by the guns in the hands of whites and their Indian employees. In the early 1860s, troops were dispatched to the Quinault River, and a blockhouse was built to restrain Indians angry with white trespassers.

With Hoh, Queets, and Quileute Indians, the Quinaults approved the Quinault River Treaty with the Indian agent M. T. Simmons on July 1, 1855. The treaty was formalized in a signing with Washington territorial governor and superintendent of Indian affairs Isaac Stevens on January 25, 1856. The Quinault Reservation, which originated with the treaty, was enlarged by executive order on November 4, 1873. On February 17, 1892, the president authorized allotments to the Quinaults on the reservation. The reservations of some other tribes signatory to the Quinault River Treaty were small and barren, and after some controversy, the government in 1907 permitted allotments to Queets and Quileute Indians, along with the Quinaults, on the Quinault Reservation. On March 4, 1911, Congress passed an act directing that Hohs and Ozettes should be allotted on the Quinault Reservation in the hope that they too would become agrarians. In 1932 the U.S. Supreme Court ruled that Chehalises, Chinooks, and Cowlitzes should be allotted as well on the Quinault. By 1933 the last of the 2,340 allotments on the reservation had been made, leaving no tribally owned land remaining there.

Joseph Burton De La Cruz (1937–2000), president of the Quinault Indian Nation from 1970 to 1994. De La Cruz was a nationally recognized Indian activist who served two terms as president of the National Congress of American Indians as well as serving as president of the National Tribal Chairman's Association and president of the Affiliated Tribes of Northwest Indians.

Courtesy of Larry Workman.

Like other Indians, the Quinaults resisted farming. They were also wary of placing their children in federal schools. One of their chiefs, Wakeenus, declared, "I would rather hang than send my children to [a government] school." But it was a sign of the growing competitive nature of the marketplace when the Quinaults established a tribally owned fish trap replete with ropes and pulleys near the mouth of the Quinault River at the end of the nineteenth century.

Government and Claims: The governing body of the tribe is the Quinault Tribe, Quinault Reservation, Washington. The tribe's Business Committee functions under bylaws adopted on August 24, 1922. The tribe voted to accept the Indian Reorganization Act of 1934 (48 Stat. 984), but did not reorganize under its terms. Indian personnel staff the reservation police force and there is a tribal court, including a chief judge and associate justices. Tribal leaders believe that their reservation would be better policed if the State of Washington were to recognize the tribe as its sole governing body. In 1975, the Quinaults adopted a new constitution, which assigned decision-making power to the eleven-member Business Committee instead of the traditional General Council of the Tribe. Then, under the Self-Governance Act of 1988, the Quinaults implemented self-rule in their affairs.

The Queets and Quinault Indians petitioned the Indian Claims Commission (Docket 242) for additional monetary compensation for the lands that both tribes had ceded to the United States under the Quinault River Treaty. The commission heard the case along with that of the Quileutes and Hohs (Docket 155), because both claims were for compensation above the $25,000 granted by the treaty for the overlapping lands. The commission found that the petitioners had had aboriginal title to approximately 688,000 acres of land as of March 8, 1858. After tribal appeals, a Claims Commission order to the Court of Claims (Docket 6-61) was dismissed, and the commission, in a compromise settlement with the

Quinault and Queets tribes on June 25, 1962, ordered a judgment against the United States of $205,172.40. After the tribes were awarded the moneys on April 17, 1973, the Quinaults voted to apply their share to community projects.

Contemporary Life and Culture: The lands of the Quinault Indian Nation consist of 208,150 acres. Nearly a third of the reservation has been alienated and is owned largely by timber and sawmilling companies. Having previously sold its timber rights, the Quinault Tribe has since begun to regain them. There remain approximately 130,000 acres on the reservation that are in an allotted-trust or otherwise restricted status. Many tribal members engage in logging, sawmilling, and allied industries. Besides a lumber mill, the Quinault Tribe has built a salmon hatchery and a fish-processing plant. It markets a considerable amount of seafood. It also operates an arts-and-crafts manufacturing plant. Socioeconomic conditions on the reservation are discouraging, however, with 80 percent of tribal members in 1996 earning $15,000 or less annually and eighty families on the reservation making less than $5,000 per year.

At one point, the tribe planned to sue the federal government because forestry practices on the reservation had proved so harmful to the environment. The situation became complicated, however, when members of about ten other tribes were allotted on the reservation, and in 1968, organized the Quinault Allottees Association. In 1971, the association filed suit in the Court of Claims, doing so without congressional authorization because they did not possess tribal status. When the Court of Claims refused to dismiss the case, the Supreme Court, on June 27, 1983, ruled that the Allottees Association could sue the United States for mismanagement of Quinault Indian resources on the reservation. There has been considerable contention between the tribe and the Allottees Association. Tribal officials fear interference from the latter group.

The tribe closed several miles of Pacific Ocean beach to the general public because of abuse of these tribal lands. In 1988 the tribe accepted 11,900 acres of Forest Service land for land omitted from the reservation in an erroneous 1892 survey by Public Law 100-638. Such land was added along both inland reservation borders. And, in 1989, the tribe accepted $26.6 million to settle a timber lawsuit filed in 1971 for careless timber cutting and for the lower prices Indians received compared with off-reservation sales. This litigation was begun under the tribal chairmanship of the late Jim Jackson, a great grandson of Chief Taholah, who was the first signer of the Treaty of Quinault with Governor Isaac Stevens in 1855. The tribe has also reached the North Boundary Settlement with the federal government, which allocated $32.2 million to the Quinaults to protect 4,207 acres of marbled murrelet habitat.

In 1990 in Taholah, the tribe built the General Store & Mercantile and in 1998 broke ground on a $750,000 convenience store and gas station located in the village of Queets. The Quinault Indian Nation operates the Quinault Beach Resort and Casino at Ocean Shores, which opened on May 22, 2000, at a construction cost of around $50 million. The resort includes 150 oversized guest rooms and a cabaret for live entertainment, while the 16,000 square feet of casino floor space includes 350 electronic gaming devices, 15 table games, poker, and keno. The tribe also operates Quinault Pride Seafood, a fish processing plant, in addition to Quinault Land and Timber Enterprises and the Maritime Resort. Quinault Mental Health opened in 1994 and in 1999 the Quinaults began the construction of a new 4,413-square-foot mental health building with a group therapy room, conference room, and individual offices for therapists. The new facility cost $354,000. In the same year, the tribe celebrated the opening of a new Natural Resources Building, put up at a cost of $4.2 million, with an executive wing that houses tribal offices and replaces five trailers previously used for administrative offices. In 2000 construction began on Moclips River Estates, an $8-million, eighty-unit housing development on the reservation.

Education is available to Quinault youth through two new daycare centers, which opened in 2001, and an elementary, middle, and high school (grades 9 to 12) operated by Taholah School District. Some students attend schools in the North Beach School District in nearby Moclips.

Though Quinaults have participated in annual paddle canoe journeys since Emmett Oliver began them in 1989, they built their first sea canoe since 1910 in the mid-1990s. Phillip Martin (whose grandfather was the sixteenth signer of the Treaty of Olympia), Emmett Oliver, and Guy Capoeman, among others, carved the boat from a 700-year-old cedar tree and named it May-ee, Quinault for "New Beginning." In 2002 tribal member Randy Capoeman carved and erected the first Quinault totem pole in over fifty years, and in 2005 bone (or slahal) games were played at Chief Tahola Days for the first time in a half century. Contemporary Quinault art style incorporates South Pacific motifs, which were introduced by a returning Quinault soldier from World War II, with Quinault motifs. The Quinault Indian Nation operates the Quinault Nation Heritage Center & Museum.

Special Events and Celebrations: The Quinault Trout Derby is held annually, usually around Memorial Day. The main feature is a cedar dugout canoe race. The tribe also holds Chief Taholah Days, a Fourth of July celebration featuring Indian dances, canoe races, and a salmon barbecue held to commemorate the signing of the Quinault River Treaty on July 1, 1855.

Suggested Readings:

Pauline K. Capoeman, ed., *Land of the Quinault* (Taholah, Wash.: Quinault Indian Nation, 1990); Philip Drucker, *Indians of the Northwest Coast* (New York: McGraw-Hill, 1955); George Gibbs, "Tribes of Western Washington and Northwestern Oregon," *Contributions to North American Ethnology*, 1 (Washington, 1877), part 2; Ronald L. Olson, *The Quinault Indians: Adze, Canoe, and House Types of the Northwest Coast* (Seattle: University of Washington Press, 1967); Jacqueline

M. Storm, et al., *Land of the Quinault* (Taholah, Wash.: Quinault Indian Nation, 1990); Charles Clark Willoughby, "Indians of the Quinault Agency, Washington Territory," *Annual Report of the Smithsonian Institution* (1886); Jacilee Wray, *Native Peoples of the Olympic Peninsula: Who We Are* (Norman: University of Oklahoma Press, 2002); Quinault Tribal Council, *Portrait of Our Land* (Taholah, Wash.: Quinault Tribal Press, 1978).

SAHEWAMISH

(Coastal Division, Salishan)

The Sahewamish lived on the innermost fingerlike reaches of southern Puget Sound in Washington State. Some of their villages were located on the lower Nisqually River and McAllister (Medicine) Creek and on several bays and inlets, including Budd Inlet, Eld (Mud) Bay, Hammersley Inlet, Henderson (South) Bay, Shelton Inlet, and Totten (Oyster) Bay. The large Sahewamish village near Arcadia, Sahéwabc or Sahéwabsh, commanded outlets of Budd and Shelton inlets and Mud and Oyster bays. Because of its prominence, the name of the Sahéwabsh village, sounding like *sahewamish,* was extended to the Natives of other villages. The Sahewamish population was estimated at 1,200 in 1780 and at 780 in 1907. After a severe smallpox plague in 1853, government officials counted 50 Sahewamish living at Eld, Hammersley, and Totten inlets. The Sahewamish were closely related to the neighboring Squaxins for whom Squaxin Island was set aside as a reservation. Yet some Sahewamish intermarried with Indians from as far away as northern Puget Sound, and some settled on reservations such as the Skokomish at the southern end of Hood Canal with other Sahewamish neighbors, the Twanas.

SALISH & KOOTENAI CONFEDERATED TRIBES

(See **Confederated Salish & Kootenai Tribes of the Flathead Reservation.***)*

SAMISH

(Coastal Division, Salishan)

The significance of the name "Samish" is unknown. The name is perpetuated in an island, a bay, a lake, and a river, all in northwestern Washington. The Samish spoke the Lkungen dialect of the Coastal Salishan language. Their winter villages were on various islands: Samish (south of Bellingham), Guemes (north of Anacortes), and Fidalgo (on which Anacortes lies). From those sites they moved throughout the San Juan Islands to numerous fishing sites. Culturally, they were closely linked with the Lummis. In the 1840s the Samish were reduced to a single village by disease and by the raids of more powerful northern tribes. On Samish Bay and Samish Island, which is joined to the mainland by a natural landfill, the Samish lived close to the once-powerful Nuwaha villagers, grouped by anthropologists with the Skagits, many of whom united with the Samish at the beginning of the twentieth century. The Samish were known for their canoe making and their gift-giving potlatches, which were attended by Indians from throughout Puget Sound, Vancouver Island, and the Fraser River country. The Samishes' last large potlatch was held shortly after 1900.

Location: Most Samish tribal members live in such communities as Anacortes, Mount Vernon, Bellingham, and Everett and in many smaller towns in northwestern Washington. A small number live on nearby reservations such as the Lummi and the Swinomish.

Numbers: The aboriginal Samish population was estimated at 1,000, including Lummis and Nooksacks. In 1850 the Samish numbered approximately 150, the same as were reported by government sources at the time of the Point Elliott Treaty in 1855. In 1930 the tribe was listed at 280 and in 1951 at approximately 350. Once considered the largest American Indian nation on Puget Sound, the Samish as of 1980 had a tribal enrollment of 590. In 2008, that number remained above 500.

History: A Nuwaha chief, Pateus (or Pattehus), was said to have signed the Point Elliott Treaty of January 22, 1855, for the Samish. Other sources allege that the Lummi chief Chowitsoot signed for them. The nineteenth-century ethnologist George Gibbs, in government employ in the Pacific Northwest at the time, stated that 113 of the 150 Samish attended the treaty council. The Samish did not appear in the final draft of the treaty, yet today's Samish claim to have documentation showing that their ancestors were included in its initial draft but were inadvertently omitted from the final draft. After the treaty was ratified, the Samish were sent to reservations such as the Lummi and the Swinomish. Refusing to leave their homelands, many left those reservations for the territory the Samish had traditionally held. Samish informants maintain that, as late as the end of the nineteenth century, American soldiers drove their ancestors to the reservations and that some of those who refused to remove were put to death while others escaped to Canada. Samish Indians of the lower classes and males suffered the most. Upper-class Samish women married to white men generally escaped such cruelties. Approximately forty-seven Samish were on the Lummi Reservation, where they were often in conflict with the Lummi and Nooksack Indians. Most of the Samish, except those who had intermarried with Lummis, returned to their tribe, which remained on Samish Island during the 1870s. Under the Point Elliott Treaty, the Samish were to have had an area set aside for them on the Swinomish Reservation. The area was to have been the western half of March's Point on Fidalgo Island (just east of Anacortes). When the Swinomish Reservation boundaries were defined by executive order on September 9, 1873, most of the Samish, the largest tribe scheduled for the reservation, found themselves outside its confines. Only a half dozen of the ninety-seven allotments on the reservation were for Samish, the latter often erroneously referred to in agency records as Skagits.

The Samish, pushed outside the protection of the U.S. government, were once again forced to move, this time to Guemes Island, which is in an area now called Potlatch Beach but was formerly referred to as New Guemes to distinguish it from earlier Samish villages on the island. The Samish built a longhouse of approximately 60 by 480 feet in which over a hundred people lived. Each of nine principal family heads was a religious leader who kept alive traditional beliefs, despite the ongoing government efforts to stamp them out on the reservations. Observers at the time referred to the Samish village on Guemes Island as the "Pagan capital."

Two Samish headmen, Sam Watchoat and Bob Syithlanoch (Citizen Sam and Bob Edwards), filed for and received trust allotments for the Guemes Island property under a homestead act. In 1883 they were issued trust patents to the lands, which protected them for a twenty-year period. The patents expired in 1903. Because the Samish had the only fresh springwater on the island, much pressure was exerted on them by their white neighbors, and by 1912 they had been forced off their lands, just as they had been forced off Samish Island by non-Indians about fifty years earlier. After the breakup of the Guemes Island village, some Samish remained as perceived squatters and others removed to various communities in Samish country such as Anacortes, Blanchard, Bay View, Edison, Bow Hill, and Summit Park. Throughout the 1890s and well into the 1900s, the Samish continued occupying fishing villages on Lopez and Cypress islands in the San Juans and traveling throughout those islands in large canoes, some thirty-six feet in length. Many took allotments on the Swinomish Reservation in 1885 and eventually (after 1900) moved onto the reservation. Other Samish received allotments there in 1905.

The late Ken Hansen (photo taken ca. 1987), a Samish Indian of northwestern Washington, was in the forefront of Samish attempts to achieve federal recognition and regain fishing and other rights for their once-powerful tribe. Hansen exemplified the many active tribal leaders of the Pacific Northwest in the 1970s and 1980s.

Authors' collections.

Government and Claims: The Samish developed a political organization as early as 1907 and met in their longhouse on Guemes Island and later in Anacortes. Later still, they held meetings on the Swinomish Reservation strictly as their own tribe. Around 1918, the Lower (Samish Flat or Stick Samish) Nuwahas merged with the Samish. In 1924 their tribal president, S. J. Kavanaugh, had also been elected president of the Northwestern Federation of American Indians, which had been founded in Tacoma in 1914 to push for fulfillment of treaty claims. In 1926 the Samish organized under a formal constitution and bylaws, which were replaced by new ones in 1951, 1965, and 1974. Today they are known as the Samish Indian Tribe. Although landless, they fought alongside their reservation allies for the greater self-governance provided under the Indian Reorganization Act (48 Stat. 984) in the 1930s, against termination of the Indians' trust relationship with the federal government in the 1950s, and against state jurisdiction. Despite all their efforts, the federal government would not recognize or acknowledge them as a tribe. In 1975 they filed a petition seeking such status, but three years later the government, without acting on it, returned it to them. In 1979 the tribe drafted and submitted a new petition under newly developed federal guidelines, but they were again denied acknowledgment in 1982.

Federal acknowledgment of the Samish as a tribe would have given tribal members the rights enjoyed by the members of the several other treaty tribes of the region. One important right pertains to fishing. In 1974 the Samish Tribe intervened in *United States* v. *Washington,* a case decided by federal judge George Boldt that clarified treaty language by reserving half the harvestable salmon and steelhead trout in the waters of Washington State for federally recognized, land-based treaty tribes. After receiving an unfavorable decision by Judge Boldt in 1979, the Samish Tribe, with four other landless tribes, appealed its case to the Ninth Circuit Court of Appeals and ultimately won back their fishing rights.

After filing its land claim (Docket 261) before the Indian Claims Commission in 1951, the Samish Tribe was awarded a settlement on October 6, 1971. The award of $5,754.96 was for lands alienated to the United States under the Point Elliott Treaty. The United States argued that, of the $17,000 to which the Samish were entitled for their lands, about $11,245.04 had already been provided them in blankets, food, and other government "services." The commission determined that the Samish had exclusively used and occupied about 9,233 acres ceded under the Point Elliott Treaty. In 1987 the BIA declared the tribe extinct, but in 1992 a federal judge ruled that the Samish were a viable entity, thus leaving the door open to the granting of federal recognition.

Contemporary Life and Culture: Having been dropped from the list of federally recognized tribes in 1969 because of a clerical error and then declared officially extinct by the U.S. government in 1987, the Samish regained recognition status in 1996. In 2001, under the leadership of the late tribal chairman Ken Hansen, the Samish purchased seventy-seven acres. Three years later, the tribe received a $3.4-million loan from the Native American Bank to help finance the $8-million Fidalgo Bay Resort Project, which includes an RV park and a clubhouse that is utilized as a conference center and currently houses the tribe's administration building and other tribal offices. By 2002 the Samish had purchased eighty acres outside of Anacortes, next to Campbell Lake, to be used for constructing the first housing development for tribal members. The Samish do not have a casino, but under state gambling compacts they lease slot machines to tribes that do, which accounts for about 20 percent of their annual operating budget.

The Samish have operated Samish Longhouse Preschool Head Start in Anacortes since 2002, and recently they started a preschool child care for those families not meeting the eligibility requirements of Head Start. Samish elementary and secondary students attend public schools in the communities in which they reside. The tribe also provides Higher Education Assistance scholarships to help students with college tuition, and their Vocational Rehabilitation Program assists adults with disabilities and those having barriers to finding employment. Medical care is available to tribal members through contracted health services as well as Indian Health Service facilities. The Samish also employ a physician and a registered nurse, who together offer a variety of services and preventive care.

In 2007 the Samish filed suit to regain fishing rights lost twenty-five years ago, specifically, fishing harvests near Bellingham and the San Juan Islands. The Samish actively support the cleaning up and restoration of Puget Sound, and in 20007 they sponsored an environmental study of Fidalgo Bay. A year later, the Samish acquired fourteen acres on Highway 20 in Anacortes; the tribe is considering the site for future hotel or casino development.

Special Events and Celebrations: In June the Samish observe Samish Cultural Day, and in January they participate in the Point Elliott Treaty Day celebration.

Suggested Readings:

> Samish Tribe, *Petition for the Federal Acknowledgement of the Samish Indian Tribe* (Anacortes, Wash.: Samish Tribal Press, 1979); Martin J. Sampson, *Indians of Skagit County* (Mount Vernon, Wash.: Skagit County Historical Society, 1972); Wayne P. Suttles, *The Economic Life of the Coast Salish of Haro and Rosario Straits,* vol. 1 of *Coast Salish and Western Washington Indians* (New York: Garland Publishing, 1974).

SAMMAMISH

(See **Duwamish.***)*

SAN JUAN TRIBE OF INDIANS

The San Juan Tribe of Indians is descended from Lummis and Samish, members of certain Canadian tribes, and even an Alaskan Indian family, all of whom have come together as a political organization.

Location: Tribal members live largely in the San Juan Islands and on the nearby mainland in northwestern Washington.

Numbers: In 1955 the tribe numbered 255.

Government and Claims: The San Juan Tribe of Indians claims aboriginal possession of approximately 120,000 acres of land in San Juan County, the county that comprises most of the San Juan Islands archipelago. The San Juans were one of several petitioning tribes of the Puget Sound area claiming that compensation was due them from the United States for alienation of their aboriginal lands. In *Duwamish et al.* v. *United States* (79 C.Cls. 530), it was decided that the San Juans had no claim for compensation because they were not recognized by the United States as a tribe, having never treated with its government. The San Juan Tribe next petitioned the Indian Claims Commission for its claim (Docket 214). The commission dismissed the case because the San Juans had no identifiable ancestry as a distinct group. They could, however, recover from any award that the Lummis (Docket 110) or Samish (Docket 261) might receive, if they could show descendency from those two tribes. The San Juan Tribe today still seeks federal acknowledgment, which among other benefits, would permit its members fishing rights guaranteed under the 1855 Point Elliott Treaty with the United States. *See* **Lummi, Mitchell Bay,** *and* **Samish.**

SANPOIL

(Interior Division, Salishan)

The word "Sanpoil" is of Native origin despite its Gallic form. The early-nine-teenth-century fur trader Alexander Henry wrote that the Sanpoils called them-selves Spoil-Ehieh (Sinpoelihuh). He also wrote that they seldom left their own lands, which were primarily along the Sanpoil River in present-day north-central Washington. Their main wintering village was near the confluence of the Colum-bia and Sanpoil rivers. They hunted game and gathered roots and berries in their

homelands and in those of their neighbors to the west, the Nespelems, as well as in lands bordering the Columbia River to the south. During salmon seasons, they fished at the mouths of the Sanpoil and Spokane rivers (the latter enters the Columbia on the east of the Sanpoil country).

With the less-numerous Nespelems, the Sanpoils developed a reputation for in-dependence among whites and Indians. Tradition has it that in precontact times Sanpoil villagers were attacked by Salish-speaking peoples like the Spokanes and Columbia Sinkiuses and also by Shahap-tian-speaking Yakamas and their allies. Sanpoils married into other tribes and carried on some trade with them. They were among the Natives who visited the

Joe James, ca. 1910, elder brother of the early-twentieth-century chief Jim James, who was known among Americans as a progressive. Before the Jameses' time, the Sanpoils, like their close neighbors, the Nespelems, had isolated themselves from the federal government, increasing the influence of the tribe's most prominent nineteenth-century figure, the Dreamer prophet, Skolaskin.

Photograph from Cull White Collection, Wash-ington State University, Pullman.

Roman Catholic missionaries François Blanchet and Modeste Demers at Kettle Falls on the Columbia River in 1838.

After the Indian wars of the 1850s, the Sanpoils, as a nontreaty tribe, remained apart from the officials of the Colville Agency under whose jurisdiction they fell. Among their nativist-isolationist responses was their refusal to provide government officials with a tribal census. Enhancing their isolationism was the influence over them of their prophet-chief, Skolaskin, who declined not only government aid but also the ministrations of Catholic priests. To control his people, he kept a pile of logs in front of his lodge with which he claimed he would save them from a flood that he predicted would destroy those who did not yield to his authority. He was incarcerated in Alcatraz for a time and became a Catholic convert shortly before his death.

In the 1880s the Sanpoils opposed settlement on the Colville Reservation with other tribes such as the Sinkiuses under Chief Moses and a Nez Perce remnant under Chief Joseph. The Sanpoil-Nespelem lands were located in the southern part of the Colville Reservation, where many Indians settled. The Sanpoils refused government aids such as tools, preferring their traditional hunting, fishing, gathering, and small-patch subsistence farming.

Anthropologists have calculated the Sanpoil population at 800 to 1,700 individuals immediately before their first contacts with non-Indians. A fur trader in 1827 listed them at 218. During the latter half of the nineteenth century various problems attending the census taken by federal officials rendered the accuracy of their numbers tenuous. The Sanpoils declined from 324 in 1905 to 202 in 1913, a downward spiral that continued during the twentieth century. In 1959, 110 full-blood-degree Sanpoils were reported on the Colville Reservation and 22 of full-blood degree beyond its borders. Today, the Sanpoil population is included with those of the Colville Confederated Tribes. *See* **Confederated Tribes of the Colville Reservation.**

Suggested Readings:

Jessie A. Bloodworth, "Human Resources Survey of the Colville Confederated Tribes," BIA Field Report, Portland Area Office, Colville Agency, Nespelem, Wash., 1959; Rickard D. Gwydir, "A Record of the San Poil Indians," *Washington Historical Quarterly* 8, no. 4 (October 1917); Verne F. Ray, "The Sanpoil and Nespelem Salishan Peoples of Northeastern Washington," *University of Washington Publications in Anthropology* 5 (1932); Robert H. Ruby and John A. Brown, *Dreamer-Prophets of the Columbia Plateau* (Norman: University of Oklahoma Press, 1989) and *Half-Sun on the Columbia: A Biography of Chief Moses* (Norman: University of Oklahoma Press, 1965).

SANTIAM

(Kalapuyan)

The Santiams, or Ahalpams, comprised at least four bands on the Santiam River that flows westward from the Cascade Mountains to the Willamette River in west-central Oregon. They spoke a dialect of the Central Kalapuyan language. At the time of contact, the Santiams and other local Indians could not identify the builders of the numerous mounds on the Calapooya River and Muddy Creek and at other locations. The mounds had been built before these Kalapuyan peoples migrated into the Willamette Valley, where the Kalapuyans were said to have replaced the tribes that some scholars have called the Multnomahs.

Like so many indigenous peoples of the Willamette Valley, the Santiams dressed lightly in summer but in other seasons wore cloaks, buckskin shirts and short trousers, moccasins, and hats fashioned of grey fox and raccoon, which contrasted with the basket hats that they wore in summer. Early non-Indian visitors found them subsisting by hunting, fishing, and gathering. They harvested grasshoppers and caterpillars as well as plant foods. The Natives who occupied the east side of the Willamette Valley, from the Santiams' lands north to those of the Northern Molalas, united in annual hunts known as "surrounds."

At times the Santiams were subject to encroachments by the Molalas and other Indians. They and others of the Willamette opposed fur traders hunting game on their lands. It was probably either Santiam lands or those of another Kalapuyan group, the Ahantchuyuks (Pudding Rivers), on which the Reverend Jason Lee established his Methodist mission in 1834 near present-day Salem. The intermittent fever of the 1830s reduced tribal populations, thus frustrating missionary efforts. By the 1840s, immigrants were entering western Oregon in increasing numbers. In 1846 some of them unjustly accused the Santiams of stealing cattle, and the Oregon Rangers of Salem were called out to recover the animals and punish the alleged thieves.

In negotiations with government agents beginning on April 11, 1851, the Santiams, under their headmen Tiacan, Alquema, and Sophan, strenuously opposed removal east of the Cascade Mountains. During the negotiations, a small band the Hanshokes that had formerly separated from the Santiams rejoined the tribe. Under pressure from white negotiators, the Santiams agreed, on April 16, 1851, to cede their lands in exchange for goods such as blankets, clothing, and calicos and a small reservation established in their homelands. At that time, they numbered 155 individuals. Aware of government opposition to Indian slavery, they denied having kept people in enslavement, even as they regarded government schools as a form of bondage. Their hopes of escaping further white encroachments were soon shattered, and in 1854 they were asked to renegotiate their treaty. In a pact with Oregon superintendent of Indian affairs Joel Palmer dated January 22, 1855 (10 Stat. 1143, ratified March 3, 1855), they consented to re-

Abe Hudson, a Santiam. His tribe, one of several in the Kalapuyan linguistic family of western Oregon, vigorously opposed government proposals to move them from the Willamette Valley to eastern Oregon to make room for settlers. The Santiams remained in western Oregon, but on the Grand Ronde Reservation.

Authors' collections.

main in the Willamette Valley until a suitable reservation could be designated as their permanent home. They agreed that they would remove to the reservation whenever it was established by the federal government. In 1856 they relocated west to the headwaters of the Yamhill River, where, in the following year, the Grand Ronde Agency was established. On the Grand Ronde Reservation the Santiam remnant was led by their headman, Jo Hutchins, who tried to help his people adjust to reservation life and non-Indian culture.

The Santiams numbered 125 on the reservation in 1870. In 1906 there were 23; and four years later there were only 9. Today, the Santiams have been absorbed into the communities of other tribal groups in the region.

Suggested Readings:

Stephen Dow Beckham, *The Indians of Western Oregon: This Land Was Theirs* (Coos Bay, Ore.: Arago Books, 1977); S. A. Clarke, *Pioneer Days of Oregon History* (Portland, Ore.: J. K. Gill Company, 1905); Leo J. Frachtenberg, "Ethnological Researches among the Kalapuya Indians," Smithsonian Miscellaneous Collections, vol. 65, no. 6 (Washington, D.C., Government Printing Office, 1916, 85–89); J. A. Hussey, *Champoeg: Place of Transition* (Portland: Oregon Historical Society, 1964); Melville Jacobs, "Santiam Kalapuya Ethnologic Texts," *University of Washington Publications in Anthropology* 11 (1945), 3–82; Harold Mackey, *The Kalapuyans: A Sourcebook on the Indians of the Willamette Valley* (Salem, Ore.· Mission Mill Museum Association, 1974); W. W. Oglesby, "The Calapooyas Indians," [188?] Manuscript P-A 82, Bancroft Library, University of California, Berkeley; James L. Ratcliff, "What Happened to the Kalapuya? A Study of the Depletion of Their Economic Base," *The Indian Historian* 6, no. 3 (Summer 1973).

SATSOP

(Coastal Division, Salishan)

The Satsops lived on the Satsop River, a tributary of the Chehalis River in south-western Washington. Some anthropologists believe that the Satsops' dialect was distinct from others in that area. Others maintain that it was a continuum of the dialect spoken by the Kwaiailks (Upper Chehalises) and other peoples as far west as the Lower Chehalises. The Satsops' political organization was like that of the Lower Chehalises and the Humptulipses and Hoquiams who were their neighbors. The Satsops occupied an intermediary position between the Twana peoples of Hood Canal on the north and the Chehalis peoples on the south. Through the Satsop lands ran the trail over which goods passed south along the Pacific Coast to Grays Harbor and from there down the coast to Willapa (Shoalwater) Bay. Through the Satsops, the Twanas obtained hemp fiber and mountain-goat hair, which were traded from east of the Cascade Mountains. Cultural activities, such as intermarriages between Satsops and Chehalises, also followed the trade routes.

In early times the Satsops fought the inhabitants of Willapa Bay and joined the Chinooks from near the mouth of the Columbia River in fighting the Quileutes, a Pacific Coast people of the Olympic Peninsula. After devastating epidemics, especially smallpox, ravaged their population, a Satsop remnant was invited by the government to remove from their ancestral lands to the Chehalis Reservation at the confluence of the Chehalis and Black rivers. Those Satsops intermarried with persons of other tribes and settled on various reservations.

With the Hoquiam band, the Whiskahs, and the Wynoochees, the Satsops numbered 350 in 1870. An 1885 census listed their population at 12, as did another census three years later. There is no Satsop tribe today.

Indians of Satsop heritage were among the Kwaiailks (Upper Chehalises), who, by an Indian Claims Commission decree on October 7, 1963, received a net sum of $754,380 for loss of ancestral lands and fishing rights. *See* **Confederated Tribes of the Chehalis Reservation.**

Besides the Satsop River, a settlement and a nuclear plant have been given the name "Satsop."

SAUK-SUIATTLE

(Coastal Division, Salishan)

Sah-ku-mehu

The River People

The Sauk-Suiattles are the descendants of peoples of the upper Skagit River watershed in northwestern Washington. In the nineteenth century they were designated as Skagits by government treaty makers and other non-Indians. Because their homelands were near the Cascade Mountains along the Suiattle River, a tributary of the Sauk (which is itself a tributary of the Skagit), their subsistence patterns and dialect varied from those of the other Skagit peoples of the lower Skagit River and Puget Sound. In precontact times, their ancestors were said to have occupied five winter houses situated from the mouth of the Sauk upstream to Sauk Prairie, an important gathering place of several tribes. They lived farther upstream in summer.

Location: Members of the Sauk-Suiattle Indian Tribe of Washington live at various places in northwestern Washington. Like the Upper Skagits, some hold scattered public-domain allotments in Skagit County. A number of their ancestors moved to reservations such as the Swinomish near the mouth of the Skagit.

Numbers: Tribal membership in 1924 numbered only 18, but by 1985 stood at 260, and in 2008, it was 233.

History: At the time of the Point Elliott Treaty (1855), the Sauk villagers among the upper Skagits were known as the Sahkumehus and Sabbu-uqus. Their headman, Wawsitkin, refused to sign the treaty because he feared that under it his people would not receive a reservation of their own. A subchief, Dahtldemin, however, did sign the document.

The upriver location of the Sauk-Suiattles did not prevent them from associating with other Indians, some of whom visited them from east of the Cascade Mountains. Tradition has it that when Roman Catholic priests first contacted the residents of the upper Skagit River, the Indians sent a delegation to near Walla Walla to a mission that had been recommended to them by Natives from east of the Cascade Mountains. On the return of the delegation, the Indians built a crude mission of their own. The advent of settlement caused the Sauk-Suiattles to abandon traditional subsistence patterns, which included hunts for such big game as elk in the Cascade Mountains. As early as 1870 surveyors entered their lands seeking a pass by which a railroad could cross the mountains. Settlers regarded as obstacles to settlement not only the living Indians but also the dead in the graveyards who had been sent there by dread diseases such as smallpox. In the mid-1880s, settlers burned a Native village of eight large cedarboard longhouses at the confluence of the Skagit and Sauk rivers. With the encroachments of outsiders, some Indians moved to the Swinomish and other reservations of the region.

Government and Claims: In 1946 the Sauk-Suiattles became a tribal entity separate from the Upper Skagits. Tribal affairs are administered by a seven-member council under a constitution and bylaws approved by the secretary of the interior on September 17, 1975. At that time the tribe received federal recognition. They were assisted in achieving that status, for which a land base is one qualification, by their ownership of a small plot of land in common with the Upper Skagits. Because it has fishing rights recognized under the Point Elliott Treaty, the tribe is a member of the Skagit System Cooperative, organized in 1976 to regulate and enhance fishing in the Skagit River system. Also participating in the cooperative are the Upper Skagits and the Swinomish Tribal Community.

To recover losses for lands taken under the Point Elliott Treaty, the Sauk-Suiattles brought suit against the United States in 1936. Their claims were submitted to the Court of Claims (82 C.Cl. 697). When they failed to receive an award, they submitted a claim (Docket 97) to the Indian Claims Commission, which dismissed it on the basis that the Sauk-Suiattles were not an identifiable tribal entity separate from the Upper Skagits at the time of the Point Elliott Treaty. As a federally acknowledged tribe, however, the Sauk-Suiattles were included in a claim with the Upper Skagits (Docket 92). For information on these claims, *see* **Upper Skagit.**

Martin Sherman of the Sauk-Suiattle Tribe, which bears the names of two streams in the upper Skagit River watershed of northwestern Washington. Although the tribe lived west of the Cascade Mountains, they and their neighbors had contacts not only with coastal groups but also occasionally with peoples east of the Cascades. The Sauk-Suiattles are among the tribes who received federal recognition in the 1970s. This image was taken in 1983.

Authors' collections.

Contemporary Life and Culture: As noted above, the Sauk-Suiattles gained federal tribal recognition status on September 17, 1975. Reservation status followed on July 9, 1984, with an original reservation consisting of fifteen acres. By 2008 that acreage had grown to eighty-four acres, of which twenty-three acres were in trust and the remainder was in the process of being placed in trust. As discussed, the Sauk-Suiattle Tribe, jointly with the Upper Skagit Indian Tribe, owns trust lands in Skagit County. Sauk-Suiattles also live on scattered individual public-domain allotments in Skagit County.

The tribe runs a daycare and preschool on their reservation. This facility offers language, nutrition, wellness, family, and educational services. The Health and Social Services Department provides health care, social services, drug and alcohol prevention, aftercare rehabilitation, and alcohol counseling. The tribe owns and operates a 611-square-foot community clinic in Darrington. Administrative, preschool, and housing offices are located in a single, multipurpose building on the reservation. A six-member police department is maintained by the tribe, and the resources of the reservation are preserved and protected by the nine staff members of the Natural Resources Department. The tribe does not operate a casino, but leases 675 slot machines to the Tulalip Tribe, raising an estimated $1.2 to $1.9 million per year, some of which goes toward purchasing school clothes for tribal-member students.

In 2004 the Sauk-Suiattles became the first Washington tribe to receive a tribal WI-FI hotspot and wireless high-speed connection. In 2008 there were nineteen HUD houses on the reservation.

The Sauk-Suiattles are active in maintaining the local mountain goat population, a staple of tribal culture. The death of Elder Katherine Brown Joseph at the age of ninety-one in 2007 marked the passing of the tribe's last Native Lushootseed speaker.

Special Events and Celebrations: The Sauk-Suiattle Powwow is held each year in August on the Darrington Bluegrass Grounds at Darrington, Washington.

Suggested Readings:

Nels Bruseth, *Indian Stories and Legends of the Stillaguamish, Sauks, and Allied Tribes* (Fairfield, Wash.: Ye Galleon Press, 1977); June McCormick Collins, *Valley of the Spirits: The Upper Skagit Indians of Western Washington* (Seattle: University of Washington Press, 1974); Barbara Lane, "Anthropological Report on the Identity, Treaty Status and Fisheries of the Sauk-Suiattle Tribe of Indians," in *Political and Economic Aspects of Indian-White Culture Contact in Western Washington in the Mid-19th Century,* May 10, 1973, manuscript in Washington State Library, Olympia; Martin J. Sampson, *Indians of Skagit County* (Mount Vernon, Wash.: Skagit County Historical Society, 1972).

SEMIAHMOO

(Coastal Division, Salishan)

The Semiahmoos, like their neighbors the Lummis and Samish and the Song-ish of southern Vancouver Island, spoke the Straits, or Lkungen, dialect of the Coastal Salishan language. The Semiahmoos lived far up on the northwest coast of the continental United States, near present-day Blaine, Washington, on Inter-state Highway 5. Their territory extended onto the southwestern British Colum-bia mainland. They have been called the Birch Bay Indians because some lived on Birch Bay. According to an Indian informant born around 1820, an ancient people, the Hulhwaluqs, lived on Birch Bay and southward to Lummi Island. The Hulhwaluqs had been attracted to that area from southern Vancouver Island by the abundant clams in Birch Bay and the elk in nearby hills. Deep middens at Birch Bay attest to the presence there of early villagers. Before the coming of white men, the Hulhwaluqs and the neighboring Skalakhans were defeated and assimilated by the Lummis, who were moving from the San Juan Islands to the mainland seeking lands and fishing places such as those on the Nooksack River.

The Semiahmoos may have been the Indians whom Spanish explorers ob-served in 1791 at Point Roberts fishing for salmon at reef-net locations, although other peoples were also known to fish there. Those Indians may not have seen white men before, but they at least had indirect contact with them, as evidenced in the brass bracelets they wore. In 1853, the usually well-informed George Gibbs could only write of the Semiahmoos: "The Shimishmoo inhabit the coast toward Frazier's river; nothing seems to be known of them whatever." He was at least aware of their population, which he reported as 250, about 50 fewer than the number given a dozen years earlier by the American naval lieutenant, Charles Wilkes. The Semiahmoos were drawn into the Hudson's Bay Company trading orbit, especially by the establishment of Fort Langley in 1827 on the lower Fraser River. A Semiahmoo chief, Kwetiseleq, was said to have become rich selling furs at the fort and purchasing slaves with his earnings. The Semiahmoos may have been among those who met the Roman Catholic missionary Modeste Demers at Fort Langley late in the summer of 1841. Demers wrote that Indians had as-sembled there from great distances to see him.

The Semiahmoos appear not to have signed the Point Elliott Treaty in 1855. Some of them located on the Lummi Reservation but, like the Nooksacks, va-cated it after a time. In the late 1850s, immediately after the treaty, most of the Semiahmoos in the United States moved north across the Canadian border. A small remnant lived in Canada into the twentieth century. A bay bordering the Washington State–British Columbia mainland bears the tribal name, as does a small Indian reserve in the latter province.

Albert Louie, a Senijextee, or Lakes Indian, who served in the American armed forces in World War II. In the nineteenth century, Indians scouted for American forces in the Pacific Northwest. They also served in World War I, but enlisted in much greater numbers in the Second World War.

Authors' collections.

SENIJEXTEE

(Interior Division, Salishan)

The Senijextees are commonly referred to as the Lakes Indians. French-Canadian fur men called them *gens des lacs* ("peoples of the lakes"). They lived along the Columbia River in present-day Washington State from Kettle Falls north to the Canadian border. They also lived along the lower Kettle River, a Columbia tributary, and in Canada in the Arrow Lakes region of the Columbia and along its tributary, the lower Kootenai. They were closely related to the Colvilles and often gathered with them at Kettle Falls during the summer and fall fishing seasons. In the nineteenth century they traded furs at the Hudson's Bay Company's Fort Colvile and worshipped at nearby Roman Catholic missions. On one occasion, a Senijextee band arrived at Fort Colvile in a fleet of about thirty canoes and offered to exchange forty prime beaver pelts for the prayers of the fort traders. Their chief, Gregoire, or Gregory, remained on good terms with white men. By protecting them from unfriendly Indians, he gained a wide reputation as a peacemaker among both whites and Indians.

Like the Colvilles, the Senijextees below the Canadian border were reluctant to leave the Colville Reservation, established east of the Columbia River in 1872 and replaced that same year by another west of that watercourse. On May 23, 1891, Senijextee and Colville chiefs signed an agreement to cede the North Half of the Colville Reservation, where many of them subsequently went to live. One of the stipulations of the agreement had allowed them to take eighty-acre allotments on the North Half. Some Senijextees moved to the South Half of the reservation to join with a Colville band there.

The 1780 Senijextee population has been estimated at 500. Their official numbers were 239 in 1870, 300 in 1882, and 294 in 1910. The last figure perhaps included some Colvilles to whom the Senijextees were closely related culturally. The members of the tribe are separated by the 49th parallel into two groups. They are also divided spiritually into activists and conservatives. There is disagreement over the identity of the hereditary leader. They united temporarily in Canada in 1991 to rebury remains of tribal ancestors returned to them by the Royal British Columbia Museum. *See also* **Confederated Tribes of the Colville Reservation.**

Suggested Readings:

David H. Chance and Jennifer V. Chance, *Kettle Falls: 1971 and 1974 Salvage Archaeology in Lake Roosevelt,* University of Idaho Anthropological Research Manuscript Series, no. 69 (Moscow: University of Idaho, 1982); David H. Chance and Jennifer V. Chance, *Kettle Falls: 1976 Salvage Archaeology in Lake Roosevelt,* University of Idaho Anthropological Manuscript Series, no. 39 (Moscow: University of Idaho, 1977); Ruth Lakin, *Kettle River Country* (Colville, Wash.: Statesman Examiner, 1976); Andrew M. Perkins, "The Lake Indians," manuscript in possession of authors.

SHASTA

(Hokan)

The Shastas resided primarily in northern California along the middle of the Klamath River in the drainage area of two tributaries, the Scott and Shasta rivers. A small portion of the tribe lived across the California border in Oregon. The name "Shasta" is believed to be derived from a well-known tribe living near the site of Yreka, California, around 1874. One ethnologist, Roland B. Dixon, gives Kaho'sadi as the Shastan name

The Shasta Tribe to which this woman belonged lived in northern California and southern Oregon. The Oregon Shastas were included in treaties with the United States in the mid-1850s and were removed north to the Grand Ronde and Siletz reservations.

Courtesy of the Smithsonian Institution's American Museum of Natural History.

for the smaller portion of the tribe in Oregon. Others say it is the name for the tribal language. Some Shasta villages in Oregon were south of present-day Ashland and Jacksonville on the northern borders of the Siskiyou Mountains and perhaps between Ashland and Table Rock in the Rogue River drainage area.

The Oregon Shastas and two other Oregon tribes, the Takelmas and Latgawas (Rogues), had a common bond in opposing encroaching miners and settlers in the Rogue River country. On one occasion, while escaping a posse of non-Indians, the Shastas hid out in the land of the Rogues. On July 21, 1852, the Rogues signed a tenuous peace treaty with American officials by which they agreed not to communicate with the Shastas, whose warriors continued to join the Rogues to avenge Shastan blood spilled by miners. In their lust for gold, the miners often ignored that some of their victims were friendly to whites. The Oregon Shastas were included in the treaties that the United States effected with the Indians of the Rogue River valley in the mid-1850s, and they were eventually removed with those Indians to the Grand Ronde and Siletz reservations of Oregon. On the Grand Ronde in 1871 they numbered fifty-one. On the Siletz Reservation that same year, along with Chastacostas and Umpquas, fifty-seven were recorded there.

Suggested Readings:

Stephen Dow Beckham, *The Indians of Western Oregon: This Land Was Theirs* (Coos Bay, Ore.: Arago Books, 1977); Edward S. Curtis, *The North American Indian* (1912; New York: Johnson Reprint Corporation, 1970), vol. 13; Roland B. Dixon, *The Shasta* (New York: AMS Press, 1983); Frederick Webb Hodge, *Handbook of American Indians North of Mexico,* pt. 2 (Washington, D.C.: Government Printing Office, 1910); C. Hart Merriam, "Source of the Name Shasta," *Journal of the Washington Academy of Sciences* 16, no. 19 (1926).

SHOALWATER BAY TRIBE, SHOALWATER BAY RESERVATION

The Canoe People of Willapa Bay

The Shoalwater Bay Tribe, Shoalwater Bay Reservation, Washington, traces its inception to the establishment by executive order on September 22, 1866, of the 334.75-acre Shoalwater Bay Reservation for about thirty or forty Indian families of Willapa (formerly Shoalwater) Bay in southwestern Washington. Members of the tribe are commonly referred to as Georgetown Indians. Their ancestors were primarily Chinook and Chehalis peoples. Like other Northwest Coast Indians, the Shoalwater Bays are rich in tradition. They told of a canoe from a "far, cold country" that carried a hundred warriors and their families south to the Columbia River. When strong winds forced them back from the

Columbia estuary, they abandoned their craft. When they returned later, they discovered that it had "grown" not only Shoalwater Bay and its environs but also its peoples.

An early people of Willapa Bay were the Willapas (Willopahs). Some ethnologists claim these were Chinookan peoples living on the lower course of the Willapa River flowing into the bay. Others maintain that since the northern limit of Chinookan speakers was the Nemah River, which lies south of the Willapa River, the Willapas were not Chinookan but possibly a branch of a nearby Athabaskan people, the Kwalhioquas. When the residents of Willapa Bay succumbed to the devastating plagues of the nineteenth century, the Lower Chehalises pushed onto their lands.

The Willapa Bay Indians favored the marine location of the Shoalwater Reservation, but since it was agriculturally unproductive, many others who were scheduled to be removed there avoided it. Some of them worked for Americans in the logging and oystering industries. Some who were entitled to allotments on the reservation were allotted instead on the Quinault Reservation farther north on the coast. Among the last of the oldtime Indians was Light-House Charley Ma-tote, or Toke, who was appointed head chief of the Shoalwater Bay people. His son, George A. Charley (chief of the Shoalwater Bay Tribe from 1889 to 1936), was one of the last of the Pacific Northwest Indians to have a flattened skull, an indication of his royal lineage. By 1879 Indians of the Shoalwater Bay Reservation spoke the Lower Chehalis dialect of the Coastal Division of the Salish language.

Location: About a half-dozen Indian families reside on the Shoalwater Bay Reservation, which fronts the northern end of Willapa Bay and the Pacific Ocean.

Numbers: Tribal membership as of 1985 stood at 64. In 1992, enrollment was 134. In 2005, the Shoalwater Bay Tribe, counted among the smallest in Washington State, had 207 enrolled members and a 1.6-square-mile reservation.

Government: The forerunners of the Shoalwater Bay Tribe, Shoalwater Bay Reservation, Washington, rejected the Indian Reorganization Act in 1934 (48 Stat. 984) but adopted a constitution and became formally organized on May 22, 1971. The tribe's executive body, the Shoalwater Bay Tribal Council, was elected shortly thereafter. In 1984 the tribe, in exchange for $1 million, renounced its claim to eight acres in Tokeland, Washington, which the government had conveyed to a citizen in 1872.

Contemporary Life and Culture: On August 23, 2008, for the first time in memory, members of the Shoalwater Bay, Chinook, and Confederated Grand Ronde Tribes participated in a six-canoe journey from Toke's Point to Bay Center. At that time, the Shoalwater Bay Tribe had not built a canoe since the late 1800s. The tribe has also been involved in repatriation efforts, and in February 2006 the

Rachel Brignone Whitish (1910–1987), a member of the Shoalwater Bay Tribe and the great granddaughter of Chief Light House Charley (Mah-tote), the head chief who assumed leadership of the tribe in 1876.

Historically, Shoalwater Bay Indians depended to a great extent on seafoods for subsistence and worked for non-Indian entrepreneurs harvesting oysters from the bay for sale in San Francisco and elsewhere. Today there is marked unemployment, and members are moving back to the 1.6-square-mile reservation where they are looking forward to establishing fishing rights and an aquaculture program. In 1981 they built a multipurpose tribal center, and in 1980 they put up six new HUD houses, with eight more constructed in 1984.

Courtesy Lucinda Shipman, Tokeland, Wash.

American Museum of Natural History in New York issued a NAGPRA notice that it held eight human remains of likely Shoalwater Bay ancestry.

Since 1998 the tribe has operated the Shoalwater Bay Casino with an RV park and gift shop just south of the community of Westport. Tribal services are provided by local, state, and federal jurisdictions. The tribe itself maintains a police force; a $365,000 learning center with a computer lab, activity room, and library stocked with an extensive collection of Native American materials; a wellness center, which was built at a cost $2 million and offers comprehensive medical, mental, and dental treatment; a $500,000 recreation center with a regulation-size basketball gymnasium; and an oyster company in nearby South Bend. Among the businesses on the reservation is a restaurant at Tokeland that features Indian fry bread and seafoods. The non-Indian community surrounding the reservation provides work for tribal members in the cranberry bogs and in the fishing, crabbing, and other industries. Children attend public schools off the reservation in the town of Ocosta.

From 1988 to 1998 the tribe attracted national attention when it was reported that an alarming number of pregnancies on the reservation—between 25 and 66 percent—were resulting in miscarriages, stillbirths, and infant deaths. Although no cause was clearly identified—though lack of prenatal care was associated with the crisis—the scourge resulted in heightened awareness and increased federal funding for health care for tribal members. In the early 1990s the Shoalwater Bay Tribe ranked among one of the poorest in the state, with 90 percent of reservation inhabitants living below the official poverty level.

Special Events and Celebrations: Each year in July the tribe hosts the Shoalwater Bay Sobriety Powwow in Tokeland, Washington.

Suggested Readings:

George A. Charley, "The Indian," *The Sou'wester* (Pacific County Historical Society) 11, no. 3 (Autumn 1976); Har Plumb, "A Happy Summer on Peacock Spit," *The Sou'wester* 13, nos. 2 and 3 (Summer–Autumn 1978); Robert H. Ruby and John A. Brown, *The Chinook Indians: Traders of the Lower Columbia River* (Norman: University of Oklahoma Press, 1976); *Seattle (Wash.) Times,* Pictorial for January 26, 1975, and April 22, 1979; James G. Swan, *The Northwest Coast; or, Three Years' Residence in Washington Territory* (1857; Fairfield, Wash.: Ye Galleon Press, 1966); Isaac H. Whealdon, "Stories and Sketches from Pacific County [Washington]," *Washington Historical Quarterly* 4, no. 3 (July 1913).

SHOSHONE

(Shoshonean of the Uto-Aztecan)

The Shoshones were popularly known as the Snake Indians, not only among whites but also among Plains tribes, presumably because they painted snakes on sticks to frighten their foes. The origin of the word "Shoshone" is unknown but is believed to have stemmed from some English name given them by whites. What has been referred to as the Shoshone Nation did not exist. The Shoshonean peoples had no composite organization or commonality of lands. In the mideighteenth century they dominated a considerable portion of the Great Plains, ranging north to the Saskatchewan River country (later Alberta Province). After a smallpox epidemic in 1782 and pressure from Blackfeet foes who had obtained firearms from white trappers, the Shoshones abandoned the Great Plains and much of the upper Missouri River watershed, but they still occupied a vast mountain and intermontaine territory in the north-central American West. In that region they comprised diverse cultural groups, although all were of the same linguistic family.

Some Shoshonean bands were highly mobile and others were not. Differences in their economic activities also militated against formation of a pan-Shoshonean political unit and pan-Shoshonean land ownership.

Because of common economic activities, the mounted Shoshone bands and their Bannock (Paiute) neighbors had developed a loose tribal organization and land-owning complex by the middle of the nineteenth century. Before they acquired horses, the Shoshone peoples were confined to smaller areas, where they subsisted on small game and seeds. Some scholars believe that the horse-riding Shoshones embodied a special class who owned these animals as hallmarks of wealth. Those with fewer horses, the academics maintain, formed another less-mobile class who participated only partially in the nomadic life of the horse-owning Shoshones. To a considerable extent this less-mobile class depended on fishing for subsistence. A third, poorer, horseless class relied on the generosity of the wealthy for their subsistence, which they augmented by consuming rodents, seeds, and insects. The Shoshone prehorse political structure was adapted to the changes occasioned by the coming of that animal.

The Shoshones have been classified into four major divisions: Southern, Western, Eastern, and Northern. We are not concerned here with the Southern division (the Utes), since they were entirely outside the Pacific Northwest. We are concerned with only the northernmost bands of Western Shoshones, who ranged north from Utah into the southwestern corner of Idaho. In the latter half of the nineteenth century they became culturally mixed and blended with western groups of the Northern Shoshones and with the Northern Paiutes in that region.

The Eastern (Wind River) Shoshones ranged over a small part of southeastern Idaho, but for the most part they were active in Wyoming. The Eastern Shoshone chief Washakie became the most powerful leader of the migratory horse-owning Shoshones at the time when his people were under the greatest stress from non-Indians late in the nineteenth century. He exerted great influence over the Northern Shoshones and was temporarily allied with such Shoshone chiefs as the noted Bannock Creek leader Pocatello (Pocataro), for whom a city in southeastern Idaho is named. For a time, Pocatello competed with Washakie for pan-Shoshonean leadership during the stressful period of white immigration. Also giving allegiance to Washakie was the Bannock chief Tahgee (Taghee) of the Northern Paiute upper class, who were affiliated with Shoshones of similar status. He later became the Northern Shoshone-Bannock head chief of the roughly 1.8-million-acre Fort Hall Reservation of southeastern Idaho, which was created on June 14, 1867. Washakie later held a similar position on the Wind River Reservation, established by treaty in western Wyoming on July 3, 1868.

The most diverse of the Pacific Northwest Shoshonean speakers were the Northern Shoshones of Idaho. They were divided into four branches: Western, Mountain, Northwestern, and Pohogwe, or Fort Hall. The Western bands of Northern Shoshones occupied the general area of southern Idaho. They included the historic Wararereekas—the sedentary fish-catching Boises and Bruneaus—who broke away from their horse-riding contingent. In the early nineteenth century, the fur man Alexander Ross described them as being under the leadership of Peiem (or Pee-eye-em, as Ross called him). In an October 10, 1864, treaty effected with Idaho superintendent of Indian affairs and territorial governor Caleb Lyon, the Shoshones of Boise Valley agreed to remove to an as-yet-undesignated reservation. On April 10, 1866, the Shoshones of the Bruneau Valley south of the Snake River made a similar treaty for their removal to an undesignated reservation. (In the 1980s, the descendants of both groups would attempt to receive compensation for their lost lands: *see* **Shoshone-Bannock Tribes of the**

Fort Hall Reservation.) Peiem's successors, Captain Jim and Bannock John, led the Boise-Bruneaus to the Fort Hall Reservation between March 12 and April 13, 1869. To survive the pressures of white immigration, a band of the Weiser Shoshones (predominately Northern Paiutes) intermarried and banded together with the Western Shoshones, sharing territory with them. They refused to leave their mountain homelands above the Payette River of western Idaho to remove to the Malheur Reservation in southeastern Oregon. Finally, they were settled on the Fort Hall Reservation and the Duck Valley Reservation (established by executive order on April 16, 1877, on the Oregon-Nevada border).

This western group of Northern Shoshones of the Boise Basin along the Snake River in southwestern Idaho was of that group called salmon fishers. Before non-Indians threatened their existence, their largest unit was the village. The Bruneau Shoshones did not adopt the horse culture or mingle with horse-riding peoples but traveled south and adopted a Western Shoshone dialect. The Boises had close ties with the Northern-Paiute Weisers, frequently mingling and eventually intermarrying with them.

The peoples who are grouped as Northwestern Shoshones had migrated to southeastern Idaho from their Utah homelands. They formerly had been part of the mounted Northern Shoshone bands, but in historic times they avoided the ambitious seasonal migratory rounds of that branch and of the mounted Bannocks. They were joined by others who shared more conservative life patterns as various branches of the Northwestern Shoshone Tribe developed from shifting alliances. During the stressful midnineteenth century, the Northwestern Shoshones came under the leadership of the Bannock Creek band chief, Pocatello. In 1850 they numbered about eighteen hundred and occupied lands stretching northward from Salt Lake Valley and the northern shores of the Great Salt and Bear lakes and the Weber, Cache, and Malad valleys. As late as 1875, when they numbered about six hundred, they still lived near where the Bear River empties into the Great Salt Lake. By the turn of the century, most of these Northwestern Shoshones were on the Fort Hall Reservation.

The Bear Lakes, the Weber Utes, the Cache Valleys, and the Bannock Creeks were four of the ten northwestern bands of Northern Shoshones. The Bear Lakes eventually allied with the Wind River Shoshones and ranged in southeastern Idaho along the river and lake that bear their name. The Weber Utes were overlooked in treaty making with the United States and were not assigned to a reservation. The Cache Valleys, ranging around the upper Bear River (Idaho and Utah), were those suffering many casualties in the Battle of Bear River in southeast Idaho on January 29, 1863. The Bannock Creeks under Pocatello ranged from the Raft River to the Portneuf River in Idaho, claiming an area that encompassed the Fort Hall Reservation at the time of its establishment. Like other bands, they suffered during the fur trade era from the devastating rendezvous when white trappers and Indians combined liquor with trading and funmaking to much excess. The three major Bannock Creek villages included Pocatello's 101

A Shoshone warrior, ca. 1890. The Shoshones, popularly called the Snake Indians, occupied vast portions of the montane, intermontane, and plains areas of the American West. In the middle of the eighteenth century, they dominated a considerable portion of the northern Great Plains.

Courtesy of the Idaho State Historical Society, Boise.

followers, Sam Pitch's 124, and Sagwitch's 158, all of whom were removed to the Fort Hall Reservation.

The Lemhis, the Agaidikas (or "salmoneaters"), and the Tukuarikas (or "sheepeaters") were among the Mountain Shoshones who lived in the mountainous country of central Idaho, where wild sheep ranged. Historically, they were more conservative than other Northern Shoshone bands. Their archaeological remains may be traced back several thousand years. Some have mistakenly concluded that they were renegades from other bands and tribes. Impoverished and disorganized in early times, with a disintegrating tribal entity, most of them became mobile after they acquired horses. Many of the Sheepeaters, for example, united with the Lemhi Shoshones; some preferred the seclusion of the mountains. In time, Bannocks also joined the Lemhis, with whom they traveled to Camas Prairie in south-central Idaho to trade buffalo meat for horses. On horseback they also went with the Eastern Shoshones to the Great Plains of Montana and Wyoming. From Indians of that region they acquired elements of the Plains culture, but they always returned to their homelands near today's Tendoy in east-central Idaho.

The Lemhis were named for Limhi, a Nephite Mormon king, after members of the Church of Jesus Christ of Latter-day Saints established a mission among them on the Salmon River at Lemhi near Tendoy, Idaho, on June 12, 1855. A Lemhi Shoshone girl, Sacajawea, after being captured by Plains Indians in 1800, accompanied the American explorers Meriwether Lewis and William Clark on their westward trek in 1805. She persuaded her people to provide the explorers with horses for their crossing of the Lolo Trail in the mountains that lay before them. The Lemhi chief at that time was her brother, Cameahwait. Succeeding Lemhi chiefs were Snag and Tendoy ("The Climber"), for whom a town is named. Tendoy managed to keep his people on their 64,000-acre Lemhi Reservation, established on the Lemhi River by executive order on February 12, 1875. On that reservation in 1878 there were 300 Tukuarikas, 190 Bannocks, and 450 Shoshones. An attempt was made to force them onto the Fort Hall Reservation by an executive order on January 7, 1879. Their resistance to removal led to a conference in Washington, D.C., from which came the agreement of May 14, 1880, mandating their removal and the cession of their reservation to the United States. Following angry protestations from the residents of the reservation, a commission recommended withdrawing that part of the agreement that called for their removal. In 1882 thirty-two Lemhis voluntarily located to the Fort Hall Reservation, and after Tendoy died in May 1907, 474 more Lemhis were moved to that reservation.

Preferring a more sedentary existence, the Tukuarikas, joining the Lemhis, continued living in the mountains, gaining their subsistence from gathering and from hunting game such as mountain sheep. They processed mountain-sheep wool into clothing and coverings and they received their name from those animals as consumers of their meat. White miners and settlers blamed the Tukuarikas for the massacre of some Chinese on February 13, 1879, and called on the military to round them up. After a series of desultory campaigns and skirmishes, the military apprehended twelve combatants from their band, which numbered only fifty-two people.

Another Northern Shoshone band, the Pohogwes, or Fort Hall Indians, was a mounted people. In the nineteenth century they became allied culturally with other Northern Shoshone bands and migratory Bannocks with whom they traveled from the Wind River Range of Wyoming to the Salmon Falls of the Snake River in Idaho and into northern Utah. They also assumed elements of Plains Indian culture. The Pohogwes signed the Soda Springs Treaty of October 14, 1863 (see below).

Settlers crossing Shoshone lands over the Immigrant Road (the Oregon Trail) were attacked by dissident warriors, who in one year, 1851, claimed to have stolen $18 million worth of their property. Shoshones were free to harass the immigrants because their ancient Blackfeet enemies were at last avoiding their lands after suffering defeats at the hands of the Shoshones. For many years after they had acquired horses and guns from white traders, the Blackfeet had held the upper hand over the Shoshones, whose raids on immigrants had usually constituted small-scale enterprises undertaken by splinter groups. In the 1850s Shoshone-Bannock combinations attacked at places as diverse as the Lemhi Mormon Mission (February 1857) and the Immigrant Road. Americans responded by sending out volunteers to patrol the road. The absence of regular army troops during the Civil War (1861–65) made it difficult to police this part of the American frontier. A volunteer force under Col. Patrick E. Conner, after several skirmishes with the Indians, inflicted the most damage on them. Four hundred Shoshones were reported dead after Connor encountered Pocatello's Bannock Creeks and other Shoshone bands, including the Cache Valleys of the upper Bear River at Battle Creek, a Bear River tributary of southeastern Idaho. The Indian losses in that engagement on January 29, 1863, were said to be the largest suffered in any confrontation between Indians and U.S. forces. Conner's victory caused white frontiersmen to breathe more easily. Pocatello was regarded as a leader of the antiwhite Shoshone factions among the Northwestern Shoshones. Non-Indians were also relieved when he failed to wrest the Shoshone leadership from Washakie, who was peacefully disposed toward the Americans.

When, shortly after the Battle of Bear River, other Shoshones suffered defeat at Salmon Falls on the Snake River, the United States effected several peace treaties with Shoshone bands, both within and outside the Pacific Northwest. One of these was the Fort Bridger (Wyoming) Treaty of July 2, 1863 (18 Stat. 685), with headmen of the Eastern, or Wind River, Shoshones under Washakie, who at the time led twelve hundred people. The treaty provided Americans safe passage through that tribe's lands. American officials effected a peace pact (13 Stat. 663) at Box Elder, Utah, on July 30, 1863, with Pocatello's Bannock Creeks and nine other bands of southeastern Idaho and northern Utah. On October 1, 1863, another peace treaty (18 Stat. 689) was negotiated with Western Shoshone bands at Ruby Valley in northeastern Nevada, guaranteeing their friendship with the United States and safe passage for the Americans. On October 12, 1863, a treaty (13 Stat. 681) was concluded with the Gosiute band of Western Shoshones of the Tuilla Valley in northeastern Nevada, also securing their friendship with the United States and safe passage through their lands for immigrants. A treaty of peace and friendship that went unratified was consummated on October 14, 1863, at Soda Springs in southeastern Idaho with the Bannocks and Pohogwes under Bannock chiefs Le Grand Coquin and Tahgee and with the chiefs of various bands of Northern Shoshones.

Government officials estimated that the United States had treated with a thousand Indians at Soda Springs. It was also calculated that the parties to the various Shoshone and Bannock peace treaties represented 8,650 Shoshonean speakers. A second Fort Bridger Treaty (15 Stat. 673) was concluded with the Eastern Shoshones under Washakie on July 3, 1868; it stipulated their removal to the 3,059,182-acre Wind River Reservation. The Bannocks had been promised a reservation by their treaty, but because the president had failed to establish the reservation they were removed to the Fort Hall Reservation, which they shared with the Shoshones.

On April 29, 1987, the Northwestern Band of the Shoshone Nation received federal recognition. Separate from the other bands of Shoshone, the six-hundred-strong Northwestern Band of the Shoshone Nation has elected tribal officials and staffs tribal offices in Pocatello, Idaho, and Brigham City, Utah, serving tribal members dispersed over southeastern Idaho and northeastern Utah. In 1989, the tribe received 184 acres from the LDS Church; these acres now constitute their reservation, and there are additional, privately owned Indian lands held in trust by the BIA. The twenty-six-acre Bear River Massacre site near Preston, Idaho, was donated to this tribe on March 24, 2003. *See* **Shoshone-Bannock Tribes of the Fort Hall Reservation.**

Suggested Readings:

W. A. Allen, *The Sheep Eaters* (Fairfield, Wash.: Ye Galleon Press, 1989); Merrill D. Beal and Merle W. Wells, *History of Idaho*, 3 vols. (New York: Lewis Historical Publishing Company,1959); W. C. Brown, "The Sheepeater Campaign," *Tenth Biennial Report of the Board of Trustees of the State Historical Society of Idaho for the Years 1925–1926* (Boise, Ida.. 1926); Ned Blackhawk, *Violence over the Land: Indians and Empires in the Early American West* (Cambridge, Mass.: Harvard University Press, 2006); Sven Liljeblad, *The Indians of Idaho* (Boise: Idaho Historical Society, 1960); Robert H. Lowie, *The Northern Shoshone,* Anthropological Papers of the American Museum of Natural History, vol. 2, pt. 2 (New York, 1909); Merle W. Wells, "Caleb Lyon's Bruneau Treaty," *Idaho Yesterdays* 13, no. 1 (Spring 1969); Brigham D. Madsen, *The Lemhi: Sacajawea's People* (Caldwell, Ida.: Caxton Printers, 1980) and *The Northern Shoshoni* (Caldwell, Ida.: Caxton Printers, 1980); Julian H. Steward, *Basin-Plateau Aboriginal Sociopolitical Groups,* Bureau of American Ethnology Bulletin no. 120 (Washington, D.C.: Government Printing Office, 1938); Omer C. Stewart, "The Western Shoshone of Nevada and the U.S. Government, 1863–1950," in Donald R. Tuohy, ed., *Selected Papers from the 14th Great Basin Anthropological Conference,* Ballena Press Publications in Archaeology, Ethnology, and History, no. 11 (Socorro, N.M., 1978) and "The Shoshoni: Their History and Social Organization," *Idaho Yesterdays* 9, no. 3 (Fall 1965); Virginia Cole Trenholm and Maurine Carley, *The Shoshonis: Sentinels of the Rockies* (Norman: University of Oklahoma Press, 1964); Deward Walker, *The Indians of Idaho* (Moscow: University Press of Idaho, 1978).

SHOSHONE-BANNOCK TRIBES OF
THE FORT HALL RESERVATION

The members of the Shoshone-Bannock Tribes of the Fort Hall Reservation, Idaho, are descendants of the two tribes who developed close ties during the nineteenth century and finally settled together on the Fort Hall Reservation.

Location: Most Shoshone-Bannocks live on the Fort Hall Reservation in southeastern Idaho.

Numbers: The combined tribal membership was 3,921 in 1984. In 1989, it was 6,617. The 2000 federal census recorded the population of the reservation at 5,762. In 2008, tribal enrollment of the Shoshone-Bannocks was approximately 5,191. Of that number 3,809 lived on the 544,000-acre Fort Hall Reservation.

History: In the second Fort Bridger Treaty of July 3, 1868 (15 Stat. 673), the Bannocks were promised a reservation on Idaho's Portneuf and Kansas (Camas) Prairie just southeast of Fort Hall. Instead, they were given the Fort Hall Reservation by an executive order on July 30, 1869. By an executive order of June 14, 1867, that reservation had also been set aside for the Shoshones of southern Idaho. The Boise Shoshones and Bruneau Shoshones moved there between March 12 and April 13, 1869. A total of 1,150 Indians lived on the reservation at that time. Other bands who signed peace treaties with the United States were also removed to Fort Hall: the Pohogwes, the Bannock Creeks, the Cache Valleys, and a few Weber Utes (of Northwestern Shoshones) and Bear Lake Indians. It was also expected that the Lemhi Shoshones, Bannocks, Tukuarikas (Sheepeaters), and other Shoshones would move to the reservation, as had been agreed on May 14, 1880 (12 Stat. 687, ratified February 23, 1889). Those latter groups would have been leaving their 64,000-acre Lemhi Reservation (established by executive order on February 12, 1875). After a September 24, 1868, treaty went unratified, thirty-two Lemhi Reservation Indians moved to the Fort Hall Reservation. The others at first refused to move but after their chief, Tendoy, died in May 1907, 474 did remove there. Absent from the Fort Hall Reservation were a few Bannocks and certain Shoshones, particularly many of the aforementioned Weber Utes, who remained in Utah, and about six families in the vicinity of Salmon, Idaho, who owned no land and received no government aid.

In August and September 1877 fifty Bannock scouts were enlisted by the U.S. military to fight Nez Perces led by Joseph and other chiefs. On May 30, 1878, the Bannock War began at Camas Prairie, Idaho (*see* **Bannock**). Because of an influx of citizens into southern Idaho Territory and consequent railroad developments, the government on May 14, 1880, reached an agreement with the Shoshone-Bannocks of the Fort Hall Reservation and the Lemhis on their reservation on the north, for removal of the latter to the Fort Hall Reservation with the Shoshone–Bannocks. The government also negotiated an agreement with the Shoshone–Bannocks for cession of 325,000 acres of the southern portion of their reservation in exchange for annuities and allotments on lands remaining within the confine. Congress was reluctant to approve the agreement, and the Lemhis eventually refused to remove. In the meantime, the Utah and Northern Railroad Company sought an east-west right-of-way across the Fort Hall Reservation for what was to become the Oregon Short Line Railway, which, like the Utah and Northern, was a subsidiary of the Union Pacific. On July 8, 1881, the Shoshone–Bannocks agreed to cede 772 acres to the Utah and Northern. Congress ratified the agreement on July 3, 1881, but legislation for cession of reservation

This man, photographed about 1890, was a forebear of the modern Shoshone-Bannocks of the Fort Hall Reservation in southeastern Idaho. Close ties between the Shoshones and the Bannocks in the nineteenth century led to their joint settlement on the same reservation.

Courtesy of the Idaho State Historical Society, Boise.

lands for white settlers was stalled in Congress. In the meantime, many settlers flocked to the site that became Pocatello, Idaho. On May 27, 1887, the government concluded an agreement with the Shoshone–Bannocks under which the two tribes ceded 1,840 acres for the Pocatello townsite. The agreement was amended and approved by Congress on September 1, 1888. Pocatello citizens were allowed rights to water from a reservation source. After citizens agitated for cession of the south half of the Fort Hall Reservation, Congress on June 6, 1900, finally approved a 416,000-acre cession from the reservation, an area much larger than that originally sought.

Seventy-nine Indians were permitted to remain, and they received allotments of 6,298.72 acres on the latter cession. The remainder of the 409,701.28 acres was opened to white settlement on June 17, 1902. A total of 1,863 Indians received allotments on 338,909 acres of the diminished reservation by congressional approval on October 28, 1914. By the twentieth century the Fort Hall Reservation, formerly composed of 1.8 million acres, had been reduced to 525,000 acres. About 45,594 acres were set aside as a timber reserve, and 36,263 acres were reserved for grazing, as approved on October 28, 1914, under the authority of an act dated March 3, 1911 (26 Stat. 1058-64).

Among later-nineteenth-century developments on the Fort Hall Reservation was the February 1880 establishment of the reservation's first boarding school. Three years later, an industrial boarding school opened. Day schools had begun operating in the 1870s. In 1881 an eight-man police force was organized, as was a tribal police court in 1888. Important early-twentieth-century milestones included the building of a hospital in 1902. Five years later the government inaugurated the Fort Hall Irrigation Project. Similar projects followed, including the introduction of the Minidoka Project in the 1920s, construction of the American Falls

Reservoir, and the development of 30,000 irrigated farmland acres at Michaud Flats in the 1930s.

Government and Claims: The Indians of the Fort Hall Reservation adopted their constitution and bylaws in 1936. On April 17, 1937, they ratified their corporate charter. Their governing body is the Fort Hall Business Council whose members are elected by secret ballot for two-year terms.

An aboriginal land claim (Docket 326-H) was filed with the Indian Claims Commission by the Shoshone Tribe of the Wind River Reservation, Wyoming, on behalf of all Eastern, Northern, and Western Shoshones and Bannocks for the lands used and occupied by those tribes. They had occupied approximately 38,300,000 acres in Wyoming, Colorado, Utah, Nevada, and Idaho. The claim, which was first litigated in the Court of Claims, resulted in an adverse decision for the petitioning tribes. The decision, which was upheld by the U.S. Supreme Court (324 U.S. 335, 1945), denied a motion for a rehearing (324 U.S. 890, 1945). A recall amendment of the Supreme Court's mandate was also denied (325 U.S. 840, 1945). All of the Shoshone, Bannock, and Shoshone–Bannock groups petitioned the Indian Claims Commission (Docket 326) to recover for multiple claims. The commission separated the various claims into separate dockets on July 5, 1957. The following tribes outside the Pacific Northwest were petitioners: the Western Shoshones of Nevada and Utah (Docket 326-A) for U.S. mismanagement of funds; the Gosiutes (Western Shoshones of Utah) (Docket 326-B) also for mismanagement of funds; the Gosiutes (Docket 326-J) for recovery of their lands; and the Western Shoshones (Docket 326-K) for recovery for their lands.

The Northern, Western, and Northwestern Shoshone petitioners included the following Pacific Northwest peoples: the Pohogwes (or Fort Halls), the Cache Valleys, the Bear Lakes, the Bannock Creeks, the Lemhis, the Boises, and the Bruneaus, along with Eastern (Washakie) Shoshones. Their claims were in Docket 326-C, which was divided into 326-C1 and 326-C2. Those dockets were transferred to the Court of Claims after dissolution of the Indian Claims Commission. Docket 326-C1 was for grazing, timber, and fiscal mismanagement and was settled for $1.6 million on October 8, 1982. Docket 326-C2 was for the government's failure to protect water rights of the tribes. A claim by the Shoshone–Bannocks of the Fort Hall Reservation (Docket 326-D) was for government mishandling of $99,323.80 for irrigation projects. A consideration in Docket 326-E was for compensation to the Fort Hall Shoshone–Bannocks for a 1900 cession of 406,864 acres of the reservation in return for the unconscionably low sum of $525,000. The Shoshone–Bannocks' Docket 326-F was for $120,000 in additional compensation for an 1889 cession of approximately 297,000 acres of the Fort Hall Reservation. Yet another claim (Docket 326-G) by the Fort Hall Tribes was on behalf of the Bannocks for the failure of the United States to provide them a reservation as promised in the Eastern Shoshone and Bannock Treaty of July 3, 1868 (ratified February 26, 1869). An identical claim, filed by individual Bannocks as an alternate representative-action claim (Docket 366), was combined with Docket 326-G. The Fort Hall tribes also placed a claim (Docket 326-H) with the Wind River tribes and the Northwest Bands of Shoshone Indians of Washakie, Utah, for loss of aboriginally owned, used, and occupied land. The Northwest Bands was a nonreservation group that included the Weber Utes and a few other Northwestern Shoshones. A separate but identical claim (Docket 367) was filed by a group of individuals calling themselves the "Shoshone Nation or Tribe of Indians" and was combined with Docket 326-H. Dockets 326-D, E, F, G, and H and Dockets 366 and 367 were consolidated for the purpose of entering a single judgment. The Indian Claims Commission on February 13, 1968, approved a total judgment amounting to $15.7 million. In Docket 326-D, E, F, and G an all-claims payment of $500,000 went to the petitioners of the Fort Hall Reservation. For Docket 326-H, the payment to the Indians of the Wind River Reservation was $7,259,699.39; the payment to the nonreservation Northwest Bands of Shoshone Indians of Washakie, Utah, was $11,375,000.00; and the payment to the Fort Hall tribes was $6,565,300.61.

A separate claim (Docket 326-I) was also heard by the commission. In 1980 the Northwest Bands of Shoshone Indians was federally recognized but without a federally approved constitution. Government services for that band were administered through the Fort Hall Agency. The Shoshone–Bannocks of Fort Hall, on behalf of Lemhi bands, sought additional monies for loss of aboriginal lands and were awarded $4.5 million by Docket 326-I.

The Wind River Shoshones filed a claim (Docket 63) for additional monies for 700,642 acres that had been ceded from their original 3,054,182-acre reservation by agreement on September 26, 1872 (18 Stat. 291), and for gold taken from those 700,642 acres between July 3, 1868, when the reservation was set aside by treaty, and the date of that cession and for offsets erroneously adjudged against the petitioner by the Court of Claims in prior action on the same issues (H-219, 82 C.Cls. 23 and 85 C.Cls. 331, 1937). The Claims Commission decided that the $27,500 paid for the cession was an unconscionably low amount and awarded the Wind River Shoshones the sum of $533,013.60 on August 20, 1954, less an offset of $100,000. That award was approved by Congress on April 22, 1957. The gold claim and the claim for offsets deducted prior to the Court of Claims' decision of June 1, 1937, were put in a separate claim (Docket 157). Decisions by the Court of Claims and the Supreme Court (304 U.S. 111, 82 L. ed. 1212, 58 S.C. 794) had established the Shoshones as the owners of underground minerals. The defending United States asked that those two causes of action be barred by res judicata. The Claims Commission found that the gold claim had not been barred but dismissed the action pertaining to the offsets as established by the Court of Claims. By a compromise settlement, the Wind River Shoshones on February 24, 1965, were awarded $195,000, less the $75,000 offset for the lost gold.

The Shoshonean-speaking peoples, including Paiutes as well as Shoshones, with twenty-four other tribes throughout the western United States, filed a claim (Docket 342-70) with the Claims Commission. The case, which was transferred to the Court of Claims, was for mismanagement of Indian Claims Commission judgment funds and for other funds such as Individual Indian Money accounts held in trust by the United States. The Shoshonean peoples were awarded $221,012.98 in 1980.

Contemporary Life and Culture: Important developments in tribal education include an alternative school where students work at their own individual pace. There is a learning lab designed for adult education. The Shoshone–Bannock Tribes also has a library and media center. There is a Fort Hall recreation department and teen center. Tribal health is advanced through the Shoshone–Bannock Tribal health department. As on other reservations, alcoholism has been a major health issue. Another related problem has been suicide, the rate among Shoshone–Bannocks being 14 percent above the national average.

Over half the people on the Fort Hall Reservation identify themselves with a Christian church. Among such churches on the reservation are Baptist, Episcopal, Roman Catholic, and Mormon faiths. Some tribal members belong to the Native American Church; in 1991, the members of this church worked for legislation legalizing peyote use in the state. That same year the Tribes negotiated the Fort Hall Water Rights Agreement with the state of Idaho and private persons over Snake River water rights. In March 1991 the BIA approved a tax code for the Indian and non-Indian businesses on the reservation, including utility companies and mining operations.

Shoshone-Bannock Tribal Enterprises manages an array of businesses for the Tribes, including the Trading Post Grocery Store, Oregon Trail Restaurant, Clothes Horse, TP Gas & Convenience Store, Bannock Peak Gas & Convenience Store, the Smoke House, the Tribal Bison Herd, and the Tribal Museum. The Tribes also operates the 40,000-square-foot Fort Hall Casino Resort with its attendant 200-room hotel, 300-seat bingo hall, 25,000-square-foot events center, meeting rooms, spa and fitness pool, water park, dining facilities, and RV park. In May 2008, the Tribes broke ground on a new 13,200-square-foot satellite casino at Blackfoot.

Among industries on the Fort Hall Reservation are a construction enterprise and a 1,500-acre farm and agricultural enterprise. An open-pit phosphate mine has operated on the reservation for some time. Indians and non-Indians engage in farming, livestock raising, and other agriculturally related enterprises. An active employment program was instituted in 1975. An important economic hub of southeastern Idaho is the 20,000-acre Fort Hall Reservation Irrigation Project. A zoning ordinance seeks to ensure clean air, water, and orderly economic growth. Recordings taken at Fort Hall have shown the reservation to be a world-class source of wind power, verifying the potential for future development of that resource.

The Lemhi Shoshones formed the Fort Lemhi Indian Community in 1995 to place before the BIA a petition seeking their formal recognition. The Public History Program at Washington State University in Pullman supported the petition with a 450-page legal and historical brief. In May 1999, Lemhi representative Rod Ariwite traveled to the White House, where he presented First Lady Hillary Clinton with a letter requesting federal restoration. As this publication was going to press, recognition had not been granted.

Special Events and Celebrations: In the second and fourth weeks of July, the Sun War Dances and Indian games are held in the Ross Fork and Bannock Creek districts. Around mid-August, the Shoshone–Bannock Indian Festival and Rodeo is held at Fort Hall. Indian Day, celebrated at Fort Hall in the latter part of September, features war dances, Indian games, and an all-Indian rodeo.

Suggested Readings:

Gregory R. Campbell, "The Lemhi Shoshoni: Ethnogenesis, Sociological Transformations, and the Construction of a Tribal Nation," *American Indian Quarterly* 25, no. 4 (2001); Clyde Hall, "A Visit with Rose Koops," *Idaho Heritage* 1, no. 10 (October 1977); John W. Heaton, *The Shoshone-Bannocks: Culture and Commerce at Fort Hall, 1870–1940* (Lawrence: University Press of Kansas, 2005); Sven Liljeblad, "Epilogue: Indian Policy and the Fort Hall Reservation," *Idaho Yesterdays* 2, no. 2 (Summer 1958) and "Some Observations on the Fort Hall Indian Reservation," *The Indian Historian* 7, no. 4 (Fall 1974); Brigham Madsen, *The Bannock of Idaho* (Caldwell, Ida.: Caxton Printers, 1958) and *The Lemhi: Sacajawea's People* (Caldwell, Ida.: Caxton Printers, 1980) and *The Northern Shoshoni* (Caldwell, Ida.: Caxton Printers, 1980); John W. W. Mann, *Sacajawea's People: The Lemhi Shoshones and the Salmon River Country* (Lincoln: University of Nebraska Press, 2004); Justina W. Parsons-Bernstein, "'I Hope We Be a Prosperous People': Shoshone and Bannock Incorporation, Ethnic Reorganization, and the Indian Way of Living Through," Ph.D. dissertation, Rutgers University, 2001; Joanna Cohan Scherer, *A Danish Photographer of Idaho Indians: Benedict Wrensted* (Norman: University of Oklahoma Press, 2006); Gregory E. Smoak, "Fort Hall and the Ghost Dance," *Idaho Yesterdays* 47, no. 1 (2006) and *Ghost Dances and Identity: Prophetic Religion and American Indian Ethnogenesis in the Nineteenth Century* (Berkeley: University of California Press, 2006); Omer C. Stewart, "The Western Shoshone of Nevada and the U.S. Government, 1863–1950," in Donald R. Tuohy, ed., *Selected Papers from the 14th Great Basin Anthropological Conference,* Ballena Press Publications in Archaeology, Ethnology and History, no. 11 (Socorro, N.M., 1978); Anna Lee Townsend, "Shoshone-Bannock Legend," *Idaho Heritage* 1, no. 10 (October 1977); Mark N. Trahant, "The Invisible Line," *Idaho Heritage* 1, no. 10 (October 1977); Virginia Cole Trenholm and Maurine Carley, *The Shoshonis: Sentinels of the Rockies* (Norman: University of Oklahoma Press, 1964).

SHOSHONE-PAIUTE TRIBES OF THE DUCK VALLEY RESERVATION, IDAHO AND NEVADA

(See **Northern Paiute.***)*

SILETZ

(Coastal Division, Salishan)

The Siletzes of the northwestern Oregon coast were the southernmost peoples of Salishan linguistic stock. A town, a river, and the reservation on which the tribe lived all bear the Siletz name, the significance of which is unknown. In aboriginal times, the tribe used the Chinook type of canoe for traveling and food gathering. They dip-netted for smelt, gathered crabs and clams, speared flounder, and gathered mussels for drying. Each spring they set large basket pots and traps near river estuaries to snare lamprey eels, which they smoked and sundried. Their hunters used sinew-backed bows, preferably of yew wood, and trapped big game, such as elk, in pitfalls. Their women dug roots and gathered berries, bracken fern, lupine, skunk cabbage, and salal. In bone, die, and shinny games the Siletzes sometimes wagered and lost all their possessions.

On their 225,000-acre reservation, the Siletzes lived among tribes of six other linguistic stocks. Like the others, they found it difficult to become the farmers that the government wished them to be. Before and during the reservation era, the relentless diseases and other consequences of white contact reduced their numbers. When officials began enumerating the peoples of the Siletz Reservation in 1857, they listed only twenty Siletzes. Perhaps because they were relatively isolated from non-Indians in aboriginal times, estimates of their populations during that period appear to be nonexistent. One source states that in 1890 the Siletzes no longer existed as a tribe. In 1930 no more than seventy-two Siletzes remained. They were plaintiffs in a suit before the Court of Claims (Case No. 45230), seeking payment for alienated ancestral lands. (*See* **Confederated Tribes of Siletz Indians; Tillamook;** *and* **Yaquina.**)

SILETZ CONFEDERATED TRIBES

(See **Confederated Tribes of Siletz Indians.***)*

SINKAIETK

(Interior Division, Salishan)

The Sinkaietks lived from around the confluence of the Columbia and Okanogan rivers north to the confluence of the Okanogan with the Similkameen River, a short distance below the Canadian border. The Sinkaietks are also called the Southern (or Lower) Okanagons, a name that is said to derive from an Indian place-name for the area near the mouth of the Similkameen River. The Sinkaietks called themselves "people of the water that does not freeze." They were closely related to the Methows, Sanpoils, Nespelems, Colvilles, and Senijextees. Among their subdivisions were the Kartars, Tonaskets, and Konkonelps.

According to elderly Sinkaietk informants, their ancestors suffered attacks by other Salish speakers like the Spokanes and Columbia Sinkiuses. The early-nine-teenth-century explorer-trader David Thompson dissuaded some Spokanes and Kalispels (Pend d'Oreilles) from attacking the Sinkaietks. Like other horse tribes of the interior, the Sinkaietks hunted, fished, and gathered for their subsistence. Sometimes they joined other Salish and Shahaptian peoples on buffalo hunts on the Great Plains. Another early-nineteenth-century fur trader, Alexander Ross, lived among them at Fort Okanogan (established August 31, 1811) at the confluence of the Columbia and Okanogan rivers. Ross wrote that polygamy was "the greatest source of evil existing among this otherwise happy people." Other Columbia Plateau peoples also practiced polygamy and, like the Sinkaietks, believed in good and evil forces. The Sinkaietks were among the Salish peoples who met the Roman Catholic missionaries François Blanchet and Modeste De-mers at Fort Colvile in November 1838. Their introduction to the Christian faith had no doubt come earlier, through contact with other Salishan peoples such as the Flatheads who had been exposed to Christianity by Iroquois Indians in the beginning of the nineteenth century. About the time of their meeting with the two Catholic missionaries, the Sinkaietks visited the Lapwai (Idaho) mission of the Reverend Henry H. Spalding of the American Board of Commissioners for Foreign Missions.

The Sinkaietks were not party to the 1855 Walla Walla Treaty with Washington territorial governor and superintendent of Indian affairs Isaac Stevens, nor did they participate in the ensuing Yakama War (1855–56), which broke out because of Indian dissatisfaction with the treaty. The Sinkaietks were influenced by one of their chiefs, Walking Grizzly-bear, to abstain from hostilities. They were, however, among those at McLoughlin Canyon near the Okanogan River south of today's Tonasket, Washington, where in the summer of 1858 Indians attacked and reportedly killed six men of a party of miners en route to Canadian goldfields. Some Sinkaietks were among those who unsuccessfully engaged U.S. Army Col. George Wright and his command in two fights in Spokane country in September 1858. In the postwar period, the tribe was angered by the establish-

Many Indians bore the name "Eneas," from the French "Ignace." This Eneas, photographed in 1905, was a Sinkaietk, or Southern Okanogon. On his tribal lands lay portions of the Colville Reservation in north-central Washington. His clothing was suitable to the rigorous climate of the reservation, where winters were cold and summer frosts were common.

Courtesy of Frank Avery.

ment of the Moses, or Columbia, Reservation in their lands and especially unhappy with the chief for whom it was named, whom they did not recognize as their leader. It was especially galling to them that Chief Moses collected grazing fees from white cattlemen running herds on Sinkaietk lands. When the Moses Reservation was terminated in 1884, some Sinkaietks remained in their homelands west of the Okanogan River and others (for example, those under the influence of the pro-American chief Tonasket) remained on their own lands in the Colville Reservation east of the Okanogan River.

Sinkaietk numbers, excluding the Northern (Upper) Okanagons in Canada, have been estimated at 1,000 in 1780 and 348 in 1906. The 1906 figure was about 187 higher than that given by a Colville Reservation agent in 1870. In 1959 there were 91 Sinkaietks of full-blood degree on their reservation and 34 outside its boundaries. Like other Indians on reservations east of the Cascade Mountains, those on the Colville retained a higher quantum of Indian blood than the tribes west of the Cascades, where white contact was more frequent. Today the Sinkaietks are amalgamated with members of the Confederated Tribes of the Colville Reservation, Washington. *See* **Confederated Tribes of the Colville Reservation.**

Suggested Readings:

Walter Cline et al., *The Sinkaietk or Southern Okanagon of Washington,* ed. Leslie
Spier, American Anthropological Association, General Series, in Anthropology,
no. 6 (Menasha, Wis.: George Banta Publishing, 1938); Lawney L. Reyes, *White
Grizzly Bear's Legacy: Learning to Be Indian* (Seattle: University of Washington
Press, 2002); Alexander Ross, *Adventures of the First Settlers on the Oregon or
Columbia River* (London, 1849); Alexander Ross, *The Fur Hunters of the Far West*
(Norman: University of Oklahoma Press, 1956); Robert H. Ruby and John A.
Brown, *Half-Sun on the Columbia: A Biography of Chief Moses* (Norman: University
of Oklahoma Press, 1965); James Teit, "The Middle Columbia Salish," *University of
Washington Publications in Anthropology* 2, no. 4 (1928).

SINKIUSE

(Interior Division, Salishan)

The name "Sinkiuse" is said to mean "between people." The Sinkiuses of the Rock
Island area of the Columbia River near Wenatchee, Washington, were called by
early French-Canadian fur traders *Isle des Pierres* ("[people of] the island of
rocks"). They called themselves Kawachens, or those "living on the banks." Another of their villages, known as "roasting place," was along the Columbia in
desert country near present-day Beverly, Washington.

Sinkiuse origins are shrouded in controversy. Some anthropologists allege that
with the introduction of horse culture in the southern Pacific Northwest interior,
the Sinkiuses and other Salishan peoples were pressured northward from the
lower Columbia River by Shahaptian peoples such as the Yakamas and the Klickitats. Other scholars dispute that explanation. Elderly Sinkiuses—or Moses Columbias as they were called in the later nineteenth century—claimed that their
ancestors had come from the north sometime in the distant past. Although the
tribe lived primarily along the Columbia, its members utilized a 5,000-square-
mile area, mostly on the Columbia Plateau south and east of the Columbia River.
The northern boundary of their lands in present-day Washington State ran along
Badger Mountain just east of the Columbia and south of Waterville, Washington, and northeast to the Grand Coulee Dam, from where the territory extended
southwest a few miles following the eastern slopes of the Grand Coulee and then
south to include Soap Lake, Ephrata, and Moses Lake. From Moses Lake, the
boundary ran south to approximately the 47th parallel and from that line southwest to the Columbia at Beverly.

In July 1811 a band of Indians that the Northwester David Thompson documented as the Sinkowarsin (Sinkiuse-Kawachen?) met the fur man at Rock Island on the Columbia just below present-day East Wenatchee. Thompson was on

Sinkiuse Chief Moses in 1890. The Sinkiuses were sometimes called the Columbia-Sinkiuses because of their location on the mid-Columbia River and the adjoining Columbia Plateau. Moses assumed leadership of the nontreaty Indians along the Columbia in the latter part of the nineteenth century. He and his people were removed to the Colville Reservation in north-central Washington.

Authors' collections.

his "Journey of the Summer Moon," searching for wider trading opportunities for the North West Company.

In the early nineteenth century the Sinkiuses were led by the powerful Sulktalthscosum, or Half-Sun, who was killed on a buffalo hunt by Plains Indians sometime around 1850. After the death of Sulktalthscosum's eldest son, Quiltenenock (Quiltomee), at the hands of white miners below the mouth of the Wenatchee River in 1858, tribal leadership passed to Quiltenenock's brother, Moses, who had received his biblical name as a boy in the school run by the American Board of Commissioners for Foreign Missions at present-day Lapwai, Idaho. Today a coulee, a lake, and the city of Moses Lake, Washington, on Interstate 90 bear his name. Moses fought Americans in the 1850s but maintained peaceful relations with them later in the postwar period. He also assumed the leadership of the nontreaty peoples on the mid-Columbia. The Columbia, or Moses, Reservation was established for him and his people by executive order on April 19, 1879. It was enlarged to the south by executive order on May 6, 1880, so that it stretched from Lake Chelan north to the Canadian border and from the crest of the Cascade Mountains to the Okanogan River. The fifteen-mile strip across the reservation's northern end was withdrawn at the insistence of miners by an executive order of February 23, 1883. Then the diminished reservation was relinquished by an agreement with Moses on July 7, 1883 (ratified by Congress on July 4, 1884). The land was restored to the public domain on May 1, 1886. Moses and his band never occupied the reservation, though the chief collected rent from white cattlemen using those lands. He and his people were removed to the Colville Reservation, established on July 2, 1872, across the Okanogan River east of the Columbia Reservation.

In 1851 the Sinkiuses numbered roughly three hundred. The 1870 population of Sinkiuse Columbias has been estimated at roughly a thousand. The increase was due to the accretion of nontreaty peoples seeking the leadership of Moses. In 1900 they were listed at around three hundred to four hundred. A 1910 census placed them at fifty-two. Tabulations as late as 1959 enumerated ninety-four of full-blood degree living on the Colville Reservation and fifty-two of full-blood degree living outside the reservation. Today a small remnant proudly asserts their Sinkiuse-Moses Columbia roots. *See also* **Confederated Tribes of the Colville Reservation.**

Suggested Readings:

Walter Cline, et al., *The Sinkaietk, or Southern Okanagon of Washington,* ed. Leslie Spier, American Anthropological Association, General Series in Anthropology, no. 6 (Menasha, Wis.: George Banta Publishing, 1938); Grace Christiansen Gardner, "Life among North Central Washington First Families," *Wenatchee (Wash.) Daily World,* May 31–December 20, 1935; Robert H. Ruby and John A. Brown, *Half-Sun on the Columbia: A Biography of Chief Moses* (Norman: University of Oklahoma Press, 1965); James A. Teit, "The Middle Columbia Salish," *University of Washington Publications in Anthropology* 2, no. 4 (June 1928) and "The Salishan Tribes of the Western Plateaus," *Forty-fifth Annual Report of the Bureau of American Ethnology* (Washington, D.C.: Government Printing Office, 1930).

SIUSLAW

(Yakonan)

The Siuslaws lived on and near the Siuslaw River along the Oregon coast, in an area of sand dunes south of the rocky cliffs of Sea Lion Caves and Heceta Head. The houses of their roughly thirty-four villages consisted of excavations beneath frame-board structures covered with earth. Two or more of these houses were sometimes joined together. Passage in and out was by ladders. Siuslaw subsistence patterns included gathering foods from the sea and hunting game. A small tribe numerically, the Siuslaws were encroached upon on occasion by peoples from as far north as the Columbia River. In 1835 the latter captured and enslaved some Siuslaw women and children. To replace their lost women, Siuslaw men reportedly journeyed south seeking wives among the Umpquas because that tribe was reportedly "most like the Siuslaws." It was also said that sometime before the middle of the nineteenth century, Siuslaw women introduced the practice of flattening the heads of their infants.

The Siuslaw homelands lay within the southern portion of the Coast Reservation, created by executive order on November 9, 1855. Before establishment of the Alsea Subagency on the southern part, the Siuslaws were under the Umpqua

Subagency off the reservation at the mouth of the Umpqua River. The Umpqua Subagency supervised the Hanis and Miluk Coos and the Kuitsh (or Lower Umpquas). There were 690 Indians under the subagency. After it closed on September 3, 1859, the Siuslaws were marched northward from their homelands to the Yachats River, where the Alsea Subagency was established in 1861. The Coos and Umpquas were also moved there. In 1862 the military Fort Umpqua was abandoned because the Indians were perceived as less of a threat. When a central strip was carved from the reservation on December 21, 1865, the northern half became the Siletz Reservation. The 620-square-mile southern portion was then named the Alsea Reservation; it had a population of 525 Indians. The removed strip, encompassing Yaquina Bay and the Yaquina River, was opened to settlers. The Alseas were living in their own homelands on the Alsea Reservation. They did not ally themselves with the Siuslaws, Kuitsh, and Coos who lived there also. An example of the friction among the tribes occurred on September 17, 1864, when the military settled an intertribal dispute over a beached whale.

The Coos, Kuitsh, and Siuslaws were invited to a congressionally ordered council to secure their consent to closure of the entire Alsea Reservation. Despite Indian opposition, the reservation was restored to the public domain by an act of Congress on March 3, 1875 (18 Stat. 420, 446). The Alsea Reservation Indians, most of whom were Siuslaws, Kuitsh, or Coos, were given the option of removing to the Siletz Reservation or resettling along the coast. Those who relocated to the Siletz were to be provided allotments and subsistence in the Salmon River area in order not to overcrowd the Siletz Valley. In 1881 a small number, sixty-seven in all, representing fifteen families, took advantage of that option and moved to the Siletz. In 1876 the government granted 160-acre homesteads to those who had not removed to the Siletz. Among the latter group, the Siuslaws settled along the Siuslaw River in the Florence, Oregon, area. The Kuitsh went to the estuary of the Umpqua River, and the Coos relocated to Coos Bay. Failing to adjust to non-Indian society in their former homelands, many Indians abandoned the Alsea Reservation. Some moved to the Siletz Reservation, only to face starvation because its agent, lacking funds, could not feed, clothe, or otherwise provide for them. Those who had organized gravitated in time to Coos Bay, where they purchased a 6.1-acre reservation, which is in nontrust status.

In 1916 a few Siuslaws joined the Kuitsh and the Hanis and Miluk Coos to form an extension of the Coos who had organized on their own at Coos Bay. Without a reservation or treaty, the four tribes in 1917 began pressing claims for the lands taken from them. They formed a new council with a chief and legal counsel. In 1929 Congress passed an act permitting them to sue the United States for their alienated lands (Case No. K-345), but on May 2, 1938, the Court of Claims ruled that by their oral testimony they had not proved ownership or title to any large acreage. The Claims Court declared that as nontreaty Indians (the treaties made with their ancestors had never been ratified), they were unable to establish titles to the lands that they claimed. One judge of the court went so far as to assert that since they had been a relatively peaceful people it was difficult to establish with any certainty their location before 1855. On November 14, 1938, the U.S. Supreme Court refused to consider their appeal. In 1947, recognizing that the BIA had constructed a large meeting hall and food-processing center a decade earlier on their 6.1-acre reservation, the Siuslaws, the Kuitsh, and the Coos in conjunction with the Lower Chinooks, filed a claim against the United States. Three years later, four petitioners—the Siuslaws, the Kuitsh, and the Hanis and Miluk Coos—were removed from the suit. The Indian claims commissioners told them that they had already had their day in court. On August 8, 1956, they filed a petition with the United Nations to renew their land claim. That international body declined to act in the matter, stating that the claim was an internal matter of the United States.

Today there are no speakers of the Siuslaw language. For recent cultural developments among the Siuslaws, *see* **Confederated Tribes of Coos, Lower Umpqua and Siuslaw Indians** *and* **Hanis Coos.**

Suggested Readings:

> Stephen Dow Beckham, *The Indians of Western Oregon: This Land Was Theirs* (Coos Bay, Ore.: Arago Books, 1977); *Indian Education,* a continuing publication of Coos County, Oregon, Intermediate Education District.

SKAGIT

(See **Lower Skagit** *and* **Upper Skagit.***)*

SKILLOOT

(Upper Chinookan Division of Chinookan)

The Skilloots spoke the Clackamas dialect of the Chinookan language. In 1805 the American explorers Meriwether Lewis and William Clark found them on both the north and the south banks of the Columbia River above and below the entrance of the Cowlitz River, in present-day Oregon and Washington. The tribe numbered about twenty-five hundred at that time. They were among the many lower Columbia River peoples who were virtually depopulated by plagues in the late eighteenth and early nineteenth centuries. Their 1780 numbers have been estimated at thirty-two hundred.

On the Oregon shore of the Columbia was the Conniac (Konnaack) Skilloot village. Its residents may have been the Chilwitses (or Hellwitses), who lived near Oak Point on the Columbia's south bank, about forty miles upstream from where the river enters the Pacific Ocean. They hunted and came to the river to fish. They numbered roughly two hundred in 1810, when the American Winship brothers (Abiel, Jonathan, and Nathan) attempted to build a fur post among them at Oak Point. If the post had been successful, it would have been the first such land-based establishment in the Pacific Northwest. It failed because of the hostility of the Chilwitses and other Indians, and also because the Columbia River, nearing its seasonal June crest, flooded out the post that the Winships were building. In 1811, men of John Jacob Astor's Pacific Fur Company established Fort Astoria downstream from the Winship site.

On August 8, 1851, Oregon superintendent of Indian affairs Anson Dart effected a treaty with what he called the "Kon-naack Band of the Chinook Tribe of Indians." In the treaty, the Skilloots ceded lands on both sides of the Columbia River north and west of the lower Cowlitz River and across the Columbia from that stream on the south and west. In exchange, they were given goods as well as the privilege of occupying their place of residence at Oak Point and the right to hunt on their ceded lands near Oak Point. *See* **Clackamas.**

SKIN

(Shahaptian)

The Skins (Skeens), or Skinpahs, lived on the north bank of the Columbia River east of the Wishrams, in what is present-day south-central Washington State. Their name derived from a word in the Tenino dialect meaning "cradle" or "cradle place." The tribal village was later named Wishram for the Skins' neighbors of that name. Later it was called Fallbridge. The Skins were believed to be the tribe whom the American explorers Meriwether Lewis and William Clark identified as the Eneeshurs in 1805–1806. At that time, they were said to number twelve hundred, a tenuous estimate since it was difficult to separate them from the large tribal groups who gathered with them to fish and trade. It is some evidence of Skin ethnic identity that they were among the fourteen groups who, at the time of their 1855 Walla Walla Treaty with the United States, formed what white officials then called the Yakama Nation. As such, they were scheduled for removal to the Yakama Reservation. Because of their location at a key passage on the Columbia River, they engaged in considerable trading and fishing for their subsistence. Like others along the Columbia, they occasionally left the river to gather roots and berries. They were one of several aboriginal peoples of the Pacific Northwest who lost their tribal identities in the nineteenth century.

SKOKOMISH TRIBE, SKOKOMISH RESERVATION

SqWuqWu'b3sh
People of the River or Big River People

The Skokomish Tribe, Skokomish Reservation, had its beginning on January 26, 1855, at the Treaty of Point-No-Point, when government officials treated with the Twana, Clallam, and Chimakum Indians. The reservation to which they were to remove was the Skokomish on the lower Skokomish River, an affluent of Hood Canal. The Skokomish name derives from one of the three Twana bands.

Location: Tribal members live not only on the Skokomish Reservation but also adjacent to it in such places as the city of Shelton, Washington.

Numbers: In 1984 the tribal population stood at 507, and in 2004 there were 745 enrolled members.

History: The Twana, Clallam, and Chimakum peoples were designated under the Point-No-Point Treaty to remove to the 3,840-acre Skokomish Reservation. By executive order on February 25, 1874, the reservation boundaries were established, and the acreage was increased to 4,986.97. Also in 1874 the Twanas, under the Medicine Creek Treaty, received allotments from their agent, Edwin Eells, thirteen years before the passage of the General Allotment, or Dawes, Act. As was often the case, government officials soon called all the Indians on the reservation by the name of one tribal group. In this case it was the Skokomish, for whom the river in their aboriginal homeland was also named.

Later in the nineteenth century an agent noted that only one-sixth of the Indians scheduled to go on the reservation ever did. Most of those who stayed away, primarily Clallams and a few Chimakums, remained in small villages along Hood Canal, Puget Sound, and the Strait of Juan de Fuca at distances of 50 to 150 miles from the reservation. Some of the Clallams who first removed to the Skokomish later abandoned it for their old homes. The scarcity of good reservation land kept them from it, as did off-reservation employment in logging, milling, and canoeing. In 1870 the Clallam headman Chitsamakkan (Chetzamokha), dubbed the Duke of York, was induced to come to the Skokomish Reservation. His bones at least came to rest in his homelands. On June 23, 1888, he was buried in the Masonic cemetery in Port Townsend.

The many works of missionary Myron Eells (who was the brother of Edwin Eells) reveal Skokomish Reservation Indians living in two cultural worlds, one Native and one white—a state that one official termed "half-civilization." Native women set aside government-introduced spinning wheels in favor of their

Mary Adams, of the Skokomish Tribe, Skokomish Reservation, ca. 1880. Her people came under the influence of missionaries and merchants in the late nineteenth and the early twentieth centuries. They lived along the shores of Hood Canal in northwestern Washington, where their reservation, the Skokomish, was established at the southern end of the canal. In October 1989, Seattle University returned to the Skokomish the remains of their ancestors that the university had obtained from the University of Washington in 1974.

Courtesy of Whitman College, Walla Walla, Wash.

own whorls. They wove socks and other clothing for settlers and for their own men who worked in the logging camps and mills. As it had to other local Indian groups, the Shaker faith spread to the Skokomish from the nearby Squaxin Island Indians, among whom it had originated in 1882. Some Squaxins moved to the Skokomish Reservation, as did their neighbors, the Sahewamish. As late as the last quarter of the nineteenth century, Indians of the Skokomish Reservation held potlatches, which were often attended by as many as ten tribes. By the end of the century, such holidays as the Fourth of July had begun to replace the traditional potlatch ceremonies.

Government and Claims: The Skokomish Tribe, Skokomish Reservation, is fully organized under the Indian Reorganization Act (48 Stat. 984). On May 3, 1938, the secretary of the interior approved the tribal constitution and bylaws. Its charter was ratified July 22, 1939. The Skokomish Tribal Council is the governing body. The tribe has established its own court to enforce its ordinances and to regulate hunting and fishing. Several kinds of services are delivered through the federal government, and some law enforcement is provided by the state through the office of the Mason County sheriff.

The tribe submitted a claim to the Indian Claims Commission (Docket 296) for compensation for the 1855 cession of Twana lands to the United States. The commission determined that the tribe originally held 355,800 acres, which on March 8, 1859, had a value of $426,960, for which the tribe had already received an unconscionably low payment of $53,383. On June 30, 1961, the commission therefore ordered an award to be made to the tribe, minus the amount already paid for the cession of their lands. The award, approved on October 14, 1966, amounted to $373,577. In 1973 the tribe spent $104,000 of the claims money on payments of $250 per capita to its members. The remainder of the moneys went into tribal development programs.

Contemporary Life and Culture: Of the enlarged Skokomish Reservation of 4,986.97 acres, nearly all of which were allotted, about 3,000 remain in Indian ownership as trust land. About 1,000 acres of bottomlands are subject to periodic flooding. Employment is available in traditional industries, such as logging, lumbering, and fishing. Some members engage in farming and cattle grazing. Like their ancestors, a few trap and hunt deer and wild fowl to supplement their diets. A program of fisheries enhancement and management is coordinated with that of the Port Gamble S'Klallam Tribe and the Lower Elwha Klallam Tribe, both of which are descended from the Clallam tribe of the Point-No-Point treaty council. The fish hatcheries installed in 1976 have been expanded. The tribe operates a fish-processing plant and in 1980 owned two fishing boats. Many tribal members, however, fish on their own.

With the Chehalis, Squaxin, and Nisqually tribes, the Skokomish belong to the Southern Puget Intertribal Planning Commission, which addresses economic problems and housing concerns. On the reservation are Indian Pentecostal and Shaker churches. Some tribal members are affiliated with a secret society that practices the traditional Native *tamanawas* religion. In the pursuit of this ancient religion, its adherents, many of them young people, blacken their faces as part of their ritual.

Opened in August 2001, the Skokomish Lucky Dog Casino underwent a nearly $4-million expansion in 2006. The construction included increasing the gambling space of the facility and adding a restaurant; however, the casino was forced to close in September 2009 because of revenue losses associated with the national recession. The Twin Totems Grocery and Deli, Skokomish Subway, and the Waterfront at Potlatch cabins, motel, and RV park number among the other tribal enterprises.

Skokomish youth attend high school in nearby Shelton. Many children attend a grade school operated by the Hood Canal school district. There is also a tribal school, called Kiikpahl, for children from kindergarten through grade 4. Skokomish Head Start and Childcare is operated on the reservation itself and serves children ages three to five. The Skokomish Tribe has also inaugurated Pathways, a program designed to increase both high school graduation rates and enrollment in postsecondary schools. The Skokomish Education Center provides students with additional support toward earning their high school diplomas, including mentoring and tutoring services, encouragement, group and individual assistance, technology, project help, planning, college preparation,

Skokomish cultural, spiritual, and educational leader Bruce Miller, or Subiyay (1944–2005). A soldier, author, artist, basket weaver, dancer, storyteller, singer, historian, botanist, linguist, teacher, advisor, and confidante, Miller worked alongside cultural regenerators like Hazel Pete and Vi Hilbert in the second half of the twentieth century, retrieving and returning to the forefront lost or nearly lost tribal practices and traditions.

Courtesy of Paul D. G. Eubanks.

and job search. The tribe retains the services of a resident anthropologist, under whose direction it has launched Native language and curriculum projects for schoolchildren. Dictionaries of the Twana language have been prepared.

Tuwaduq Family Services delivers programs and services designed to promote the social, mental, emotional, and spiritual well-being of present and future generations. Comprehensive medical, nutritional, and dental care is provided through Skokomish Health Clinic. Public safety on the reservation is preserved by the Skokomish Department of Public Safety, a five-officer around-the-clock police force. The tribe publishes the monthly *Skokomish Sounder*, their tribal newspaper. To maintain and preserve the cultural resources of the Twana people, the Skokomish Tribe funds and operates its own Tribal Historic Preservation Office. In 1980 a basketry project was begun in cooperation with the Chehalis, Suquamish, and Nisqually Indians. The Skokomish have been active in repatriation efforts, retrieving the remains of their ancestors from Seattle University in 1989. In the summer of 2009, tribal spiritual leaders were ceremonially reclaiming ancestral names for the lands containing longhouses, village sites, and burial grounds that were being returned to them. As the late Skokomish cultural leader, Bruce Miller, commented, "We were dismembered. Our culture was taken away. Our language was taken away. Our way of life was taken away. The only way to cure dismemberment is to remember."

Special Events and Celebrations: On the weekend nearest January 26, the tribe annually holds Treaty Days, recalling the Point-No-Point Treaty signed on that day in 1855. First salmon runs are also observed on the reservation, and the intertribal bone game, the Slahal, is played during the summer. The tribe hosts the annual Elders' Picnic in August. A naming ceremony, in which ancestral names are taken, is held in winter. The public is not invited to this event. *See* **Twana;** **Clallam;** *and* **Chimakum.**

Suggested Readings:

George P. Castile, "Edwin Eells. U.S. Indian Agent, 1871–1895," *Pacific Northwest Quarterly* 72, no. 2 (April 1981) and *The Indians of Puget Sound* (Seattle, 1985); Myron Eells, *The Twana, Chemakum, and Klallam Indians of Washington Territory* (1887) and "The Twana Indians of the Skokomish Reservation in Washington Territory," *United States Geological and Geographical Survey* (a bulletin of the U.S. Department of the Interior), vol. 3, no. 1 (April 9, 1877); W. W. Elmendorf, *The Structure of Twana Society,* Monograph Supplement no. 2 (Pullman: Washington State University, 1960) and *Twana Narratives: Native Historical Accounts of a Coast Salish Culture* (Seattle: University of Washington Press, 1993); Gordon James, *StuxWa?scH3Ia: Keep the Knowledge and Memories of Our Ancestors Alive* (Shelton, Wash.: Skokomish Indian Tribe, 1993); Michael D. Pavel, et al., "Too Long, Too Silent: The Threat to Cedar and the Sacred Ways of the Skokomish," *American Indian Culture & Research Journal* 17, no. 3 (1993); Robert H. Ruby and John A. Brown, *Myron Eells and the Puget Sound Indians* (Seattle: Superior Publishing Company, 1976), in which is contained a list of the published works of Eells; Nile Thompson, *What Is Twana?* (Shelton, Wash.: Skokomish Indian Tribe, 1979).

SKYKOMISH

(Coastal Division, Salishan)

The Skykomish, who originated as a subdivision of the Snoqualmies, lived in what is present-day Washington State. Their primary villages were on the Skykomish River, formerly called the North Fork of the Snohomish River. They also resided in the drainage area of the Snoqualmie River. Their land base at the time of the first white contacts comprised about 974,822 acres, of which roughly 538,048 were drained by the Skykomish River and about 436,744 by the Snoqualmie. In the Point Elliott Treaty of 1855, which two Skykomish subchiefs signed, the tribe appeared as the Skai-whamish. They had been mentioned earlier in the journals of white men, such as the Hudson's Bay Company traders at Fort Nisqually, which was established in 1833 on southern Puget Sound, The Skykomish traded at that fort, as did their neighbors and allies, the Snoqualmies. Today the river along U.S. Highway 2 bears the Skykomish name, as does a Cascade Mountain town along that route.

A riverine mountain people, the Skykomish subsisted mainly from the land. They hunted, fished, and gathered roots and berries on the western slopes of the Cascade Mountains. They were also found at times on the shores of Puget Sound on the west, where they went to trade. From the Snohomish and the Clallams they obtained dog hair, which, with goat wool, feathers, and fireweed, they wove into blankets. On occasion, they confronted other tribes, such as the Klickitats and the Clallams. In May 1849, some of their warriors, with those of the Snoqualmies, attacked Fort Nisqually. In the Indian War of 1855–56 in which some Puget Sound Indians fought Americans, they remained neutral under their pro-American (though anti-British) Snoqualmie headman, Patkanin, who at an earlier time had opposed all whites. The close Skykomish ties with the Snoqualmies caused anthropologists to disagree as to whether or not the Skykomish were a Snoqualmie subdivision.

On June 30, 1960, the Indian Claims Commission handed down its decision in a claim (Docket 93) that had been filed by the Snoqualmies on behalf of the Skykomish. Contrary to the Snoqualmie position, the commission ruled that the Skykomish had been a separate, identifiable people. The Snoqualmies appealed to the commission to modify its order in hopes that the commission would look into the matter further once the commissioners had consulted Indians of Skykomish descent in the Snoqualmie tribe. Again, the commission denied the petitioners' claims to recover compensation on behalf of the Skykomish. The Snoqualmies then appealed to the Court of Claims on August 27, 1965 (178 C.Cls. 570, 372 F. 2d 951). That court reversed the commission's decision, and on September 23, 1968, a final judgment was entered in favor of the Snoqualmies for a settlement of $257,698.29 for themselves and the Skykomish.

In 1849 the Skykomish population was listed at 410, and in 1852 at 175. In the 1860s many Skykomish were living on the Tulalip Reservation on Puget Sound near the mouth of the Snohomish River. On that reservation, their last reported census enumerated them under their headman, William Stechlech, at 49 men, 44 women, and 51 children, for a total of 144. After 1871, statistical reports from the reservation did not record them as a separate people, because of the individual-allotment process there and because of their intermarriage with other Native peoples and assimilation with whites. Thus the Skykomish no longer exist as an identifiable tribe. *See* **Tulalip Tribes of the Tulalip Reservation** *and* **Snoqualmie.**

SNOHOMISH

(Coastal Division, Salishan)

Sdoh-doh-hohbsh
The Lowland People

The Snohomish were sometimes called the Sinahomish (or Sneomuses). Their name is said to mean "a large number of people" but has also been rendered as "a warrior tribe." They lived near the mouth of the Snohomish River, a Puget Sound affluent in northwestern Washington State, north of today's Marysville; on the southern tip of Camano Island; on Whidbey Island opposite the present-day city of Mukilteo; and up the Snohomish River as far east as today's Monroe. Among the Snohomish subdivisions in those locations, besides the Snohomish proper, were the Sdohobcs of the lower Snohomish River and Whidbey Island and the Sdocohobcs on the Snohomish River between Snohomish and Monroe. Other Snohomish subdivisions were the N'Quentlamamishes (or Kwehtlamamishes) of the Pilchuck River. Besides the river and the city, a county bears the tribal name.

Location: About 93 percent of the enrolled members of the Snohomish Tribe of Indians live within seventy-five miles of their ancestral lands. About 4 percent live out of state. The residences of the other 3 percent are unknown.

Numbers: In 1844 the Snohomish numbered 322. A decade later, their population stood at 350, indicating perhaps that a smallpox plague of that time did not strike them as severely as it did other Natives of the region. In 1980 there was a Snohomish membership of about 700, a population that had expanded to approximately 1,200 by 2008.

History: When the Snohomish met the Hudson's Bay Company trader John Work in their country in December 1824, they believed his party had come to attack them. They had long been in conflict with tribes such as the Clallams of the Strait of Juan de Fuca and the Cowichans of southeastern Vancouver Island. One Snohomish warrior demonstrated for Work's party how to kill the Cowichans if that tribe were to attack. The Snohomish were among the various peoples who traded at the Hudson's Bay Company's Fort Nisqually, which was established in 1833 at the southern end of Puget Sound. They were also among those who met the Roman Catholic missionaries in their lands in the early 1840s. At the time of those contacts, the Snohomish were governed by headmen, with one such leader having influence over several villages.

Nine Snohomish headmen signed the Point Elliott Treaty, for which the council was held in 1855 in the Snohomish country near present-day Mukilteo. At

Charles Jules, a Snohomish Indian, ca. 1905. His people occupied the vicinity of present-day Everett, Washington, and the watershed of their namesake river, the Snohomish.

Authors' collections.

the council, about 350 Snohomish and their allies, the Snoqualmies, were represented by Chief Patkanin, who had been hostile to Americans in pretreaty times but had become impressed with their potential power. With a small band, Patkanin was allied with the Americans during the Indian War of 1855–56. During that conflict, most of the other Snohomish remained neutral, which prompted an Indian agent in February 1856 to recommend to Washington territorial governor and superintendent of Indian affairs Isaac Stevens that the tribe be disbanded, since they were "doing nothing for us." They were among the neutral Indians who were removed by government officials to such places in Puget Sound as Fox and Whidbey islands and Port Gamble on the Kitsap Peninsula.

The Tulalip (formerly the Snohomish) Reservation had been authorized under the Point Elliott Treaty and was enlarged by executive order on December 23, 1873, from 22,489.91 acres to 24,320 acres. It lay in Snohomish lands but was also intended for occupancy by the Skykomish, the Snoqualmies, and the Stillaguamish. Early in the reservation period the agent, Rev. Eugene Casimir Chirouse, O.M.I., employed various means to help the Indians survive the difficult transition that they were experiencing. During this time, because of their small population, the retaliations of the Indians against white encroachments took the form of isolated, unorganized attacks. Many Snohomish vacated the reservation because of the severe overcrowding that taxed their ability to subsist there. In the 1870s, many more left because of oppressive government policies that opposed their traditional religious practices and the use of their language. Out-migration continued during the allotment period, 1883 to 1901, when it became evident that the reservation lands were too limited for individual occupancy.

Government and Claims: The Snohomish Tribe of Indians claims to have had continuous political authority over the centuries. Its members are descendants of those Snohomish who refused to move or to return to the Tulalip Reservation as agreed to in the Point Elliott Treaty. Since the 1920s the tribe has used the committee system of governance and has operated under councils and chairpersons. It was first incorporated under state law in 1927 and again in 1974. It functions under bylaws written in 1928 and a constitution written in 1934. Although the federal government recognizes the Snohomish tribe as a political entity (because the forebears of tribal members signed the Point Elliott Treaty), it has not acknowledged the Snohomish as a tribal entity. In October 1977 the tribe adopted a comprehensive plan for restoration, and they continue to seek acknowledgment and a land base in the form of a reservation in the Snohomish River valley between Snohomish and Monroe, Washington.

The Snohomish filed a claim (Docket 125) with the Indian Claims Commission for the lands that they ceded to the United States in 1855, including the southern reaches of Whidbey and Camano islands, all of Gedney (Hat) Island, and a portion of the mainland that confronts Puget Sound and stretches from Mukilteo north to Warm Beach. The east boundary extended from Granite City (Falls) south to the intersections of the Snohomish, Snoqualmie, and Skykomish rivers, and to Granite City on the north. It was within this 164,000-acre tract that the Tulalip Reservation was established. The commission determined the 1859 value of the land at $180,700 and issued an award after considering offsets. On August 13, 1964, the commission found that the total consideration paid to the Snohomish for their aboriginal lands had been $44,534.21. The tribe therefore had $136,165.79 coming to it. *See* **Tulalip Tribes of the Tulalip Reservation.**

Contemporary Life and Culture: In 2008, the Snohomish Tribe appealed the latest decision, handed down in 2004, that denied them federal acknowledgment.

Special Events and Celebrations: The Snohomish Tribe holds its annual June powwow at Fort Flagler State Park on Marrowstone Island.

Suggested Readings:

Rick Carter, "The Invisible Indians," *Snohomish County Tribune,* June 8, 1972; Gustav B. Joergenson, *History of the Twin Cities* [of Stanwood and East Stanwood, Washington], *Twin City (Wash.) News,* April 1, 1948–October 27, 1949 (70 issues); Nancy L. McDaniel, *The Snohomish Tribe of Indians: Our Heritage . . . Our People* (self-published, 2004); Colin Ellidge Tweddell, "A Historical and Ethnological Study of the Snohomish Indian People," in *Coast Salish and Western Washington Indians,* vol. 2 (New York: Garland Publishing, 1974), 475–694; William Whitfield, *History of Snohomish County, Washington,* 2 vols. (Evansville, Ind.: Unigraphic, 1979).

SNOQUALMIE

(Coastal Division, Salishan)

S·Dukwalbixw

People of the Moon

The Snoqualmies lived in two main villages in the Snoqualmie River valley, which is between Puget Sound and the Cascade Mountains in western Washington State. One of their villages was at the mouth of the Tolt River, and the other was about a mile below the spectacular Snoqualmie Falls. The Snoqualmie name is also perpetuated in a town near Interstate 90 and in a mountain pass that is traversed by Interstate 90.

The Snoqualmies are said to have carried the designation "people of the moon" and also "crowned with snow." They believed themselves to have been transformed from the mythical Beaver. Unlike most other peoples of the Puget Sound basin, they were well organized, but the degree of organization allowed less individual freedom for their people. Like their neighbors, the Skykomish, the Snoqualmies hunted in the Cascade Mountains. Among their quarry were goats, whose wool their women wove into blankets, along with fireweed, feathers, and dogs' hair, which they obtained from peoples such as the Clallams and the Snohomish. The Snoqualmies intermarried with the Yakamas (who lived just east of the Cascade Mountains), and they obtained horses from them. Snoqualmie summer houses were constructed of poles and mats, with one side open to an outside fireplace.

Location: Today most individuals of the Snoqualmie Tribe live on non-Indian land in the Snoqualmie River valley and at other places in the Puget Sound basin.

Numbers: As of 1982, Snoqualmie tribal membership stood at 505. In April 2008, tribal enrollment was estimated at 650.

History: The Snoqualmies' usually peaceful routines were interrupted by conflicts with other tribes like the Cowichans of southeastern Vancouver Island in Canada, the Clallams, and the Nisquallis. The Snoqualmies' headman, Patkanin, was initially hostile to Americans. After an attack on the Hudson's Bay Company's Fort Nisqually on May 1, 1849, in which an American was killed, six men under Patkanin's leadership were brought to trial in the white men's court, and two of them were hanged (including, reportedly, Patkanin's brother, a Skykomish). One who escaped punishment was an innocent slave, whom, in keeping with an ancient practice, the Indians had tried to substitute for one of the guilty parties. Changing his disposition toward Americans, Patkanin signed

The woven blanket worn here by David Delgard was typical of the Snoqualmies and their neighbors in the hills and Cascade Mountains of western Washington.

Courtesy of the Everett (Wash.) Public Library.

the Point Elliott Treaty of 1855. At the treaty council, he reportedly said, "Our hearts are with the whites," though he did not mean all whites, for he was said to have remained anti-British. Proving his loyalty to the Americans, he led sixty warriors as American allies in the Indian war that broke out shortly after the signing of the Point Elliott Treaty. For delivering the slain bodies of their foes to government officials, he and his followers received money, blankets, and other goods. At the conclusion of the war there were several homicides committed by younger Snoqualmies who had been inflamed by liquor obtained from non-Indians.

Patkanin was buried on the Tulalip Reservation, to which his people had been removed. They numbered 301 on that reservation in 1870 under their headman, Sanawa. In succeeding years they intermarried with Tulalip peoples and others and were slowly assimilated into neighboring white communities. After the Point Elliott Treaty, the Snoqualmies tried unsuccessfully to secure a reservation in their ancestral lands in the vicinity of the Tolt River.

Since there was no longer an identifiable Skykomish tribe, the Snoqualmies filed a claim on their own behalf and that of the Skykomish (Docket 93) to recover for lands ceded to the United States under the Point Elliott Treaty. On June 30, 1961, the Indian Claims Commission ruled against the petitioners. The Snoqualmies had maintained that the Skykomish had been absorbed within their own tribe and thus that the Skykomish lands belonged to the Snoqualmies. The Snoqualmies subsequently appealed to the commission to modify its order in hopes that it would look further into the matter after consulting Indians of Skykomish descent in the Snoqualmie Tribe, but the commission denied the petitioners' claim to recover compensation on behalf of the Skykomish. When the Snoqualmies appealed to the Court of Claims on August 27, 1965 (178 C.Cls. 570, 372 F.

2d 951), the court reversed the commission's decision. On September 23, 1968, a final judgment was entered in favor of the Snoqualmies and the Skykomish, and a settlement of $257,698.29 was offered. As one of the tribes signatory to the Point Elliott Treaty, the Snoqualmies had already received $25,889.75 as a consideration for the loss of their lands.

The tribe seeks to prevent power and other development on or near Snoqualmie Falls, which it regards as sacred.

Contemporary Life and Culture: On October 6, 1999, the Snoqualmie Tribe was granted formal federal recognition and that date is now commemorated each year as the Snoqualmie National Holiday. Another milestone occurred on November 1, 2008, with the opening of the Snoqualmie Casino alongside Interstate 90, twenty-seven miles east of Seattle near the town of Snoqualmie, a $70-million, 170,000-square-foot facility sitting on fifty-six acres. The casino operates with a staff of 850 who support 1,650 slot machines, 52 Vegas-style gaming tables, five restaurants, four bars, a wine cellar, a cigar lounge, a 1,000-seat special events center, a cabaret lounge, and a gift shop, all completely owned and operated by the Snoqualmie Tribe. To monitor the casino area, the tribe is seeking to establish its own police force, and it hopes to eventually have tribally operated fire and emergency services.

The Snoqualmies do not have a reservation other than the casino land, but they maintain tribal offices and health clinics in the towns of Snoqualmie and Carnation as well as a drug-and-alcohol-recovery treatment center in Snoqualmie. The Snoqualmies recently bought the old Nespelem Hospital in Snoqualmie. The hospital sits on four acres and includes a house that is being renovated into apartment units. The tribe is also considering purchase of the Snoqualmie Valley Hospital for $30 million. This is a forty-eight-acre complex that they envision transforming into a regional health care facility available to all American Indians and Alaska Natives, regardless of affiliation. The tribe is assisting its students with tuition and other college expenses and is planning to allocate casino money for that purpose. Language reacquisition classes have been introduced, and two young Snoqualmies have learned the Lushootseed dialect, which they are in turn teaching to other Snoqualmies.

In 1989 the tribe participated in the Washington State centennial celebration, and in 1991 they held a ceremony in which elders conferred traditional names on members of the tribe. In December 2007 the tribe opened Paddle, a Native crafts store. There are hopes of building a museum or cultural center in Snoqualmie so that the tribe can bring its history to the public. The Snoqualmies continue to litigate issues surrounding Snoqualmie Falls, one of their most sacred ancient sites.

Special Events and Celebrations: Since 1997 the Snoqualmies have participated in Canoe Journey, an annual trek from the sacred Snoqualmie Falls to various tribal locations throughout the Pacific Northwest. Its purpose is to build camaraderie and mutual respect among tribal youth and to foster friendship among tribes.

Suggested Readings:

Arthur C. Ballard, et al., *Mythology of Southern Puget Sound: Legends Shared by Tribal Elders* (North Bend, Wash.: Snoqualmie Valley Historical Museum, 1999); Daniel L. Boxberger and Bruce G. Miller, "Evolution or History? A Response to Tollefson," *Ethnohistory* 44, no. 1 (1997); Edmond S. Meany, "Chief Patkanin," *Washington Historical Quarterly* 15, no. 3 (July 1924); Martha D. Murphy, *The Snoqualmie People* (Issaquah, Wash.: M. D. Murphy, 1976); Robert H. Ruby and John A. Brown, *Indians of the Pacific Northwest: A History* (Norman: University of Oklahoma Press, 1981); Kenneth D. Tollefson, "The Snoqualmie: A Puget Sound Chiefdom," *Ethnology* 26, no. 2 (1987); "Cultural Survival of the Snoqualmie Tribe," *American Indian Culture & Research Journal* 16, no. 4 (1992) and "The Snoqualmie Indians as Hop Pickers," *Columbia: The Magazine of Northwest History* 8, no. 4 (1994-95); Kenneth D. Tollefson and Martin L. Abbott, "From Fish Weir to Waterfall," *American Indian Quarterly* 17, no. 2 (1993).

SPOKANE

(Interior Division, Salishan)

The Spokanes (Spokans) maintain that their name originated when a Native beat on a hollow tree inside of which a serpent made a noise that sounded like "Spukcane." One day, they say, as their chief pondered the noise, vibrations radiated from his head, which gave the word the vague meaning "power from the brain." In early times, the Spokanes called themselves the Spukanees, which is translated "sun peoples," or more freely, "children of the sun." Others maintain that the tribal name derived from that of one of their chiefs and from nothing else.

The tribe lived in the general area of the Spokane River in three primary bands: the Upper Spokanes, whose general area extended from Spokane Falls east to around the present-day Washington-Idaho border; the Middle Spokanes, who were west of Spokane Falls in the vicinity of the Little Spokane River; and the Lower Spokanes, whose territory was farther west, as far as the confluence of the Columbia and Spokane rivers. Although they comprised three groups, the Spokane peoples coalesced during times of emergency. No Native people of the Pacific Northwest had stronger family ties than the Spokanes did. Their successors are known officially today as the Spokane Tribe of the Spokane Reservation, Washington.

A city and county are but two of the many entities bearing the Spokane name.

Location: Among the various locations where Spokane Indians may be found is the 157,376-acre Spokane Reservation established by executive order on January 18, 1881, northwest of the city of Spokane. The greatest number of the tribal membership live here on the reservation. But they also live on other reservations such as the Flathead (formerly the Jocko) and the Coeur d'Alene, and they are found in off-reservation locations, among which the city of Spokane is important.

Numbers: Authorities disagree in their estimates of the Spokane population in the immediate precontact period, their calculations varying from 1,400 to 2,500. A Hudson's Bay Company trader reported their number at 704 in 1827. A U.S. census in 1910 placed them at 643. In 1985, tribal membership stood at 1,961; four years later there were 1,248 enrolled members and in January 2006, 2,441.

History: The Spokanes generally lived at peace with their Interior Salish neighbors, but were known to fight them at times. Conflicts were usually of short duration, lasting only until grievances were settled. With the acquisition of horses in the eighteenth century, the Spokanes, especially the Upper Spokanes, joined the Flatheads, the Kalispels, the Nez Perces, and others in trading and buffalo-hunting expeditions across the Rocky Mountains to the Great Plains. The Spokanes' association with the Kalispels was so close that in the middle of the nineteenth century a government official stated that the Kalispels were an amalgam of Kalispels, Spokanes, and Flatheads. Occasionally, conflicts erupted between the tribes from west of the Rocky Mountains and the Blackfeet and other Plains tribes, who regarded the former as poachers on their lands.

The Spokanes came to be significantly involved in the commercial fur trade at least by 1810 with the establishment of the North West Company's Spokane House, which was followed the next year by the rival Pacific Fur Company's Fort Spokane. After the failure of the Pacific Fur Company and the merger of the North West and Hudson's Bay companies in 1821, the Spokanes had a trading post in their lands until 1826, when the post was removed north to Fort Colvile.

The Spokane tribe's first major confrontation with Christianity occurred around 1830 with the return of Spokane Garry (later Chief Garry) to his people from an Anglican mission school at Red River (later Winnipeg). Between 1838 and 1848, the Reverends Elkanah Walker and Cushing Eells were active missionaries among the Spokanes, having been sent by the American Board of Commissioners for Foreign Missions. The presence also of Roman Catholic missionaries, including Rev. Pierre De Smet, S.J., and his successors, further widened the divisions among the Spokane peoples.

The Spokanes became involved in wars with whites by joining the Coeur d'Alenes and other Salish speakers, along with the Shahaptian-speaking Palouses, in fighting American troops under Maj. Edward Steptoe in May 1858 and Col. George Wright in September of the same year. Their defeat in two key encounters with Wright's troops opened the interior of the Pacific Northwest to American settlement. Despite pleas by the younger Chief Joseph that the Spokanes enter the Nez Perce War of 1877 against the United States, they remained neutral, like their Coeur d'Alene neighbors.

There were two major agreements between the Spokanes and the federal government. On August 18, 1877, the Lower Spokanes consented to move by November 1, 1877, to a tract of land that was established as the Spokane Reservation by executive order on January 18, 1881. Then, on March 18, 1887, the Upper and Middle Spokanes agreed to relocate to one of three reservations: the Colville, the Flathead, or the Coeur d'Alene. That agreement was ratified July 13, 1892, and Congress later extended its benefits to the many Upper and Middle Spokanes who had removed to the Spokane Reservation. In 1897 there were 145 Spokanes on the Coeur d'Alene Reservation and 91 on the Flathead Reservation. In the meantime, trouble had broken out between the white citizenry of the rapidly growing city of Spokane and its Indians who had not removed to reservations. Several Spokanes, including Chief Garry, were involved with whites in disputes over land titles.

Among various acts pertaining to the Spokane Reservation was a joint congressional resolution of June 19, 1902, providing that the secretary of the interior make allotments in severalty to Indians. In 1906 a total of 651 members of the Spokane tribe were allotted 64,750 acres. Among subsequent acts was that authorizing the secretary of the interior to sell surplus unallotted and agricultural reservation lands.

In its earlier period the Spokane Reservation retained its primarily Protestant orientation. After the removal of Chief Enoch and his Catholic followers from the reservation in 1896, the religious picture shifted greatly: of an estimated six hundred reservation inhabitants, about half were of the Catholic faith. Helping Spokanes to adjust to non-Indian culture was Chief Lot, who favored white teachers for reservation children. After Fort Spokane, at the confluence of the Columbia and Spokane rivers, was abandoned in 1898 by the military, a government boarding school was established there. In the early twentieth century, when the reservation was under the Colville Agency, its chief executive, Capt. John McA. Webster, worked diligently on behalf of the Spokanes to prepare them for entry into the modern world. Ironically, many of the technical advances that he sought for them benefited the white community.

Traditionalism remained strong among the Spokanes. They opposed termination of their reservation and of their relationship with the federal government throughout the 1960s. In 1973, when militants of the American Indian Movement came on the reservation, they made little headway with the Indians. A 1961 study of Spokane assimilation patterns indicated that there had been closer assimilation with white culture in the latter half of the nineteenth century than there was a half century later.

Government and Claims: Initially, the Spokane Agency operated as a subagency under the Colville Agency and was located at Chewelah. In 1887 it was moved to the Spokane Reservation, which is across the Spokane River from Fort Spokane. In 1902, the subagency was relocated across the river to Fort Spokane and occupied abandoned buildings next to the boarding school. In 1912 the Spokane Subagency became a full agency. At that time, it moved to the city of Spokane, but in the same year it was returned to the old agency grounds on the Spokane Reservation. Because its facilities were in a dilapidated condition, the agency returned in November 1913 to Spokane, where it remained until 1915, when it was reestablished at Wellpinit on the Spokane Reservation. In 1925 the agency was reduced once more to the status of a subagency under the Colville Agency.

After the passage of the Indian Reorganization Act in 1934 (48 Stat. 984), it was not until May 12, 1951, that the Spokane Tribe of the Spokane Reservation, Washington, approved its formal organization by a vote of 95 to 34. Its constitution and bylaws were approved by the commissioner of Indian affairs on June 27, 1951. In 1970 the Spokanes again had their own agency at Wellpinit. In 1973 the administration of the Kalispel Reservation, formerly under the Northern Idaho Agency at Lapwai, was transferred to the Spokane Agency.

On August 10, 1951, the tribe filed a petition with two claims (Docket 331) with the Indian Claims Commission. One claim alleged that the cession of the tribe's land to the United States under the agreement of March 18, 1887 (27 Stat. 120, 139; ratified July 13, 1892), had been for an unconscionably small consideration. A second, separate claim, filed by amended petitions for accounting purposes, became Docket 331-A. The tribe alleged that the United States, which, as the tribe's guardian and trustee, held certain of its moneys and properties in trust, had failed to properly account for their management, handling, and disposition. On February 3, 1969, the tribe and the United States filed a joint motion with the Indian Claims Commission, requesting that the two dockets (331 and 331-A) be consolidated. The commission approved a settlement of $6.7 million for both dockets. The final judgment was rendered on February 21, 1967, after the tribe had voted the previous December 155 to 3 to accept the compromise offer. About half the moneys received were distributed to the approximately sixteen hundred tribal members, with shares for minors placed in trust. The other half of the moneys was spent for various tribal programs, such as land acquisition, scholarships, resource development, credit, and financing.

Later, the Spokanes filed claims (Dockets 523-71 and 524-71), which were subsequently transferred to the Court of Claims, for mismanagement of the Indian Claims Commission judgment funds and for other funds, such as Individual Indian Money accounts held in trust by the United States. In 1981, the tribe was awarded $271,431.23.

Contemporary Life and Culture: With reestablishment of the Spokane Agency on the Spokane Reservation in 1970, health facilities were greatly expanded.

Alcohol- and drug-abuse programs were put in operation. Under BIA funding, the tribe sponsored a summer work-experience program for its youth, who made trails and did cleanup work on the reservation. Under BIA control, an Indian Action program trained tribal members in carpentry, heavy-equipment operation, electrical installation, clerical work, and other fields. For instance, Spokanes on the reservation engage in logging, stock raising, and farming. In 2006 the Spokane Tribe received approval to participate in the U.S. Department of the Interior's 477 Demonstration Initiative, a comprehensive employment, training, and welfare program for federally recognized tribes to address economic and workforce needs in their communities.

The tribe, as well as some individual Spokanes, has benefited from sales of the uranium ore that was discovered on the reservation in 1953. When the Dawn Mining Company had exhausted the Midnight Mine

A Spokane couple, Alex and Margaret Sherwood, ca. 1967. The Spokane Tribal Cultural Center on the Spokane Reservation at Wellpinit, Washington, bears his name. The reservation lies northwest of Spokane, which is named for the tribe. Customarily, Indians were shunted onto unwanted lands. Ironically, rich uranium deposits were discovered on the Spokane Reservation; however, the mining of this ore has threatened the health of tribal members.

Authors' collections.

after extracting uranium ore from 1955 to 1981, it began processing low-grade ore. Another mine, the Sherwood open-pit uranium mine, which is completely on tribal land, began operations in 1976 under Western Nuclear, Inc. It too processed low-grade ore, and from its operations, the tribe received a small dividend until its closure in 1984. In 1992 the tribe considered a state order for a nuclear cleanup of the abandoned Dawn mine and the twenty-eight-acre, seventy-foot-deep tailings pond of its mill, located eighteen miles away at Ford, Washington. The cleanup project is estimated to cost up to $40 million and to last twenty years. In 1998, the Environmental Protection Agency took on Western Nuclear and the Sherwood Uranium Mill Project site on the reservation as a superfund site for restoration and cleanup of pollutants in the land and water. The tribe was also to be part of a study of health effects caused by emissions at midcentury from an off-reservation nuclear facility at the Hanford Nuclear Reservation. Seven other tribes were to take part.

In August 1982, the tribe purchased from heirs of an allottee a quarter section of land near Colville, Washington, for commercial development. Held in trust for the tribe, it is known as the Chewelah Homestead Allotment. Plans for the raising of fruit on the reservation have failed to materialize. A wood-veneer plant near the town of Ford on the eastern edge of the reservation was closed down in 1979, but the Spokane Indian Reservation Timber Products Enterprise continues to be a source of income for the tribe. SPOKO Fuel, a tribal enterprise, opened in Airway Heights, Washington, in 2006.

The first reservation-established casino in Washington opened on the Spokane Reservation. The Two Rivers Casino, located at the confluence of the Spokane and Columbia Rivers, has an adjoining 7,000- to 12,000-seat open-air amphitheatre. More recently, the tribe constructed the Chewelah Casino on trust land near the town of Chewelah in Stevens County. And in the summer of 2009, plans were announced for the establishment of a new casino in the Spokane suburb of Airway Heights. A gaming compact between the tribe and the State of Washington was approved by the U.S. Department of the Interior in 2007, setting limits for the size and scope of gaming for the Spokane Tribe and bringing its gaming operations within the state's regulatory structure. In 2007, Spokane tribal chairman Richard Sherwood observed, "With the additional funds from gaming, our Tribal Council will work to improve health care to our Elders, provide for higher education for our children and build an infrastructure which will improve our Reservation economy for generations to come."

From an agreement for rehabilitation of Spokane lands that was negotiated in connection with the construction of Grand Coulee Dam on the Columbia, a project completed in 1940, the tribe has gained a $6-million irrigation system from which it is able to water two thousand acres of cropland located on benches along the Spokane River on the southern edge of the reservation.

Like other tribes, the Spokanes have been involved in disputes with state and federal agencies over jurisdictions on the reservation. They seek compensation for the water stored behind Grand Coulee Dam and other dams on the Spokane River. From Little Falls Dam on the Spokane River, they also seek a percentage of the revenues from power production. The tribe won its fight for the waters of Chamokane Creek on the eastern edge of the reservation when the State of Washington was forbidden to approve the tapping of new wells in the aquifer of that creek.

The Alex Sherwood Memorial Center, dedicated June 7, 1975, fosters Spokane Indian culture. It is a large two-story stone structure housing tribal offices, a short-order food service, a library, and a museum. In 1979 a longhouse was dedicated near Wellpinit. The Cultural Preservation Program was started on the Spokane Reservation in 1995 to preserve cultural sites and history within the Lake Roosevelt Recreational Area. As part of the Cultural Preservation Program, the tribe maintains a repository, an archives, and a library. Among the classes offered in the Wellpinit school is a course on the Spokane language, and public schools

George Flett is a prominent artist of the Spokane Tribe. His art has been featured in galleries and exhibits throughout the United States. Born in Nespelem, Washington, on the Colville Reservation, Flett graduated from Wellpinit High School on the Spokane Reservation. He is an Army veteran, has studied at the Institute of American Indian Arts in Santa Fe, and is a graduate of the University of Colorado.

Courtesy of Larry Reisnouer, *(Spokane) Spokesman-Review.*

in the city of Spokane, which has a sizable Indian population, conduct classes that include Indian culture. "Inner Tribal Beat" is a radio program produced by a Spokane tribal member and broadcast over a station located in the city of Spokane.

The Spokane Tribal College opened in 1995 on the reservation and has since expanded into the city of Spokane. The college specializes in providing culturally appropriate higher education for Native American students and offers two-year liberal arts and vocational degrees. It maintains an articulation agreement with Gonzaga University and Whitworth College in Spokane and Eastern Washington University in Cheney.

In June 1991 the tribe dedicated their $2.5-million fish hatchery, developed and constructed as partial mitigation for the loss of salmon and steelhead, as well as habitat, to hydroelectric power development on the Columbia River, namely, the Grand Coulee Dam. The hatchery annually produces kokanee salmon, which is a land-locked form of sockeye salmon, and rainbow trout for release into Lake Roosevelt, Banks Lake, and reservation inland lakes. The Little Falls

Sherman Alexie (b. 1966) is one of the premier American fiction writers, having won the 2007 National Book Award in Young People's Literature and in 2010 the Pen/Faulkner Award for fiction. Of Spokane and Coeur d'Alene heritage, Alexie is also involved in the movie industry, having written screenplays for the acclaimed *Smoke Signals* (1998) and *The Business of Fancydancing* (2002). When not writing, Alexie is a stand-up comedian in the Seattle area.

Courtesy of Larry Reisnouer, *(Spokane) Spokesman-Review.*

Agreement of 1994 between Washington Water Power (now Avista Utilities) and the Spokane Tribe recognized the sovereignty of the Spokane Tribe and Avista's responsibility to the welfare of the Spokane River within the boundaries of the reservation.

The Water & Fish Program, which began in 2001, combines EPA and tribally funded water quality programs with the Bonneville Power Administration (BPA)-funded Joint Stock Assessment stream and lake assessment project, the goal being the protection and improvement of water quality and fisheries. In late 2003 the Lake Roosevelt White Sturgeon Recovery Project began, managed by the tribe as a multiagency project responsible for assessing the white sturgeon population in Lake Roosevelt. The project receives funding from the BPA through the authority of the Northwest Power Act and the Northwest Power and Conservation Council's Columbia Basin Fish and Wildlife Program to recover native populations of fish and wildlife in hydropower impacted regions. The 109th Congress of the United States in 2005 passed H.R. 1797 entitled, *Spokane Tribe of Indians of the Spokane Reservation Grand Coulee Dam Equitable Compensation Settlement Act.* The act addresses the significant harm having been done by the construction and operation of Grand Coulee Dam.

The year 2005 also saw initiation of the tribe's Temporary Assistance to Needy Families Program, which was devised to protect and benefit tribal children and their families; respect and preserve the culture, values, and traditions of American Indians; provide families access as well as input into the full range of programs and services needed; and promote self-esteem, independence, and self-sufficiency.

Today the reservation hosts Roman Catholic, Presbyterian, and Assemblies of God churches, all of which have attempted to harmonize as much as possible the

Christian faith with Native traditions and ceremonials, such as root festivals.

Special Events and Celebrations: The Centennial Powwow is staged in January on the Saturday that falls closest to January 18 each year, the day marking the establishment of the Spokane Reservation by presidential executive order. The Spokane Tribal Labor Day Celebration is held each year over the four-day Labor Day weekend.

Suggested Readings:

> Sherman Alexie, *The Absolutely True Diary of a Part-Time Indian* (New York: Little, Brown, 2007); David H. Chance, *People of the Falls* (Kettle Falls, Wash.: Kettle Falls Historical Center, 1986); Cary C. Collins, "Forged from Federal Indian Policy: Wellpinit, Washington, 1915–1985," *Journal of the West* 36, no. 4 (October 1997); Clifford M. Drury, *Nine Years with the Spokane Indians: The Diary, 1838–1848, of Elkanah Walker* (Glendale, Calif.: Arthur H. Clark Co., 1976); William S. Lewis, *The Case of Spokane Garry* (Fairfield, Wash.: Ye Galleon Press, 1987); John W. W. Mann, "'No More Out': The Deep Creek Colony of Spokane Indians, 1878–1888," *Pacific Northwest Quarterly* 98 (Fall 2007); Prodipto Roy and Della M. Walker, *Assimilation of the Spokane Indians,* Washington Agricultural Experiment Station Bulletin no. 628 (Pullman: Washington State University, Institute of Agricultural Science, 1961); Robert H. Ruby and John A. Brown, *The Spokane Indians: Children of the Sun* (Norman: University of Oklahoma Press, 1970, 2005); David C. Wynecoop, *Children of the Sun: A History of the Spokane Indians* (Wellpinit, Wash.: David C. Wynecoop, 1969) and *The Way It Was according to Chick: Growing Up on the Spokane Indian Reservation* (Spokane, Wash.: Tornado Creek Publications, 2003).

SQUAXIN ISLAND

(Coastal Division, Salishan)

The People of the Water

The Squaxins, or Squaxons, lived between Hood Canal and Case Inlet on the southern reaches of Puget Sound in Washington State. Their name is said to stem from a word meaning "alone." The Squaxins had ties with neighboring peoples— like the Twanas of Hood Canal—with whom they intermarried. Successors of the original Squaxins are known officially today as the Squaxin Island Tribe, Squaxin Island Reservation, Washington.

Location: Under the December 26, 1854, Medicine Creek Treaty, Squaxin Island in southern Puget Sound was set aside as the Squaxin Reservation, which originally totaled 1,494.15 acres. (The island is five miles long and three-quarters of a mile wide.) Today, however, the Squaxins live off their island reservation, primarily in the area of Kamilche and Shelton.

Numbers: With their neighbors on Hood Canal, the Squaxins were estimated to have had a population of 1,000 in 1780. In 1856 they were listed officially at 375; in 1901, at 98; and in 1937, at 32. In 1984, tribal membership was 302, which increased to 1,022 by 2010.

History: After the Medicine Creek Treaty and the establishment of the Squaxin Island Reservation, government officials tried to adapt the Squaxins to an agrarian mode of subsistence. The task was difficult, partly because the island was largely timbered and did not lend itself to that type of economy. During the Puget Sound Indian War (1855–56), the Squaxins were confined on Squaxin Island, but at the end of the conflict they scattered to various places around southern Puget Sound. By then, most of them had abandoned their traditional dress. Yet in the early 1860s, they refused to live in small houses that the government built for them, and many continued such practices as shamanism and head-flattening. In 1874 the reservation was patented in severalty to twenty-three Indians. The difficulty of obtaining subsistence there continued to keep many Squaxins away. After the Skokomish Reservation was set aside on February 25, 1874, about thirty Squaxins moved there and became assimilated into the Twana community. Although they both spoke their own dialects, the Squaxins and the Twanas could understand one another. Some Squaxins were allotted on the Quinault Reservation, and many Squaxins have inherited interests there.

In 1882, the Squaxin John Slocum, on becoming ill, believed that he had died. Failing to enter heaven, he related that he was told to go either to hell or back to earth and preach to the Indians. Returning to earth, he discovered that his soul had returned to his body, and he began the Indian Shaker Church, which stressed strict morality, sobriety, and honesty. Shaker services were implemented by paraphernalia derived from Roman Catholic and Protestant churches and the Native religions. In his drive for moral living, Slocum was stimulated by his own and his people's exposure to immoral lumberjacks and whiskey peddlers. The Shaker faith spread throughout the Pacific Northwest and has had many Indian adherents down to the present. Within the Shaker organization, a division developed between those who emphasized the importance of the Bible and those who believed that faith and inspiration derive through nonwritten means.

Government and Claims: The governing body of the Squaxin Island Tribe, Squaxin Island Reservation, Washington, is the tribal council. The tribe voted to accept the Indian Reorganization Act of 1934 and adopted a constitution, which the secretary of the Interior approved on July 8, 1965.

After filing a claim (Docket 206) with the Indian Claims Commission, the

Calvin Peters, former Squaxin tribal chairman, photographed at the dedication of the Yakama Indian Nation cultural complex in 1980. Squaxin Island in lower Puget Sound is the reservation for the tribe.

Authors' collections.

tribe was awarded $7,661.82 on July 31, 1974.

Contemporary Life and Culture: The Squaxin Island Tribe is predominantly Protestant, possibly because of its ancestors' opposition to Catholic priests and because of the Protestant influence in the Puyallup Agency, where the Squaxins were assigned during the President Ulysses S. Grant Peace Policy era of the 1870s. The income of tribal members is derived from lumbering, fishing, and other industries. Because of the saltwater environment of Squaxin Island, the State of Washington has established a park there, and it leases tidelands near the park.

A third of the island is in non-Indian ownership. The tribe is reluctant to subdivide its roughly 827.89 acres of remaining trust lands on the island. Just off the Kamilche exit on U.S. Highway 101 is the tribal center, which serves as a recreation center and meeting place. The tribe operates a chum and coho salmon hatchery on a creek behind Taylor Towne. Marine scientists from the University of Washington advise and assist the tribe in clam raising on the Squaxin Island beaches. On the western shores of the island there is a salmon farm consisting of a series of holding pens.

In the early 1970s the Squaxins bought lands, including the school district of Kamilche, which the Department of the Interior agreed to accept and hold in trust status. Squaxins had moved into the Kamilche Valley many years before.

The Squaxin Island Tribe became Washington State's first commercial cigarette manufacturer when it inaugurated Skookum Creek Tobacco Company in April 2005, selling Complete and Premis brands as well as loose pouch tobacco and a line of cigars made in the Dominican Republic. In 2007 the tribe expanded its distribution to stores operating off reservation and tribal lands. Cigarette profits help fund a 100-student reservation daycare.

In mid-2006 the tribe broke ground on a new golf course attached to its

47,400-square-foot Little Creek Casino & Resort, which had opened in September 1995, and it announced plans to construct an events center and add one hundred rooms to its hotel. Other tribal businesses include a hotel, the Kamilche Trading Post gas station/liquor store/convenience store, a shellfish farm, and the Harstine Oyster Seafood Company with its 4,000-square-foot processing facility. The tribe has considered constructing a railroad through the reservation in order to repackage and distribute propane gas, and it has conducted negotiations with an entrepreneur in Japan to manufacture sunglasses on the reservation. In 2007, with the casino drawing four thousand to five thousand customers a day, the tribe was the largest employer in Mason County.

In 1999 the ancient tribal village of "qcw up" was unearthed at Mud Bay near Olympia, revealing a large number of artifacts dating back five hundred to fifteen hundred years. Two years later, the tribe dedicated the new Squaxin Island Museum Library and Research Center. Built at a cost of $3 million and named "The Home of Our Sacred Belongings," the museum features the grand "Hall of Seven Inlets," which represents the seven ancestral villages of the Squaxin people.

Special Events and Celebrations: SalmonFest is held the third weekend in August in Shelton to celebrate and preserve the salmon. Sa'Heh'Wa'Mish Days is a gathering of tribes for three days in February on the Squaxin Island Reservation to share knowledge, teachings, and values.

Suggested Readings:

> Susan Olsen and Mary Randlett, *An Illustrated History of Mason County, Washington* (Shelton, Wash., 1978); SuAnn M. Reddick and Cary C. Collins, "Medicine Creek to Fox Island: Cadastral Scams and Contested Domains," *Oregon Historical Quarterly* 106, no. 3 (2005); Archie Satterfield, "The Squaxin Tribe: 'This is Our Home,'" *Seattle Times*, pictorial, June 7, 1970.

STEILACOOM

(Coastal Division, Salishan)

Scht'ilaqwam

The Steilacoom, or Steilacoomamish, were a Salish-speaking tribe on Steilacoom (now Chambers) Creek in the southern Puget Sound region of Washington. Their name derives from a flower growing near the mouth of the creek. Some ethnologists claim that they were once part of the Nisqually tribe; others maintain that they were a subdivision of the Puyallups. Their homeland was a 10,900-acre strip approximately two miles wide and eight miles long. Descendants ar-

Joan Ortez, Steilacoom tribal chair, ca. 1978. Contrary perhaps to popular belief, women have always played important roles in Pacific Northwest tribes. Among the programs in which Ortez's people are engaged is the establishment of an activities center near Tacoma, Washington.

Courtesy of N.E.W.S. Photo N. W.

gue that their original tribal territory included that set out by Washington territorial governor and superintendent of Indian affairs Isaac Stevens in the Medicine Creek Treaty of 1854, to which the Steilacooms were a party. The area was on the southern shores of Puget Sound and its adjacent inlets, specifically from the Nisqually Flats north to Commencement Bay. Although the Steilacooms traveled with neighboring peoples over the area of the treaty, their homelands were confined to the environs of Steilacoom Creek, especially the lower parts of that stream, which flowed through their village of Tchtelcab. Today a city bears the tribal name.

Oriented toward the waters of Puget Sound, the Steilacooms fished with other Indians around Anderson, Fox, and McNeil islands in southern Puget Sound. They hunted but little and never adopted horses as did the Nisquallis, who had close ties with the horse-riding Yakamas and Klickitats. The Steilacooms' political and land-holding units were autonomous villages, which were mainly exogamous and for the most part patrilocal. Social and economic activities united them in the winter. In the summer their families united with Natives of other villages with whom they had kinship and friendship ties.

Because non-Indian institutions were established among them at an early date, some anthropologists believe that the Steilacoom culture was suppressed sooner than that of many other peoples of the Pacific Northwest. Today many of the tribe's members trace their lineage to the Steilacooms of the 1850s.

Location: The Steilacooms, who were thought to have numbered five hundred in precontact times, are a nonreservation tribe. Many live in the area occupied or visited by their ancestors in Pierce, Kitsap, and Thurston counties.

Numbers: In 1853 the population of the Steilacooms was 175. In 1854 they were reported to number only 25. The reduction may have been due to the smallpox that was sweeping the region in 1853. In 1986 there were 615 tribal members, a number that had increased to 665 in 2003 and to over 800 in June 2008.

History: The Steilacooms followed a pattern similar to that of other Pacific Northwest Natives in their relations with whites. In the contact period they met explorers and traders. Among places where they encountered fur traders was Fort Nisqually, the Hudson's Bay Company post that was established in 1833 on the southern shores of Puget Sound. It was because of Indian-white friction in that area that the United States in 1849 built Fort Steilacoom about six miles north of Fort Nisqually. Dr. William F. Tolmie, who was in charge of the Puget Sound Agricultural Company, a Hudson's Bay Company subsidiary, demanded and received $600,000 for fifteen years as rent for the Fort Steilacoom area, claiming that the land belonged to his firm. The lands included in this claim lay not only in the Steilacoom homeland but also in that of the Nisquallis, Puyallups, and Squaxins.

The Indians again felt the presence of white men when Port Steilacoom was built at the main Steilacoom village in 1850 and when Steilacoom City was founded in 1851. The two entities became known as Upper and Lower Steilacoom. By 1853 a sufficient number of whites had settled among the Steilacooms to support the construction of a store and hotel and, shortly thereafter, a school and a church, which were followed by a sawmill and a gristmill, both built by Thomas Chambers on Steilacoom Creek, which he renamed Chambers Creek. During the Puget Sound phase of the 1855-56 Indian War, Steilacooms were among the thirty Indians whom Acting Agent J. V. Weber removed to Fox Island to separate them from the Indians who were hostile to Americans.

Government and Claims: The Steilacoom Indian Tribe has a constitution and by-laws that evolved from its original government, which was organized in the 1930s. The governing body is a nine-member council under the direction of a chairperson, secretary, and treasurer. There is also an honorary chieftain. When the federal government closed down the Fox Island reserve, the Steilacooms refused to move to the Puyallup or Nisqually reservations. The Steilacoom Indian Tribe has not yet received official acknowledgment from the federal government.

It has been estimated that payments to the tribe for lands alienated under the Medicine Creek Treaty have amounted to $10,727.57. The Steilacooms submitted a claim (Docket 208) to the Indian Claims Commission for additional compensation for their ceded lands. The commission decided that their value in the middle of the nineteenth century was $20,000. With the previous estimated payment deducted and an offset of $126.11, there remained $9,146.32, and that amount was awarded to the tribe in a final order on July 31, 1974. The tribe prepared a resolution asking the BIA to hold those funds in a trust to be used for a land-replacement program.

Contemporary Life and Culture: In June 1981, the tribe signed an agreement to lease from the Pierce County government five acres in Fort Steilacoom Park that are on aboriginal Steilacoom grounds near the city of Steilacoom and fifteen miles from Tacoma. On that land the tribe is creating an activities learning center dedicated not only to the Steilacoom but to the general public. An important part of the center is the Steilacoom Institute of Appropriate Technology, featuring not only traditional Indian technology but also modern scientific endeavors such as energy conservation. The educational programs are emphasized and coordinated with those of Fort Steilacoom Community College. The institute is also geared to fulfill the economic and social needs of the tribe. Some of its services will be available to the general public. The tribal cultural center, which opened in 1989 in the community of Steilacoom, houses the tribal administrative office, a museum, a snack bar, an archive, and a café. The tribe administers several different programs, including food and nutrition, employment, and cultural activities.

In 2010 the Steilacoom Tribe remained unrecognized by the federal government, having been declared officially extinct by the BIA in January 2000.

STILLAGUAMISH TRIBE OF INDIANS

(Coastal Division, Salishan)

The name "Stillaguamish," or Stillaquamish, stems from a word meaning "river people." The tribe lived in about twenty-nine villages, which were mainly on the river bearing their name in present-day northwestern Washington but also on its branches between the Skagit River on the north and the Snohomish River on the south. An important gathering place for the Upper Stillaguamish was southwest of today's Darrington. The Lower Stillaguamish often gathered near the modern-day settlements of Silvana, Trafton, Milltown, Hazel, and Florence. Descendants of the Stillaguamish claim that their ancestral lands exceeded 300,000 acres along the Stillaguamish River, from Stanwood east to Darrington. They were closely related to the Snohomish, the Sauk-Suiattles, and the Skagits. They also intermarried with Natives from points as far distant as Oregon and California. Their tribal identity has been acknowledged by the Indian Claims Commission. The successors of the original Stillaguamish are known officially as the Stillaguamish Tribe of Indians.

Location: The people of the Stillaguamish Tribe of Indians live mostly in Snohomish County, Washington, but some reside as far away as Arizona and Alaska.

Numbers: In 1853 Stillaguamish estimates were officially given as between 150

Esther Ross (1904–1988). More than any other person and for most of her adult life, Ross fought for federal recognition of the Stillaguamish Tribe. Combining toughness with persistence, she possessed the ability to make adversaries shudder in her presence and was an effective advocate both at home and in Washington, D.C.

Courtesy of Jim Lee, *Everett (Wash.) Herald*

and 200, though there is evidence that their population was larger before a smallpox plague struck that year. In 1984 the Stillaguamish Tribe numbered 156 and in 2008 there were 200 enrolled members.

History: At the time of white contact, the Stillaguamish were apparently an independent people with no more than subtribal status. The observations in 1850 of Samuel Hancock, who is believed to have been the first non-Indian to follow the course of the Stillaguamish River, reveal much about these people. It was clear that they were involved in intertribal conflict, for they believed that he and his party of Native canoemen were on an expedition against them. Like other northern Puget Sound Indians, they were occasionally attacked by other peoples, such as the Clallams. At the time of Hancock's journey, they had had some knowledge of Christianity, for a headman in one of their villages of about three hundred made the sign of the cross. The Reverend Eugene Casimir Chirouse, O.M.I., who established a mission in the lower Snohomish River country in 1857 and later supervised the nearby Tulalip Indian Agency, exerted considerable influence on the Stillaguamish.

When Samuel Hancock visited them, they possessed few firearms and had never seen a revolver. Their women wore clothes manufactured of cedar bark. In the nearby Cascade Mountains they hunted goats, and they traded the skins to other Indians or to whites for groceries and other items in such places as Victoria on lower Vancouver Island. Dogs, which they kept for their hair, were the measure of a woman's wealth. They buried the bones of animals in the belief that their spirits would return, make new bodies, and live in the hills. They ate salmon and other seafoods, roots, and berries. After contact, they raised potatoes in small patches on bottomlands. Later they worked for settlers at such jobs as clearing land and harvesting crops. Their winter houses were built with cedar planks supported by large poles. These buildings housed several families. Their portable summer dwellings were often constructed of cattail matting placed over wooden frames. They fished mainly with two-pronged spears or with nets. Sometimes they bobbed with pronged spears across the river currents.

Government and Claims: Prior to receiving federal recognition on February 7, 1979, Stillaguamish tribal members created a considerable stir by marching in Fourth of July parades with the American flag upside down in order to call attention to their drive for federal acknowledgment. Chief Esther Ross was one of the Stillaguamish who for many years had worked diligently to obtain such status.

The Stillaguamish filed a claim (Docket 207) with the Indian Claims Commission for payment for lands ceded to the United States under the Point Elliott Treaty of 1855. On January 8, 1970, pursuant to a settlement between the parties, the commission entered a final judgment in the amount of $64,460 for the tribe's 58,600 acres of aboriginal lands, less the consideration that had been paid it under the treaty. The net award was $48,570.

Contemporary Life and Culture: Tribal members are employed in various communities, especially in Snohomish County. The tribe operates fish-hatching facilities on Jim Creek. Tribal members are deeply interested in their tribal heritage and have cooperated with those assembling a tribal history.

With the backing of a $36-million loan, the Stillaguamish Tribe opened the Angel of the Winds Casino near Arlington in the fall of 2004. Late in 2008 the casino underwent expansion from 22,000 to 106,000 square feet, which includes a 150-seat, full-service restaurant, a 50-seat lounge with an entertainment stage, and a gift shop. Since the expansion, the casino has produced sufficient profits that the tribe has been able to purchase approximately $20 million in additional acreage on which it hopes to expand tribal services and projects. The renovation cost $44 million for a facility that generates $30 million in revenue annually, welcomes some 800,000 patrons per year, and provides jobs to more than five hundred full-time employees. In keeping with the terms of its compact with the State of Washington, the Stillaguamish distributed $181,132 to local nonprofit organizations. Eventually the tribe would like to build a hotel adjacent to the casino as well as open a gas station and convenience store nearby.

The tribe operates dental, wellness, and counseling clinics. As a way to encourage a healthy diet and combat diabetes among tribal members, the Stillaguamish brought a small bison herd to their reservation in May 2008. In 2009 the Stillaguamish sent out its first fishing fleet since 1985 and celebrated its first formal First Salmon Ceremony in more than a quarter century.

Special Events and Celebrations: The Stillaguamish Tribe hosts the annual Stillaguamish Festival of the River, which is held the second week of August as a means to strengthen understanding and knowledge of water quality and salmon habitat.

Suggested Readings:

Nels Bruseth, *Indian Stories and Legends of the Stillaguamish, Sauks, and Allied Tribes* (Fairfield, Wash.: Ye Galleon Press, 1977); Samuel Hancock, *The Narrative of Samuel Hancock, 1845–1860* (New York: R. M. McBride, 1927); Gustaf B. Joergenson, *History of the Twin Cities* (Stanwood and East Stanwood, Washington), published in seventy issues of the *Twin City News,* April 1, 1948–October 27, 1949; Barbara Lane, "Anthropological Report on the Identity, Treaty Status and Fisheries of the Stillaguamish Indians," in *Political and Economic Aspects of Indian-White Culture Contact in Western Washington in the Mid-19th Century,* May 10, 1973, manuscript in Washington State Library, Olympia; Robert H. Ruby and John A. Brown, "The Indian Chief and the Wagon Train," *Columbia: The Magazine of Northwest History* 10, no. 4 (1996–97) and *Esther Ross: Stillaguamish Champion* (Norman: University of Oklahoma Press, 2001); Marian Smith, "The Coast Salish of Puget Sound," *American Anthropologist,* n.s., 43, no. 2, pt. 1 (April 1941): 197–211; William Whitfield, *History of Snohomish County, Washington* (Evansville, Ind.: Unigraphic, 1979), 2 vols.

SUQUAMISH

(Coastal Division, Salishan)

D'Suq'Wub

People of the Clear Saltwater

The Suquamish name is derived from that of the ancient Native village that lay along the shores of Agate Passage, near the town of Suquamish, on the eastern Kitsap Peninsula of western Washington State. The Snohomish, who lived across Puget Sound from the Suquamish on the east, called them "mixed people."

The Suquamish lived from Gig Harbor north to Appletree Cove, between Hood Canal and Admiralty Inlet as far south as Case and Carr inlets, and on Black, Bainbridge, and Whidbey islands. Between Hood Canal and Admiralty Inlet they occupied at least three autonomous villages. It was in the village of Suqua that the famed "Old-Man-House" stood. It was about 500 feet long and 60 feet wide and accommodated several families. In the 1870s a federal agent ordered the burning of this physical and spiritual center of the Suquamish community.

Suquamish life revolved around the seasonal harvests of fish, shellfish, roots, and berries. As fall neared, the Suquamish traded with neighboring tribes for such items as whale oil, razor clams, salmon, basketry, and beadwork. During the winter they repaired their utensils, tools, and weapons. In that season they also carried on carving, weaving, and basket making in their longhouses. Winter was a time when tribal elders taught the young through song, dance, story, and ceremony. Today the successors of the aboriginal Suquamish are known officially as the Suquamish Tribe, Port Madison Reservation, Washington.

Location: Roughly two hundred tribal members live on or adjacent to the Port Madison Reservation, which was established under the Point Elliott Treaty of 1855 for the Suquamish, Duwamish, and Skekomish (Muckleshoot) Indians. Other tribal members live primarily in nearby communities, such as Sequim, Bremerton, Port Orchard, Seattle, and Tacoma.

Numbers: In 1844 the Suquamish were listed at 525; in 1856 at 509 and, in other records, 441. In 1909, they numbered 180. In 1985 the Suquamish tribal membership stood at roughly 577. Today there are 950 enrolled members, half of whom live on the Port Madison Indian Reservation.

History: The Suquamish remained mostly at peace with non-Indians but not always with other tribes. Their famous chief, Sealth, or Seattle (after whom the city was named), reportedly was born on Blake Island around 1786. He was born from the union of Schweabe, a Suquamish leader, and a Duwamish woman. According to Suquamish tradition, Schweabe was involved in wars with the Chimakums, who tried to encroach on Suquamish lands. The Suquamish also confronted the Duwamish, whose lands they sought to possess. The population of the two tribes was reduced partly because of Suquamish aggression. Schweabe encouraged activities such as wood carving and the building of canoes. The Suquamish journeyed in these craft to places as far distant as Vancouver Island. They traded with surrounding tribes and with the Hudson's Bay Company at Fort Nisqually, which the Bay Company established in 1833. The Suquamish came under the influence of Roman Catholic missionaries in the late 1830s and early 1840s, and they have remained predominately Catholic to the present day.

They were, as noted, party to the Point Elliott Treaty, which was signed by their headman and six subchiefs. According to the treaty, they were scheduled to live on the 7,284.48-acre Port Madison Reservation, which was also at times called the Suquamish, Seattle, or Fort Kitsap Reservation. Their headman, Kitsap, had taken issue with the terms of the treaty and chose not to live on the reservation.

Of the total acreage of the Port Madison Reservation, 5,909.48 acres were allotted to thirty-nine Indians. The remaining 1,375 acres went unallotted. Despite some government assistance, the Suquamish were forced to leave the reservation in order to subsist. Complicating their problems were the continuing encroachments of Canadian Indians. For example, in 1859 the Suquamish attacked a party of Haidas on the western shores of Bainbridge Island in retaliation for Haida raids on Puget Sound. Living in the midst of hundreds of miles of poorly policed Puget Sound shorelines, the Suquamish were especially vulnerable to the inroads of whiskey peddlers. In October 1862, while attending a large Indian gathering at

Port Madison to receive presents from the Duwamish, the Suquamish headmen seized and burned a boat belonging to rum dealers who were selling their wares to the assembled Indians.

The Suquamish worked for settlers, especially the owners of the mills that sprang up around Puget Sound in the 1850s. At one Port Madison mill, they were paid in inch-square brass pieces that represented twenty-five and fifty cents, which they could use to purchase goods at a store.

By act of Congress on October 24, 1864, the reservation was enlarged and re-defined. Its lands lay on two projections separated by a body of water. On one of these is the Suquamish Reservation proper, on which today is located the tribal center. The other, referred to as the Indianola Tract, was added to the original reservation. Indians were often coerced into selling their reservation lands, un-til over half of the reservation had passed into non-Indian hands. In 1980 over eight hundred non-Indians lived on the reservation, and three times that num-ber lived adjacent to it.

In the early twentieth century the village of Suqua was acquired for a mil-itary post. The villagers were uprooted, as families were required to settle on individual allotments scattered across the reservation. On their allotments, the Suquamish, contrary to the government's mandates, farmed very little. They re-tained their fishing and hunting lifestyles. Some families moved off the reserva-tion rather than send their children to government boarding schools, thus relin-quishing claims to its lands. By 1920 non-Indian fishing and canning industries were threatening the salmon runs not only in Suquamish waters but all over Puget Sound.

Some indication of the American influence among the Suquamish was the 1923 visit of their baseball team to Japan, where they sought to introduce the American game.

Government and Claims: The Suquamish Tribe, Port Madison Reservation, Washington, by the constitution and bylaws adopted on May 23, 1965, operates under an elected seven-member council. The large number of non-Indians on the Port Madison Reservation has posed some problems for the tribe. The tribe received little satisfaction from the U.S. Supreme Court ruling in *Oliphant* v. *Suquamish Tribe, et al.* (Case No. 76-5729, decided March 6, 1978), in which the court ruled that "Indian Tribal Courts do not have inherent criminal jurisdiction to try and to punish non-Indians, and hence may not assume such jurisdiction unless specifically authorized by Congress to do so."

The Suquamish filed a claim (Docket 132) for additional compensation for lands ceded to the United States under the Point Elliott Treaty of 1855. The In-dian Claims Commission found that the tribe had ceded 87,130 acres, exclusive of the 1,280 acres that were set aside for the reservation under the treaty, and that the fair market value of that land was $78,500 in 1859, the year that the treaty was ratified. To determine what sums were due the tribe, it was necessary, how-

Jack Adams, a Suquamish of the Kitsap Peninsula in western Washington. Important developments among his people included the completion in 1980 of a beautiful tribal center which houses Squamish heritage artifacts.

Courtesy of the Smithsonian Institution.

ever, to ascertain how much of the consideration that it had received from the treaty was chargeable against the $78,500. The Suquamish were one of eleven tribes that petitioned the commission (*Upper Skagit Tribe of Indians et al. v. U.S.,* 1964) to determine the amount that had already been paid to the Suquamish. The Point Elliott Treaty had provided a consideration for the entire cession but had failed to stipulate that the payment be made in specific proportionate amounts to the respective tribes. In a final judgment, dated October 22, 1970, the commission ruled that the Suquamish should have received a total consideration of $36,329.51 for the aboriginal lands that they ceded to the United States, or 46 percent of the fair market value. Consequently, the commission decided on January 21, 1966, that they were entitled to an additional $42,170.49.

Contemporary Life and Culture: Of the original 7,284.48 acres of the Port Madison Reservation, there remain but 2,849.42 acres in trust or in Indian ownership. The remaining acreage has gone into fee status.

Several members of the tribe work in reservation management. Some are engaged in logging, and others receive income from trust lands. A number are employed in the nearby Trident Nuclear Submarine Base, on which construction began in 1975. Others perform seasonal farmwork and are fishermen. The tribe operates hatcheries as part of its fisheries enhancement program. Besides fishing, clamming is an important activity of tribal members. The revenues derived from the sale of cigarettes have been reduced by federal court decisions requiring the payment of state taxes on reservation sales. Suquamish children attend local public schools. Welfare services are provided by federal and local governments.

In 1977 the Suquamish Tribe created the Suquamish Tribal Cultural Cent nonprofit organization dedicated to the reconstruction and preservation of the tribe's culture and history. Six years later, in 1983, the Suquamish constructed the 8,500-square-foot Suquamish Museum & Cultural Center, the second American Indian museum opened in Washington State. A new 9,000-square-foot museum and arts center is currently being built across from the tribal center. The new facility will include an auditorium, an archives and research room, a gift shop, a public meeting room, and an ADA-compliant public restrooms.

Part of the cultural resurgence taking place on the Port Madison Reservation includes plans to construct a new 13,169-square-foot Suquamish community house in the tradition of Old-Man-House, the ancestral Suquamish winter village on the shoreline of Agate Passage. In 2009 the Suquamish hosted the Coast Salish Exhibit from the National Museum of the American Indian as well as Canoe Journey. The first modern Canoe Journey event was a one-day pull from Suquamish to Seattle in 1989 in recognition of the Washington State centennial year. In 2007 the Burke Museum of Seattle returned to the tribe the remains of eleven adult Suquamish men and women.

Among Suquamish business enterprises are Suquamish Clearwater Casino Resort, which includes an eighty-five-room hotel, the historic Kiana Lodge, Agate Pass Business Park, and several retail stores. In 2008 the Suquamish employed a government workforce of approximately 240 in a variety of departments, including health care, low-income housing, and employment assistance, as well as programs for elders, for domestic violence, and for community fitness and nutrition. Its total employment of approximately one thousand makes the Suquamish Tribe one of the largest employers in Kitsap County.

Special Events and Celebrations: In the third week of August, the tribe holds its annual Chief Seattle Days, which features canoe races, meals of baked salmon and clams, Native artwork, traditional dancing, and a pageant portraying the history of local Indians, including the lives of Chiefs Seattle and Kitsap. The celebration is held with help of the American Legion, which sets the date. *See* **Suquamish Tribe, Port Madison Reservation**.

Suggested Readings:

Jerry L. Clark, "Thus Spoke Chief Seattle: The Story of an Undocumented Speech," *Prologue* 17, no. 1 (1985); Albert Furtwangler, *Answering Chief Seattle* (Seattle: University of Washington Press, 1997); Hermann Haeberlin and Erna Gunther, "The Indians of Puget Sound," *University of Washington Publications in Anthropology* 4, no. 1 (1930); Denise Low, "Contemporary Reinvention of Chief Seattle: Variant Texts of Chief Seattle's 1854 Speech," *American Indian Quarterly* 19, no. 3 (1995).

SUQUAMISH TRIBE, PORT MADISON RESERVATION

The Suquamish and the Duwamish were assigned to the Suquamish, or Port Madison, Reservation under the Point Elliott Treaty of 1855. Its Indians are known today as Suquamish Tribe, Port Madison Reservation. *See* **Suquamish** *and* **Duwamish**.

SWALLAH

(Coastal Division, Salishan)

Some ethnologists have grouped the Swallahs (or Swalish) with the Lummis of present-day northwestern Washington, because both peoples spoke the Lkungen dialect of their Salishan language. The Reverend Myron Eells, who in the late nineteenth and early twentieth centuries wrote voluminously about the Indians of Hood Canal and the Strait of Juan de Fuca, listed the Swallahs as living in the San Juan Islands, which lie between Vancouver Island and the U.S. mainland. The ethnologist John R. Swanton documented them as having lived in four villages in the San Juan Islands, located as follows: on the southeastern shores of Orcas Island; on the east side of San Juan Island; and in two villages on Waldron Island. They are also listed as having lived on Orcas Island, on which stands Mount Constitution, which bore the name Swelax, from which the name "Swallah" possibly derives.

SWINOMISH

(Coastal Division, Salsihan)

According to Swinomish tradition, the tribe originated when a headman's son wandered from camp with his dog and suffered many hardships. Through purification of the spirit, he obtained great powers that enabled him to convert his dog into a beautiful princess, who became his wife and the mother of the peoples whom he created by sowing (or throwing) rocks on the earth.

In early days, whites tended to group the Swinomish with the Lower Skagits, but they were a distinct people, claiming occupancy of separate territory in present-day northwestern Washington. Their lands included portions of north Whidbey Island and all of the islands in Similk Bay and northern Skag

Robert Joe, 1987, chairman of the Swinomish Indian Tribal Community, Swinomish Reservation. He is an example of modern American Indian administrators who are equally comfortable in the cultures of both Indian and white America.

Authors' collections.

including Hope, Skagit, Kiket, Coat, and Ika, as well as Smith Island on the west coast of Whidbey and Hat Island in Padilla Bay. A small, related band, the Squinomish, occupied the mouth, estuary, and delta of the Skagit River on the north, forming a buffer between the Swinomish and the Lower Skagits. The Swinomish spoke the northern Lushootseed dialect of Coastal Salish.

The Swinomish were a marine-oriented people. As much as 70 percent of their subsistence came from fish and other marine life. They also gathered berries and, after contact with white fur traders, raised potatoes. They maintained permanent villages during the winter months. At other seasons, they traveled within reasonable distances of those villages to outlying fishing and camping sites of varying degrees of permanency. From precontact times well into the nineteenth century, the more-or-less contiguous Swinomish villages, which were not totally autonomous in a political sense, enjoyed a certain measure of independence from each other. These villages were composed of several families under leaders whose positions were determined by material wealth and standing. None of them had complete control over all of the villages. There were strong kinship ties among the villages because they shared a common culture and language. Social contacts with neighbors living at some distance came through such ceremonies as the potlatch. This gift-giving feast, so common among Pacific Northwest coastal peoples, enabled its hosts to achieve social status.

Epidemics are believed to have struck around 1800, seriously reducing the Swinomish populations. In some areas, deaths ran as high as 80 percent. Government officials in 1855 placed the Swinomish numbers between 150 and 200. The Swinomish were among the tribes who located on the Swinomish Reservation, which was set aside near the mouth of the Skagit River under the Point Elliott Treaty in 1855, which their headmen signed. The reservation's northern boundaries were clarified by an executive order dated September 9, 1873, which, in essence, permanently established the 7,448.80-acre reservation. The Indian Claims Commission determined that the Swinomish were an identifiable tribe when they presented a claim (Docket 233) for compensation for the aboriginal lands that they had ceded under the Point Elliott Treaty, for which the United States had paid them an unconscionably low consideration. The Swinomish requested the difference between the amount already paid them and the fair market value of the land. On July 6, 1972, they were awarded $29,000. *See* **Swinomish Indian Tribal Community, Swinomish Reservation.**

SWINOMISH INDIAN TRIBAL COMMUNITY, SWINOMISH RESERVATION

Most members of the Swinomish Indian Tribal Community, Swinomish Reservation, Washington, are descendants of the Swinomish proper, the Skagits, and the Samish peoples.

Location: Tribal members live primarily on the Swinomish Reservation in Skagit County, near the mouth of the Skagit River on northern Puget Sound. The reservation lies adjacent to the Swinomish Slough, a channel forming the eastern boundary of the reservation. Across from the slough is the town of La Conner. Other members live in the farming, fishing, and lumbering region surrounding the reservation.

Numbers: In 1909 the tribe numbered 268. In 1937 the population was 285. In 1985 it was 624 and in 2002, 778.

History: The Swinomish Reservation was created through the authority of the Point Elliott Treaty of 1855, which Swinomish headmen signed. An executive order of September 9, 1873, clarified the ill-defined northern boundary and added 59.73 acres, in essence, permanently establishing the 7,448.80-acre reservation. Having come under Roman Catholic missionary influences, the ancestors of the Swinomish Indian Tribal Community were under the Tulalip Agency, which was assigned to Catholics under the President Ulysses S. Grant Peace Policy. Under that policy, it was hoped that the Swinomish would become agrarians, but they did so only reluctantly. During the 1860s they scattered to various points around Puget Sound, seeking employment. They clashed with white settlers over lands until the reservation boundaries were defined. In 1884 about three-fourths of the Indians on the Swinomish Reservation were engaged in farming, logging, and milling. The remainder were following traditional subsistence patterns.

Annie McLeod of the Swinomish Indian Tribal Community, Swinomish Reservation, ca. 1900. Her people came under the influence of Roman Catholics during the
era of the Ulysses S. Grant Peace Policy when Indian reservations fell under church
control.

Courtesy of the Skagit County Historical Museum, La Conner, Wash.

Government and Claims: The Swinomish Indian Tribal Community operates
under a constitution that was adopted by its members after they accepted the
Indian Reorganization Act (48 Stat. 984) on November 16, 1935. They approved
their constitution on January 27, 1936, and their charter, which was ratified on
July 25 of that same year and later amended. Their governing body is the Swinomish Indian Senate, from which the principal tribal officers are elected. A Swinomish agent, O. G. Upchurch, believed that the introduction of formal demo-
cratic government among them simply reduced to written form a traditional
expression of the will of the people.

The Swinomish Indian Tribal Community is composed of Swinomish, Kikiallus, Suquamish, Samish, and Upper and Lower Skagit peoples. The Community
filed a claim (Docket 293) for an alteration in its reservation, claiming it was not
as promised to them during the Point Elliott Treaty negotiations in 1855, though
it had been enlarged. On June 21, 1971, the Indian Claims Commission ordered
that the petition be dismissed.

Contemporary Life and Culture: On the Swinomish Reservation in 1950 there were 5,395 acres of allotted land, 40 acres of unallotted land, and 85 acres reserved by the federal government. In 1978 there remained 3,430.76 acres of allotted land held in trust or otherwise restricted and about 263 acres of tribally owned land in trust. Since 1934–35, when the Swinomish installed modern fish traps, they have engaged in commercial fishing, despite conflicts with the State of Washington over fishing jurisdictions. Among other enterprises, the Tribal Community owns the Swinomish Fish Company, whose facilities were installed in 1973. Its operations provide not only revenues but also employment for the Community's members. The Community belongs to the Skagit System Cooperative, which was organized in 1976 to regulate and enhance fishing in the Skagit River system. Also involved in the cooperative are the Upper Skagit and Sauk-Suiattle tribes. The income of most members of the Community derives from fishing, farm labor, and lumbering. Some supplement their incomes by the sale of Native goods that are woven, knit, or carved. A center dedicated in August 1964 injected new spirit into the Community. Socioeconomic services are provided through local, state, and federal agencies. After closure of the Tulalip school in 1932, Swinomish children attended school in nearby La Conner, where cooperation exists between school and tribal officials. Much-needed improvements in housing have been made. The Community's religious preference is Roman Catholic.

Since 1994 the Swinomish have operated the 43,000-square-foot Swinomish Northern Lights Casino at Anacortes. Built at a cost of $4 million, the casino includes, in addition to gaming, the Two Salmon Café, a lounge, a delicatessen, the Aurora Showman (with a capacity of six hundred), a cabaret (with a capacity of three hundred), and an RV park with thirty-five sites. The tribe's other major enterprise is the Swinomish Chevron gas station-convenience store. Reservation safety is provided through the Swinomish Police Department. The tribe operates a daycare, a Head Start program, and an Indian child welfare program. Health care is delivered through the 1,375-square-foot Swinomish Tribal Health Center, while *Gathering of Wisdoms* provides a traditional approach to mental health. Graduating high school seniors receive college tuition assistance.

Active in managing the cultural resources of their reservation, the Swinomish are especially involved in ongoing salmon recovery efforts. The tribe is planning to build a marina on the north end of the reservation as well as a cultural center and museum. In November 2008, PBS aired "March Point," a digital media project created by three Swinomish teenagers investigating the effects of the Shell and Tesoro oil refineries that operate on the reservation.

Special Events and Celebrations: On Memorial Day the Tribal Community holds the Swinomish Festival. Activities include ball-and-stick games, dances, and a salmon bake. Tribal members also observe the Treaty Days Celebration on the weekend that falls nearest January 22, on which date in 1855 their Point

Elliott Treaty was signed. The Swinomish hold their Blessing of the Fleet and First Salmon Ceremony each year in late May, marking the beginning of the fishing season and also honoring and protecting their members who fish. Other special events include the honoring of veterans each Memorial Day, the annual Elders Intertribal Luncheon, and Native American Day, which is observed on the fourth Monday of September.

Suggested Readings:

Herman Haeberlin and Erna Gunther, "The Indians of Puget Sound," *University of Washington Publications in Anthropology* 4, no. 1 (1930); Anne Brooks Middleton, "Enduring Traditions: The Education of Two Swinomish Women," master's thesis, Western Washington University, 1994; Natalie Andrea Roberts, "A History of the Swinomish Tribal Community," Ph.D. dissertation, University of Washington, 1975; Martin J. Sampson, *Indians of Skagit County* (Mount Vernon, Wash.: Skagit County Historical Society, 1972); O. C. Upchurch, "The Swinomish People and Their State," *Pacific Northwest Quarterly* 27, no. 4 (October 1936).

TAITNAPAM

(Shahaptian)

The Taitnapams (Titon-nap-pams) were a Shahaptian group speaking the Klickitat dialect, or one very closely related to it. By the middle of the nineteenth century, they had moved west of Washington's Cascade Mountains into the upper Cowlitz Valley, where their women often married into Salish-speaking Cowlitz Indian families. Some ethnologists identify the Taitnapams as Upper Cowlitzes whose original band had absorbed sufficient numbers of Western Klickitats to form a new group (the Eastern Klickitats lived east of the Cascade Mountains). The Taitnapams retained much of the Cowlitzes' culture and the Klickitats' Shahaptian language.

The name "Taitnapam" derives from the Tieton River, a Yakima River tributary, which was probably their home before they migrated west. One of their bands lived at what is today Mossyrock on the Cowlitz River, and their lands extended eastward up the Cowlitz watershed on the southern flank of Mount Rainier. Another band lived south of Mount Saint Helens in the Lewis River watershed. Both the Cowlitz and the Lewis are tributaries of the Columbia. In their hilly and mountain homelands, the Taitnapams hunted such game as elk, deer, and sheep. They also raised horses. Taitnapams on the upper Lewis River were perhaps the band that a North West Company fur trader in 1814 noted as living near Mount Saint Helens, from which they descended to hunt in the Willamette Valley of Oregon. The ethnologist George Gibbs noted that the Taitnapams had a certain mystique among lower Cowlitz River Indians, who circulated tales that the Taitnapams stole and ate children and traveled invisibly. Eastern Klickitats called them "wild," or "wood," Indians.

In 1853, Gibbs listed their numbers at around seventy-five. With some Klickitats they had been estimated at six hundred in 1780. They joined Puyallups and Nisquallis in combat against Americans in the Puget Sound Indian War of 1855–56. In 1907 a Tacoma newspaperman wrote an article, entitled "Whole Tribe of Indians Is Dead," on the passing of what he termed the "Peniyah" Indians, sometimes identified as Klickitats who had formerly lived in the lonely foothills southwest of Mount Rainier. Some Taitnapams were eventually driven back east over the Cascade Mountains to the upper Kittitas Valley, where they joined a tribe of similar dialect, the Pshwanapams, a Kittitas band of Upper Yakamas. Their descendants lived among not only the Pshwanapams but also the Micals of the upper Nisqually River on the west below Mount Rainier. There were still Taitnapams living off-reservation in their traditional territory in the 1970s. *See* **Cowlitz** *and* **Klickitat.**

Suggested Readings:

Melville Jacobs, "A Sketch of Northern Sahaptin Grammar," *University of Washington Publications in Anthropology* 4, no. 2 (1931): 87–98; Leslie Spier, *Tribal Distribution in Washington,* American Anthropological Association, General Series in Anthropology, no. 3 (Menasha, Wis.: George Banta Publishing Co., 1936).

TAKELMA

(Takilman)

The Takelmas (or Dagelmas) were one of the Rogue River tribes who inhabited the Rogue River watershed on the east side of the Coast Range in southwestern Oregon. They were one of two major Takilman-speaking tribes in that area. The western, or Lowland Takelmas, lived in villages along the middle Rogue River and its southern tributary, the Illinois River. Their name meant "those living alongside [the Rogue] river." The other Takilman-speaking tribe, the Latgawas, lived farther east on the upper Rogue River in the foothills of the Cascade Mountains. The name ascribed to them meant "those living in the uplands." The two tribes spoke virtually the same language, but with dialect differences. Some linguists believe that Takilman speakers and those of Kalapuyan linguistic stock stemmed from a common language family. The name "Rogue" was applied to all people of the Rogue River valley by the early fur and mountain men, who regarded as unprincipled the Natives' alleged hostile acts against the strangers on their lands.

The Takelmas were said to be larger in stature than the Latgawas, but less aggressive and less accustomed to raiding other tribes for food and other valuables.

The Takelmas were sold as slaves by the Latgawas to the Klamaths on the east. The Latgawas, much to the disgust of the Takelmas, ate crows, ants' eggs, lice, and insect larvae. Among the staple foods eaten by the Takilman peoples were acorns, manzanita berries (which they mixed into a drink by adding mashed pine nuts), and several varieties of seeds. They hunted deer and elk, often approaching the former with dogs in surrounds. The Takelmas also caught eels and fish in the Rogue River and fish in other streams. Their housing included small brush shelters at their mountain fishing places and permanent winter homes of split sugar-pine boards. They were said to have traded wives to the Shastas for basket hats. They traversed their watercourses in canoes. To protect themselves from their foes, they wore double-layered elkskin armor fastened at the sides with sticks. Although sleeveless, these cuirasses were resistant to arrows. Their wearers believed that the symbolic designs on them also provided protection from enemy missiles. They used dentalia shells for ornamentation, and both men and women tattooed themselves. The women often accompanied the men to war.

The Takelmas believed that a person would die if a rattlesnake struck his or her shadow and that eagle cries heralded death by arrows. They prized very highly obsidian, which they secured in trade and used in weaponry. Their culture exhibited traits of northern Californian Indians as well as those of northwest coast tribes. They appear to have had no concept of the guardian spirit that was so common in the traditions of Pacific Northwest peoples. Some ethnologists classify the Rogue River peoples as members of the Lower Klamath cultural complex. Their village units were virtually autonomous units.

As noted, the Takelmas resisted intrusions on their lands by outsiders, such as the Hudson's Bay Company fur brigades, which, in 1829, began traversing their country en route to California. For several years thereafter, as travel increased through the Takelmas' land, they and the Latgawas tried to run off intruders by firing arrows into their parties. The cattle drovers en route to the Willamette Valley from California in the 1830s were among those who came under the attacks of these Natives. The Takelmas harassed immigrant parties and, in 1846, the Scott-Applegate road-building party. Their greatest hostility to newcomers came after the 1848 discovery of gold at Sutter's Mill in the Sacramento Valley of California. Rogue bands attempted to match the firepower of these travelers by various means and built up a considerable arsenal of weaponry through theft, depredation, and murder. However, they also extended favors and provided services to strangers.

In May 1850, Oregon territorial governor Joseph Lane, in company with fifteen Klickitats under their chief, Quatley (Quarterly), set out to the south to effect a treaty with the Rogues. During their meeting, the Natives tried to attack Lane but were repulsed by the Klickitat chief and his men. One Rogue River chieftain, impressed with Lane's bravery, asked to take the governor's name and subsequently called himself Joe (or Jo). Despite the ensuing treaty, conflict continued between the Rogue Indians and settlers. On June 17, 1851, Maj. Philip Kearney,

U.S.A., with a detachment of mounted regulars en route to California, engaged the Rogues in battle near Table Rock in Takelma country. In that encounter, the troops lost a captain and the Rogues lost eleven men, with several more wounded. When the conflict resumed on June 23, the Indians sustained several more casualties in a four-hour skirmish with the troops. Refusing to make a peace treaty, the Rogues fled. Some of their captured women and children were eventually delivered to the new Oregon territorial governor, John P. Gaines. In order to retrieve their families, the Rogues signed a treaty, the terms of which obligated them to keep the peace and restore stolen properties, but again they reneged on the agreement. Their plight was rendered more acute by the discovery of gold in their valley in 1851, when their assaults on immigrants increased. After one attack by the volunteers, Rogue Chief Sam and his people, who were wintering in the Big Bar area, were surrounded and forced to sue for peace. In a July 21, 1852, treaty, the Rogues agreed not to communicate with the Shastas on the south, whom settlers blamed for numerous depredations. The Rogues also promised to respect the property of non-Indians in their valley. These agreements were difficult to accept because the gold miners muddied the streams, ruined the salmon runs, killed game, and committed numerous other depredations on the lands where they settled and ran their cattle.

New towns such as Jacksonville, Oregon, meant more misery for the Rogues. After they had been attacked by regulars and volunteers from the towns and had lost thirty women and children to the troops of Major Kearney, the government detailed Alonzo Skinner into the Rogue Valley to serve as Indian agent. In the meantime, miners continued to pour into the Rogue, Illinois, and Applegate river valleys. After a year's lull, conflict resumed. The Rogues, Shastas, and Klamaths formed a coalition but were decisively defeated in August 1853. Eight were killed and twenty wounded, though their warriors were better armed than that of their enemies. Typical of the American groups hostile to Indians was the Crescent City, California, Guard, who carried a banner bearing the word "EXTERMINATION." Because they respected former Governor Lane, who led the troops, the Indian combatants requested a council at Table Rock after the signing of a peace treaty on September 4. At the council, about seven hundred armed Indians faced troops and Oregon superintendent of Indian affairs Joel Palmer, who was charged with the responsibility of effecting a long-term treaty with the Indians. The document signed on September 10, 1853 (ratified April 12, 1854), preserved the peace for about two years. Under its terms, a reservation was established at Table Rock to which chiefs Sam, Jim, and Jo moved their people. Opposite the reservation on the Rogue's south bank was a military post that operated until 1856, when the Indians were removed to a reservation. By the treaty, the Rogue bands ceded to the United States about twenty-five hundred square miles of their valley above Applegate Creek. In exchange, they received $60,000, of which $15,000 was retained to pay settlers for properties that Indians had destroyed. Before leaving the area, Lane made an informal peace arrangement with

Shasta Chief Tipsu. On November 18, 1854, Palmer treated with the Chasta-costas (Shasta Scotons) and Grave Creek Umpquas. The latter ceded lands that extended from south of Cow Creek to the Oregon-California border.

The Oregon-California border was relatively peaceful despite occasional conflicts between nonreservation Indians and non-Indians, including so-called "squawmen" who fought the Shastas and spread rumors of Indian outbreaks. Reprisals and counterreprisals continued into 1855, however, involving Indians and posses out to revenge the killing of miners. In July, after Indians had slain eleven white miners along the Klamath River between Humbug and Horse creeks in California, whites fired indiscriminately at the Indians and hanged twenty-five of them in what was known as the Humbug War. These conflicts between Shastas and miners on the Klamath River spread to the Rogue Valley because settlers blamed the Indians on the Table Rock Reservation for their troubles. White volunteers, ignoring the army and agency personnel among the Rogues, stormed Indian camps, killing women and children. On October 8 twenty-three Rogues were killed by volunteers near the mouth of Butte Creek. The next morning, roving Indians killed sixteen miners and settlers. Several Indians of a large force lost their lives in an October 17 fight with volunteers on Galice Creek.

By the fall of 1855, the Takelmas were no longer fighting to defend their homes but for their survival. On October 31 and into November they confronted a combined volunteer and regular army force at Hungry Hill in the Grave Creek watershed. This last battle of the year, from which the white attackers withdrew, did little to help the Takelmas, who were without food, clothing, and shelter. With hope exhausted, 314 of the Indians turned themselves in to the U.S. Army at Fort Lane for protection, while 300 others waited on the Umpqua for a decision about their fate. Superintendent Palmer ordered the Umpqua Valley Yoncallas and Southern Molalas to the future Grand Ronde Reservation on the Yamhill River, to which they departed in January 1856. On February 22, 1856, the Takelmas and Latgawas from Table Rock also set out for that same reservation. Most traveled afoot except for thirty-four of the aged and infirm. There were orphans in the party, which lost several of its members along the way, mostly children or the elderly.

Skirmishes between whites and Takelmas and Latgawas continued in the aftermath of that exodus. Most of this later conflict took place on the coast and in mountainous stretches of the Rogue Valley and involved regular army forces. In the interior, volunteer troops did most of the fighting. After Rogues, Shastas, and a few Umpquas engaged volunteers in March 1856 near Eight Dollar Mountain in the Umpqua Valley, the Indians escaped to regroup on a bar below Little Meadows on the Rogue River. Forced to flee in mid-April, most of them got away into woods ahead of the troops. After several Indian prisoners were sent to lure in the holdouts, the chiefs, on May 21, 1856, met at the camp of Col. Robert Buchanan at Oak Flat on the right bank of the Illinois. On May 27 the Indians arrived a day late at a proposed council and surrounded a small military force.

Princess (or Lady) Oscharwasha, also known as Jennie, was one of the last of her tribe of Takelmas of the Rogue River region. She died in May 1893 in Jacksonville, Oregon, where she performed domestic work. She was buried in the robe shown here, which she had made of buckskin many years earlier. It weighed nearly fifty pounds and was decorated in the most costly, elaborate manner. It appears to be fashioned in Plains Indian design and is atypical of the clothes worn by Indians of the Rogue River.

Courtesy of the Southern Oregon Historical Society, Medford.

In the ensuing Big Bend fight, which continued until May 29, the Indians, led by chiefs John and George, were defeated by a regular army-volunteer combination. Following that setback, the Indians began their march downriver on June 10, 1856. Ten days later, at Port Orford, they boarded the steamer *Columbia,* which held about six hundred Rogues, including Takelmas and Tututnis, along with Chetcos, Chastacostas, and Mishikhwutmetunnes. They were shipped up the Pacific Coast and the Columbia and Willamette rivers to Oregon City, from where they were taken to the settlement of Dayton and then to what was supposed to be their new home, the Grand Ronde Reservation. A November 1856 census revealed that those who were congregated there numbered 1,925, of whom 909 were of the Rogue and Shasta bands. By May 1857, nearly all of the Rogues and Shastas had been moved again, this time to the Siletz Reservation. Only Chief Sam, a neutral during the war, remained on the Grand Ronde, with fifty-eight followers.

The Umpqua Valley Kalapuyan speakers on the Grand Ronde numbered 262 in 1857. There were 600 Kalapuyan peoples from the Willamette Valley there. Figures for the Siletz Reservation in 1857 showed 554 Rogues and Shastas whose treaties had not been ratified. With other tribes of their area, the Takelmas in

1852 numbered 1,154. Two years later their population stood at 523, an indication of the devastating effects of their war and the confinement of reservation life, which furthered their decline and eroded their culture. In 1884 there were no more than twenty-seven still living. In 1935 there were reportedly only three or four elderly women on the Siletz who spoke the Takelman language, and but two women on the Grand Ronde, who spoke its upland dialect. By the early twentieth century, any evidence of Takelma tribal viability had disappeared. Until then, the few survivors had communicated mainly in the Chinook jargon, broken English or some Athabaskan dialect. In the late 1970s, archaeologists excavated Takelma village sites before they were covered by the waters behind a dam on the Applegate, a Rogue tributary.

Suggested Readings:

Stephen Dow Beckham, *Requiem for a People: The Rogue Indians and the Frontiersmen* (Corvallis: Oregon State University Press, 1996); Nathan Douthit, *Indians and Whites at Peace and War in Southern Oregon, 1820s–1860s* (Corvallis: Oregon State University Press, 2002); Frederick Webb Hodge, *Handbook of American Indians North of Mexico,* vol. 2 (Washington, D.C.: Government Printing Office, 1910); Edward Sapir, "Notes on the Takelma Indians of Southwestern Oregon," *American Anthropologist,* n.s., 9, no. 2 (April–June 1907); "Religious Ideas of the Takelma Indians," *Journal of American Folklore* 20 (1907): 33–49; and "Takelma Texts," *University of Pennsylvania Museum of Anthropology Publications* 2 (1909): 1–263; Dorothy Sutton and Jack Sutton, eds., *Indian Wars of the Rogue River* (Grants Pass, Ore.: Josephine County Historical Society, 1969); Frank K. Walsh, *Indian Battles along the Rogue River, 1855–56* (Grants Pass, Ore.: Te-cum-tom Publications, 1972).

TALTUSHTUNTUDE

(Athabaskan)

The Taltushtuntudes lived along Galice Creek, an upper-middle Rogue River tributary that enters that stream from the south in southwestern Oregon. Because of their location, the Taltushtuntudes were also known as the Galice Creek Indians. They spoke a dialect similar to that of the Dakubetedes, another Athabaskan people who inhabited another Rogue tributary, the Applegate River, on the east. Culturally, the Taltushtuntudes became assimilated with the Takelman-speaking Takelmas. They were with them at the middle of the century, and shortly thereafter both tribes failed to expel the white intruders from their lands.

On the Siletz Reservation, under the classification "Galice Creeks," the Taltushtuntudes were reported to number eighteen in 1856 and forty-two in 1937. For an account of their confrontations with settlers and the history of their treaties, wars, and ultimate removal to the Siletz Reservation, *see* **Takelma.**

TENINO

(Shahaptian)

The Teninos were composed of four bands: the Teninos proper; the Tukspush (Dockspuses), commonly called the John Day Indians for the river of that name; the Wyams (Waims); and the Tyighs (Tyghs). A valley in north-central Oregon bears the name "Tygh."

When the American explorers Meriwether Lewis and William Clark visited the Teninos in 1805–1806, the tribe's villages were located on the north bank of the Columbia River, but they hunted and fished on the south side. The first Tenino village on the south side was believed to have been established in 1815 near the mouth of the Deschutes River, a Columbia River tributary. South of the Columbia, the Teninos appropriated the Tygh Valley and a fishery (Sherar's Bridge), which was about thirty miles up the Deschutes from its mouth. Around 1820 they drove the Molalas westward across the Cascade Mountains and appro-priated lands from the Columbia south to the Mutton Mountains. They shared territory with the Paiutes in a buffer zone between the two peoples. They then established two villages on the south side of the Columbia. One was about two miles east of what was later known as Big Eddy and two miles east of the main Wasco Indian village. The other was six miles inland on what today is known as Fifteen Mile Creek. The Wyams established a village on the Columbia's south bank near present-day Celilo, and another a few miles up the Deschutes. A few miles up the John Day River, on opposite shores, were two villages of Tukspush. In treaty times (circa 1855) the Wyams extended up the John Day River as far south as today's Clarno, Oregon.

Individuals and families of one Tenino village would freely affiliate with those of another village, though they tended to marry within their own bands. Each band owned its own fishing grounds. Besides being fishermen, the Teninos were mercantilists. They controlled vital places at Celilo Falls on the Columbia, where they imposed tolls on passersby and portaged their goods. In the 1840s, they exacted "dollars" from Oregon-bound white travelers passing their stretch of river.

Lewis and Clark observed that the Tenino peoples, more than others whom they met on their trek, demanded more for their horses, which they acquired by raiding other tribes. They were not skilled horsemen like the Cayuses and Nez Perces on the east, and they did not geld their animals; yet they too regarded them as symbols of wealth and a means by which to exploit large areas.

In 1780 the population of the Tenino bands was estimated at 1,400. In 1854 they numbered 500, and in 1858, 450. In 1962, 250 of their descendants were reported in Oregon. Formerly, the Teninos were strong enough to substantiate their boast that they had killed 500 Paiutes and Klamaths and had captured 40 Paiute women and young girls. During the Cayuse War of 1848, the Cayuses

A Tenino warrior whose
people waged wars against
such tribes as the Klamaths,
the Molalas, and the Northern Paiutes.

Authors' collections.

attempted to pressure the Teninos into fighting volunteers of the Oregon provisional government. Two Tenino bands rendered half-hearted aid to the Cayuses,
but others went into hiding in the Yakama country. The Teninos temporized
their support of the Cayuses even to the point of meeting with the commissioners sent out to negotiate with the Cayuses. They also returned livestock stolen
from the whites.

On June 25, 1855, the Tenino bands signed a treaty (12 Stat. 963, ratified
March 8, 1858, and proclaimed April 18, 1858) with Oregon superintendent of
Indian affairs Joel Palmer. By its terms, they alienated their lands in return for
assignment to the Warm Springs Reservation in north-central Oregon. Some
Tukspush avoided the Warm Springs until 1878, when they left their homes in
the area of Clarno. During the Yakama War (1855–56), some Teninos burned
agency buildings on the Umatilla River, but in an attack on The Dalles they were
unable to elicit the assistance of the preoccupied Cayuses.

The Paiutes raided the Teninos and their allies on the Warm Springs Reservation until well past the middle of the century. Aware of intertribal animosities,

the U.S. military in the 1860s recruited Tenino scouts from the Warm Springs Reservation in its war against the Paiutes, and it also enlisted them in a war against the Modocs in 1873. On the Warm Springs the Teninos became incorporated within the Warm Springs Confederated Tribes. For additional information and readings, *see* **Confederated Tribes of Warm Springs**.

TILLAMOOK

(Coastal Division, Salishan)

The Tillamooks were formerly called by other names, such as the Calamoxes. They lived on the Pacific Coast of Oregon between Nehalem and the Salmon River and from the crest of the Coast Range to the Pacific Ocean. The Tillamooks had been separated in precontact times from other Salish peoples to their north by Chinookan peoples around the mouth of the Columbia River. Consequently, their cultural traits varied somewhat from those of other coastal Salish peoples, exhibiting California tribal influences. The word *"Tillamook"* is said to mean "land of many waters." The anthropologist Franz Boas said it means "people of Nekelim, or Nehalem." An Oregon county and a city on U.S. Highway 101 bear the tribal name.

Some ethnologists have identified four groups within the Tillamook tribe: the Nehalems, the Tillamooks proper, the Nestuccas, and the Nechesnes (who are often called the Salmon River Indians). In the middle of the nineteenth century, government officials referred to the Nehalems and the Tillamooks proper as Northern Tillamooks as opposed to the Nechesnes, who were misnamed Southern Tillamooks along with the Alseas, Yaquinas, and Siletzes. Linguistic studies have not confirmed the classification of the four Tillamook groups as a single tribe, though their dialects are similar. Until recently, the Nehalems and Tillamooks proper were regarded as bands of a single tribe because they had come together to petition the federal government for claims awards since the late nineteenth century. At the time of the first white contacts, each of the four groups may have been composed of multiple villages. Subsequently, the Tillamook peoples were generally reduced to a single village by diseases such as syphilis and smallpox and through abuse of liquor and firearms. Each group was a tribal entity only in that it was autonomous.

The Tillamook peoples tended to be short of stature with broad, thick, flat feet, thick ankles, and crooked legs. They flattened the heads of their aristocracy by applying pressure to their skulls in infancy. Before the nineteenth century, the Tillamooks practiced tattooing. They held slaves in the manner of most northwest coast peoples. They subsisted on waterfowl such as ducks and geese, which they caught by wading into the water wearing pitch-and-feather-covered baskets

Maggie Adams and her daughter, Lizzie Adams, ca. 1890. The ancestors of these Tillamook women had contact with Meriwether Lewis and William Clark. The basket in Lizzie's hands was used for carrying various goods but sometimes the Tillamooks also wore feather-covered baskets over their heads as decoys to snare waterfowl.

Courtesy of the Pioneer Museum, Tillamook, Oregon.

as decoys over their heads. With great dexterity they also hunted game in the nearby hills with bows and arrows. They caught fish and gathered shellfish, some of which they carried over the Coast Range into the Willamette Valley to trade to residents of the Tualatin country for goods such as the wappato root, which they also dug for themselves at Wapato Lake. Sometimes the Tillamooks canoed up the coast and the Columbia River to trade. Among the goods that reached them from great distances were the highly prized dentalia shells from Vancouver Island. When they first met non-Indians, Tillamook men wore animal skins and their women petticoats or skirts of cedar bark, silk grass, plant flags, and rushes. The Tillamooks adopted EuroAmerican dress at an early date. They lived in plank-and-mat houses, many of which had pitched, shedlike roofs.

It is uncertain when the Tillamooks first encountered white maritime traders. Some Nehalems had Caucasian features, suggesting white contact before 1775, when Spanish explorers were along their coasts. Beeswax found on Nehalem shores is believed to have been washed up from a wrecked Spanish ship, such as those that, beginning in 1560, sailed between Manila and Acapulco. On August 10 and 11, 1788, the Nestuccas traded warily with the American Capt. Robert Gray. On August 15 in Tillamook Bay, in exchange for sea otter and boiled and roasted crab, they received from Gray and his crew knives, axes, and adzes. They knew the value of metal knives, which they already possessed. When Gray's crew came ashore, the Natives offered them food, but when one crewman grabbed a cutlass that another had carelessly left sticking in the sand, a skirmish ensued, leaving three Indians and a crewman dead. In their canoes, the Natives failed to head off Gray's ship, *Lady Washington*. After firing her guns on the Natives and their plank houses ashore, the ship sailed out of what Gray called "Murderers Harbour."

Meriwether Lewis and William Clark were probably the first Americans to reach Tillamook country overland. When Clark visited the Tillamooks in January 1806, they had just processed the flesh and meat of a 105-foot whale that had washed up on their beaches. Soon the Tillamooks had contact with traders of John Jacob Astor's Pacific Fur Company and their successors of the North West Company. Duncan McDougall, a North West Company trader from headquarters at Fort George (Astoria, Oregon), called the Tillamooks the "most roguish" people of the region.

Guns, liquor, and disease took their toll on the Tillamook peoples, as outsiders continued to encroach on their country by land and sea. The passage of Hudson's Bay Company men and their trade goods along their coasts to their villages further broke down their society. On one occasion they were punished by company officials, even though in 1828 they had befriended and escorted the American Jedediah Smith to Fort Vancouver after the attack on his party by Kuitsh (Lower Umpqua) Indians.

The greatest usurpation of Tillamook lands was by American settlers stimulated by the Donation Land Act of 1850. In the ensuing years, non-Indians literally crowded Tillamooks off their beaches. Kilchis, the headman of the Tillamooks proper and a friend of the outsiders, helped minimize racial confrontations. Yet he was a bitter foe of Chief Kotata of the neighboring Clatsops on the north. Oregon superintendent of Indian affairs Anson Dart negotiated with Kilchis in the unratified treaty of August 7, 1851. On the previous day, the Nehalems had also signed a treaty to cede their lands. On August 11, 1855, all of the tribes and bands south of the Tillamooks along the Oregon coast, who were misnamed Southern Tillamooks, treated with Oregon superintendent of Indian affairs Joel Palmer. During the Indian wars of the 1850s, when pressured by Klickitat Indians to enter into hostilities, the Tillamooks obeyed Kilchis's order that they bring in their guns to prove to Americans their peaceful disposition. Kilchis also sought to maintain some semblance of Tillamook tribal identity, which had been threatened by population loss. Lewis and Clark had estimated the Tillamooks at twenty-two hundred. By 1841, that number had dropped to four hundred. Thirty years later there were but twenty-eight Nehalems, fifty-five Nestuccas, and eighty-three of Kilchis's Tillamooks proper. In 1950 between two hundred and three hundred petitioners were able to prove Tillamook descent.

By act of Congress on June 7, 1897 (30 Stat. 67), the Nehalems were awarded a $10,500 settlement for their unratified 1851 treaty. On August 24, 1912 (37 Stat. 578), the Tillamooks proper were also awarded $10,500 for settlement of their claims. On August 27, 1962, they and the Nehalems shared an Indian Claims

Commission award of $169,187.50 after offsets for another claim (Docket 240). From this award, each eligible member received $620. The Nechesnes received an award by the Court of Claims (Case No. 45230) as the Alsea Band of Tillamooks et al. *See* **Yaquina.**

Suggested Readings:

Franz Boas, "Notes on the Tillamook," *University of California Publications in American Archaeology and Ethnology* 33 (1923): 3–16; Franz Boas, "Traditions of the Tillamook Indians," *Journal of American Folklore* 11 (1898): 23–28; Elizabeth Derr Jacobs, *Nehalem Tillamook Tales* (Eugene: University of Oregon, 1959); Ada M. Orcutt, *Tillamook: Land of Many Waters* (Portland, Ore.: Binfords and Mort, 1951); John Sauter, "History of Tillamook Indians," *Tillamook Times,* 5, issue 1, n.d.; John Sauter and Bruce Johnson, *Tillamook Indians of the Oregon Coast* (Portland, Ore.: Binfords and Mort, 1974); Herbert C. Taylor, Jr., "Anthropological Investigation of the Tillamook Indians Relative to Tribal Identity and Aboriginal Possession of Lands," 1953, photocopy of manuscript in Tillamook County Pioneer Museum, Tillamook, Oregon.

TUKUARIKA (SHEEPEATER)

(See **Shoshone-Bannock Tribes of the Fort Hall Reservation** *and* **Shoshone.***)*

TULALIP TRIBES OF THE TULALIP RESERVATION

People of the Salmon

The name "Tulalip" stems from a Native word meaning "almost land-locked bay," referring to Tulalip Bay just north of present-day Everett, Washington. The name came to be applied to the nearby Tulalip Reservation as well as to its Indian residents, who came to be known as the Tulalip Tribes of the Tulalip Reservation. They were Coastal Salish peoples, mostly Snohomish, Stillaguamish, Snoqualmie, Skykomish, Skagit, and Samish Indians (see also the entries for those tribes).

Location: Members of the Tulalip Tribes live on their reservation and in its environs in northwestern Washington. The reservation is located just north of Everett and west of Marysville and is bounded on the south and west by Puget Sound. Reservation roads connect with Interstate 5, which is along the reserva-

Stanley Jones, Sr., former Tulalip tribal chairman, ca. 1980. The Tulalip Reservation, where most of the tribe live, is located just west of Marysville, Washington. Jones or Scho-Itallem (No. 1. Warrior) served forty-four years on the Tulalip Tribes Board of Directors, overseeing an expansion that saw his tribe grow from three employees in 1966 to 3,600 in 2010.

Authors' collections.

tion's eastern boundary, along with the main north-south line of the Burlington Northern Railway.

Numbers: In 1985 the Tulalip Tribes had 1,099 members, most of whom lived on the reservation. In 2008 the Tulalip Tribes had about 3,700 enrolled members, all but 1,100 of whom lived on the reservation, which experiences some 13,000 visitors per day.

History: The beginnings of the Tulalip Tribes were at the Point Elliott Treaty of January 22, 1855, under which provision was made for the establishment of the 22,489.91-acre Tulalip Reservation (formerly called the Snohomish), which by executive order was enlarged to 24,300 acres on December 23, 1873, when its boundaries were defined. It was intended for the Snohomish, Snoqualmie, Stillaguamish, and Skykomish tribes and remnants of others.

During the 1840s and 1850s, Indians of the Tulalip area came under the influence of Roman Catholic missionaries, some of whom, such as the Reverend Eugene Casimir Chirouse, O.M.I., actively ministered to the reservation's peoples. During the Peace Policy era of President Ulysses S. Grant in the 1870s, during which religious denominations managed the various Indian agencies, the Tulalip was administered by Catholics, of whom the most influential was Father Chirouse, who served as agent. In his efforts to make the Tulalip Indians farmers, Chirouse faced innumerable problems. The Indians did not quickly adapt to agriculture, as the federal government had hoped they would. The heavily timbered reservation was poorly suited to farming; moreover, the Indians did not wish to alter their ancient means of livelihood: fishing, hunting, and gathering.

Many were forced from the reservation to find subsistence elsewhere. Several cultivated small patches, and some engaged in logging and in other tribe-related enterprises to supply not only their own needs but also an expanding market among non-Indians. At the same time, the Tulalip Indians became victims of foreign diseases and the omnipresent threat posed by liquor. The dream of Chirouse, like that of other agents in the same situation, was frustrated by a growing secularism, which eventually produced a return to government control of the agencies in the post-Peace Policy era.

Allotting was conducted on the Tulalip Reservation between 1883 and 1909. Since the reservation's acreage was limited and the land poorly suited to agriculture, some Indians failed to obtain allotments.

Government and Claims: The Tulalip Tribes of the Tulalip Reservation operate under a constitution and bylaws that were approved January 24, 1936, and a charter that was ratified on October 3, 1936. Both documents have since been modernized. Tribal affairs are supervised by a board of directors, which employs a business manager and other officials. Active committees administer lands and leasing, loans, education, enrollment, water resources and roads, hunting and fishing, and recreation.

The Tulalip Tribes did not file a petition with the Indian Claims Commission for any claim as the successor of any of the tribes sent to the reservation.

Contemporary Life and Culture: By the 1970s more than half the Tulalip Reservation (13,995 acres) had been sold to non-Indians. Of the Indian-owned lands at that time, 4,571 acres remained in trust or some other restricted status; 3,845 were tribally owned in trust; and 80 were owned by the Tulalip Tribes in fee-patent status. Tribal members continue to live on allotments throughout the reservation.

Since the virgin timber has been logged, the Tulalip Tribes has shifted to other sources of income, such as the leasing of waterfront sites. The Tribes owns an industrial site and manages and operates a fish hatchery to generate income for Indian and non-Indian alike. Children in the upper grades attend schools in nearby Marysville. Three buildings on the Tulalip are on the National Registry of Historic Places: the Tulalip Shaker Church, St. Anne's Catholic Church, and the Tulalip agency building. The following faiths are represented on the reservation: Catholic, Mormon, Indian Shaker, Church of God, and Pentecostal. As part of the Tribes' efforts to perpetuate ancient crafts, an artist has been employed to teach wood carving.

Seeking to increase its funds, the Tulalip Tribes in June 1983 opened its Entertainment Center, which features computerized bingo games, and in June 1991 entered into the first state-tribe casino gaming compact. In 1992, it became the first Washington tribe to open a casino, a 12,000-square-foot facility near the 1,400-seat bingo parlor. In 2002, gaming proceeds made up nearly 90 percent

Johnny Moses is a foremost cultural and spiritual leader of the Tulalip Tribes. Born on Vancouver Island, he learned much of his knowledge of Native traditions and healing from his grandparents with whom he lived as a young man. His traditional name is Whis.stem.men.knee (Walking Medicine Robe).

Courtesy of Paul D. G. Eubanks.

of the Tribes' annual budget. Today the Tulalips operate two casinos, the Tulalip Resort Casino and the Quil Ceda Creek Nightclub and Casino. The Tulalip Tribes is the owner of a twelve-story, 370-room, $130-million luxury hotel as well as Quil Ceda Village, a sprawling retail complex and business park with 169 employees and $720 million in annual revenues, Tulalip Liquor & Smoke Shop, Tulalip Broadband, and Tulalip Marina. It is host to 157 designer outlet shops on the reservation in addition to Home Depot and Walmart stores. In March 2007, the Tribes broke ground on a new $28-million, 75,000-square-foot administrative building (the old structure will be converted into a community and youth center) that will house most of the Tulalip government's sixty-five departments. Also under construction is a new $1.5-million data services building.

The Tulalip Tribes maintains health and dental clinics, family and senior housing, a utility, tribal police and fire departments, and tribal and elder courts. The Tribes operates restaurants, golf courses, and a 2,300-reserved-seat open-air amphitheatre. KANU-TV is the Tulalips' cable channel, the first and only nationally broadcast tribal network and the first to transmit live worldwide via the Internet. Since 2003, the Tulalips have hosted *NorthWest Indian News*.

The Tribes' net income was estimated in 2000 at $38 million and at $102 million in 2005. The Tribes employed 350 people in 1990; by 2006, that number had risen to 2,400. In 2006 the Tribes contributed $2.3 million to local charities and law enforcement groups and since 1993 has given away more than $22 million, donating, for example, $200,000 to help rebuild the Tulalip Indian Shaker Church in 2007. As of July 2006, the Tribes had $450 million earmarked in planned or approved development, which now includes an investment in wind energy projects on other reservations.

The cultural values and spiritual beliefs of the Tulalip Tribes are to be preserved through the newly completed $19-million, 35,000-square-foot Hibulb Cultural Center, which sits on fifty-two acres and join a 10,000-square-foot curation facility. In the summer of 2010, a natural history preserve will be added to the complex.

Education for tribal members is delivered through local public schools, such as those of the Marysville School District, and the Tulalip Heritage School (grades 6 through 12), which has partnered with Everett Community College to provide college classes to high school seniors. Tulalip Heritage School was one of the first schools selected by the Bill & Melinda Gates Foundation to allow students an opportunity to earn a high school diploma and two years of college credit in four years of study. The Tribes also operates both a Montessori school and the Tulalip Adult Training and Education program, maintains a Lushootseed Language Department, and supports and administers *beda?chelh,* or "Our Children," a program designed to promote and protect the welfare and health of tribal children and families. This program also includes early childhood education and art therapy groups for elementary and middle school students. For those tribal members pursuing higher education, the Tulalip Tribes pays tuition and provides a fixed stipend for books and living expenses.

In August 2003 the Tribes opened a state-of-the-art health clinic and pharmacy and operates a dental clinic that provides hygienist care and orthodontics. Tribal members are also participating in Housing Hope, the first self-help housing construction project introduced on tribal lands in the state of Washington, while the Elder's Home Replacement Program is substituting new homes for those of about four tribal elders per year.

The Tulalip Tribes maintains an aggressive environmental preservation program. In 2008, it donated $50,000 to the Native American Rights Fund, an organization dedicated to preserving the rights of American Indians. In 1979, the Tribes revived the return of Big Chief Salmon, or the First Salmon Ceremony, an event celebrated annually ever since. The Lushootseed language has been introduced into the local public elementary schools, and, by the fourth grade, some students are writing and speaking sentences. In May 2008, Catholic Mass was celebrated for the first time in the Lushootseed language on the reservation. The Tribes has contributed financially to totem carving in Salish Sea (Puget Sound) schools and has filled its hotel and other businesses with pieces from Tulalip and other Indian artists. This art has been estimated to have a total value of $1 million. "Generations: The Art & Culture of the Tulalip Tribes," an exhibit at the Arts Council of Snohomish County in 2008, featured baskets, carvings, paintings, metal work, and other exemplars of Tulalip craftsmanship. In addition, the Tribes has opened an art studio for those wishing to practice and learn carving and other Native forms.

In the planning stages is a $10-million tribal museum. Tulalips participate each year in Canoe Journey, a multitribal event held throughout Oregon, Washington, and British Columbia; in 2003, they hosted the event. The Tribes opposed the construction of an interpretive center at a site on Camano Island after archeologists uncovered human remains and other Indian artifacts that date back sixteen hundred years.

Special Events and Celebrations: Like other tribes under the Point Elliott Treaty, the Tulalip Indians observe Treaty Days on the weekend nearest January 22. This event, though held on the Tulalip Reservation, is also attended by other tribes who lack adequate facilities for Smokehouse (religious) ceremonies. During these ceremonies, tribal elders remind younger members of the lands that once belonged to their ancestors, exhorting them to protect those that remain. A smoked-salmon feast is also held. Non-Indians may attend the event, and artists may portray it, but cameras and other recording devices are not permitted. Other important events include the annual Veteran's Powwow, held the first weekend of June, and the Salmon Ceremony, celebrated the third week in June in conjunction with the Marysville Strawberry Festival.

Suggested Readings:

Scott Jenkins, "A Contemporary View of Arts and Crafts on the Tulalip Reservation," master's thesis, Western Washington University, 1993; Gustaf B. Joergenson, *History of the Twin Cities* (Stanwood and East Stanwood, Washington) in seventy issues of *Twin City News,* April 1, 1948–October 27, 1949; Bobby R. Pressley, "In Search of the Cultural Center: Defining a Process for Designing with the Tulalip Tribes," master's thesis, University of Washington, 1994; Beckye Randall, *The Tulalip Tribes: We Are the People of the Salmon: By Our Ancestors, We Remember, Tulalip, Washington* (Marysville, Wash.: Marysville Globe, 1996); Lita Sheldon, *Tulalip Tribal Bibliography* (Marysville, Wash.: Tulalip Indian Tribes, 1990); *Tulalip Tribes: Looking toward the Future through the Past* (Marysville, Wash.: Marysville Globe/Arlington Times, n.d.); Ben Smith, *Two Paths: Emmett Oliver's Revolution in Indian Education* (Seattle, Wash.: Salish Press, 1995); Colin Ellidge Tweddell, "A Historical and Ethnological Study of the Snohomish Indian People," in *Coast Salish and Western Washington Indians,* vol. 2 (New York: Garland Publishing, 1974), 475–694; William Whitfield, *History of Snohomish County, Washington* (Evansville, Ind.: Unigraphic, 1979), 2 vols.

TUTUTNI

(Athabaskan)

The Tututnis (or Tututnnes), the meaning of whose name is unknown, were popularly called the Coast Rogues. Their several bands lived in what is now southwestern Oregon along the Illinois and the lower Rogue rivers and near the Pacific Coast between the Coquille River on the north and the Chetco River on the south. There were as many as seven Tututni groups, who were culturally related and had kinship ties. They did not, however, constitute a typical tribe because the usual sociopolitical organization, involving headmen and governmental authority, was lacking. Their houses were twelve-to-sixteen-foot excavations, on the sides of which stood eight-foot puncheons beneath board-and-thatch roofs. Round holes at the gable ends served as entryways, and descent was made down notched poles.

The Tututnis burned grassy headlands near river mouths in the belief that the practice ensured the return of salmon from the sea. They also harvested acorns, which they sometimes traded. From peoples of the Oregon interior they obtained highly prized obsidian, which, as evidence of wealth, they fashioned into blades that measured as much as twenty centimeters in length.

In the spring of 1792, the Tututnis paddled their canoes out to meet the British explorer Capt. George Vancouver. A quarter century later, they met a white fur trader, Peter Corney, who recorded them as wearing dressed-deerskin garments and small, tight-fitting hats. To Corney's North West Company ship they brought baskets, fish, and berries to trade. On June 27, 1828, they fled their villages on both sides of the Rogue River at the approach of a north-bound American party under Jedediah Smith. Two years later, after a storm beached a Russian whaling ship, the Tututnis succumbed to a disease that they blamed on the Russians, unaware of the presence of the intermittent fever that some Indians believed had been brought by American maritime traders.

During the 1850s, Tututni game trails and hunting grounds were destroyed by settlers clearing lands for farms, while white ferrymen preempted their river-crossing businesses. In September 1849, after the *William G. Hagstaff* ran aground near the mouth of the Rogue River, Indians stormed and burned her and salvaged her chain plates to fashion into knives. Her captain, Charles White, and eighteen men wandered along the coast for three weeks. In June 1851, some Tututnis were killed and wounded by shots from a small cannon that had been fired by men coming ashore from the steamer *Seagull*. White men established a beachhead on the Tututni lands, on which they laid out the town of Port Orford, which in August already numbered sixty souls. The security of the town was strengthened that month by the arrival of Lt. August V. Kautz, U.S.A., with twenty troops, and by the arrival of other soldiers from Fort Orford. The Tututnis were further pressured when more settlers came to Port Orford after the gold discoveries in the Rogue River valley in 1852.

In November 1855 the Tututnis threatened the non-Indians at Port Orford, while other Tututnis up the Rogue River urged the lower-valley Natives to join them in war against the whites. On February 22, 1856, the Tututnis attacked the Gold Beach Guards, who were encamped opposite the large Tututni village at Port Orford. Moving through the forests, the Indians fired on the cabins of miners and others who were attending a George Washington's Birthday celebration

Martha Johnson, a member of the Tututni tribe of southwestern Oregon, popularly known as Coast Rogues. Such beadwork was valuable not only for adornment but also for trading.

Authors' collections.

at Gold Beach, and they killed a number of whites. Prominent among the reported twenty-six who perished was an Indian agent named Ben Wright, who had been betrayed, it was said, by his common-law Indian wife, Chetco Jennie. He was felled by an axe wielded by one Enos, an Indian of mixed heritage from the East, who urged the Indians to destroy white men. The conflict continued as the Tututnis burned most of the settlers' homes between Port Orford and Smith River. About 130 settlers escaped to Fort Miner, which was on the Rogue's north bank, near its mouth. From the south bank of the river, the Tututnis attacked for ten miles down the coast. It was a help to them that Maj. John F. Reynolds, U.S.A., was needed to protect Port Orford and was therefore unable to dispatch an expedition to help the beleaguered Americans, who were rescued five weeks later by army regulars from Fort Humboldt, California.

The Tututni resistance was both the cause and the effect of their treaties with the United States. By an unratified September 1851 treaty, various Tututni bands had surrendered 2.5 million acres in return for $28,500. Further anguish was thrust on them by the treaties that they entered into in August and September 1855 with Oregon superintendent of Indian affairs Joel Palmer, and by Congress's failure to ratify those documents. In the final phase of what was known as the Rogue wars, many Tututnis fled upriver to join the Takelmas, the Latgawas, and their allies. By June 1856, those Tututnis who had remained and other inhabitants of the Rogue Valley had been rounded up at Port Orford. The moaning and the wailing of these nearly naked unfortunates and of those who were resisting capture could not have escaped the ears of their foes. In February 1857, 152 more were collected. On June 20 about 600 Tututni, Chetco, Coquille, Chastacosta, Takelma, and Latgawa Indians and a few Shastas were herded aboard a steamer, as were nearly 600 more shortly thereafter. The captives were shipped up the coast and up the Columbia and Willamette rivers to Dayton, Oregon. From there, they were marched over the Coast Range to an alien home on the Grand Ronde Reservation. They remained there for a year and then moved to the Siletz (first called the Coast Reservation), which was established by executive order on November 9, 1855. That they had no treaty with the United States made little difference to their captors.

Because of the harshness and the strangeness of reservation life, only 141 Tututnis remained in 1930. By 1964 there were just 6 who spoke their Native tongue. In 1854, during the turbulent decade of their demise, they had numbered roughly 1,311.

With certain other western Oregon tribes, the Tututnis were plaintiffs in a case (No. 45230) tried in the Court of Claims, in which the tribe sued for the loss of lands that were taken from the Coast Reservation by executive order on December 21, 1865, and by act of Congress on March 3, 1875. (For details of the case, see **Yaquina.**) They appealed their award to the U.S. Supreme Court, which on November 25, 1946, upheld the April 2, 1945, ruling of the Court of Claims. The final award was $465,225.60 for the Tututnis.

Suggested Readings:

Stephen Dow Beckham, *Requiem for a People: The Rogue Indians and the Frontiersmen* (Corvallis: Oregon State University Press, 1996); Percy T. Booth, *Valley of the Rogues* (Grants Pass, Ore.: Josephine County Historical Society, 1970); Edward S. Curtis, *The North American Indian* (1912; New York: Johnson Reprint Corporation, 1970), vol. 13; Cora DuBois, "The Wealth Concept as an Integrative Factor in Tolowa-Tututni Culture," in *Essays in Anthropology, Presented to A. L. Kroeber* (Berkeley: University of California Press, 1936).

TWANA

(Coastal Division, Salishan)

The name "Twana" is said to mean "people from below." In the Point-No-Point Treaty with the United States of 1855, they appear as the Toanhooches. Today a state park at the southern end of Hood Canal near U.S. Highway 101 bears the name Twanoh.

The Twanas originally occupied both sides of Hood Canal in Washington State. In the nineteenth century, the missionary Myron Eells divided them into three bands: Duhlelips, Skokomish, and Kolsids (or Quilceeds). The largest of these bands was the Skokomish, whose name is based on a Twana word meaning "people of the large river," which refers to the Skokomish River, an affluent of Hood Canal. Others have identified five permanent Twana villages. The anthropologist William Elmendorf located them in nine permanent villages, most of

A young, full-blood-degree Twana man, ca. 1880. His short hair and clothing show the influence of missionaries. His ancestors lived in a society with strong class distinctions. When Capt. George Vancouver visited Puget Sound in 1792, the Twanas presented the British explorer with bows and arrows.

Courtesy of Whitman College, Walla Walla, Wash.

which were at the mouths of salmon streams along Hood Canal. The modern-day descendants of these Twana peoples are members of the Skokomish Tribe, Skokomish Reservation.

Location: Tribal members live not only on the Skokomish Reservation but also adjacent to it in such places as the city of Shelton.

Numbers: Two hundred years ago, with the neighboring Squaxins, the tribe was said to have numbered about a thousand. Official estimates in the 1850s placed the Twana at between two hundred and three hundred individuals.

History: Socially, the Twanas had three classes: a high and a low free class and slaves. Although the village structure was informal and lacked true governing offices, considerable prestige and influence adhered to the high-ranking men of each village. As among other Salish speakers, religion played a significant role in the Twanas' lives. Individuals acquired guardian spirits, which were ceremoniously revealed in winter dances. The Twanas sought peace despite attacks on them by Natives of the Olympic Peninsula and Puget Sound. They had commercial ties with the Clallams and the Makahs on the north and west and with the Kwaiailks and Satsops on the south. They rarely undertook extensive trading expeditions, but did obtain such items as hemp fiber and mountain-goat hair from the east through intermediaries, such as the Satsops. From the Makahs and the Vancouver Island tribes they acquired, often through Clallam intermediaries, implements and ornaments of shell, bone, stone, fiber, wood, and, later, metal. In 1792 they presented members of Capt. George Vancouver's British expedition with bows and arrows. Some of the latter were iron-tipped, indicating that the Twanas had had contact with white mariners other than Vancouver or had traded with Natives who had obtained metals directly or indirectly from foreign explorers. The metals may have come from wrecked ships, possibly from Asia. The Twanas were among those who traded at the Hudson's Bay Company's

Fort Nisqually, which was established in 1833 on the southern reaches of Puget Sound.

Today the Twanas belong to the Skokomish Tribe, Skokomish Reservation. That tribe may be said to have originated when Twana, Clallam, and Chimakum headmen signed the Point-No-Point Treaty on January 26, 1855. At the treaty council, some Twanas opposed selling their lands. They were aware of their commercial value because settlers were logging them for poles and lumber. They also opposed removal to any reservation that might be established on Clallam lands instead of on theirs. Eventually, the three tribes were designated to remove to a 3,840-acre reservation carved from Twana lands along the lower Skokomish River. *See* **Skokomish Tribe, Skokomish Reservation.**

Suggested Readings:

W. W. Elmendorf, *The Structure of Twana Society,* Monograph Supplement no. 2 (Pullman, Wash.: Washington State University, 1960, 1992).

UMATILLA

(Shahaptian)

The Umatillas lived on the lower reaches of the Umatilla River, a Columbia River tributary in northeastern Oregon, and along both banks of the Columbia from present-day Arlington, Oregon, east to the mouth of the Walla Walla River of southeastern Washington. The tribal name derives from a village name meaning "many rocks." It is also the name of a county and a town in Oregon. The Umatillas were estimated to have been 1,500 in 1780, 272 in 1910, 145 in 1923, and 124 in 1937. One estimate of the number of Umatillas in Oregon in 1962 varied from between 10 and 100.

Before acquiring horses early in the eighteenth century, the Umatillas depended primarily on salmon and other fish for survival. Like many Columbia River peoples, they caught the salmon with an assortment of spears, nets, traps, and weirs. They sought bountiful catches by performing strict first-salmon ceremonies before the season began. They also gathered mussels from the river. Away from the river, they harvested camas, berries, pine nuts, seeds, bark, and sap. They roasted food in earthen ovens and boiled it in water heated by hot stones. They lived in multifamily lodges constructed of poles and mats over shallow excavations. Some of their houses measured as large as sixteen by sixty feet. Like other interior peoples, they used sweat lodges for spiritual purposes. Their horses made them mobile, which facilitated their hunting of game.

The Umatillas had few intertribal political ties; yet, under threats by their most feared enemy, the Paiutes, they formed a war alliance with the Nez Perces on

Amy and Saul Webb, photographed in 1968 at Thornhollow, Oregon, on the eastern half of the Umatilla Reservation.

Authors' collections.

the east. When McNary Dam was built on the Columbia River, its backwaters covered Blalock Island, which was their stronghold against mounted Paiute raiders. In 1848 they dispatched warriors to join their Cayuse neighbors after the Whitman Massacre of the previous year. These Umatilla warriors remained with the combatants throughout most of the Cayuse War, which was fought against a volunteer army from the Willamette Valley.

Living along the Immigrant Road (the Oregon Trail), as it broke westward to the Columbia, the Umatillas, like their Cayuse neighbors, were alarmed at the increasing numbers of immigrants passing over that route in the 1840s. Ignoring the unrest that white immigration had instilled among the Indians, Congress passed the Donation Land Law on September 29, 1850, allowing settlers to homestead lands in Oregon not yet ceded by the Indians. Aware that the local tribes were restive, the government in 1851 established the Utilla (Umatilla) Agency on the Lower Crossing of the Umatilla River near present-day Echo, Oregon. The Roman Catholic mission of St. Anne (later named for St. Joseph and today for St. Andrew) had been founded in 1847 near Pendleton, Oregon, but was abandoned in 1848 after the killing of Marcus and Narcissa Whitman and the advent of the Cayuse War. In 1851 it was reestablished. Like the Cayuses, the Umatillas frequented the Utilla Agency to obtain not only food but also intelligence concerning non-Indian activities. They suffered at the hands of incompetent agents, one of whom encouraged them to steal immigrant cattle, which he later purchased from them.

Fearing war, white cattlemen fled the Umatilla Valley in October 1855, the year that the Tenino Indians burned the agency building. The Yakama War of 1855–56 broke out in that same month. In May and June 1855, the Umatillas met the Washington and Oregon superintendents of Indian affairs, Isaac Stevens and Joel Palmer, in the Walla Walla treaty council. Along with the Cayuses and the Walla Wallas, they signed a treaty on June 9 (12 Stat. 945, ratified March 8, 1859, and proclaimed April 11, 1859), yielding their land to the United States in return for a reservation north and south of the middle Umatilla River. Early in the Yakama War, volunteer forces had manned Fort Henrietta on the Umatilla River at Lower Crossing, as they tried to control the hostile Umatilla and Cayuse elements. At that time, those two tribes faced war against not only the Americans but also their ancient Paiute foes. On one occasion at the height of the Yakama War, when the Umatillas were in council with the Cayuses and the Yakamas in the Grande Ronde Valley, they were attacked by Paiutes and forced to flee, abandoning their old, young, and crippled.

As noted, the Umatillas' numbers were given variously as from ten to one hundred in 1962, but like their reservation allies, the Cayuses and Walla Wallas, they had by then lost most semblances of independent tribal identity. *See* **Confederated Tribes of the Umatilla Indian Reservation.**

Suggested Readings:

Robert H. Ruby and John A. Brown, *The Cayuse Indians: Imperial Tribesmen of Old Oregon* (Norman: University of Oklahoma Press, 1972, 2005); Joel L. Shiner, "The McNary Reservoir: A Study in Plateau Archaeology," *Bureau of American Ethnology Bulletin no. 179* (Washington, D.C.: Government Printing Office, 1961).

UMATILLA CONFEDERATED TRIBES

(See **Confederated Tribes of the Umatilla Indian Reservation.***)*

UPPER CHEHALIS

(See **Kwaiailk.***)*

UPPER SKAGIT

(Coastal Division, Salishan)

People of the River

The Upper Skagit Tribe of Washington comprises four of the eleven aboriginal bands of the Skagit River in northwestern Washington, where a river and
a county also bear the tribal name. The meaning of the name "Skagit" seems to
have been lost. The ancestors of the Upper Skagits were hunting, fishing, and
gathering peoples. Among the neighbors with whom they had close cultural ties
were the Sauks of the river of that name, a Skagit tributary, and the Suiattles
of the Suiattle River, a Sauk tributary. On occasion, the Skagits traveled east of
the Cascade Mountains to visit the Natives there, and the latter traveled west to
visit the Skagits. Their relative remoteness from the peoples of the lower Skagit
River is reflected in differences in their dialects. The secret society that was so
important among the Natives of Puget Sound appears to have been much weaker
among the Upper Skagits.

Location: Upper Skagit tribal members live throughout northwestern Washington, but mainly in Skagit County.

Numbers: Around 1855 the residents of the upper Skagit River numbered about
300. In 1984 there were 223 Upper Skagits. In 1994 the tribe had grown to 600
and in 2008 to 1,031 members.

History: Headmen of the upper Skagit Basin were among the signatories to the
Point Elliott Treaty of 1855. One who attended the treaty council but did not
sign the document was the prophet-cultist Slaybebtkud, who came from east
of the Cascade Mountains to join the Skagits. After the treaty, he exerted great
authority by uniting about ten extended and autonomous village bands of the
upper Skagit River and its tributaries. For sixty years after the treaty, the federal
government claimed that the Indians of the upper Skagit River did not constitute
a single tribe because they lived in villages as bands.

The lands of the Upper Skagits were crossed by the surveyors of the Northern
Pacific Railroad in 1870 and shortly thereafter by settlers. The Indians were angered when the whites encroached on lands that held the graves of their dead.
On one occasion, settlers burned a village of eight large cedarboard houses at
the confluence of the Skagit and Sauk rivers. Residents of the upper Skagit suffered from the inevitable diseases that were a consequence of contact. In 1889,
for example, the bodies of the dead lay unburied after a smallpox epidemic. Initially, the Natives of the upper Skagit River were suspicious of Roman Catholic

Knuckle Boome, former leader and chairman of the Upper Skagit Tribe of Indians, ca. 1980. Leaders such as Boome directed the tribe's campaign for recognition by the federal government. As a member of the Skagit System Cooperative, the Upper Skagit Tribe sought to restore and maintain fish runs in the Skagit River system.

Authors' collections.

priests, but later the friendly disposition of Slaybebtkud to missionaries of that faith helped them to minister to his people.

Government and Claims: The Upper Skagits asserted that they had a right to federal acknowledgment as a tribe stemming from a 1913 congressional appropriation to them and from the Sauk-Suiattles' purchase of a piece of their land for a cemetery. This was proof, they claimed, of congressional recognition of the Indians of the upper Skagit Valley as a single tribal unit. The Upper Skagits operate under a constitution and bylaws approved by the secretary of the interior on December 4, 1974. Their governing body is the seven-member Upper Skagit Tribal Council. Its chairperson is elected annually from among the tribal members by popular vote.

In January 1951 the tribe filed a claim (Docket 92) alleging that the consideration it had received for lands acquired by the United States under the Point Elliott Treaty was unconscionably low. The 1,769,804 acres that the tribe claimed from Mount Vernon (the county seat of Skagit County) to the Canadian border overlapped with the acreage claimed by the Lower Skagit Tribe (Docket 294). An amended petition filed on October 17, 1958, modified the boundaries of the Upper Skagits' land claim and also changed their name from Skagit Tribe of Indians to Upper Skagit Tribe of Indians. On September 23, 1968, a final judgment was ordered for the tribe, by which it was awarded $385,471.42.

Contemporary Life and Culture: The Upper Skagits received federal tribal recognition in 1974. During the period from 1977 to 1982, the tribe applied for

The late Upper Skagit storyteller, linguist, author, and educator Vi Hilbert, or Taqwsheblu (1918–2008), spent a lifetime dedicated to the study, promotion, and preservation of her tribe's Lushootseed language and culture. Like Hazel Pete, Hilbert attended the Tulalip boarding school and Chemawa Indian School and held an honorary doctoral degree from Seattle University, given in recognition of her significant contributions to the Upper Skagit culture.

Courtesy of Paul D. G. Eubanks.

and received several federally funded grants and contracts, which it utilized to purchase land. A twenty-five-acre tract on Bow Hill north of the former tribal headquarters in Burlington was purchased over a four-year period, partly from tribal members who owned individual allotments in that area. In 1981 a seventy-four-acre parcel east of Sedro-Woolley was purchased from a local resident, taken into trust status by the government, and declared reservation land (along with the Bow Hill holding). Tribal members live in numerous scattered public-domain allotments in Skagit County, and they are employed in the surrounding communities.

With the Swinomish Indian Tribal Community and the Sauk-Suiattles, the Upper Skagit Tribe is a member of the Skagit System Cooperative, which was organized in 1976 to regulate and enhance fishing in the Skagit River system. In December 1990 the tribe signed a pact with the state Wildlife Department to adopt "comprehensive internal hunting regulations, sharing them with the state in a timely fashion," by which the tribe would set seasons, report kills, and issue hunting and identification requirements, much to the displeasure of non-Indian sportsmen. The tribe was joined by the Suquamish, Stillaguamish, and Sauk-Suiattle in this pact.

Sixteen acres of land along Interstate 5 near Burlington is now the site of their 65,000-square-foot Skagit Valley Casino Resort. Built at a cost of $24 million and opened in 1995, the resort has an associated outdoor amphitheatre with a seating capacity of twenty-seven hundred, three restaurants, and a 103-room deluxe hotel that opened in March 2002 at a cost of $11 million. The casino attracts 1 million visitors annually and employs 450 people. In 2003 the Upper Skagits entered into a consulting agreement with Trillium Corporation to manage the Resort Semiahmoo near Blaine, the largest such facility in the state.

The Upper Skagit Tribe is a member of the Northwest Washington service unit of the Indian Health Service, along with the Lummi, Nooksack, and Swinomish tribes. The 4,500-square-foot Upper Skagit Tribal Health Facility opened in 1995 and provides limited primary care and a variety of social services. To protect and sustain the resources of their reservation, the Upper Skagits maintain fisheries management, timber resources, and natural resources departments. The tribe operates a hatchery on the Skagit River, having begun a chum enhancement program in 1990. In 2008, coho salmon returned to the Upper Skagit reservation for the first time in a half century. And in 2009 the Upper Skagits received a $105,000 grant to help restore 140 acres of salmon habitat on waterways located near their reservation.

In March 2001, the tribe received a $90,000 EPA grant to assist them in reaching compliance with tribal, state, and federal environmental laws. In July 2004 a HUD block grant of $1,369,611 was issued to the tribe to promote affordable housing on the reservation.

Special Events and Celebrations: Each year in August the Upper Skagits host the Upper Skagit Celebration and Stick Game Tournament at Sedro-Woolley, Washington.

Suggested Readings:

> June McCormick Collins, *Valley of the Spirits: The Upper Skagit Indians of Western Washington* (Seattle: University of Washington Press, 1974); Paul C. Pitzer, *Building the Skagit: A Century of Upper Skagit Valley History, 1870–1970* (Portland, Ore.: Galley Press, 1978); Martin J. Sampson, *Indians of Skagit County* (Mount Vernon, Wash.: Skagit County Historical Society, 1972).

UPPER UMPQUA

(Athabaskan)

The Upper Umpquas lived in what is now southwestern Oregon in the valley of the south fork of the Umpqua River, an affluent of the Pacific Ocean. The name "Umpqua" has been variously interpreted to mean "high and low water," "thunder," and a Native call, "A-i-e! Ump-sa-qua!" meaning "Boat, bring over the water!"

In the middle of the nineteenth century the Upper Umpquas were divided into five bands: Miwaletas, Augunsahs, Quintiousas, Targunsans, and Wartahoos. The Miwaletas, who lived on Cow Creek, an Umpqua tributary, have also been called the Nahankhuotanas. The Upper Umpquas had a population estimated at about 200 to 400 in the middle of the nineteenth century. On the 60,000-acre Grand Ronde Reservation (established by executive order on June 30, 1857, in the Yamhill country north of the Upper Umpqua lands), the Upper Umpquas numbered 84 in 1902, 109 in 1910, and 43 in 1937.

Incarceration on the reservation was traumatic for the Upper Umpquas, who had been a fiercely independent people. In historic times their men had entered combat wearing thick, almost impregnable two-piece elkskin cuirasses, which were laced at the sides and ornamented with figures and designs. Other ceremonial elements in their battle dress were single white eagle tail feathers. Among the first non-Indians whom they met were the Astorian fur hunters who entered the Umpqua homelands from the Willamette Valley. These were the southernmost Astorian fur probes. Late in the fall of 1818, the Upper Umpquas were visited by the Nor'Wester Alexander Roderick McLeod leading a party of sixty, who crossed from the Willamette to the Umpqua and proceeded to the coast. The Upper Umpquas opposed trafficking with whites. Their disposition did not change after the killing of about fourteen Natives on the Umpqua River in 1818, a deed that was believed to have been perpetrated by Iroquois in the employ of the North West Company. When the Hudson's Bay Company pushed its fur trade into the upper Willamette and Umpqua valleys in 1826, the Kuitsh (Lower Umpquas), remembering the 1818 killings, repulsed a free trapper who was working his way down the Umpqua. Ten years later, the Hudson's Bay Company established a fur-gathering station, Fort Umpqua, near today's Elkton, Oregon, about fifty miles from the coast on the south bank of the Umpqua, which was the western boundary of Upper Umpqua country. At that post, Umpqua Natives saw fur traders cultivate the land and raise stock before the post was abandoned in 1852. Since 1829, Bay Company brigades had traversed Umpqua country, hunting, trapping, and trading en route to the Sacramento River. They followed a line that was roughly that of today's Interstate 5.

Abandonment by fur-trading brigades after 1843 did not reduce the number of outsiders crossing Umpqua lands. The opening of the Scott-Applegate Road in 1846 facilitated their passage. On the heels of those early settlers came gold seekers traveling to and from California. Restive under such trespasses, the Natives on the south (most likely the Takelmas, a Rogue people) sought to recruit the Upper Umpquas to help repulse the invaders, but the latter refused. With the outbreak of the Rogue wars in the early 1850s, an Upper Umpqua headman, Napesa (Nez-zac), or Louis (who lived near where the Little River joins the North Umpqua River, near Glide, Oregon) moved his bands in fear that soldiers, assuming them hostile, would kill them. In 1855 a peaceful Umpqua band, moving to Flournoy Valley (two miles west of Lookingglass, Oregon) to encamp, was attacked by panicky whites, with a resultant loss of life.

On November 29, 1854, a treaty (10 Stat. 1125, ratified March 3, 1855) was signed between the Upper Umpquas of the middle Umpqua Valley and Oregon superintendent of Indian affairs Joel Palmer. By this treaty, the Umpquas

Tirzah Trask, an Upper Umpqua Indian, photographed by the well-known photographer Lee Moorhouse about 1900. Trask's people lived in southwestern Oregon in the valley of the south fork of the Umpqua River. In the fashion of the Indians of that region, she is seen here in the elaborate attire that evolved from the simpler clothes of earlier times.

Courtesy of the Smithsonian Institution.

and the Yoncallas of the Umpqua Valley ceded their lands. In exchange, they were given a temporary 67,820-acre reservation in their valley near the mouth of Calapooya Creek on lands that they had ceded about twelve miles downstream from the fork of the Umpqua River. They resided there until the October 8, 1855, renewal of the Rogue wars, when the government decided that they should be removed to the Grande Ronde Valley.

In rounding up the Indians in southwestern Oregon Territory during the Rogue wars, Superintendent Palmer made a treaty with several villages of the nomadic Indians of Cow Creek, a tributary of the south fork of the Umpqua River. In the treaty making, Palmer lumped together some Miwaletas and Targunsans with some Takelmas and a few other Indians who were thought to be Southern Molalas. He called these combined peoples the Cow Creek Band of Umpqua Tribe of Indians and concluded a treaty with them on September 19, 1853 (10 Stat. 1027, ratified April 1, 1854), by which they surrendered all claims to the Umpqua Valley in return for a small temporary reservation. They remained on that reservation until moved elsewhere by the government. For their cession, the government promised them $12,000 and houses.

Seventeen of that Cow Creek Band and about thirty Southern Molalas signed a treaty on December 21, 1855 (12 Stat. 981), ceding their claims to the Umpqua Valley and agreeing, with Upper Umpqua and Yoncalla approval, to remove with the latter two tribes to the Yamhill country on the north, where the Grand Ronde Reservation was to be established. The three tribes were first relocated with the main body of the Upper Umpquas to the latter's temporary reservation, where roughly thirty Molalas and Yoncallas were consigned to one camp with Upper Umpquas. When the Cow Creeks were rounded up in November 1855, many fled to the hills, where they were joined by others leaving the Yamhill country to which they had been removed from the south fork of the Umpqua River. When the time came for the Umpquas to leave their temporary reservation for the Grand Ronde Reservation, Chief Napesa refused to abandon the Umpqua Valley. He and twenty of his band were permitted to remain in their homeland. With Napesa's death early in 1856 and his burial in that land, a headman known as The Captain assumed leadership of the band.

On January 10, 1856, a total of 337 Cow Creeks, Yoncallas, and Upper Umpquas began their trek northward with a funeral chant and then trudged through snow and freezing weather to the Yamhill country, where they arrived on February 2. En route, many lacked food and clothing, and others were too ill to travel. With but eight teams and wagons to transport them, most were forced to walk to their place of confinement. Once there, troubles continued to plague them as they tried to adjust to a new way of life in an alien land. The many deaths revealed how unsuccessful they were. The survivors were later moved to the 225,000-acre Siletz Reservation (established by executive order on November 9, 1855). Others made their way back to the Umpqua Valley to rejoin The Captain. Authorities made several attempts to round up his elusive band.

The Cow Creeks were plaintiffs in Case No. 45231 tried before the Court of Claims, in which that court decided on April 3, 1950, that they were not to be allowed recovery of money for their ceded lands. They were not so entitled, the court ruled, because an award would not have exceeded the $12,000 in installments already paid them under the treaty. Descendants of other Umpqua bands, along with those of twenty Yoncallas whose ancestors had lived in the Umpqua Valley, were awarded a judgment of $377,177.16 on April 3, 1950, for the loss of the reserved area in the Umpqua Valley from which they had been removed in 1856. The award represented the principal of $67,820 plus interest and deductions for offsets. *See* **Cow Creek Band of Umpqua Tribe of Indians**.

Suggested Readings:

Lavola J. Bakken, *Land of the North Umpquas: Peaceful Indians of the West* (Grants Pass, Ore.: Te-cum-tom Publications, 1973); Stephen Dow Beckham, *Requiem for a People: The Rogue Indians and the Frontiersmen* (Corvallis: Oregon State University Press, 1996); Joel V. Berreman, *Tribal Distribution in Oregon*, Memoirs of the American Anthropological Association, no. 47 (Menasha, Wis.: George Banta Publishing Co., 1937); Leo J. Frachtenberg, *Lower Umpqua Texts and Notes on the*

Kusan Dialect, Columbia University Contributions to American Anthropology, no. 4 (New York, 1914); Leslie Spier, "Tribal Distribution in Southwestern Oregon," *Oregon Historical Quarterly* 28 (December 1927).

WAHKIAKUM

(Upper Chinookan Division of Chinookan)

According to the anthropologist Franz Boas, the Wahkiakums spoke the Cathlamet dialect of Upper Chinookan. Yet, living on the lower Columbia River, they were culturally related to two Lower Chinookan peoples, the Chinooks proper and the Clatsops, whose culture was primarily that of the coastal Pacific Northwest peoples but modified by contacts with peoples east of the Cascade Mountains. Washington Irving had access to Astorian fur-trader notes of about 1811 that have since been lost. In writing his *Astoria* (1837), he stated that the Wahkiakums and the Chinooks were initially one and the same people and that, about two generations before non-Indians entered their lands, a quarrel erupted between their ruling headman and his brother, Wahkiacu, who then seceded with his people to form the Wahkiakus, or Wask-i-cums. In a similar vein, Abbé Domenech, in *Seven Years' Residence in the Great Deserts of North America* (1860), stated that the Wahkiakums were one of four "clans." The others were the Cathlamets, Chinooks, and Clatsops, who splintered off around the middle of the eighteenth century because of infighting among village headmen. After the separation, the Wahkiakums visited and intermarried with other tribes in the lands where they went to fish, gather seafoods and berries, and hunt.

The principal Wahkiakum village lay in present-day Washington State on the Columbia's north bank east of the Chinook lands, which they bordered at Grays River, an affluent of Grays Bay on the Columbia's north bank. Boas stated that the Wahkiakums lived in two main villages, of which one, Tlalegak, was located a little below Pillar Rock, a short distance above Grays Bay, and the other, Chakwayalham, was farther down the Columbia. At least one of the important Wahkiakum villages lay near present-day Cathlamet, Washington, in Wahkiakum County.

Although they fished off islands in the Columbia River opposite Grays Bay and upstream, the Wahkiakums lived primarily by the chase. Their hunting territory extended north from the Columbia to the Chehalis River watershed and west and south to the western end of Grays Bay.

Irving stated that there were sixty-six Wahkiakum warriors, a figure that supports the estimate of the American explorers Meriwether Lewis and William Clark of a total of two hundred Wahkiakums in 1805–1806. En route down the Columbia in 1805, the explorers purchased fish and dogs from the Wahkiakums whom they called the "best canoe navigators." In 1841 the American naval explorer Lt. Charles Wilkes noted that the Wahkiakum headman, Skamakowa (Skumahqueah), had formerly led a large tribe that had become very small since the intermittent fever outbreak of 1829–30 had nearly destroyed it. Government officials estimated that there were 185 Wahkiakums, Cathlamets, and Chinooks living in thirty-seven houses at the time of those tribes' treaties with the United States. The ethnologist George Gibbs, writing shortly thereafter, stated that the chief was almost the last survivor of those peoples.

One provision of the treaty that the Wahkiakums signed on August 8, 1851, was that, in exchange for their lands, they were to receive a $700 annuity for ten years. The short period of time was dictated by their fears of becoming extinct. They were to be given $100 in cash and the remainder in goods. They retained rights to occupy their places of residence, fish in the Columbia and two small streams, cut timber for building and for fuel, and hunt. They also obtained the usual clothing, hardware, and miscellaneous items. Chief Skamakowa was to receive a fifty-dollar rifle. The treaty was similar to those concluded with other tribes and bands of the area at that time, but was never ratified by the United States Senate.

On August 24, 1912, Congress passed legislation to compensate the Wahkiakums, Chinooks, Clatsops, and Cathlamets for the loss of their lands in accordance with the decision of the Court of Claims. The Wahkiakums' share of the award was $7,000. The Chinook tribes, including the Wahkiakums, petitioned the government for additional compensation for the loss of aboriginal lands, in the case of *Duwamish et al.* v. *The United States* (79 C.Cls. 530). The Court of Claims dismissed the case on grounds that compensation had already been made to the tribes with whom the government had treated. Descendants of the Wahkiakums, who had been assimilated within other tribes, were among petitioners bringing claims before the Indian Claims Commission and sharing in any awards made. The Wahkiakums also filed suit in federal court, along with the Lower Chinooks and the Cowlitzes, seeking protection of their fishing rights in southwestern Washington, but they were excluded in *United States* v. *Washington* (384 F. Supp. 312, 1974) because they had tried too late to enter that litigation. It is unlikely that the Wahkiakums could be successful in any such case brought against Washington State, since they are not a federally acknowledged tribe, a prerequisite for the guarantee of fishing rights.

In January 1979 descendants of the Wahkiakums, as the Wahkiakum Indian Tribe, having been excluded from earlier landmark treaty-rights cases, filed in the U.S. District Court of Oregon, asking that their "federally guaranteed right to take fish" in the Columbia River be recognized. The Wahkiakums acted separately from the Chinook Indian Tribe of Chinook, Washington, in initiating the fishing rights litigation, though the descent of the two groups is intermixed, and both were identified as Chinooks for allotment purposes on the Quinault Reservation. The Chinooks, nevertheless, maintain a separate tribal identity from the Quinaults, as do the Wahkiakums who are included on the membership rolls of the Chinook Indian Tribe. In May 1980, a ruling by the U.S. District Court, which was upheld in September 1981 by a U.S. Circuit Court of Appeals, denied the claim of about fifty Wahkiakums that their Columbia River fishing rights were guaranteed by the 1855–56 Quinault River Treaty. Nonreservation Wahkiakums had also shared in a November 4, 1971, award to the Chinook Nation (*see* **Chinook**). Some Indians of Wahkiakum descent have joined a conglomerate that includes Kwalhioquas, Lower Chinooks, Cathlamets, Clatsops, Tillamooks, the Conniac Band of Upper Chinookan Skilloots, and Willapas, all of whom are organized under the name Confederated Treaty Tribes of Tansey Point.

Suggested Readings:

> Melville Jacobs, "Historic Perspectives in Indian Languages of Oregon and Washington," *Pacific Northwest Quarterly* 28, no. 1 (January 1937); Albert Buell Lewis, "Tribes of the Columbia Valley and the Coast of Washington and Oregon," *Memoirs of the American Anthropological Association* (1906), vol. 2, pt. 2; Fred Lockley, *History of the Columbia River Valley from The Dalles to the Sea* (Chicago, 1928), 2 vols.; Verne F. Ray, "Lower Chinook Ethnographic Notes," *University of Washington Publications in Anthropology* 2, no. 2 (1938) and "The Historical Position of the Lower Chinook in the Native Culture of the Pacific Northwest," *Pacific Northwest Quarterly* 28, no. 4 (October 1937).

WALLA WALLA

(Shahaptian)

The Walla Wallas lived along the Columbia River in the area of its confluence with the Walla Walla River, and east along the Walla Walla to its junction with the Touchet River.

There is a dispute over the meaning of the name "Walla Walla." Linguist Bruce J. Rigsby asserts that the name, meaning "flow" and "stream," was used by a neighboring tribe, the Umatillas, to refer to the Walla Wallas, and that from that source it became the name that the Walla Wallas applied to themselves. The ethnologist John R. Swanton stated that it meant "little river." John Keast Lord, a naturalist with the British Boundary Commission who visited the Walla Walla country around 1860, stated that it meant "ever-bright and sparkling." Because of their proximity and repeated exposure to their traditional enemy, the Shoshones, the Walla Wallas had close ties with other Shahaptian speakers, such as the Nez Perces and the Umatillas, as well as with the Waiilatpuan-speaking Cayuses.

In 1805–1806 the Walla Wallas met Meriwether Lewis and William Clark. Five years later and for several years thereafter, they encountered personnel of the fur-trading companies traveling up and down the Columbia River. In 1818, Fort

This Walla Walla war-rior, photographed in the early 1900s, bore the name Piopio-Maksmaks. He was a relative of the famous Walla Walla chief, Peopeomox-mox, slain in an engagement with white volunteers in the late 1850s.

Photograph by Edward S. Curtis from Curtis's "List of Large Plates Supplementing Volume 8," *The North American Indian* (Plate 267).

Nez Perces, later Fort Walla Walla, was built in their lands near the confluence of the Columbia and Walla Walla rivers. Later, a military post in the Walla Walla Valley also bore the Walla Walla name.

In 1836 the Walla Wallas came under the ministrations of the Reverend Marcus Whitman and his wife, Narcissa, of the American Board of Commissioners for Foreign Missions. In 1838 they met two Roman Catholic missionaries, Rev. François Blanchet and Rev. Modeste Demers. Because the resident Cayuses declined to do so, Walla Walla women worked at the Whitman Mission, which was established in 1836 in the Walla Walla Valley. The Cayuses regarded the Walla Wallas as an inferior people descended from slaves. In 1844, when the son of Walla Walla chief Peopeomoxmox was killed by a white man at Sutter's Mill in the Sacramento country of California, the Americans there geared up for defense, fearing that a "thousand Walla Walla" would return to retaliate. In that figure the Californians included Cayuses and Umatillas, as well as Walla Wallas. A band of those northern Indians did return to California two years later, but they were too weak from disease and too few in numbers to wreak any kind of vengeance.

Some Walla Wallas were said to be among those who joined Capt. John C. Frémont's California Battalion in the fighting that led to the annexation of California by the United States. The Walla Wallas did not participate in the November 29, 1847, Whitman Massacre, which was carried out by their Cayuse neighbors and Indians of mixed heritage married to Cayuse women. However, some Walla Wallas joined the Cayuses in their ensuing war against the Americans in 1848.

The Walla Wallas attended the treaty council in the valley that bears their name. Under provisions of the treaty that they signed on June 9, 1855, they, the Cayuses, and the Umatillas were scheduled to remove to the Umatilla Reservation in present-day northeastern Oregon. During the Yakama Indian War in the fall of 1855, after the Walla Wallas had pillaged the fort that bore their name, Chief Peopeomoxmox was shot and killed, and his body was mutilated by white volunteer troops. There was no rush of Walla Wallas to the Umatilla Reservation after that, but they slowly began locating there as whites increasingly came to occupy their former lands.

Prereservation estimates of the Walla Walla population ranged from five hundred in 1836 to eleven hundred in 1841 and to two thousand in 1848. In 1962 their descendants in Oregon numbered between a hundred and two hundred. On the Umatilla Reservation, where the Cayuses' ties were with the Nez Perces, the Walla Wallas associated more with the Umatillas and the peoples of the Warm Springs Reservation farther west in north-central Oregon. By the early twentieth century, tribal distinctions on the Umatilla had blurred. Today descendants of the Walla Wallas, along with those of Cayuses and Umatillas, form the Umatilla Confederated Tribes. Yet their original tribal name is perpetuated in many things, including a river and its valley, a city, and a county. *See* **Confederated Tribes of the Umatilla Indian Reservation.**

Suggested Readings:

Angelo Anastasio, "Intergroup Relations in the Southern Plateau," master's thesis, University of Chicago, 1955; T. W. Davenport, "Recollections of an Indian Agent," *Oregon Historical Quarterly* 8 (March-December 1907); Robert H, Ruby and John A. Brown, *The Cayuse Indians: Imperial Tribesmen of Old Oregon* (Norman: University of Oklahoma Press, 1972, 2005); J. F. Santee, "Pio-Pio-Mox-Mox," *Oregon Historical Quarterly* 34 (March-December 1933).

WANAPUM

(Shahaptian)

River People

The Wanapums were composed of several groups, one of which was called "Sokulks" by the American explorers Meriwether Lewis and William Clark. They lived along the Columbia River, or "Enche Wana," as they called it, in the area of the Priest Rapids, which today have been obliterated by the backwaters of the dam bearing that name in central Washington State. About fifteen miles upstream from Priest Rapids Dam, the Wanapum Dam takes the name of these peoples.

This Wanapum woman, photographed in the 1960s, holds her tribe's chief source of food, the salmon. Special laws passed by the Washington State legislature permitted the Wanapums to catch fish for ceremonial and noncommercial purposes.

Authors' collections.

History: Priest Rapids was named by fur traders, who on August 18, 1811, encountered a Native priest there. A strong spiritual influence remained among the Wanapums, especially that exerted by the prophet Smohalla, whose Dreamer religion gained momentum around 1800. Smohalla is said to have been badly hurt in a fight with another Columbia River chief, Moses. He was then supposed to have wandered for a time before he returned to his people a greater prophet than ever. He preached the sacredness of the earth and its final restoration to aboriginal purity. Through his ceremonials, which included flags, drums, and certain nativist and Christian forms, he was able to attract to his rush-mat lodge in P'na ("fish weir") village those traditionalists who avoided reservations and were called "renegades" by the whites. Under Smohalla's influence and leadership, the Wanapums maintained their independence, despite the efforts of Indian agents to confine them to reservations. The Wanapums were successful, partly because of the difference of opinion between Indian agents and army officials, who disagreed on the proper distribution of the tribe, and partly because of the poor soils of their Priest Rapids homeland, which did not attract white settlement. After his death in March 1895, Smohalla was succeeded by his son, Little Smohalla, who froze to death in 1917. A direct descendant, Puck Hyah Toot (Johnny Buck), was a Wanapum leader until his death on September 11, 1956.

A Washington State law of 1939 allowed a tribal remnant to take fish for personal and ceremonial use, but not for commercial purposes. When the laws were recodified in 1949, the one permitting the Wanapums to so fish was erased from the books. Therefore, in 1981 the state enacted another law allowing them to obtain permits to take fish for ceremonial and subsistence purposes.

During World War II the Wanapums, still living in mat dwellings as they always had, were removed from the area that had been set aside for the Atomic Energy Reservation at Hanford, Washington, to the foot of the Priest Rapids.

Rex Buck, Jr., a descendant of Smohalla and the spiritual and civic leader of the Wanapum Tribe. Buck, who works for the benefit of indigenous peoples everywhere, has been a key figure in repatriating Plateau ancestors back to their tribes. In recognition of his leadership, he was the 2008 recipient of the Peace and Friendship Award bestowed by the Washington State Historical Society on individuals who have advanced public understanding of the cultural diversity of Washington State. Today between seventy-five and one hundred Wanapums live year-round on a thin sliver of land on the west side of the Priest Rapids Dam.

Courtesy of Don Seabrook, *Wenatchee (Wash.) World.*

The Wanapums maintain that they have never signed any treaty with the federal government, but that four tribal members entered into an agreement, dated January 15, 1957, with Washington's Grant County Public Utility District. The Federal Power Commission required such a pact to protect the utility from future claims on the site of the Priest Rapids Dam. By the terms of the agreement, the utility agreed to pay the tribe a $20,000 cash settlement, most of which was to be divided among the surviving Wanapums. The utility retained $1,300 to finance feasts and religious ceremonies for the tribal remnant and their guests at the damsite. The Wanapums were also assured the right to hunt and fish on the lands and waters of the project and were assured lifelong housing in individual dwellings, electricity and water for the houses and yards, a longhouse, and employment on the dam. The utility agreed to move some petroglyphs from Whale Island in the Columbia River to the Wanapum burial grounds. The utility also agreed to provide a livelihood in coming years for the three families remaining at Priest Rapids.

Contemporary Life and Culture: The Wanapums remain a federally unrecognized, nontreaty tribe. Today some fifty to seventy-five Wanapums live year round in their thirteen-home village on the west side of the Priest Rapids Dam on the Columbia River. In 1870 the Wanapums had numbered about three hundred, a significant reduction from the estimated eighteen hundred of a century earlier. Approximately 25 percent of Wanapums are employed by the Grant County Public Utility District. Many surviving Wanapums are enrolled in other inland northwest tribes.

Rex Buck, Jr., who is a direct descendant of Smohalla, serves as a spiritual leader and advisor to the Wanapums and other Pacific Northwest tribes. In 2008 he received the "Peace and Friendship" medal from the Washington State Historical Society for his advancement of public understanding of the cultural diversity of the peoples of Washington State.

The Wanapums are very active in their culture, digging traditional roots, wearing traditional clothing, and participating in their annual First Food Feast. Wanapum youth are learning fish catching, hemp-rope weaving, ancient tool construction, and other traditional skills. Through their Living Cultures Program, Wanapums gave sixty-seven presentations in local public schools and fairs in 2007, while the Wanapum Native American Discovery Unit is a traveling diorama with artifacts and photographs exhibited in a customized forty-foot motor home that brings Wanapum history and culture to schools and community events. In 2000 the Wanapums constructed a tule-mat longhouse in their village at Priest Rapids, a significant cultural and sacred achievement. Tribal culture and history is also preserved through the Wanapum Heritage Center, a major museum located at the Wanapum Dam on the Columbia River, where visitors can steer a steamboat, view historical artifacts and beadwork and basketry, and watch videos on Wanapum history and culture.

Special Events and Celebrations: The Root Festival is held every spring.

Suggested Readings:

E. L. Huggins, "Smohalla, the Prophet of Priest Rapids," *Overland Monthly,* 2d ser., vol. 17 (January-June 1891); Maj. J. W. MacMurray, "The 'Dreamers' of the Columbia River Valley in Washington Territory," *Transactions of the Albany Institute* 11 (1887): 241–48; James Mooney, "The Ghost-Dance Religion and the Sioux Outbreak of 1890," *Fourteenth Annual Report of the Bureau of American Ethnology* (Washington, D.C.: Government Printing Office, 1896); Click Relander, *Drummers and Dreamers* (Caldwell, Ida.: Caxton Printers, Ltd., 1956); Robert H. Ruby and John A. Brown, *Half-Sun on the Columbia: A Biography of Chief Moses* (Norman: University of Oklahoma Press, 1965) and *Dreamer Prophets of the Columbia Plateau* (Norman: University of Oklahoma Press, 1989); Margery Ann Beach Sharkey, "Revitalization and Change: A History of the Wanapum Indians, Their Prophet Smowhala, and the Washani Religion," Ph.D. dissertation, Washington State University, 1984.

WARM SPRINGS FEDERATED TRIBES

*(See **Confederated Tribes of Warm Springs.**)*

WASCO
(Upper Chinookan Division of Chinookan)

The name "Wasco" stems from that tribe's own word meaning "cup" or "small horn bowl," a reference to a cup-shaped rock near The Dalles, Oregon. The Astorian Robert Stuart called the Wascos the Cathlascos, a variation of that being Calascos. Another fur man, Alexander Ross, referred to them as the Wisscopams. They have also been designated as Wascos proper and Dalles Wascos. Among the places bearing their name are a county and a town in north-central Oregon, where they occupied the south bank of the Columbia River from The Dalles downstream to Hood River.

In 1822, about seven years before the outbreak of the intermittent fever, the Wascos numbered about 900. In 1853 a U.S. military census placed their population at 300. By 1855 their membership had dropped to 252, possibly because of the smallpox plague of 1853. Having once been the strongest of the Upper Chinookan peoples, they, like others of their linguistic family, declined in numbers, as well as in power, under pressure from the non-Indians and their attendant diseases.

History: The Wascos' standing was to a great extent due to their geographic position along a key stretch of the Columbia River, where they became the foremost traders among the Upper Chinookan peoples. Their primary village, Winquatt, was the gathering place for many tribes. They owned and traded slaves and horses, but their main exchange item was the several species of salmon that they caught and prepared between May and October, sometimes in baskets that could hold as much as a hundred pounds. After processing, some of the fish were consumed locally, not only by the Wascos but also by Indians who gathered from hundreds of miles around. The Wasco country was possibly the most important locus of aboriginal trade in the Pacific Northwest interior. Fishing stations were individually controlled, and they were assigned first to family members, then to neighboring villagers, and finally to friendly visitors from farther away. In the later part of October, the Wascos often journeyed downstream to the mouth of the Willamette River to dig wappato roots. They also dug camas roots in the valley of the White Salmon River, a Columbia affluent from the north. By the 1840s, when white travelers en route to the Willamette Valley were entering the Wasco lands, the Wascos and their neighbors wanted "dollars" for the goods that they traded to the immigrants and for the portaging services that they provided them.

Wasco culture somewhat resembled that of the peoples of the northwest coast. For example, they lived in plank houses of the coastal type. Although they were also exposed to the cultures of the Columbia Plateau in the interior, they were not influenced by them to the same extent that the nearby Upper Chinookan Wishrams were. Except for brief intervals, the Wascos warred against the North-

These Wasco Indians, photographed in the early 1900s, were, from left to right, Da-wa-da-tha (Peter Jackson), Wa-bi-ga, and Wa-lik-sma (Susan Seymour). The Wascos lived at The Dalles of the Columbia River, one of the Pacific Northwest's most important Native fishing and trading places.

Authors' collections.

ern Paiutes of the interior on the south. In one skirmish in 1811, the Paiutes attacked some Wascos in their canoes on the Columbia River. The conflicts between the two peoples were aggravated by the barrenness of the Paiute lands, on which the Chinookan speakers encroached, seeking to improve their own means of subsistence. During conflicts, the Wascos imprisoned Paiute women and children and then sold them in village marts.

In 1838 Methodist missionaries began their Wascopam Mission at The Dalles in Wasco country. Later, they sold out to the Roman Catholics, who began St. Peter's Mission there in 1848. After the Whitman Massacre on November 29,

1847, the Cayuse Indians threatened some Wascos into joining them in their war against the Oregon provisional government, but most Wascos refrained from hostilities. After 1850, The Dalles area was a center of American military operations against the Indians in the war that broke out in 1855. The latter war was precipitated by dissatisfaction with the June 25, 1855, treaty with the United States, which was signed by Wascos and other Upper Chinookans from the Columbia River as far inland as the Cascades and Hood River, as well as Sahaptian-speaking Teninos. Under the treaty, these peoples relinquished about 10 million acres for the Warm Springs Reservation, which was 464,000 acres before boundary adjustments in the Indians' favor. Removal from their homes to the soil-poor Warm Springs would rankle that reservation's Indians for many years to come. Fortunately for them, Congress did not ratify a treaty (14 Stat. 751) signed on November 15, 1865, which would have rescinded their rights to fish in their traditional places along the Columbia River, which had been guaranteed by the 1855 treaty. On February 9, 1929 (45 Stat. 1158), about seven acres were set aside for a village at the old tribal fishing campsite near Celilo Falls on the Columbia for a small band of Indians living there who had been assigned to the Warm Springs Reservation. The vagueness of that reservation's northern and western boundaries also angered the Wascos and other Warm Springs Indians.

After occupying multiple-family dwellings, sometimes called longhouses, the Wascos moved onto small plots on the Warm Springs Reservation between the agency headquarters and the Deschutes River. There they began clearing and farming the land. In 1866 they and the Teninos were recruited by the American military as scouts in a war with the Paiutes. The Wascos also served as scouts in the Modoc War of 1872–73. A Paiute remnant, who were victims of the Bannock-Paiute War of 1878, were eventually removed to the Warm Springs Reservation, where they were located about fifteen miles south of agency headquarters. Unlike the Wascos, who assumed tribal leadership roles on the reservation, the Paiutes remained leery of federal policies and administrators.

In the 1870s, the Wascos and other Warm Springs peoples came under the influence of the Presbyterians, who administered the reservation during the President Ulysses S. Grant Peace Policy era under the agent, Capt. John Smith. The captain tried zealously to raise what he believed were poor moral standards brought on by previous military governance of the reservation. He also attempted to eliminate Native healings, polygamy, and other practices, such as slave-holding. On the reservation in 1869, the Wascos held some Achomawis and Atsugewis, or Pit River Indians, whom they had bought from Klamaths several years before. Under the General Allotment Act of February 8, 1887 (24 Stat. 388), 140,529 acres were allotted to 968 Indians on the Warm Springs Reservation, and 1,195 acres were set aside for agency, school, and church purposes.

Today the Wascos are largely assimilated with the other peoples of the Warm Springs Reservation. In 1946 there remained only twenty who spoke the Native language. *See* **Confederated Tribes of Warm Springs.**

Suggested Readings:

David French, "Wasco-Wishram," in Edward H. Spicer, ed., *Perspectives in American Culture Change* (Chicago: University of Chicago Press, 1961); Frederick Webb Hodge, *Handbook of American Indians North of Mexico,* pt. 2 (Washington, D.C.: Government Printing Office, 1910); Gordon MacNab, *A History of the McQuinn Strip* (Portland, Ore., 1972); Ralph M. Shane and Ruby D. Leno, *A History of the Warm Springs Reservation, Oregon* (Portland, Ore., 1949); Robert H. Suphan, "Ethnological Report on the Wasco and Tenino Indians," *Oregon Indians,* vol. 2 (New York: Garland Publishing, 1974), 9–85.

WATLALA

(Upper Chinookan Division of Chinookan)

The Watlalas (or Wahlalas), also known as the Cascade Indians, were called the Shalala Nation by the American explorers Meriwether Lewis and William Clark, who encountered them in 1805–1806. Lewis and Clark described them as living in three subdivisions: the Yhehuhs, above The Cascades of the Columbia River; the Clahclellahs, below those rapids; and the Wahclellahs, on the Columbia at Beacon Rock, a few miles upstream from present-day Skamania, Washington. In fact, there were as many as six subdivisions of the Watlalas living where the Columbia breaks through the Cascade Mountains. Their dialect originally differed but slightly from that of the more dominant Wascos upstream with whom the Watlala remnant joined after the ravages of the intermittent fever in the 1830s. The tribe then became known by the name of one of its subdivisions, the Watlalas. Sometimes they were called the Cascade Wascos. Their villages lay on both the north and the south banks of the Columbia near present-day Cascade Locks, Oregon.

At the beginning of the nineteenth century, like the Wascos and the Chilluckittequaws (Hood Rivers) who were also Upper Chinookan speakers, the Watlalas were a sedentary people who combined a basically northwest coast culture with elements from the Columbia Plateau of the interior. Like other Upper Chinookans, they fished and traded. During the fishing season from May to October, they caught several species of salmon. Fishing stations were controlled and were assigned first to family members, then to neighboring villagers, and finally to friendly peoples from farther distances. When Lewis and Clark met them they did not have horses. In the early nineteenth century white travelers feared passage around The Cascades of the Columbia, where the Native mausoleums and steep bluffs hiding the sun added to the gloom of the place. The Indians of The Cascades had a reputation for thievery because they appropriated the goods of travelers along that vital stretch of the river, exacting tolls from passersby and serving as their porters.

Under the designation "Wahlalas," the Watlalas signed with Kalapuyan tribes a treaty with Oregon superintendent of Indian affairs Joel Palmer on January 22, 1855 (10 Stat. 1143, ratified March 3, 1855), ceding to the United States their lands west of the Middle Cascades of the Columbia. Under the designation "Kigaltwallas," they surrendered their lands east of the Middle Cascades in a treaty of June 25, 1855, that the United States effected with the tribes of "Middle Oregon." In March 1865, they were lured into anti-American hostilities, apparently by a Klickitat-Yakama Indian coalition. Ironically, despite their pleas of innocence, some Watlalas were subsequently hanged by the victorious American military.

With the Wascos, the Watlalas were estimated to have been 3,200 in 1780, 2,800 in 1805–1806, and 1,400 in 1812. In 1855 they numbered about seventy, nearly twice as many as in the 1830s, when the epidemic had raged. Today no one speaks their language and the members of the tribe have been absorbed into the populations of other tribes.

Suggested Readings:

Frederick Webb Hodge, *Handbook of American Indians North of Mexico,* pt. 2 (Washington, D.C.: Government Printing Office, 1910).

WAUYUKMA

(Shahaptian)

The Wauyukmas lived on the Snake River below the mouth of the Palouse River in modern-day Washington State. They are believed by some to have been closely related to the Palouse Indians of that region and by others to have been a band of the Palouse tribe. The name "Wauyukma," meaning "old salmon trap," is appropriate for them, since salmon fishing provided much of their subsistence. The Wauyukmas' 1780 population, apparently including the Palouses, has been estimated at eighteen hundred. It seems that they occupied a single village.

Suggested Readings:

Melville Jacobs, "A Sketch of Northern Sahaptin Grammar," *University of Washington Publications in Anthropology* 4, no.2 (1931); Verne F. Ray, "Native Villages and Groupings of the Columbia Basin," *Pacific Northwest Quarterly* 27, no. 2 (April 1936).

———————————

WENATCHI

(Interior Division, Salishan)

P'squosa

The name "Wenatchi" (or Wenatchee) is derived from a Shahaptian word loosely meaning "water coming out." The opening from which the water came was possibly Tumwater Canyon on the Wenatchee River near today's Leavenworth, Washington, on U.S. Highway 2. In the early nineteenth century, the Wenatchis comprised five bands that lived primarily in the Wenatchee River watershed and the area near its mouth, and for a short distance up and down the Columbia River to which the Wenatchee is a tributary. Some anthropologists maintain that in early times other Wenatchis lived south in the Kittitas Valley of the upper Yakima River country. The residents of the Kittitas Valley, the Kittitas band of Upper Yakamas, were, according to these anthropologists, absorbed by Shahaptian peoples who imposed their language upon them. These Upper Yakama peoples camped with the Wenatchis at fisheries on the Wenatchis' lands about twenty-five to thirty miles up the Wenatchee River from its Columbia confluence.

The Wenatchis first appeared in print as "Wahnaachee" in the maps and journals of Meriwether Lewis and William Clark. The Wenatchis called themselves the Pisquows (Pisquoses), the name by which early-day fur men referred to them and their river. They depended more on their river valley and its environs for subsistence than did the Sinkiuses (Moses Columbias), their neighbors across the Columbia River. Yet the Wenatchis were known to travel as far away as The Dalles and across the Cascade Mountains to the Puget Sound to trade.

In 1841 the Wenatchis met Lt. Robert Johnson, a member of Lt. Charles Wilkes's U.S. Navy expedition, near the mouth of the Wenatchee River. Johnson reported that the Natives were growing potatoes in turf enclosures, an evidence of fur-trader influence. A dozen years later, Indians there entertained Capt. George McClellan of the Pacific Railroad Survey and later of Civil War fame by racing horses.

Wenatchi chief Tecolekun was one of fourteen signers of the Yakama treaty at the Walla Walla council in 1855. Some Wenatchis joined the Yakamas in their war against the Americans, which broke out that fall. During the conflict, troops attacked and killed innocent villagers on White River, a Lake Wenatchee tributary. In August 1858, soldiers engaged in a punitive expedition to the Wenatchee River hanged four Natives without any semblance of a trial, in the belief they had attacked white miners. Earlier that summer, miners en route to the Canadian goldfields, after skirmishing with Wenatchi Indians at the mouth of their river, killed an Indian man, Quiltenenock (Quiltomee), whose brother, Moses, assumed leadership of the scattered mid-Columbia bands. Tecolekun was re-

Pete Judge, a Wenatchi Indian, ca. 1910. Judge's people lived along the Wenatchee River in central Washington. The Wenatchis were forced off their lands by settlers. Some relocated to the nearby Colville Reservation.

Courtesy of the North Central Washington Museum Association, Wenatchee.

portedly killed that May during fighting between Indians and the troops of U.S. Army Col. Edward Steptoe near present-day Rosalia, Washington, south of Spokane Falls.

The Wenatchis came under the influence of the missionary efforts of Roman Catholic priests such as Rev. Urban Grassi, S.J., whose journey to the Wenatchee River in the summer of 1873 led to the establishment of the St. Francis Xavier Mission near present-day Cashmere (formerly, Mission) about ten miles from the mouth of the Wenatchee River. After a major earthquake in 1872, Grassi sought to convert to his faith the powerful Wenatchi prophet, Patoi, who was attracting many followers by his nativist preachings.

During the reservation era, the Wenatchis refused to take allotments on the Yakama Reservation. Because of their associations with the Upper Yakamas at such places as the Wenatshapam Fishery, which was reserved for Indian use under the Yakama treaty, the Wenatchis were confederated by government officials with the Yakamas. The Indians were angered when their fisheries were sold for $20,000 on January 8, 1894, at the urging of the Yakama agent L. T. Erwin. The funds from their sale were used to build the Erwin Ditch for irrigation on the Yakama Reservation. In 1911, some Wenatchis, who were scheduled for removal, took homesteads on their ancestral lands. But these lands, which were valuable for irrigation, only caused problems for the Wenatchis holding them, and they were soon alienated from their original owners. In the spring of 1911, some of those Wenatchis relinquished their holdings to join others of their people already on the Colville Reservation, taking allotments there. By 1915, twelve quarter sections originally allotted to Indians near Cashmere were subdivided into nearly two hundred tiny tracts.

In 1959 about 153 Indians on the Colville Reservation were classified as Wenatchis and 115 more were listed as living off the reservation. Those 1959 figures may have included some of the Sinkiuses. In 1970 only 33 Wenatchi-Sinkiuses were reported. They and their close neighbors were estimated to have numbered over 1,000 in 1780.

For Wenatchi claims, *see* **Confederated Tribes of the Colville Reservation.**

Contemporary Life and Culture: In May 1987, in an East Wenatchee orchard along the banks of the Columbia River, the nation's most complete, undisturbed deposit of Clovis artifacts was accidentally discovered. The subsequent dig was only partially completed and has since been closed, partly due to the opposition of the Wenatchi Indians, who view the site as a sacred ceremonial or burial location. In 2005, a bill was introduced in the Washington State legislature that would allow up to fifty Wenatchi tribal members a year to fish at a ceremonial fishery established on the Wenatchee River or Icicle Creek.

The Wenatchi Band continues to push for what they believe are their negotiated rights (Treaty of 1855 and an 1894 agreement) to a reservation and to hunt, fish, and gather in the Wenatchee River basin. The Wenatchi are also lobbying to acquire some 20,000 acres of the Wenatchee National Forest near Cashmere that includes ancient burial grounds. Though these efforts have not been successful, the tribe has been granted fishing rights in the Wenatchee River. In 2002, in support of Wenatchi claims, a film was produced called "False Promises: The Lost Land of the Wenatchi," which aired on Northwest Public Television.

In 1999, at a powwow held in Cashmere, the Wenatchi Band reclaimed their Salish tribal name of "P'squosa" over "Wenatchi," the latter a Yakama word given by that tribe.

In 2003, approximately fifteen hundred people living on the Colville Indian Reservation considered themselves of Wenatchi descent.

Mathew Dick, Wenatchi. Dick is the great-grandson of the last chief of the Wenatchi Tribe and former council chairman of the Colville Tribal Business Council. He is chairman of the Wenatchi Indian band's advisory committee and has been a strong advocate of Wenatchi fishing rights on the Wenatchee River.

Courtesy of Jefferson Robbins, *Wenatchee (Wash.) World.*

Special Events and Celebrations: On a periodic basis, the Wenatchis gather in Cashmere for a powwow or for other festivities.

Suggested Readings:

> Walter Cline et al., *The Sinkaietk, or Southern Okanagan, of Washington,* ed. Leslie Spier, American Anthropology Association, General Series in Anthropology, no. 6 (Menasha, Wis.: George Banta Publishing Co., 1938); E. Richard Hart, "The History of the Wenatchi Fishing Reservation," *Western Legal History* 13, no. 2 (2000); John Hermilt and Louis Judge, "The Wenatchee Indians Ask Justice," *Washington Historical Quarterly* 16, no. 1 (January 1925); Robert H. Ruby and John A. Brown, *Half-Sun on the Columbia: A Biography of Chief Moses* (Norman: University of Oklahoma Press, 1965); Cashmere, Wash., Pubic Schools, *The Wenatchi Indians: Guardians of the Valley,* ed. Richard D. Scheuerman (Fairfield, Wash., Ye Galleon Press, 1982); Richard Scheuerman, *The Wenatchee Valley and Its First Peoples* (Pullman: Washington State University Press, 2005); James A. Teit, "The Middle Columbia Salish," *University of Washington Publications in Anthropology* 2, no. 4 (1928).

WHISKAH

(Coastal Division, Salishan)

The Whiskahs lived in present-day southwestern Washington. Although autonomous, they were perhaps tied linguistically to the Lower Chehalises, and they shared with them a similar history. They were also closely related to the Wynoochees. They were classified by the ethnologist John R. Swanton as a village of the Humptulipses only because of their location near that tribe. (*See* **Humptulips**; **Lower Chehalis;** *and* **Wynoochee**.)

WILLAMETTE VALLEY CONFEDERATED TRIBES

The Willamette Valley Confederated Tribes of Indians was composed of descendants of the tribes who signed a treaty with the United States on January 10, 1855. The confederation included all the Kalapuyan peoples, except the Yoncallas, plus the Molalas, the Clackamases, the Clowwewallas, and the Watlalas. The confederation, which no longer exists, was primarily a political organization formed to seek compensation for their lost lands.

WILLAPA

(See **Shoalwater Bay.***)*

WISHRAM

(Upper Chinookan Division of Chinookan)

The Wishrams were the "Echeloots" whom the American explorers Meriwether Lewis and William Clark visited on their westward trek in 1805. Their name is derived from a Yakama word. The lands of this Upper Chinookan tribe extended along the Columbia's north bank from about ten miles above The Dalles to about ten miles below them. Their main village was at Spearfish (today's Wishram, Washington), where in 1906 the Spokane, Portland & Seattle Railway established a siding called Spedis for a Wishram chief.

By the estimates of Lewis and Clark and others, near the beginning of the nineteenth century the Wishrams proper represented between 6 and 10 percent (an estimated one thousand to sixteen hundred people) of the total Upper Chinookan population. It has been reported that the 1782–83 smallpox epidemic killed about half the Wishrams. With other Chinookans, they also suffered population losses from other diseases such as the intermittent fever that broke out in 1829.

For their subsistence, the Wishrams depended heavily on the salmon that they caught where the Columbia River narrows at The Dalles. They preserved the fish in baskets containing up to a hundred pounds each, not only for their own consumption but also for trade with the other peoples who flocked there in salmon seasons, making it perhaps the foremost Native mart and the mecca of the Pacific Northwest. Like other Columbia River peoples, they observed strict "first-salmon" rituals.

Located between the coastal and the interior regions of the Pacific Northwest, the Wishrams exhibited cultural traits from both regions. Around the middle of the eighteenth century, they showed evidence of integration with the Shahaptian peoples on their east by utilizing mat-covered lodges as well as their own lodges constructed of planks, which were typical of the coastal peoples. In winter they lived in the semisubterranean houses that were common among the peoples of the interior whose dress they also came to emulate. Like others of the lower Columbia River and the northwest coast, the Wishrams paid considerable attention to disposing of their dead, whom they placed in rectangular grave-houses of planks and poles on islands in the Columbia River. The class distinctions among Wishrams resembled those so evident among the coastal peoples, who were grouped into upper, middle, and lower ranks. Included in the lower class

A Wishram girl, Eagle Feather, in traditional dress. The photograph was one of many taken of Indian people by Lee Moorhouse around the turn of the twentieth century. Some Wishrams were confederated with other Indians on the Yakama Reservation of south-central Washington.

Authors' collections.

were slaves, whom Wishrams held not only to enhance the position of their owners but also, and as importantly, to exchange for goods which were carried to them over routes stretching from the Rocky Mountains to the Pacific Ocean and from Canada to the Spanish-Mexican borderlands. Even before they had seen EuroAmericans, the Wishrams had obtained their goods in trade.

The unfriendliness of Wishrams to non-Indians developed, it appears, in proportion to the presence of outsiders on the Columbia River, where they threatened the mercantile dominance of the tribe. In 1811, the tribe was hostile to Astorian fur traders who sought their services as porters over a ten-mile stretch around Celilo Falls. The following year, they attacked an Astorian party, nearly killing one of its members. Wishram resistance to non-Indian incursions weakened as the Hudson's Bay Company increased its control over the Columbia, as their population declined and the emigrant population increased, and as they came under the influence of the Methodist Wascopam Mission founded in 1838 on their lands. The Wishrams' hostility was not entirely directed toward whites; for ages they had opposed the Natives raiding them from up and down the Columbia River and the Northern Paiutes from the southern interior.

Under leaders such as the Dreamer chief Colwash, the Wishrams rejected removal to a reservation. In contrast to the Natives of the Columbia's south bank, who relocated to the Warm Springs Reservation in north-central Oregon, some Wishrams between 1860 and 1865 moved to the Yakama Reservation in Washington Territory, though at times they returned to their former homes in order to have access to the fisheries. Several families, avoiding the reservation, remained in their homelands along the Columbia.

A 1910 census listed 274 Wishrams. In 1962, 10 were reported in Washington.

Suggested Readings:

> David French, "Wasco-Wishram," in Edward H. Spicer, ed., *Perspectives in American Indian Culture Change* (Chicago: University of Chicago Press, 1961); Leslie Spier and Edward Sapir, "Wishram Ethnography," *University of Washington Publications in Anthropology* 3, no. 3 (1930).

WYNOOCHEE

(Coastal Division, Salishan)

The Wynoochees lived on the river bearing their name, a tributary of the Chehalis River in southwestern Washington State. The Wynoochees and their Whiskah neighbors have been classified on occasion as belonging to the Lower Chehalis tribe because of their linguistic and cultural closeness. Washington superintendent of Indian affairs Samuel Ross stated in a September 1870 report that the Wynoochees and the Whiskahs, like others of the Chehalis watershed, were probably once a single people who, over time, had divided to form two separate tribal identities. Ross counted the Wynoochees and the neighboring Hoquiams, Satsops, and Whiskahs at 350 under a headman named Sam. The ethnologist John R. Swanton classified the Whiskahs as a village of the Humptulips Tribe, while Frederick Webb Hodge categorized them as a Chehalis subdivision. The ethnologist George Gibbs noted that in 1853 Wynoochees had had few associations with whites, but after the period of United States and Indian treaty-making between 1854 and 1856, they received gifts from government officials and worked for wages in oyster companies on Willapa Bay.

Today the Wynoochees have been absorbed into the populations of other tribes.

YAHUSKIN

*(See **Northern Paiute** and **Klamath Tribes**.)*

YAKAMA

(Shahaptian)

The Yakamas were one of the most numerous of the Shahaptian-speaking peoples. Their 1780 population was estimated at three thousand. Later censuses recorded by early-nineteenth-century observers, however, were likely inflated because they included other Native groups.

According to John R. Swanton, the name Yakama means "runaway." Another ethnologist, Frederick Webb Hodge, stated that the Native name of Yakamas was Waptailmin, or Pakiutlema, meaning "people of the gap." Union Gap, south of present-day Yakima, Washington, was the site of their main village, Pa'kiut ("hills together"). An authority on the Yakamas, L. V. McWhorter, asserted that Spokane and Nespelem Natives conferred the name "Yah-ah-kima" on the portion of the tribe known as the Upper Yakamas, who were frequently also called the Kittitas ("rock people"). Some believe that Yakama is a modification of Yah-ah-ka-ma, meaning "a growing family" or "a tribe expansion." Other meanings ascribed to the tribal name were "black bear," "big belly," or "the pregnant ones." Some elderly Yakamas believe the last meaning derived from the spectacle of female refugees during the Yakama War of 1855–56.

The Yakamas lived in the watershed of the Yakima River, their primary watercourse in central and south-central Washington. The Yakima River begins in the Cascade Mountains and is joined by other streams such as the Tieton, the Cowiche, the Toppenish, and the Satus as it flows southeast to join the Columbia near Richland, Washington. Besides the Upper Yakamas on the north, the Lower Yakamas, or Yakamas proper, occupied the lower Yakima watershed from the ancient Selah village (just north of present-day Yakima) south to today's Prosser. The Upper Yakamas, also called the Kittitas, occupied the upper Yakima Valley north of Selah and the Kittitas Valley. Besides the river and an Indian reservation, a county and a city on U.S. Highway 97 and Interstate 82 bear a derivation of the Yakama name.

When elderly Yakamas were asked about their origins, they replied that red men were the first on earth and that they were followed by water and finally by wood. Among the Yakama traditions are stories of the Flood and of prophets dying for three days and returning to earth. Tradition also carries predictions of the coming of the black-robed Roman Catholic priests. All of those indicate an early familiarity with Christianity such as could have come through direct or indirect ties with the American Southwest, where Spanish priests had established missions. Christianity may also have come to the Yakamas from Salish speakers who had contacts with Catholic Iroquois Indians or French-Canadian Catholics in the early nineteenth century.

The Yakamas came into direct contact with outsiders in 1805–1806 when they met Lewis and Clark. Soon after that, other non-Indian travelers and traders

"Yakima Indian Doctors"
Maj. Moorhouse

Yakama healers, photographed by Lee Moorhouse, ca. 1900. The populous Shahaptian-speaking Yakamas have produced many prophets, shamans, and other religious leaders. Native religions such as the Pompom, the Feather, and the Shaker continued into the twentieth century alongside those introduced by non-Indians.

Courtesy of the Yakama Indian Nation Cultural Center, Toppenish, Wash.

passed through the Yakamas' lands and in the late 1830s and 1840s they came under the ministrations of Catholic priests.

Among both Indians and whites, the Yakamas possessed a reputation for stressing individuality in their society. Fishing was perhaps their most important means of subsistence followed by gathering roots and berries and hunting. Some historians claim that the Yakamas obtained horses from the peoples of the Great Basin through Cayuse Indian intermediaries sometime around 1730. In any event, with horses they were able to hunt buffalo on the plains, though they did not pursue them to the same extent that the interior Salish peoples did or as much as the Nez Perces who were also Shahaptian speakers. The Yakamas did not hunt buffalo at the expense of their traditional food gathering.

As white settlement of the interior progressed, the Yakamas were among Indians who treated with Washington territorial governor and superintendent of Indian affairs Isaac Stevens at the Walla Walla council. The Yakama headmen who signed the Yakama treaty on June 9, 1855, represented various lower-middle Columbia River bands. Despite opposition to the treaty, fourteen tribes under the Yakama standard ceded to the United States about 10 million acres of present-day central Washington in return for their main reservation, which was less than 1,250,000 acres. They were also to receive the usual goods and services from the government in exchange for their lands. Designated under the treaty as the

Virginia Beavert (b. 1921) is the only surviving Yakama elder who knows the sacred songs and parables of the Waashat religion and one of only a few who practices and teaches its principles. Beavert serves as a member of the Yakama Indian Nation and the General Tribal Council. A graduate of Central Washington University in Ellensburg, with a bachelor's degree in anthropology, and the University of Arizona, with a master's in bilingual and bicultural education, Beavert was recipient of the Governor's Heritage Award in 2005, Washington State's highest artistic honor.

Courtesy of Chris Pietsch, *(Ore.) Register-Guard.*

head chief of the Yakamas, Kamiakin led a coalition of interior tribes against the Americans in what became known as the Yakama War of 1855–56. Despite some initial victories, the Yakamas and their allies were defeated in a key fight early in November 1855 at Union Gap. During the war, Yakama unity was disrupted by friction between Kamiakin's Lower Yakama faction and that of the Upper Yakamas who regarded this son of a Palouse father as an outsider.

After the treaty was ratified on March 8, 1859, the fourteen confederated tribes formed what Yakamas called the Yakama Nation. From then on, the story of the Yakamas is interwoven with that of those tribes who composed the Yakama Nation of the Yakama Reservation under the Yakama, or Simcoe, Agency. *See* **Confederated Tribes and Bands of the Yakama Nation.**

Suggested Readings:

See the readings under **Confederated Tribes and Bands of the Yakama Nation.**

YAKAMA TRIBES OF THE YAKAMA RESERVATION
(See **Confederated Tribes and Bands of the Yakama Nation.***)*

YAMEL

(Kalapuyan)

The Yamels, or Yamhills, comprised six bands who spoke the Tualatin-Yamhill dialect, one of three Kalapuyan dialects. Their name originated from a Native word meaning "a ford." The Yamhill River flows east through Yamhill County to the Willamette River in northwestern Oregon. A town and a county also bear the tribal name Yamhill.

The Yamels suffered the severe population losses experienced by other Kalapuyan speakers. In 1849, when non-Indians had taken most of their lands, Oregon territorial governor Joseph Lane visited the Yamels and counted only ninety members of the tribe. By 1910 they had been reduced to five. On April 24, 1851, they met in council with commissioners authorized by Congress to treat with them for their lands. At that time they numbered fifty-four persons. They refused the commissioners' proposal that they move east of the Cascade Mountains, as did other Kalapuyan peoples, expressing instead their wish for a reserve in their homelands where for generations they had gathered native grains and roots from the soil, lakes, and marshes. At that time about thirty Yamel families lived on the tribal lands. Government agents promised that houses would be built for them on a proposed reserve. Apparently, the commissioners did not make a similar commitment to other Kalapuyan peoples.

After a treaty was signed on May 2, 1851, Oregon superintendent of Indian affairs Anson Dart tried to resettle the Yamels and their fellow Kalapuyans on the agreed-upon reservation, though the treaties directing them to do so remained unratified. When the treaties failed to become ratified, operations to resettle them out of the way of settlers came to an end. In 1854, however, under pressure from the increasing number of immigrants, the tribe was asked to

The Yamels, popularly called Yamhills, spoke a dialect of the Kalapuyan language. This male adult Kalapuyan speaker was sketched in the early 1840s by A. T. Agate, who was among the U.S. Navy explorers under Lt. Charles Wilkes.

Reproduced from Charles Pickering, *The Races of Men and Their Geographical Distribution* (1863). Courtesy of Harold Mackey.

negotiate a second treaty. Along with the Molalas and a few Clackamasas, they met at Dayton, Oregon Territory, on January 4, 1855, with Oregon superintendent of Indian affairs Joel Palmer to sign a treaty (10 Stat. 1143). By its terms, the Yamels agreed to live in the Willamette Valley until the government established a suitable reservation for them. Such a reserve, the 60,000-acre Grand Ronde, was created on June 30, 1857, in the tribe's ancestral homelands in the upper Yamhill River country. There were forty-seven Yamels on the reservation in 1870.

Suggested Readings:

S. A. Clarke, *Pioneer Days of Oregon History* (Portland, Ore., 1905); Leo J. Frachtenberg, *Ethnological Researches among the Kalapuya Indians,* Smithsonian Miscellaneous Collections 65, no. 6 (1916); J. A. Hussey, *Champoeg: Place of Transition* (Portland: Oregon Historical Society, 1964); Harold Mackey, *The Kalapayans: A Sourcebook on the Indians of the Willamette Valley* (Salem, Ore.: Mission Hill Museum Association, 1974); W. W. Oglesby, "The Calapooyas Indians" (188?), Mss. P-A 82, Bancroft Library, University of California, Berkeley; James L. Ratcliff, "What Happened to the Kalapuya? A Study of the Depletion of Their Economic Base," *The Indian Historian* 6, no. 3 (Summer 1973).

YAQUINA

(Yakonan)

The Yaquinas occupied territory along the central Oregon coast on the river that today bears their name. A bay also bears the tribal name. Like so many coastal and riverine peoples of the Pacific Northwest, their tribal organization was informal. There were several villages in which one or two headmen held positions because of their wealth, which was measured primarily in dentalia shells and slaves. The headmen's authority was weak, but each village had long-standing rules, traditions, values, and attitudes that bound the leaders and followers together. Shamans sought powers not only to cure but also to divine the causes of threats such as poor salmon runs, which they attempted to remedy by entering streams with poles to stimulate the runs.

Although the Yaquinas had seen white men and had traded with them, most of their EuroAmerican goods were obtained indirectly. Trade increased with the presence of Hudson's Bay Company traders along the Yaquinas' coasts in the 1820s.

With the Upper Coquilles, Tututnis, Chetcos, Siletzes, Nechesnes, and Alseas, the Yaquinas as Siletz Reservation inhabitants were in the first group of nontreaty Indians to be awarded claims by the United States. In 1888 and 1893, a Senate subcommittee on Indian Affairs recognized the Siletz Indians' claim, but it was not until August 26, 1935, that legislation was passed (49 Stat. 810) enabling them to bring suit in the Court of Claims against the government (Case No. 45230). In instituting that suit, the tribes presented every possible shred of documentary evidence that they could assemble to prove that their claim was based on an involuntary and uncompensated appropriation of lands by the government. In their presentation they applied lessons learned from the Miluk and Hanis Coos, the Siuslaws and the Kuitsh (Lower Umpquas), who in a 1938 ruling had lost an award for their alienated lands because of improper presentation of the evidence, which had rested largely on the oral testimony of individual Indians. The Yaquinas and other tribes on April 2, 1945, received an award of $3,128,900. Because of a Supreme Court ruling on April 6, 1951, they were, however, disallowed interest monies. The Coquilles received $847,190.40 of that award; the Tututnis, $465,225; and the Chetcos, $489,085. As confederated "Tillamook" tribes, the Nechesnes, Siletzes, Yaquinas, and Alseas shared $1,327,399.20. Their claim for $10 million was settled with that award.

In 1910 the Yaquinas numbered but nineteen members. No one today speaks the Yaquina language.

Suggested Readings:

Stephen Dow Beckham, *The Indians of Western Oregon: This Land Was Theirs* (Coos Bay, Ore.: Arago Books, 1977); J. O. Dorsey, "Indians of the Siletz Reservation," *American Anthropologist* 2 (1889); William Eugene Kent, "The Siletz Indian Reservation, 1855–1900," master's thesis, Portland State University, 1973.

YONCALLA

(Kalapuyan)

The Yoncalla dialect was one of three Kalapuyan dialects. The modern tribal name, "Yoncalla," is derived from their name for themselves. The tribe was divided into two bands. Their homelands lay south of the Willamette Valley on Elk and Calapooya creeks between present-day Oakland and Drain, Oregon. Elk and Calapooya creeks are tributaries of the Umpqua River, an affluent of the Pacific Ocean. A town near Drain today bears the name Yoncalla.

Like other Kalapuyan speakers, the Yoncallas were pressured not only by non-Indians entering their lands but also by Klickitat Indians from north of the Columbia River who entered the Willamette Valley and pushed as far south as the Umpqua Valley after the 1830s. During the 1820s, the Yoncallas were visited by the Hudson's Bay Company fur men Alexander R. McLeod and Thomas McKay and by brigades of their firm.

394

This Yoncalla posed for a photographer who may have provided non-Indian clothing for the sitting.

Authors' collections.

On November 29, 1854, the Yoncallas and Umpquas signed a treaty with U.S. officials (10 Stat. 1125 ratified March 3, 1855). They agreed to remove to a reservation where and when the government deemed best and to receive allotments there at the president's discretion. Moneys received from improvements in their homelands were to be spent on permanent improvements on their reservation. In the fall of 1855, during the later stages of the Rogue wars, Oregon superintendent of Indian affairs Joel Palmer gathered together the noncombatant tribes in southern Oregon. The Yoncallas and the Upper Umpquas agreed to confederate with the Southern Molalas, who in turn consented to the association in a December 21, 1855, treaty (12 Stat. 981, ratified March 8, 1859). Palmer then ordered those three tribes removed north to the headwaters of the Yamhill River, where the Grand Ronde Reservation was to be established for them. They began their trek to that place on January 10, 1856, arriving on February 2 after enduring hardships. Not all of them relocated. Those under Chief Halotish and a few Upper Umpquas under their headman, Napesa, remained in their Umpqua Valley homelands under the protection of white settlers, especially Meshak Tipton and Jesse Applegate, who set aside portions of their farms for them. Three decades later, a small Yoncalla remnant still farmed there, living in the manner of the Americans and sending their children to local schools. Descendants of those Yoncallas, with those of the Upper Umpquas, were awarded $377,177.16 by a decision of the Court of Claims, on April 3, 1950, for the loss of their homelands (Case No. 45231). This award represented the principal of $67,820, plus interest and deductions for offsets.

In 1910 the original Yoncallas had numbered only ten members.

Suggested Readings:

S. A. Clarke, *Pioneer Days of Oregon History* (Portland, Ore., 1905); Leo J. Frachtenberg, *Ethnological Researches among the Kalapuya Indians,* Smithsonian Miscellaneous Collections 65, no. 6 (1916); Anne Applegate Kruse, *The Halo Trail: The Story of the Yoncalla Indians* (Drain, Ore., 1954); Harold Mackey, *The Kalapuyans: A Sourcebook on the Indians of the Willamette Valley* (Salem, Ore.: Mission Mill Museum Association, 1974); W. W. Oglesby, "The Calapooyas Indians," [188?] mss. P-A 82, Bancroft Library, University of California, Berkeley; James L. Ratcliff, "What Happened to the Kalapuya? A Study of the Depletion of Their Economic Base," *The Indian Historian* 6, no. 3 (Summer 1973).

Index

Page numbers in **bold** refer to main entries in the guide. Page numbers in *italics* refer to illustrations.